Russia in
the Twentieth Century

SIXTH EDITION

Russia in the Twentieth Century

M. K. DZIEWANOWSKI
University of Wisconsin, Milwaukee

Prentice
Hall

Upper Saddle River, New Jersey 07458

Library of Congress Cataloging-in-Publication Data

Dziewanowski, M. K.
   Russia in the twentieth century / M.K. Dziewanowski.—6th ed.
     p. cm.
   Rev. ed. of: A history of Soviet Russia and its aftermath. 5th ed. 1997.
   Includes bibliographical references and index.
   ISBN 0-13-097852-3
   1. Soviet Union–History. I. Title: Russia in the 20th century. II. Dziewanowski, M. K.
   History of Soviet Russia and its aftermath. III. Title.

DK246.D9 2002
947.084—dc21

                    2002021129

Acquisitions Editor: Charles Cavaliere
Associate Editor: Emsal Hasan
Editorial Assistant: Adrienne Paul
Marketing Manager: Claire Rehwinkel
Editorial/production supervision: Barbara Christenberry
Manufacturing Buyer: Sherry Lewis
Cover Art Director: Jayne Conte
Cover Designer: Bruce Kenselaar

This book was set in 10/12 New Baskerville by A & A Publishing Services, Inc. and was printed and bound by RR Donnelley/Harrisonburg. Cover was printed by Phoenix Color Corp.

Photo credits appear on page 403.

This is the sixth edition of book formerly titled A HISTORY OF SOVIET RUSSIA AND ITS AFTERMATH, 5th Edition.

© 2003, 1997, 1993, 1989, 1985, 1979 by Pearson Education, Inc.
Upper Saddle River, New Jersey 07458

Printed in the United States of America

10 9 8 7 6 5 4 3

ISBN 0-13-097852-3

Pearson Education LTD., *London*
Pearson Education Australia PTY. Limited, *Sydney*
Pearson Education Singapore, Pte. Ltd.
Pearson Education North Asia Ltd., *Hong Kong*
Pearson Education Canada, Ltd., *Toronto*
Pearson Educación de Mexico, S.A. de C.V.
Pearson Education—*Japan, Tokyo*
Pearson Education Malaysia, Pte. Ltd.
Pearson Education, Upper Saddle River, New Jersey

To my Harvard teachers of things Russian and Soviet:

Professors Michael Karpovich and Merle Fainsod

Contents

4   *The Russo-Japanese War and the Revolution of 1905*   42

5   *The Aftermath of the Revolution of 1905: The Constitutional Experiment*   58

6   *World War I and the Revolutions of 1917*   72

PART II   COMMUNIST RUSSIA

7   *Utopia at the Creation*   91

13 *The Industrialization Debate and the Five-Year Plans*   169

14 *The Purges*   185

15 *A New Nationality Policy and the Soviet Cultural Revolution*   197

16 *From Isolation to Collective Security*   209

HALF PRICE BOOKS®

Half Price Books
3860 LA REUNION PKWY
DALLAS, TX 75212
OFS OrderID 3473769

Thank you for your order, Millies Books Ref# 3613545!

Thank you for shopping with Half Price Books! Please contact service31@hpb.com, if you
have any questions, comments or concerns about your order (59170717)

SKU	ISBN/UPC	Title & Author/Artist	Shelf ID	Qty
S162761601	9780130978523	Russia in the Twentieth Century (6th Edition) Dziewanowski, M. K.	HIST 11.3	1

SHIPPED STANDARD TO:
Millies Books Ref# 3613545
2805 Duke Parkway
Aurora IL 60569-4587

ORDER# **59170717**
Alibris

Preface

The twentieth century was the most turbulent period of Russia's millennial history. Even at its start, the country's impressive economic progress, achieved at great human cost, was profoundly affected by the humiliating defeat in the 1904–1905 war with Japan. The war, followed by a revolution, resulted in the establishment of a quasi-representative but not quite democratic constitutional regime. The painfully slow political evolution of the Tsarist empire was interrupted by the bloody and exhausting World War I, which started in 1914 and ended for Russia in 1917 largely as a result of the double revolution; the first one, which took place in March, overturned the autocratic Tsarist regime and replaced it with the democratic Provisional Government. The second revolution occurred in November 1917, when the democratic regime was overthrown by the Bolshevik *coup d'état*, which established the Communist dictatorship, headed by Vladimir Lenin. The Bolshevik *coup* was followed by a cruel, protracted civil war (1918–1921) and a radical Communist experiment that laid the foundations of a centralized economy.

The experiment involved the forcible industrialization and the collectivization of a still traditional, but tolerably functioning, agricultural system. Both experiments involved enormous suffering affecting millions of human beings, especially in Ukraine and Kazakstan. The brutal political, social, and economic changes imposed by Joseph Stalin were paralleled by the ubiquitous terror that culminated in the Great Purges of the 1930s: millions of people were incarcerated in labor camps, and up to one million executed. World War II and the German attack on the Soviet Union in 1941 resulted in multiple millions of military and civilian casualties and vast economic devastation.

The triumphant end of the war in 1945 did not bring about preservation of the meager political and religious liberties which Stalin felt necessary to concede to the Soviet people in order to stimulate the effort necessary to win "the Great Patriotic War." Quite the contrary, soon after its end, Stalin, by then master of a vast satellite empire, reimposed his terror involving large-scale arrests and frequent executions of individuals suspected of disloyalty to the Communist system. As a result of World War II, the Soviet Union became the second superpower, threatening

its rival, the United States, with nuclear annihilation. Despite some brilliant achievements
in military technology, rocketry, and space
travel, the masses of the Soviet people continued their miserable existence, and were
driven by their Communist rulers to more
and more ruinous sacrifices in the name of
distant, utopian objectives. At the same time,
nationality problems proved to be a time
bomb implanted at the foundation of the
Soviet empire.

The forty-year long military arms race with
the United States, known as the "Cold War,"
lasted from the late 1940s to the late 1980s,
impoverished the Soviet masses and resulted
in the undermining of the already obsolete,
grossly inefficient economy. The effort to
project Soviet power into the Caribbean,
Middle East, and Africa further weakened
the overcentralized and increasingly mal-
functioning system. Its back was finally broken by the debilitating, fruitless war in
Afghanistan that finally exposed the weakness of the outwardly impressive but ineffective Soviet military machine. The deepening
psychological exhaustion and dissatisfaction
with the oppressive regime, unable to satisfy
many of the most basic needs of the broad
masses, resulted in a series of sudden
upheavals.

First, the increasingly restless satellite
empire fell apart in 1989. This was followed
by the breakup of the Soviet Union in 1991,
which was replaced by the Commonwealth of
Independent States. The demoralization and
disintegration of the central Communist
Party system and governmental machine was
paralleled by civil disorder, a painful economic crisis and two bloody and humiliating
wars against the breakaway republic of
Chechnya, conducted by the real heir of the
former Soviet Union, the Russian Federation.

The Federation has suffered not only
from a near permanent political and economic crisis, but also from a psychological
malaise among Russia's political elites. As a
consequence of the disintegration of the
Soviet Union, Russia's frontiers dramatically
shrank: loss of the Baltic republics, Lithuania, Latvia, and Estonia, deprived Russia of
access to the Baltic Sea; the establishment of
an independent Ukraine barred the Federation from the Black Sea; and the rise of three
Caucasian states and five Central Asian
republics limited Russia's role in the Euroasiatic area. All these setbacks, so painful to the
national pride, left the Russian political elite
frustrated. If one adds the environmental
and demographic problems left behind by
the vanished Communist system, the tragic
situation of Russia at the end of the twentieth century could hardly be underestimated.

The book is divided into three unequal
parts. Part I, besides providing some basic
information about Russia, deals with the last
declining period of the Tsarist regime (Chapters 1–6). The second part (Chapters 7–24)
covers the seventy-four years of the Communist rule. Part III deals with the fall of the
Soviet state and the formation of the Russian
Federation in 1991 (Chapters 25–26).

The story of the Communist rule over this
vast Euroasiatic space, some one-sixth of the
earth, makes up the bulk of the book. There
are some basic, distinctive features that are
discernable throughout the entire narrative.

The story of the Communist Party's evolution away from Marxist orthodoxy in the
direction of Great Russian nationalism is one of
the predominant themes of the book. In all
editions I have tried to show how the initial
Communist evangelic ardor was gradually
fused with traditional Muscovite nationalism
and how it was carefully camouflaged by
Marxist verbiage. This thesis has been fully
vindicated by subsequent developments,
especially those following the disintegration
of the Communist regime. I have also tried to
illustrate how the geopolitical origins of the
Muscovite-Russian state have been increasingly visible throughout the Soviet and post-
Soviet phases of Russian history. One of the
most characteristic features of this return to
the past has been the revival of the historic
and religious roots of Russian culture.

Another distinctive feature of the book
has been the stress on the multinational features of the former Soviet empire and the

largely unsuccessful attempts to Russify the other ethnic groups under the guise of creating "a new Soviet man." These attempts at disguised Russification have been increasingly opposed by the many other ethnic groups of which the USSR was composed. That is why this book has paid a great deal of attention to the centripetal, as well as centrifugal, trends within the former Soviet empire.

A large part of the book is devoted to the twenty-nine-year period of 1924–1953, to the phantasmagoric era of Stalin, who influenced much of the political reality of the Soviet Union, and even its aftermath, the Russian Federation as well as the Commonwealth of Independent States (CIS).

Any history of Russia that has to straddle the imperial and the Soviet periods faces many problems. Among them is the unavoidable issue of the calendars. Until February 1918, Russia used the Julian calendar, which in the twentieth century was thirteen days behind the Western, or Gregorian, calendar. Hence, the Russians speak of the "February Revolution" when referring to the downfall of the Tsarist regime in Petrograd (February 27), while for us it is the revolution of March 12, 1917. The abdication of Tsar Nicholas II, which according to the old-style calendar took place on March 2, for us occurred on March 15. Lenin returned from Switzerland to Petrograd on April 3, according to the Julian calendar, but on April 16, according to ours. Finally, the "Great October Proletarian Revolution," which, according to the Julian calendar, was carried out on October 25, for us was accomplished on November 7. In order to avoid confusion, both dates are given for events prior to January 1918, when the Western calendar was introduced in Russia.

Another problem is that of the spelling of Russian words. There is, unfortunately, no universally accepted system of transliteration of Russian into English. On the whole, the book favors transliteration rather than phonetic transcription, but tends to accept well-established traditional spelling of East Slavic names as easier on the student.

While preparing my book, I was ably and unselfishly assisted by Bill Myers, my former graduate student at Boston University. I am also grateful to my former student from the University of Wisconsin, Charlie Schaefer, for proofreading parts of the book, and my wife, Ada, for helping me with the preparation of the sixth edition. My warm thanks go to my friend and colleague, Professor of geography at the U.W.M., Dr. Paul E. Lydolph, for kindly allowing me to use statistical tables from the supplement to his excellent *Geography of the U.S.S.R.* My editor, Barbara Christenberry, greatly helped me in correcting this version of the manuscript and I wish to thank her for her efforts.

I am also greatly indebted to the Russian Research Center of Harvard University, with which I was connected from 1949 to 1968. The stimulating atmosphere of the Center and the contacts provided by it have been most helpful for preparing this book.

M. K. DZIEWANOWSKI
University of Wisconsin-Milwaukee

Chapter 1

The Geopolitical Personality of Russia and Its Hegemonial Sphere

Modern science and technology have considerably liberated contemporary Western civilization from subjugation to the forces of nature and geography. But this freedom from natural environment is far from complete, even in the era of computers and jumbo jets. In backward Russia, dependence on geography has always been of great importance. A book devoted to Russian history logically begins, then, with an introductory chapter on the physical environment and its persistent influence on that history.

Size, Shape, and Resources

First, one must start with the size and shape of the Russian Federation. Throughout the twentieth century, whether in its imperial, communist, or post-Soviet incarnations, Russia has been the largest country of the world, more than twice as large as the United States. One of Russia's paradoxes is that about three-fourths of its inhabitants have lived in Europe, while nearly three-fourths of its territory has been situated in Asia. The distance separating the Far Eastern end of the Russian realm and its European heart-

land is staggering. It takes about nine hours to fly from Moscow to Vladivostok at the shore of the Pacific Ocean. A unique sign-post in Vladivostok reads: 9,329 kilometers (5,789 miles) to Saint Petersburg (from 1924 till 1991 called Leningrad).

The enormity of the Russian Federation is perhaps the most striking feature of its geopolitical personality. It takes the Trans-Siberian express ten days and eleven time zones to cover the distance between St. Petersburg and Vladivostok. To cross from the western to the eastern extremity, the traveler had to span nearly 7,000 miles and reset his watch ten times. When the long summer day draws to an end on the Baltic shore of Russia, it is already dawn of the next day on its Pacific coast.

Covering over six-and-a-half million square miles, the Federation encompasses more land than all of North America. Indeed, it is about as large as the United States (3.6 million square miles), China 3.7 million), and India (1.2 million) *combined*. The size and continental character of the United States and Russia are common features of the two countries. Space (and hence colonization) has been an important geohis-

1

torical phenomenon in both. It provided what had once seemed an ever-receding frontier, and one that engendered certain common attitudes toward space. Russia's eastward march to the Pacific was similar in both execution and purpose to America's westward march to its Pacific shores. Both countries provided an outlet for the restless, energetic strata of each society and opened new lands for an excess population. The job of conquering foreign lands, integrating them, and keeping them subdued proved to be a heavy drain on the Great Russian people, the founders and real masters of the Muscovite-Russian-Soviet imperial structure.

The Russian Federation, though the largest, is not the most populous country in the world. With some 140 million people, it is well behind China with over one billion, and India with some 700 million, and the United States. The Russian Federation, as established in 1992, with over 100 ethnic groups, is far less ethnically homogeneous than the United States or even China, and has one of the lowest population densities in the world (ten persons per square kilometer).

The chief successor of the Soviet Union, the Russian Federation, has inherited much of the heterogeneity of its predecessor.

Russia's size is matched by its potentially huge resources. It has on its territory every raw material it needed for its economic development, except natural rubber and quinine. It is estimated that about one-half of the known deposits of iron and one-fifth of the world's hard-coal deposits are located within its territory. It is one of the largest producers of oil in the world. It also contained 33 percent of the world's water power, 25 percent of the world's forests, and 10 percent of the world's known oil reserves. Thus, potentially, Russia is the richest country in the world.

Yet traditionally the resources of Russia have been poorly managed. In addition to their mismanagement, the resources of Russia suffer from several handicaps. First, most of the soil, especially in ethnic Russia, is of inferior quality. Second, rainfall has been erratic, coming usually not in the spring but in the summer, during harvest time. Third, Russia has the highest percentage of marshland in the world; marshes and extensive peat bogs covered roughly one-fifth of its land surface. Finally, a large percent of the total area is unsuited for cultivation because of rain shortages, severe subarctic climate, and the nature of the soil. As a consequence, the agricultural season has been on the whole as short as it is hectic. Where Western European farmers enjoy a farming season of eight to nine months, their Russian counterparts have only four to six. This short season has traditionally resulted in low yields and a low level of animal husbandry.

In addition, the resources of the Russian Federation are located largely (with the exception of the Urals and Siberia) on its periphery. Furthermore, a considerable part of the water power is in the frozen wastes of northern Siberia where it can not effectively be used. The valleys of the great Siberian streams—the Yenisei and the Lena, for instance—contain large deposits of coal and iron ore, but for the most part they are buried in a frigid area where the earth, permanently frozen to a depth of several hundred feet, makes exploitation uneconomical. Hence, besides its persistent structural and organizational troubles, the Russian economy had to cope with difficulties inherent in the nation's geographic and climatic conditions.

Another characteristic feature of the Russian Federation is its northern location. The southernmost harbor of the Russian Far East is due west of Portsmouth, New Hampshire. Most of the Russian Federation is on the same latitude as Canada; next to it, Soviet Russia was the northernmost country in the world. Moscow is north of Edmonton, Alberta; St. Petersburg (formerly Leningrad) lies as far north as Anchorage, Alaska. Not surprisingly, then, the Russians had to develop agriculture and industry in the north to a far greater extent than have the Canadians.

Nearly three-quarters of the Russian Federation has an extremely cold winter. The average January temperature in the Eurasian heartland is below zero degrees Fahrenheit.

Natural Regions of the Russian Federation

3

During the late autumn and winter, icy, biting winds, unchecked by mountain ranges, sweep from that gigantic icebox, the Arctic Ocean, through the vastness of Siberia and over the East European plain.

The relative flatness of European Russia—its amorphous, sprawling boundlessness—has been another characteristic of its geopolitical personality. By and large, the Russian realm is one huge plain that extends from Central Europe deep into Asia. This broad stretch of land, where for hundreds of miles one may search in vain for high hills, let alone a mountain, has also profoundly affected the mentality of the Russian people.

Geographic Regions

Contemporary Russia could claim a greater variety of geographic regions and climates than any other country in the world. It has been the only land that harbored both tigers and polar bears. Actually, the Russian heartland has been characterized by a certain uniformity; the variety is situated on its fringes. The territory of the Russian Federation could be divided into four main climatic and botanical zones or regions. Running essentially east to west, these were: the subarctic tundra, the forest, the steppe and desert, and the mountain region.

The subarctic tundra is the northernmost; it spreads along the Arctic Ocean from Finland to the Bering Sea. Frozen most of the year, it is a bleak region of marshes, moss, crawling shrub, dwarf trees, and grass. Its soil yields practically no crops, and its subsoil is perpetually frozen. To the hunter and trapper, however, the tundra is a paradise, for it is rich in fur-bearing animals, including polar fox, sable, and ermine.

The tundra, which covers a large part of the Russian subarctic territory, merges with the taiga, or the coniferous forest. Here spruce, pine, cedar, and fir predominate, with a sprinkling of ash, aspen, and birch. St. Petersburg lies not far to the south of the tundra zone. With well over 5 million inhabi-

tants, the city is the second largest and most important in the Russian Federation. A great port at the juncture of the Baltic and the Neva and a vital railway terminal, St. Petersburg continues to be a cultural and industrial center of considerable importance. Culturally, it is the most Western city in Russia.

Further south, beyond the taiga, lies the zone of forests and fields, some 5,000 miles long and 1,200 miles wide. Most of the woodlands are mixed: a blend of coniferous and deciduous trees. They contain one-quarter of the world's forest preserves. The capital city of Moscow, with over 12 million inhabitants, is situated in the middle of this zone, near the sources of the Western Dvina, the Dnieper, and the Volga, in approximately the same latitude as Labrador. Historically the main focus of the Russian life, Moscow remains a major industrial center. It is also an important communication center of all of Eastern Europe. Eleven main railways converge on the city.

Forests have played a considerable role in Russian history. The early civilization of Russia, and for that matter of Eastern Europe, as a whole, has been profoundly affected by the extensive forests that once covered areas much larger than they do now. Timber has always been widely used throughout Northern and Eastern Europe. Besides serving as fuel, the forests have provided material for weapons and ploughs, for dwellings, palisades, furniture, and for all sorts of domestic utensils. Moreover, forests provide meat and fur-bearing animals, berries, honey, wax, and mushrooms. The northern regions of Russia have an abundance of timber, but they do not produce enough food, especially grain. On the other hand, some former integral parts of the Tsarist Empire and its successors, the Soviet Union and the Russian Federation, have yielded sufficient food but possess relatively little timber.

The contrast between the forest and the steppe has been significant not only geographically but historically as well. The open fertile spaces have been an invitation both to invaders and to those seeking land and freedom. The nomadic tribes of Asia—the Polovtsy, the Petchenegs, the Tatars—have often invaded Eastern Europe by passing through the open flat gap between the Urals and the Caspian Sea. These Asian invaders undermined the existence of the Kievan Rus, which both the present-day Ukrainians, as well as the Russians, consider as their cradle. These invasions ruined Kiev and the entire valley of the Dnieper. For centuries the lush grassland of the Ukrainian steppe has attracted adventurous souls bent on escaping tyranny. It was the steppe that produced the typical frontiersmen of Eastern Europe, the Cossacks. The superb horsemanship and daring of these people were largely the result of the challenge of their geographical environment. In the long run, however, the steady, tough, and hard-working inhabitants of the forest prevailed over the mercurial, less reliable people of the steppe, and Muscovy conquered Ukraine in the seventeenth and eighteenth centuries and kept it until the disintegration of the Soviet Union in 1991.

As the steppe extends south and southeast toward the Caspian and Aral seas, the amount of rainfall diminishes. Here dry winds from the east often bring severe droughts. In many parts of the steppe zone, cultivation without a great deal of artificial irrigation is risky. This requirement is particularly vital around the northern end of the fast-shrinking Caspian Sea, which is now well below sea level, where the dry steppe is giving way to the advancing sand dunes of Central Asia. The enormous desert region, larger than the state of Texas, is interspersed with oases and pasture land. It stretches eastward beyond the Caspian Sea toward Turkestan and Mongolia and ends only at the Chinese border, in Manchuria. As has been already noted, European Russia is a huge, flat saucer with few hills and no mountains worth climbing. Western Siberia has the same terrain. The Ural Mountains, picturesque and rich in mineral wealth, are really a chain of gently sloping hills. They form a purely conventional and symbolically low frontier between the European and Asiatic segments of Russia.

Russian Asia

The broad lowlands to the north of the central Asiatic mountains are deserts punctuated by river valleys, oases, and three large bodies of water: the Caspian Sea, the Aral Sea, and Lake Balkhash. In the north, these deserts gradually merge with the western Siberian upland, which is traversed by the basin of the River Ob. Further to the northeast, between the sources of the Irtysh and the Ob rivers, are the northwest-southeast oriented Altai Mountains, which reach heights of about 16,000 feet. Rich in mineral resources, these mountains continue eastward along the borders of the Russian Federation, Mongolia, and China, and encompass the Sayan, Yablonoi, and Stanovoi ranges, which stretch along the Amur River. Lake Baikal, believed to be about 25 million years old, is one of the deepest lakes in the world; it contains nearly one-fifth of the globe's lake water. More than 1,000 varieties of plants, fish, and animals are unique to the lake. To its north, sandwiched between the Sayan and Yablonoi ranges and the Yenisei and Lena rivers, is the broad central Siberian plateau. Although its altitude is generally about 2,000 feet above sea level, it occasionally rises to 6,000 feet. The plateau is dissected by numerous mighty rivers, including the 2,500-mile-long Ob and the 2,300-mile-long Yenisei.

Further to the east, along the eastern Arctic Ocean and the Sea of Okhotsk, in the valleys of the Lena, Kolyma, Amur, and Ussuri, stretches eastern Siberia, or the Russian Far Eastern Region. Eastern Siberia, the traditional destination of large numbers of Russian political and criminal exiles, has become an area of growing strategic importance. It has been a source of discord between China and Russia since the 1960s. The Far Eastern Region, on which China has made sizable territorial claims, is the largest territorial unit of the Russian Federation. It includes southern Sakhalin and the Kurile Islands (seized from Japan after World War II), as well as the autonomous republic of Biro-birdzan, where Stalin tried to establish the Jewish Autonomous Region in 1928. The northern tip of the Russian Far Eastern Region is within 20 miles of Alaska; the southern tip comes close to the Japanese islands and borders on China. The chain of the Kuriles, stretched between the Sea of Okhotsk and the Pacific, forms a stepping stone between the Kamchatka peninsula and Japan.

The Far Eastern Region is the land most distant from the main centers of Russia. To link it with Moscow, the double-tracking of the Trans-Siberian Railroad was completed in 1937; the 1970s saw the Baikal-Amur branch connect Lake Baikal with the Pacific coast. The development of jet-plane communication has also helped to diminish the isolation of the Far Eastern Region. Even so, its strategic position—because of its proximity to the United States, Japan, and China—and its underpopulation make its status rather precarious. Twelve times the size of France, the region is still populated by about 8 million people.

The dwindling numbers of the original inhabitants of Siberia and the Far Eastern Region have been overtaken in the twentieth century by the Russians and Ukrainians. The Chinese, once found throughout the Amur and the Maritime Territory with its 4,000 miles of Pacific seaboard, were expelled at the end of World War II to Manchuria and other parts of China, but are now gradually returning. The population is unevenly distributed and tends to be centered in large towns like Khabarovsk, Komsomolsk, and Vladivostok. The population concentration in the industrial centers is due to the same conditions that make agriculture very difficult throughout most of the Russian north: permafrost, scarcity of rain, and brevity of the agricultural season. The only large expanses of cultivated land in the region are the Amur Basin and the southern Pacific coastal area. Despite some economic progress, the Far Eastern Region is still far from self-supporting in terms of either manufactured goods or food, with the exception of fish. The maritime region has the largest fisheries of the Russian Federation.

The Far Eastern Region also contains considerable mineral wealth, which the Russians have tried to develop, not infrequently with the help of foreign capital. Besides huge resources of timber, oil, water power, furs, and fish, the region contains diamonds, gold, mercury, mica, tin, and tungsten. The USSR was the second largest producer of gold after South Africa. Since the fragmentation of the Soviet Union in 1991, most of this wealth has been inherited by the Russian Federation. The inaccessibility of many of these minerals and the high cost of their production, however, reduce their practical value.

Rainfall and Crops

The dearth of rainfall is one of the most serious natural handicaps of the area of the Russian Federation. More than a third of its territory has an average annual rainfall and snowfall considered insufficient for agriculture or successful stock-rearing. Indeed, few districts enjoy the average North American rainfall. As a consequence, in many places even a slight shift of the moisture is not well distributed. In the south, where the soil is good, much of the desperately needed rain comes in the form of heavy thunderstorms, which cause short, lush springs that soon fade into hot, arid summers. Throughout most of the extreme north, especially in the tundra regions, the cold and lack of rain are the two climatic enemies of the region's inhabitants. Verkhoyansk, in northern Siberia, is the coldest human settlement on earth; the thermometer there often drops to minus 120 degrees Fahrenheit. Only where a chain of mountains blocks off the arctic winds and intercepts the rain clouds does the climate change dramatically, as in the Crimea and the Caucasus.

Climate and soil have shaped the mentality of the people and the character of farming. The long severe winters mean short growing periods and so dictate the nature of the crops. Winter wheat, for example, is grown in the region of Rostov-on-Don and along the northwestern coast of the Caspian Sea; in eastern Siberia there are no winter crops whatsoever. Some 40 percent of the soil of the Russian Federation lies within the permafrost zone where the subsurface soil is permanently frozen to a depth of several hundred feet.

Each geographical zone has its own form of vegetation. In the tundra there is neither forest nor agriculture; only primitive cattle breeding (mostly reindeer farming) is possible. Likewise, in the northern forest zone there is little agricultural development. In contrast, the black soil belt, which has its widest expanse in Ukraine and from there stretches eastward in a narrowing triangle into western Siberia, is blessed with fertile humus, rich in organic matter and minerals. A wide variety of crops have been cultivated throughout this belt: wheat, beet roots, flax, tobacco, sunflowers. There are large deposits of minerals—iron ore and coal. The steppe is more favorable to cattle breeding because agriculture would require intense irrigation.

Seas and Waterways

The Russian Federation is surrounded by ten seas, most of them frozen over during a good part of the year. The Baltic gives the northwestern part of European Russia indirect access to the North Sea and thus to the Atlantic Ocean. The main Baltic ports are now St. Petersburg and the enclave of Kaliningrad, the broader access to the Baltic Sea being blocked by the three independent states: Estonia, Latvia, and Lithuania. Through the Turkish straits (the Bosporus and the Dardanelles), the Black Sea, the northern shore of which went to the Ukrainian Republic in 1991, connects the southwest-

ern part of the Russian Federation with the Mediterranean. Through the Suez Canal, it connects with the Indian Ocean. Five seas of the Arctic Ocean touch its northernmost lands and three of the Pacific Ocean (Bering, Okhotsk, and the Sea of Japan) wash Russia's Far Eastern maritime frontiers. There are also the two landlocked seas—the Caspian and the Aral—but they are, for all practical purposes, large salty, shallow lakes. The principal Caspian ports are Astrakhan, Krasnovodsk, and Baku.

The long coastline of the Russian Federation is rather deceptive, for the bulk of their territories is located far from seas and oceans. Paradoxically, despite the ten seas that surround it, the Federation is the most landlocked country in the world, because of the loss of the three Baltic Republics, Lithuania, Latvia, and Estonia, as well as the Ukraine and the Caucasian states.

The maritime coast of the Federation is split into four main sectors: the Black Sea, the Baltic, the Arctic and its subsidiary, the White Sea, and the Pacific Ocean. The Arctic Ocean and the White Sea have been a negligible factor, both politically and economically, in Russia's development. And it was not until the eighteenth century that the Russians reached both the Baltic and the Black seas. Maritime communications between the Black Sea and the Baltic were difficult enough, but between them and the Pacific the problems were formidable.

It is a severe strategic and economic handicap that most of the Russian ports are icebound for a considerable part of the year. Oddly enough, Murmansk, the northernmost Russian harbor, is an exception, for the benign Gulf Stream washes this sector of the Arctic coast and makes it generally accessible. On the other hand, the shores of the Gulf of Finland, including the ports of St. Petersburg and Kronstadt are frozen from November to April. As a rule, the harbor of Sevastopol, on the Black Sea, where the Russian Federation has retained a naval base in the midst of the Ukrainian sovereign terri-

Seas and Rivers of Eurasia

tory, is also ice-blocked throughout January and February. Vladivostok, precariously suspended at the end of the long Trans-Siberian railroads and situated in a region claimed by China, is icebound for four months in the winter.

If until the 1960s the seas played a relatively small part in Russia's history, the rivers have not. They have had a decisive influence on the destiny of the entire Euroasiatic area and the formation of the Muscovite-Russian state. All told, the area has about 180,000 miles of rivers. The intricate system of rivers that intersects the Eurasian plain has been an important channel of communication. In the past, long, swift, navigable rivers have enabled the Russians to travel more widely than the people of Central or Western Europe. By cutting through forest and marshes, the rivers have deprived these natural obstacles of much of their forbidding character. They have always provided highways for boats and barges in the summer and for skis and sleds in the winter. The main rivers of the European part of Eurasia (the Dvina, Dnieper, Don, Donets, and Volga) all radiate from the Great Russian plain, not far from Moscow; they originate from either the Valdai Plateau of some 1,000 feet or the marshes and lakes of the central region. Most of them flow in a north-south direction. The city of Moscow started its fantastic imperial career as a settlement at the crossroads of the two greater waterways and trunk lines of trade: the Caspian-Baltic axis of rivers and portages and the west-east route from the western Dvina to the Volga. Thus the city eventually became a natural pivot of the Eurasian empire that its rulers founded.

Of the half-million rivers and streams of the Euroasiatic area, the longest are the Amur (2,900 miles), which stretches along most of the Russian-Chinese frontier and empties into the Sea of Okhotsk, the Lena (2,860 miles), the Ob (2,287 miles), and the Yenisei (2,300 miles). The longest of Russia's European rivers, the Volga, is about the same length (2,300 miles). Most Russian streams, with their western banks higher than the

eastern, meander lazily through the plains. When the snows melt, the rivers often flood the low-lying areas and cause much damage. In European Russia, the economic value of the main rivers is largely curtailed by the nature of the seas into which they empty: The northern Dvina flows to the icy White Sea, the Don empties into the Black Sea, whose outlets are controlled by Turkey, and "Mother Volga" reinforces the dwindling water resources of the Caspian. The Volga has more than a thousand tributaries and drains an area the size of Germany, France, and England combined. As Russia's Mississippi, it winds leisurely from the Belorussian forests to the shores of the Caspian, and through its tributary, the Kama, it extends far to the east, beyond the Urals, and approaches the proximity of the powerful west Siberian river, the Ob.

Slavic Family of Nations

The absence of serious natural obstacles in European Russia has permitted an easy flow of people and invites control by the strongest, best organized, and most enterprising group. The Russians are the largest branch of the Slavic race, which altogether numbers well over 200 million people. The next largest Slavonic peoples are the Ukrainians and the Poles, with over 52 million and 39 million people, respectively. The Slavs belong to the Indo-European family. The origin of the Slavic settlements in Europe is a controversial issue because conclusive evidence is still lacking on the date of the settlements and on the areas the Slavic tribes initially occupied. For our purposes, it is enough to say that by the sixth century they lived in an area of Europe bounded by the Carpathians, and Dnieper, and the Elbe.

The Russians, together with the Ukrainians, Belorussians, Serbs, and Bulgarians, constitute the eastern segment of the Slavonic family. Their ethos, mores, and mentality have been deeply permeated with the Eastern, Greek Orthodox brand of

Christianity coming from Constantinople. For more than a millennium, the eastern Slavs have been using a modified Greek alphabet while the western Slavs—the Poles, Slovaks, Croats, Slovenes, and Czechs—have clung to the western variety of the Christian religion (mostly Roman Catholicism) and use Latin script.

The cultural split of the Slavonic race has had a substantial impact on East European history. It has lent a specific coloring to the rivalry between the two most dynamic and ambitious Slavic nations, the Russians and the Poles. For a thousand years each has viewed itself as the champion of its respective brand of civilization and way of life. For a thousand years Russians and Poles have argued and fought not so much over the territory between them, for these two antagonists are not, and never have been, immediate neighbors. They have always been separated, by a chain of four peoples: the Letts (or Latvians), the Lithuanians, the Belorussians, and the Ukrainians. The perennial question has been which country shall control, organize, and lead the peoples of the transition zone: the land at the Baltic area, as well as Belorussia and Ukraine.

The Russians' feud with the Poles, of course, has not been the sole source of unrest and wars in Eastern Europe. Another great conflict has been that between the Russians and the restless and mercurial Ukrainians, the second largest Slavic group that controls vast natural resources and is placed in a highly strategic location along the northern shores of the Black Sea.

Since the sixteenth century the Muscovite-Russian state has been a multinational structure. For as Kliuchevsky stresses in his monumental *History of Russia*, migration, colonization, and conquest have been fundamental facts of Russian history. When faced with open "frontiers," or large empty spaces such as Siberia in the sixteenth and seventeenth centuries or Ukraine (which literally means "frontier") in the eighteenth and nineteenth centuries, Russian expansion has been both swift and dramatic. The same applies to the expansion toward the south, on the shores of the Black and Caspian Seas in the Caucasus and in Central Asia.

No single factor can adequately explain this steady, truly phenomenal Russian expansion. Neither the relative weakness of the neighboring peoples, nor the lack of natural barriers confronting the Russians, nor their compulsion to reach the sea and acquire warm-water ports, nor even the Muscovite sense of messianic mission, tells the whole story. The restless, elemental impulses that have compelled the Russian people to wander further and further in search of new lands and fresh conquests are among the most controversial subjects of modern geopolitics as well as psychohistory.

As a result of their imperial expansion, the Russian people formed a large empire that incorporated many peoples alien to Russian cultural tradition; it lasted for almost four centuries. Despite all the painful territorial losses suffered as a result of the disintegration of the multinational Soviet Union in 1991, the Russian state, now called a Federation, is also a conglomeration of a variety of ethnic groups. Besides the Russians, who form over 80 percent of the Federation's population, there are about one hundred other ethnic groups, the most numerous being the Tatars. There are three Tatar entities: Volga Tatars, the Siberian Tatars, and those of Crimea. All three Tatar groups are descendants of the various hordes that invaded the Ukrainian-Russian lands in the thirteenth century and exercised a sort of overlordship for more than two hundred years. The Volga Tatars are to be found along the middle reaches of the Volga and around the city of Kazan. The Siberian Tatars live in the western parts of Siberia near Tomsk and in the Tyumen, Tobolsk, and Tara regions. The Crimean Tatars lived in Crimea until World War II, when Stalin ordered them deported to various distant parts of the USSR because of their alleged pro-German sympathies. Only after 1957 did they begin to return individually to Crimea, now settled mostly by Russian colonists yet belonging to the newly established Ukrainian Republic.

Summary

What, then, is the gist of geopolitical personality? Peninsularity and mosaics of land and sea mark the western extremities of this Euroasian land mass. But the outstanding features of its Russian heartland are its northern location, its massiveness, its position astride Europe and Asia, and its continental isolation from direct maritime routes.

Russia is the only major country of Europe that was never even temporarily a part of the Roman Empire, and it has less in common with the cultural and spiritual heritage of the West. Russia is a typical frontier country and has always lived on the margin of the Western world. In the global view, and in the terminology of the great British political geographer Sir Halford MacKinder in his *Democratic Ideal of Reality*, Russia might be said to be a pivotal part of the "World Island" of which Europe forms merely a fringe. Culturally, the Russians have absorbed both European and Asiatic influences, and in so doing they have produced a unique politico-cultural world of their own that is distinct from both Europe and Asia.

Suggested Reading

For a list of the basic books, atlases, and bibliographic references about the history and geography of Russia and the former Soviet Union, see Paul L. Horecky (Ed.), *Russia and the Soviet Union: A Bibliographic Guide to Western Language Publications* (Chicago: University of Chicago Press, 1965); and Horecky, *Basic Russian Publications: A Selected and Annotated Bibliography on Russia and the Soviet Union* (Chicago: University of Chicago Press, 1965).

More specific information may be derived from the following books:

BOBRICK, BENSON, *East of the Sun: The Epic Conquest and Tragic History of Siberia*. New York: Poseidon Press, 1992.

CHEW, ALLEN F., *An Atlas of Russian History: Eleven Centuries of Changing Borders*. New Haven and London: Yale University Press, 1970 and 1994.

DUBINSKAYA, LIDIYA, *The Soviet Union: A Guide and Reference Book*. Moscow: Raduga Publishers, 1985.

FORSYTH, JAMES, *A History of the Peoples of Siberia: Russia's North Asian Colony 1581–1990*. Cambridge: Cambridge University Press, 1992.

GREGORY, JAMES, *Russian Land, Soviet People*. London and New York: Pegasus, 1968.

HOLZNER, LUTZ AND JEANNE M. KNAPP (EDS.), *Soviet Geography Studies in Our Time. A Festschrift for Paul E. Lydolph*. Milwaukee: The University of Wisconsin, 1987.

HOOSON, DAVID J.M., *The Soviet Union*. Belmont, CA.: Wadsworth Publishing Company, 1966.

JACKSON, WILLIAM A.D., *The Russo-Chinese Borderlands*. Princeton, NJ: Princeton University Press, 1962.

KAISER, J. ROBERT, *The Geography of Nationalism in Russia and the USSR*. Princeton, NJ: Princeton University Press, 1962.

KARASIK, THEODOR W. (ED.), *Russia and Eurasia: Facts and Figures Handbook*. Gulf Breeze, Florida, 1994.

KATZ, ZEV, R. ROGERS, AND F. HARNED (EDS.), *Handbook of Major Soviet Nationalities*. New York: Free Press, 1975.

KOZLOV, VICTOR, *The Peoples of the Union*. Bloomington, IN.: Indiana University Press, 1988.

LYDOLPH, PAUL E., *Geography of the U.S.S.R.*, 5th ed. Elkhart Lake, WI: Misty Valley Publishing, 1990.

MELLOR, ROY, *The Soviet Union and Its Geographic Problem*. New York: Macmillan, 1982.

MIKHAILOV, NIKOLAI N., *Glimpses of the USSR: Its Economy and Geography*. Moscow: Foreign Language Publishing House, 1960.

MILLER, WRIGHT, *Who are the Russian People?* New York: Taplinger, 1973.

MOTYL, ALEXANDER (ED.), *The Post–Soviet Nations: Perspective on the Demise of the USSR*. New York: Columbia University Press, 1992.

Oxford Regional Economic Atlas: U.S.S.R. and Eastern Europe. New York: Oxford University Press, 1963.

PARKER W.H., *An Historical Geography of Russia*. Chicago: Aldine Publishing Company, 1969.

SHABAD, THEODORE, *Geography of the U.S.S.R.: A Regional Survey.* New York: Columbia University Press, 1951.

SHOW, DENIS J. B., *The Post-Soviet Republics.* New York: Wiley, 1995.

———, *Russia in the Modern World.* Oxford: Blackwell, 1999.

WESSON, ROBERT G., *The Russian Dilemma: A Political and Geopolitical View.* New Brunswick, NJ: Rutgers University Press, 1974.

WIXMAN, RONALD, *The Peoples of the USSR.* New York: M.E. Sharpe, 1988.

Chapter 2

The Russian State Tradition

Human beings are shaped not only by their physical environment, but also by generations of history. Without entering into intricate controversies about the origins of Russia as a state, one may say that the first large-scale organization to function on the territory of the former Soviet Union was the work of the Norman warrior-traders (known as Vikings), interacting with local Slavic and Finnish elements.

By 862, the Vikings or Varangians, whom the Finns called *Ruotsi* and the local Slavs *Rusi*, had managed to organize the hitherto rather amorphous host of Slavic and Finnish tribes along the Volkov–Dnieper waterway into a loose federation of towns and trading stations. This unique structure actually more resembled the East India or Hudson Bay Companies of a latter era than it did a medieval feudal state. The federation, often called by its Finnish-Normal name of *Rus*, centered around the most important commercial emporium, the city of Kiev, strategically situated at the junction of the Dnieper and the Desna rivers. The Volkov–Dnieper waterway was a major trade route that connected the Baltic and Black seas, and thus linked Scandinavia with the most powerful center of the early medieval world—the East Roman or Byzantine Empire. The Byzantine Empire, with its capital, Constantinople, was at that time a large market for furs, wax, hides, amber, and slaves, thus attracting merchants from all over the world. Among them were the adventurous Norman Vikings, who tried to get there from Scandinavia not only through the Mediterranean, then largely controlled by the Arabs, but also through the combined overland and water route leading from the Gulf of Finland through the Volkov and the Dnieper to the Black Sea. The Slavs and Finns through whose area the Vikings passed must have been impressed by the superior skills and discipline of the Scandinavian warrior-traders, because in 862 they finally submitted to their rule without much opposition.

Kievan Rus

One of the crucial events in the early period of Rus was the acceptance of Christianity in 988 by Prince Vladimir, a descendant of Rurik, the Varangian prince and ruler of Novgorod. Unlike the route of Christianity to the Western Slavs, the Gospel came to Kiev not from Rome, which was becoming an important cultural and political center of the Western world, but from the Eastern Greek or Byzantine Empire, which was already involved in early stages of an ecclesiastic schism with Rome. Along with Greek or Orthodox Christianity, Kievan Rus acquired from Constantinople its written language, its art, and its philosophy of government and State-Church relations. These relations were based on the concept of the unity of secular and religious authority, symbolized in the person of an autocratic ruler, who was both head of the State and of the Church. This unity was the essence of the theory and practice of what is known as *Caesaropapism*. The language the Greek missionaries brought with them to Kiev was a Bulgarian-Macedonian dialect of the region of Saloniki and a modified Greek alphabet. The dialect, which the two chief missionaries of the Southern Slavs, Cyril and Methodius, used in preaching the Gospel to the Slavic tribes in the Balkans and Moravia, soon became the literary and ecclesiastic language of the Kievan state, the present-day Church Slavonic.

The Kievan state was a loose federation of Finnish and Slavic towns and trading stations stretching through the region between the Baltic and Black seas along the Volkov-Dnieper waterway. The Kievan state structure and its establishment were controlled by an oligarchic elite, which was largely of Norman-Varangian stock. The Norman rulers considered Rus as their property and stressed their exercise of power by the collection of tribute. Soon the Viking pirate-traders settled down, intermarried, gradually merged with the natives, and produced the upper social stratum of Kievan nobility. Only they were entitled to own land and to bear arms. Gradually, they also came to supply candidates for higher ecclesiastic offices that initially had been overwhelmingly occupied by Greeks. The northern segment of the Kievan federation, centering around Novgorod, developed a mixture of urban oligarchy and participatory democracy exemplified by popular assemblies of all free citizens; this system, after the Mongol invasions of the thirteenth century, was largely limited to Novgorod and a few cities in the north like Pskov. Kiev, more under Byzantine influence and in danger of constant raids by the nomadic tribes of Asia, stuck to a more autocratic system of government.

In the eleventh and twelfth centuries, Rus reached a high level of economic and cultural development. While agriculture and handicraft played some role in the life of the federation, trade with Byzantium, Persia and Scandinavia was the life blood of the Kievan state. Trade, however, especially with the south, was constantly hampered by raids by the barbarian tribes that emerged from the steppes of Central Asia, one wave after another. During the twelfth century, these constant attacks by the nomadic tribes undermined the Kievan federation's commerce and depopulated and ruined its eastern approaches. Consequently, the population of Kievan Rus began to migrate in two directions. One stream flowed west, toward the region of the western Bug and the upper Dniester, to Volhynia and Galicia; another migratory movement flowed northward toward the lands of the Oka, the Moskva, and the upper Volga. There marshes and forests provided a natural shelter against the devastating raids of the nomads. The nomadic invasions chased the population from the ravaged southern regions and thereby contributed to the settlement of the central forest lands, destined to be the heartland of the future Muscovite-Russian state.

The final blow to the decaying Kievan federation was dealt by the Mongol or Tatar invasions of the thirteenth century. The Tatars, who originally inhabited the Mongolian plateau north of the Gobi desert, were a savage, fast-growing group of horsemen, herdsmen, and hunters. One of the Tatar chieftains, Ghengis Khan, united the quarreling tribes and marched against his overlord, the Emperor of China. The Tatars broke through the Great Wall and captured Peking in 1215. After having enlisted the services of Chinese military and administra-

The Tatar Empire in Europe from Thirteenth to Fifteenth Centuries

tive experts, the Tatars turned toward Central Asia, Iran, Northern India, and, finally, Europe. In 1236, they appeared on the Volga, and in the spring of 1237 invaded the Dnieper valley. Kiev was captured and razed in December 1240, while most of its people were slaughtered. The Tatars devastated the land—burning, pillaging, and taking thousands of slaves, mostly women and children. Only the main city of northern Rus, Novgorod, was spared—through the payment of tribute.

After having destroyed Kievan Rus, the Mongols proceeded westward toward Poland, Bohemia, and Hungary. In April 1241, they crushed a mixed Polish-Bohemian-German force at Legnica (Liegnitz) in Silesia. In 1242, a struggle for succession after the death of Ghengis Khan prevented the Tatars, who had meanwhile reached the Adriatic Sea, from exploiting their unprecedented victories. The Mongol invaders withdrew to their base in Mongolia, abandoning Poland, Bohemia, and Hungary, but not the bulk of the Kievan Federation.

The Emergence of Moscow

The Tatar raids were one of the worst plagues that Eastern Europe as a whole suffered during the Middle Ages. For the lands of Kievan Federation, they were a catastrophe. Wasted and depopulated for generations, contacts with the west were made very difficult. As a result, the lands of the Dnieper valley, as well as the territories to their northeast around Vladimir and Moscow, stagnated under the Tatar yoke. The Tatars, who themselves converted to Islam only in the fourteenth century, were tolerant in religious affairs but greedy for tribute and slaves, especially women and children. Many survivors of the Tatar raids fled to the north and northeast. As a consequence of the catastrophe that had ruined the Kievan Rus, during the thirteenth and fourteenth centuries the lands around present-day Moscow were gradually settled by refugees from the south who sought shelter in the northern forests from the repeated Tatar raids. The city of Moscow stood on the Moskva River, which had great economic importance because it connected the river system of the middle Oka, with that of the upper Volga. The population attracted to its lands and the large volume of trade on the Moskva River brought in taxes and customs duties.

The princes of Moscow, although also vassals of the Tatar rulers, skillfully profited from the location of their capital at the intersection of two important migration and trade routes that went from the north to the northeast and from the north to the south. To facilitate the collection of tribute, the Tatar Khans would appoint one of the native princes to act as their instrument in administering the conquered lands on behalf of the Tatars. Since the princes of Muscovy struck the Khans as the most willing and obsequious of the princes of Rus, they were appointed tax collectors and administrators of justice on behalf of the Tatars. This gave to the Muscovite princes definite advantages over the other regional rulers and descendants of Rurik and thus launched them on an unprecedented imperial career.

While enjoying the favors of the Tatars as their agents, the rulers of Muscovy took advantage of their position to enhance their power and enlarge their domain. Their policy combined shrewd marriages with conquest and purchase of surrounding territory. While princely domains around them were subdivided, Muscovite rulers as a rule willed their inheritance to the oldest son. Freedom from Tatar raids and relative prosperity attracted settlers, commerce, and gave Moscow prosperity as well as political prestige. In the fourteenth century, the privileged and sheltered city also attracted the metropolitans of Kiev, who eventually settled in Moscow. They enjoyed the relative safety of the city and the protection of its rulers. Thus, by the end of the fourteenth century, Moscow had emerged as the most important political and ecclesiastic center of the Tatar-controlled portion of the former Kievan state.

The other parts of the now atomized former Kievan federation had a different fate. The city-republic of Novgorod, far away to the north and sheltered from the Tatar raids through its location behind the belt of forest and marshes, developed into an affluent trading center. The city soon joined the powerful German commercial league, the Hansa, and prospered on fur, hides, wax, and all sorts of naval stores, until the close of the fifteenth century. The westernmost fringes of the former Kievan federation—present-day Belorussia, western Ukraine, or Volhynia, and

Podalia—fell under the influence of Lithuania and Poland, both better able to protect their inhabitants from Tatar encroachments. At the end of the fourteenth century, Poland and Lithuania established a personal union, and set up a confederation known as the Polish-Lithuanian Commonwealth. The Commonwealth was to last for about four centuries, until its partition at the end of the eighteenth century. Meanwhile, during the fourteenth and fifteenth centuries, by skillfully combining dynastic marriages and conquests, the Lithuanians and Poles acquired most of the Dvina-Dnieper waterway. The Grand Duchy of Muscovy and the City republic of Novgorod, however, remained outside their reach.

Muscovy as Heir of the Tatars and Byzantium

The middle of the fifteenth century opened great vistas to the ambitious Muscovite rulers. The Turks captured Constantinople in 1453, while the decaying Golden Horde split into three Khanates: Kazan and Astrakhan on the Volga, and Crimea, the black Sea Peninsula. Each of these splits was in turn exploited by the princes of Moscow. By far the most important was the final disintegration of the Golden Horde. Seeing the growing weakness of the Tatars, Ivan III (1440–1505) simply refused to pay his annual tribute and homage in 1480. The Tatars, divided among themselves, were unable to reassert their power. Thus the "Mongol yoke" undramatically disappeared overnight. Yet it left as lasting an imprint on the people and lands that had been under their overlordship as any other single factor in Muscovite-Russian history. The Mongol yoke lasted in Rus for some 240 years, roughly from 1240 to 1480, longer than any other epoch in the history of the land. (The subsequent Muscovite period lasted only 223 years, from 1480 to 1703; the imperial era stretched for 214 years, from 1703 to 1917, while the Soviet period existed a mere 74 years, from 1917 to 1991.)

The "yoke" has had a far-reaching and lasting effect on Muscovite-Russian mentality and institutions. First, Rus, isolated from Western influences, never used Roman law or partook in the great religious movements of the West. It was not affected by the Renaissance, the Reformation, and the development of flourishing urban centers and universities. Second, for nearly ten generations the Russian princes watched with awe, envy, and admiration the military skills and political efficiency of the Tatars. They tended to ascribe the Tatar successes primarily to the iron discipline and slavish obedience enforced by the Khans not only on their conquered peoples, but also on their own subjects. This bolstered the latent autocratic tradition taken over from Byzantium. Medieval Muscovite society was overwhelmingly dependent on the autocratic ruler who, following the Tatar patterns, subjugated all social and ethnic groups and made them serve his purposes.

Moveover, the Muscovite rulers took over from their Tatar masters many political and administrative institutions. For instance, the census, tax collection, and postal system of the Muscovite state, as well as its methods of spying and torturing were borrowed from the Mongol Tatars. Since they admired Tatar military efficiency, the Muscovite princes tried to imitate their pattern of army organization, training, and tactics. Up to recent times these traditions were still visible, for example, in the scouting tactics of the Cossacks. The Tatar influence could for centuries also be observed in a variety of details: in the long, oriental dress of the Muscovite people, in their cooking, in their vocabulary. For instance, the Russian words for whip, shackles, inn, horse, money, and treasury are of Mongol origin; so too is the word "cossack." Finally, during centuries of coexistence, a great deal of Tatar blood has been injected into Muscovite veins. A considerable segment of the Russian aristocracy traced its origins to the Tatar princes.

After the overthrow of the Mongol domination in 1480, Muscovite rulers continued to follow the Tatar examples: They regarded the persons and possessions of their subjects as their property, and the entire land as a source of tribute and recruits. The tribute the Muscovite rulers used to levy for the Tatars was now collected for their own benefit. The main purpose for their despotic regime was to continue squeezing the maximum income out of the people, as the Tatars had done. The relations of the Muscovites with the conquered ethnic groups were also shaped by Tatar patterns. Thus, Tatar rule molded a society deficient in those political, economic, and cultural institutions the existence of which is a precondition of a pluralistic body politic of the Western type. These deficiencies in civil institutions were felt by all Muscovites, both the rulers and the ruled.

The second important event of the fifteenth century was the capturing of Constantinople by the Ottoman Turks in 1453 and the subsequent downfall of the Byzantine Empire. Moscow's connections with Constantinople were largely limited to the acceptance of the traditional primacy of its patriarchate over all other regional Orthodox Churches. With passing generations, the umbilical cord uniting the Orthodox Church of the Rus-Muscovy had become weaker. The cultural-spiritual dependence of Moscovy on Constantinople was largely channeled through the Orthodox hierarchy; traditionally, the bishops and metropolitans, although actually chosen by the Grand Prince, were endorsed by the Byzantine Patriarchs. This began to change after 1439, when the Muscovite Church rejected the accord of the Union of Florence between the Greek Orthodox Church of Constantinople and Rome as an act of apostasy. The Grand Duke of Muscovy immediately took advantage of the break and began to appoint his own bishops without any reference to the Patriarch of Constantinople. The last vestiges of traditional dependence on the senior Orthodox patriarchate disappeared almost automatically when the capital of the Byzantine Empire, Constantinople, fell into the hands of the "infidel" Turkish Sultan in 1453.

As a consequence of the capture of Constantinople and the overthrow of the Tatar yoke, the Grand Dukes of Muscovy emerged as the only fully sovereign Orthodox rulers of importance. Ivan III married a daughter of the last Emperor of Byzantium, took over his coat of arms, the black double-headed eagle, and assumed the title of "Caesar," or *Tsar* in Russian. The old theory that the church could not exist without active state support was now reemphasized in Moscow with increased vigor. The Grand Dukes of Muscovy reasserted their role as heads of the Orthodox Church, the secular vicars of Christ on earth. Thus, the Caesaropapist theory was revised and reemphasized.

After 1453, Muscovy came to regard itself as the sole citadel of the Orthodoxy, beleaguered by infidels, heretics, and apostates, while the Grand Duke of Muscovy was its sole secular shield. This was immediately acknowledged by the Muscovite hierarchy, eager to assure itself a protector against internal and external dangers: a reform movement at home, and the Catholic Church of Poland-Lithuania in the west. In return for this protection, the Muscovite clergy, brought up in the centuries-old tradition of Byzantine Caesaropapist submission, gave the autocrat its full support. The popular saying, "One God in Heaven, one Sovereign on Earth," was strongly backed by the hierarchy. As a Muscovite monk, Joseph of Volokolamsk, put it: "In his mortal form [the Tsar] resembles all men, but in his power he is like unto Almighty God." Moreover, the Orthodox Church provided the Muscovite monarchy with a whole array of convenient legends, one of which traced Rurik's ancestry to Emperor Augustus of Rome. The crowning piece of this mythmaking was the allegation that Moscow was the "Third Rome." This was suggested in the greetings sent to Basil III around 1515 by Monk Philotheos, Abbot of Pskov monastery:

The Church and ancient Rome fell because of the Apollinarian heresy; as the second Rome, the Church of Constantinople, it has been hewn by the axes of Ishmaelites; but this third new Rome, the Holy Apostolic Church, under Thy mighty rule, shines throughout the entire world more brightly than the sun. All the Orthodox Christian realms have converged into their own. Thou art the sole Autocrat of the Universe, the only Caesar of the Christians. . . . Two Romes have fallen, but the Third stands, and no fourth can ever be. . . .

Soon the Messianic message of Abbot Philotheos, combined with the dynastic claims of the Rurik dynasty and Slavic nationalistic urges, became the program of the Muscovite Tsars, and later of the Russian Emperors. Gradually, the doctrine of Moscow as "the Third Rome" evolved into a highly complex national and religious philosophy and survived to modern times, accompanied by various historically conditioned interpretations. Up to the time of the Revolution of 1917, all Russian rulers—autocratic heads of State as well as secular heads of the Orthodox Church of the Empire—embodied the Caesaropapist concept of power, both spiritual and temporal.

The Muscovite System

The second half of the fifteenth century produced in Muscovy a unique political system, a blend of Mongol despotism, Byzantine Caesaropapism, and local Slavic-Finnish tradition. This peculiar system was already striking at the time of Basil III (1505–1533), son and successor of Ivan III, and father of Ivan IV, or "the Terrible" (1533–1584). This phenomenon puzzled Baron Sigmund Herberstein, who traveled to Russia as the Ambassador of Holy Roman emperors Maximilian I and Ferdinand I. Herberstein noted in his diary that the Tsar had unlimited control over the lives and property of his subjects. Nobody dared to oppose him. His will was God's will. "These people enjoy slavery more than freedom," noted the German observer. The perceptive Frenchman, Marquis de Custine, who went to the Russia of Nicholas I in 1839, summed up his observations by concluding that "The political state of Russia may be defined in one sentence: it is a country in which the government says what it pleases, because it alone has the right to speak. . . ."

Parallel to the consolidation of Tsarist theocratic absolutism was the shaping of social system, the foundation of which was the attachment to the land of most of the rural population. The primitive conditions of Russia's economy resulted in a shortage of ready cash. This made the rulers of Muscovy pay their servants not in money but in landed estates. As officers and officials, servants would be granted by their rulers landed estates on the condition of service, which terminated only by death or severe illness of the grantee. The estates could be sold, exchanged, or even passed from father to son only with the prince's permission, and only on condition of continuing service by the new owner. To allow this new class of landed gentry to serve the sovereign, the gentry had to be assured that their lands would be duly cultivated. Hence peasants were assigned to the estates and obliged to cultivate the master's land. In return, the masters would leave a certain amount of that land to the peasant for his family's support.

The right of freedom to roam about had been firmly rooted in the customary law of the early Kievan Rus. The Russian peasant could go where he pleased at a time when his Western counterpart was still tied to the land. But as Tatar raids and exactions caused a severe scarcity of manpower, the princes and landowners resorted to all sorts of tricks to limit the right of movement and fix the fluid population to the land. Ultimately, this came to be applied not only to the peasants but also to the members of the prince's retinue, who had customarily been free to enroll in the service of a prince of their choice. The enserfment of the peasants was closely intertwined with the attachment of the gentry to their estates. Since the masters were also magistrates for their peasants, the power of the lord over his "souls" (as the serfs were called) was for all practical purposes complete, despite the vestigial legal limitations.   By the middle of the seventeenth century, the serfs were already treated like chattel; they were bought and sold, exchanged and pawned; they lost the right to appeal to the state against the injustices of their owners.   The only exception to this was high treason.   Since they owned serfs, the Muscovite gentry were in turn bondsmen of the all-powerful Autocrat.   As his vassals, they were at the mercy of the despot; they owned the land only as long as they served their sovereign; like the serfs, they also could be deprived of land, moved from one job to another, or transferred to a different place.

Thus, the peculiarities of Muscovy's social development were largely shaped by a mixture of Byzantine and Tatar traditions.   The forces that opposed the rise of royal absolutism in the West were either very weak or altogether absent in Muscovy-Russia.   The Church was shackled by its Greek Caesaropapist heritage; unlike the Western Church, it never claimed equality with, let along superiority over, secular rule.   The Orthodox hierarchy never produced its Gregory VII or Innocent III.   It had experienced neither its struggle for investiture nor its Canossa.[1]   This political dependence had far-reaching consequences. Pressed by Islam and by Roman Catholicism, the Orthodox Church became withdrawn, intolerant, xenophobic, and largely ignorant.   It did not develop an intense intellectual life or a deeper involvement in vital social issues. Unlike the Western churches, it never founded universities. As early as the sixteenth century, it was no longer an autonomous body that could counterbalance the growing power of the state, but meekly submitted to it and eventually came to act like its agency.   Until the end, in Muscovy-Russia the Church was the subservient instrument of the State.

The feudal lords were another social force that could have challenged the autocracy, but in Muscovy the nobles were never as strong and well organized as in Central or Western Europe.   Hereditary property in landed estates existed for a short period of time in Muscovy prior to the consolidation of the grand ducal absolutism at the close of the fifteenth century. After 1480, as soon as Ivan III strengthened his power, he proceeded to replace private property with tenure conditional on service. Between the end of the fifteenth century and 1785, Russian squires held their land on the Tsar's sufferance. Consequently, the Muscovite-Russian nobility was largely composed of shifting elements without deeper local roots; the "serving gentry" was moved from place to place in accordance with the needs of the state or simply at the whim of the Autocrat.

Another social stratum that played a considerable role in the West—the merchants—constituted in Muscovy, an overwhelmingly rural society, a relatively small and weak group.   Moreover, they were also compelled to serve the State, or, more exactly, its ruler, who treated the State as his property.   The only two independent trading communities with an oligarchic tradition, the northern, largely commercial city-republics of Novgorod and Pskov, were overwhelmed and ruthlessly destroyed in the fifteenth century by their Muscovite rival.   The rest of the Russian merchant class did not reveal much appetite or ability for self-government, even when offered it during the eighteenth and nineteenth centuries. Alliances between burghers and other social groups or the Crown, so characteristic of Western European development, were never seriously attempted in Muscovy-Russia. The weakness of the Russian bourgeoisie, the historical proponent of liberalism, was striking. This weakness was evident during the period of the "Great Reforms" of the late nineteenth century and during the constitutional period of 1905–1917. This phenomenon may be traced to the traditional weakness and passivity of the Russian merchant class, and its subservience to the Autocrat.

---

[1] A humble pilgrimage to get papal forgiveness was made by the Holy Roman Emperor of the German nation, Henry IV, to Canossa in 1077.

Muscovite Expansion

Besides the quick consolidation of Tsarist absolutism and the enserfment of the peasants, another characteristic feature of Muscovite-Russian development was the phenomenal territorial expansion of Muscovy in all directions. With the annexation of the Tatar city-states Kazan and Astrakhan during the sixteenth century, Muscovy acquired its first major non-Slavic territory. From the Volga bases a rapid, largely spontaneous, movement developed; it proceeded eastward beyond the Urals and toward the Caspian Sea, Central Asia, and the Pacific Ocean. Siberia, a subcontinent larger than the United States, was conquered in a short sixty-two years by groups of Cossack adventurers and common criminals. By 1643, the Muscovites were already on the Pacific coast. Muscovy's territorial expansion was unprecedented in history. In 1300 the Duchy of Muscovy covered approximately 20,000 square kilometers; in 1462, when Ivan III ascended the throne, it reached 430,000 and continued to grow at the rate of 35,000 square kilometers a year for the next century and a half. As early as 1600 it was as large as the rest of Europe, and by the middle of the seventeenth century—even before the conquests of Peter the Great—Muscovy was the largest country in the world. Thus, the Russians managed to build a huge empire before they became a nation in the modern sense of the term. This priority of foreign, colonial expansion over domestic problems has been one of the striking features of Russia's historic evolution.

There are many reasons for Muscovy's expansion that go far beyond the desire to "gather the hereditary lands of Rurik," often proclaimed by many Russian historians, or the overrated "urge to the sea." Not the least important of these was the perpetual hunger for fresh resources, especially agricultural; in a primitive, extensive economy, more and more land was needed. Every new conquest was usually followed by the deportation of large groups of the local population usually to the northern parts of the land, and by

Muscovite peasant colonization. As the great Russian historian, Vasily O. Kliuchevsky, bluntly put it: "Colonization is the essence of Russian history." Colonization and also colonialism were accompanied by distribution of landed estates to deserving officers, officials, and Orthodox monasteries. Of some 800,000 serfs whom Catherine II (1762–1796) presented as gifts to her supporters and lovers during her reign, well over half came from the lands seized from the partition of Poland-Lithuania. These expansive and centralistic tendencies were paralleled by the desire to proselytize and spread the Russian language and culture and the Greek Orthodox faith to the farthest Tsarist domains.

By the beginning of the nineteenth century, with the incorporation of Finland (1809) and central Poland (1815), about half of the Empire's population was composed of ethnic minorities. Yet the autocracy insisted on treating the Empire as if it were a unitary state and tried to impose its absolutist system on all its subjects. Whatever special powers St. Petersburg was compelled to concede to certain parts of the Empire (like the constitutions of the Grand Duchy of Finland between 1809 and 1899 or of the Kingdom of Poland between 1815 and 1831) were reluctantly given and only under pressure. In 1462 the Grand Duchy of Muscovy extended over 24,000 square kilometers, while the Tsarist Empire in 1914 ruled over 3.5 million square kilometers. The speed of expansion of the Russian state was without precedent in history.

Largely as a result of its westward expansion, by the second half of the sixteenth and the beginning of the seventeenth century, Muscovy—like Japan in the nineteenth century—came into ever closer contact with the more advanced outside world, especially Sweden and Germany. The Tsars' realization that Western civilization was technologically superior made them launch a series of reforms aimed mainly at modernizing their backward instruments of power and imperial expansion. Consequently, most reforms were limited to military and naval matters and rejected Western ideas and the political institutions that stood behind them.

The most striking representative of the new dynasty that ascended the Muscovite throne in 1613—the Romanovs—was Peter I, known as "the Great," (1682–1725). Peter was bent on quick modernization of his domain. Impatient, restless, and often reckless, Peter brought a large number of Western teachers and technical experts to Muscovy, and with them embarked upon a policy of streamlining his backward state by introduction of Western technology. His reforms were not so much introduced as inflicted on his subjects. Those who opposed them, he punished harshly. He reorganized the old Muscovite Army and founded the Russian Navy. Peter fostered education by means equally as ruthless as those he employed in his other reforms. It was he who laid the foundation of modern Russian industry. The brunt of his reforms was borne by the peasant masses already firmly shackled by serfdom and assigned to the land to serve the gentry. Peter went one step further and put all of the peasant's property, as well as his body, at the master's disposal. He also granted to the gentry the right to increase the peasant's obligations at will, and even to send him to penal servitude. Beards, a symbol of the old mores, were forbidden or taxed if tolerated.

The rule of Peter the Great marked the last stage in the process of chaining the Orthodox Church to the State. In 1721, Peter abolished the office of the Patriarch and substituted a Church Council, the Holy Synod, composed of bishops, but headed by a lay official appointed by the Tsar. The clergy became simply a part of a huge bureaucratic machine by means of which Peter ruled his expanding realm. The treatment of Russian Orthodox clergymen as government officials continued after Peter's reign. This included the payment of salaries as well as the award of ranks and orders. Until 1863, junior members of the clergy were submitted to flogging, like enlisted men in the armed forces.

Peter's desire to obtain access to the sea, to

Peter the Great

open "a window to the West," implied a challenge to Sweden, then the master of the Baltic. The protracted conflict, known in history as the "Great Northern War" (1699–1721), was concluded by the Treaty of Nystadt (1721). As a result of his triumph over Sweden, Peter acquired the entire south coast of the Gulf of Finland, including Ingria, Estonia, and Livonia. Peter, who hated Moscow as a symbol of the old, largely medieval traditions, built a new capital in the Finnish marshes at the mouth of the Neva River on the land newly conquered from Sweden. From 1703 to 1918, St. Petersburg, not "Holy Moscow," was the capital of the Empire. After the end of the Great Northern War, the Tsardom of Muscovy was officially renamed the "Russian Empire," the new term "Russia" being the Latinized form of "Rus."

The rule of Peter the Great imposed upon the still backward Russia a full-scale cultural revolution. Not only was the country reshaped politically, but even their vocabulary was profoundly reshaped by the forcible imposition of over 3,000 foreign words of German, Dutch, English, Swedish, French, and Latin words, one-fourth of them naval, one-fourth military and the rest of administrative, commercial, medical, or architectural terms. Most of them have survived up to our times.

Peter's Successors

Under Peter's successors, reformatory zeal slackened considerably for two generations or so, but was felt strongly by Catherine II (1762–1796). Her long rule, most successful in the international arena, was marred, however, by her neglect of socioeconomic issues, especially of the soaring peasant problem. By the close of the eighteenth century the issue of serfdom became the dominant issue of the Tsarist Empire. Elevated to the throne by a camarilla of aristocratic officers, Catherine freely distributed estates and serfs to her supporters and lovers. Since peasants working on the estates belonging to the Crown enjoyed a better legal and economic status, their transfer to private hands meant a considerable worsening of their lot. During Catherine's reign, the lot of the serf population and its legal and economic situation hit bottom, for Catherine not only confirmed the decrees of Peter the Great, but enlarged upon them. For all practical purposes, the status of the serfs was equalized with that of slaves. No wonder, therefore, that from 1773 to 1775 her Empire witnessed the greatest and most horrible of all the peasant rebellions so characteristic of Muscovite-Russian history. The uprising, led by a veteran Cossack, Yemelian Pugachev, shook the very foundation of the Empire, and only the use of a large army crushed the rebellion.

While Peter the Great established Russia firmly on the shores of the Baltic, Catherine II wrested from the Turks the northern littoral of the Black Sea, including the Crimea. During two brilliant campaigns, the Russian fleet roamed the Mediterranean. Catherine was the first Romanov ruler to proclaim loudly that Constantinople was her goal and to claim openly a protectorate over the Christians of the Ottoman Empire. The acquisition of Crimea at the end of the eighteenth century was followed by the establishment of the protectorate over Georgia in 1801 and the gradual conquest of Turkmenistan during the years 1801–1886. Meanwhile Uzbekistan and Kazakstan were crushed and incorporated into the Empire. While establishing their rule astride the Caucasian range, the Russian troops encountered an especially tenacious resistance on the part of a Chechen tribe of uniquely stubborn and courageous guerilla fighters.

A special feature of her reign was her Polish policy. While Peter the Great considered Poland-Lithuania as Russia's protectorate and as a buffer in the West, Catherine partitioned the ancient Commonwealth three times (in 1772, 1793, and 1795), in partnership with Prussia and Austria. The two Teutonic powers annexed most of ethnographic Poland, while Catherine appropriated not only the lands that had formed part of the old Kievan state, like Belorussia and the Ukraine, but also ethnic Lithuania, which had never belonged to "Rurik's patrimony" and was ethnically as well as religiously different from the Russian stock.

In 1815, after the Napoleonic Wars, the acquisition of Central Poland by Alexander I (1801–1825) created a "Polish problem," which became one of the endemic issues of the Tsarist Empire. A series of Polish uprisings (in 1794, 1830–1831, and 1863–1864) had an adverse effect on Russia's domestic stability as well as on its international relations. First, the existence of the highly explosive Polish question created a certain community of interest with the other partitioning powers, Prussia-Germany and Austria, thus strengthening within the Empire the conservative, Teutonic elements. The German influence became very powerful in Tsarist Russia beginning at the time of Peter the Great with his acquisition of the Baltic provinces and their rich and influential German landowning and merchant class. All this created internal tensions and affected Russia's freedom of movement on the international scene, especially toward united Germany. Second, Russia's rule over most of ethnographic Poland, the hotbed of revolu-

Expansion of Russia under Catherine II and the Partitions of Poland 1772, 1793, 1795

tionary, irredentist movements, hampered the Empire's internal evolution; one of the chief arguments of reactionary forces against any liberalization was that national minorities, especially the restless Poles, would seize such an opportunity to claim autonomy and thus undermine the unity of the Empire. Meanwhile, in 1809, Russia annexed Finland and, in 1812, Romanian Bessarabia. As a result, the Tsarist Empire came to control a belt of territories on its western periphery that stretched from the Gulf of Finland to the mouth of the Danube. Most of these lands had a much higher level of civilization than Russia, and their people were reluctant subjects of St. Petersburg, eager either for independence or at least broad autonomy. Thus, by hindering the process of peaceful reform, nationality problems pushed Russia toward a violent upheaval.

For all practical purposes, up to the middle of the eighteenth century the tsars claimed all the lands of their realm as their patrimony and all its inhabitants as servants of the State. This began to change in the second half of the eighteenth century as far as the nobility was concerned. The succession crisis that followed the death of Peter the Great in 1725 allowed the gentry, through a series of palace revolutions, to strengthen its position. By placing on the Tsarist throne several immature and unexperienced monarchs, mainly women and adolescents, the Russian nobility wrested from them important concessions which somewhat limited imperial absolutism. In 1762, the gentry was formally exempted from obligatory state service by Peter III. They were allowed to pursue their private interests and even to travel abroad. Nearly all the monopolies on trade and industry were abolished. In 1785, Catherine II allowed the gentry and the townsmen to form their respective corporate organizations. Moreover, the noblemen were given full and unconditional title to their estates.

Despite these concessions, and despite the influence of the unwieldy bureaucratic machine, the old authoritarian and patrimonial system never disappeared completely.

Although allowing many of its subjects to become rich and educated, the autocracy insisted on preserving its monopoly of political power and refused to share it in the form of truly representative institutions. This rigidity created a paradoxical situation: An increasingly enlightened and prosperous society was forced to tolerate a paternalistic state that rejected any freely elected representative institutions of the Western type. This basic contradiction was a source of tension between the politically minded members of the society and the authorities. By the end of the eighteenth century the Russian gentry, more economically secure, freer from being constantly ordered about, and better informed as a result of exposure to Western ideas, began to think for itself.

Under Catherine's rule, the abolitionist movement was born. In 1790, the son of a gentry family and a customs official, Alexander Radishchev (1749–1802), published his critical volume *Journey from St. Petersburg to Moscow*. In the form of letters to an imaginary friend, Radishchev presented the tragic lot of the serfs and urged abolition of the immoral, inefficient, and degrading institution. The book was confiscated and its author imprisoned and sentenced to death. Eventually the verdict was commuted to ten years of exile in Siberia. Radishchev's *Journey* greatly influenced all subsequent radical and socialist writings of the nineteenth century. He is generally considered a forerunner of the peculiarly Russian phenomenon called *intelligentsia*.

Unlike the Soviet definition of intelligentsia, which equated it with the white-collar class, the old term, which had become a household word by 1860, had a more restricted meaning. Prior to the Bolshevik triumph, the term *intelligentsia* comprised only those critically minded and educated people who were in opposition to the establishment and dedicated to selfless social and educational work on society's behalf. Both missionary spirit and a critical attitude toward the powers that be were regarded as essential features of an intelligentsia. Inspired by a guilt complex and a preoccupation with the messianic, promethean idea of social redemption, members of the intelligentsia often devoted themselves to the cause of social revolution. The revolutionary movement of the Tsarist Empire was inspired, organized, and led overwhelmingly by the intelligentsia. It is impossible to underrate the role of this group in Russia's modern history.

Summary: Imperial Russia in Perspective

Like the Golden Horde or the Ottoman Empire, the old Muscovite state was organized more for warfare than welfare. A sense of responsibility for public well-being came very late, only at the end of the nineteenth century. Unlike Western or Central Europe, no reception of Roman law ever took place in Russia. Following the Tatar example, law was equated with the will or whim of the ruler. Until the Great Reforms of the 1860s, Tsarist jurisprudence did not distinguish between laws, decrees, and administrative ordinances. Only in the nineteenth century was Russian law codified, and even then the codification was inadequate. Until the judiciary reform of 1864, justice was a branch of the administration, and its first concern was not defense of the individual but protection of state interests and enforcement of public order, as interpreted by an autocratic ruler.

The Tsarist Empire was established rapidly, but at the cost of wasting vital resources that should have been invested for constructive domestic purposes. This squandering of both people's energy and money weakened their ability to establish a civil society as well as their ability to form a compact heartland of the sprawling, multiethnic colonial complex in form of a compact national state.

The Russian autocratic system, as it existed with some modification in 1905, until March 1917, made one individual the central pillar of the Empire. The Tsar was not only the symbol of state sovereignty and unity but also its absolute ruler, its supreme executive of government. In this task he was assisted by cabinet ministers who were merely his personal agents. The Emperor was also the supreme legislator, the sole source of law. In this task he was assisted by the Council of State, an institution modeled on the French by Tsar Alexander I in 1810. The Council was composed of high administrative officials and legal experts appointed by the Tsar to help him in drafting legislation. The existence of the Council, like that of the ministers, did not limit the absolute power of the Emperor. The ministers did not share in his power: They were called in only to assist with advice and legal-administrative technicalities. Besides being the supreme executive and the only source of law until 1905, the Russian monarch was also the supreme judge. All verdicts in the Empire were pronounced in his name. In his capacity as supreme judge, the Emperor was assisted by the Senate. In addition to its judicial functions, the Senate exercised supervision over the administrative machinery. Thus the Russian Senate combined some of the functions exercised in the United States by the Supreme Court with those of the administrative tribunals provided for by some European constitutions. The Tsar was also the Supreme Commander-in-Chief of the armed forces, the army and navy. As if all these powers were not sufficient, the Tsar was also the secular head of the Orthodox Church of his Empire. His person was regarded as sacred, and on state occasions he was surrounded by a semireligious ceremony. The Tsar was also the richest landowner of the country: on the eve of the Revolution of 1917, the crown properties covered some 20 million acres of land.

Imperial Russia was not a totalitarian state as we understand the word. It lacked both the will to become one, largely because of its lingering respect for traditional Christian values and for private property, as well as the technical means available to modern dictators. Russia, before 1917, was rather an autocratic, repressive multinational Empire. One of its congenital weaknesses was that it remained purblind to the difficulties of integrating territories that were alien to Russian cultural traditions. A constant struggle to repress irredentist as well as revolutionary ferment was a serious drain on the Empire's resources.

The scope of the Tsarist reprisals against the opposition was on a relatively small scale by contemporary standards. Between 1823 and 1861 only a dozen or so people were executed and only some 14,000 to 15,000 people exiled for political reasons. From the hanging of the five leaders of the "Decembrist" revolt against Nicholas I in 1826 to the downfall of the Tsarist regime in 1917, the number of all death sentences actually carried out on the territory of the Empire amounted to 4,410, according to official statistics. Many of these executions took place under the martial law prevailing between September 1, 1906, and May 3, 1907, when the regime was fighting the unprecedented wave of terrorism that was responsible for the death of 1,969 state officials and 2,535 private individuals. In 1880 there were in the whole Russian Empire only about 1,200 people exiled for political crimes. In 1901 the total number of political exiles amounted to 4,113, and most were living in relative comfort in faraway places assigned to them by the police. After the cruel and despotic rule of Peter the Great, mass executions without trial or mass deportations to Siberia or other remote places were unknown to the prerevolutionary Russian regimes. From a historic perspective the Tsarist regime was an autocratic one, a strange mixture of backwardness and progress, of inherited, deep-rooted conservatism and reluctant, slow reform. The regime suffered from the lack of autonomous political, socioeconomic institutions, the absence of any adequate give-and-take relations between State and society until the constitution of 1905. Consequently, the Tsarist regime was a poor political and civic school for the Russian people. The intolerant attitude of the autocracy rejected any idea of compromise. This all-or-nothing approach was taken up by opponents of the regime, who organized various revolutionary groups to overthrow the Tsarist regime.

Suggested Reading

BILLINGTON, JAMES, *The Icon and the Axe: Interpretive History of Russian Culture.* New York: Random House, 1970.

BLUM, JEROME, *Lord and Peasant in Russia.* Princeton, NJ: Princeton University Press, 1961.

CLOWES, EDITH W. AND OTHERS (EDS.), *Between Tsar and People: Educated Society and the Quest for Public Identity in Late Imperial Russia.* Princeton, NJ: Princeton University Press, 1991.

CUSTINE, ASTOLPHE L. L., *Journey for Our Times.* New York: Pellegrin and Cudahy, 1951.

DANIELS, ROBERT V., *Russia: The Roots of Confrontation.* Cambridge, MA and London: Harvard University Press, 1985, Chs. 1–4.

GEYER, DIETRICH, *Russian Imperialism: The Interaction of Domestic and Foreign Policy, 1860–1914.* New Haven, CT: Yale University Press, 1987.

KLIUCHEVSKY, VASILY O., *Peter the Great.* New York: St. Martin's Press, 1958.

LEDONNE, JOHN, P., *The Russian Empire and the World, 1700–1917: The Geopolitics of Expansion and Containment.* New York: Oxford University Press, 1996.

LIEVEN, DOMINIC. *Russia's Rulers under the Old Regime.* New Haven: Yale University Press, 1989.

MADARIAGA, ISABEL DE, *Russia in the Age of Catherine the Great.* London: Weidenfeld and Nicholson, 1981.

MARTIN, MALIA, *Russia Under Western Eyes: From the Bronze Horseman to the Lenin Mausoleum.* Cambridge, MA: Belknap for Harvard, 1999.

MASSIE, ROBERT K., *Peter the Great.* New York: Knopf, 1980.

MILIUKOV, PAVEL N., *Outlines of Russian Culture* (Michael Karpovich, Ed.). Philadelphia: University of Pennsylvania Press, 1942. 3 vols.

———, *Russia and Its Critics.* New York: Collier Books, 1962.

PIPES, RICHARD, *Russia under the Old Regime.* London: Weidenfeld and Nicholson, 1974.

PUSHKAROV, SERGEI, *The Emergence of Modern Russia, 1801–1917.* New York: Holt, Rinehart and Winston, 1963.

RADZINSKY, EDWARD, *The Last Tsar: The Life and Death of Nicholas II.* New York: Doubleday, 1992.

RAEFF, MARC (ED.), *Russian Intellectual History: An*

Anthology. New York: Harcourt Brace Jovanovich, 1966.

ROGGER, HANS, *National Consciousness in Eighteenth Century Russia.* Cambridge, Mass.: Harvard University Press, 1960.

SETON-WATSON, HUGH, *The Russian Empire, 1801–1917.* New York: Oxford University Press, 1967.

STARR, FREDERICK S., *Decentralization and Self-Government in Russia, 1830–1870.* Princeton, NJ: Princeton University Press, 1972.

STEINBERG, MARK D., *The Fall of the Romanovs.* New Haven: Yale, 1995.

VUCHINICH, VANE S. (ED.), *The Peasant in Nineteenth Century Russia.* Stanford, Calif.: Stanford University Press, 1968.

WALLACE, DONALD M., *Russia on the Eve of War and Revolution.* Princeton, NJ: Princeton University Press, 1984.

WARE, TIMOTHY, *The Orthodox Church.* New York: Penguin Books, 1963.

WOROBEC, CHRISTINE D., *Peasant Russia: Family and Community in the Post-Emancipation Period.* Princeton, NJ: Princeton University Press, 1991.

WREN, MELVIN C., *The Western Impact upon Russia.* New York: Holt, Rinehart and Winston, 1971.

ZERNOV, NICHOLAS, *Eastern Christendom.* New York: G. P. Putnam's Sons, 1961.

Chapter 3

The Russian Revolutionary Tradition

The revolutionary movement played an overwhelming role in the history of twentieth-century Russia. The first instance of a modern Russian revolutionary group fighting the Tsarist regime in the name of a more or less coherent program was the revolt of a handful of aristocratic guard officers against the autocracy and the iniquities of the traditional, antiquated socioeconomic system. Since the revolt took place in December 1825, its members are known as *Decembrists*.

The uprising should be viewed against the background of its epoch. The Napoleonic wars saw Russia deeply involved in the affairs of Europe. A grandson of Catherine II, Alexander I (1801–1825), had ambitious plans for restructuring the European community in accordance with his visionary, idealistic, but impractical schemes. Preoccupied primarily with international affairs, Alexander had abandoned his early plans for enlightened domestic reforms. This shift in policy deepened the dissatisfaction of the expanding, restless intelligentsia with Russia's backwardness and fostered their further alienation from the system based on privilege, serfdom, repression, and censorship. The young Russian officers roaming Europe during the campaigns against Napoleon brought home the liberal and revolutionary ideas of the West and formed a number of secret societies dedicated to the implementation of these ideas.

In December 1825, within a month of Alexander's death, a group of officer-conspirators staged a coup d'état, the aims of which were the abolition of autocracy and serfdom and the introduction of either a liberal constitution or a centralized republican system of government. The improvised revolt was promptly and ruthlessly suppressed by Alexander's younger brother, and successor, Nicholas I (1825–1855). The five ringleaders of the conspiracy were hanged and several other conspirators banished to Siberia.

The Decembrists' uprising was the first Russian revolt directly inspired by Western liberalism and the first to have a political program. Hastily organized, deprived of determined and experienced leadership, and with no support from the masses, it was doomed to failure. The Decembrists were trying to reap before they had sown, to stage a revolution before they had organized a revolutionary movement. But the revolt of the Decembrists provided the mounting opposition to the Tsarist autocracy with two important elements: a revolutionary legend and a group of martyr-heroes to worship.

Shaken by the revolt of the Decembrists, who were mostly guard officers enjoying all the privileges of their class, the sulking Tsar Nicholas sought safety by suppressing even the idea of fundamental reform. Soon after the conspirators' trial, he established a corps of gendarmes of some 10,000 men and a new branch of the secret police, the "Third Section" of his personal chancery, to deal with political problems and the repression of dissent. In 1845, Tsar Nicholas also promulgated a new criminal code, which became a milestone in the evolution of Russia as a police state. The new Criminal Code of 1845 made all attempts to limit the authority of the Tsar, to alter the existing system of government, or even to fail to denounce anyone guilty of these offenses, criminal offenses carrying the death penalty and the confiscation of all property. In practice, the propagation of ideas that in any way spread doubt about the authority of the Tsar was mostly punishable by the loss of civil rights, from four to twelve years of hard labor, and, in addition, corporal punishment and branding. The Criminal Code of 1845 made politics a monopoly of the establishment and gave to the Third Section and its auxiliary organs a perfect instrument for the arbitrary repression of all forms of political dissent.

The system of Nicholas I was undermined not so much by domestic political opposition as by foreign adventures. The Tsar wanted to extend Russia's influence over the Balkans and the Middle East and eventually to partition the Ottoman Empire, causing him to stumble into a war against a powerful coalition centering around Great Britain and France. Apprehensive of his adventurous designs, they supported Turkey as a dam against further Russian encroachments in the area. The ensuing war, which took place in the Black Sea region largely on the Crimean peninsula from 1853 to 1855, resulted in a humiliating defeat for the Russian forces. They were badly armed, indifferently commanded, and composed of sulking serfs unable to match technologically superior Western contingents.

The Great Reforms

Nicholas's son and successor, Alexander II (1855–1881), ended the Crimean War with the Treaty of Paris (1856) and turned his attention toward neglected domestic issues. Alexander's *Great Reforms* were extensive. The educational system was liberalized; access to higher education was granted to all classes, primary as well as secondary education was expanded, and in 1863 institutions of higher learning were granted a measure of autonomy. Preventive censorship was abolished. By the Imperial decrees of 1861 and 1864, the serfs (both those privately owned and those belonging to the State) were emancipated from the power of their masters. The peasant was to remain a member of the existing local village communal exploitation of land, or *mir*, organized on the basis of the collective ownership of land. The landowners were to be compensated from State funds, while the peasants were to repay the State over a period of forty-nine years. The liberation of the Russian serfs, parallel to the emancipation of the slaves in the United States, involved a huge mass, about 50 million people. Unlike the American slaves, the Russian peasants retained most of the land they were cultivating at the time of the emancipation.

Following the liberation of the serfs in 1864, Alexander established elected self-governing bodies on the communal, district, and provincial levels. Although the landowners were largely in control, the peasants also participated. Soon these local bodies, or *zemstvos*, became schools for responsible, day-to-day, grass-roots civic work. The only outlet for semi-independent social activities, the zemstvos soon became a breeding ground of liberal and reform sentiments. In addition, in the same year independent judiciary and public trial by jury were introduced. In 1870 a measure of municipal self-government was granted. Four years later, the antiquated structure of the military service (in which a man had to serve for twenty-five years) was streamlined, somewhat humanized, and the length of service shortened. The principle of universal military service was introduced. During the period of the Great Reforms, Alexander II attempted to put an end to the arbitrary rule of the police and to transform his Empire into a state grounded in law. The Great Reforms, carried out against the bitter opposition of the conservatives and the well-entrenched bureaucracy, were considered by Russian liberals as a significant step toward eventual establishment of a constitutional system of government, or a "crowning of the edifice" of a reconstructed, modernized Russia.

Yet the reforms of the 1860s not only did not eliminate the tension between State and society, but rather, they intensified it. While conceding its people significant economic opportunities, basic civil rights, and some intellectual freedoms, the autocracy insisted on keeping its monopoly of political power and continued to regard itself as the only legitimate source of authority. The growing disappointment with the shortcomings of the Great Reforms, especially the stiff terms of the emancipation of the peasants, caused a great deal of vocal criticism and public manifestation during the early 1860s. This social ferment resulted in the birth of the Russian agrarian socialist movement, *Populism*.

Russian Agrarian Socialism

One of the earliest Russian socialists was Alexander I. Herzen, a brilliant debater. Through his voluminous and persuasive writing, Herzen, in exile after 1847, tried to adapt the European socialist concepts to the conditions of his native country. His London-based periodical *Kolokol (The Bell)* attempted to demonstrate that backward, agrarian Russia was actually riper for socialism than advanced, industrialized Western Europe. Influenced by Herzen, the Russian agrarian socialist of the 1860s and 1870s believed that if the peasants could be educated to socialists' ideas, the native Russian form of agrarian cooperative, the mir, would be transformed into the basic cell of a new society. In this way, backward Russia could escape the miseries of capitalism and pass in a relatively short period of time from a feudal state to socialism.

Populism was based on two premises: first, faith in the significance of the commune as a key institution of the socialist transformation of Russia; and, second, mistrust of liberalism and capitalism. Both assumptions were connected with the belief that Russia's social and economic backwardness was an advantage over capitalist Western Europe and a way of bypassing the capitalist stage of development. Yet Herzen and his followers believed that Russia was essentially a part of the Western world. Unlike their opponents, the Slavophiles, who wanted to preserve the traditional Russian institutions, the Westernizers rejected the uniqueness of their country's civilization and regarded Russia merely as a retarded segment of Europe, the segment that should try to catch up with the rest of the Western world.

Paradoxically, it was the emancipation of the serfs and other progressive reforms that gave birth to the revolutionary activities of the Populists. There were numerous reasons for the spread of their protest movement. First, emancipation gave the peasants too little land, saddled them with high redemption payments, subjected them to special, discriminating laws, and thus left them on the margin of the society. Second, some of the reforms—such as those of the press and the education system—were abandoned halfway. Moreover, the educational reform, which gave access to higher education to sons of peasants and merchants, soon produced a considerable body of fairly well-educated people of radical political views without prospects of gainful employment.

One characteristic phenomenon of the 1870s was the emergence of the *going-to-the-people* movement, or a tendency of the Populist intelligentsia to live and work with the peasantry in order to help in its education and eventual emancipation. The movement reached its peak in the "mad summer" of 1874. Thousands of young and not-so-young members of the intelligentsia flocked to the villages to preach the gospel of social revolution. Yet the peasants were indifferent to abstract political ideas and hostile to those who wanted to inculcate them with strange concepts. The main preoccupation of the peasants was the acquisition of more land and the betterment of material conditions in general. The idea of a revolutionary overthrow of the Tsar, whom the peasants tended to view as their father and protector against the greedy landowners and corrupt officials, was alien to the rural masses. In many cases the peasants simply handed over the strangers from the cities to the local police as dangerous agitators against the Tsar. The foolishly idealized image of a "good peasant" was shattered almost overnight. The going-to-the-people movement ended in failure.

Disappointed in their pet dream of galvanizing the peasant masses into revolutionary action by means of propaganda and agitation, the radicals turned to terror. Violent protests involving the use of pistols and bombs were started in 1878 by a small body of some thirty or forty people who called themselves the *People's Will*. They conducted their terror and sabotage with breathtaking, reckless courage for some three years. The terrorist activities aimed at shattering the bureaucratic machinery and inciting the peasants to rebellion by exposing the Tsar's helplessness and his unwillingness to carry out more radical land reform ("the black partition"). The radicals hoped to summon a Constituent Assembly representing the real desires of the people, or the "people's will."

Failures to achieve international goals soon added to domestic tensions. The humiliating setbacks of Russian diplomacy at the Congress of Berlin that ended the Russo-Turkish War of 1877–1878 were bitterly resented by Slavophile public opinion at home. The dismantling of Greater Bulgaria, sponsored by St. Petersburg but opposed by London, Berlin, and Vienna, was followed by the occupation of the Slavic provinces of Bosnia and Herzegovnia by Austria-Hungary; these were bitter pills for the increasingly Panslavic-inclined Russian patriots to swallow. Soon a more politically minded outgrowth of the Slavophiles began to preach the idea of Russia as leader and future unifier of all the Slavic peoples, who should eventually merge into one huge Slavonic Empire.[1]

The mood of patriotic enthusiasm generated by the war against the Turks, considered a traditional enemy of the Orthodox Slavs, had temporarily silenced domestic opposition against the soft-pedaling of the Great Reforms. In 1878, after the Congress of Berlin, the revolutionaries, especially the terrorists of the People's Will, redoubled their efforts. The battle of wills between the Tsarist security apparatus and the terrorists lasted for three years. Finally, on March 13, 1881, a bomb thrown by one of the terrorists in St. Petersburg killed the man who had emancipated over 50 million serfs, often called "Tsar Liberator." A few hours before Alexander was killed, he had signed a quasi-constitutional project devised to involve elected representatives of a consultative assembly in legislative tasks.

The Birth of Russian Marxist Socialism

The assassination of the "Tsar Liberator" was the peak of the activities of the People's Will. Alexander III (1881–1894), the embittered son of Alexander II, never published his father's quasi-constitutional charter. Quite the contrary: acting under the influence of his narrow-minded, reactionary advisor, Constantine Pobedonostsev (1827–1907), the new Tsar proclaimed his

[1] The Panslavic school of thought was greatly stimulated in 1869 by the publication of a theoretical study, *Russia and Europe*. Its author, Nicholas Y. Danilevsky (1828–1885), was an eloquent exponent of Russian nationalism who advanced a theory of the unique and superior character of youthful Slavonic peoples as compared with the aging Western nations..

unmitigated devotion to absolutism in his accession manifesto and initiated a repressive course of action. Its main victims were not only the radical and liberal opposition, but also religious and national minorities, especially the Jews, who suffered numerous pogroms. The press was muzzled, the zemstvos hampered in their activity, and intellectual life stifled by censorship.

To the terror of the People's Will, the government carried out a series of systematic counterrevolutionary measures. One of them, already taken in 1878, empowered the Corps of Gendarmes to detain and even exile administratively (without trial by a law court or permission of the Attorney General) anyone suspected of a political crime. Whereas under the Criminal Code of 1845 a citizen had to actually commit a subversive act before being liable to exile, now a suspicion of subversion was enough to have him suffer that fate. Trial by jury was done away with in political cases; now all political cases were to be dealt with by "administrative methods," that is, by the gendarmes and police, to the exclusion of the law courts. In addition, Alexander III reorganized the branches of the police dealing with political crimes by giving them further arbitrary powers. The law of August 1, 1881, introduced two institutions: the state of "Reinforced Safeguard," which corresponded to a minor state of siege, and that of "Extraordinary Safeguard," which in the West would equal a major state of siege. The new law gave the police and administrative authorities powers unparalleled in the civilized world. The law placed the fate of the people in the hands of uncontrolled police officials and made them dependent on their whim, thus making Russia a full-blown police state. From then on, a majority of the Tsarist Empire was under the state of Reinforced Safeguard with occasional recurrence to Extraordinary Safeguard, as, for instance, during the revolution of 1905 and its aftermath.

As a consequence of this series of measures, the opposition was temporarily paralyzed. Soon, however, the revolutionary movement revived. The revival was caused by the excess of burgeoning, unrestricted Russian industrial development; the plight of a peasantry suffering from excessive taxes, stiff redemption payments, and high-handed governmental paternalism; the oppressive though erratic censorship; the spread of Great Russian chauvinism—all these produced increasing resentment and, at the close of the century, gave birth to several new revolutionary groups.

One reason for the upsurge of revolutionary activities was the deteriorating economic situation of the peasant masses. Agricultural production, hampered by the mir, was lagging. According to an official census of 1877, the average landholding of a Russian peasant family was about thirty-five acres; in France the average size of a peasant farm was about nine acres. But the colder, drier, and more capricious climate, in addition to the backward cultivation methods, made the position of the rapidly increasing Russian peasantry incomparably worse. Since the shortage of land was relative, it was technological backwardness that was mainly responsible for Russia's agricultural retardation. The threat of periodic land repartition hampered initiative and prevented peasants from investing in land that could be taken away at any time. All these factors inhibited productivity and resulted in the progressive impoverishment of the peasant masses during the second half of the nineteenth and beginning of the twentieth century.

The plight of the Russian worker, largely an unwilling and homesick migrant from his native village, was equally bad. Fascinated by the machine and the profit it provided to those who mastered it, the Russian entrepreneurial class, like its Western counterpart at the early stages of the industrial revolution, was largely blind to the human side of economic progress. At the end of the century, the workers' barracks-like living conditions were quite similar to those Marx's collaborator Engels had observed in England in the 1840s. Wretched working conditions, long working days of about twelve to sixteen hours, arbitrary fines, compulsory workers' canteens run by the factory owner—these were commonplace phenomena in Russia in the 1880s and 1890s. To this one should add the shortage of labor inspectors to check on the rudimentary labor legislation hastily enacted in the 1880s, and a ban on strikes, although not on lockouts. Workers' grievances were sullenly nurtured by the rapidly growing industrial working class, who could not express them in a legitimate way, let alone much improve their wretched condition.

The task of defending the interest of the laboring masses of the Tsarist Empire was taken over by a small group of the increasingly radical intelligentsia. This new revolutionary mood was more directly inspired by the followers of Marx and Engels than by the events of the 1860s and 1870s. The Russian translation of *Das Kapital* was published in Russia in 1872, five years after its German edition, but earlier than in any other foreign country. Marxism spread among the Russian intelligentsia like wildfire. This was in part because the doctrine gave to the people who had rejected religious dogma a sense of moral certitude for which they had been longing, and also because it represented what seemed a scientific panacea for the ills of contemporary society. The classic Marxist ideas, however, which were formulated on the basis of West European experience, were hardly applicable to the condition of a heterogeneous and overwhelmingly rural-pastoral Tsarist Empire. Transplanted to Russia, the Marxist theories had, of necessity, to be adapted to suit the new, strange environment.

George Plekhanov

The transformation of orthodox Marxism into the Russian type of Communism was a long, gradual, and involved process. The first systematic explanation of Marxist doctrine in Russian was given by a repentant nobleman, George Plekhanov. As a student at the Mining Institute of St. Petersburg, Plekhanov had participated in the going-to-the-people movement of the 1870s. Disappointed with the passivity of the peasants and the fruitless terrorist activities of the radical wing of Populism, he emigrated to Switzerland and began to study Marxism. Plekhanov, together with three former Populists, Paul Axelrod, Lev Deutsch, and Vera Zasulich, was the founder of the first Russian Marxist group, "Liberation of Labor" (1883).

During his forty years of exile, Plekhanov wrote many books and pamphlets. Owing to his intellectual capacities, he soon became the leader of the slow forming Russian Social-Democratic movement. Plekhanov believed that the main failing of the Populists lay in their uncritical worship of the passive peasant masses. The chief strength of Marxist Socialism, on the other hand, lay in its intellectual discipline and its "scientific" formulation of a program of political as well as social action. Along with Marx and Engels, Plekhanov argued that, rather than the amorphous peasant masses spread over the vastness of the Tsarist Empire, the workers concentrated in the strategic points of modern industrial societies should form the core of a modern revolutionary movement. The working-class movement, acting in a still semifeudal country, argued Plekhanov, should proceed through two phases: a bourgeois upheaval followed by a socialist revolution. First, a political revolution should destroy the Tsarist autocracy and establish a liberal bourgeois regime; such a regime would create conditions more favorable for the proletarian masses (an eight-hour working day, trade unions, social security, educational facilities, and so on). After an indeterminate period, the working class, by then well prepared for its historical role, would strike out, abolish bourgeois rule, and establish the "dictatorship of the proletariat." The revolution would place control of the means of production in the hands of the workers and establish a socialist system, a stepping stone toward the final goal of the historic process, which is Communism.

To achieve these objectives, argued Plekhanov, it was necessary to create an

Karl Marx

instrument that would lead the struggle, that is, a regular Social-Democratic Party. The party would be composed essentially of workers but led, at least in the beginning, by a small group of intellectuals. Following the tradition of Marx and Engels, and in accordance with the pattern set by the largest and most prestigious Social-Democratic Party in the contemporary world, the German party, Plekhanov emphasized democratic principles and minimized the leadership role of the intellectuals. Their function was merely to serve the working-class movement. Plekhanov stressed that a socialist revolution should wait until the working class was educated enough to assume its high responsibilities, which is to say, when "objective" socioeconomic conditions would be ripe for the introduction of a complex socialist system suitable only to highly developed industrial societies. Thus, Plekhanov was a rather scrupulous interpreter of orthodox Marxism and wanted to

transplant it to his native country gradually but without major adaptations.

The Shaping of Socialist Mass Parties

While Plekhanov was laboring abroad to lay down the theoretical foundations of the Russian Marxist movement, the industrial revolution in the Tsarist Empire was advancing rapidly. Actually, the first socialist parties of the Empire were formed on its multinational periphery, in Russian Poland, and in the socioeconomically more advanced western provinces of the Tsarist domains. As far back as 1882, an early socialist party called "Proletariat" was organized in Warsaw. Ten years after its suppression by the police, a group of Polish intellectuals and workers who were forced to emigrate to Paris formed there the Polish Socialist Party (1892). The next year a splinter group, protesting its native party's emphasis on patriotism, established a party of its own, the Social-Democratic Party of Poland (soon to be renamed Social-Democratic Party of Poland and Lithuania). This was the party of Rosa Luxemburg, Feliks Dzerzhinsky, and Karl Radek. And it was in the Lithuanian regions of the Tsarist Empire, in Vilna (Wilno, now Vilnius), that in 1897 the delegates of various Jewish Marxist debating clubs and underground cells gathered to set up the "General Jewish Workers' Union" in Lithuania, Poland, and Russia. This representation of the Jewish, Marxist proletarian masses was to be known by its colloquial Yiddish abbreviation of *Bund*. Owing to the high educational level of its membership, the qualities of its leaders, and the oppressive conditions under which the Jewish proletariat suffered in the towns and cities of the *Pale of Settlement*, to which they were limited by the authorities, the Bund developed into a mass party sooner than the socialist organizations of other ethnic groups. In Livonia and Kurland, the Lettish Social-Democratic movement achieved considerable influence among the local workers, both in the urban centers and in the countryside. At the same time, in the Transcaucasia, especially among the Georgians and the Armenians, various socialist groups were also formed. Everywhere, lack of political freedom continued to favor conspiratorial activity.

In 1898, on the initiative of the Jewish Bund, nine delegates of these scattered socialist conspiratorial cells congregated in the Belorussian city of Minsk and proclaimed the foundations of the Russian Social-Democratic Workers' Party (RSDWP). While the immediate objective of the party was the establishment of a constitutional regime, its ultimate goal was to be a Socialist system with public ownership of the means of production, including land. Soon after this meeting, declared to be the first congress of the new party, most of the delegates were arrested by the Tsarist police. Thus the seemingly stillborn party suffered its first heavy blow, which seemed to spell its end. Yet the unrest that prompted the formation of these groups was a symptom of deep seated socioeconomic and political malaise that proved impossible to extirpate. The ferment was soon to be aggravated by the severe economic depression of the years 1899–1903. Since the famine of 1891, which had brought widespread death from starvation in many regions of the Empire, unrest among peasants had also worsened.

The plight of the peasantry was a challenge to the Populist-inclined intelligentsia. A few former members of the agrarian socialist groups Land and Liberty and the People's Will, began to re-form their scattered ranks, and at the close of 1901, they formed the *Social Revolutionary Party*, or the SRs, as they were colloquially called. The SRs were primarily dedicated to the defense of the peasant interests and insisted on the necessity of public ownership of the land as the main source of the peasantry's livelihood. While preaching close cooperation between workers and peasants, they rejected the hegemony of the urban proletariat in an overwhelmingly agrarian society. This factor, as well as the distinctive mentality of the village people, argued the Social-Revolutionary leaders, necessitated a specifically Russian interpretation of the Socialist doctrine involving acceptance of a leading role for the peasantry. Moreover, argued the SRs, the elemental land hunger of the peasant, his fierce attachment to the soil he tilled, ought to be respected. Hence the agrarian program of the SRs provided for nationalization of the land that should be owned by the State; the State, however, would lease the land to local peasant communities, which would in turn sublease it to individual peasant families for long periods of time.

While devoting the bulk of their energies to grass-roots work among the peasants (as social workers in the ranks of the local zemstvos, as teachers, doctors, or agrarian instructors), the Social Revolutionaries preached the theory of propaganda by acts of terror. Whenever Tsarist officials were especially obnoxious and all other means of persuasion and pressure failed, such representatives of the oppressive regime had to be assassinated in the name of the higher interest of the people. The SRs were convinced that such a punishment of hated officials, often called "propaganda by deeds," would spur on the revolutionary spirit of the masses and eventually frighten the regime into concessions. Thus the doctrine of the SRs was a compromise between Socialist collectivist doctrine and common sense, between the going-to-the-people movement and the terrorist traditions of the People's Will.

The SRs, despite their loose organization, were spontaneously appealing not only to the peasant masses but also to many students and intellectuals. Soon the Social Revolutionary Party became the largest and the most deeply rooted political party of pre-Soviet Russia.

Legal Marxists

Meanwhile, the already differentiated Marxist revolutionary movement began to undergo further evolution. By the end of the nineteenth century, the revisionist, gradualist ideas of a prominent member of the German Social-Democratic Party, Edward Bernstein, had also penetrated into Russia. Bernstein questioned the necessity of a violent upheaval to achieve Socialism. By the close of the century some early, more scholarly Russian students of Marxism, like Peter Struve and Sergei N. Bulgakov, began to formulate a theory of nonviolent social change similar to that of Edward Bernstein. Struve, in his *Critical Notes on the Problem of the Economic Development of Russia,* published in 1894, had come to the conclusion that capitalism would offer to backward Russia a great many practical advantages, and that his countrymen should learn from Western liberalism. The Tsarist authorities did not suppress the writings and activities of this type of scholarly Marxist, and tended to regard such people as "thieves falling out." Despite these hopes, the ideas of the "legal Marxists," as they were called, found a considerable following among intellectuals and university students. By and large, however, gradualism had no significant appeal to the masses of the Russian people. In a society shaped by the forces described in the previous chapter, any idea of a partial adjustment, of give and take, tended to be regarded with suspicion and often even with contempt.

Watching legal Marxists, an ingenious secret police officer, Sergey Zubatov, convinced Tsarist authorities that they should fight the revolutionaries by infiltrating the labor movement. He advocated spreading slogans that would stress economic demands and thus would be attractive to the workers, yet largely harmless to the government. As a consequence of this strategy, the wrath of the workers would be directed against the local factory owners and other capitalists, who were largely foreigners or Jews. The idea of channeling and deflecting the wrath of the workers was temporarily accepted by the regime. For a number of years the movement, soon to be called "police socialism," spread in a series of urban centers, including St. Petersburg and Moscow. Some of the Zubatov methods were soon taken over by a son of a Ukrainian peasant, a Greek Orthodox priest named Gregory Gapon, to form his Assembly of Russian Workingmen, a nucleus of a Christian Socialist movement.

The Emergence of Lenin

Among the members of the lingering Russian Social Democratic Workers' Party was the son of a school inspector, Vladimir Ulianov, whom we know better by his revolutionary pen name of Lenin. Vladimir Ulianov was a gold medal graduate (which would correspond to our summa cum laude) of the University of Kazan on the Volga. Together with his older brother, Alexander, Vladimir Ulianov joined a Marxist conspiratorial cell early on. Soon his brother became involved in an attempt on the life of Alexander III. While Alexander was sentenced to death, Vladimir was exiled to Siberia, and later, in 1900, expelled from Russia. His revolutionary experience had taught Ulianov the specific weaknesses of his countrymen: anarchic tendencies, proclivity to loose talk, endless theoretical hairsplitting, lack of discipline, and inability to keep secrets. All this he contrasted against the skillful and ruthless operations of the Tsarist secret police. The story of the First Congress of the RSDWP was a good example of this contrast. Vladimir Ulianov concluded that under the circumstances, the revolutionaries had little chance of success unless they radically changed their methods.

Analyzing in exile the existing situation and the prospects for the future, Ulianov wrote a book that he published in 1902 under the pseudonym Lenin, entitled *What Is to Be Done?* In this polemical book directed against the reformist trend of the Russian Socialist movement, Lenin forcefully stated his views. The only remedy to the many ills of the Russian revolutionary movement would be to set up a tight, hierarchically organized party composed of dedicated people devoted body and soul to the task of the proletarian

Vladimir Ulianov Lenin

The concept of a small, select revolutionary party was not a novelty in the Russian revolutionary tradition. There had been in the past some Russian Populists of a Jacobin variety who advocated a similar approach. The most significant were Pyotr Tkachěv and Sergey Nechayev; both preached violent overthrow of the Tsarist order and establishment of a revolutionary dictatorship. In 1868–1869 Nechayev together with Tkachěv drafted a "Program of Revolutionary Action" which spoke of "social revolution as our final aim, and political revolution as the only means of achieving this aim." The essence of Russian Jacobinism was the insistence on the dictatorship of a minority group with the object of carrying out by force the socialist transformation of the country's political and socioeconomic system. Nechayev, in his booklet *Revolutionary Catechism*, stressed the need for total dedication, and wrote: "The revolutionist is a doomed man. He has no personal interests, no affairs, sentiments, attachments, property, not even a name of his own. Everything in him is absorbed by one exclusive interest, one thought, the revolution."[2] Lenin's spiritual links with Nechayev and Tkachěv were close. With Tkachěv, Lenin shared three vital concepts: (1) the belief in the decisive role of a disciplined, hierarchically organized conspiratorial elite; (2) the necessity of a violent revolution to be launched as soon as possible, irrespective of socioeconomic conditions as prescribed by Marx and Engels; and (3) the insistence on the establishment of a determined minority dictatorship that would introduce socialism, imposing their reforms by force if necessary. Nechayev and Tkachěv, but especially the latter, form a vital link

revolution; they must be a match for the repressive instruments at the disposal of the establishment. The nucleus of the party, he argued, should be a small compact core united by the bonds of reliable and hardened workers connected by strict secrecy. Only such a strong and disciplined organization could prevent the danger of premature outbreaks before the ferment and anger of the workers had ripened. He argued that, because of the need for restraint and secrecy, democratic management was inapplicable to a revolutionary organization in Russia. According to *What Is to Be Done?* the proposed party should act as a "vanguard of the revolutionary forces," or a small detachment of soldiers preceding a larger body of troops and doing scouting work for them. This quasi-military formula chartered the elitist and antidemocratic course of the movement Lenin established.

---

[2] The very title of Nechayev's work, *Catechism,* has obvious religious connotations, and a mixture of religion and politics permeated with Byzantine traditions has been a part of the Russian ethos. The advice to abandon permanently one's name while entering a revolutionary conspiracy was observed by many followers of the movement, including Ulianov-Lenin himself. Iosif Djugrashvili soon became Joseph Stalin, and Lev (or Leon) Bronstein, Leon Trotsky.

between revolutionary Populism and Bolshevism. This makes Lenin a continuer of the native Jacobin trend.

Menshevism versus Bolshevism

Lenin's seminal book, *What Is to Be Done?* was published in 1902. The next year the resurgent Marxist groups decided to resume their broader organizational activities and arrange for the RSDWP's Second Congress. It gathered some fifty delegates, first in Brussels, and then, again detected by the Russian police, the group moved its deliberations to London. During the crucial Second Congress, two main issues agitated the delegates: that of the party structure and organizations, and that of its affiliations and allegiances.

The first problem focused on two issues: who can be a member of the party, and what should be his duties? Some delegates, like Yulii O. Martov, Lenin's associate and coworker from the émigré paper *Iskra (The Spark)*, advanced a broad formula: Every person who agreed with the movement should be considered a member. According to Lenin, the acceptance of this formula would make the party a broad, amorphous mass movement with many people loosely connected but not really belonging to it. His counter formula was: A member of the party is one who, besides paying his dues, submits to its discipline and actively works in one of the party cells, doing a job assigned to him.

Despite Lenin's vigorous opposition, the supporters of the broad definition, who were in the majority, prevailed. Soon, however, another difference polarized the reborn Social-Democratic movement. Everyone realized that the working class of the Tsarist Empire, then numbering about two and a half million people, was still too weak to gain power single-handedly and had to have allies in its struggle. The question was, with which social stratum should the workers cooperate in their struggle against the autocracy allied with the capitalists? Plekhanov and Martov and most of their followers, true to the teachings of Marx and Engels, were for enlisting the support of the most progressive and educated segment of the middle class, the liberal bourgeoisie. On this point they again clashed with Lenin. He rejected Marx's condemnation of the peasantry as a petty bourgeois class and advocated close cooperation with the poor and landless peasants. Lenin claimed that the latter were actually closer to rural workers, hence, for all practical purposes, also proletarians like the urban workers. According to Lenin, while the liberal bourgeoisie at the decisive moment always would side with the autocracy against the socialists, the rural proletariat, land-hungry and revolutionary by instinct and tradition, was the only reliable ally of the workers. And here Lenin found supporters among most of the Congress delegates. Delighted to be finally in the majority, despite his contempt for the democratic process, he called his followers the "majority faction"—*Bolsheviki* in Russian. Lenin's adversaries, actually a numerically stronger group on most other issues, meekly gave up this term while accepting the psychologically debilitating name of *Mensheviki*, or members of the "minority faction." The nicknames stuck.

The Second Congress of the RSDWP, besides voting the party rules, also formulated its program. The immediate or "minimum" program dealt with the short-range goals of the movement, those objectives to be achieved before the establishment of socialism. The minimum program comprised the overthrow of Tsarist authority and the establishment of a democratic republic that would abolish all remnants of serfdom in the countryside and the introduction of progressive social reforms benefiting both workers and peasants, including an eight-hour working day. The original program of the RSDWP included a point about an agrarian reform that would allot more land to the peasants. Later, however, the Bolsheviks replaced this postulate with a demand for the outright confiscation of all farms, while the Mensheviks came to advocate control of the land by local, freely elected peasant committees.

As a consequence of its Second Congress, the RSDWP split into two factions, which soon solidified. They established themselves into two separate and antagonistic parties, each with a different program, leadership, methods of operation, and a contradictory vision of the future. While the Bolsheviks represented a centralist, elitist, authoritarian concept, the Mensheviks were inclined to model their party after the Social-Democratic movements of Central and Western Europe, especially the German Social Democratic Party. The Mensheviks were gradualist in their mentality and methods of operation; they attached considerable importance to trade unions and to democratic and parliamentary activities. They were motivated by the desire to work gradually with and for the masses. Until the crisis of the autumn of 1917, they had more of a mass following than the Bolsheviks. The Bolsheviks, on the other hand, were more efficiently organized, more firmly led, and inclined more toward clandestine, revolutionary activities.

The programmatic clashes that split the RSDWP had their origins in the difficulties of adapting Marxist doctrine, which was a product of West European thought and environment, to specific Russian conditions. The Menshevik theories, which tried to follow rigidly Marxist doctrine and West European patterns, were to prove more alien to the Russian working masses than the simpler, often highly demagogic, teachings of Lenin, whose dogmatic and authoritarian approach was so much closer to the native Russian mentality.

Summary

The compulsive revolutionary, as some of his biographers called Lenin, rejected the two-stage concept as unnecessary procrastination incomprehensible to the simple-minded people of Russia. During the revolution of 1905, he jettisoned the orthodox Marxist two-stage scheme and decided that the workers and peasants of Russia should seize power as soon as possible, and thus break the capitalistic chain at its weakest point as the first step toward the world proletarian revolution. Thus, while paying lip service to Marxism, Lenin proceeded to construct a doctrine that was actually a revision of the original theory. The three most significant aspects of Lenin's "revisionism" were (1) his attempt to make Marxism applicable to rural Russia by preaching an alliance of industrial workers with the landless and poor peasantry; (2) his theory of the hierarchic, centralist, authoritarian party as an indispensable tool of the proletarian revolution or "the vanguard of the proletariat," which was unable to fulfill its historic role alone; and (3) the rejection of a two-stage revolution.

As we have seen, at the beginning of the twentieth century the Russian revolutionary movement represented a plethora of clandestine parties, factions, and small debating circles. The Bolsheviks, although very vocal and active, were merely a minor segment of the movement. Most of the revolutionaries shared with the mass of the Russian intelligentsia its characteristic features: a principled, abstract, often highly doctrinaire approach to many crucial issues at stake and the rejection of any compromise with the hated Tsarist regime. It was not to be reformed, but destroyed.

Suggested Reading

ASCHER, ABRAHAM, *Pavel Axelrod and the Development of Menshevism.* Cambridge, MA: Harvard University Press, 1972.

AVRICH, PAUL, *Anarchist Portraits.* Princeton, NJ: Princeton University Press, 1990.

BARON, SAMUEL H., *Plekhanov: The Father of Russian Marxism.* Stanford, CA: Stanford University Press, 1966

BERDYAEV, NICHOLAS, *The Origins of Russian Communism.* Ann Arbor: University of Michigan Press, 1960.

BILLINGTON, JAMES H., *Mikhailovsky and Russian Populism.* New York: Oxford Press, 1958.

BROOKS, JEFFREY, *When Russia Learned to Read: Literacy and Popular Literature, 1861–1917.* Princeton, NJ: Princeton University Press, 1988.

FISCHER, LOUIS, *Lenin.* New York: Harper and Row, 1965.

GALILI, ZIVA, *The Menshevik Leader in the Russian Revolution.* Princeton, NJ: Princeton University Press, 1989.

HAIMSON, LEOPOLD H., *The Russian Marxists and the Origins of Bolshevism.* Cambridge, MA: Harvard University Press, 1955.

KILLER, JOHN D., *Imperial Russia's Jewish Question, 1855–1881.* Cambridge: Cambridge University Press, 1995.

KROPOTKIN, PETER, *Mutual Aid.* Boston: Porter Sargent, 1976.

MALIA, MARTIN, *Alexander Herzen and the Birth of Russian Socialism, 1812–1855.* Cambridge, MA: Harvard University Press, 1961.

MEYER, ALFRED G., *Leninism.* Cambridge, MA: Harvard University Press, 1957.

NAIMARK, NORMAN M., *Terrorists and Social Democrats. The Russian Revolutionary Movement under Alexander III.* Cambridge, MA: Harvard University Press, 1983.

POSSONY, STEPHEN, *Lenin—A Compulsive Revolutionary.* Chicago: Regnery, 1964.

PUTNAM, GEORGE F., *Russian Alternatives to Marxism.* Knoxville: University of Tennessee Press, 1977.

RADKEY, OLIVER, *Agrarian Foes of Bolshevism.* New York: Columbia University Press, 1958.

RIASANOVSKY, NICHOLAS V., *A Parting of the Ways: Government and the Educated Public in Russia, 1801–1855.* New York: Oxford University Press, 1976.

ROGGER, HANS, *Russia in the Age of Modernization and Revolution.* New York: Longman, 1983.

RUUD, CHARLES A., AND SERGEI A. STEPANOV, *Fontanka 16: The Tsars' Secret Police.* Montreal: McGill-Queen's University Press, 1999.

SERVICE, ROBERT, *Lenin: A Political Life.* Volume I. *The Strengths of Contradiction.* Bloomington, IN: Indiana University Press, 1985.

STITES, RICHARD, *The Women's Liberation Movement in Russia: Feminism, Nihilism, and Bolshevism, 1860–1930.* Princeton, NJ: Princeton University Press, 1991.

SZAMUELI, TIBOR, *The Russian Tradition.* London: Secker and Warburg, 1974.

TUCKER, ROBERT C., *Stalin as a Revolutionary, 1879–1929.* New York: W. W. Norton, 1973.

ULAM, ADAM, *The Bolsheviks.* New York: Collier, 1965.

———, *In the Name of the People.* New York: Viking Press, 1977.

VENTURI, FRANCO, *Roots of the Revolution: A History of the Populist and Socialist Movements in Nineteenth Century Russia.* New York: Knopf, 1960.

WILLIAMS, ROBERT C., *The Other Bolsheviks: Lenin and His Critics, 1904–1914.* Bloomington: Indiana University Press, 1986.

WOLFE, BERTRAM D., *Marxism: 100 Years in the Life of a Doctrine.* New York: Dial Press, 1967.

YARMOLINSKY, AVRAHM, *Road to Revolution (A Century of Russian Radicalism).* New York: Collier Books, 1986.

Chapter 4

The Russo–Japanese War and the Revolution of 1905

When Tsar Nicholas II ascended the ivory throne of Ivan the Terrible in 1894, he inherited a huge empire of some 130 million people composed of well over 100 ethnic groups, it was beset by a host of pressing problems. His economically fast-progressing realm was saddled with an obsolete centralistic structure unsuited for a dynamic country inhabited by a host of ethnic groups, many of them craving political and human rights as well as national autonomy, and some of them, like Finland and Poland, striving for independence. By the end of the nineteenth century it was obvious that most of the politically minded subjects of the new Tsar, irrespective of their origin, had outgrown the existing political structure and were eager to establish a legal order based on civil liberties and human rights. Also, the geopolitical situation of the Russian Empire was deteriorating rapidly, and the Euroasiatic realm of Nicholas II had to face two aggressive powers on its western and eastern extremities: a united Germany and a modernized Japan.

The new monarch possessed many features praiseworthy in an ordinary citizen but fatal in an autocratic ruler. He was modest, frugal, and very polite, a good son, husband, and father; yet he was weak, moody, had an untrained mind, and lacked the primal energy of will so essential in a leader. At the same time, Nicholas II was a fatalist; he believed that, since he was born on May 6 (Old Style) May 18 (New Style) 1868, on the day of St. Job the Sufferer, his life was bound to be marked with tragedy. Politics inspired him with aversion. He disliked serious discussions of theoretical problems because he could not cope with them. His former tutor, Konstantine P. Pobedonostsev, the Ober-Procurator of the Holy Synod, a reactionary Slavophile and narrow-minded fanatic who firmly believed in the traditional autocratic system and in Russia's historic mission, inculcated Nicholas with a profound suspicion of the dynamic forces of the epoch, those of liberalism and democracy. Pobedonostsev's influence strengthened the native conservatism of the young monarch and his belief in the divinely ordained mandate of the autocratic Tsar: he was determined to preserve his power intact. Consequently, in the liberal and progressive ideas of the times Nicholas saw nothing but stupidity and malevolence—vain, unhealthy dreams of intellectuals, manipulated by international Jewry allied to Freemasonry.

Tsar Nicholas II (sitting on the left) and his family on a visit to their cousin, King Edward VII of Britain.

Nicholas II was married to a German princess, Alexandra of Hesse, a granddaughter of Queen Victoria. His wife was a striking contrast to him, intense and ambitious. Nicholas was dominated by his spouse and often tended to follow her capricious, erratic advice in matters of the highest importance. As one of his critics, Leon Trotsky, put it, he was a henpecked husband and a chicken-headed monarch.

The Peasant Problem

The man so badly equipped to exercise his office was confronted with a host of stupendous problems, the most important of which was the land question. It was crucial because

of its magnitude and age-old neglect; it affected nearly 80 percent of the population, or over 100 million peasants. Yet for centuries the Tsarist regime had considered the issue from the point of view of its own fiscal and military interests and that of the nobility, the class regarded as the main support of the throne. The Emancipation Decrees of 1861 and 1864 were the first breach in the traditional neglect of the peasantry. The decrees freed the peasants from their masters but not from the village commune; if anything, the commune's hold over its members was strengthened. The village commune existed throughout most of ethnic Russia, but not in the multinational borderlands of the Empire. The commune had three characteristic features. First, within the commune the land belonged not to individuals but to all its members collectively; individual peasants had no right of property, but merely a right to use it as determined by the commune. The land was allotted not to individuals but to families, and was periodically repartitioned in accordance with the changing size of the families. Second, the commune was collectively responsible for taxes. This necessitated restriction of the peasant's right of withdrawal from the commune; the right was to be granted only if the departing peasant would undertake to continue paying his share of taxes. Third, the peasant was subject to a form of paternalism embodied by the state-appointed officials called "land captains," who were usually retired army officers. Moreover, the peasant was subject not to the general laws of the country but to local custom and was liable to receive corporal punishment. Consequently, the village commune hampered peasant economic initiative, inhibited experimentation, and kept the peasantry as a class apart.

To the inferior legal status, one must add the gradually worsening economic situation of the large masses of the peasantry. Heavy taxes and high redemption payments set up by the Emancipation Decrees compelled a large percentage of the fast-multiplying peasantry to hire themselves as farm labor, to seek outside earnings, or simply to migrate to the cities in search of gainful employment. The population explosion that followed the Emancipation was not paralleled by technical progress or the introduction of modern cultivation methods. This was due to a lack of capital and to an attachment to the communal system that tended to reinforce the traditional farming methods, like the scattered-strip or three-field system, in which one field lay fallow each year. This, more than the shortage of land, was mainly responsible for peasant poverty. The land hunger was only partly alleviated by migration to distant parts of the empire like southern Siberia, where village communes did not exist, or by purchase of land from the rapidly disintegrating large estates.

The Nationality Problem

The second most important problem confronting Nicholas was the nationality question. Nearly half of the Empire was composed of ethnic minorities. Prudence dictated a cautious and conciliatory policy toward ethnic groups, especially those constituting large and compact segments of the Empire like Finns, Poles, or Ukrainians. Tsar Alexander III launched a vigorous policy of Russification of the western borderlands of the Empire; it was conducted by means of administration integration, placing many native Russians into administrative and professional positions in the Baltic provinces and Poland, encouragement of exclusively Russian education and even building more and more onionlike Orthodox churches in those largely Lutheran and Catholic regions, like Poland. This policy was not abandoned by Nicholas II. Following his father's slogan, "Russia for the Russians," Nicholas II pursued a policy of centralization and Russification. For instance, the autonomy of the Grand Duchy of Finland, respected by the previous rulers, was restricted in 1898. In 1901 the Finnish Army was disbanded and military conscription into the Russian armed forces was extended to the Grand Duchy of Finland. The Finns, hitherto loyal to the Empire but fiercely attached to their constitutional privileges, resented these encroachments. The centralizing policy boomeranged and eventually turned the hitherto peaceful Finns into supporters of the revolutionaries. The Finns provided them with shelter and assistance while nurturing their own irredentist aspirations. In the Empire's ten Polish provinces, the policy of Russification initiated after the uprising of 1863–1864 continued unabated.

The Tsarist regime did not recognize the existence of a separate Ukrainian nationality or Ukrainian language. According to official doctrine, there was only one Russian nation composed of three branches: Great Russians, Little Russians (Ukrainians), and White Russians (Belorussians). Also, the endemic anti-Semitism of the Russian autocracy continued under Nicholas II in a more virulent form. Legislation concerning the Pale of Settlement, where some 3 million Jews were located, was tightened. Their access to higher education and liberal professions was restricted; they were also discriminated against in economic life and subject to special taxes. The authorities tolerated vicious forms of anti-Semitism, including violent pogroms. The most infamous took place in Kishinev in April 1903, in Gomel in August 1903, and the largest in 1905 in Odessa. No wonder, therefore, that Jewish emigration from Russia to the United States, Palestine, and Western Europe continued to increase, while at home the Jews constituted a considerable segment of the revolutionary movement. At the same time, treatment of other national minorities, especially the Caucasian peoples and the Baltic Germans, was harsh and often trampled on their ethnic feelings unnecessarily. These policies tended to alienate large strata of the non-Russian majority of the Empire's population; the percentage of non-Russians in the revolutionary movement was remarkable high.

Industrial Expansion

The close of the nineteenth century saw the first phase of the industrial revolution in Russia. Large deposits of coal and iron were discovered in the Ukraine, especially in the basin of the Donets River, and oil was found in the Caucasus. From 1880 on, the output of iron and steel showed a remarkable increase. The Civil War in the United States made cotton export difficult and thereby stimulated its production in Russia, where the newly acquired Central Asiatic provinces supplied ample quantities of raw material. In northern Russia, production of flax grew by leaps and bounds. Soon Moscow and Lódz in Russian Poland became important centers of the textile industry. The rapid expansion of industrial production was par-

alleled by the mushrooming of private trade, banking, and insurance companies. The swift growth of industry, trade, communication, and various services resulted in the appearance of a large mass of urban workers and in the quick expansion of the stratum of professional people.

Economic development of the Tsarist Empire was given a powerful stimulus in 1892 with the appointment of Sergius Witte to the key post of Minister of Finance. This resourceful, self-made former railroad engineer proved to be a technocrat with great energy and a clear vision of Russia's future as an industrial giant. As Minister of Communication, he had already greatly developed the Empire's infrastructure, beginning with the railroad system—a precondition for industrialization. The climax of the railroad building came in the years 1896–1900, when over 10,000 miles of rails were laid. Witte who controlled the Ministry of Finance for eleven years until August 1903, laid down the foundation of capitalistic development of Russia. For a decade he was the most powerful man in Russia. Through his administrative empire-building, the Minister of Finance managed to control education and agriculture as well as foreign policy. Witte saw Russia as a part of European, indeed, world economy. Although a fierce patriot, he nevertheless believed that for a decade or so Russia should forego its great power pretentions in order to devote its energies and resources to the vital task of modernization.

Witte realized that to remain a great power the Empire had to modernize, which meant to him to industrialize at all costs. To this objective he was determined to subordinate other considerations. He was, for instance, in favor of a highly protectionist trade policy that would allow infant Russian industries to develop and mature. Consequently, he set up stiff tariffs and introduced heavy taxes on such articles of common use as alcohol, matches, tobacco, and kerosene. Witte was aware of the scarcity of Russia's native capital. Consequently, he tried to attract foreign investment with prospects of high profit and financial stability. Arguing that all major powers including Japan had adopted the gold standard, at that time a symbol of respectability, he introduced it in Russia in 1896. As advantageous as Witte's policy was for industrialization, however, it was a deterrent to agrarian progress; high tariffs, while protecting big industrial trusts and syndicates, drove the price of agricultural machinery and other products needed for modernization of the backward Russian farms to prohibitive heights.

On the other hand, under Witte's leadership Russian industry increasingly attracted foreign credits and investments. The alliance with France, concluded in 1892–1893 under Alexander III, was followed by a rapid influx of French capital. With its aid, the Trans-Siberian Railroad connected St. Petersburg with Vladivostok, although initially with only a single line. Soon British, Belgian, and American capital, lured by lavish connections and hugh profits, followed the French example.

As a consequence of rapid yet uneven progress and of rural overpopulation, the number of industrial workers was expanding rapidly. By the end of the nineteenth century they numbered over two and a half million, and well over three million on the eve of the Revolution of 1917. Their economic position was unenviable: they had to subsist on one of the lowest wages in Europe. They lived mostly in wretched, barracks-like dwellings or in miserable wooden cottages, where the lack of sanitation and pure water caused frequent outbursts of dysentery and typhoid fever. In 1897 the standard working day was eleven and a half hours. Because the workers had no right to association and no right to strike, they often had to suffer abuses by foremen as well as by factory owners. Only in 1912 would a rudimentary security system for industrial workers be introduced by the government. Attempts at strikes were ruthlessly suppressed.

In view of these actions, the proletarians of Russia felt that the Tsarist government was not their protector but their coexploiter,

who tended to side not with the workers but with the capitalists, many of whom were foreigners. Initially the workers' restiveness was not explosive; however, gradually stimulated by revolutionary agitation, they awakened to the value of group action, and industrial strikes and riots soon paralleled the traditional sporadic peasant mutinies. The situation worsened in 1901–1903 when Russia passed through an economic depression that resulted in widespread unemployment and a rapid fall in stocks, in bank capital, and in prices. In 1902, for instance, no less than 2,400 enterprises went bankrupt and over 90,000 workers lost their jobs.

Political Ferment

The second half of the nineteenth century, marked by rapid socioeconomic transformation and freer access to education in Russia, produced an expanding group of professional people. By the close of the century, they numbered some half a million. The industrial revolution, the expansion of the bureaucratic machine and of educational facilities, the functioning of rural self-government, all provided this group with broader political vistas. The growing aspirations and expectations of these people were bound to clash with the autocracy's monopoly of political power. To close the gap between the establishment and the educated, and hence politically minded, strata of the population seemed logical. This was not the case, however. The autocracy, after a brief period of relative liberalization that lasted for over a decade from 1855 to 1866, returned to tighter controls on intellectual activities; the autonomous status of institutions of higher learning was abolished and censorship of publications tightened. Constant administrative interference with the often enlightened and beneficial work of the local self-governments, which had been functioning in the countryside since the 1860s, heavy-handed censorship, tight control of the otherwise neglected educational institutions, and frequent arbitrary arrests irritated the Russian liberals. As a consequence, many members of the educated classes, denied legitimate active participation in political life, increasingly assumed the radical attitudes characteristic of the hard core of the intelligentsia. Many intellectuals, professional people, and even some of the gentry supported the working classes' demands for shorter hours, social security, and the right to organize. The early hopes that the Great Reforms initiated in the 1860s would be brought to their logical conclusion, that the autocratic regime would be gradually transformed into a constitutional monarchy, were cruelly disappointed under Alexander III. In 1896, Nicholas II also condemned these aspirations as "vain dreams."

The Russian liberal movement began to crystallize at the beginning of the twentieth century. In 1901, the progressive zemstvo circles established in Stuttgard, Germany, a journal called *Liberation*, under the editorship of a former Social Democrat, later a "legal Marxist," Peter Struve. The journal's first issue expressed the hope of "uniting all those groups of Russian society that cannot find an outlet for their feelings of indignation either in class or in revolutionary struggle." In 1903 some of the readers of the journal formed a *Union of Liberation* led by an eminent professor of history, Paul N. Miliukov, author of the impressive *Studies in the History of Russian Culture*.[1] Miliukov postulated that the subjects of the Empire should not be treated in a less favorable manner than the people whom they helped to free. He argued that the Russians, no less than the Bulgarians liberated by Russian arms from the Turks in 1878, deserved a bill of rights, including *habeas corpus*, and a constitutional charter granting political representation with representatives elected by universal suffrage. However, the program was rebuked by

the Government as unsuitable to Russia. This intractable attitude tended to push the frustrated Russian liberals to the left, toward the radicals and socialists. Consequently, to the ferment among the politically more advanced ethnic groups (the Jews, the Finns, the Poles), as well as the peasants and the workers, now were added many frustrated Russian liberals.

By 1902 the Empire was experiencing an economic depression and industrial unrest flared markedly. That summer the Ukrainian provinces witnessed the worst outbreak of peasant violence since 1880. The highly explosive situation alarmed Tsarist authorities. The reactionary Minister of the Interior, Vyacheslav von Plehve, talking to Witte in 1903, said bluntly: "The country is on the verge of revolution. The only way to avert it is to make a small victorious war." The tense situation in the Far East soon provided the military–bureaucratic clique at the Court with opportunities to engineer such a military venture as an outlet for domestic troubles.

Russian Foreign Policy

To understand the Russo-Japanese war of 1904–1905, once must outline Russia's international position. At the Congress of Berlin in 1878, the united front of Britain, Austria, and Germany deprived Russia of the main fruit of her victory over Turkey. Rebuffed in the Balkans, the Russians turned their energies toward Central Asia and the Far East, where they continued to press against the decaying Empire of China and gained considerable stretches of territory along the Amur River, as far as the Pacific. Drive in that direction was urged not only by a group of Russian thinkers and writers of the Eurasian school, who preached Russia's expansion in Asia, but also by a cousin of Nicholas II, the German Emperor William II. He was anxious to divert Russia's energy from the Balkans, where her Pan-Slavic ambitions conflicted with the interests of Germany's chief ally,

---

[1] The work appeared in English as *Outlines of Russian Culture*, edited by Michael Karpovich (Philadelphia: University of Philadelphia Press, 1942), 3 vols.

Austro-Hungary, while in Asia Russia was bound to clash with Britain, Germany's chief commercial and naval competitor.

Prussia had been Russia's traditional ally since the end of the eighteenth century, and the two countries were linked by a network of royal intermarriages as well as by a common fear of the twin dynamic forces of the modern era: nationalism and social revolution. Germany, united under Prussian leadership in 1871, continued to be Russia's chief trading partner and main provider of technical know-how. Nevertheless, the requirements of the European balance of power, the fear of the growing might of a powerful Germany allied with Austro–Hungary, pushed the Tsarist Empire toward France, then sulking after her defeat by Prussia in 1870–1871.

The spectacular German naval, commercial, and colonial expansion at the turn of the century also threatened the British. As a consequence, London gradually abandoned its traditional mistrust of the French and established an informal understanding with them known as *Entente Cordiale*. Yet even the *Entente* was not sufficiently strong to counterbalance the might of Germany and Austria, and Russian aid was considered indispensable by the French.

Rapprochement between autocratic Russia and liberal French Republic was not a simple matter. It was opposed in Russia by many conservatives, including Witte, who favored alliance with Germany, as well as by some economic vested interests. Nevertheless, believing Russia to be isolated and menaced by the growing German ambitions, Alexander III was increasingly leaning toward the French. The Russian need for French capital and the generous loans offered by Paris to St. Petersburg paved the way toward a political understanding in 1893–1894. The military agreement between Russia and France provided that, if France were attacked without provocation by Germany or by Italy supported by Germany, Russia would use all its available forces to fight Germany. On the other hand, if Russia were attacked by Germany, or by Austro-Hungary supported by Germany, France would launch an offensive against the aggressor with all its forces.

The signing of the alliance with France was designed to protect the Tsarist Empire from both Germany and Austro-Hungary. Vienna and Budapest, however, resented Russia's close ties with the Greek Orthodox Balkan Slavs, especially with small but ambitious Serbia, whose leaders dreamed of unifying all southern Slavs under their wing and thus creating a large Yugoslav state. In view of the circumstances under which World War I broke out, it is worth bearing in mind that the French promised to help the Russians against Austro-Hungary only in case the latter were supported by Germany. The alliance with France was the cornerstone of St. Petersburg's policy from 1894.

Russian Expansion in the Far East

Meanwhile, the progressive disintegration of the Chinese Empire, which essentially created a power vacuum in the Far East. This tempted Russia and Japan to fill the gap. Tsar Nicholas II believed in Russia's "Asiatic mission," and circumstances seemed to favor the idea. The Trans-Siberian railroad brought the Pacific within eight days' journey from Moscow. Russia's export of textiles and metallurgical products to Far Eastern markets expanded. Southern Siberia and the Maritime Provinces around Vladivostok were gradually settled with the surplus population from the Empire's European provinces. The Trans-Siberian railroad passed along southern Siberia but made a great detour around Manchuria's northern frontier in order to reach the main Russian port of the Pacific, Vladivostok, which in Russian means "Rule of the East."

China's growing weakness was an invitation to Russian expansion. Largely spontaneous, the drive that had begun in the sixteenth century assumed a more systematic character around the end of the nineteenth century. At the same time, however, the reformed and revitalized Japan was nurturing imperial ambitions around Manchuria and Korea—so close and hence believed to be vital to Japan's security. Since meanwhile, the Russians had also developed a foothold in Korea, the interests of these two dynamic powers clashed with those of the Chinese trying to protect their old hegemonic sphere.

In 1894 an armed conflict broke out between China and Japan over Korea. The freshly modernized Japanese army and navy easily prevailed over the antiquated Chinese forces. In 1895 Peking was compelled to cede to Japan the island of Formosa (now Taiwan), the Pescadores Islands, and the peninsula of Liao-Tung, which has two important harbors: Port Arthur and Dairen (known in Russian as Dalny). Both powers now recognized Korea's independence. Soon, however, an international conference summoned by Nicholas II deprived the Japanese of the strategic Liao-Tung peninsula. Instead the Japanese were given a considerable indemnity and kept Formosa and the Pescadores. China's territorial integrity was otherwise guaranteed by Russia. For its alleged services to China, Russia extracted an important concession for the construction of a railroad running from China across Manchuria to Vladivostok. The concession put a considerable strip of Chinese territory under Russian administration for a period of eighty years. Russian troops organized as an "international defense force" were to protect the "East Chinese Railway."

Meanwhile, the Russians were also trying to replace China as Korea's protector. Simultaneously with the penetration of both Manchuria and Korea. St. Petersburg extracted from Peking another concession in the form of the right to keep Russian warships in Port Arthur and Dairen. This gave the Russians unhampered, ice-free access to the Pacific through the Yellow Sea, outside the enclosed Sea of Japan. As a consequence of these encroachments, China's patriotic feelings were aroused and a wave of xenophobia swept the country. In November 1897, two German missionaries were killed by a mob in Shantung. To this the European powers replied by wholesale despoliation of China. Germany, Great Britain, and France each annexed a port city, while Russia, guarantor of China's integrity, imposed on Peking another of those "unequal treaties," about which the Chinese have been complaining ever since, and wrested Port Arthur. The annexation was camouflaged as a "lease" for twenty-five years.

The humiliated and desperate Chinese replied to this vivisection with another outburst of xenophobia and a revolt led by a military organization known as "Boxers." In 1900 numerous massacres of the "foreign devils" were perpetrated throughout the Middle Kingdom. The Western quarter in Peking was besieged. The European powers retorted with a naval and military expedition and a cruel revenge. Now the Chinese were compelled by St. Petersburg to prolong the "lease" of Port Arthur from twenty-five to ninety-nine years. The harbor was connected with the Trans-Siberian railway through the "Chinese Eastern Railway" running through Manchuria.

Meanwhile, at the Russian capital two factions were fighting over the best course of action to be taken in the Far East. One was headed by Witte, who argued that Russia should take into consideration Japan's vital interest at least in Korea and slow down its headlong expansion. In a memorandum presented to the Tsar in 1902, he urged him to strive for a rapprochement with Japan on the basis of mutual economic advantages in developing the resources of the Far East. Witte advised Nicholas to strike a bargain with Tokyo that would consolidate Russian influence in rich and strategic Manchuria while leaving Korea to Japan. This cautious policy of "peaceful penetration" was opposed by a group of the Tsar's advisors, who played on the Emperor's proclivity toward spectacular schemes and on the greed of some Grand Dukes who had been involved in a timber concession on the Yalu River, while looking on the Japanese as a sort of short-tailed monkies. Supported by the influential Minister of the Interior, von Plehve, the hawks won the day. In August of 1903, Witte was dismissed from the key post of Minister of Finance and appointed to the largely nominal post of Chairman of the Council of Ministers. His economically inspired pacifism was only one of many disagreements between the Tsar and Witte, who was a paragon of efficiency and an often brutally frank opponent of some of the Emperor's hare-brained schemes.

While recklessly pursuing an expansionist policy and rejecting Japanese overtures, St. Petersburg neglected adequate military and naval preparations in the Far East. The Russians were looking down on the "yellow monkies," as inferior, incapable of challenging the superior Slavs.

The Russo–Japanese War of 1904–1905

After completing their preparations, the Japanese, without declaring war, launched a surprise attack on the Russian Pacific squadron lying at anchor off Port Arthur on the night of January 26 (February 8 NS), 1904. Several Russian vessels were destroyed and several others damaged. The remnant of the crippled fleet was compelled to seek shelter in the inner harbor, there to be blockaded for months. This early version of "Pearl Harbor" left the strategic initiative in the hands of the Japanese.

In view of this disaster, it was decided in St. Petersburg that the Russian Baltic squadron should be sent to Far Eastern waters to restore the naval balance there. The squadron, unable to sail through the Suez Canal controlled by Japan's ally, Great Britain, had to travel almost nine months; they covered 18,000 miles, or three-fourths of the earth's circumference. Sailing around the Cape of Good Hope, the Baltic squadron finally reached the Far Eastern theater of war in May 1905. There in the straits of Tsushima that separate Korea from Japan, the naval battle of Tsushima was fought on May 27–29. The encounter of the two fleets, in which nearly a hundred ships took part, lasted only about forty-five minutes. The more maneuverable and better commanded Japanese fleet annihilated the Russian Baltic Squadron almost completely.

Having seized command of the sea, the Japanese transported their superbly trained troops, full of patriotic fervor, onto the Asian mainland. Fighting with reckless bravado, they proceeded to inflict on the Russians a series of humiliating defeats, first in the valley of the Yalu River and then in Manchuria. Meanwhile, the Russian Far Eastern military stronghold, Port Arthur, surrendered in December 1904 after 148 days of siege.

Despite the catastrophe of Tsushima and the capitulation of Port Arthur, and despite the defeats in Manchuria, the total potential resources of Russia were still far superior to those of Japan, exhausted by her costly victories. What prevented Nicholas II from continuing the war was the situation at home. From the very beginning the distant Far East war was almost as unpopular among the Russian people as the war in Vietnam was to be in the United States. By the summer of 1905, large-scale political manifestations and mutinies by soldiers, sailors, peasants, and workers, acts of terror, and sabotage assumed menacing proportions. Under the circumstances, Tsar Nicholas decided to accept United States President Theodore Roosevelt's suggestion of peace. Witte was sent to the United States to negotiate a settlement. At the presidential summer home in Portsmouth, New Hampshire, the peace treaty between Russia and Japan was signed on August 23 (September 5 NS), 1905. Witte acknowledged Korea and southern Manchuria as part of Japan's sphere of influence. The Japanese annexed the southern part of the island of Sakhalin. Russia ceded to Japan the rights it had recently acquired in Port Arthur and Dairen on the peninsula of Liao-Tung. Northern Manchuria, however, with its important Chinese Eastern Railway, remained within the Russian orbit.

Territorial Expansion of Russia, 1550–1917

The underlying cause of Russia's defeat was its failure to match its imperial drive in the Far East with adequate diplomatic planning and to balance its new commitments with adequate military resources. Blinded by their racist mentality, the Russians had underestimated the power of Japan. While provoking Tokyo by encroaching on Japan's spheres of influence in southern Manchuria and Korea, the Russians had failed to draw proper conclusions about the possible consequences of their acts. Lack of adequate military supplies, antiquated training, obsolete transport facilities, and the corruption and inefficiency of the Russian civil military administration were all significant factors that hampered the Russian war effort. But political and social unrest played a crucial role in the Russian acceptance of the Japanese peace terms.

Unrest at Home

From the very beginning, the politically conscious Russian people suspected that the foreign adventures had been engineered by the Tsarist bureaucrats as a substitute for domestic reforms. Yet as long as there was a chance for a military victory, the population of Russia proper did not protest very actively. Initially, it was in the nationally heterogeneous borderlands—where ethnic grievances were compounded by political and socioeconomic issues—of the Baltic provinces, Ukraine and of Russian Poland that the opposition to the war assumed very threatening proportions from the very beginning.

In Russia proper, the first major symptom of discontent came somewhat later; the assassination of the unpopular Minister of the Interior, von Plehve, in July 1904 by a member of the Social Revolutionary Party was one of the first signals of the unrest. Von Plehve was replaced by a mild liberal, Prince Sviatopolk-Mirsky, who immediately made a series of minor concessions. These failed however, to satisfy mounting opposition. From late autumn of 1904, most of the educated politically active middle and upper classes were in an uproar, loudly condemning the war and urging immediate reforms. When in December 1904 the fortress of Port Arthur capitulated under humiliating circumstances, a wave of protest against the war spread to the proletarian masses in the cities and to the countryside. When four members of a labor group were dismissed from the Putilov Steel Works in St. Petersburg in December 1904, several thousand workers went on strike. Soon other factories in the capital joined them. By the beginning of January 1905, the number of strikers had reached 140,000. Most of the industrial life of the capital was paralyzed.

Aware of inflation and unemployment among the workers of the capital and sympathizing with their plight, the hitherto loyal Christian Socialist Assembly of the Russian Factory Workers, led by an Orthodox priest, Father Gapon, decided to stage a mass demonstration. His idea was to submit the grievances of the workers in the form of a humble petition to the Tsar, asking for an eight-hour workday, an increase in workers' wages up to one ruble per day, a bill of rights, and free universal education. Despite police warnings that the planned mass demonstration would not be tolerated in the vicinity of the Palace and that the delegation would not be received by the Tsar, Gapon insisted on carrying out his original plan.

On Sunday, January 9 (22 NS), 1905, large crowds of workers singing patriotic and church songs and carrying pictures of the Imperial family and holy icons converged on the Winter Palace. On the order of Grand Duke Vladimir, military governor of the capital, the police and some 20,000 soldiers barred all roads leading to the Palace. When, despite two successive warnings to disperse, the demonstrators pressed their march forward, several volleys were fired into the crowd. Then a cavalry charge dispersed the demonstrators. According to the official figures, 96 people were killed on the spot and 333 wounded, of whom 34 died subsequently.

Prior to that bloody Sunday, often called

President Theodore Roosevelt with S. J. Witte and Baron Roman Rosen of Russia and the Japanese Delegates before the signing of the Treaty of Portsmouth.

"the Gaponade," the old myth of the Tsar as "Little Father" had lingered among the people. The massacre of January 22 dealt a severe blow to the legend of the "good Tsar" separated from his children by the "bad bureaucrats." The expulsion of a large number of unemployed people from the capital ordered by authorities after the massacre merely helped to disseminate the news about the carnage to the remote corners of the Empire. This resulted in an epidemic of strikes, mutinies, and other violent demonstrations that soon spilled over the Tsarist domains.

Meanwhile, in March 1905, the Russian forces were beaten at the eight-day battle of Mukden, in Manchuria, the bloodiest battle of the war, and lost nearly 100,000 men. Again the Government offered some concessions to appease the people and issued a series of partial concessions. In April a toleration edict was issued: Religious teaching was declared free, and dissenters from Greek Orthodoxy were allowed to abandon the established church. Jews were also given some minor concessions. When news of the Tsushima catastrophe reached the capital, the government outlined a scheme for a consultative assembly to be elected on a limited franchise in four stages.

The opposition took advantage of this scheme, which seemed to foreshadow elections to a consultative *Duma* (assembly), to form open political parties, trade unions, and other associations. From the "Mukden Spring" on, hitherto secret groups, like the Constitutional Democrats (or Cadets), the Social Revolutionaries, the two Social-Democratic factions, as well as innumerable minor groups and trade organizations, operated quite freely. On the initiative of these parties, pamphlets and leaflets were published, and meetings and mass demonstrations were organized. All the while, political unrest was spreading and numerous mutinies in the armed forces took place; for instance, the sailors of the battleship *Potemkin* rebelled in Odessa in June 1905. During the spring and summer of 1905, Russian, Ukrainian, and Latvian peasants began to help themselves to the landlords' estates, to cut timber, and to appropriate grain, cattle, and implements. There were numerous cases of the peasants paying off old scores with bludgeon and torch.

The St. Petersburg Soviet and the Constitutional Manifesto

It was in the midst of this ferment that Witte returned home with the Treaty of Portsmouth in his pocket. This meant that now the Tsarist regime would be able to withdraw most of the Far Eastern contingent of troops and assume a stiffer posture toward the opposition. By October the Government regained its self-confidence and ordered the entire Congress of Railroad Workers, then deliberating in St. Petersburg, to be arrested. In protest against this move, nearly all the railroads went on strike. As a result, many factories had to stop work because of the lack of supplies. In a few days the strike had spread and paralyzed most communication, industry, trade, education, and even entertainment within the Empire. It was especially effective in St. Petersburg, essentially a northern frontier city overwhelmingly dependent on transport for food, fuel, and other necessities.

Amidst the mounting wave of protest was born the idea of a working-class coordinating council to direct the originally spontaneous protest movement. The nucleus of the first such council (*soviet* in Russian) was set up by the strikers of some fifty printing shops in the capital. They elected deputies to represent them in dealing with the authorities. These deputies, joined by delegates from other similar bodies, formed a Council, or Soviet, of Workers' Deputies composed of some 122 members; 26 of them were delegates of the organized trade unions, while 96 represented various industrial plants. The St. Petersburg Soviet elected an Executive Committee. Its vice-chairman was a young member of the Russian Social-Democratic Workers' Party, Leon Bronstein (best known by one of his pen names Trotsky). The St. Petersburg Soviet of Workers' Deputies issued a manifesto that not only repeated the demand for a Constituent Assembly, but also appealed for unity of the working class under "the glorious Red Flag of the proletarians of all lands," an echo of the Communist Manifesto of Marx and Engels.

The majority of the St. Petersburg Soviet belonged either to the Menshevik faction of the RSDWP or, like Trotsky, were close to it; the rest were affiliated either with the Bolsheviks, the Social Revolutionaries, or various minor revolutionary groups. Overthrow of the autocracy and setting up a democratic republic in Russia were their common objectives. For this purpose, the Soviet urged the workers to form fighting squads, or "Red Guards." Soon similar Soviets were formed in several hundred provincial places. From the very beginning there were differences of opinion between various groups as to the course to be followed. The Bolsheviks and some of the Social Revolutionaries considered an armed uprising as the only means of overthrowing the Tsarist regime; the Mensheviks saw a possibility of at least a temporary accommodation with the liberals and were less inclined to plot an armed uprising. At the bottom of this attitude of the Mensheviks was the classic Marxist theory of a two-stage revolution and a hope for a legal workers' party modeled after the German Social-Democratic movement.

Frightened by the general strike, Tsar Nicholas surrendered. On October 17 (30 NS), 1905, he decided upon a step that he regarded as a betrayal of the promise he had made to his father on his deathbed: to preserve the autocratic power intact. He reluctantly issued a manifesto that promised most of the concessions demanded by the liberal opposition. The concessions included a bill of rights and a Legislative Assembly, without which no law would be passed. The assembly was to comprise two houses. The lower house, or *Duma*, was to be composed of deputies elected for five years on a fairly broad franchise; the upper house, the old but now reshaped Council of State, was to be composed of an equal number of appointed and elected representatives. Cabinet ministers were to be appointed by and responsible to the monarch.

According to the supplemental Fundamental Laws, the monarch—not the people—was the source of sovereignty. The budget rights of the Duma were strictly limited, with certain segments exempted from its control, including the budget of the Imperial House and certain sections of the armed forces appropriations. Budget and foreign policy were to be controlled largely by the sovereign. Article 87 of the Fundamental Laws granted the Government the right to issue decrees in case of emergency or when the Duma was not in session. Such decrees, however, were technically invalid unless confirmed by the Duma within three months. In short, the Russian system was a crossbreed between Western constitutionalism and Russian autocracy. Significantly, the Tsar not only retained numerous prerogatives but also his title of "Autocrat of all the Russias."

The last major revolutionary event of that fateful year was another general strike proclaimed by the Moscow Soviet in December to protest against the reprisals. Soon the strike turned into an armed uprising in the working-class Presna district of Moscow and was brutally suppressed. It took two years and a series of stern measures to bring the minor, smoldering fires of 1905 under control. Peasant unrest continued throughout 1906 and was only suppressed by large-scale summary executions of the rebellion's ringleaders. But with the collapse of the Moscow rebellion, the task of breaking the back of the revolutionary movement was accomplished.

Summary: The Balance Sheet

The balance sheet of the crisis of 1905 is complex. Was it a real revolution? As a result of it, no new ruler ascended the throne, no socioeconomic upheaval took place, no power was transferred from one class to another, and no radical shift in Russia's foreign policy was brought about. The revolt of the workers and peasants was suppressed without the achievement of their final objectives. The widespread unrest and the series of mass demonstrations, mutinies, and acts of terror resulted merely in a partial reshaping of the autocratic system, which became a halfway house between Western liberalism and Russian authoritarianism, a hybrid combining Western constitutionalism with native autocracy. The compromise reflected the balance of political forces that existed within the Empire at that time.

It was true that under pressure of the protest movement, the autocracy had had to make some concessions to the opposition, but the opposition was not strong enough to make absolutism capitulate unconditionally. The two pillars of the regime, the armed forces and the bureaucracy, although badly shattered, remained basically loyal to the Tsar. The peasants, previously frightened by the punitive expeditions, were now temporarily bribed by the abolition of the redemption payments. The revolutionaries proved to be weak because of their division among at least three major groups, the Social Revolutionary Party, the Mensheviks, and the Bolsheviks, each advocating different tactics.

Nevertheless, the events of 1904–1905 should be looked upon as a "dress rehearsal for 1917," as Lenin put it. The crisis of 1905 brought about a series of novel phenomena that foreshadowed future events. One of them was the active participation of millions of people in political life. Another novelty was the emergence from the underground of the first legal political parties in Russian history; the most important were the Cadets, the SRs, and the Social Democrats, by that time already irrevocably split into two rival factions, the Bolsheviks and the Mensheviks.

The revolution of 1905 saw also the appearance of the organized right wing political parties, like Russian Monarchist Party or the Union of the Russian People. The Monarchist Party was permeated with vague Slavophile ideas: They idealized the ancient *Zemsky Sobor*, and longed for the return of the stern authoritarian methods of Aleksander III with his Russification program and emphasis on Orthodoxy as a state religion. With their antiquated ideas the Monarchist Party remained a small group. The Union of the Russian People, on the other hand, became a large-scale political movement. Led by energetic people like Dr. A. I. Dubrovin and V. M. Puryshkievich, they declared as their goal to "unify Russian people of all estates and statuses in order to work together on behalf of our beloved fatherland Russia, one and indivisible," and vowed to fight for this goal they regarded as a secret crusade. With the slogans "For Tsar, Faith, and Fatherland" and "Russia is for Russians," they were determined to use all methods, fair and foul to impose their xenophobic, anti-Semitic program on the highly ethnically differentiated Empire. Not avoiding parliamentary activities, the union emphasized "direct action" and organized fighting squads for this purpose. Soon the example set by the Union was imitated by numerous other rightist groups that mushroomed during the turbulent years 1905–1907. Like vigilantes, these rightist groups intimidated and even killed their political opponents.

From now on these parties, together with other emerging organizations like the legalized trade unions and other professional associations, made Russia a different place. Finally, October 1905 saw the appearance of the St. Petersburg Soviet, a broadly representative council of the working class. The institution of Soviets was to play a significant role in the more serious crisis of 1917.

The crisis of 1904–1905 also gave a powerful stimulus to the more developed and restless ethnic groups of the Empire to express their own dissatisfaction. As a result, the Poles and the Baltic peoples, and to a lesser extent the Jews, gained some religious and cultural concessions. The revolutionary events of 1904–1905 also hastened the evolution of the national consciousness of the Ukrainians and the Muslim peoples of the Caucasus and Central Asia. Consequently, the crisis of 1904–1905 was also an ethnic upheaval.

The crisis of 1905 had, moreover, considerable impact on the outside world. Besides stimulating the growth of radical and socialist forces in Europe, the Russian storm contributed substantially to the subsequent awakening of nationalism and the development of constitutional regimes in Turkey, Persia, and China. The Russo-Japanese War was fought largely on Chinese territory; in Manchuria, and around the Liao-Tung peninsula. This further stressed the helplessness of the Manchu dynasty, accelerated its downfall in 1911, and prepared the way for the proclamation of the Chinese Republic with Sun Yat-Sen as President.

The Russo-Japanese War, which represented the first major defeat of a great European power at the hands of an Asian nation, was also a major stage in the process of undermining the supremacy of the white man on the globe. The Russian storm of 1905 contributed significantly toward preparing the ground for a tidal wave of anti-white, anticolonial sentiment, which spread from Asia to Africa and in our day has swept away most of the colonial regimes.

Suggested Reading

BECKER, SEYMOUR, *Russia's Protectorates in Central Asia: Khiva and Bokhara*. Cambridge, MA: Harvard University Press, 1968.

BONNELL, VICTORIA, *Roots of Rebellion, Workers' Politics and Organizations in St. Petersburg and Moscow, 1900–1914*. Berkeley and Los Angeles: University of California Press, 1986.

BUSHNELL, JOHN, *Mutiny Amid Repression: Russian Soldiers in the Revolution of 1905–1906*. Indiana-Michigan Series in Russian and East European

Studies (Alexander Rabinowitch and William G. Rosenberg, Eds.). Bloomington: Indiana University Press, 1985.

CONNAUGHTON,, R. M., *The War of the Rising Sun and the Tumbling Bear: A Military History of the Russo-Japanese War, 1904–1905.* New York: Routlege, 1988.

DZIEWANOWSKI, M. K., *The Communist Party of Poland: An Outline of History.* Cambridge, MA: Harvard University Press, 1976, Chs. 1–3.

GRANT, JONATHAN A., *Big Business in Russia: The Putilov Company in Late Imperial Russia, 1868–1917.* Pitt Series in Russian and East European Studies. Pittsburgh: University of Pittsburgh Press, 1999.

GREENBERG, LOUIS, *The Jews in Russia: The Struggle for Emancipation.* New Haven, CT: Yale University Press, 1965, 2 vols.

HARCAVE, SIDNEY, *First Blood: The Russian Revolution of 1905.* New York: Macmillan, 1964.

HOSKING, GEOFFREY, *Russia: People and Empire 1552–1917.* Cambridge, MA: Harvard University Press, 1997.

KILLER, D. JOHN, *Imperial Russia's Jewish Question.* London: Cambridge University Press, 1995.

LAQUEUR, WALTER, *Black Hundred,* New York: Harper Collins, 1993.

MALAMAZOFF, ANDREW, *Russian Far Eastern Policy, 1881–1904.* Berkeley: University of California Press, 1958.

PAVLOVSKY, GEORGE, *Agricultural Russia on the Eve of the Revolution* (reprint). New York: Howard Fertig, 1968.

RAWSON, DON, *Russian Right and the Revolution of 1905.* London: Cambridge University Press, 1995.

ROMANOV, BORIS A., *Russia in Manchuria, 1892–1906.* Ann Arbor, MI: J. W. Edward, 1952.

RUBINOW, ISAAC MAX, *Economic Conditions of the Jews in Russia.* New York: Arno, 1975.

SABLINSKY, WALTER, *The Road to Bloody Sunday.* Princeton, NJ: Princeton University Press, 1976.

SCHWARZ, SALOMAN M., *The Revolution of 1905: The Workers' Movement and the Formation of Bolshevism and Menshevism.* Chicago: University of Chicago Press, 1967.

SPECTOR, IVAR, *The First Russian Revolution and Its Impact on Asia.* Upper Saddle River, NJ: Prentice-Hall, 1962.

TROTSKY, LEON, *1905.* New York: Random House, 1971.

TROYAT, HENRI, *Daily Life in Russia under the Last Tsar.* New York: Macmillan, 1962.

VERNER, ANDREW, M., *The Crisis of Russian Autocracy: Nicholas II and the 1905 Revolution.* Princeton, NJ: Princeton University Press, 1990.

VON LAUE, THEODORE, *Sergei Witte and the Industrialization of Russia* New York: Columbia University Press, 1963.

WITTE, SERGEI, *Memoirs of Count Witte.* New York: M. E. Sharpe, 1990.

WOOD ALAN (ED.), *The History of Siberia: From Russian Conquest to Revolution.* New York: Routledge, 1991.

Chapter 5

The Aftermath of the Revolution of 1905: The Constitutional Experiment

The crushing of the Moscow uprising set the stage for the elections to the first Duma. Meanwhile, fortified by a large loan of 400 million rubles that France had granted to bolster its tottering ally, and with the aid of the troops returning from the Far East, Witte gradually proceeded to pacify the rebellious western and central provinces. The peasants were appeased by the abolition of the redemption payments and the soldiers by an increase in allowances to privates and non-commissioned officers and the payment of bonuses to those who participated in police duties. The main centers of the rebellion thus were repressed. Although some acts of terror and agrarian disturbances and riots, especially in the western borderlands, continued for over a year, the exhausted country was gradually settling down to a more normal existence.

Having restored a semblance of order, Witte made his bid to the liberals. He issued a decree that made the franchise for the Duma practically universal; it was to include all taxpayers, nearly all lodgers, and all factory workers. Unimpressed by the October Manifesto, the Fundamental Laws, and Witte's gambit, the Cadet leader Pavel Mil-

iukov rejected a ministerial post and declared, "Nothing has changed, the struggle goes on." He believed that no reform short of the establishment of a parliamentary system of the British type would be good enough for Russia. Many of his colleagues did not share that view, however. Consequently, the Cadet party split; its right wing seceded and formed a party of its own led by a moderate liberal businessman, Alexander I. Guchkov. The new party represented the progressive stratum of the upper middle class, which approved of the October Manifesto and was determined to implement it; hence their colloquial name, the *Octobrists*.

The First Duma and Witte's Dismissal

The Duma elections were an unprecedented phenomenon in Russian history. For the first time the people were allowed to participate in the political process. Voting took place in March 1906, in a tense and uncertain atmosphere punctuated by acts of terror. Because both the reactionaries and the radicals had been discredited by their excesses, public opinion favored the middle-of-the-road parties. Moreover, a boycott of the elections by most of the socialist groups benefited the well-organized Cadets, whose slogan, "Political Freedom and Social Justice," appealed to many people. And indeed they won well over one-third of all the seats and emerged as the largest party in the Duma. The Cadets were the only nonsocialist group that had vitality, vision, and good organization. Consequently, they dominated the first Duma.

As soon as Witte had completed the tricky task of transition from autocracy pure and simple to a half-autocratic, half-constitutional regime, he was dismissed by the Tsar, who disliked him because of his liberal leaning and his condescending attitude. Witte did not hesitate to drop such critical remarks about his master like, for instance: "Can't you understand this? Even the Tsar understands it!" Witte was the dominant personality of Russia's politics in the late nineteenth and early twentieth century, its virtual Prime Minister for over a decade, from 1892 to 1903. A man of great energy and considerable political skill, he was determined to push industrialization at all cost. He boldly tried to overcome Russia's backwardness by modernizing her economy from above. Under his administration the Empire's industrial production more than doubled. He was convinced that enlightened, modernized absolutism was more suitable for Russia than Western parliamentary systems. Yet once the constitutional remedy appeared to him as an expedient necessity, he did not hesitate to sponsor it with the zeal so characteristic of all his undertakings. With the dismissal of Witte passed one of the rare statesmen of the Empire's twilight.

The business of the first Duma, which gathered in the Tauride Palace in St. Petersburg in May 1906, was largely in the hands of the Cadets. On their initiative the House put forward a program of comprehensive reforms, including a scheme for agrarian reform that provided for segments of private large estates to be expropriated at a fair market price and divided among peasants under state supervision. However, the program was rejected outright by the Government as "inadmissible" and

Count Sergious J. Witte
(1849–1915)

violating "the sacred right of private property." In reply, the House declared its lack of confidence in the Government, a move contrary to the Constitution. This provoked the Government to issue a statement warning the country not to trust the Duma. To this the House replied by passing an appeal to the people denouncing the Executive. Unable to work with the Duma, Tsar Nicholas dissolved it in July 1906 after less than three months.

The night of the dissolution some two hundred deputies, most of them Cadets, crossed the Finnish border to Viborg. There, under the protection of Finnish autonomy, they drew up another public appeal urging passive resistance, including refusal to pay taxes and supply recruits to the armed forces until the Duma was restored. The opposition also disclaimed responsibility for all foreign loans secured by the Executive without the Duma's approval. The Government denounced the Viborg Manifesto as a revolutionary step and disenfranchised its authors. The manifesto fell flat because the apathetic country would not respond to its appeal.

The Ascent of Stolypin

Piotr Stolypin, Minister of the Interior, was now appointed as Premier. Although a moderate constitutionalist by conviction, Stolypin was determined to interpret the October Manifesto and the Fundamental Laws in a restrictive sense and refused to go any further because he believed that Russia was not yet ready for a fully parliamentary system. Another Duma was called for March 1907, within the legal time limit of nine months. Stolypin used the intervening period for accomplishing two tasks: to restore "law and order" and to implement moderate reforms. The pacification, however, he considered as priority number one.

Both tasks were to be accomplished by means of extensive use of Article 87 of the Fundamental Laws, which allowed the Government to issue decrees when the Duma was not in session. In September 1906, Stolypin instituted special military tribunals to deal with flagrant violations of the law. The proceedings of these tribunals were to be completed within four days. In case of conviction, the standard sentence was death, usually by hanging. Where the disorder assumed threatening proportions, as in Russian Poland or in the Baltic provinces, large-scale "punitive expeditions" were dispatched. From the day of their institution in September 1906 to the day of their cancellation in May 1907, these tribunals executed 1,144 persons. Hence the hangman's noose became known as "Stolypin's necktie." To understand the severity of Stolypin's reprisals, one has to bear in mind the violence and scope of the lingering revolutionary ferment and the acts of terror perpetrated. During the year 1906 alone, no fewer than 738 state officials and 645 private individuals were murdered by revolutionaries and common criminals, while, 1,719 were wounded. In 1907 about 3,000 people all told were killed and nearly 1,734 wounded. Only in 1908 did these figures drop dramatically.

The terrorist activities of the leftist groups were matched by the extreme right-wing groups, who set up armed squads of all sorts and perpetrated numerous acts of violence. The "Fighting Squads" of the right became known under the blanket name of *Black Hundreds*. The rightists were convinced that the Constitutional Manifesto of 1905 was an unwarranted mistake, a concession wrested from the Autocrat in a moment of weakness by the revolutionary movement secretly instigated by the Jews. The Black Hundreds unleashed vitriolic anti-Semitic propaganda and staged several pogroms. Soon the rightists founded a political party called *The Union of the Russian People*, which insisted on the revocation of the Manifesto. In 1907–1908, at the peak of its activity, the Union had about 200 branches with some 30,000 members.

The Russian conservative movement, of which the Black Hundreds was merely a lunatic fringe, was shaped largely by the negative qualities of its left-wing opponent. The conservatives shared with the leftists their preference for physical violence, their contempt for Western liberalism, and their all-or-nothing attitude. Both groups were, in different ways, authoritarian and intolerant. If one adds the elements of racism inherent in their glorification of their own people, their anti-Semitism, and their love of terror, called "direct action," the Black Hundreds were in many ways forerunners of Fascism.

Stolypin's Agrarian Reforms

The new strong man of the constitutional period, Piotr Stolypin, a landowner of gentry origin, was also for modernization; unlike Witte, however, he emphasized modernization of Russia's agrarian structure. Stolypin was by education a natural scientist with a strong interest in agriculture. He acquired extensive administrative experience as an efficient governor of Grodno and Saratov, on the Volga. Despite his social origins, Stolypin was aware that an inept, indolent, and impoverished rural nobility could not be a sufficient base for the Imperial regime. Even the addition of the bureaucracy and the small, largely foreign, entrepreneurial and merchant groups could not sufficiently broaden the social base of the regime. Stolypin understood that the welfare of the largest stratum of the country was a prerequisite for its overall economic well-being and political stability. To rebuild the prosperity of

Piotr A. Stolypin (1862–1911)

peasant Russia, a task neglected by Witte, now became Stolypin's main objective.

Simultaneously with the repressive measures, between September and November 1906 Stolypin issued a series of decrees that constituted a virtual agrarian revolution. First, he made large tracts of Crown and State land available for sale at moderate prices to the peasants. Second, he allowed them to leave the village communes and claim their allotment in a private property consolidated in one parcel outside the mir, and thus become individual farmers, like those of Western and Central Europe. Finally, Stolypin swept away most of the vestiges of feudalism still affecting the peasantry, like special domestic passports, arbitrary jurisdiction of the land captains, and degrading corporal punishment. The peasants were now eligible for offices in local administration. Thus the peasantry was made equal with other classes.

Stolypin's objective was to encourage the more enterprising, hard-working, thrifty peasants, those who had enough savings and energy to take advantage of his reform, which, under Russian conditions of inveterate collectivism, had a rather revolutionary tinge. "The sober and the strong," as he put it, were to remain in the countryside, set up their individual farms, and become the backbone of the new, orderly, prosperous, and powerful Great Russia. Those who had neither resources nor skills to accommodate themselves to the new conditions were either to be driven to the cities to provide a surplus labor force for fast-growing industry or be left in the countryside as cheap hired labor available to the squires and the prosperous peasants, or *kulaks*.

Of all the Russian political parties, only the Octobrists backed Stolypin's enlightened reforms. For opposite reasons, both the conservatives and the revolutionaries desired to maintain the village commune. The former, permeated with the Slavophile concept of an idealized mir, wanted to preserve this decaying institution as an alleged embodiment of the old Russian tradition. The socialist parties, on the other hand, wanted to keep communal ownership of the land because, they calculated, it would be easier to transfer to State ownership the already collectively owned land than to wrest it from millions of individual farmers. Both factions of the Social Democrats rejected the Stolypin reform because they realized that the creation of a strong stratum of yeomanry would imperil their chances of grabbing political power. The Social Revolutionary Party held that the land was to be handed over to the local organs of self-government for lease to peasant families. The Cadets criticized the reform as not radical enough; it avoided the crucial issue of the compulsory division of private large estates against proper compensation to the owners.

Thus only the masses of the peasantry enthusiastically responded to the decrees of the Premier. The response was strongest in the Ukraine on the right bank of the Dnieper, where the tradition of individual ownership was strongest. There about half of the former communal land soon passed into private ownership. Between 1907 and 1915, when the reform was suspended because, as it was explained, of the absence of huge numbers of drafted men, over two million peasant households left the collective exploitation of the land, or the mir, and became individual owners of their allotments. This amounted to 22 percent of the total number of commune members. Since, in addition to that, there were over 2.8 million peasant families, mostly in the western and southwestern provinces of the Empire, who owned their plots as individual farmers before Stolypin's reform, by 1915 about half of the whole peasantry was already free of its debilitating collectivist fetters.

The Second Duma

While pacifying the country and reshaping its agrarian structure, Stolypin was at the same time engineering the elections to the second Duma. This was a difficult task because, for the first time, various socialist parties decided to participate in the elections. The Senate, by arbitrary interpretation of the Electoral Law, disenfranchised large categories of voters. This included the 200 signatories of the Viborg Manifesto. The attempts at influencing the election to the second Duma by "administrative means" backfired, however, and the second Duma was considerably to the left of the first. Although the Cadet representation was reduced by one-third, various socialist groups entered the second Duma in force; together they represented an impressive force of about two hundred deputies. The two factions of the RSDWP, together with their sympathizers, had sixty-five votes, of which thirty-five were Mensheviks or their hangers-on, while the Bolsheviks had only eighteen deputies. The Populist Labor Party, or the *Trudoviki*, was the largest segment, numbering 104 deputies. While the Mensheviks plunged into parliamentary activity with gusto, the Bolsheviks regarded the Duma merely as an arena for the dissemination of revolutionary propaganda. By blocking orderly legislative activity, the Bolshevik Duma faction persistently interfered with the enactment of various reforms.

The life of the second Duma was no smoother than that of the first. The question of terror and sabotage and the measures to be undertaken to curtail them soon resulted in another political stalemate between the Duma and the Government. While the opposition denounced Stolypin's method of pacification, the Government in turn indiscriminately condemned most of the Duma factions for stirring up civil disobedience. Stolypin, who was an authoritarian personality, found it difficult to establish a working compromise with a popular representative body. Unable to achieve a modicum of cooperation, in June 1907 he dissolved the three-month-old second Duma under the convenient pretext that a group of deputies had participated in a plot against the life of the Emperor.

Before the Duma's dissolution, a new electoral law had been carefully prepared by the Ministry of the Interior. The law was a violation of the Constitution, which provided that no change relating to the status of the Chambers was to take place without the consent of the Duma. But Stolypin, bent on having a more cooperative legislature, proceeded to engineer elections to the third Duma to suit his purpose. The original electoral law had been framed in a way that would assure a large peasant representation. Stolypin firmly believed that the peasants were essentially conservative, loyal to the Tsar, and should be made the foundation of the system. In the first and second Dumas, however, the peasant deputies surprised the Government by their advocacy of several radical schemes, including the abolition of large private estates. Consequently, the new electoral law was so constructed as to give predominance to the gentry and the upper middle class, as well as to reduce the representation of ethnic groups. On Stolypin's instruction, the local governors were given a free hand in manipulating the electoral process. The slightest failure to observe the formalities of a complicated registration system was used by the authorities as an excuse to cancel the voting rights of those suspected of supporting the opposition. The main victims of the "administrative measures" were among the leftist groups; thirty-one Social-Democratic deputies were arrested and sent to Siberia.

The Third Duma

Elections to the third Duma, conducted in an atmosphere of repression, finally satisfied Stolypin's expectations. The uncooperative Cadets obtained only about half of their former representation and had only about fifty votes. On the other hand, the number of deputies belonging to conservative groups increased considerably. Under the able leadership of the Octobrists' Guchkov, they would dominate the third and also the fourth Duma (elected in 1912). Representations of the multinational borderlands, like the Ukrainians and the Poles, were cut down drastically; for instance, the Polish Circle was reduced from thirty-four to fourteen deputies. The Octobrists, with 153 deputies, took over the role of the Cadets in the previous two Dumas. The third Duma was as cooperative as the previous ones were rebellious.

The bold, resolute, and incorruptible Stolypin had many enemies within his own administration, and even among the Imperial family; Nicholas II considered him too progressive and too much bent on experimentation. To his numerous political enemies, one should add his personal enemies, for his bluntness did not make him popular in government circles. At the court, Stolypin had numerous enemies because he antagonized those who supported a charlatan named Grigory Y. Rasputin. Rasputin had come to St. Petersburg at the end of 1903 from the Siberian city of Tobolsk, posing as a wandering saintly hermit. He was actually an uneducated peasant, wandering from place to place and living by his wits. Grand Duke Alexis, the only male in the Imperial family

and hence heir to the throne, was suffering from acute hemophilia, and Rasputin was the only man who could stop the frequently recurring bleedings. These treatments gave the alleged miracle worker ascendancy over the anxious mother and, through her, considerable political influence. Stolypin early perceived that Rasputin was an unscrupulous and self-seeking crook and repeatedly warned the Emperor against him.

On September 14, 1911, under mysterious circumstances, Stolypin was fatally shot. Stolypin's record was ambivalent. He was the first Russian statesman since the emancipation to pay serious attention to the plight of the peasantry. He favored modernization of the government. Yet he held steadfastly to his concept of bureaucratic paternalism and made only token concessions to popular desires. On the other hand, he recognized the importance of improving education and the standard of living. He was not opposed to a modicum of popular participation in government, but firmly believed that the locus of political power ought to reside in the central administration. He always treated the Duma with a mixture of suspicion and condescension. He would declare from time to time his willingness to find a workable compromise but only on his own terms. Being a Great Russian nationalist, he dreamed about a powerful and centralized but economically progressive Empire. Turning to the socialist deputies of the second Duma, Stolypin said: "You want a Great Change, while I want a Great Russia." He was the last statesmanlike figure of prerevolutionary Russia, and his policies represented a desperate effort to stabilize and bolster the Imperial regime by providing it with a broader social base.

The Record of the Third and Fourth Dumas

The third Duma was the only one to die a natural death (in 1912), and the first that was permitted to examine the budget and engage in systematic parliamentary work.

Although both the third and fourth Dumas were based on a very narrow foundation and were grossly unrepresentative, simply the fact that the Chamber was the only forum where elected deputies could voice popular grievances and desires gradually made many people forget its limitations. One of the instances when public opinion rallied behind the Duma was the bill voted in 1908 to provide for universal free, obligatory education for children aged eight to eleven. The scheme also provided for the reorganization and expansion of teacher training and school construction so as to eliminate illiteracy in Russia by 1922. The whole plan was to be financed by the Treasury. Whether the scheme was realistic, in view of the shortage of funds and competent personnel, is doubtful. Yet considerable progress was made. By 1914 almost every populous settlement in European Russia had some type of primary school, and between 1907 and 1914 the number of children in the elementary schools more than doubled. While in 1894 the incidence of literacy among military recruits was 38 percent, in 1913 it improved to 73 percent, which was roughly equivalent to that of Italy at that time. During the period of 1907–1914, enrollment in institutions of higher learning more than tripled, while the number of students in secondary schools nearly quadrupled.[1]

The "Silver Age" of Culture

The life of the third and fourth Dumas coincided with a renewed phase of economic progress and considerable artistic and scientific creativity. At the close of the nineteenth century, Russia entered a period usually referred to as the "Silver Age." This era was characterized by a general rise in the cultural level and the expansion of an intelligent and often highly appreciative public. Unlike the present-day Soviet policies, Tsarist censorship was purely negative and limited in focus. It tended to suppress material the authorities considered either directly offensive or subversive, but it did not exact positive conformity to a set of ideological, let alone esthetic, principles. The censors concentrated their attentions mainly on political books, pamphlets, and periodicals, while treating fiction, poetry, and literary criticism more lightly. Consequently, while Tsarist censorship hampered the expression of radical political views, it did not seriously interfere with most artistic creation.

Although the great genius of Russian prose Leo Tolstoy lived until 1910, the religious experience he had undergone in 1880 separated him from the main current of the Russian literary scene. But meanwhile a number of talented writers arose in various corners of the vast Empire. The most prominent and best known in the West was Anton P. Chekhov (1860–1904). Chekhov came from a family of former serfs. Brought up in Taganrog on the Sea of Azov, he graduated from the Moscow University medical school. Soon, however, he deserted his profession for literature and published a series of sketches about peasant life that often contained subtle humor. Later he moved from short stories to theater and developed an extraordinary gift for penetrating psychological insight and for portraying moods and attitudes characteristic of the Russian intelligentsia. The two most striking examples of his mature work are the plays *The Seagull* (1896) and *The Cherry Orchard* (1904). A mixture of quiet pessimism and subtle irony permeates his later works. They usually end on a minor key—"not with a bang but a whimper."

The first director to become interested in Chekhov's plays was Konstantin S. Stanislavsky (1863–1938). He launched Chekhov's early plays in Moscow on the stage of the newly created Moscow Art Theater.

---

[1] "The social mobility accompanying the growth of the higher education is reflected in the fact that the proportion of children of peasants, craftsmen, and workers enrolled in the universities grew from 15.7% in 1880 to 38.8% in 1914, and in the higher technical institutes was 54% in the latter year. The officer corps was no doubt the most conservative branch of the bureaucracy, but it appears that by the end of the Empire a majority of the new officers came from non-noble families, as did some of the leading generals in the First World War." C. E. Black, "The Nature of Imperial Russian Society," *Slavic Review*, 20 (December 1961), 579.

Anton P. Chekhov (1860–1904)

Rejecting established routine and repertoire, Stanislavsky insisted upon staging only plays of the highest artistic value and originality. Experimenting with various methods, he finally arrived at an approach that he called "psychological realism." His was the theater of moods, capable of projecting subtle psychological nuances. Stanislavsky's dramatic school provided new cadres of Russian theater and has had many followers in the West.

In 1890, Russia witnessed the rise to fame and great popularity of a self-educated worker, Alexis M. Peshkov (1868–1936), who became known under his pen name of Maxim Gorky (or Maxim the Bitter). This initially little known provincial journalist soon produced a series of books and stories, some of them autobiographical, like his trilogy *Childhood*, *In the World*, and *My Universities*. Gorky ran counter to the predominant trend of nineteenth-century literature. Many of his heroes are rough but dynamic daredevils, reckless tramps, and resourceful revolutionaries, some of them forerunners of the "positive heroes" of Soviet literature. By the beginning of the twentieth century, Gorky had achieved world fame, having become perhaps the most popular prose writer of Russia.

The close of the nineteenth century witnessed the appearance of a neoromantic trend in Russian letters. Its ideals and aims were best expressed by the group known as *Symbolists*. The Russian Symbolists were inspired by the French group of the same name (Mallarmé, Verlaine, Rimbaud) and also by the American writer Edgar Allen Poe. Nevertheless, native inspiration was not lacking.

It should be stressed that the neoromantic movement started as a protest against the established standards of artistic naturalism, realism, or "civic art" so fashionable during the 1860s to 1890s and so popular with many revolutionaries, including Lenin himself. *Civic art* was initially introduced by such nineteenth-century writers as Vissarion G. Belinsky, Nicholas G. Chernyshevsky, Nikolay A. Dobroliubov, Dmitri I. Pisarev, and Nicholas A. Nekrasov, who considered all forms of artistic expression as mere tools of social reform. In the field of plastic art, one of the main instruments of civic art was the Society of Circulatory Exhibitions, which tried to propagate all forms of artistic creativity, especially painting, among the masses. Some of the pictures of Ilya I. Repin, for instance his well-known *Volga Boatmen* or his *Arrest of a Revolutionary*, are typical examples of this trend, so influential among the radicals at the close of the nineteenth century.

The fundamental reason for the neoromantic revolt was psychological. It was a protest by the more romantically inclined younger artists, fed up and frustrated by the often drab, dreary, moralizing civic art of the older ones. The most significant among the Russian Symbolists were Dmitri S. Merezhkovsky, Andrey Bely (Boris N. Bugayev), and Alexander A. Blok. In 1892, Merezhkovsky, who was also a literary critic and a poet, wrote a book entitled *Symbols*, which revealed the influence of the poetic concepts of Charles Baudelaire and Edgar Allen Poe. Merezhkovsky saw as the goal of history the synthesis of the Hellenic principle of the beauty of the flesh with the Judeo-Christian principle of the purity of the spirit. He was also one of the prominent figures in the religious revival, or "God-seeking," that became prominent in the early twentieth-century Russian intellectual life. Merezhkovsky and Nikolai A. Berdiaev, a talented philosophical writer, were among the first in Russia at that time to devote themselves to the search for a new form of ecumenical Christianity.

Another contributor to the neoromantic trend, Andrey Bely, was a rather esoteric and extravagant writer of a "symphonic" poetry full of ingenious but often puzzling polyphonic experiments. He is best known for his surrealistic novel *St. Petersburg* (1913) and for the four volumes of his memoirs, which are a valuable record of the Symbolist movement. The most original and outstanding of the group however, was Alexander A. Blok, a philogist by training. Blok quickly gained renown because of his musical poems, lyrical dramas, and a cycle of historical verses that sprang from his deep mystical love of Russia, which he alternately addressed as his mother, wife, and lover. Although Blok reached the peak of his creativity and fame after the Bolshevik upheaval with the publication of two allegorical poems, "The Twelve" and "The Scythans" (1918), the bulk of his work belongs to the preceding period. Like most of the Symbolists, Blok was initially sympathetic to the revolutionary movement but was quickly alienated from the Bolshevik regime. He died of hunger in 1921, a bitterly disillusioned man full of tragic forebodings for the future of Russia.

A powerful stimulus was given to the neoromantic movement by the appearance of a richly illustrated artistic magazine called *The World of Art (Mir Iskustva)*. Although it lasted for only five years (1899–1904), *The World of Art* helped considerably to popularize the ideas of the Symbolists and to refine the artistic tastes of the general public. In particular, the magazine contributed to the advancement of graphic art, book illustration, and stage design. While the group of gifted and imaginative people who gathered around the paper did not neglect native Russian sources of inspiration, they were also in touch with the West as well as with the Orient. Generally, *The World of Art* had a stimulating effect on all branches of the arts, generating public interest, and popularizing Russian artistic achievements abroad.

Of the artistic-literary schools of prerevolutionary Russia besides the Symbolists, the *Acmeists* should also be mentioned. This group was both an outgrowth of the Symbolists and at the same time a reaction against them. The name of the group comes from the Greek word *acme*, which means a high stage of perfection. By 1911, the Acmeists had rebelled against the Symbolists' affected estheticism and often excessive verbosity. The Acmeists urged a return to precision and simplicity in the use of words; in short, to a greater harmony of artistic expression. The leading Acmeists were Nicholas S. Gumilev, Anna A. Akhmatova, and Osip E. Mandelshtam. All three were highly individualistic poets who emphasized a sensual and nostalgic perception of the world. All of them continued to create during the Soviet era, until they were ravaged by the Stalinist terror.

The neoromantic trend quickly spread from literature to other artistic media, including music and dance. One of the most prominent and influential musicians of the twentieth century was Igor Stravinsky. His versatility, originality, and endurance were amazing. His innovative works comprise operas, ballets, orchestral pieces (including several symphonies), concertos, and chamber and piano music. Three of his well-known ballets produced during the prerevolutionary period are "The Firebird" (1910), "Petrushka" (1911), and "The Rite of Spring" (1913). Stravinsky's teacher at the St. Petersburg Conservatory of Music was Nicholas Rimsky-Korsakov, himself a famous composer who wrote some fifteen operas, numerous cantatas, and choral pieces. His best-known operas are "Sadko" (1895) and "The Tsar's Bride" (1898). Rimsky-Korsakov also relied on native sources; he collected

Russian folksongs, which were an important source of his creativity. Perhaps the most popular of the Russian composers of the pre-revolutionary era was Alexander N. Scriabin. He wrote numerous piano concertos and orchestral works, among them "The Poem of Ecstasy" (1908) and "Prometheus" (1909–1910). Scriabin aimed at a synthesis of all the arts that would transform the world of creativity. He worked in the mystical vein of many of Russia's writers and was a believer in the philosophy of Dmitri Merezhkovsky.

The beginning of the twentieth century also marked a new epoch in the history of the Russian ballet, which culminated in the achievements of an ingenious and resourceful impresario and director, Serge Diaghilev. Diaghilev's central idea was to bring about an organic integration of ballet, music, and scenery, including costumes. The roster of pictorial talents that Diaghilev employed in his twenty-year career (1909–1929) is most impressive: it includes Picasso, Braque, Derain, and Rouault. This integrative concept was the basis of the remarkable dancing ensemble known as the *Ballets Russes*, which Diaghilev organized, directed, and took to Paris and London in 1910, there to score great artistic successes. Diaghilev was the first to present to the Western public Stravinsky's "Firebird," "Petrushka," and "The Rite of Spring." The Ballets Russes had many stars, but Vaslav Nijinsky (Wacław Niżyński) and Anna Pavlova were perhaps the most brilliant. The Ballets Russes was not only the first modern ballet company; it also embodied for a whole generation of European intellectuals the very essence of the rich and refined, yet largely decadent, culture of pre-revolutionary Russia. Thus, at the turn of the century, the Russian intelligentsia made an effort to turn their country not only into an

Russian Prima Ballerina, Anna Pavlova. Portrait by Dorothea Cordes

importer, but also an exporter of cultural values to the Western world.

To complete the picture of the artistic scene of prerevolutionary Russia, we should mention a small but highly vocal group of writers and painters known as the *Futurists*. In the years 1909–1913 the manifestoes of the Italian founder of the Futurist movement, F. T. Marinetti, were published in Milan. They were translated in Moscow in 1914. This publication stimulated the growth of artistic groups that identified themselves with Futurism. Never in their history were the Russian educated strata so close to Europe as on the eve of World War I. The leading representative of Russian Futurism was a young poet, Vladimir V. Mayakovsky. Born in Georgia, he started his career, together with Boris Pasternak, Andrey Bely, and Alexander Blok, just before World War I. Influenced by the Italian pioneers of Futurism, Mayakovsky sympathized with the Bolsheviks and revolted against all established traditions and accepted artistic forms. He tried to experiment with words as pure sound apart from their meaning, often shocking the "bourgeois" public by unexpected, brutal associations, bizarre metaphors, and startling alliterations. In the plastic arts, the Futurists toyed with geometric designs that expressed the massiveness and speed of the machine age. They attempted to create a "dynamic art of the future." They were, in a way, the forerunners of abstract art. Of these Russian pioneers of abstract art, Vasily V. Kandinsky is the most important. He emphasized the significance of color and form, regardless of subject matter. He taught for a time during World War I at Moscow University and the Moscow Academy of Arts, but then he settled in Germany and became an active member of the German group known as the Bauhaus. Another painter, Kazimir Malevich (Kazimierz Malewicz), starting as a follower of the impressionists, passed through expressionism, fauvism, cubism, and eventually evolved a style of his own. The pictures of this new style, which Malevich called Suprematism, consisted of arrangements of geometrical elements. Malevich attempted to re-create the two-dimensional spirituality of icons through the medium of abstract painting. After the 1917 revolution and the Bolshevik *coup*, when many painters accepted utilitarian social functions of art as the only true ones, Malevich continued to insist on the priority of the spiritual values of abstract paintings. Unlike Kandinsky or Marc Chagall and many other émigré artists, Malevich remained in Russia. Neglected and forgotten, he died there in 1935, but is considered a prominent figure in twentieth-century art.

By the late nineteenth and early twentieth centuries, Russian scholarship had reached a respectable level and also maintained close ties with the West. In 1869, Dmitri I. Mendeleyev compiled his periodic table of chemical elements, corrected the atomic weight of nine elements, and predicted the existence of four new ones. Perhaps the most famous Russian scientist at the end of the Imperial regime was Ivan P. Pavlov. In 1904 he won the Nobel Prize for his theory of conditioned and unconditioned responses. He advanced his theory on the basis of experiments with dogs, in which Pavlov discovered that a conditioned response could be established by applying sound stimuli over a period of time to an animal before it ate. He noted that the dogs would salivate when the stimuli were reapplied, even if food was no longer offered to them. Pavlov also made contributions to medical science and chemistry; for instance, he discovered the existence of fermenting enzymes in gastric juices. His findings became a cornerstone in the field of psychology and the study of the learning process. Another Russian scientist, Ilya Metchnikov, was awarded the Nobel Prize for medicine in 1916 for his achievements in bacteriology. He was the first to postulate that white corpuscles and leukocytes devour bacteria in the blood, and that inflammation in infected parts of the body is caused by the struggle between white corpuscles and germs.

Vassily Kliuchevsky, the great Russian historian, produced at the turn of the century a monumental five-volume synthesis of his country's early history and a number of excellent monographs comparable to the best Western works. But no Russian social scientist has reached greater fame than the jurist and historian Pavel G. Vinogradov. In 1903 he left the University of Moscow because of a conflict with the Tsarist authorities, went to England, and was appointed Professor of Jurisprudence at Oxford. There he introduced the seminar system and produced the nine-volume *Oxford Studies in Social and Legal History* (1902–1907), as well as numerous other works. The already mentioned Paul Milivkov (1859–1943) was not only an active politician, but also a productive scholar, whose *Outlines of Russian Culture* became a standard work on the subject for a couple of generations; he also widely lectured throughout Europe and the United States on political as well as cultural subjects.

The Tsarist Empire on the Eve of World War I

This artistic and scientific creativity during the twilight of the Empire blossomed against the background of an expanding economy and a latent revolutionary movement. The movement resurfaced, however, in 1912 after the violent Lena gold mine mass strike during which some two hundred workers were killed. The crest of the new wave of protest and rebellion was reached on the eve of the war. Yet the surface seemed to be fairly placid. There had been several good harvests, per capita agrarian production had scored sizable gains, and the Empire was able to export a substantial quantity of food products, especially grain. Industrial growth, while not as spectacular as under Witte, was impressive enough. Both the metallurgic and textile industries were advancing rapidly. Only the production of oil was lagging behind, and this was due partly to the ravages wrought in the Baku region by the revolutionary events of 1905–1907 and partly to the depletion of the oil wells there. The Empire's fast economic progress was a result

of several factors; the most important of these were a huge population living within a single customs area, the general advance of science and technology following the rising educational level, and a considerable inflow of foreign investments.

After 1907–1908, with the pacification of the country under Stolypin, an influx of foreign—mostly French—capital again became a significant factor in the process of industrialization. By 1914 French investors owned 22 percent of the stocks of the major privately owned Russian banks. About one-quarter of the total French income from long-term investments came from Russia. In 1913 about one-third of all capital in private industries was foreign. By 1914 Russia was saddled with the largest foreign debt of all the great powers. Her dependence on foreign creditors was often embarrassing and occasionally even humiliating.

The years 1907–1913 were marked by a measure of prosperity and a modicum of freedom; it was very modest by Western standards, but considerable when compared with conditions prior to October 1905. The Constitutional Manifesto had granted a bill of rights and thus assured a limited measure of freedom of press, speech, and association. The insurance law of 1912 was rather insufficient: it provided for payment by the plant of from two-thirds to three-quarters of the normal wage in case of sickness or accident. Yet it covered a majority of the industrial workers employed in large enterprises. While workers' unions were treated with sullen suspicion, they were at least tolerated. On the other hand, it is important to realize that the Russian trade-union movement was rather small and weak. In 1907 there were only about 652 unions with about 200,000 members, or 5.5 percent of all industrial labor. Most unions were only local, and only twenty-two of them numbered over 1,000 members. The largest and strongest of them was the Union of Metal Workers in Petrograd (St. Petersburg had been given the Russian name of Petrograd in 1914). In case of a labor conflict, the Tsarist government was always on the side of the entrepreneurial class, which increased the alienation of the workers from the regime.

During the last decade of the nineteenth century and the beginning of the twentieth, the Tsarist Empire was undergoing rapid economic expansion. Using an array of measures, starting with high customs barriers, tax reductions, national defense contracts, state orders, and profit guarantees, the Government tried to protect heavy industry. All this encouraged the formation of numerous trusts and cartels. The percentage of enterprises employing more than 1,000 workers was as large in prerevolutionary Russia as in Germany. Some mighty tycoons, like Sava Morozov, who controlled large textile plants, and Alexis Putilov, owner of numerous metallurgical enterprises, banks, and railroads, exercised considerable influence on the affairs of state through their personal connections with cabinet officials and members of the Imperial family.

It is obvious that the antiquated political system, largely based on a rusty, and unwieldy bureaucratic machine, was hardly suitable to the needs of a modern economy. The Empire's real income per capita was lower than Italy's. Many vital industries were either lacking (the automotive industry, for instance) or in their infancy (the electric and chemical industries). Most of the more complicated industrial equipment had to be imported. While Russia's rate of growth was spectacular, it was starting from a very low base, and in 1913–1914 the country was far behind Western nations in per capita production. For instance, Russian steel production at that time amounted to some 4.5 million tons, while Germany, with half the population of the Tsarist Empire, produced about 17 million tons in the same period. Although Russia had a population four times larger than that of France, both produced approximately the same amount of steel. In 1913, in terms of per capita gross national product, Russia ranked fifteenth out of the world's twenty-three industrial nations.

Russia's economic progress was impressive; its growth averaged about 6 percent per year between 1886 and 1917, which was faster than in most Western countries except Germany, the United States, and Japan. Yet, on the eve of World War I, despite seven-league strides, the Tsarist Empire was a bizarre mixture of inherited backwardness and rapid, yet uneven modernization. It was still a largely rural, pastoral society in which modernization based on the latest technology coexisted with semifeudal methods of production, especially in agriculture. It was this half-modern, half-medieval Russia, with gradually reviving revolutionary ferment, that was to clash on the battlefields of World War I with a formidable coalition centering around Germany, the most technologically advanced country in Europe.

Suggested Reading

BLACK, CYRIL E., *Dynamics of Modernization*. New York: Harper and Row, 1966.

CHMIELINSKI, EDWARD, *The Polish Question in the Russian State Duma*. Knoxville: University of Tennessee Press, 1970.

DRUMUND, JOHN, *Speaking of Diaghilev*. New York: Faber & Faber/Farrar, Straus & Giroux, 1999.

EDMONTON, LINDA (ED.), *Women and Society in Russia and the Soviet Union*. London: Cambridge University Press, 1992.

GRAY, CAMILLA, *The Great Experiment: Russian Art, 1863–1922*. London: Thames & Hudson; New York: Abrams, 1962.

HAIMSON, LEOPOLD H. (ED.), *The Politics of Rural Russia, 1905–1914*. Studies of the Russian Institute, Columbia University. New York: Columbia University Press, 1979.

HOSKINS, G. A., *The Russian Constitutional Experiment*. Cambridge: Cambridge University Press, 1973.

KINGSTON-MANN, ESTHER AND TIMOTHY MIXTER (EDS.), *Peasant Economy, Culture, and Politics of European Russia, 1800–1921*. Princeton, NJ: Princeton University Press, 1990.

KOKOVTSOV, VLADIMIR N., *Out of My Past: The Memoirs of Count Kokovtsov, Russian Minister of Finance, 1904–1914, Chairman of the Council of Ministers, 1911–1914*. Stanford, CA: Stanford University Press, 1935.

LEVINE, ALFRED, *The Second Duma.* New Haven, CT: Yale University Press, 1966.

MASLENIKOV, OLEG, *The Frenzied Poets: Andrey Bely and the Russian Symbolists.* Berkeley: University of California Press, 1952.

MASSIE, ROBERT, *The Romanovs: The Final Chapter.* New York: Random House, 1995.

MILIUKOV, PAUL, *Memoirs, 1905–1917.* Ann Arbor: University of Michigan Press, 1967.

PIPES, RICHARD, *Struve: Liberal on the Left (1870–1905),* Cambridge, MA: Harvard University Press, 1970.

———, *Struve: Liberal on the Right (1905–1944),* Cambridge, MA: Harvard University Press, 1980.

———, *Russia Under the Old Regime.* London: Weidenfeld and Nicholson, 1974.

POGGIOLI, RENATO, *The Poets of Russia, 1890–1930.* Cambridge, MA: Harvard University Press, 1960.

RICE, TAMARA TALBOT, *A Concise History of Russian Art.* New York: Praeger, 1963.

RIHA, THOMAS, *A Russian European: Paul Miliukov in Russian Politics.* Notre Dame, IN: University of Notre Dame Press, 1969.

ROGERS, HANS, *Jewish Policies and Right-Wing Politics in Imperial Russia.* Berkeley and Los Angeles: University of California Press, 1986.

ROGGER, HANS, "Russia," in *The European Right,* Hans Rogger and Eugene Weber (Eds.). Berkeley and Los Angeles: University of California Press, 1965.

ROSENTHAL, BERNICE G., *Dmitri Sergevich Merezhkovsky and the Silver Age: The Development of a Revolutionary Mentality.* The Hague: Martinus Nijhoff, 1975.

SITES, RICHARD, *Russian Popular Culture. Entertainment and Society Since 1900.* London: Cambridge University Press, 1992.

SMITH, JAY C., JR., *The Russian Struggle for Power, 1914–1917.* New York: Philosophical Library, 1956.

Chapter 6

World War 1 and the Revolutions of 1917

On June 28, 1914, Archduke Francis Ferdinand, heir to the throne of Austria and Hungary, was assassinated by a Serbian terrorist in the Austrian-controlled town of Sarajevo in Bosnia. Although at the time there was no irrefutable evidence of the Serbian government's complicity in the crime, Vienna and Budapest in response presented Belgrade with a stiff ultimatum that included demands considered humiliating by the Serbians. The acceptance of most of the demands by Serbia, an ally of Russia, did not satisfy either the Austro-Hungarians or the Germans. The military leaders of both countries assumed that this would be the right moment to launch a war that would establish their sphere of influence in the Near and Middle East and give them a steppingstone toward broader, worldwide ambitions.

St. Petersburg correctly anticipated that Austro-Hungary, encouraged by Germany, would want to use the assassination as a pretext for crushing Serbia. Since this would undermine the Russian position in the Balkans, the preservation of Serbian independence was considered by Tsarist diplomats to be vital not only to Russia's position in the area, but also to the balance of power in Europe. Russia's leaders believed that because they had twice urged the Serbian leaders to give way to Austro-Hungarian demands (in 1909 and 1913), they could not do it a third time. If the Russians again insisted upon surrender, ran the argument in St. Petersburg, they would abdicate their Great Power status and indicate that they were not to be trusted as allies. The establishment of an Austro-German sphere of influence in the Balkans would be a vital step forward in the realization of those powers' ambitious scheme to control the markets, bases, and energy resources of the Middle East.[1] The disastrous war with Japan of 1904–1905 had severely undermined Russia's image as a Great Power. Could it allow a further erosion of its position?

[1] A German scholar, Franz Fischer has demonstrated how Germany's expansionist ambitions were not limited only to Europe and Africa. He also pointed out that these ambitions could only succeed through a war that would smash the great power positions of all its principal opponents, Great Britain, France, and Russia; Franz Fischer, *Germany's Aims in the First World War* (New York: W. W. Norton, 1967).

Russia and World War I

Seeing the Russians determined to stand up to the Teutonic powers, the French promised to support their main ally and to fulfill their obligations deriving from the alliance of 1893–1894. Great Britain, although united with France by an informal agreement, refused to commit itself to the French side until the Germans had violated Belgian neutrality. In this way, Europe drifted into a war in which Russia, France and Britain fought Germany and Austro-Hungary or the "Central Powers."

Russian propaganda represented the war as one of liberation that would rescue the Slavic peoples from the Teutonic and Magyar yokes. Many Czechs, Slovaks, Serbs, and even some Poles responded to these appeals. The Bulgarians, however, ignored St. Petersburg's urgings, and after some hesitation, joined the Central Powers in 1915. Italy, a formal member of the Triple Alliance, deserted it in the same year and eventually entered the war on the side of Russia, France, Great Britain, and Serbia.

To keep the Russians in the war, in September 1914, the Western allies offered them all the Polish lands then in the hands of Germany and Austria, and promised the Czech throne to a Russian grand duke. The signatories pledged themselves not to sign a separate peace. In March 1915, after the entry of the Ottoman Empire into the war, Great Britain accepted Russian demands concerning the Black Sea Straits and Constantinople. A month later the French acknowledged Russian claims to Turkish Armenia, as well as to a part of Turkish Kurdistan. In return for these promises, the Russians agreed to support various British and French claims to certain parts of the Ottoman Empire, as well as French plans concerning the Rhineland. Moreover, St. Petersburg agreed to the transformation of the central, neutral zone of Persia into a British sphere of influence. The texts of these agreements were kept secret, but soon various details leaked out and became public knowledge.

Imperial Russia entered the war as a loyal ally of France and Britain and repeatedly proved its loyalty to the common cause. To relieve German pressure on Paris, the Russian armies launched a hastily prepared counteroffensive in East Prussia and Galicia. While most of Eastern Galicia was occupied by Russian troops for nearly a year, the East Prussian offensive proved to be a disaster. Two Russian armies, badly commanded, were surrounded and annihilated in the Masurian lake district.[2]

In the summer of 1915, the Russians had to evacuate their Polish provinces and withdraw far to the east, abandoning most of Lithuania and large stretches of Belorussia and the Ukraine to the Central Powers. Serbia could not be reached by the Russians and was overrun by the enemy. By the end of 1916, Russian casualties (killed, wounded, prisoners of war, and missing) amounted to about 7 million men, or nearly half of the entire force originally mobilized in 1914. Despite Russia's temporary occupation of Eastern Galicia and its successful 1916 offensive on the southern front, the balance sheet of the war for Russia was negative. At the same time, France and Britain were fighting a life-and-death struggle, the outcome of which hung in the balance until the summer of 1918, when the massive entry of American troops finally tipped the scales and forced the Germans to capitulate on November 11, 1918.

Effects of the War on the Tsarist Empire

In Russia, from the beginning, the war produced a deep crisis that worsened as the bloody conflict progressed. The outburst of patriotic enthusiasm that swept throughout most of Russia in July and August 1914 did not last long. Like a heap of straw thrown into a burning stove, the enthusiasm burst

[2] The Russian army's defeat at Tannenberg and the Masurian lakes in East Prussia has been brilliantly chronicled by Alexander Solzhenitsyn in his novel *August, 1914.*

Europe During World War, I, 1914–1918

with a bright flame, but burned out quickly. The protracted struggle imposed an unbearable strain on the resources of a fast developing but still backward country and exposed the very fabric of Russian society to a gruesome ordeal. The mobilization of 15 million men dislocated the Russian economy. Withdrawal of these young men from the country's economy was a heavy burden, especially on industry, which chronically suffered from a shortage of skilled workers. Agriculture, always plagued by surplus manpower, was much less affected. The situation was relieved to some extent, but never completely remedied, by the employment of women and nearly 400,000 prisoners of war. The armed forces created new demands, not only for military equipment, but also for foodstuffs, leather, and textiles, which the Russian economy could not satisfy.

By 1915, Russian exports had sunk to half of their 1913 level. On the other hand, imports had risen considerably, since the country needed not only large quantities of military equipment and munitions, but also machinery for the reorganization of its armament industry. Another debilitating factor was the almost complete isolation of Russia from the outside world. The closing of major trade routes through the Baltic and Black Seas resulted in a blockade of Russia by the Central Powers. The weak Russian navy was unable to break the blockade. This situation necessitated a fundamental change in Russia's trade routes and in the volume and nature of its exports and imports. All supplies from the outside had to be transported through two extended lines, via the more than 5,000-mile-long, one-track Trans-Siberian railroad or through a 1,200-mile-long line built especially for this purpose between Petrograd and the Arctic port of Murmansk. The shift of Russian industry to war production resulted in a shortage of consumer goods. This in turn unleashed inflationary pressures. By the beginning of 1917, the amount of paper money increased by some 600 percent, several times more than the rate of any other belligerent power.

To the problem of inflation was added the dislocations that resulted from the evacuation of Russian forces from the most economically advanced western part of the Empire, like Central Poland. The scorched earth policy, the forced removal of a large part of the population from the abandoned territories resulted in the overburdening of transport caused grave problems to military and civilian authorities. Moreover, the administration had to feed and house millions of refugees who were only partially absorbed into the economy. The maldistribution of food, inflation, and worsening living conditions caused serious disaffection among the workers. The was especially true in the case of Petrograd, located in the Empire's exposed northwestern corner. Industrial strikes, so prominent during the first half of 1914 and temporarily silenced by the mood of patriotic elation, were more and more frequent by the end of 1915 and in 1916. The left-socialist movement, initially embarrassed by the nationalistic fervor, began to reassert itself and caused considerable trouble for the Tsarist security apparatus.

Widespread military incompetence and corruption in the civil and military administrations affected the morale of the Russian people. Many of the setbacks suffered by the Russians were due to lack of equipment and supplies, especially heavy artillery and machine guns. Even ordinary rifles were in short supply. In 1914 the entire Tsarist army had only 244 war planes, 70 of them bombers. The provisioning of the troops, as well as of the civilian population, was often inadequate.

Responding to the challenge, the public offered its help to the government by forming a series of "Voluntary Organizations," like the Union of Zemstvos, the Union of Municipalities, and the War Industry Committees. The committees helped to mobilize industries serving the war machine. Chairman of the Central War Industry Committee was the leader of the Octobrist Party, Alexander I. Guchkov, in cooperation with Prince George Y. Lvov, a veteran among the Zemstvo notables.

The defeats of the crucial summer of 1915, dramatically exposed the inadequacy of Russian leadership. In August of that year, the Tsar, at the suggestion of Rasputin, dismissed the Commander-in-Chief, Grand Duke Nicholas Nikolayevich, and assumed supreme command himself. This was a dangerous step, since from that time on the Emperor assumed personal responsibility for the conduct of the war. Leaving the capital for his front headquarters in Mogilev on the upper Dnieper, the Emperor delegated his power to the Empress. Surrounded by a clique of courtiers, Alexandra decided the most important State issues. She would regularly receive from the Prime Minister—first Goremykin, and then B. V. Stuermer—reports on the work of the government. She interfered with the upper bureaucracy's appointments and dismissed cabinet ministers and other high dignitaries.

The military disasters of 1915, the inefficiency of the leadership, and the growing strain on the economy revealed a deep split in Russian public opinion. The liberals, the radicals, and the right wing of the socialist movement were generally pro-Entente; they hoped that Russia's struggle shoulder to shoulder with the Western democracies would contribute to the eventual liberalization of its domestic system after the war. On the other hand, many Russian conservatives regretted that their country was compelled to fight alongside the liberal democracies against its traditional former allies, with whom the Tsarist Empire had been connected by so many ties, including profitable trade relations. In addition to problems caused by this split, the public was systematically flooded with false rumors about alleged treason at the top, negotiations for a separate peace, and scandals in court circles, many of them involving Rasputin. Exaggerated rumors about his role at the Court filtered down to the front and undermined the soldiers' morale.

Activities of the Opposition

The mounting crisis was taken advantage of by the Duma opposition parties craving for power. In August 1915 they organized a coalition known as the *Progressive Bloc*. This parliamentary grouping included deputies from three moderate parties: the Cadets, the Octobrists, and the Progressive Nationalists. These parties constituted about three-quarters of the fourth Duma. The Bloc, dominated by Professor Miliukov, called for elimination of "the distrust of public initiative" and enforcement of the rule of law, and urged the Tsar to remove the incompetent bureaucratic government and appoint a new cabinet that was representative of public opinion.

Initially, the government was inclined to strike a deal with the moderate opposition, but the uncompromising stance taken by the Bloc made it impossible. When the Tsar rejected their unconditional demands, the Bloc parties, which earlier in a show of patriotic enthusiasm had supported the government, now launched a merciless antigovernment campaign. Many members of the Bloc became involved in conspiratorial and even openly subversive activities. Some opposition leaders planned a palace revolution that would place on the throne one of the grand dukes, who would pursue the war with more vigor and prove more amenable to the Bloc's demands.[3]

As has been already mentioned, the Russian people started the war in a patriotic mood. With the exception of the Bolsheviks and a few minor leftist groups, most socialists followed the example of the veteran socialist Plekhanov and took a pro-war stand. Even the spokesman of the Populist Labor Party, Alexander Kerensky, urged the working people first "to defend our country and then set it free." Such an attitude was motivated by the conviction that a Central Powers victory would mean a triumph of reaction and militarism and would spell control of Europe by Germany. Soon, however, when initial wrath toward the Central Powers had cooled down and the first major setbacks had occurred, the war was carefully scrutinized. Many Cadet

---

[3] For a conspiratorial interpretation of the overthrow of the Tsarist regime, with an emphasis on the role of the masonic lodges, see George Katkov, *Russia 1917* (New York: Oxford University Press, 1957).

leaders came to see the war as an opportunity to seize power by overthrowing the Tsarist regime. The diverse leftist groups embraced a variety of attitudes toward the war. They stretched from the "defensism" of Plekhanov, Kerensky, and most Social Revolutionaries, through the pacifism of many Mensheviks, to Lenin's outright defeatism, with its insistence on "turning the imperialistic war into a civil war."

Lenin presented this program at two international conferences of the socialist left in Switzerland, the first at Zimmerwald in 1915, and the second at Kienthal in 1916. Lenin's extreme defeatist views were, however, rejected even by these radical leftist gatherings. Only a small minority supported his stand that it was impossible to attain social revolution without wishing for the defeat of one's government and actively working for such a defeat. Undisturbed even by the opposition in the ranks of the leftist socialists, Lenin continued to work for the realization of his ideas with his characteristic ruthlessness.

Meanwhile, both Berlin and Vienna were eagerly following the domestic situation in Russia, especially the defeatist stand of the Bolsheviks. They were hoping to eliminate Russia by unsuccessfully trying to negotiate a separate peace with Petrograd and then dealing a mortal blow to the Western allies. Unable to achieve this objective, they turned to political warfare. Consequently, the German and Austrian authorities readily allowed the Bolsheviks to circulate their leaflets and pamphlets among Russian prisoners of war. Worsening economic conditions and the mood of dejection that had been spreading throughout the Tsarist Empire since the summer of 1915 helped the defeatist propaganda to gain momentum. From the beginning of 1916 the country experienced a wave of industrial strikes that inhibited the war effort and threatened the stability of the Tsarist regime. The general mood of the country was little affected by the offensive started by General Alexis Brusilov against the Austrians in Galicia. His initially brilliant drive recaptured western Wolhynia and parts of Galicia, but failed to reach Lvov (Lviv). In the summer of

General Alexis Brusilov (1852–1925)

1916, the Austrians, reinforced by German contingents, managed to stabilize the southwestern Russian front. Rumania, which entered the war on the side of the Allies, encouraged by the successes of Brusilov, soon capitulated, and even the spectacular advance of the Russian forces on the Caucasian forces against Turkey did not improve much the mood of the average Russian.

In December 1916, in the midst of the mounting political and economic crises, a small conspiratorial group killed Rasputin, falsely considered to be a German agent. The Tsar returned from the front to attend Rasputin's funeral and banished those who participated in the plot. Then he returned to the front and sank back into apathy. He remained in this state for several weeks, unmindful of all the warnings of the gathering storm.

Downfall of the Tsarist Regime

While the liberal circles were trying to exploit the domestic crisis, a series of strikes broke out in Petrograd at the end of February in 1917. They were the result of a dramatic rise in the prices of necessities, particularly of food. As a result of faulty distribution, there were acute bread shortages in the capital. Faced with rising prices, the workers at the Putilov locomotive and machine factory demanded a 50 percent wage increase; the management turned them down. To this refusal the workers responded with a sit-down strike. On February 22 (March 7) the management retaliated by declaring a lockout, which left about 40,000 workers jobless. The Putilov men appealed to their fellow workers in Petrograd to help them out of their plight. As a consequence, a wave of sympathy strikes swept the capital. By February 23–26 (March 8–11), some 200,000 workers left their factories in the capital.

On February 23 (March 8), housewives staged mass protests against food shortages. They were joined by the locked out Putilov factory workers; the police fired on the crowds. By Saturday evening February 25 (March 10), Petrograd was in a state of general strike and turmoil. On Sunday, February 26 (March 11), huge crowds protesting the shortage of bread again marched with flags and slogans through the main thoroughfares of Petrograd. In some cases the soldiers, when ordered to shoot, executed their orders; but in other instances they refused to obey and even joined the marchers. The next day, Monday, February 27 (March 12), the whole Volhynian Guard Regiment, largely composed of Ukrainian recruits, joined the demonstrators. Soon most of the Petrograd garrison had followed the example of the Volhynians. Thus, the worker demonstrations turned into a soldier mutiny.

In the meanwhile, the Tsar, who was still at the front, postponed the meeting of the Duma. The deputies, who were afraid that this meant a disguised dissolution, were determined to resist and met on February 27 (March 12), in defiance of the monarch, to review the situation. Until that time the revolt had been largely spontaneous and leaderless. It consisted mostly of anonymous workers, soldiers, and students fired by revulsion against military and bureaucratic inefficiency and angry at the indifference of Tsarist authorities to the lot of the common people. Only on February 27 (March 12), when the people learned about the defiant attitude of the Duma, now deliberating against the explicit wish of the Tsar, did delegations of various regiments and civilian institutions begin to arrive at the Tauride Palace, the seat of the Duma, to offer their support and cooperation. Emboldened by this popular support, the Duma appointed a Provisional Committee under the Octobrist Speaker of the House, M. V. Rodzianko.

When he was informed about the mutinies and manifestations, the Emperor called them a stab in the backs of the fighting men and ordered their immediate suppression. Meanwhile, however, the revolt spread. The demonstrators captured depots of weapons and began to distribute arms to the mob. Prisons were opened and inmates released. Police headquarters were set on fire. On March 1 (March 14), the Provisional Committee of the Duma proclaimed itself the Provisional Government. The fifty-six-year-old landowner Prince George Y. Lvov, chairman of the Union of Zemstvos, a man with no experience in public administration, was selected as its Prime Minister. The leader of the Progressive Bloc, the Cadet politician Professor Miliukov, assumed the portfolio of Foreign Affairs. It was he who became the driving force behind the Provisional Government. Suddenly, the people who, until 1917, had no experience in running the machinery of state, took upon themselves to lead a great empire. Thus the passengers of the train took upon themselves the role of the drivers of the locomotive.

The Provisional Regime versus the Petrograd Soviet

The setting up of the Provisional Government was a challenge to the socialists, who were very imperfectly represented in the fourth Duma. Hasty elections were arranged in various factories and barracks, and by seven o'clock on the evening of February 27 (March 12), a rival proletarian body, the Petrograd Soviet of Workers, Peasants, and Soldiers, gathered to question the legality and credentials of the bourgeois Provisional Government. Symbolically enough the Soviet met in the left wing of the Tauride Palace, while the Provisional Government deliberated in the right wing. Most members of the Soviet were Mensheviks and Social Revolutionaries, with the Bolsheviks numbering some 10 percent of the delegates.

Although the two rivals for authority and power were linked by their criticism of the fallen regime, they operated from different theoretical premises, used different methods, and aimed at different objectives. Considering the Provisional Government to be an unrepresentative, bourgeois body, the Soviet forbade any of its members to participate in the Government's work. An exception was made in the case of Alexander Kerensky, an able young lawyer of thirty-five and a gifted orator and Duma deputy representing a mildly socialist Labor Party. He alone among the leftist politicians was allowed to accept a ministerial post, the Minister of Justice, to watch over the bourgeois rival on behalf of the Soviet. Since he was at the same time vice-chairman of the Petrograd Soviet, he was the only personal link between the two rival groups.

Throughout the eight months that separated the downfall of Tsardom from the Bolshevik coup d'état, the relationship between the two bodies competing for power was of crucial importance. After some hesitation, on March 2 (March 15) the Soviet agreed to give conditional support to the Provisional Government. The Government was to summon, as soon as possible, a Constituent Assembly to be elected on the basis of universal suffrage; the Government was to allow all local governing bodies to be elected on the same franchise; all civil rights were to be shared by soldiers, while discipline was to be maintained at the front; finally, the garrison of Petrograd was not to be removed from the capital. The conditional support granted the Provisional Government by the Petrograd Soviet was in accordance with the classic Marxist theory of a two-stage revolution. The Menshevik and Social Revolutionary leaders of the Soviet were convinced that the semifeudal country was not ready for socialism and needed a transition period between the bourgeois and the proletarian stages of the revolution to allow the working class to prepare for the future socialist phase.

Meanwhile, however, contrary to the agreement that left the executive power with the Provisional Government, the Soviet, anxious to win over the armed forces to its side, began to circulate a set of instructions addressed to the soldiers. These instructions, which came to be known as *Order Number One*, freed the soldiers from the old fetters of discipline. The death penalty was abolished: political commissars were to be instituted in each unit from the company level on; problems of a nonmilitary nature were to be settled by majority vote; committees in which officers had the same vote as privates were to be elected in each unit; and the saluting of officers was dropped. Order Number One removed actual control of the troops from the hands of the officers and dealt a fatal blow to the cohesion of Russia's armed forces. The Order was motivated by the Soviet's fear of the armed forces, commanded largely by conservative-minded generals and admirals. The Soviet suspected that they would sooner or later stage a counterrevolutionary coup and restore the old order in one guise or another. Consequently, decomposition of the old fighting force was considered as a major and worthy objective of the Soviet. From then on, the politicized soldiers became one of the chief focuses of the struggle for power between the Soviet and the Provisional Government. Few people understood the nature of the struggle better than Lenin, then still in Switzerland, but closely watching the events in Russia.

Most military commanders tried to evade the strict application of the Order to their units and limit the powers of the Soldiers' Committees to strictly nonmilitary matters (education, provisioning the canteens, and the like), but the Committees tended more and more to encroach on all fields of activity. Soon they even insisted that their sanction was necessary to order soldiers to the front line. For the Russian army, composed largely of semi-illiterate peasants, the Order, which went well beyond what the most liberal mind could regard as compatible with military efficiency, had disastrous consequences. It gradually crippled its fighting capacity beyond repair.

The Abdication of Nicholas II

As these events were taking place in Petrograd, Tsar Nicholas was at his General Headquarters near Pskov, trying to mount some countermeasures. Meanwhile, the Provisional Government telegraphed principal army commanders asking for support. Practically all of them sided with the Provisional Government, hoping that it would pursue the war with more vigor and determination. Only when he had failed to muster enough troops to suppress the revolt in the capital, had been deserted by his supporters, and was helpless did the Tsar decide to abdicate in favor of his younger brother, Grand Duke Michael. The drama of abdication took place on the night of March 2 (15) at a little railroad station that, symbolically enough, bore the name Dno (which in Russian means *bottom*). The act of the abdication was, characteristically enough, addressed to the Army, which the Tsar considered as the embodiment of Russia. Before giving up his Imperial powers in his own name and that of his adolescent, hemophiliac son Alexis, the Tsar confirmed the Provisional Government and asked the people to support it in order to carry the war to a victorious conclusion. Immediately after the abdication Nicholas was put under house arrest.

In the Provisional Government there were two ministers who had monarchist inclinations: Miliukov and Guchkov. They wanted to offer the vacant throne to Grand Duke Michael, brother of Nicholas. But when the Grand Duke asked for a guarantee of his personal safety and the Government was unable to grant it, he declined the offer. Thus, after 304 years, the Romanov dynasty fell without much resistance.

In a historic sense, the collapse of the Romanov dynasty in Russia is an important turning point not only in Russian but in world history and is comparable to the downfall of the French monarchy at the end of the eighteenth century. The struggle caught the Tsarist Empire in the middle of a process of transformation (agrarian, educational, and military), at a point when most of the reforms undertaken during the constitutional period were beginning to produce their first results. Among the principal reasons for the fall of the Tsarist government was its failure to overcome Russia's backwardness by modernizing the antiquated structure rapidly enough to adapt to fast-changing social and economic conditions. Although the Tsarist Empire was developing rapidly, its socioeconomic progress was more accelerated than its political evolution. Industrialization was suffering from many drawbacks. First, it was undertaken too late and was handicapped by heavy dependence on foreign capital. Foreign investors required high interest rates and drained much of the country's resources. The Tsarist regime's age-long neglect of the peasant problem and the consequent alienation of the rural masses (which comprised some 80 percent of the population) also played a role. Stolypin's reforms, as beneficial as they were, also came too late and were interrupted by the war. The same was true for the educational reform begun in 1908. All belated attempts at reform undertaken by imperial Russia were, as a rule, hampered by shortage of funds that were channelled into foreign expansion at the cost of domestic needs.

Alienation of enlightened members of the society was another cause of the crisis that crippled Imperial Russia. Lack of a representative institution at the top level deprived the educated strata of a chance to develop a sense of political responsibility and coparticipation in the affairs of state. In due time, this political involvement might even have filtered down to other social groups. By the middle of the nineteenth century, there was a striking need for an institutional framework that would allow the educated and increasingly articulate intelligentsia, landowners, and professionals to express legally their grievances and aspirations. Such institutions would have gradually associated these classes with the undertakings of the regime, given them a sense of participation, and thus would have constituted a school of civic activities. The failure to gradually transform the absolutist regime into a consultative and, later, participatory one was a grave mistake. In the absence of such a system, a large mass of educated, progressive people was pushed into the ranks of the revolutionary movement. The Imperial Duma, granted under pressure in 1905–1906, came much too late. What would have been sufficient a generation before seemed not enough to the Miliukovs or the Rodziankos.

Another cardinal mistake of the Tsarist regime was its failure at mass communication and mass mobilization. The regime was incapable of persuading the millions of gray-coated soldiers, furrowed into muddy trenches stretching for over 2,000 miles from the Baltic to the Black seas, that their endless, bloody battles had any real meaning. The alienated masses of soldiery came to regard the war as meaningless and hopeless.

To the socioeconomic, political and psychological causes of the collapse, one should add the mediocrity of leadership. The last generation of Imperial politicians was perhaps the weakest and least talented in modern Russian history. There is no doubt that at the time of World War I the Russian ruling team, including the Emperor, showed striking ineptitude and passivity. The last phase of the Imperial regime could boast of only three strong men: Pobedonostsev, Witte, and Stolypin. It is characteristic that the first, whose influence was on the whole pernicious, was allowed to linger for two generations and advise both Alexander III and Nicholas II. Witte was twice dismissed and died an embittered man, while Stolypin was assassinated under mysterious circumstances.

It was this Russia, led by confused and hesitant mediocrities, that for the second time in a generation stumbled into a war against much stronger, technologically superior adversaries. For such a protracted, murderous war, Russia was insufficiently prepared—militarily, economically, and politically.

Consequences of the Abdication

The triumph of the revolution, evident in Petrograd by the middle of March, had speedy repercussions throughout the Empire. By the close of the month the new revolutionary order had won the day, although at the cost of some 2,000 lives. The bureaucracy, the army, and the navy quickly accepted the Provisional Government. The police and the extreme right-wing parties either vanished or went underground.

The fall of the Tsardom caused a profound anxiety among the Western allies, who were still desperately struggling for survival. They had made plans for a great concerted offensive on both fronts in the spring of 1917. As soon as the Provisional Government reaffirmed its loyalty to the Alliance, the Allied Powers recognized the Government. In the United States the overthrow of the autocracy in Russia was greeted enthusiastically. President Woodrow Wilson hailed the new liberal government with the words, "Does not every American feel that assurance has been added to our hope for the future peace of the world by the wonderful and heartening things that have been happening in Russia? Here is a fit partner for the league of honor."

While Paris, London and Washington viewed the Russian upheaval mainly in terms of their own military objectives, for the peoples of Russia the Revolution was a far greater event than the war, and they were increasingly preoccupied with domestic questions. Should the country be a constitutional monarchy or a democratic republic—or perhaps a federation of her component ethnic parts? What social and economic reforms ought to be introduced? Here the issue of land distribution loomed largest.

At this point one should stress that the Provisional Government, from the beginning, revealed an amazing lack of leadership. The old Tsarist administration had collapsed with the abdication of the Tsar, from whom they had claimed all authority. Now Prince Lvov had the extraordinary idea of inviting local self-governing bodies to organize themselves as they chose. The police had been swept away by a tidal wave of anger and replaced by a voluntary militia incapable of coping with the mounting problems generated by the new situation. The commissars sent by the new Government to replace the old provincial governors were largely inexperienced as administrators and never acquired any real authority. Consequently, the country witnessed a rapid breakdown of the existing obsolete but functioning structure. The Provisional Government selected by the highly conservative and unrepresentative fourth Duma was aware of its weakness and inclined to procrastinate. Lacking in self-confidence and without a clear mandate, the cabinet soft-pedaled the issue of fundamental domestic reform and repeatedly shifted the burden of decision to the future Constituent Assembly, which was expected to be a panacea for all ills.

The Petrograd Soviet, rival body of the Provisional Government, also suffered from many handicaps. It was a loose, fluctuating body of between 1,000 and 3,000 deputies who had been hastily elected, primarily by acclamation, in the factories and barracks of the capital. The Soviet claimed to represent not the narrow stratum of the bourgeoisie, like the Duma, but the broad masses of working people, and styled itself an organ of "revolutionary democracy." Although its deputies were elected only by the workers and soldiers of the capital, the Petrograd Soviet arrogated to itself the right to make decisions affecting the whole country. As a rule, no agenda was prepared for deliberations of the Soviet in advance for its meetings; interminable debates were often interrupted by the arrival of delegates or telephone messages. Decisions were often made on the spur of the moment, without a clear understanding of their implications. Actual policy making was in the hands of the Executive Committee, a body of fifty to sixty delegates elected by the Soviet. Under these circumstances, a small, well-organized group of people could easily sway the Soviet one way or another. Unlike the Mensheviks and the SRs, the Bolsheviks, until Lenin's return from Switzerland, played a minor role in the first Petrograd Soviet and tended to follow its "social-patriotic" majority, which, on the whole, supported the Government. The Petrograd Soviet was a model for about 900 similar provincial bodies that mushroomed throughout the country in the spring of 1917.

The Provisional Government repeatedly submitted to the Soviet's pressures, for fear that it would withdraw its precarious conditional support. The shaky cooperation with the Soviet symbolized, in the eyes of the Government, the backing of the broad masses of the population, with whom the amiable, well-intentioned, but socially isolated members of the Provisional Government had little contact. Thus from February (March) to October (November), Russia, with no head of state, had two governing bodies: one enjoyed formal authority without real power, and the other power without formal authority.

Lenin's Return to Russia

Events in Russia were studied systematically by the Central Powers, especially in Berlin. In the spring of 1917, with the declaration of war against Germany by the United States, the situation of the Central Powers was becoming increasingly critical, in view of the food shortage, mounting casualties, and growing political tensions. Under the circumstances, the Germans decided to help the chief Russian defeatist Lenin, then living in Switzerland, to return home. The purpose of his trip was the Germans hoped to create the greatest possible chaos within Russia, so that internal collapse would compel Russia to withdraw from the war. Berlin offered Lenin and twenty of his close coworkers, including such prominent Bolsheviks as G. Y.

Zinoviev, L. B. Kameniev, Karl Radek, and A. V. Lunacharsky, free passage through Germany to Sweden.

After crossing through Germany, Sweden, and Finland, the Bolshevik team disembarked at the Finland station in Petrograd on April 3 (16). Lenin was greeted with distrust not only by the Provisional Government, which suspected him of being a German agent, but also by the Petrograd Soviet, which was dominated by his opponents, the Mensheviks and SRs, and was afraid of him as its fierce critic and competitor. When Lenin returned to Petrograd, he was forty-eight years old. He immediately embarked upon feverish, relentless activity on three fronts. His first aim was to win over the Bolshevik party to his policy aiming at grabbing power at any price, even at the cost of Russia's defeat. His second was to capture the Petrograd Soviet and turn it into a tool of his party. Third, with the support of the Soviet, he wanted to overthrow the Provisional Government and establish the Bolsheviks in power.

Under Lenin's influence the Bolshevik Party, whose platform had hitherto been only slightly more radical than that of the Mensheviks or the Social Revolutionaries, was thoroughly reshaped. On April 7 (20), Lenin published his program of action known as "The April Theses." Lenin's platform rejected the classic Marxist concept of a two-stage revolution and insisted on the immediate seizure of power by his Party so as to implement his slogan, "Peace, land, bread, and all power to the Soviets." "Land" meant not the agrarian reform to be voted in due time by the future Constituent Assembly, but the immediate radical distribution of state and landowners' land among the peasants. "Bread" was a blanket term for a variety of socioeconomic reforms in a socialist spirit. The first step was to be achieved by immediate seizure of the factories and establishment of workers' control over them. "Peace" meant not the negotiated, or "white" peace "without annexations or indemnities" advocated by most of the moderate socialists. Lenin advocated an immediate end to the war, which he condemned as imperialist on both sides, in order to overthrow the bour-

geoisie—first in Russia, and then throughout all of Europe. "Turn the imperialist war into a civil war" was Lenin's battle cry. To foster revolutionary activities on a worldwide scale, the old "social-patriotic," defensist Social–Democratic Second International, discredited by its passivity toward the war, should be scrapped, Lenin said, and thrown into the garbage can of history. The Bolshevik Party should shed its old name and assume the adjective "Communist." A new communist international organization should be established. Behind Lenin's ambitious peace program was an optimistic concept of the potentialities of the revolutionary forces in Europe, especially of the Spartacist groups in Germany, who were determined to seize power in Berlin and act hand in hand with their Russian comrades.

The Provisional Government denounced Lenin's program as "destructive" and "anarchistic" and branded its author as a German agent and spy paid by secret funds of the enemy intelligence.[4] Despite these accusation, Lenin was not arrested, which is another indication of the Government's impotence. Meanwhile, in May, Trotsky returned to Russia from the United States and soon sided with Lenin. Consequently, that spring was a major turning point of the first phase of the Revolution. Until then, both the Provisional Government and the Soviet had lacked strong leaders. No political party had will to act vigorously. With the return of Lenin, one small group, with about 20,000 members that controlled only about

---

[4] The problem of the extent of German aid to the Bolsheviks is no more a controversial question. According to former Soviet sources, the Bolshevik Party published some eighty periodicals in 1917. The Party had about 20,000 members, and no large native resources, while the Germans did spend considerable sums of money for psychological warfare in Russia. Most of the money went to the Bolsheviks who, thanks to them, could publish forty-one newspapers, most of them in Russian and Ukrainian, with a daily circulation of 320,000 copies. For a discussion of the problem see Katkov, *Russia, op.cit.*, and Z. Zeman, ed., *Germany and Revolution in Russia 1915–1918* (New York: Oxford University Press, 1958); also W. B. Scharlau and Zbynek A. B. Zeman, *Merchant of Revolution: A Life of Alexander Helphand (Parvus)* (New York: Oxford University Press, 1965).

10 percent of the Soviet deputies and thus far had not been particularly active or outspoken in its opposition to the Government, underwent a radical change. It was now headed by a determined and able leader who was bent on achieving a definite program.

The July Crisis and the Kornilov Affair

While in domestic affairs the Provisional Government constantly displayed lamentable weakness, it was initially more assertive in foreign and military matters. Despite the dwindling discipline and morale of an army profoundly affected by war weariness and undermined by Order Number One, the Government decided to reaffirm its intention and willingness to continue the war "to a victorious conclusion." In the spring of 1917 the Western allies were hard-pressed by the Germans. Kerensky, since May the Minister of War, and representatives of the Mensheviks and SRs in the cabinet resolved to launch a new large-scale offensive on the Galician front, where the Russians were facing weaker Austro-Hungarian forces. In June and July the Russian offensive scored some spectacular initial successes, but it was soon turned into a retreat and eventually became a rout. The failure of the offensive was promptly followed by a governmental crisis over the issue of autonomy for the Ukraine and by a Bolshevik attempt to seize power. At the beginning of July some units of the Petrograd garrison, afraid of being sent to the front to support the sagging offensive, revolted. The Bolsheviks decided to take advantage of the mutiny to seize power. On July 3–5 (16–18), large-scale violent battles took place between the rebels and the units loyal to the Government. Several hundred people were killed. Order was finally restored by troops brought in from the vicinity of Petrograd. The rebellion was put down and the Government ordered the arrest of other Bolshevik leaders. Lenin managed, however, to escape to Finland.

The suppression of the July Bolshevik riots in Petrograd gave the Provisional Government a fresh lease on life, but it was not utilized properly. Soon another crisis followed. On July 7 (20), Prince Lvov resigned his premiership because his cabinet could not agree on three vital issues: whether to proclaim Russia a republic; whether to sanction the spontaneous seizure of land by the peasants, who were impatiently waiting for the promised land reform; and what to do about the increasingly restless Ukraine demanding wide autonomy. When the Cadet ministers resigned as a protest against granting autonomy to that vital part of the former Empire, a new coalition government was formed by Kerensky, with the Mensheviks and the Social Revolutionaries dominating the cabinet, but unable to coordinate properly the activities of the Government with those of the reluctant Soviets.

By far the most crucial problem was the civilian-military tension that precipitated another crisis. The failure of the July offensive was followed by recriminations and bickering in military quarters. A scapegoat was found in the person of the Commander-in-Chief. General Alexis A. Brusilov was dismissed and replaced by Kerensky's nominee, General Lavr G. Kornilov, then commander of the southwestern front. Kornilov was a man of great energy and courage, but he had little understanding of political issues. His former Chief of Staff, General M. V. Alexeyev, called him a "man with a lion's heart and the brain of a sheep." Kornilov firmly believed in Russia's capacity to win the war. He insisted on the necessity of restoring order at home and on strict military discipline at the front if the Russian forces were to regain their fighting capacity. He was inclined toward immediate dissolution of the Soviets and suppression of the Bolshevik Party. These requests were rejected, however, by the Socialists, who were suspicious of him as a potential military dictator. Also, they were loath to apply stern measures against fellow Socialists and former co-victims of Tsarist reprisals, however misguided they might appear to outsiders. The Socialists insisted on more rapid "democratization" in domestic and foreign policies. Nevertheless, Kerensky did make some gestures to placate Kornilov—for instance, free-

General Lavr Kornilov (1870–1918)

understood that Kerensky had agreed to accept him as the future dictator. Acting under this assumption and without clarifying the issue, Kornilov decided to act on his own. On August 25 (September 7), he ordered his troops to march on Petrograd.

The shocked and threatened Kerensky reversed his stand. He denounced "the Bonapartist threat" of a self-styled dictator, allegedly bent on restoring Tsardom and summoned all supporters of "revolutionary democracy" to fight against him. The Government virtually suspended the ban on the Bolshevik Party, released its leaders on bail, and distributed some 40,000 rifles to the workers, mostly to the Bolshevik-controlled Red Guards. The Petrograd Soviet, facing the immediate menace of an occupation of the capital by Kornilov's troops, was quick to forget the memories of the July Days. A Committee for Struggle with Counterrevolution, which included the Bolsheviks, was set up. The Bolshevik tactics for this important turn of events were summed up by Lenin's dictum: "We shall support the Provisional Government as a rope supports the hanged man." The emergency created by Kornilov's attempted coup allowed the Bolsheviks to re-create their own fighting squads, now armed with weapons supplied by the Government. The arms were never to be returned. The initial opposition of organized rightist groups disappeared almost completely.

As a result of these measures, the advance of Kornilov's troops was checked. Meanwhile, the morale of his soldiers was undermined by agitators, mainly Bolsheviks, dispatched for this purpose by the Soviet. The coup collapsed. Kornilov and most of his top assistants were arrested. The coup further eroded the prestige of the Government while bolstering the Bolsheviks, who could from now on invoke with some credibility the specter of a "Bonapartist" dictatorship. By September the Bolsheviks had gained control of the Petrograd and Moscow Soviets and achieved success in various local Soviets throughout the country. At the end of September, Trotsky was elected Chairman of the Petrograd Soviet, which he skillfully manipulated to enhance the Bolshevik position.

dom of the press was somewhat curtailed, and the death penalty for desertion and treason was reintroduced at the front.

These measures corresponded to the slowly changing mood of a considerable segment of the Russian population. By the summer of 1917 a large part of moderate public opinion, in agreement with Kornilov, concluded that no strictly democratic measures could arrest the drift toward catastrophe. Kerensky himself was increasingly inclined toward sterner measures but was too shy and unskillful in their application. Afraid of the growing Bolshevik threat, he secretly ordered Kornilov to keep crack troops in readiness for a march on Petrograd to smash another possible Bolshevik revolt. While both wished to check the Bolsheviks, each visualized the outcome differently. Kornilov

In the wake of the aborted coup, disorder and anarchy assumed ever larger proportions. Army deserters, who by October numbered about two million, were returning home, often committing acts of violence and robbery on their way. The peasants, who had lost patience with the Provisional Government's procrastination, continued to seize large estates. The land, together with cattle and implements, was divided, the manor houses burned, and the landowners often murdered. In the cities the ignorant wantonness of the mob was rampant. Shops were looted; hundreds of attacks on officers, officials, and private individuals were recorded every day; and many factory owners and managers were being lynched by the workers. The entire communication system began to break down. Famine in the cities was spreading. At the same time, German forces were pushing relentlessly eastward. In September they occupied most of Latvia, including Riga. Evacuation of Petrograd and shifting of the capital to the more secure Moscow was seriously contemplated.

The Bolshevik Coup D'État

Lenin quickly grasped that the moment for decisive action was at hand. In October he returned in disguise to Petrograd and began to prepare the ground for the planned Bolshevik armed insurrection. The Bolshevik Party, however, was still far from being a monolithic force and it took a great deal of persuading to push it to immediate action. It was on Lenin's insistence that the Bolshevik military organization intensified its training and its infiltration of various military and naval units of the Petrograd garrison, especially the Kronstadt naval base. Yet despite his exhortations, the majority of the Bolshevik leaders initially took a pessimistic view toward Lenin's slogan. "All power to the Soviets through armed insurrection." Mindful of the disastrous July Days, most of the Bolsheviks overestimated the strength and resolution of the Government. Moreover, they were still bothered by vestigial democratic scruples and wanted to be sure of a majority

in the All-Russian Congress of Soviets, to assemble at the end of October in Petrograd. Finally however, as a result of his stubborn persuasion and support by Trotsky, Lenin managed to galvanize his party into action by October 21–22 (November 3–4).

The Provisional Government, although vaguely aware of the Bolshevik preparations, remained passive. Only on October 24 (November 6) was an order issued to ban the Bolshevik Party and arrest its leaders. Loyal troops were to be brought from the vicinity of the capital to deal with the imminent coup. But these measures came too late. On October 25 (November 7) the Bolsheviks began their operation. Meanwhile, the cabinet was in permanent session but was unable to act effectively in time to cope with the mounting Bolshevik menace. With little resistance, the Kronstadt sailors, the Lettish Sharpshooters, and the Red Guards occupied key points of the capital one by one, starting with the crucial central telephone and telegraph building. Then came the offices of the general staff, various ministries, and banks.

The Provisional Government once more revealed its helplessness. Barricaded in the Winter Palace and protected by a few companies of officer cadets, a battalion of women volunteers, and a handful of cavaliers of the order of St. George, the Government was drafting and redrafting a proclamation to the people of Petrograd, summoning them to oppose the Bolshevik threat. By midday of October 25 (November 7), however, most of the city was already under Bolshevik control. The Winter Palace was the last visible citadel of the Government; therefore, it was vital for Lenin to announce its capture at the Second Congress of the Soviets then gathering in the capital and to get its stamp of approval for the seizure of power by his party.

Most Bolshevik historians, including Trotsky, as well as many Soviet films, gave a highly romanticized version of the final assault on the Winter Palace. They stress the alleged grandeur of the master plan and the mastery of its execution. But in reality, the capture of the huge Palace was an almost bloodless series of scattered skirmishes interspersed

Iosif V. Djugashvili, known as Stalin, as Commissar for Nationalities, 1917–1923

Shliapnikov, one of the few genuine proletarians among the Bolshevik leaders; Military and Naval Affairs were directed by a triumvirate of A. Antonov-Ovseenko, N. V. Krylenko, and F. M. Dybenko; Popular Education went to A. V. Lunacharsky; and Foreign Affairs to L. D. Trotsky. As Commissar for Nationalities, a relatively little-known Georgian Bolshevik by the name of Iosif V. Djugashvili, better known to us as Stalin, was appointed.

While the Bolshevik victory in Petrograd was almost bloodless, Lenin's supporters in Moscow encountered much stronger resistance. There the bitter cost, until the capitulation of the garrison of the Kremlin, was about five hundred people killed on the Bolshevik side alone. The triumph in Moscow was followed promptly by similar but much easier victories in most of the Great Russian provincial centers. In the non-Russian periphery of the former Tsarist Empire, the resistance to Bolshevik encroachments was considerably stiffer, and some three years of civil war would be needed to overcome it.

The Bolshevik Victory in Historic Perspective

with chaotic negotiations with its confused defenders. Finally, the defenders were convinced of the uselessness of further resistance and surrendered. The whole operation involved only six casualties. As Lenin said, "We found the power lying in the streets, and we picked it up."

The seizure of the Winter Palace and the arrest of thirteen members of the Provisional Government (Kerensky had escaped the siege to seek the help of loyal troops) consummated the Bolshevik triumph in Petrograd. The capture of the Palace was followed by Lenin's proclamation of the Bolshevik victory and the formation of the first Soviet Government, the Soviet of People's Commissars. The term "minister" had been discarded as a reactionary, bourgeois title. The composition of the Council was as follows: Chairman of the Council was Lenin himself; Commissariat of the Interior was entrusted to A. E. Rykov; that of Labor went to A. G.

The victory of the Bolsheviks in Russia has proved to be one of the decisive events of the twentieth century. According to Soviet historiography, the October Revolution was the product of a clearly discernible, irresistible trend in Russian history. Official Soviet history maintained that the capture of power was meticulously planned by the Party, acting under the guidance of the omniscient, infallible Lenin. Party historians insisted that the Bolshevik triumph was the inevitable consequence of Russian domestic conditions and at the same time an integral segment of the international struggle of the proletariat against the bourgeoisie, with the Russian comrades acting as a vanguard of the world proletarian forces. This view held that the Communists were victorious in Russia because, under the stubborn leadership of Lenin and his Bolshevik Party, they dealt a timely blow to the weakest link in the "chain of capitalism."

Independent historians, on the other hand, are inclined to see the coup largely as a result of circumstances; the weak Provisional Government, the victim of its own errors, was overthrown by the ruthless, cold-blooded determination of a small group of criminal conspirators. Whatever the shortcomings of the Government, argue the non-Communist writers, it represented the only democratic alternative, and gave Russia the only democratic interlude before the disintegration of the Communist dictatorship in 1991. The Government ended racial and religious discrimination, adopted progressive social legislation, including the establishment of factory committees and an eight-hour working day, and introduced basic freedoms, including as large a scope for self-expression as ever existed anywhere in the world. Never did the peoples of Russia enjoy greater political liberty than between February–March and October–November of 1917. Lenin himself admitted that in the spring of 1917 Russia was "the freest country in the world." Independent historians regard the Bolshevik coup as a reckless but successful gamble of a dictatorially minded minority group. Its triumph resulted in a rather unfortunate reversal of what was presumed to be Russia's painfully slow evolution toward civic society and constitutional democracy. According to them, Lenin was carried to power by a wave of anarchy that he exploited ruthlessly without any moral scruples.

The weakest point in the reasoning of many historians of the liberal and even conservative schools is their ambivalence toward the Provisional Government, failing to acknowledge that Government's inherent weaknesses. From the very beginning the Provisional Government was deeply divided, hesitant, lacking in self-confidence, and unable to cope not only with long-range issues but even with everyday problems. The downfall of Tsardom brought no relief to the working masses as inflation continued to spiral. While food prices increased by 500 to 600 percent after the war, wages went up only by 300 to 400 percent. In all three critical periods—May, July, and September—the Provisional Government revealed its inability to cope with these difficulties.

The abdication of political leadership on the part of the educated, civilized forces revealed the shallow roots of Russian liberal democracy. Courageous, vociferous, and often brilliant in criticizing the abuses of Tsarist autocracy, they lacked practical experience and were unable to act positively and decisively when exercising political power. Kerensky, "the Hamlet of the Russian Revolution," "the conjurer-in-chief," was perhaps the best example of these shortcomings of the Russian intelligentsia. An able and dedicated lawyer, he was in love with his own flowery oratory but was unable to grasp the practical issues and cope with them resolutely. His faith in the miraculous power of revolutionary phraseology proved disastrous.

There were two phases of the Revolution: the liberal one that overthrew the Tsarist regime and the Bolshevik coup that destroyed the weak and hesitant, yet basically liberal and democratically inclined Provisional Government. The first upheaval was a revolt of the people against the inefficient, corrupt, and discredited government of Nicholas II. Most testimonies agree that the revolt was a popular one, a largely spontaneous and bloodless uprising from below, greeted with joy by most politically articulate people. The role of the Bolsheviks in the first phase of the Revolution was marginal. A great majority of contemporary observers as well as latter-day historians agree that the Bolshevik seizure of power, on the other hand, was a conspiratorial coup d'état. It was launched by a small but determined, brutal, demagogic minority that took advantage of the war-weariness and demoralization of the masses and the helplessness of the Provisional Government. It was, therefore, a typical conspiratorial *coup d'état.*

The crisis of 1917 propelled onto the political stage millions of war-weary, uprooted soldiers, most of them semiarticulate peasants and workers in uniform, desperately looking for effective leadership amidst the monumental confusion caused by the erosion and sudden downfall of traditional institutions. The unexpected, complete, and truly unparalleled freedom suddenly bestowed upon the masses turned their heads and pushed them toward anarchy and license. The Bolsheviks were the only party able to channel this discontent for their purposes. Their skillful propaganda dramatically widened the dangerous rift between the two societies hitherto uneasily coexisting behind the facade of the Tsarist autocracy. The Westernized, civilized, and often liberally inclined thin crust of the Russian polity for generations had been profoundly alienated from the largely illiterate, primitive peasant masses. These masses, traumatized by the seemingly endless war, were unable to comprehend the lavish freedom suddenly granted to them by the benevolent yet highly unrealistic Provisional Government. The Government was, moreover, discredited by the Bolshevik demagogic agitation as representing only the age-old "oppressors." In a few days, Russia jumped over several stages of political evolution—from a long tradition of submission and apathy to modern democracy. This was obviously too much for the Russian masses to assimilate overnight.

While the leaders of other parties, mostly prisoners of democratic scruples, were busy arguing with each other about fine points of theory, the Bolsheviks were catering to the instincts and hatreds of the masses. In the most confused situation, the Bolsheviks were the only group that grasped the true meaning of what was going on and were able to harness those longings for their own objectives. Here they proved master organizers, skillful manipulators of modern mass politics, and imaginative leaders. The Bolsheviks' vigorous organizational effort and grass-roots work were very effective. For instance, they were the first to form fighting squads—the Red Guards, Army and Navy committees, factory committees, and so forth. Realizing how elemental was the desire for peace, they put that slogan at the head of their program. They printed a special paper for the front soldiers, *Pravda of the Trenches*, that encouraged the soldiers to abandon the trenches and fraternize with the enemy and to "vote with their feet."

They encouraged the spontaneous division of large estates that had been taking place in the countryside since the summer of 1917. To gain the support of ethnic minorities, the Bolsheviks, although at heart rigid centralists, loudly proclaimed the slogan of national self-determination, including the right to secession.

The Provisional Government had failed on most counts as an effective executive power. It was unable either to extricate Russia from the war or to continue the struggle to achieve victory. It proved incapable of convincing the alienated, sulking masses that it was going to offer them the fundamental reforms desired by the people, especially radical land reform. On the other hand, one must admit that the task of the Provisional Government was exceedingly difficult. Russia had more than three years of war behind it and had suffered some seven million casualties. The new Government could neither go on with the war, because of the growing disintegration of the armed forces, nor sign a separate peace for fear of mortally endangering its Western Allies and helping Germany to establish a hegemonial position in Europe, with all that it would imply for Russia's political position in the future. The land and war issues were interconnected. The elemental longing for peace conditioned all other aspects of soldiers' behavior. "What good is land to me if I am dead?" was a typical question asked by the rank-and-file people at the front. Besides the legal scruples the Government felt concerning the peasants' spontaneous seizure of the land, the anarchic, often violent redistribution was all too quickly diminishing dwindling food supplies. The situation in the factories, with their ineffective, often quarreling, workers' committees, was similar.

The failure of the Provisional Government spelled the first tragic failure of infant liberal democracy in Russia. The withdrawal of Russia from active association with the West and the militant proclamation by its new leaders of demagogic slogans, radically opposed to everything the liberal West stood for, were bound to have far-reaching global repercussions. Consequently, the triumph of the Bolsheviks over one-sixth of the earth opened a new era in the history of the twentieth century.

Suggested Reading

CHAMBERLIN, WILLIAM H., *The Russian Revolution.* Vol. 1. New York: Macmillan, 1935.

CHERNOV, VICTOR, *The Great Russian Revolution.* New Haven, CT: Yale University Press, 1936.

DANIELS, ROBERT V., *Red October.* New York: Scribners, 1967.

DZIEWANOWSKI, M. K. (ED.), *The Russian Revolution: An Anthology.* New York: T. Y. Crowell, 1970.

FIGES, ORLANDO, *A People's Tragedy: A History of the Russian Revolution.* New York: Viking, 1997.

FITZPATRICK, SHELIA, *The Russian Revolution.* New York: Oxford University Press, 1982.

FRANCIS, DAVID R., *Russia from the American Embassy.* New York: Scribners, 1922.

FRANKEL, EDITH ROGOVIN, ET AL. (EDS.), *Revolution in Russia. Reassessment of 1917.* New York: Cambridge University Press, 1992.

FULLER, JR., WILLIAM C., *Civil–Military Conflict in Imperial Russia, 1881–1914.* Princeton, NJ: Princeton University Press, 1985.

HOSKINS, GEOFFREY, *The Russian Constitutional Experiment, Government, and the Duma, 1907–1919.* New York: Cambridge University Press, 1973.

JAHN, HUBERTUS F., *Patriotic Culture in Russia during World War I.* Ithaca and London: Cornell University Press, 1995.

KATKOV, GEORGE, *Russia 1917.* New York: Oxford University Press, 1967.

KEEP, JOHN L. H., *The Russian Revolution: A Study in Mass Mobilization.* New York: Norton, 1976.

KENEZ, PETER, *The Birth of the Propaganda State: Soviet Methods of Mobilization, 1917–1929.* New York: Cambridge University Press, 1985.

KERENSKY, ALEXANDER, *Russia and History's Turning Point.* New York: Duell, Sloan and Pierce, 1965.

KOENIKER, DIANE P. AND WILLIAM G. ROSENBERG, *Strikes and Revolution in Russia, 1917.* Princeton, NJ: Princeton University Press, 1989.

LIEVEN, O.C.B., *Russia and the Origins of the First World War.* New York: St. Martin's, 1983.

MANDEL, DAVID, *The Petrograd Workers and the Fall of the Old Regime from the February Revolution to the July Days, 1917.* London: Macmillan, 1983.

MASSIE, ROBERT K., *The Romanovs: The Final Chapter.* New York: Random House, 1995.

MAYZEL, MATITISHU, *An Army in Transition: The Russian High Command, October 1917–May 1918.* Tel-Aviv: Russian and East European Research Center, Tel-Aviv University, 1976.

MELGUNOV, S. P., *The Bolshevik Seizure of Power* (Ed. and abridged by Sergei G. Pushkarev in collaboration with Boris S. Pushkarev). Santa Barbara, CA, and Oxford, England: ABC Clio, 1972.

MENNING, BRUCE W., *Bayonets before Bullets: The Russian Imperial Army, 1861–1914.* Bloomington: Indiana University Press, 1992.

MORENSHIELDT, DMITRI VON (ED.), *The Russian Revolution: Contemporary Accounts.* New York: Oxford University Press, 1971.

PALEOLOGUE, MAURICE, *An Ambassador's Memoirs.* London: Hutchinson, 1923–1935. 3 Vols.

PERRIE, MAUREEN, *The Agrarian Policy of the Russian Socialist–Revolutionary Party.* New York: Cambridge University Press, 1976.

PIPES, RICHARD (ED.), *Revolutionary Russia.* Cambridge, MA: Harvard University Press, 1968.

———. *The Russian Revolution.* New York: Alfred A. Knopf, 1990.

RABINOVITCH, ALEXANDER, *The Bolsheviks Come to Power.* New York: Norton, 1977.

STEINBERG, MARK D., AND VLADIMIK KHRUSTALEV, *The Fall of the Romanovs: Political Dreams and Personal Struggles in a Time of Revolution.* New Haven: Yale University Press, 1995.

STOCKDALE, MELISSA KIRSCHKE, *Paul Miliukov and the Quest for a Liberal Russia, 1880–1918.* Ithaca: Cornell University Press, 1996.

SUKHANOV, N. N. (N. N. HIMMER), *The Russian Revolution, 1917: A Personal Record.* Princeton, NJ: Princeton University Press, 1984.

WILDMAN, ALLAN K., *The End of the Russian Imperial Army.* Princeton, NJ: Princeton University Press, 2 Vols., 1980 and 1987.

ZEMAN, Z. A. B. (ED.), *Germany and the Revolution in Russia, 1915–1918.* New York: Oxford University Press, 1958.

Chapter 7

Utopia at the Creation

One of the first steps of the Soviet Government was to publish the Peace Decree of November 8, (Nov. 21 N.S) 1917. The decree was actually an appeal to all belligerent powers to start immediate negotiations for ending the hostilities and concluding a peace without annexations or indemnities. The Entente, mainly France and Britain, encouraged by the United States' entry into the war, was reluctant to talk about an end to the war, but the Central Powers agreed to the Soviet suggestions. On December 5 (Dec. 18 N.S.) an armistice was concluded between the Soviets and the Germans, and between Austro–Hungary and the Ottoman Empire. Soon peace talks were opened at Brest-Litovsk.

Anxious as it was to secure peace, the Soviet Government never forgot during its negotiations with the Central Powers that fomenting social revolution was its primary task. Immediately after publishing their Peace Decree, the Bolsheviks started sending out fiery radio appeals addressed "to all, all People of the World," urging them to struggle for peace through every available means including civil war. At that time the expectation of a social revolution in Germany and Austro-Hungary was Lenin's main hope for the survival of the weak, infant Soviet regime. Consequently, the Bolsheviks sent agitators among the soldiers of the Central Powers urging them to revolt against their officers. The German soldiers were told to throw down their arms and go home or, better yet, to turn their weapons on the exploiters and oppressors and change the "imperialistic war" into a European civil war.

Domestic Measures of the Bolsheviks

One day after the publication of the Peace Decree, the Soviet regime took its next important step, publication of the Land Decree. This decree ordered immediate partition of large estates—whether belonging to private individuals, members of the former imperial family, or the church—and their distribution to the peasants. All livestock and implements were also to be seized and shared by the rural populace. The land was to become the property of the State, and only those willing to cultivate it themselves were to be permitted to use it. In this way the Bolshevik leaders gave their legal blessing to splitting up the land into some 25 million small holdings. They acquiesced to this for tactical reasons, but they did not abandon their ultimate goal of the collectivization of agriculture. When and how it was to be collectivized would depend on later circumstances. Thus the Land Decree was a stopgap measure; another agrarian revolution would follow when circumstances warranted.

On the heels of these two momentous decrees came the establishment of an eight-hour working day, followed by a series of measures that reasserted Communist egalitarian principles and reshaped the privilege-ridden social structure of Tsarist Russia. All titles were abolished. Individuals were to be addressed as "citizen" or, if a member of the party, as "comrade." A similar principle was introduced into the militia, which was to replace the old armed forces. The militia was to be composed of citizen volunteers; again, all titles and ranks were to be eliminated, and commanders were to be elected by the rank and file.

The struggle against religion, considered by Marx to be "the opiate of the people," was not forgotten. For a long time the Church has been subservient to the State; since 1721, when Peter the Great abolished the office of Moscow Patriarch, it had been administered as a government department. This subservience had had a crippling effect upon its spiritual life and had made the church bureaucratic, ossified, and heavily dependent on secular authorities. In fact, the hierarchy became largely identified with bureaucratic authorities, thereby rendering Orthodoxy useless as an instrument of social and political reform. As a tool of the autocracy, the Church had automatically become a major target in the struggle against the Tsarist State.

As early as February 15, 1918, a decree of the Council of People's Commissars declared the separation of the State from the Orthodox Church. The same decree proclaimed freedom of worship insofar as it did not "violate public order." The term "public order" was arbitrarily interpreted by the new regime. At the same time, all Church property was confiscated and all religious instruction in the schools abolished. Religious, or "bourgeois," marriages were ridiculed and sexual promiscuity encouraged. Only civil marriages were recognized by the State. Divorce could be obtained at once by a simple declaration of agreement; when one side objected, the procedure would be longer. Many traditional cultural patterns were also altered. The old Cyrillic alphabet was simplified, and on February 14, 1918 (February 1, old style), the Julian calendar was abandoned and the West's Gregorian calendar introduced. Teaching of religion to minors was forbidden. These measures brought the party into bitter conflict with all churches and religious groups, but especially with the Orthodox Church. The Patriarch of Moscow denounced the Bolshevik regime and its leaders as "monsters of the human race" and "madmen." These anathemas made the Bolsheviks redouble their vicious reprisals. Arrests, deportations and executions of the clergy multiplied. According to estimates at least twenty-eight bishops and some 1,000 priests of the Orthodox Church had perished by 1923.[1]

The new rulers of Russia were determined to implement as quickly as possible a radical socialist organization of the country and to impose a centrally planned economy. The state was to control all economic activity: it was to fix priorities, allocate resources, and determine prices and wages. Thus, from the beginning, the Soviet economy was a "command economy," one based on instructions issued from above and not on the law of supply and demand. These hasty, radical reforms precipitated chaotic conditions that resulted in shortages of basic necessities. Soon, urban centers were threatened with starvation. Consequently factory workers began leaving the cities in search of food, while rampant inflation paralyzed the economy. The workers who remained in the cities continued to seize factories, mines, and other enterprises and to administer them through elected factory committees, which were to be the chief

---

[1] As a result of the Communist reprisals a part of the Orthodox hierarchy and clergy had fled the country by 1921 and established a separate Church organization outside of Russia that came to be known as either "the Russian Orthodox Church Abroad" or "Bynodal Church."

instrument of "workers' control." The often genuine enthusiasm of the workers, however, was no match for the expert knowledge of their former managers and engineers, and industrial production sank lower and lower.

The factory committees finally proved not only ineffective, but harmful to production, and were eventually suppressed. The workers were ordered to join the new government trade unions, and all strikes were outlawed. As a result, the Bolshevik Party's authoritarianism also became firmly entrenched in the economy.

All banks, insurance companies, and means of communication were taken over by Soviet authorities immediately after the Bolshevik seizure of power. On June 28, 1918, the Bolsheviks went one step further and nationalized most of Russia's large industries (some 1,100 joint stock companies). For the time being, all former administrative personnel were ordered to remain at their jobs or face prosecution for "sabotage." Private trade was gradually extinguished, and the State undertook to distribute food as far as it was available. Consequently, by the summer of 1918, "the commanding heights of the economy," as Lenin put it, were in the hands of the State (see Chapter 9). In 1914, the Imperial regime controlled about 10 percent of the national economy; by 1921–22 the new regime controlled 80–90 percent of it.

Neither the nationalization decree nor the other regulations that kept pouring from the government presses—along with paper money—could stem the rising tide of chaos or provide the cities with food and other necessities. The spreading famine increasingly caused a great many people of all classes to abandon the cities and search for food in rural areas. Many workers who had maintained ties with their native villages returned home. The result of this mass migration from the urban areas was an acute shortage of manpower. The new regime tried to counter the situation by establishing a system of compulsory labor and by introducing a strict system of rationing in which workers were given priority. One of the Communist slogans was "Those who do not work, should not eat."

The Cheka and the Dissolution of the Constituent Assembly

The Bolshevik triumph in the two capitals was far from ending the struggle for power. Even before the outbreak of the civil war in the winter and spring of 1918, the Mensheviks and most of the SRs tried to oust the Bolsheviks from power by regaining majorities in the city soviets, and the new rulers of Petrograd and Moscow often suffered resounding defeats in the local elections. On December 20, therefore, in a move to protect the new regime from its actual and potential enemies, the government set up the Extraordinary Commission to Combat Counterrevolution—colloquially called the *Cheka*, which is its Russian acronym. The organization was given complete autonomy and could carry out searches, arrests, and death sentences. The Cheka was described by one of its prominent members as "the eyes, ears, and the mailed fist" of the proletariat and as "the naked avenging sword of the Revolution." At the beginning of 1918, when the capital was shifted from Petrograd to Moscow, the headquarters of the dreaded Cheka were established in the Lubianka, home of a respectable insurance company. An old co-worker of Lenin's, Felix Dzerzhinsky, was placed at its head. With fanatic zeal, Dzerzhinsky dedicated himself to the task of eradicating all enemies of the new regime.[2]

[2] The Tsarist secret police, known as *Okhrana*, had relied on the Special Corps of Gendarmes, a force of some 15,000 men. By mid-1921, the *Cheka* amounted to some 250,000 (seventeen times larger than *Okhrana*) and was constantly growing. While the *Okhrana* had exercised virtually no extra judicial powers and the number of executions carried out during the last fifty years of the Tsarist regime amounted to some four to five thousand, those affected during the first six years of the Soviet rule, according to Lenin's estimate, were no less than 200,000. George Leggett, *The Cheka: Lenin's Political Police* (New York: Oxford University Press, Clarendon Press, 1981), pp. 56–57 and Epilogue. As Lenin put it on April 3, 1920, "A good Communist is at the same time a good Chekist." In October 1918, he declared, "The revolutionary dictatorship of the proletariat is power secured and sustained through coercion of the bourgeoisie by the proletariat, a power unrestricted by any laws."

When the Constituent Assembly was dispersed in January 1918 and the Brest-Litovsk Treaty signed in March of that year, opposition intensified, and so did the terror.

The convocation of a democratically elected assembly had been awaited for so long that its sudden dismissal came as something of a shock. To view the issue of the Assembly in its proper perspective, it is necessary to recall the action taken in the late summer of 1917 by the Provisional Government. At that time the Kerensky regime finally fixed November 25 (December 8) as the date for elections to the Assembly. The date itself was a factor in precipitating the Bolshevik coup, as Lenin's apprehension that the voting might go against the Bolshevik Party helped him to persuade his comrades to act without further delay. Once in power, however, the Bolsheviks decided that it would be too risky for the new regime to ignore public opinion by abrogating the election. Consequently, despite serious misgivings about the final outcome, Lenin decided that the elections should be allowed to take place without further postponement or hindrance. Consequently, with the exception of some meddling with the results of a few districts, peaceful elections took place without gross interference on the part of the Bolsheviks.

The voting represented the first free, unfettered, and democratic elections in Russian history. And as Lenin had presaged, the results proved highly unsatisfactory from the Bolshevik point of view. Out of the total 703 deputies elected, only 168 were Bolsheviks, while 380 were Social Revolutionaries. The Party made the strongest showing in big cities, where the working class was relatively large; but the masses of the peasantry supported the Social Revolutionaries. Even if the Left SRs had joined in a government coalition as allies of the Bolsheviks, together they would have constituted less than one-third of the deputies.[3]

Once having allowed the elections to take place, the Bolsheviks found it difficult to prevent the Assembly from convening. On January 5 (18), 1918, the vicinity of the Tauride Palace, where the inaugural session of Russia's first full-scale parliament was taking place, resembled an armed camp. The Bolsheviks had taken rigid precaution of distributing admission tickets to the public by the Cheka. Baltic sailors and Latvian sharpshooters crowded the corridors and galleries of the former Imperial residence and threatened the non-Bolsheviks with lynching.

Despite these threats, the Social Revolutionaries and the Mensheviks, who together dominated the Assembly, managed quickly to adopt four measures. They elected the moderate Socialist Revolutionary Victor Chernov, former Minister of Agriculture in the Provisional Government, as Speaker. They proclaimed Russia a democratic federal republic; they disregarded the negotiations of Brest for a separate peace and issued an appeal for an international socialist conference that would achieve a "general democratic peace." Ignoring measures already passed by the Bolsheviks, they proclaimed the basic principles of a Land Law that would affect land redistribution in accordance with Socialist Revolutionary agrarian programs. The land would be nationalized and would be equally accessible to all who wished to till it.

All these measures were regarded by Lenin as a challenge to the authority of the Soviet regime. When it became apparent that the Assembly would persist in its deliberations and that it refused to legitimize the Bolshevik rule, it was more than Lenin could tolerate. At five o'clock on the morning of January 19 (February 1) he ordered the sailors to clear the hall.

---

[3]According to an American scholar, of the total 41 million votes cast, the Social Revolutionaries (Russian as well as Ukrainian) polled 17 million; the Bolsheviks, 9.8 million; the Cadets, 2 million; the Mensheviks, less than 1.4 million. Of the 703 deputies, 380 were Social Revolutionaries; 39, Left Social Revolutionaries; 168, Bolsheviks; 18, Mensheviks; 17, Cadets; 4, Popular Socialists; and 77 represented various ethnic minorities. Oliver H. Radkey, Jr., *The Election to the Russian Constituent Assembly of 1917* (Cambridge, Mass.: Harvard University Press, 1950), pp. 15–16.

Thus ended in less than twenty-four hours the first democratically elected parliament in Russian history.

Peace Negotiations

Meanwhile, the Bolsheviks had to confront the hard facts of international life. The armistice of December 15 (28) was followed by protracted peace negotiations at Brest-Litovsk. The Soviet delegation, led first by Adolf Joffe and then by Foreign Affairs Commissar Trotsky, and the Central Powers delegation could not agree on the basic premises of the settlement. The Soviet side insisted on peace "without annexations or indemnities," whereas the Central Powers demanded territorial concessions and reparations in cash as well as large supplies of food produce. The upshot was that at the end of December the Soviet delegation broke off the talks and left Brest-Litovsk. But not for long, for with their army in shambles and facing the formidable war machine of Germany and Austro-Hungary, the defenseless Bolsheviks were in a desperate situation. Semiofficial contacts were established with Western representatives in Petrograd to try to induce the Allies to join the Soviet Government at the peace table. There was some loose talk that the Allies would lend the Soviets military assistance. Mutual distrust, however, prevented any agreement, and the Soviet Government was left to its own resources, face to face with Germany, Austro-Hungary, Bulgaria, and Turkey.

In the annals of diplomatic history the negotiations of Brest-Litovsk represent the beginning of a new diplomatic style, one that no doubt contributed to the mistrust between the Soviets and the Allies. When he broke off the talks on December 29, Trotsky issued an appeal urging the workers of the West to rise. They remained by and large loyal to their leaders, however. Meanwhile, the armies of the Central Powers resumed their slow but relentless march toward Petrograd, Moscow, and Kiev.

Within days of breaking off the talks, the

Leon Trotsky as Commissar for War, 1918–1925

helplessness and full gravity of their situation was brought home to the Bolshevik leaders. On January 9, 1918, they returned to Brest. As soon as the Soviet delegation reappeared, Trotsky was faced with new, stiffer demands by the Central Powers. The Germans brushed aside Trotsky's verbosity and insisted on a prompt settlement in which the Russians would provide indemnities and agree to territorial concessions. To break Soviet resistance to these stiff demands and obtain grain supplements from the Ukraine, the Germans ingeniously bypassed the Soviet representatives and invited a delegation of the Ukrainian Central National Council of Kiev, or the Central Rada, to Brest, an offer the anti-Bolshevik Ukrainians eagerly accepted.

The Bolsheviks, driven into a corner, were split. A large segment of the Party, led by Nicholas I. Bukharin, continued to favor defiance. Remembering the French Revolution and still hoping for a social upheaval throughout Europe, Bukharin preached a revolutionary war against the Central Powers. However, the minority, headed by Lenin and supported by Zinoviev, Kameniev, and Stalin, were for immediate peace, whatever the conditions imposed by the victors. Between those two factions stood Trotsky, who wanted to adhere to the terms of the armistice but sign no formal peace treaty.

The Bolsheviks' revolutionary oratory failed to impress the Central Powers, and on February 18 their troops resumed their eastward march. First the Germans occupied unresisting Latvia and Estonia; then they threatened Petrograd. This grim reality (which forced the removal of the capital to Moscow), combined with Lenin's determination, made the Soviets declare, six days later, their readiness to sign the peace agreement. Meanwhile, the Turks had put forward new demands for restitution of the regions lost to Russia at the Congress of Berlin of 1878—the Armenian cities of Kars, Batum, and Ardahan. The helpless Bolsheviks had to capitulate.

The Treaty of Brest-Litovsk

The day the Soviet delegation arrived at Brest-Litovsk (February 28, 1918), a strange scene took place at the railroad station. On the platform stood a group of officials: diplomats in top hats and swallowtail coats and officers dressed in their gold-braided uniforms. When the Soviet representatives detrained, the self-assured bureaucrats of the Central Powers found to their astonishment that they were facing a motley gang of shabby, long-haired bohemians, cigarettes in their mouths and their pockets full of revolutionary leaflets. As the bureaucrats formally greeted the Soviet delegates, Bolshevik Karl Radek drifted over to the amazed onlookers and began to distribute pamphlets urging the violent overthrow of the very governments with which the Soviets were about to start peaceful relations.

The scene marked a transition in international behavior. Heretofore, discussions between nations had been conducted in secret by professional, old-school diplomats. In the past, the function of diplomacy had been to influence top political circles. Brest-Litovsk initiated a new era in which diplomatic intercourse would be carried on largely in the open in an effort to influence masses of people through propaganda. This new approach to diplomacy later was made easier with the advent of mass media.

By the terms of the Brest-Litovsk Treaty, the Soviet Government agreed to recognize the independence of the Ukraine, Finland, and Georgia. Moreover, the Soviets agreed to accept the status that the Central Powers had bestowed on Poland, Lithuania, Latvia, and Estonia in the name of national self-determination. These countries would be vassal states ruled by German princes. The Russians also lost a strip of Transcaucasia to the Ottoman Empire. The treaty reduced Soviet territory by 1,267,000 square miles and its population by 62 million. Furthermore, the peace cost the Russians 32 percent of their arable lands, 26 percent of their railroads, 33 percent of their factories, and up to 75 percent of their coal mines. The Soviet Government also had to accept a commercial treaty that committed it to supply the victors with large quantities of food. The German and Austrian press greeted Brest as "bread peace," that would allow the Central Powers, especially Germany and Austria, to win the war.

The *diktat* of Brest was the final act of Russia's withdrawal from World War I; it was the most humiliating treaty in modern Russian history. It took away the acquisitions of more than two centuries of territorial expansion. As a result, European Russia was reduced to about the size of the old Grand Duchy of Muscovy as it existed before Peter the Great. If the human losses suffered during the war (1.3 million killed, 3 million wounded, and 2.5 million prisoners of war) are added to the territorial concessions, the price the Russians paid for their participation in the struggle is staggering.

The signing of the treaty ended the most precarious period in the history of Russia's Bolshevik regime. At that time the Soviet state was practically defenseless. In early 1918 the forces of the Central Powers could easily have reached Petrograd and Moscow. They could have set up whatever government they wished. Even the Romanians, who had been crushed by the Central Powers, could afford to annex the province of Bessarabia. Thus, from the point of view of the regime's survival, Lenin's decision to make immediate peace was farsighted. Any other policy would have brought disaster. The position Lenin took on the issue further enhanced his prestige. It helped to make him the uncontested leader and arbiter of the Communist Party. After Brest-Litovsk, he came to be recognized not only as the founder of the Soviet State, but also as its savior in an hour of mortal danger.

Trotsky and Bukharin, on the other hand, the chief opponents of Lenin's decision to sign the treaty, lost in stature. Almost immediately after the passions aroused by the February-March 1918 intraparty debates had subsided, it became obvious to everyone that the two had advocated an adventurous and potentially catastrophic line of conduct.

The Brest-Litovsk negotiations represented for the Bolsheviks their first major confrontation with the harsh realities of international life. They had started the discussions in a high-spirited, utopian mood, persuaded that the proletarian revolution was just around the corner and that it would be possible to bluff their way to diplomatic success with slogans. They ended by signing the treaty in a sober mood, aware of the value of military power.

The treaty lasted no more than a few months (March-November 1918), for it was invalidated by November 11, 1918, as a result of the surrender of Germany to the Western powers. Moreover, the Brest agreement was never fully implemented because the Bolsheviks signed it with a firm determination to evade it, and the Central Powers, temporarily masters of Eastern Europe, interpreted it in such a way as to make a mockery of it. The treaty was even more significant than the later Allied intervention: It represented the most brutal attempt by a

foreign power to intervene in the domestic affairs of postrevolutionary Russia. The German-Austrian occupation covered an incomparably larger segment of the former Tsarist Empire than the much publicized yet limited intervention of the Entente. The troops of the Central Powers, totaling some 100 divisions, stretched from Estonia in the north to the Caucasus in the south. The Central Powers managed to set up in these lands a series of vassal states. The most important was the Ukrainian puppet state, with Pavlo P. Skoropadsky, a former Tsarist general, serving as *Hetman*, or head, of this quasi-monarchic regime. Short-lived though the occupation by the Central Powers was, it was marked by intense exploitation of the natural resources of Ukraine, which was despoiled not only of its crops, but even of its black soil, exported by the Germans to fertilize the suburban gardens of their cities. The spectacular success of Germany's diplomacy seemed to open dazzling vistas for Berlin in Eastern Europe. The chief of the German general staff, Erich Ludendorff, even toyed with the idea of a large-scale deportation of the native populations of Poland and Ukraine to Siberia in order to make living space (*Lebensraum*) for German war veterans and other settlers from Germany.

The Aftermath of Brest-Litovsk

Not surprisingly, the surrender at Brest-Litovsk precipitated an acute crisis, domestic as well as international, that contributed to the outbreak of civil war and to Western Allied intervention. The Entente powers, hitherto opposed to the idea of armed intervention in Russia, used the separate peace between its former ally and its enemies as further proof of Soviet-German collusion that should justify open involvement on the side of the anti-Soviet opposition. At home Lenin was accused—not only by the opposition but also by many of his followers—of selling Russia's birthright to the imperialistic Central Powers. The Left Social Revolutionaries withdrew their support from the

Bolsheviks and recalled their representatives from the Council of People's Commissars. From then on the SRs were in the forefront of the opposition to Russia's Communist regime. Hoping to provoke a renewal of hostilities, one member of the Social Revolutionary Party assassinated the German ambassador in Moscow, Count von Mirbach. Another, Dora (Fanny) Kaplan, shot Lenin on August 30, 1918, wounding him in the neck and shoulder.

Despite mounting reaction against the Brest-Litovsk settlement, Lenin remained firm. On March 6, he made his report to the Seventh Party Congress and underlined the fact that the treaty offered the infant Soviet regime a breathing spell indispensable for its consolidation and survival. Moreover, he was still hoping for a proletarian upheaval in Germany. But, as he put it: "Germany is now pregnant with revolution; in our country we already have a healthy baby—the Socialist Republic—which we will murder by resuming war." He urged his comrades to accept the peace and to abandon their ideological antimilitarism and devote more attention to the issue of forging a new instrument of action, the Red Army. Under his pressure, the Seventh Congress approved the motion to accept the peace treaty.

The Seventh Congress moved the Party one step further along the path of authoritarianism by asserting that "there can be no question of freedom for the bourgeoisie. . . . The Party must mercilessly suppress all attempts of the opposition to return to power. And this is what is meant by a dictatorship of the proletariat." The Congress renamed the Russian Social Democratic Workers' Party (Bolshevik) the Communist Party.

The Birth of the Red Army

The aftermath of the Brest-Litovsk Treaty, then, marked a turning point in the evolution of the Communist regime in Russia. The Party reluctantly shed its pacifist illusions and antimilitarist notions; it also became more ruthless and intolerant of opposition.

Slowly the Bolsheviks began to rescue from the chaos the few surviving organized units of the army and navy—the regiments of the Lettish Sharpshooters, for instance. Even so, these small units were helpless against the massive, disciplined legions of the Central Powers. The Bolsheviks' dire military situation vis-à-vis the Germans was made even worse by the armed resistance of the White detachments, which began to appear at various scattered points in Russia in the spring of 1918. White Russian resistance contributed to the further expansion of regular Bolshevik fighting units.

In April 1918, Trotsky, who had left the Commissariat for Foreign Affairs and was now Commissar for War, set out to reorganize the existing militia into a more tightly organized and disciplined conscripted force. Compulsory military training was ordered for all able-bodied workers and for those peasants who did not hire labor and were considered poor or medium peasants. Rich peasants (*kulaks*) and members of the bourgeoisie, mistrusted as class enemies, were denied the privilege of bearing arms in defense of the Revolution; instead, they were to serve in the auxiliary labor battalions. Officers were no longer elected. The old bonds of authority and discipline were not immediately reintroduced, for it was believed that strict, systematic ideological indoctrination would suffice. Nevertheless, the death penalty was restored for "military crimes," and the term was applied arbitrarily. Because trained officers of Communist persuasion were in very short supply, Trotsky ordered the conscription of officers from the old Imperial Army, provided they would conform politically and do their professional duty conscientiously. Many of them obeyed that order, including some of the prominent leaders like, e.g., General Brusilov.

In its organization, motivation, and objectives, the Red Army was a new type of armed force. Its regulations stressed the principle of equality at every step, a principle reflected in simple, Spartan uniforms, in the attitude of the commanders toward their rank and file, and in the everyday behavior of the officers.

Hierarchy was determined solely by function. The title of officer was replaced by that of commander (*komandir*). To this single acceptable title was added a definition of the officer's function, like company commander, regimental commander, divisional commander, and so on, up to the top. The hated Tsarist badges of rank, especially the gold and silver braided shoulders straps, were done away with altogether and replaced by simple, austere symbols—a few red squares, stripes, or triangles. Another distinctive feature of the Red Army was the duality of its command; to the authority of the regular field commanders was added that of the political commissars, the party's eyes and ears within the armed forces. The commissars' tasks were manifold and complex, and included bolstering discipline, supervising the political reliability of the field commander, carrying out educational functions, and watching over the ideological indoctrination of the soldiers. They combined the functions formerly performed by educational officers and chaplains.

The new Red Army was to be motivated not by traditional Russian patriotism, semi-religious and semi-nationalistic in nature, but by "proletarian internationalism"—the solidarity of workers in all lands united through their hatred of the capitalist system and fired by devotion to the revolutionary cause. Nor were the objectives of the Red Army similar to those of its Tsarist predecessor. Besides being proclaimed by the official declaration as "the sword of the first Socialist State," as well as of the Bolshevik Party, the Red Army was to be an instrument of the world proletarian revolution. It was to be ready to defend its bulwark, the Soviet State, and to intervene, when necessary, on behalf of other revolutionary movements all over the world. The models for Red Army soldiers were not the old marshals Suvorov, Kutuzov, or Prince Alexander Nevsky, but the leader of the mutiny of Roman slaves, Spartacus, the fanatical leader of the French Revolution, Marat, and the heroes of the Paris Commune of 1870–1871. The cosmopolitan mood of the early Soviet state was also reflected in the adoption of the "Internationale" as its first anthem.

The First Soviet Constitution

The Bolsheviks did not hide their profound contempt for "bourgeois legality," as they demonstrated by their brutal dispersal of the democratically elected Constituent Assembly. Yet the necessity for some sort of formal framework could not be entirely disregarded. On July 19, 1918, therefore, the first Soviet Constitution for the Russian Socialist Federated Soviet Republic was officially promulgated. According to its ambitious preamble, the chief goal of the Communist regime in Russia was "the pitiless suppression of the exploiters, the socialist organization of society, and the victory of socialism in all countries." The Constitution repudiated all secret treaties and colonial policies; it granted independence to Finland and the right of self-determination to Armenia. The Declaration of Rights of Toiling and Exploited People, which had been one of the initial acts of the new regime, was now included in the charter. The Declaration guaranteed, but only to the working class, freedom of speech, press, and association, as well as free access to education. Members of the former ruling groups and the bourgeoisie in general were disenfranchised.

The first Soviet Constitution guaranteed to urban residents a five-to-one preponderance in suffrage over those who lived in the countryside; in addition, deputies from rural constituencies were to be elected indirectly. The pyramid of local and regional councils, or soviets, was to be the basis of the whole political hierarchy, at the apex of which would be the All-Russian Congress of Soviets. The Congress was to have supreme authority. Between meetings of the Congress, supreme power was to be exercised by the Central Executive Committee, a large, unwieldy body elected by the Congress and composed of more than 200 members. The Central Executive Committee was to appoint the Cabinet, or Council of People's Commissars. The principle of the dictatorship of the proletariat, was written into the charter. Strangely enough, the first Constitution failed to mention the driving force of the revolutionary changes—the Communist Party. The old national flag, introduced by Peter the Great (three long stripes, white, blue, and red) was abolished and from then on; the official banner of the Soviet State was to be a red flag with a gold star surmounting a hammer and sickle placed in the upper left corner. The hammer represented the workers and the sickle the peasants, while the star was a symbol of a bright future.

The Soviet Constitution was a fiction completely divested of political reality. The document tended to obfuscate the real state of things, e.g., like failing to mention the decisive role of the Party. In practice the Constitution was an instrument by means of which the Party exercised an unaccountable and unlimited dictatorial power; this reality was camouflaged by a quasi-democratic phraseology.

While the first Soviet Constitution was being promulgated and the new regime was being challenged by Russians and foreigners alike, the living symbols of the old regime were eliminated. In the summer of 1917, Nicholas II and his family had been deported to Tobolsk, and then to Ekaterinburg (renamed Sverdlovsk) in the Urals. In July 1918, with the Civil War developing in Siberia, the local soviet resolved that the Imperial family should not be allowed to fall into the hands of opponents of the Communist regime, to become a symbol of anti-Communist resistance. During the night of July 16–17, 1918, Nicholas II, his family, his doctor, and servants were taken to the cellar of the house where they lived under arrest and shot to death. Their bodies were sprayed with chemicals and burned in a nearby mine and the ashes scattered in a swamp.[4]

---

[4] It is worthwhile to note that when the Chinese Communists seized power in 1949, the last emperor of the Manchu dynasty, Pu-Yi, was not executed; after several years spent in prison and rehabilitation camp, he was allowed to work as a gardener and, later on, was even elected as a member of the State Council of Nationalities.

Suggested Reading

BOROVKIN, VLADIMIR N., *The Mensheviks after October*. Ithaca, NY: Cornell University Press, 1987.

CHAMBERLIN, WILLIAM H., *The Russian Revolution*, Vol. 1. New York: Macmillan, 1935.

CLEMENTS, BARBARA EVANS, *Bolshevik Feminist: The Life of Aleksandra Kollontai*. Bloomington: Indiana University Press, 1979.

DAVIS, R. W., ET AL. (EDS.), *The Economic Transformation of the Soviet Union, 1913–1945*. New York: Cambridge University Press, 1993.

DEGRAS, JANE T. (ED.), *Soviet Documents on Foreign Policy, 1917–1941*. New York: Oxford University Press, 1951–1953, 3 vols.

FARNSWORTH, BEATRICE, *Aleksandra Kollontai: Socialism, Feminism, and the Bolshevik Revolution*. Stanford, CA: Stanford University Press, 1980.

GARDER, MICHEL, *History of the Soviet Army*. New York: Praeger, 1966.

GERSON, LEONARD D., *The Secret Police in Lenin's Russia*. Philadelphia: Temple University Press, 1976.

GOLDMAN, WENDY, *Women, the State and Revolution: Soviet Family Policy and Social Life, 1917–1936*. New York: Cambridge University Press, 1995.

KEEP, JOHN L. H., *The Russian Revolution: A Study in Mass Mobilization*. London: Weidenfeld and Nicholson, 1976.

KENNAN, GEORGE F., *The Decision to Intervene*. Princeton, NJ: Princeton University Press, 1989.

———, *Soviet-American Relations, 1917–1920*, Vol. 1, *Russia Leaves the War*. Princeton, NJ: Princeton University Press, 1989.

LEGGETT, GEORGE, *The Cheka: Lenin's Political Police*. New York: Oxford University Press, 1981.

NOVE, ALEC, *An Economic History of the U.S.S.R.* London: Allen Lane, Penguin Press, 1969.

PIPES, RICHARD, *Russia Under the Bolshevik Regime*. New York: Alfred A. Knopf, 1993.

RADKEY, OLIVER H., *The Elections to the Russian Constituent Assembly of 1917*. Cambridge, MA: Harvard University Press, 1950.

RANSEL, DAVID L., *Mothers of Misery: Child Abandonment in Russia*. Lawrenceville, NJ: Princeton University Press, 1990.

SAUL, E. NORMAN, *Sailors in Revolt: The Russian Baltic Fleet in 1917*. Lawrence: Regents Press of Kansas, 1978.

SHAPIRO, LEONARD, *The Origins of the Communist Autocracy, 1917–1922*, Cambridge, MA: Harvard University Press, 1955.

SMITH, MICHAEL G., *Language and Power in the Creation of the USSR, 1917–1953: Contributions to the Sociology of Language,* vol. 80. Berlin: Mouton de Gruyter, 1998.

WALICKI, ANDRZEJ, *Marxism and the Leap to the Kingdom of Freedom: The Rise and Fall of the Communist Utopia.* Stanford, CA: Stanford University Press, 1995.

WHEELER-BENNETT, JOHN W., *The Forgotten Peace: Brest-Litovsk, March 1918.* New York: Macmillan, 1939.

Chapter 8

The Ordeal of the Civil War, 1918–1921

Initially, the Bolshevik coup d'état was accepted by the great majority of Russian people without much active opposition. Absorbed in the routine of making a living amidst mounting chaos and threatening starvation, exhausted by everyday cares and chores, they did not at first grasp all the implications of the upheaval. Only after the doors of the Constituent Assembly had slammed shut and the Bolsheviks bowed to the humiliating terms of the Treaty of Brest-Litovsk, while the harshness of Bolshevik rule became increasingly apparent, was the opposition galvanized into action.

During the first weeks of Bolshevik rule, in December 1917, General Lavr Kornilov and several other senior officers who had been involved in his attempted coup escaped from house arrest. Most of them went to the Don Cossack territory, an area where Communist rule had not yet been established. There they contacted former chief of staff General Mikhail Alexeyev and began to organize the first armed groups to fight openly against the Bolsheviks. To the military was soon added a handful of politicians such as Cadet leaders Miliukov and Rodzianko. Around this nucleus was organized the Anti-Soviet Volunteer Army, at first composed almost exclusively of officers and numbering only 3,000 men.

In one of the early skirmishes in March 1918, General Kornilov was killed, and a month later General Alexeyev died. As a result, the leadership of the Volunteer Army fell to its highest ranking officer, Anton I. Denikin. Denikin was at the start of the war a divisional commander, later on became commander of the entire southern and southwestern fronts. A man of peasant stock, he was a fairly moderate republican. He lacked the skill and experience necessary to lead a group of people that was not only a fighting unit but also represented a politically motivated movement.

The Allied Intervention

Although Denikin's army eventually became the greatest threat to Bolshevik rule, it was not destined to deal the first serious blow. That came almost by accident from a group of Czech and Slovak prisoners of war who had either surrendered earlier to the Tsarist armies or had simply deserted their Austro-Hungarian units. These prisoners, most of them seething with anti-Hapsburg sentiment, were organized into a Czecho-Slovak brigade stationed in the Ukraine. By the close of the war, they numbered approximately 30,000 well-organized officers and soldiers. After the Treaty of Brest-Litovsk and the collapse of active Russian resistance to the Germans, the Czecho-Slovak National Committee of Paris, headed by Tomaš G. Masaryk, decided to transfer the former POWs from Ukraine to France. The Soviets, trying to prove that despite their abject surrender at Brest they were not "German agents," gave their consent to the plan.

In March 1918, the former prisoners left their camps, located mostly in the Ukraine, for Vladivostok. Their journey along the Trans-Siberian Railway was often slowed by clashes with the local Red authorities and partisan units. Rumors spread among the POWs that the Soviets were constantly delaying the convoys in order to incorporate the well-armed Czecho-Slovak Legion into the Red Army. In this tense atmosphere, a minor skirmish triggered a major crisis. On May 14 at Chelyabinsk, a fight between the soldiers of the Legion and some Hungarian pro-Communist POWs ended in a Czecho-Slovak victory. Trotsky, then Commissar for War, declared the Legion a counterrevolutionary force, and ordered its soldiers to be disarmed or, if they resisted, shot.

The Legion almost unanimously decided to continue to Vladivostok, even if it meant shooting their way there. Their decision resulted in a series of armed clashes and pitched battles between the Legion and Red units as the convoy advanced toward the Pacific. The well-organized and disciplined Legion, commanded by French officers, proceeded to inflict one defeat after another on the Reds. In the process, the convoy, often acting in tactical alliance with local anti-Bolshevik forces, captured several Siberian towns and cities. On June 29, the Legion triumphantly reached Vladivostok.

Thus it was a body of foreign soldiers that dealt the first major, spectacular-armed blow to the Soviet regime. The long series of victories compiled by a small group of POWs over the Red units had an electrifying effect on Paris and London. To the leaders of the Entente, the establishment in Russia of a "dictatorship of the proletariat" dedicated to opposing practically everything the West believed in was totally abhorrent. That this regime immediately repudiated all financial obligations of the Tsarist government only served to aggravate further the situation. Finally, the signing of the Brest-Litovsk Treaty, construed by Western diplomats as an unconditional surrender, if not an alliance with the Central Powers, was more than the statesmen of Paris and London could take. Their reaction to the situation in Russia was no doubt partially colored by the fact that these were the crucial moments of the war; the German army was closer to Paris than ever before, and the transfer to the west of more troops by the Central Powers, now that the Eastern Front was quiet, seemed likely to tip the scale. Furthermore, the victories of the Czecho-Slovak Legion over the Bolshevik regime, regarded in the West as barbarous and treacherous, now proved it to be weak as well. It looked as if it needed merely a push to be toppled. The temptation to act, therefore, was overwhelming. On July 2, 1918, the Allied Supreme War Council decided to give military support to the forces of resistance against the Bolshevik regime.

This declaration notwithstanding, the Allies were still locked in a life-and-death struggle on the Western Front and postponed direct action against Russia until the armistice was signed with Germany on November 11, 1918. In the meantime, the Allied powers dispatched their troops to secure vast stores of war materiel that had previously been dispatched to the Tsarist authorities to bolster Russian resistance. The main locations of these stores were the ports of Murmansk, Archangel, and Vladivostok. After the Brest-Litovsk Treaty was signed, wild rumors circulated that these depots were falling to Germans. In March 1918 a small detachment of British troops followed by French and American ones, landed first in Murmansk and Vladivostok and then in Archangel solely to protect the military stores there.

Soon the Japanese, who had their own interests in mind, joined the Allied intervention. The presence of a considerable body of Japanese soldiers at that strategic point made President Wilson suspicious, and soon an American Expeditionary Corps was dispatched to Vladivostok. Within a year some 7,000 American soldiers had been dispatched to counterbalance, at least partially, the 72,000 Japanese already in the Maritime Territory around Vladivostok. The small garrisons at Murmansk and Archangel were, meanwhile, also reinforced by the Western Allies. In addition, the British sent a squadron of the Royal Navy to the Baltic soon after the armistice and supplied some aid to the small White Army operating from Estonia under the command of General N. N. Yudenich. At the end of November, the British and French cooperated in dispatching a ship to Novorossisk in the Black Sea, loaded with arms and munitions for General Denikin and his Volunteer Army. Also during this flurry of activity, in April 1919, a French infantry division landed in Odessa, and the British transferred some of their troops from their sphere of influence in Persia to the Caucus, to Batum, and to Baku. By 1919, the Allied intervention in Russia was in full swing.

The Emergence of Kolchak

When the various Western attempts at mediation between the Whites and the Reds failed, the Entente powers decided to press on with their efforts to bolster the anti-Communist forces. These forces were centered in four principal areas: (1) in Ukraine where Denikin's Volunteer Army was deployed; (2) Estonia, where General Nikolay Yudenich operated; (3) the far north at Murmansk and

Archangel, two ports where some small White units were organized with the support of the Allied detachments; and (4) in the vast territories east of the Volga River and in Siberia, where numerous White groups were operating independently, at least initially. On September 8, 1918, the White groups around Samara on the Volga combined resources with those of various Siberian centers of anti-Communist resistance and formed an executive body known as the *Directorate.* The Directorate, based in the city of Ufa in the Bashkir region south of the Ural Mountains, was the result of a shaky political compromise; the body was composed of two SRs and three Liberals.

However, a compromise over the Directorate contrived under foreign pressure satisfied no one. Quarrels erupted frequently, and for all practical purposes the Directorate resembled Krylov's fable in which a chariot is drawn by a swan, a crab, and a pike, with each pulling in a different direction. Especially indignant were some of the Tsarist officers who unjustly suspected the Socialist Revolutionary members of the coalition of secretly sympathizing and even conspiring with their former socialist comrades, the Bolsheviks. The absurd situation could not last long. And indeed, by mid-November a group of officers had overthrown the Directorate and proclaimed the reluctant Admiral Alexander V. Kolchak Supreme Ruler and Commander-in-Chief of all Russia.

Kolchak was a competent naval officer and a former commander of the Black Sea Squadron. A scholarly person, he had little interest in politics and none of the qualities necessary for leadership in the midst of a vicious civil war. Hesitating, procrastinating, and lacking good judgment of character, he was unable either to choose the proper coworkers to whom he could delegate authority or to act as a true dictator himself. Yet, with British support, Kolchak soon established his authority in Siberia west of Lake Baikal. (The region east of Baikal was in the hands of a Japanese puppet.)

For a time—at the close of 1918 and the

The Russian Civil War, 1918–1921

beginning of 1919—the Entente believed that Kolchak might become the head of the future government of Russia. As a consequence, Allied support was given mainly to him, although other White groups were not totally neglected. Kolchak's forces in the winter of 1918–1919 numbered about 120,000 well-trained and well-equipped soldiers. Pressed by the allies, the other White leaders accepted Kolchak's leadership and started preparing a combined offensive for the spring of 1919. They hoped to overthrow the Bolsheviks, who controlled most of the heartland of the old empire.

The offensive was to be a three-pronged drive by White forces with Allied assistance. Kolchak's units were to strike from their Siberian bases against Moscow. At the same time, Denikin's army was to attack from the south, while Yudenich, operating from Estonia, was to execute a diversionary attack on Petrograd in order to pull Bolshevik forces away from the defense of the Red capital. Paris and London took it for granted that by the end of 1919 the Bolsheviks would be swept into the garbage bin of history.

The Kolchak Offensive

The offensive was opened by Kolchak, who by April had reached the Volga cities of Samara and Kazan. Despite these successes, he had not been able to establish direct contact with Denikin, who was operating far to the south. Kolchak's weaknesses soon came to the fore. The peasants did not trust a leader who refused to confirm their possession of the land. Behind his rapidly advancing troops, riots and mutinies broke out constantly. Most of his own soldiers were "peasants in uniform," and not too reliable. Red partisans were also active in sabotaging the advance of his army. By June Kolchak's victorious march was stopped dead in its tracks and reversed by an able Red Army commander of Kirgiz origin, Mikhail V. Frunze.

Kolchak's retreat was even more spectacular than his advance. Leaving supplies behind, he hastily abandoned Ufa in June; in July he was already east of the Urals and had to evacuate the Siberian city of Omsk. From then on, his forces disintegrated with astonishing rapidity. Not only was Kolchak incapable of controlling his own soldiers; he also quarreled with the leaders of the Czecho-Slovak Legion. In January 1920 he fled further eastward, resigned his post as Supreme Ruler and Commander, and appointed Denikin his successor. Arms and food provided Kolchak by the West became a windfall for the Bolsheviks. Forsaken by his followers, Kolchak was soon handed over by the Czechs to the Bolsheviks. In February 1920 he was executed. Now all of Siberia west of Lake Baikal was under Communist rule, although there were still some White groups, as well as some American and Japanese detachments, east of Baikal.

The victory over Kolchak was only one aspect of a civil war that was not so much a succession of separate campaigns as a conglomeration of offensives, retreats, and counteroffensives. Many events took place simultaneously, and the complex situation changed like a kaleidoscope. In May and June 1919, while Kolchak was still fighting, Denikin's Volunteer Army launched a victorious drive from its southern bases. One of the major objectives of the White offensive was to secure a junction of their two most important armies, Kolchak's and Denikin's. This was never achieved because at Tsaritsyn or the Volga (subsequently named Stalingrad and then Volograd) the Red units commanded by Kliment E. Voroshilov (assisted by his chief political commissar, Joseph Stalin) put up a successful resistance to the Whites' attacks. In the west, however, the small, self-confident Volunteer Army, together with the local Ukrainian nationalist forces and irregular local bands, took Kharkov and went on to capture Kiev on August 30. Unfortunately for the Whites, their initial victories in Ukraine came too late to save Kolchak from being routed beyond the Urals into Siberia.

Denikin's forces soon encountered the same difficulties that had plagued Kolchak's troops: their base of operations and rear

General Anton Denikin (1872–1947)

manded the army of the Ukrainian Directorate, there were dozens of smaller guerrilla chieftains fighting the Bolsheviks, the strongest and the most colorful of whom was Nestor I. Makhno. Makhno, a former convict, was an anarchist who was not above changing sides. For the most part, though, he collaborated with the Bolsheviks, who skillfully took advantage of his political instability and personal vanity. The result was that Makhno's, as well as several other bands harassed the Volunteer Army, sapping its strength and diverting its fighting units from their main objective.

The Decisive Phases of the Civil War

Despite all these obstacles, Denikin, emboldened by his initial successes, was eager to plunge northward and capture Moscow. By the middle of October, his advanced cavalry units were in Orël, some 250 miles south of the capital. The Bolshevik leaders, fearing defeat, prepared to go underground once again, and Lenin ordered false passports to be manufactured for them. But Denikin was fighting too many enemies simultaneously. He had failed to make satisfactory compromises with the Ukrainians, and he was not able to reach a workable agreement with the Poles, who insisted on a guarantee of their newly won independence as a precondition for their cooperation. Consequently, Denikin, who had spread his forces too thinly, had to face not only the Bolsheviks but also the Ukrainians and other restless ethnic groups. His rear was soon penetrated by Red cavalry detachments led by Semyon M. Budyenny, the able former sergeant major of a Tsarist dragoon regiment. By autumn, Denikin's lines of communication and supply were impossible to defend, and at the end of October his offensive suddenly collapsed. Like Kolchak's, his retreat also soon became a rout.

flank were not secure. There were two main reasons for this insecurity. The first was a series of peasant revolts; another can be traced to the inscription on all the White generals' banners—"Russia: one, great, and indivisible." This slogan made Denikin an anathema to the Ukrainian nationalists, who were dreaming of independence. To Denikin, the Ukrainians were simply a branch of the Russian nation. Even the very name "Ukraine" was rejected by the Whites, who used the terms "Little Russia" or "Southern Russia." Some of the Ukrainian nationalists might have considered a federation with Russia, but any return to the old centralism preached by Denikin was totally unacceptable to most of them.

Because the Ukrainian forces were fragmented and independent of one another, their mutual jealousies could be exploited. In addition to Simon V. Petlyura, who com-

Certain aspects of Yudenich's story closely parallel Kolchak's and Denikin's, but his political stubbornness is more striking. During Denikin's offensive on Moscow,

Yudenich—at the head of 20,000 men, Estonians as well as Russians—advanced toward Petrograd. The Soviets, unable to spare troops from the main southern sector, were contemplating the evacuation of the city. At the gates of Petrograd by the middle of October and convinced that the city might fall at any minute, Yudenich declared: "There is no Estonia. It is a piece of Russian soil, a Russian province. The Estonian government is a gang of criminals." The shocked Estonians withdrew their detachments and understandably, returned home. Yudenich, no longer strong enough to attack Petrograd, had to halt his offensive. This crisis gave the Bolsheviks a much needed breathing spell. Trotsky managed to rally the local Red Guard, arm some workers, and stop Yudenich's attempts to advance further. Meanwhile, events in the south—the defeat of Denikin—took away the significance of Yudenich's diversionary attack. By mid-November, Yudenich had to fall back to his base in Estonia. Denikin's rout and Yudenich's retreat marked the turning point of the armed struggle for power in Russia.

By the end of 1919, the battered remnants of the Volunteer Army were being forced to seek shelter in the Don Cossack region but failed to strike a compromise with them. At the end of March 1920, 35,000 of Denikin's soldiers had to be evacuated by the British Royal Navy from the Don region to the Crimea. To compound his troubles, Denikin lost the confidence of his subordinates and resigned his command; he then left for the West.

The new commander of the Volunteer Army, General Baron Piotr N. Wrangel, was the most capable and energetic of the White military leaders, but he came to power too late in the day. In addition to lowered morale, he had to contend with the relative consolidation and stiffening of the Bolshevik rule over the Great Russian hinterland and hesitation in the French and British capitals over whether to continue supporting the anti-Bolshevik cause.

The interventions that had started with such high hopes suffered one setback and disappointment after another. France was exasperated with the political and military ineffectiveness of the Whites, who were obviously unable to use to their advantage the large sums of money, weapons, and equipment supplied by the British and French. Displeased, the French decided to withdraw most of their forces from Russia. Meanwhile, the British had become anxious to lift the Allied blockade and to resume trading with the area that traditionally had been one of their sources for grain and lumber supplies. As Lloyd George bluntly put it in replying to criticism by one of his opponents, "One can trade even with cannibals. . . ." The British outposts in Transcaucasia and Central Asia were abandoned. In September and October 1919, the bulk of the Allied detachments were withdrawn from the Far East. By January 1920, most Allied forces, except the Japanese, were out of Russia.

With the Allies gone, the situation of the remaining White detachments operating in the south became critical. The Polish victories over the Red Army in the spring of 1920 and the occupation of the right bank of the Dnieper Ukraine seemed to augur well for Wrangel's cause, yet there was no effective cooperation with the Poles. By the autumn of 1920, victorious but exhausted, the Poles decided to quit; in October, Soviet-Polish peace negotiations opened in the Latvian Capital of Riga. This event finally convinced Wrangel that his situation was hopeless. His soldiers and their families, some 135,000 people, were evacuated from the Crimea to Constantinople and soon merged with the large mass of Russian émigrés.

The Western Borderlands

The effects of the Russian Civil War were not only limited to Russia. In a sense the conflict was a cyclone the impact of which could be felt indirectly in many parts of the world. The struggle directly affected neighboring countries, but its force was greatest on the multiethnic fringes of the former Tsarist empire. Anti-Bolshevik elements were strongest in the western and southern borderlands where the tendency toward autonomy and even independence had been stimulated by the fear of the Bolshevik regime. In some cases the events taking place on the periphery had considerable effect on the contest for power between the Reds and the Whites. But to understand this aspect of the Civil War, it is necessary to ask what impact the downfall of the Tsarist regime had on the non-Russian nationalities and what response they had to the Soviet challenge of Communism.

To many ethnic leaders of the Tsarist empire, the 1917 February-March liberal revolution in Petrograd had seemed like a turning point in human history, another "Spring of Nations." Many people were convinced that a new era of liberty and justice was dawning for all. For a full six months, it had seemed as if the empire of Nicholas II might be transformed into a democratic federation, but the triumph of the Bolsheviks in Petrograd and Moscow altered the situation overnight. Many of the nationalities, including Ukrainians, Lithuanians, Latvians, Estonians, and Caucasians, might have been initially willing to have autonomous regions within a democratic, federal Russian republic. But most of the ethnic groups were suspicious of the Bolsheviks. It was not so much class struggle as it was national liberation that preoccupied the majority of the leaders of the smaller nationalities on the western and southern fringes of the old empire. In the liberal phase of the upheaval, the ethnic groups saw a chance to escape from the domination of the Great Russians. The authoritarian strivings of the Bolshevik revolution, however, augured nothing but danger to the diverse cultures on the edges of the empire.

Indeed, following Germany's capitulation in the west, the pressure of revolutionary forces could be felt all along the empire's other reaches. As the Germans withdrew from the territories they had occupied in Eastern Europe after the Brest-Litovsk Treaty, the Bolsheviks promptly tried to recapture them; with a mixture of military pressure and political subversion, they extended their rule to the west. The westward movement of the Red Army began on November 17, 1918, less than a week after the Germans capitulated to the Western Allies on the Western Front. By the end of the year Soviet troops, supported by local Communists, had occupied a large part of Belorussia and Lithuania, plus portions of Latvia and Estonia.

The latter two countries were invaded on November 29 by local Communist detachments supported by Moscow. An Estonian Workers' Council was set up in Communist-occupied territory and claimed authority over the entire country. By December 10, more than half of it was in Red hands. On December 25, *Izvestia*, the official newspaper of the Soviet Government, wrote, "Estonia, Latvia, and Lithuania are directly on the road from Russia to Western Europe, and are a hindrance to our revolution because they separate Soviet Russia from revolutionary Germany." It was only through a valiant effort by the Estonian people, aided by the Allies (mainly the Royal Navy), that the immediate danger to the very existence of their tiny country was staved off.

In Latvia, things were quite different. There, because of an unbalanced social structure that was a result of the survival of a number of large estates and an abundance of rural proletarians, the Communists could command substantially more popular support. In January 1919, Latvia's capital, Riga, was captured by the Red Army. Further to the south, the Lithuanian capital of Vilnius (Wilno), previously evacuated by the Germans, was taken by the Bolsheviks on January 5. By the middle of January, three-fourths of Latvia and a large slice of historic Lithuania were under Communist rule. These successes gave the Bolshevik regime a precious foothold on the Baltic Sea and the only access to it south of Petrograd.

Communist successes in the Baltic area were generally viewed as part of the revolutionary upsurge throughout Central and Eastern Europe. In March 1919, Communists seized power in a prostrate Hungary, set up a Soviet regime in Bavaria, and attempted a coup d'état in Berlin. Communist agitation mounted in Westphalia and Württemberg, and unrest spread in Austria. So in 1919, as the First Congress of the Communist International Party was gathering in Moscow, the situation in Eastern Europe was fluid, and Communism was on the offensive.

The Soviet-Polish Clash

The revolutionary turmoil in Russia, together with the chiliastic aspirations of its new rulers, elicited active opposition from Poland the bulk of which had belonged to the Tsarist Empire since the partitions (1772, 1793, 1795). To the leaders of Poland, which had been re-created in 1918, after the more than a century of subjugation, the apparent weakening of central authority in Russia seemed like a splendid opportunity to reverse the wheel of history and reassert Poland's former position in Eastern Europe. During the sixteenth and seventeenth centuries, the area between ethnographic Poland and Russia proper—Lithuania, Belorussia, and the Ukraine—had been an object of bitter contention. Now, with the old empire disintegrating, the Poles felt they had an excellent chance to regain at least some of their historic patrimony. The main proponent of the idea that Poland should establish a belt of buffer states between itself and Russia was the old socialist fighter Joseph Piłsudski. A man of Lithuanian stock. Piłsudski was a firm believer in the restoration of the old Polish-Lithuanian federation in a modernized shape. He considered the Dnieper Ukraine to be the key to the balance of power in Eastern Europe; he argued that whoever controlled this crucial area and its resources would be able to organize Eastern Europe. Piłsudski found a partner in Simon Petlyura, the Ukrainian Socialist military leader. Petlyura, as commander-in-chief and leader of the Ukrainian democratic government, called the Directorate, was the most serious antagonist of Bolshevik rule on the Dnieper. In the autumn of 1919, after the defeat of Ukrainian nationalist forces by the Bolsheviks and by Denikin, Petlyura sought shelter in Poland. In the spring of 1920, he signed a treaty of alliance with Poland, providing for a cooperative effort against Soviet Russia to establish an independent democratic Ukrainian Republic.

The campaign launched by Polish-Ukrainian forces on April 25, 1920, scored impressive initial successes. In May, the Polish troops captured Kiev and most of the lands on the right bank of the Dnieper. There Petlyura started to reconstruct the Ukrainian state. But in June the Red Army launched a long-prepared counteroffensive, and the Poles and Petlyura's forces had to retreat.

The battle for Kiev, which took place at the beginning of June 1920, could be called the second battle of Poltava. The first was in 1709, when Charles XII of Sweden, supported by the Ukrainian Cossacks, was defeated by Peter the Great. Both battles decided the fate of the Ukraine for a long time to come. The victory opened new vistas for Communism in East Central Europe. When the Red Army launched its counterattack that June, Stalin, who was not only the Soviet Peoples' Commissar for Nationalities but also the Chief Political Commissar of the Western Front, was already exchanging letters with Lenin on the nationality question in the future Soviet hegemonial sphere in East Central Europe. With Stalin at the army's headquarters were groups of Serbian and Hungarian Communists who dreamed of returning to their own countries as Communist dictators in the event of a Soviet victory over Poland. However, the battle of Warsaw in August 1920 made Soviet plans for East Central Europe irrelevant. The Red Army, commanded by M. N. Tukhachevsky, was decisively defeated. Realization of the Soviet's plans was delayed a quarter of a century, until the end of World War II.[1]

[1] The British Ambassador in Berlin, Lord D'Abernon, considered the first major defeat of the Red Army as an important turning point of history. In his book he called the battle of Warsaw one of the decisive battles in world history and concluded that, had the Poles "failed to arrest the triumphant march of the Soviet Army at the Battle of Warsaw, not only the world Christianity would have experienced a dangerous reverse, but also the very existence of western civilization would have been imperilled." (Lord D'Abernon, *The Eighteenth Decisive Battle of World History,* London, 1931, pp. 8–9.)

Poland won the war militarily, but it was not strong enough to exploit its victory politically. The compromise Treaty of Riga in March 1921 divided both the Ukraine and Belorussia into two segments: Western (Polish) and Eastern (Soviet).

The Caucasus and Central Asia

The Soviet-Polish contest, a crucial aspect of the vast panorama of the Civil War, was only one component of the gigantic sociopolitical struggle for mastery of an area that covered one-sixth of the earth. Another was the battle fought almost simultaneously in the south, in the Caucasus, on the border between Europe and Asia. Shortly after the Communist takeover in Petrograd and Moscow, the Caucasian peoples—Georgians, Armenians, and Azerbaijanis—broke away from Russian rule. Like the Ukrainians, these nations, with their strong native movements were motivated by a mixture of national sentiment and revolutionary zeal. Most of their leaders being Mensheviks opposed the spirit and practice of Bolshevism. On April 22, 1918, the three groups set up a Transcaucasian Federal Republic with a Georgian Menshevik as its president. The endemic ethnic, political, religious, and personal rivalries among the main partners, however, were difficult to control. After only a month, the federation fell apart. From then on each nationality tried to fend for itself and follow an independent path in search of outside aid and protection against powerful neighbors.

Georgia, with its Menshevik Party in power and afraid of the Bolsheviks whom it had outlawed, turned to Germany for support. The Germans were willing to extend their protectorate over Georgia, but were loath to do the same for the Armenians because of Berlin's alliance with the Turks, the traditional enemies of Christian Armenians. The Armenian Republic, ruled by a party of radical nationalists, was initially successful in defending its sovereignty against the Turks. But unable to rid themselves of the fear of their perennial persecutors and

exterminators, the Armenians threw their support behind the then seemingly triumphant General Denikin. In so doing, they trusted that a strong Russia would not allow their absorption into the Ottoman Empire, for the earlier massacres of their conationals did not betoken a bright future there. After the collapse of the White Army, the desperate Armenians sought help from the United States and appealed for protection to the newly established League of Nations.

After the Central Powers surrendered in November 1918, the Georgians tried to seek British protection. Once Azerbaijan—Muslim, Turkish-speaking, and rich in oil—declared its independence, the British found themselves competing fiercely in that region with the Bolsheviks and the Turks. After the November 11 armistice with the Germans, the British were able to establish their protectorate over Azerbaijan. Because of the devastation and chaos created by the Civil War, however, Western oil firms found it difficult to exploit the deposits, and the British Government soon lost its enthusiasm for Azerbaijan's independence.

The Entente Powers were willing to grant de facto recognition to all three Transcaucasian republics but, absorbed in their own postwar problems, they did little to help the republics defend themselves against the Bolsheviks. In the spring of 1920, after Denikin's defeat, the Bolsheviks turned their attention farther south, to the quarreling Georgians, Armenians, and Azerbaijanis. In April the Red Army conquered Azerbaijan and began to make military and political preparations for an offensive against Georgia and Armenia. The Polish-Ukrainian offensive of April-May 1920 temporarily upset their timetable. Meanwhile, the overconfident Armenians became imprudently involved in a war with the Turks over an Armenian-speaking region in eastern Anatolia. Taking advantage of this, Moscow issued an ultimatum on December 2, 1920, and the Armenians capitulated. In February and March of 1920 the Bolsheviks, again, matching military force with political subversion, finally conquered the Republic of Georgia. Thus by the spring of 1921, Transcaucasia was under Communist control. In December 1922, the region was declared the Transcaucasian Soviet Socialist Republic.

Conquest of the vast Muslim areas of southeast and central Asia took the Bolsheviks somewhat longer. Stalin's Commissariat of Nationalities, taking into account the highly explosive nature of local racial and religious problems in this region, paid considerable attention to the sentiments of the Muslim peoples, bordering on Turkey, Iran, and Afghanistan. Moscow used not only political subversion and infiltration to neutralize the pan-Islamic groups, but also made generous promises in matters of religion, culture, and economics. For instance, Stalin, himself a Georgian, set up a Central Muslim Commissariat, recognized the existence of an independent Muslim Communist Party, and even allowed, for a time, the organization of the Muslim Military College directed by a Volga Tatar, Mirza Sultan Galiev. Sultan Galiev, Stalin's right hand in the Commissariat of Nationalities, was a pioneer of "national Communism" among his brethren. At one time a large segment of Red Army units facing Kolchak were Muslim. It was Sultan Galiev who applied Lenin's concept that imperialism was the highest stage of capitalism to the Muslim world and proclaimed that all classes of the colonial nations, being oppressed by their Western masters, should cooperate with the Bolsheviks by forming "national liberation movements." This initially Soviet thesis was, later on, developed by Mao Tsetung and Ho Chi Ming as well as other Third World Marxist leaders. After Kolchak's defeat, the largest Muslim area, Turkestan, was gradually subdued. Local partisan units, known as *Bahmachi*, operated sporadically until the middle of 1920, but by 1923 Turkestan was for all practical purposes a part of the Soviet Union. The two former Tsarist central Asian protectorates, the Khanates of Khiva and Bukhara, along with other minor central Asian territories, were also reconquered and incorporated into the expanding Soviet state. Once the Bolsheviks were securely in power, the separate Muslim Communist Party was suppressed, and Sultan Galiev was arrested in 1923; in 1928 he was sent to a concentration camp in Solovki, on the White Sea.

Reasons for the Bolshevik Triumph

By the beginning of 1921 the Bolsheviks had won the Civil War with the exception of a series of sporadic peasant uprisings that would pester them for years to come. After more than two years of fighting, with luck, pluck, ruthlessness, and cunning, they had emerged as masters over most of the old Romanov Empire. The reasons for this Bolshevik triumph are varied and complex.

The first reason for their victory was their unity of purpose. All their enemies were hopelessly divided among themselves by political and ethnic differences. The Bolsheviks, on the other hand, formed a single, highly centralized, dictatorially led team. Their rivals, on the other hand, were a loose, heterogeneous, and precarious coalition of political groups. The White camp included reactionary military circles at one end of the political spectrum, and some SRs and the Mensheviks at the other. These differences were perhaps best reflected in the attitude of these groups toward Russia's number one problem—land. The reactionaries advocated that the land the peasants had seized be returned outright to its former owners, whereas the Socialists were in favor of recognizing the legitimacy of the seizure. The middle-of-the-road Cadets procrastinated and insisted upon relegating all fundamental reforms—including those involving land, nationalities, and constitutional issues—to the Constituent Assembly, which would be reconvened after the victory over the Bolsheviks. The SRs and Mensheviks were ready to accept the division of the land among the peasants, but were too weak to make their point of view prevail.

Next in importance to the land question was the ethnic problem. Most of the armed attempts to overthrow Bolshevik rule originated in the non-Russian areas of the old empire. Yet, ironically, all the leaders of the

White armies were Great Russian nationalists, intolerant of ethnic plurality. The ethnic minorities made repeated attempts to strike a bargain that would reshape the old centralized structure of the Russian state, but their efforts were in vain. The Whites would listen only to their own battle cry. "Russia: one, great and indivisible." They assumed an especially scornful attitude toward the largest, and hence potentially most powerful of the nationalities, the Ukrainians.

In their ethnic policies, the Bolsheviks were much more subtle than the Whites. As early as November 28, 1917, the Council of People's Commissars solemnly proclaimed the right of national self-determination, including the right of secession. But the Bolsheviks did not equate the *right* of self-determination with a *demand* for actual separation and insisted that the principle be interpreted dialectically, according to the interests of the proletarian revolution. Prior to the revolution, the Bolsheviks had opposed any attempt by a Tsarist government to retain by force any national group that wanted to secede from the empire. Once they seized power, however, they reversed their stand. They argued that because economic exploitation and ethnic oppression did not exist in the Soviet Republic, all reasons for secession had been eliminated. Yet throughout the Civil War the Soviet Government loudly proclaimed the lofty principle of self-determination, all the while trying by both agitation and brutal coercion to keep all the former empire's ethnic groups within the Soviet Republic.

The Bolshevik treatment of the Ukrainian problem is a good example of their approach to the nationality issue. A few weeks after the March 1917 revolution, the Ukrainians demanded home rule and set up a Central National Council, or Central *Rada*, in Kiev. Insisting upon broad local autonomy and planning for federation with the All-Russian Democratic Republic, the Rada shunned secession. Complete independence was proclaimed only after the Bolsheviks had triumphed in Petrograd and Moscow. On December 17 (30), 1917, the Council of People's Commissars formally and unconditionally recognized the Ukraine's independence from Russia. At the same time, the Soviets sent Kiev an ultimatum demanding free passage over Ukrainian territory for Red troops marching south to fight the Volunteer Army. Also simultaneously, a rival prefabricated Communist government was set up in Kharkov—the eastern, more industrial, and hence more proletarian and Russianized, segment of the Ukraine. The government was headed by a Bulgarian Communist, Kristian Rakovski. Through subversion and military aggression, this Soviet Ukraine government was soon planted in Kiev. Ousted from the Dnieper Ukraine by Denikin in August 1919, the Reds returned at the end of that year. Chased from Kiev by the Piłsudski-Petlyura offensive of April-May 1920, the Bolsheviks again conquered the Dnieper valley in June and reestablished their rule.

As previously noted, similar attempts by the Soviet Union to intervene militarily in the affairs of its neighbors were made in Finland, Estonia, Latvia, Lithuania, and Belorussia. With the exception of Belorussia, they all failed because of the resistance of local anti-Communist forces, who were often assisted by the West. There is no doubt that Soviet "revolutionary intervention" in neighboring countries was far more systematic, extensive, and forceful than Western intervention in Russia, which was very limited, sporadic, and halfhearted.

Paradoxically, the party that had so vociferously condemned both the old Imperial regime and the Whites for centralistic and chauvinistic policies was the one that most successfully managed to suppress most of the irredentist strivings. Against extraordinary odds, the Bolsheviks managed to capture not only all of the historic Great Russian lands but also most of the Ukraine, the entirety of Transcaucasia and Siberia, including the Pacific Maritime Territory, and the Central Asian regions of the Tsarist Empire. In historic perspective, the Bolsheviks appear as the watchful guardians of the multinational heartland of the Russian Empire. If they were unable to reconquer Finland, Estonia,

Latvia, Lithuania, Poland, Bessarabia, and the western fringes of Belorussia and the Ukraine, it was not for lack of serious effort.

There was yet another aspect of the Bolshevik victory: the scope and nature of Allied intervention. Slow in arriving, it was badly planned, limited in scope, and clumsily executed. Allied intelligence was often misinformed about Soviet strength and objectives; on the whole it underestimated what it initially called "the Bolshevik bands." The Entente Powers also underestimated the xenophobic and anti-interventionist sentiments of the Russian masses and the pacifistic mood of their own people, who, after the terrible bloodbath of World War I, were eager to end all fighting. The rivalries between France and Great Britain in Europe, and Japan and the United States in the Far East, were also a factor in undermining the Allied venture. Each nation had its own reasons for intervening and different methods for carrying it out. Different policies were advocated at various times and at different theaters of operation by the same power. In the oil-rich Caucasus near the British sphere of influence in Iran, for example, London was far more willing to support irredentist tendencies than in the Ukraine, where French economic interests predominated.

The intervention also constituted a negative psychological factor; the Whites depended so heavily on foreign aid that they failed to pay attention to generating enough domestic support. The Bolsheviks, who relied mainly on native support, avoided this mistake. In some ways, the intervention helped rather than hindered the Bolshevik cause, by arousing popular xenophobia and turning the Reds into unwitting champions of Great Russian nationalism.

From a military point of view, the Bolsheviks had a great advantage because they controlled the Great Russian heartland with its internal lines of communication and such vital industrial centers as Petrograd and Moscow. True, the industries of these centers were dislocated by the revolutionary upheaval. But under the ruthless discipline of "war Communism," they still supplied the Reds far more adequately than the erratic Western Powers did the Whites. Its internal lines of communication, coupled with its enemies' lack of coordination, allowed the Red Army to carry out strategic redeployments from one front to another; some divisions were transferred during the Civil War from one sector to another four and five times, according to the demands of the military situation. Another secret of the Bolshevik victory was a wiser, more economic use of their always scarce and often primitive resources. The Bolsheviks were frequently innovative in their use of the materiel they did have. They mounted machine guns on horse-drawn carriages, for example, which made the guns highly mobile and always ready for use. This simple device allowed Budyenny's Cavalry Army to break the White's resistance several times.

The Bolsheviks were also imaginative in their use of demagogic propaganda and skillful political warfare. Here they were infinitely superior to the Whites, whose propagandistic efforts were almost invariably crude, clumsy, and often counterproductive. The White leaders, being mostly old fashioned military men, without political experience, were inept at the art of persuasion and ignorant of the elementary principles of political tactics. The Bolsheviks, on the other hand, were experts when it came to modern propaganda and agitation methods. They made use of secret presses and numerous radio stations, and they published several thousand newspapers and bulletins. The posters of the Bolsheviks—simple, suggestive, exhortative—are an excellent example of their demagogic skills.

Another crucial and controversial aspect of the struggle was the use of terror. There is no doubt that both rivals for power acted ruthlessly and committed many atrocities. The vindictive hatred on both sides made the maxim "Two eyes for one eye, all teeth for one tooth" the prevailing rule of the Russian Civil War. The Bolsheviks were much more cruel and perpetrated atrocities on a more massive scale. On the other hand, their acts of terror were better calculated to exact political benefit. By and large they were not as often unpremeditated acts of blind fury, as were most anti-Jewish pogroms and other acts of reprisal perpetrated by some of the White detachments.

The last though not least element of importance in the Civil War was the quality of the leading elites. On the whole the Bolsheviks demonstrated far greater energy, singleness of purpose, and political skill than their opponents. And in evidencing these qualities, the Communist Party was an essential factor. While the Whites represented a plethora of quarreling political groups, the Bolsheviks were directed by one closely knit, utterly ruthless team. While on the White side there was a dire shortage of political talents, the Reds had one highly gifted ruthless leader who enjoyed unquestioned authority—Lenin. Around him was a band of able and dedicated people, many of them, particularly Trotsky, distinguished by their organizational as well as political skills.[2] On both sides, the Civil War was decided by a relative handful of people. The masses, exhausted by the trials of the previous grim half decade, were neutral and often apathetic. In such life-and-death struggle, it was a small but highly integrated and centrally directed team of leaders that played the crucial role. The opponents of Communist rule had little to match the Bolshevik elite. Some anti-Bolshevik leaders were benevolent prophets of the past, some could be classified as anachronisms, and others were merely narrow-minded reactionaries; enlightened people, like General Wrangel or Boris Savinkov, were exceptions to the rule. Numerous acts of individual heroism the part of many of the Whites could not counterbalance the more systematic efforts by the Reds.

The Civil War devastated Russia. It turned it into a swamp of misery and human degradation. The War was an unforgettable, horrifying experience for all who lived through it. It not only left the homeland in blood and ruins, but it chased a large part of the educated elite abroad, thus impoverishing the Russian culture. Many leading intellectuals emigrated and permanently settled abroad. Among them were such historians as Michael Karpovich, George Werudsky, Paul Milinkov, and Gleb Struve, writers like Vladimir Nabokov and Ivan Bunin, literary critic and linguist Roman Jakobson, sociologist Pitirim Sorokin, economist Vassili Leontiev, singer Fyodor Shalapin, painters Marc Chagall, Vasili Kandinski, and Chaim Soutine; also the composers like Sergei Prokofiev and Igor Stravinsky, as well as Sergei Diagilev with his world famous *Ballet Russe*, decided to remain abroad. Bunin was the first Russian writer to receive the Nobel Prize for Literature in 1933.

The Civil War also profoundly altered future Soviet relations with the outside world. Finally, the intervention in which France, Britain, and the United States took part on the side of the Whites, contributed to the further deterioration of relations between the Soviet Union and the Western world.

Suggested Reading

ADAMS, ARTHUR, *The Second Ukrainian Campaign of the Bolsheviks.* New Haven, CT: Yale University Press, 1963.

BENVENUTI FRANCESCO, *The Bolsheviks and the Red Army, 1919–1922.* Cambridge, Eng.; New York; New Rochelle, NY: Cambridge University Press, 1989.

BRADLEY, JOHN, F. N., *Civil War in Russia, 1917–1920.* New York: St. Martins, 1975.

———, *Allied Intervention in Russia, 1917–1920.* Lanham, MD: University Press of America, 1984.

BRINKLEY, GEORGE, *The Volunteer Army and the Allied Intervention in South Russia, 1917–1921.* Notre Dame, IN: University of Notre Dame Press, 1966.

CHAMBERLIN, WILLIAM H., *The Russian Revolution, 1917–1921*, Vol. 2. New York: Macmillan, 1935.

DANIELS, ROBERT V., *Russia: The Roots of Confronta-*

[2] Trotsky managed, by various means, to enlist the services of some 75,000 ex-Imperial officers (including 775 generals) to serve in the Red Army (Richard Pipes, *Russia Under the Bolshevik Regime.* New York, 1993, p. 55).

tion. Cambridge, MA: Harvard University Press, 1985, Ch. 6.

DAVIS, NORMAN, *White Eagle & Red Star: The Polish-Soviet War, 1919–20.* New York: St. Martin's Press, 1972.

DENIKIN, ANTON, *The Russian Turmoil.* London: Hutchinson, 1922.

———, *The White Army.* London: Johnston Gate, 1930.

DEUTSCHER, ISAAC, *The Prophet Armed—Trotsky: 1879–1921.* New York and London: Oxford University Press, 1954.

DZIEWANOWSKI, M. K., *A European Federalist: Joseph Pilsudski, 1918–1922.* Stanford, CA: Stanford University Press, 1969.

FOGLESONG, DAVID S., *America's Secret War against Bolshevism: U.S. Intervention in the Russian Civil War, 1917–1920.* Chapel Hill: University of North Carolina Press, 1995.

FOOTMAN, DAVID, *Civil War in Russia.* New York: Faber, 1962.

KAZEMZADEH, FIRUZ, *The Struggle for Transcaucasia, 1917–1921.* New York: Philosophical Library, 1951.

KENEZ, PETER, *Civil War in South Russia, 1919–1920: The Defeat of the Whites.* Berkeley: University of California Press, 1977.

KENNAN, GEORGE, F., *The Decision to Intervene.* Princeton, NJ: Princeton University Press, 1989.

LIBICH, ANDRÉ, *From the Other Shore: Russian Social Democracy after 1921.* Harvard Historical Studies 125. Cambridge, MA: Harvard University press, 1997.

LINCOLN, BRUCE W., *Red Victory: A History of the Russian Civil War.* New York: Simon & Schuster, 1990.

MORLEY, JAMES W., *The Japanese Thrust into Siberia, 1918–1920.* New York: Columbia University Press, 1957.

MOYNIHAN, BRIAN, *The Claws of the Bear: The History of the Red Army.* Boston: Houghton Mifflin, 1989.

PIPES, RICHARD, *The Formation of the Soviet Union: Communism and Nationalism.* Cambridge, MA: Harvard University Press, 1964.

RESHETAR, JOHN S., JR., *The Ukrainian Revolution, 1917–1920.* Princeton, NJ: Princeton University Press, 1952.

RODKEY, OLIVER, H. *The Unknown Civil War in Russia.* Stanford, CA: Hoover, 1976.

ROSENBERG, WILLIAM, G. *Liberals in the Russian Revolution: The Constitutional Democratic Party, 1917–1921.* Princeton, NJ: Princeton University Press. 1974.

SCHILD, GEORGE, *Between Ideology and* Realpolitik*: Woodrow Wilson and the Russian Revolution, 1917–1921.* Westport, CT: Greenwood Press, 1995.

SMELE, JONATHAN D., *Civil War in Siberia: The Anti-Bolshevik Government of Admiral Kolchak, 1918–1920.* Cambridge: Cambridge University Press, 1996.

UNTERBERGER, BETTY M., *America's Siberian Expedition, 1918–1920.* Durham, NC: Duke University Press, 1956.

WRANGEL, PIOTR N., *The Memoirs of General Wrangel.* London: Williams And Norgate, 1929.

Chapter 9

From War Communism to the New Economic Policy

The Bolsheviks inherited from the Provisional Government an economy in shambles. The Government was able to stem neither the rebelliousness of the peasantry, the restlessness of the workers, nor the suspicion of the business establishment. Wartime inflation amounted to nearly 600 percent, with wages trailing far behind prices. Production was falling rapidly, and by the autumn of 1917 had sunk to between 30 and 40 percent of the 1913 level. Transport was disorganized, and as early as the summer of 1917, shortages of food and fuel were critical.

The Bolshevik leaders had no concrete program for the rehabilitation of the country. The platform of the RSDWP adopted by its Second Congress in London in 1903 had made general reference to "replacing private property in the means of production and exchange by social property and introducing planned organization of the social-productive forces." Now the Soviet Communists attempted to experiment by plunging headlong into the utopia of an instant, radical political and socioeconomic system known as War Communism.

War Communism

War Communism had three main characteristics. The first was the nationalization of banking, transport, foreign trade, and large-scale industry; this meant that economic power was concentrated in the hands of the State, which administered all four of these through its highly centralized bureaucratic system. The second aspect of War Communism was a shift away from commercial and monetary forms of exchange and distribution and toward the rationing of basic goods and services. The third feature was the widespread application of naked force whenever exhortation and persuasion failed to supplant the usual economic stimuli.

War Communism had two principal aims: to prevent the total collapse of the economy and to mobilize the existing resources for the struggle against domestic and foreign enemies of the new regime. To most of the Party leaders, however, War Communism was not only expedient, but it also represented a daring attempt to reshape radically the socioeconomic structure of the country through a rapid transformation from capitalist to communist patterns. The economic policies of War Communism were implicit in the Bolshevik practice and were largely an expression of the doctrinaire zeal of Russia's new rulers. A market economy, in which production was carried out essentially by independent, autonomous producers for exchange on the open market, was to be replaced by a centrally planned, state-controlled economy. In June 1918, about half a year after the takeover of all banks, other credit institutions, and insurance companies, the Soviets nationalized most large industrial enterprises. Despite the survival of small and medium-size enterprises and of individual control of land by the peasantry, the Government had obtained a firm grip on what Lenin called "the commanding heights" of the Soviet economy. By the close of 1920, most of Russian industry was run by the State.

To manage this, a vast bureaucratic machinery, with the Council of the National Economy at the top, was set up in December 1917 and endowed with vast powers. It was empowered to confiscate, reorganize, and run all industries, and also to coordinate and plan the country's future economic expansion. The central Council of the National Economy in Moscow had its provincial and local counterparts, which were to control individual enterprises and plan for the future. The turbulent conditions of the Civil War, however, were not conducive to long-range planning. Yet planning was such a Marxist axiom that in 1920 the first steps in that direction were taken under the guise of the State Commission for Electrification. Lenin's hopes regarding the Commission were reflected in his statement, "Electrification plus Soviets equals Communism." Hydroelectric stations were to provide power for industry and transport, as well as for the villages. In 1921, the task of long-term planning was transferred to a specialized institution, the State Planning Commission, or *Gosplan.*

Marx considered buying and selling as parasitic. The Government's prohibition of free trade, however, placed on it the burden of rationing food to the urban population and supplying the peasants with industrial goods. This system theoretically rendered money unnecessary. During War Communism, the Soviets constantly toyed with the idea of abolishing money, and the period was crowded with fantastic ideas concerning a moneyless economy. However, the concept failed completely; it merely contributed to the chaos and rampant inflation that made the Soviet ruble worthless.

Meanwhile, in view of the general economic breakdown, the Soviet Government was faced with many urgent objectives in fighting the Civil War. The most important was to make the industrial workers—many of whom had fled to their villages in search of food—return to the factories and increase productivity. Unable to cope with these tasks because of the failure of food rationing, the Bolsheviks resorted to state impressment and, in 1920, introduced a system of labor conscription. The ineffective workers' councils were abolished. The old functions of the trade unions were declared superfluous, since private capitalists had been wiped out by the Revolution, and the factories now belonged to the workers. Membership in trade unions was obligatory, and the unions were turned into government-controlled organizations whose purpose was no longer to organize strikes, but to prevent them; not to defend workers' rights, but to bolster production. This caused bitter criticism from a Party faction called the Workers' Opposition. Strikes, though not specifically forbidden, were condemned as "sabotage" by official propaganda. The right to strike was not included in the Soviet Constitution of 1918.

At the same time, wage incentives and bonuses (mainly in the form of food and money) were gradually reintroduced. While imposing iron discipline, the Government made efforts to kindle a new kind of enthusiasm by propagating a "Socialist competition of labor," as well as by means of various honorific titles and awards. For instance, individuals able to produce more than the norm were granted such titles as "shock worker" (those who exceeded the prescribed norms), and were given other honorary awards. To obtain extra unpaid labor, the Party and the Soviet mass media exercised pressure upon laborers to "volunteer" an extra day of work for the sake of "building Socialism."

Another critical task was to compel the reluctant peasants to supply food to the starving cities. Nowhere was compulsion more visible than in the countryside. It should be made clear that the spontaneous seizure of the large landed estates that had taken place in the summer and autumn of 1917 did not end rural inequalities. Again, "the sober and the strong" usually acted more quickly than the rest of the peasants. Consequently, the *kulak* segment of the peasantry was strengthened. This frightened the Bolsheviks. They promptly organized committees of poor peasants to promote "class struggle in the countryside"; the main target of these committees were the *kulaks*. These most industrious and productive farmers were now often forcibly deprived of their surplus produce for the benefit of the poorer peasants and the urban workers. The term *kulak* was applied very broadly; theoretically, anybody who hired labor was automatically denounced as an exploiter—a *kulak*. Yet often the disparaging label was applied to any peasant who did not submit willingly to the confiscatory measures of the new regime.

To remedy the desperate shortage of food in the cities, it was decreed that all peasants had to supply to the State all their produce above the specified subsistence minimum. The regulation assumed that the peasants, in turn, would be supplied by State enterprises with what they needed. This proved unachievable because of the low productivity of the workers and the needs of the Red Army fighting the Civil War. In view of the peasants' passive resistance, in May 1918 the so-called "grain dictatorship" was set up. To make the peasants "disgorge" their alleged surpluses and deliver the compulsory food levy to the cities, semimilitary detachments, known as the "Food Army," were organized to force them to do so. By 1919, they numbered some 45,000 armed workers.

Failure of War Communism

The procurement of food was not only a critical emergency measure required to forestall urban starvation and promote the survival of the Soviet regime; the principle of confiscation of surplus was also an essential point of the War Communism's program. The theoretical justification of requisitioning was that it was in accordance with the socialist tenet of the equal distribution of basic resources. There was still another long-range goal behind the forced seizure of food: to compel individual peasants to abandon their homesteads and join the collective farms. For this purpose the Soviet authorities had preserved some of the more advanced large estates to establish model agricultural collectives, or Soviet State farms.

To encourage at least a segment of the peasantry to give up their private allotments, pool their equipment, and accept collective forms of land exploitation, the peasants were given various incentives; they were promised loans, cattle, and agricultural implements. Yet the first drive toward collectivization fell flat because the overwhelming majority of Russian peasants were reluctant to join either the collective farms (*kolkhozy*) or the State farms (*sovkhozy*). The term *kolkhoz* is an abbreviation of the words *kolektyvnoe khoziaistvo*, which means "collective farm." Theoretically, a *kolkhoz* was an agricultural cooperative controlled and operated by its members, who pooled their land, cattle, and equipment in order to work together. Each member of the cooperative shared in its output proportionate to the number of labor days contributed.[1] Some of the annual output was delivered to the State, while the rest was either divided among the members or sold for the benefit of all the members of the collective farm. The term *sovkhoz* is an abbreviation for *Sovietskoe khoziaistvo*, or Soviet farm; this was a State-owned and -operated agricultural enterprise. In such an enterprise,

---

[1] The labor day unit did not correspond to a day's work, but to a particular amount of work, with different, often quite arbitrary, yardsticks for different kinds of work.

everything—the land, equipment, and cattle—belonged to the State, while the peasants were employed as mere field workers and paid a fixed wage.

In an overwhelmingly agrarian country, where some 80 percent of the population was still living in the countryside and responsible for more than 50 percent of the national income, the attitude of the countryside was of decisive importance for War Communism. Widespread fierce resistance, expressed in innumerable peasant uprisings, served as a warning to the Government. By the beginning of 1921, peasant resistance was overwhelming.

Another major difficulty facing the Soviet regime was the continuous flight of starved workers to the villages in search of food. The workers, together with speculators known as "bagmen," wandered from village to village trying to buy and/or beg for food. By August 1920, Moscow has lost about half of its population and Petrograd nearly two-thirds. Even those who remained could hardly be fed in view of the peasants' reluctance to deliver food to cities that had virtually nothing of value to offer them in return.

Other difficulties facing the Government included the state of the railways, which were largely in ruin. As a result most factories, deprived of raw materials, could operate only part-time; some establishments had to close down completely. By the end of 1920 total industrial production had dropped to about one-fifth of the 1913 level. The output of consumer goods, especially shoes and clothing, was actually lower than that. Labor productivity sank to less than half of its prewar level. By the beginning of 1921, many factories had to close down altogether for lack of fuel, which was as scarce as food. On January 22, 1921, the meager bread ration in large population centers was cut by one-third. By February, fuel shortages in the large cities had become catastrophic, and that month workers of sixty-four large factories in Petrograd, including the Putilov metal works, went on strike.

However, starvation was not limited to the cities. To the ruinous effects of War Communism were added the natural disasters that had plagued the country for centuries: drought, dust, and locusts. The peasants also suffered from the confiscatory measures outlined above; very often even grain seed had been taken away from them. As a consequence, in 1920–1921, there were large-scale peasant uprisings in western Siberia, in the Ukraine (where Makhno was still active), and in Central Russia, mainly in the province of Tambov, where some guerrilla leaders, such as Antonov, waged a successful partisan war against the Soviet authorities. During February 1921 alone, there were no less than 118 major peasant risings in various parts of the country. There were also numerous strikes and riots in the various urban centers, all of them suppressed with merciless cruelty.

The Kronstadt Revolt

Dissatisfaction also penetrated the ranks of sailors and soldiers, most of them recruited from the countryside. Of these outbursts of discontent, the most important and dramatic was the uprising at the naval base of Kronstadt. Situated in the Gulf of Finland on the long, narrow, and rocky island of Kotlin some twenty miles west of Petrograd, Kronstadt had originally been built by Peter the Great to protect the capital from the open sea. With its garrison of 15,000 sailors and soldiers, Kronstadt had a long revolutionary tradition dating back to 1905. The rowdy "blue jackets" played a prominent part both during the ferment of those days and in the overthrow of the Tsarist regime. Throughout the Civil War, the Baltic sailors were in the forefront of the struggle against the Whites and suffered heavy losses.

The end of the Civil War, however, brought about a change of mood even among the "pride and glory of the Revolution," as Trotsky called the Kronstadt fighters. For three years they had been struggling, hoping to abolish the hateful rigors of War Communism. The sailors resented that the end of the war had brought about nothing of the sort. Quite the contrary. The iron discipline Trotsky had reimposed on them (abolition of ship's committees, appointment of political commissars from outside) was compounded by the continuation of old privations: poor rations, inadequate clothing, and cold, unheated barracks. At the end of 1920 there was an epidemic of scurvy in the Baltic fleet.

With the end of the Civil War, home leaves, previously practically nonexistent, were now granted more liberally. These were an eye-opener to the "peasants and workers in uniform," for they acquainted the sailors and soldiers first-hand with the often desperate conditions of the country. Their rate of desertion increased. By the middle of February 1921, tensions in the Baltic squadron, stimulated by the wave of strikes sweeping the factories of Petrograd, reached the boiling point. The garrison of Kronstadt elected a Provisional Revolutionary Committee and voted a resolution. While expressing sympathy for the strikers' demands, it declared a lack of confidence in "the present Soviet" because it did "not express the will of the workers and peasants." The resolution insisted on immediate free elections open to all left socialist parties and that the peasants be granted "full freedom of action in regard to the land" as long as they did not use hired labor. The resolution did not ask for the overthrow of the regime, but rather for its democratization. The Kronstadt sailors acted as the conscience of the Bolsheviks: They appealed to them to live up to their old slogans and grant political power to the freely elected Soviets. The resolution turned the Kronstadt sailors into spokesmen for the sentiments of the broad popular masses smarting under the senseless, coercive policies of War Communism.

The Soviet government promptly denounced the Provisional Revolutionary Committee and its acts of defiance as "counterrevolutionary" and asked for the unconditional surrender of the rebels. When this was rejected, an attack was ordered by War Commissar Trotsky; the rebels who would not surrender were to be "shot like ducks." The military drive against the heavily fortified island opened on March 7 during a heavy blizzard and lasted for over ten days. On March 18 the attackers crushed the last centers of resistance. Many defenders, including some of the principal leaders, managed to flee across the solid ice to Finland. In violation of the conditions of capitulation, all the captured leaders and many other rebels were shot. Those who remained were sent to distant forced labor camps.

The Kronstadt uprising represented an attempt to reshape the Bolshevik dictatorship by appealing to the Soviet masses in the name of a return to the original but by then discarded battle cry, "All power to the Soviets." Most of the rebels understood this to mean local committees, freely elected by leftist parties only, that would operate autonomously, under the supervision but without the blatant interference of central Party authorities. To the rebels the Soviets represented the spirit of the old village communes in revolutionary garb. The Bolsheviks had skillfully manipulated this essentially populist myth and used the Soviets as an instrument for the destruction of the old order. In Lenin's scheme, however, the Soviets were always to be controlled by the Party, which was to remain the sole locus of power. Soviets independent of the Party represented to the Bolsheviks a spontaneous, uncontrollable, and hence dangerous, force. That is why, immediately after the Revolution, the Bolsheviks reduced the Soviets' role to a purely symbolic one, and they operated under firm Party control.

The impact of the uprising was considerable, both at home and abroad. Abroad, the revolt delayed international recognition of the Soviet regime. At home, the uprising touched off several mutinies and local disturbances, and compelled the Bolsheviks to replace the bankrupt War Communism by a new set of policies. The failure of War Communism had been obvious for months to all sober-minded Bolshevik leaders. On February 24—five days before the beginning of the rebellion—Lenin had already presented a draft of new economic directives to the Central Committee of the Communist Party for inclusion on the agenda of its Tenth

Congress, which was to gather in Moscow on March 8. There is no doubt, however, that the Kronstadt affair, by dramatizing the desperate plight of the masses, helped Lenin overcome the resistance of the left wing of the Party still hellbent on enforcing radical measures.

When one analyzes the end result of War Communism, one must admit that it contributed a great deal to breaking down the old capitalist system, but very little positive to building a new, stable socioeconomic order. In the nationalized industries, a slow beginning had been made toward the establishment of self-government in the form of workers' councils, but the lack of proper personnel and adequate know-how pushed the Bolsheviks toward a policy of strict control of the trade unions and sui generis state capitalism with pronounced militaristic features. The peasantry, temporarily neutralized by the redistribution of the landed estates, was soon driven into sullen hostility toward the regime by the indiscriminate requisitioning of their produce. In the field of procurement, little was achieved beyond the extension of the grain monopoly (which had been established by the Provisional Government) and the introduction of rationing. Both institutions functioned in as spotty and perfunctory a manner as the chaotic circumstances of the Civil War and famine dictated.

Thus War Communism was ultimately a utopian experiment. It was a violent but futile attempt to drive the country at full speed toward socialism-communism, despite the unreadiness and unwillingness of the masses to submit. As we have seen, the experiments of War Communism greatly contributed to deepening the widespread chaos and famine into which Russia had been plunged by World War I, the Revolution, and the Civil War.

The New Economic Policy (NEP)

By 1921, most of the Soviet leaders realized that they had overreached themselves and must embark on a new policy. They under-stood that the transition from a capitalist to a socialist economic order could not be achieved overnight, in one great leap forward. The task had to be faced in a more realistic manner, stretched over long years, and performed by different methods. This was the rationale behind the steps Lenin took in March 1921 at the Tenth Congress of the Communist Party, which was one of the most dramatic gatherings of this type in the annals of Communism.

Lenin's report to the Congress did not hide the extreme gravity of the domestic situation. Arguing against the opponents of the new course with a frankness that often shocked his comrades, he admitted that the danger of peasant revolt constituted a far greater menace to the Soviet regime than the White armies had ever been. Consequently, he urged a radical departure from the principles and practices of War Communism and the adoption of a set of new economic policies. While insisting on holding on to "the commanding heights," that is banking, transport, large-scale industry, and foreign trade, Lenin urged that positions of secondary importance be left in private hands, and that the peasants be placated by means of a series of concessions. Instead of the food levy, which forcibly wrested from the peasants all their surplus produce and often their means of livelihood, a definite tax was introduced. Initially levied in kind (mostly in food produce), the tax was later converted into cash. The decree specified that the tax should not exceed half of the former requisition. It was calculated progressively, and was to fall more heavily on the *kulaks* than on the poor or middle-income peasants. The rest of his surplus the peasant could sell on the open market. The decree spelled the end of arbitrary requisitioning, the peasants' nightmare during the preceding three years.

The launching of the *new economic policy*, usually referred to as NEP, came too late and did not prevent a large-scale famine. While the NEP was unfolding, the famine was spreading during 1921 and part of 1922.

Large stretches of the countryside had been ravaged and abused for years. The famine hit especially hard in the Volga region and the Ukraine, and millions there were on the verge of starvation. Extreme and urgent measures were needed to remedy the situation, yet the Moscow government, desperately short of resources, was unable to undertake them. In July 1921, the writer Maxim Gorky wrote a plea addressed "To All Honest People" of the world, imploring them to help Russia in its predicament. One of the first to respond was the United States. For twenty-two months (August 1921–June 1923), about 180 foreign, mostly American, relief workers operated in Soviet territory, feeding some 22 million people. The Vatican and the Quakers, as well as many other organizations, followed with their own relief missions.[2]

The NEP did not develop in accordance with a preconceived plan; it evolved spontaneously in accord with its own internal logic. One of the consequences of the freedom to sell food produce was the reestablishment of freedom of trade in general. Initially, the government hoped to organize, and thus control, the entire system of distribution; however, lack of financial resources as well as qualified personnel made it impossible. Consequently, the peasants themselves proceeded to sell the surplus of the bumper harvest of 1922 to the buyers who offered them the best price. This resulted in a rapid revival of small traders and of thousands of marketplaces, bazaars, and traditional fairs. The middlemen, who under War Communism had a precarious existence as black marketeers, or "enemies of the people," now reappeared and started openly to apply the skills hitherto used in shadowy operations.

[2]The resolution of the Council of People's Commissars of July 10, 1923, paid tribute to "an enormous and entirely disinterested effort of the American Relief Administration," that "rescued from death . . . millions of people of all ages." It is estimated that between 5 and 6 million people died of starvation before the foreign relief measures were applied.

Consequences of the NEP

One step led to another; from trade the new economic system expanded to industry and then affected property relations. If the peasant was to produce more food, he had to be granted a measure of security in the form of reasonably long land tenure. This was done via a series of concessions to the peasants, which in 1922 were embodied in the Land Code. While the principle of land nationalization was reaffirmed, the peasant was declared a long-term tenant. Leasing of the land was allowed; later, even the hiring of additional labor (previously condemned as an evil capitalistic practice) was permitted under certain conditions.

Moreover, the NEP could not be limited only to the countryside and small trade. Once the countryside returned to the market economy, industry was bound to be affected. If the peasants were to sell their surpluses to the cities, the industries had to have something to offer in return. This would inevitably influence the entire economic system. And indeed, licenses soon had to be granted for private enterprise. Development of consumer industries, commercial enterprises, and service shops was soon tolerated, and even encouraged. Many small industrial enterprises, previously nationalized, were now returned to their previous owners or leased on certain strictly defined conditions to these "Nepmen." With astonishing rapidity, the industries revived. Small-scale, light industries, especially leather and textiles, mushroomed in response to the enormous demand for shoes, clothing, harnesses, and the like, products that had hardly been manufactured for years.

The confusion of the NEP created opportunities for quick and easy profit. Soon large fortunes were made by some of the Nepmen. The speed with which small private companies and speculators reestablished themselves and prospered was shocking to diehard, orthodox Communists.

Simultaneous with the limited and selective toleration of private initiative, significant

Russian women selling fruit and vegetables at a Kiev bazaar.

changes were introduced into the management of socialized enterprises. The State industries were reorganized into approximately 500 trusts; each enterprise was to be run on a commercial basis and submit its plans and accounts to the Supreme Economic Council for approval and supervision of their expenditures and revenues. Other than that, managers of individual factories were allowed considerable scope for initiative. The huge, unwieldy bureaucratic machinery that was to manage them was decentralized, somewhat streamlined, and provided with individual managers who replaced the previously predominant but usually cumbersome committees. Strict cost accounting was reintroduced. At the same time, wage incentives (piece rates and bonuses) replaced "socialist competition." The Labor Code of 1922, which included compulsory work, was abolished; it was to be applied only in cases of national emergency or as a punishment for offenses against the State. Trade unions, although still controlled by the State, regained some of their autonomy and were now called the spokesmen of "true, proletarian democracy." Strikes were reluctantly allowed—and even encouraged—when they were directed against private entrepreneurs.

The rapid increase in the food supply permitted the abolition of food rationing. The NEP also affected the country's foreign relations. The end of foreign intervention was followed by the lifting of the Allied blockade and a gradual resumption of international trade. Soon concessions were granted to foreign capitalists on the basis of partnership with the Soviet Government. The promulgation of NEP coincided with the signing of the first Anglo-Soviet trade agreement.

Through the German-Soviet agreement of Rapallo (April 1922), the Weimar Republic followed Great Britain's example and had soon overtaken it and established itself as Soviet Russia's best customer. (See Chapter 10 on early Soviet foreign policy.)

The growth of a money economy increased the demand for credit. From 1922 on, a network of State banks for financing commercial as well as industrial enterprises was organized. Soon the banks were followed by State insurance agencies. A vodka monopoly was reintroduced together with a variety of old indirect taxes and excises. All of these steps required a stable currency. The first Soviet ruble had become worthless as a result of the spiraling inflation and therefore had to be replaced by a currency that would command confidence. Meanwhile, the Soviet State Bank was reorganized in 1922 and empowered to issue a new ruble based partially on gold. In 1925, the old, worthless currency was withdrawn and exchanged for a new ruble. This in itself was a major reversal of the original tenets of Bolshevism. Before the seizure of power, Lenin had treated gold with the utmost contempt. Now his attitude changed and he declared, "When we conquer power on a world scale, we shall use gold to build lavatories. Meanwhile we must save gold . . . sell it at the highest price. When living among wolves, let's howl like wolves."

Contradictions of the NEP

From a historic perspective, there seems to be no doubt that the abandonment of War Communism was a necessity if the Communist Party wanted to preserve its power. The introduction of the NEP was a tactical, temporary retreat from positions the Soviets found impossible to defend at that moment, but which they were determined to recapture later on. In the meantime, the paramount need was to embark upon the long-run task of rehabilitating the starved and ruined country and of creating a rational, workable economy.

The NEP represented a painful rethinking by the Bolsheviks of the practical consequences of their seizure of power in the backward, agrarian country. By 1921–1922 the millennial, maximalist mentality had had to give way to a more evolutionary-reformist mood. In the mixed economy established by the NEP, the State sector included the central banking system, large industrial enterprises, foreign trade, and communication. The private sector comprised most agriculture, most of the retail and part of the wholesale trade, and all the handicraft. The predominance of the State sector was overwhelming. While private business accounted for 88.5 percent of the total number of enterprises, it employed only 12.4 percent of the industrial labor force. On the other hand, State-controlled companies employed 84.1 percent of the nonagricultural labor force.

Some 24 million peasant households were the main beneficiaries of the NEP. The peasantry gained three things: security of land tenure, freedom from requisitioning, and a free hand in selling agricultural surpluses. By making these concessions, Lenin admitted that, in the long run, the Soviet regime could ill afford to disregard the interests of some 80 percent of the population and had to win their cooperation. This also meant the return, under duress, to his original concept of the alliance of workers and peasants. The decision "to retreat in order to jump higher" in the future was essentially a political one. It represented a temporary capitulation by the Soviet Government to the peasantry, "a peasant Brest-Litovsk," as a leftist opponent put it.

The NEP, based on a precarious balance of two sectors, private and public, represented a shaky compromise between communism and capitalism, between collectivism and individualism, between private initiative and State control. From the very beginning, the NEP's mixed structure suffered from a variety of contradictions and paradoxes. The Communists were to coexist competitively with the small capitalists, learn from them how to be efficient and productive, and eventually demonstrate the superiority of the socialist system. In everyday practice, however, the capitalists proved their superior efficiency and flexibility. They were producing and distributing better goods more quickly and cheaply, despite being hampered at every step by high taxes, an intricate net of regulations, and a variety of discriminatory administrative practices. The State-controlled industries, on the other hand, were lagging behind both in volume of production and in quality. The fact that the private initiative represented by the Nepmen was doing relatively better then the nationalized sector was insufferable in the long run, because it disproved, by daily practice, the basic tenet of the doctrines on which the Bolsheviks based their claim to power. It was obvious that either the forces unleashed by the NEP would corrode the Soviet system or the system would have to destroy them in order to survive.

The preparation for a showdown was visible in a variety of political measures undertaken by the Party. While retaining control of the "commanding heights" of the economy, which is to say, banking, large-scale industry, transportation, and the monopoly of foreign trade, the Party kept the reins of political power tightly in its hands. Despite the pressure of a group of Party members headed by Alexander D. Shliapnikov and Alexandra Kollontai, a faction known as the Workers' Opposition, Lenin rejected the idea of granting freedom of speech and the press to other Socialist parties like the Mensheviks and the SRs. On the contrary, it was during the NEP that the surviving representatives of these groups were either imprisoned or driven abroad, and the remainder compelled to join the ruling party or abstain completely from any political activity. By 1922, most of the surviving leaders of the former opposition, including the Mensheviks like Martov and Chernov, had to emigrate. Step by step, Communist authoritarianism was assuming increasingly rigid features.

The Tenth Party Congress reemphasized the ban on all factionalism and reinforced the rigid inner Party discipline. In the midst of general confusion, Party members were to rekindle their "revolutionary vigilance" and to remain the bulwark of the system. In the summer of 1921 the Party went through its first mass purge, which reduced its membership by one-third. In 1922, the Cheka, or the Extraordinary Commission for Fighting Counter-Revolution and Sabotage, was reorganized and given a new, more innocuous name, that of *GPU (Gosudarstvennoe Politicheskoe Upravlenie,* or State Political Administration). Thus from an *extraordinary* institution it became an *ordinary,* standing institution of Soviet reality. Moreover, its jurisdiction was expanded; the new organization was granted the right to arrest Party members, a privilege not enjoyed by the Cheka. Thus, the drift from authoritarianism toward totalitarianism continued.

The period of the NEP coincided with the emergence of Stalin as the most influential figure of the regime. In May 1922, he was entrusted with the post of Secretary General of the Central Committee. Initially, few Party people attached much importance to the appointment of a man whom many considered simply as an efficient, harmless bureaucrat, apparently without political ambitions. At that time, Stalin was known in inner Party circles as "Comrade Card Index."

Meanwhile, the Party directed more violent measures against religious freedom. By 1920, 673 monasteries were closed and despoiled. In 1921, religious instruction to the young was forbidden; all parochial schools closed; Church lands and treasures were confiscated. The Criminal Code of 1926 prescribed forced labor as the punishment for any religious teaching. Under penalty of deportation, all religiously oriented writings were banned, and seminaries and monasteries closed. Any resistance to these measures was regarded as "sabotage" and "counterrevolution." Well over a thousand bishops, monks, and priests either were deported to hard labor camps or executed, and many surviving clerics, including the Patriarch of Moscow, were arrested. Atheistic propaganda was greatly intensified.

The NEP and Culture

The first socioeconomic changes brought about by the Communist victory were reflected in the field of education and culture. As we have previously discussed, the war was preceded by a period of artistic vitality and intellectual experimentation. The Bolsheviks seized power determined to reshape the country's cultural and educational patterns to serve their goals, but they had their priorities.

Popular education was the first target of the new regime. It was to be treated as an instrument of class struggle, as a propagandistic tool of the Communist Party. As Lenin so bluntly put it, "an illiterate person is outside politics"; this meant that he could not be effectively reached by the Party. At the end of the Civil War, all schools were placed under State control. A large-scale campaign to teach reading and writing to the masses was effectively organized. At the same time, the old high schools, or *Gymnasia*, were eliminated. The new Soviet secondary school, Lenin asserted, was to be a composite of "basic scientific knowledge of both nature and society and the world outlook of scientific materialism, Communist morality, physical exercise for good health." Moreover, close links were to be established between study and productive labor. This was the concept of "polytechnization." It meant two things: First, pupils were to combine general education with practical vocational training; second, this stress on vocational training in turn implied an emphasis not on the humanities, but on the natural sciences. Simultaneous with "polytechnization," the new regime embraced certain ideas of progressive education, and during the 1920s most Soviet schools abolished textbooks, examinations, and grading systems.

Institutions of higher learning also suffered bitterly from Soviet Russia's cultural revolution. It was during the Civil War that academic instruction received its heaviest blows; most professors of "bourgeois" origin who did not emigrate were either dismissed or arrested. While such scholars as Nicholas Berdiaev, Mikhail I. Rostovtsev, Pitirim Sorokin, and George Vernadsky had to leave the country, the Marxist historian Michael Pokrovsky became virtual dictator of the "academic sector" and ran it with an iron fist. The traditional university ceased to function. To repopulate technical schools with working class students, new institutions known as Workers' Faculties, loosely affiliated with the old polytechnical institutions and universities, hastily furnished college preparatory instruction at times and places convenient to working people and the ruling Party.

Parallel with the transformation of the educational system, the new regime nationalized all publishing houses and organized a central State publishing and coordinating agency. Gradually, strict censorship of all printed material was enforced. Nevertheless, during the NEP era, Soviet literature continued to be characterized by a variety of attitudes and modes of expression. All this was tolerated for the time being, provided it did not openly contradict the basic principles of the regime.

The Bolsheviks realized that the education of society does not take place exclusively in school and soon made provisions for youth organizations dedicated to Communist goals—the "All-Union Leninist–Communist Children's Organization," known as the Young Pioneers, and the "All-Union Leninist-Communist Youth Organization," better known as *Komosomol*. The Young Pioneers included children from the ages of ten to fourteen; the Komosomol included young people up to their early thirties. Both organizations were under the close ideological supervision and intense indoctrination of the Communist Party, which regarded them as nurseries for its future members.

Fine Arts and Literature

While focusing their attention on education, publishing, and other mass media, the Bolsheviks were less strict with regard to fine arts and literature. Their initial leniency toward the arts was partly due to their initial preoccupation with politics and economy, and partly with the cultivated and sensitive personality of the first Commissar for Education, Anatoli V. Lunacharsky, a prominent Marxist critic and an old Bolshevik who enjoyed Lenin's confidence. After the Bolshevik coup, Lenin put him in charge of education and intervened only sporadically, when he suspected that Lunacharsky's tolerance might threaten the guiding role of the Party in the field of culture. Lunacharsky, supported by some moderate leaders like Bukharin, pursued a somewhat permissive policy toward artists, including those of the avant garde.

Many leading Russian writers who strongly disapproved of the Communist regime, emigrated. Those who did remain, such as Akhmatova, Blok, Biely, Briusov, Mandelshtam, Mayakovsky, and Pasternak, continued to write, trying to adapt to the new regime. Some of them, like Blok and Mayakovsky, lent their support to the new rulers. Blok even greeted the Bolshevik coup with an ecstatic poem, "The Twelve" (1919). This poem is a symbolic vision of Christ crowned with a wreath of white roses leading twelve Red Guardsmen who shoot their way to victory. Blok survived the Revolution by two more years, but his progressive disillusionment and despair made him artistically sterile. He died of starvation in 1921. Another writer who had started his career before the war as a Futurist, Boris Pasternak, soon developed a personal style both in prose and poetry. In addition to producing several volumes of original and often brilliant verse, he translated into Russian many works of Shakespeare, Goethe, and Verlaine, as well as some of the leading Georgian poets.

But perhaps the most significant Bolshevik writer of the period was Mayakovsky. Besides writing poetry, prose, drama, and political satire attacking the opponents of Communism and eulogizing the new regime, he also designed posters for Party propaganda campaigns. His poem "The Left March" was an enthusiastic welcome to the dawn of the new Communist era. Initially, Mayakovsky persuaded Soviet authorities to lend support to the Futurists as pioneers of a new "revolutionary" style, not only in literature but also in painting, graphic art, and architecture. This short-lived decision proved beneficial to Russian artists. For the first time in their national history, Russian architects created during the postrevolutionary decade a school of design and urban planning equal to the best Western models. The graphic artists, especially poster designers, also profited from the stimulus given them by Futurism and Cubism, as well as the German movement known under the name of *Bauhaus*, led by Walter Gropius.

Soon, however, Futurism fell from official favor, and hesitant government support was temporarily shifted to the "Proletarian Cultural and Educational Organization," known as *Proletkult*. The Proletkult united a large body of 2,000 to 3,000 artists and writers, brought together by the desire to educate the workers in the arts as well as in Marxist ideology. These artists were organized in a number of clubs spread throughout the Soviet Union. The main theorist of the Proletkult was Alexandr A. Bogdanov (Malinovsky), a philosopher and economist as well as a physician. A man of original and independent mind, he argued that the new art and literature that were to express the proletarian revolution would be created not solely by people of proletarian stock. He insisted that the treasures of the old culture be preserved and passed on to the coming generations as a foundation for new achievements. Lenin soon came to suspect that the Proletkult harbored too many ideologically alien elements that might constitute a threat to the Soviet regime. He insisted that no organization be independent of the Party and ordered the group to be subordinated to it. By 1928, an organization of Communist writers known as RAPP (the Russian abbreviation for "Russian Association of Proletarian Writers") assumed a quasi-dictatorial position in the literary field.

Meanwhile, however, other groups still enjoyed limited freedom. To these independent artists and writers belonged the talented, lyrical peasant poet, Sergei A. Yesenin, a sentimental Slavophile and author of melodious verses idealizing the old Russian countryside and its folklore. Under the Soviet regime, however, Yesenin's verses soon came to reflect the mood of despair and resignation that led him to suicide in 1925. Another writer, Yevgeny I. Zamyatin, in a surrealistic novel entitled *We* published in 1924, described a small clique of ruthless people establishing a state that controls all aspects of human activity. Zamyatin's vision anticipated George Orwell's nightmarish society of the future by a generation. Soon, Zamyatin had to emigrate. The NEP era saw also the debut of the most widely read of Soviet novelists, Mikhail A. Sholokhov. By the late 1920s, he had achieved great renown with the appearance of his great novel *And Quiet Flows the Don*. This panoramic epic describes the life of the Don Cossacks on the eve of World War I and during the revolutionary period.

The 1920s also saw the emergence of a number of brilliant new writers, among them Isaac E. Babel, a former political commissar of Budyonny's Cavalry Army. Babel described with savage realism his impressions of the Civil War and of the Soviet-Polish campaign of 1920 in a series of stories published under the title *Red Cavalry* (1926). Babel also wrote novels and theater plays, the best of which is probably *Benya Krik* (1928), the story of a Jewish gangster in the author's native Odessa. Another, initially tolerated novelist and playwright was Mikhail Bulgakov, one of the sharpest postrevolutionary satirists. Bulgakov's most successful work of this period were his epic novel *White Guards*, describing the struggles of the Civil War, and the play entitled *The Days of the Turbins*.

Performing Arts

The NEP also witnessed remarkable innovations in the field of performing arts. With the exception of the ballet, which was largely left alone, the Bolshevik regime tried to manipulate the performing arts, especially theater and cinema, to serve their objectives. While Stanislavsky continued to direct more or less as before, his two pupils Yevgeny B. Vakhtangov and Vsevolod E. Meyerhold tried to make the old plays more understandable to the now largely proletarian audiences, and even tended to subordinate esthetic considerations to the dictates of ideology. Using teams of young, enthusiastic actors, Vakhtangov successfully integrated often highly stylized folklore with grotesque buffoonery and even acrobatics. The activities of Vakhtangov and Meyerhold gave a powerful stimulus to a number of similar but more modest local enterprises organized by various trade unions, cultural clubs, schools, and ethnic groups. During the 1920s there were numerous people's theaters functioning in various Soviet republics, including the newly established Central Asian Republic, but especially in the Ukraine, which was then witnessing an outburst of creativity, a veritable national cultural renaissance. One of the most original people's theaters was the Jewish Theater of Moscow. During this period, the cultural Russification of ethnic groups was discouraged and anti-Semitism officially condemned.

The most remarkable progress during the 1920s, however, was made in the cinema. To Lenin, movies were "the most important of all arts" because of their far-reaching propagandistic potential and especially their influence on the still largely illiterate masses. And, indeed, immediately after the Civil War the Soviet Government rapidly expanded the seven movie studios and approximately 1,000 theaters inherited from the old regime. Within the decade they had covered the country with a network of movie theaters supplied with films produced by numerous State-controlled production centers. Two early Soviet directors who reached high artistic levels were Sergei M. Eisenstein and Vsevolod I. Pudovkin. Both scored their most brilliant successes in the late 1920s and the 1930s. Both Eisenstein and Pudovkin are best remembered as cinematic iconographers of the historic revolutionary era. The middle of the 1920s brought Eisenstein's film *Battleship Potiomkin,* which dramatized to the Soviet spectator the story of the revolt of the Black Sea sailors in the summer of 1905. The tenth anniversary of the Bolshevik revolution was celebrated by two major films, Pudovkin's *Last Days of Petersburg* and Eisenstein's *Ten Days that Shook the World* (an adaptation of John Reed's book under a similar title).

The NEP: A Balance Sheet

The NEP represented a baffling combination of economic and cultural liberalization with political repression. During the years 1921–1928, the Party, as well as artists and economists, was groping for new solutions in the quickly changing society emerging from the turmoil. Despite the painful losses that Russian culture had suffered during the preceding traumatic period, and despite its increasing regimentation, the first decade after the Revolution represents the freest, richest, and most creative period of the Soviet era. While the last races of political pluralism were gradually disappearing, they were still precariously surviving in the field of culture, which showed remarkable vitality. Economic recovery was speedy, and by 1925–1926 the standard of living of an average worker probably exceeded the prerevolutionary level. An average peasant, seemingly secure owner of his enlarged plot of land, also lived better than ever. On the other hand, the authoritarian features of the Soviet system were already quite pronounced. The chief instrument of repression was the expanded and reorganized political police that kept close watch on all aspects of life. Consequently, in historic perspective, the NEP represents a period pregnant with possibilities. During the mid-1920s it was not quite clear in which direction the Soviet system would develop—toward greater freedom, more private enterprise and the development of what was later termed "socialism with a human face," or toward totalitarian control and repression.

Suggested Reading

AVES, JONATHAN, *Workers against Lenin: Labour Protest and the Bolshevik Dictatorship.* International Library of Historical Studies. London: I. B. Tauris Publishers, 1996.

AVRICH, PAUL, *Kronstadt 1921.* Princeton, NJ: Princeton University Press, 1970.

BAILES, KENDAL E., *Science and Russian Culture in the Age of Revolutions.* Bloomington: Indiana University Press, 1990.

FARNSWORTH, BEATRICE, *Aleksandra Kollontai: Socialism, Feminism, and the Bolshevik Revolution.* Stanford, CA: Stanford University Press, 1980.

FISCHER, HAROLD H., *The Famine in Soviet Russia, 1919–1923: The Operations of the American Relief Administration.* New York: Oxford University Press, 1927.

FITZPATRICK, SHEILA, *The Commissariat for Enlightenment . . . 1917–1921.* New York: Cambridge University Press, 1970.

FITZPATRICK, SHEILA (ED.), *Cultural Revolution in Russia, 1928–1931.* Bloomington: Indiana University Press, 1984.

FITZPATRICK, SHEILA ET AL. (EDS.), *Russia in the Era of NEP: Exploration of Soviet Society and Culture.* Bloomington, IN: Indiana University Press, 1991.

GETZLER, ISRAEL, *Kronstadt 1917–1921: The Fate of a Soviet Democracy.* New York: Cambridge University Press, 1983.

HOLMES, LARY E. *The Kremlin and the Schoolhouse: Reforming Education in Soviet Russia, 1917–1931.* Bloomington, IN: Indiana University Press, 1991.

KINGSTON-MANN, ESTHER, *Lenin and the Problem of Marxist Peasant Revolution.* New York: Oxford University Press, 1983.

KOLLONTAI, ALEXANDRA, *The Workers' Opposition in Russia.* Lioudou: Solidarity, 1977.

KOPP, ARISTOTLE, *Soviet Architecture and City Planning, 1917–1935.* New York: George Braziller, 1970.

LIH, LARS T., *Bread and Authority in Russia, 1914–1921.* Berkeley, CA: University of California Press, 1989.

PIPES, RICHARD, *Russia under the Bolshevik Regime.* New York: Alfred A. Knopf, 1993.

POGGIOLI, RENATO, *The Poets of Russia, 1890–1930.* Cambridge, MA: Harvard University Press, 1960.

PUSHKAREVA, NATALIA, Women in Russian History: From the Tenth to the Twentieth Century. M. E. Sharpe, 1997.

SERGE, VICTOR, *Memoirs of a Revolutionary, 1901–1941.* New York: Oxford University Press, 1963.

SHAPIRO, LEONARD, *The Origins of the Communist Autocracy Political Opposition in the Soviet State,* *1917–1922,* 2nd Ed. Cambridge: Harvard University Press, 1977.

SOLOMON, SUSAN G. AND HUTCHISON, JOHN H. (EDS.), *Health and Society in Revolutionary Russia.* Bloomington, IN: Indiana University Press, 1990.

Chapter 10

Between the Comintern and the Narkomindel: Early Soviet Foreign Policy

As Marxists, the Bolsheviks had based their ideas about relations among states on two assumptions. The first was that international conflicts were merely an outward manifestation of the inner contradictions of capitalism and would therefore be bound to disappear with its downfall and subsequent triumph of Communism. Second, Soviet leaders took it for granted that since "workers have no country," international solidarity would replace the proletarians' loyalty to their respective nation-states.

The latter assumption suffered its first heavy blow from 1914 to 1918. Most of the socialist parties in Europe, starting with the Social Democrats in Germany, basically supported the war efforts of their respective governments. Throughout the war, moreover, the proletarians of the belligerent countries slaughtered each other like everybody else. Finally, by the end of the war, the workers had failed to turn "the imperialistic war into a civil war," and thus aid the Bolsheviks. All this made Lenin condemn the Social Democratic parties as "social traitors," "renegades," and "Judases" to the proletarian cause. Consequently, he resolved that the Second Socialist International, which had united the

socialist parties since 1889, should be scrapped, and that all truly revolutionary proletarian parties should be modeled on the Bolshevik example and grouped into a new, more militant, international organization.

The Communist International (Comintern)

When Lenin was still in exile he could do little. His chance came only after November 1917, when he became undisputed head of the Soviet government. As a result of the Bolshevik triumph, most working-class movements began to split and their extreme left wings, one by one, began to form "parties of the new type," modeled on the Bolshevik party and calling themselves Communists. Initially, however, there were only sporadic contacts between them. The decision to set up a Communist International was precipitated early in 1919 by the news that the Social Democratic (or Second) International, shocked by the eagerness of the socialists to support the war effort of their respective countries, had decided to update its structure. There was no time to lose, argued

Lenin. Early in March some thirty representatives of leftist parties sympathetic to the Bolshevik point of view met in Moscow.

It was a strange gathering, and many among the motley crowd of delegates had dubious credentials. For instance, the fledgling American Communist movement was represented by John Reed. Christian Rakovsky, a French-educated Bulgarian, former Romanian citizen, and at that time head of the new Soviet Ukrainian government, claimed to represent the fictitious Balkan Revolutionary Federation. Most other delegates were members not of political movements but of tiny leftist splinters of the existing Social Democratic movements. The only sizable Communist Party, besides that of Soviet Russia, was the German. Yet its leadership, inspired by Rosa Luxemburg, was afraid that a Communist International set up at that time in Moscow would be nothing but a *Russian* International.

Despite German objections, and at Lenin's insistence, on March 4, 1919, the conference proclaimed itself the First Congress of the Communist International and promptly elected an Executive Committee. Lenin's close co-worker, Grigori Zinoviev, became its Chairman, while Karl Radek was selected as its Secretary. The *Comintern*, as the new organization came to be called, immediately issued an appeal "To the Workers of All Countries," urging them to follow the Bolshevik example, overthrow their bourgeois governments, and establish the dictatorship of the proletariat. The rebels were promised aid from the "first Socialist Government" of the world.

Soon after its foundation, the Comintern suffered a severe setback. Although in December 1918 the left wing of the German Social Democratic Party, known as the Spartacists, had succeeded in setting up the Communist Workers' Party of Germany, the party was too weak to stem that country's drift to the right. When in January 1919 the Communists staged an uprising in Berlin, the revolt was ruthlessly suppressed by the German Army. The two leaders of the Spartacists, Rosa Luxemburg and Karl

Liebknecht, were shot, and the Spartacist party banned. In May 1919, the Communist regime in Bavaria collapsed, while the Communist government of Bela Kun in Hungary went down in August of that year, undermined by its own ineffectiveness and swept away by the rightist forces led by Admiral Nicholas Horthy. At the same time in Russia the situation was critical; the White Armies of Denikin and Yudenich were converging on Moscow. Only at the close of 1919, with the destruction of Denikin's army, did the Bolsheviks' self-confidence revive.

Watching the changing European scene, Lenin decided in 1919 that while the Bolsheviks should persist in their revolutionary attempts, other approaches should not be neglected. Abandoning his previous diatribes against the democratic process and trade unionism, he wrote his pamphlet *Left Communism—Infantile Disease of Communism*. The booklet took to task those foreign comrades who were reluctant to exploit the opportunities provided them by existing trade unions and parliamentary institutions in their own countries. This rigid attitude was mistaken, naive, and childish, Lenin admonished. By participating in parliamentary or trade union activities, a revolutionary party would not necessarily become a parliamentary reformist party. Tactical alliances with non-Communist groups were permitted, provided the Communists retained their organizational as well as ideological identity intact. Flexible tactics adapted to changing local conditions were to be used by all foreign Communist parties. But above all, the politics of foreign comrades ought to be guided by one objective, that of helping the infant Soviet State by promoting class war throughout the world.

The Second Congress of the Comintern

The slow rate of the postwar European economic recovery led to social ferment. This unrest was reflected in the mushrooming of Communist parties throughout Europe. Consequently, when the Second Congress of the Comintern gathered in Moscow in July 1920, it was a much more impressive affair than the first; this time some 200 delegates represented forty-one Communist parties. They stressed not only defending the Soviet State, but also carrying the revolution abroad through Poland to Germany. The Congress exhorted the Red soldiers, then fighting the Poles, to capture Warsaw and not to lay down their arms until Poland had become a member of a world federation of Soviet republics.

While deliberating about such distant goals as the future "International Soviet Republic," the Congress laid down the organizational foundations of the world Communist movement; this took the form of twenty-one conditions for admission to the Comintern. They were molded by the Leninist assumption that a small, doctrinally pure, hierarchically structured party would be preferable to a broad, loosely organized mass movement. To be admitted to the Comintern as a section, each party had to have its platform approved by the Comintern. Each platform had to denounce colonial exploitation and actively work for the destruction of colonial empires. Each party had to carry out periodic purges and expel from its ranks all reformists and gradualists and introduce the Bolshevik principles of "democratic centralism" in its functioning. This meant, first, election to all leading party organs from lower to higher bodies, from primary cells to top executive committees; second, periodic reports of the elected party organizations; third, complete subordination of the minority to the majority; fourth, the absolutely binding character of decisions of higher bodies upon lower bodies. Outwardly, the formula was to strike a balance between authority and autonomy, between central control and local initiative. In fact, however, democratic centralism as practiced by those brought up in the rigid Bolshevik school of centralism meant stressing authority over democracy: this emphasis resulted in the strict subordination of the lower bodies to the will of the self-perpetuating, increasingly co-opted, and nonelected leadership.

By imposing their own specifically interpreted principles of democratic centralism upon the national sections of the Comintern, the Soviet leaders had started the process of eliminating from the newly formed Communist parties the still lingering Social-Democratic spirit and gradually assimilating the member parties to the Soviet patterns. This conscious and systematic "Bolshevization" soon resulted in a far-reaching unification of the international Communist movement. As a consequence, the Comintern soon became not a federation of autonomous parties, but a tightly integrated organization spreading its branches to each and every country. This was reflected in the terminology used by the Comintern. Each member party was to bear the uniform title "The Communist Party of . . ." (a given country), invariably followed by the words, "Section of the Communist International."

In addition to these authoritarian measures undertaken by the Soviet leadership, further strict control over the Comintern was to be exercised through the establishment of its General Headquarters in Moscow. This advantage was further enhanced by the composition of the Executive Committee on the Comintern. Of the twenty-one seats, five were reserved for "the country in which the Executive Committee is located," while no other national section was to be represented by more than one delegate. Thus by 1920 the infant Soviet State had already managed to erect an institution, the Executive Committee, which for over twenty years would function in Moscow parallel with the Commissariat for Foreign Affairs, or *Narkomindel*.

Duality of Soviet Foreign Policy

When the Red Army offensive was smashed at the Battle of Warsaw (August 14–18, 1920), the Comintern's original mood of jubilation gave way to one of frustration. Trotsky's slogan of "permanent revolution" proved to be rather Utopian The Comintern now had to settle down and face reality. The frontal offensive on Western capitalism had to cede its place to a long tortuous series of shifting skirmishes.

This strategy of indirect approach was reflected in the Third Congress of the Comintern, which again took place in Moscow, in June and July 1921. Following the proclamation of the NEP, Soviet Russia badly needed technical and financial aid from the West and could hardly afford to unduly offend the capitalist powers, especially Great Britain. This was one of the reasons the Third Congress played down the colonial problem. The main slogan of the Third Congress was "To the masses." Since the industrial working masses were largely controlled by the Social Democrats, a rival "Red International of Trade Unions" was set up. Its purpose was to split up the existing International Federation of Trade Unions run by the Second Social-Democratic International, and assure to the Communists direct access to the workers over the heads of their leaders. Later a Moscow-controlled international peasant organization was established to carry out a similar mission.

With the founding of the Comintern and its subsidiaries, the Soviet State assumed a dual character in world affairs. On the one hand, despite its strikingly novel socioeconomic and political structure, it tried to present itself to the outside world as a state like any other. Through the People's Commissariat of Foreign Affairs (*Narkomindel*), it tried to conduct more or less conventional relations with other nations. On the other hand, Moscow was the general headquarters of a supranational, universalistic, militant movement (the Comintern) devoted to subverting all other non-Communist states. Both organizations were masterminded by the same center of disposition, the Bolshevik Party, and both operated out of Moscow. This was, however, repeatedly denied by Soviet State leaders, who pretended to be unaware of the activities and objectives of the Comintern, which was allegedly a private organization.

Comintern policy was conducted in the spirit of permanent ideological holy war against the "capitalist encirclement"; despite tactical oscillations, Moscow never accepted more than a temporary truce with their enemies. This compelled the Western powers to respond in kind. Soviet foreign policy was an unprecedented phenomenon in international relations. Sporadic mutual encouragement of internal subversion among rival nation-states was not a novel phenomenon in history. What was without precedent, however, was the Comintern's challenge to all existing states, as well as the worldwide scope of its activity in the fields of propaganda, subversion, and intelligence gathering.

Conventional Diplomatic Relations

Initially, Soviet leaders regarded their more traditional and largely improvised diplomatic activities as a temporary but necessary activity. Trotsky, the first Foreign Commissar, was convinced that after issuing a few revolutionary declarations, he would "close the shop" and shift his energies to more important matters. Following the Brest-Litovsk Treaty, however, and faced with the harsh realities of the international arena, the Bolsheviks had to revise their views. Gradually, the Narkomindel had to develop more systematic activities and establish conventional diplomatic, consular, and trade relations.

From the very beginning, Germany represented to Soviet Russia the most important country in Europe. Since the time of Peter the Great, Russians had been fascinated with things German, as if to illustrate the maxim about the attraction of opposites. This fascination was inherited by the Russian Marxists for a variety of reasons. Both Marx and Engels were German. The strongest and most prestigious Marxist Party in the early twentieth century was that of the German Social-Democrats. Germany was the most advanced industrial state on the European continent. In addition, it was Berlin that had sent Lenin back to Russia in 1917 and initially lent him considerable support. It was on the German proletariat that Lenin focused his hopes during the early moments of the Bolshevik regime. And it was with the Germans and their allies that the first formal diplomatic agreement was signed at Brest-Litovsk by the Bolsheviks in March 1918. Not surprisingly, therefore, the German language became the first *lingua franca* of the Comintern, only gradually replaced by Russian.

As Lenin had anticipated, however, the Brest-Litovsk Treaty was soon swept away by the revolutionary event that took place in Germany in November 1918. The overthrow of the German Imperial regime brought to power a provisional government composed largely of Social Democrats. The reformist and gradualist German Social Democrats, however, refused to resume diplomatic relations with Moscow. Relations had been broken off the same year when the first Soviet envoy, Adolf Joffe, was ordered out of Berlin soon after his arrival shortly before the end of the war for having indulged in secret, subversive propaganda. In January 1919, as mentioned earlier, the attempted Communist uprising in Berlin had been ruthlessly crushed by the German army and a number of Communist leaders executed.

Soviet relations with the sponsors of the Treaty of Versailles, France, Great Britain, and the United States, were worse still. The Civil War in Russia and the role played in it by the British, French, and American troops had not exactly endeared these powers to the Bolsheviks. According to the Bolsheviks, the British and French had won the "imperialistic" and "predatory" war and were busy dividing the spoils: markets and mandates, military bases and economic concessions. The newly created League of Nations was vitriolically denounced by Moscow as the "League of Robbers," an instrument of the French and British power for the preservation of the post-Versailles system and the stabilization of capitalism, a "capitalist International" with its seat in Geneva, Switzerland.

Nevertheless, the Bolsheviks had to negotiate more or less conventional agreements with various components of the "capitalistic encirclement." During 1920 and 1921, having failed to subvert and conquer its western neighbors, Soviet Russia signed, one by one, peace treaties with Estonia, Latvia, Lithuania, Finland, and Poland. Romania was an exception because Moscow never recognized the incorporation of Bessarabia by Bucharest. Then came a trade agreement with Britain, followed by similar arrangements with Norway, Austria, and Italy.

The May 1921 trade agreement with London was of particular significance for the new rulers of Russia. To the Bolsheviks of the early 1920s, Britain still appeared as the great world power, the impressive center of a vast colonial empire, the main bastion of capitalism, and therefore the ultimate enemy of Communism. At that time the City of London, and not Wall Street, was the symbol of international capitalism. The trade pact was only a small break in the wall of isolation, since it was not immediately followed by *de jure* recognition of Russia's new regime and the resumption of full-scale diplomatic relations. However, the modest trade agreement with Great Britain was a significant step in the direction of normalizing relations with the capitalist world. The pact was signed largely on Soviet terms. Moscow did not reverse its repudiation of the pre-1917 debts and did not indemnify British investors. It was true that both sides pledged to "refrain from hostile acts and measures against the other party" and that the Soviet Government promised to "refrain from any attempt or incitement . . . of any Asiatic nations to activities hostile to British interests," but Moscow undertook these obligations with firm determination not to honor them. Yet the moral significance of the treaty was unmistakable; it spelled the gradual loss of the revolutionary zeal of the vanguard of world Communism.

Next to Great Britain, France was regarded by Bolshevik leaders as the major enemy of the Soviet State and world Communism. During the Civil War, it was Paris that had been in the vanguard of the intervention. During the 1920s, it was France that managed to construct in Eastern Europe a network of treaties of alliance with Poland, Czechoslovakia, Romania, and Yugoslavia. The purpose of these alliances was twofold: The French clients were not only to watch over a defeated, but restless and still potentially dangerous, Germany, but also to contain Communist Russia by forming a *cordon sanitaire*, or quarantine line, against Bolshevism. Thus, the hostility and suspicion of the French and British toward these two outcasts of the Versailles system gradually tended to push them toward each other.

The Rapallo Treaty

The first step toward breaking through the wall of isolation surrounding Soviet Russia was the international conference of April 1922 in Genoa, Italy. The conference was an attempt by the European countries to deal collectively with their postwar economic problems. The two outcasts, Russia and Germany, were invited because it was widely believed that their cooperation would be indispensable to Europe's economic rehabilitation.

The Genoa Conference was a memorable event in Soviet history; it could be compared to the first appearance of Communist Chinese delegates at the United Nations in 1972. For the first time since the Bolshevik Revolution, a large Soviet diplomatic delegation appeared outside its native land at an important international gathering. The delegation was led by the second Soviet Commissar for Foreign Affairs (after Trotsky), Grigori Chicherin, dressed—surprisingly—like all the other delegates, in top hat and cutaway. Of aristocratic origin, he displayed impeccable manners and spoke fluent French. The attitude of the Russians toward the Genoa Conference was mixed. On the one hand, they saw an opportunity to secure Western economic aid for their country; on the other, they suspected that their capitalist creditors might form a united front and again raise the issue of the old Tsarist debts. While participating in the official activities of the conference, Chicherin never lost sight of his main aim, that of inducing Germany to help Russia economically and militarily, thereby permitting Russia diplomatically to reenter the international area hand in hand with a potentially powerful partner. Chicherin's cause was helped by Allied claims for German war reparations, amounting to approximately 132 billion gold marks. The Germans had anticipated the stiffening of the Western powers' attitude in this matter. Since the Russians were also afraid of the renewal of Western pressure concerning the Tsarist debts, the Allied claims against Germany—combined with the existing social boycott of the two pariahs of Europe—automatically created a strong community of interests between Moscow and Berlin. Almost immediately after the opening of the conference, secret negotiations between the two delegations began at a nearby Italian resort town, Rapallo.

From the Soviet point of view, Germany was a large reservoir of unemployed military personnel and a source of the advanced technical know-how so badly needed for the reconstruction of the Soviet armed forces and their devastated war industry. The Soviet economy also needed German civilian engineers to speed its rehabilitation. Berlin's goal, on the other hand, was to evade the disarmament clauses of the Treaty of Versailles,

Grigori Chicherin, People's Commissar for Foreign Affairs, 1918–1930

which limited the German Army to 100,000 men and forbade the manufacturing as well as the maintaining of tanks, planes, and poison gas. Chicherin suggested that this manufacturing could be done on Soviet soil.

The events that eventually pushed Germany into the Soviets' arms were precipitated by German fears of Western demands for strict execution of the peace treaty's reparation clauses. One should remember that the French had inserted Article 116 into the Treaty of Versailles, signed in June 1919, at a time when the Entente Powers were anticipating a speedy White victory in Russia. Article 116 reserved for Russia, which did not attend the Paris Peace Conference, the right to obtain reparations from Germany. The clause was inserted with the expectation that the reconstruction of Russia, and hence the repayment of prewar Tsarist debts, especially the French investments, would be greatly facilitated by German war indemnities. However, the article boomeranged, for it frightened the Germans and made them more susceptible to Chicherin's offer. He suggested the cancellation of mutual debts and a close cooperation in defiance of the Western powers.

On April 16, 1922, at Rapallo, Chicherin and his German counterpart, Walter Rathenau, signed a Treaty of Friendship and Cooperation. The agreement provided for resumption of normal diplomatic relations between the two countries; both sides renounced all war reparations and granted each other preferential treatment in trade relations. The pact also provided for mutual consultation prior to all important international agreements. The Treaty of Rapallo, despite its modest title and outwardly innocuous content, covered a variety of cooperative Soviet-German ventures, including secret military arrangements. The Treaty was an important turning point in the diplomatic annals of Soviet Russia and a significant factor in European diplomacy for well over a decade. The treaty formed the foundation for a partnership between the two great losers of World War I, who were now bent on sharing their isolation in order to overthrow the Versailles system and jointly overcome their temporary weaknesses. For Soviet Russia, Rapallo was a great diplomatic victory; it represented Moscow's return to an active role in the diplomatic arena on terms of equality.

For the Western powers, Rapallo came as a shock. In Paris, Rapallo caused alarm lest it be followed by the evasion of the disarmament clauses of the Versailles Treaty by Germany and threaten France's East European allies from the east, thus effectively neutralizing their role as anti-German instruments.[1]

The Aftermath of Rapallo

The consequences of the Soviet-German agreement of 1922 were far-reaching. German experts began to build their war planes and submarines, as well as to manufacture poison gas, on Russian soil. Such German firms as Krupp, Daimler, and Rheinmetal established branches in Russia and began to produce tanks in cooperation with Soviet technicians. These collaborative ventures in manufacturing war material were paralleled by the exchange of military, but not naval, personnel. German officers were sent to Russia to attend military training courses; Soviet officers, including such aces as Tukhachevsky, were dispatched for the same purpose to Germany. Three secret German military training grounds were established in Russia: one for tanks, another for chemical warfare, and a third for aviation. The foundations of German rearmament were laid down on Soviet soil, thanks to Rapallo. Military collaboration was accompanied by economic cooperation between the two partners. From 1926 on, Berlin gave guarantees to German firms that sold goods to the Russians on credit. Soon Germany regained its position as Russia's major economic partner. The close collaboration between the

---

[1] For an introduction to Soviet-German dealings during the Weimar Republic, see Gerald Freund, *Unholy Alliance: Russo-German Relations from the Treaty of Brest-Litovsk to the Treaty of Berlin* (New York: Harcourt Brace Jovanovich, 1957).

two countries continued until 1934, after Hitler's seizure of power.

Despite the pact's mutual benefits, Soviet-German relations were characterized by a strange ambivalence. On the one hand, the Narkomindel considered Berlin its main partner in the field of international relations. On the other hand, highly industrialized Germany, with its vast masses of proletarians and the largest Communist movement outside Soviet Russia, was still considered the key target of the Comintern's revolutionary strategy. Here the Soviet quest for security through an alliance with a strong, stable partner clashed with its hope of subverting this very partner in order to gain a jumping-off point for further Communist expansion.

The best example of this dichotomy occurred in 1923. At that time Germany was suffering from a disastrous economic depression, acute social unrest, and resulting chronic political instability; inflation had spiraled to an unprecedented extent. Only a wheelbarrow full of money would suffice for the daily shopping. The situation was aggravated by the problems of war reparations and the feverish agitation for a revision of the Treaty of Versailles. In January 1923, the German government refused to pay the current installment on its reparations. Paris replied by militarily occupying the Ruhr basin, a vital industrial area on the Rhine. This in turn precipitated a wave of passive resistance, sabotage, and acts of terror, not only in the Ruhr but throughout the entire Rhineland, then still under inter-Allied military control. Moscow believed that occupation of the Ruhr might be the first step toward a French-British conflict and, eventually, the beginning of a European general war. The "revolutionary situation" created by the Ruhr crisis was a temptation to Comintern strategists, convinced that the hour of the proletarian revolution in Germany was at hand.

Almost simultaneously, another radical but right-wing and nationalistic leader, Adolf Hitler, seized on the prevailing confusion and staged his rightist revolt in Munich. The suppression of his attempted *coup d'état*, or *putsch* in German, cost him an imprisonment in the fortress of Landsberg. There he wrote his main work, *Mein Kampf* (*My Struggle*), the bible of his National Socialist movement. One of the book's main themes was the author's deep hatred for the non-Aryan, "inferior races," not only for Jews, but also for Slavs, and his vision of a vaster living space (*Lebensraum*) for the Germans to be found on plains of the Soviet Union, mainly in Ukraine.

The failure of the Comintern's German strategem had its repercussions in the incipient struggle for power then beginning in Russia. (This is discussed in the next chapter.) The defeat of the German Communists dramatically diminished the role of the Comintern and adversely affected the prestige of its head, Zinoviev. The failure also undermined the position of Trotsky, whose theory of "permanent revolution" was discredited first by the defeat in Poland in 1920 and then in Germany in 1922–1923.

Soviet Russia and Asia

Next to Germany, the most important foreign policy item on the agenda of the Soviet leadership in the 1920s was the problem of the colonial and semicolonial countries of Africa and Asia, especially China. Russo-Chinese relations extended back to Peter the Great, who by the Treaty of Nerchensk of 1689 expanded the Muscovite boundary in southern Siberia at China's expense. This aggressive drive, slowed down under his successors, was resumed around the middle of the nineteenth century, when the antiquated Chinese Empire was weakened by various European encroachments like the annexation of Hong Kong by Britain. In the chaotic situation of the 1860s, Russian pioneers (frontiersmen) wrested large regions from China. The first of them was the present Chinese province of Sinkiang between the Aral and Caspian seas, which was then called Turkestan. The second was Outer Mongolia, and the third included the present Russian maritime provinces on the Pacific Ocean.

These enormous territories covered all the area east of the Ussuri and north of the Amur rivers, amounting to some 580,000 square miles, a region as big as Alaska. Tsarist control of Outer Mongolia—which in 1911 declared itself an "autonomous republic" but was actually a protectorate of St. Petersburg—pushed the Russian holdings within approximately 400 miles of Peking.

The revolutionary events in Russia of 1905 were closely watched by Sun Yat-sen, head of the Chinese nationalists. The downfall of the Manchu dynasty in 1911 plunged China into anarchy. Sun Yat-sen was unable to consolidate his hold on the country torn by a civil war. Greatly impressed by the Bolshevik Party and its techniques for the seizure of power, he resolved to apply some of Lenin's methods, if not his ideology, to his own party, the *Kuomintang*, devoted to social reform. Sun Yat-sen considered the Bolshevik Party to be both an ally and an organizational model, but he rejected Communist authoritarian doctrine, while accepting its anticolonialism. Moreover, he welcomed whatever technical and military help Moscow would send him to free China from foreign overlordship and to modernize his country.

From the Soviet point of view, cooperation with the *Kuomintang*, the strongest political movement in Asia and a staunch opponent of "Western imperialism," was of considerable value. To Lenin, the Western colonies were the weakest link in the capitalist chain and anticolonialism was a fundamental principle of the Comintern. One of its early proclamations appealed to the "colonial slaves of Africa and Asia" to rise, and promised them that "the hour of proletarian dictatorship in Europe will also be the day of your own liberation." The chief purpose of this propaganda was to undermine the hold the Western powers, Great Britain and France, had on their overseas possessions, and thereby weaken their economic and consequent military potential. The British, whom Bolshevik leaders still considered as their main enemies both in Europe and in Asia, were singled out by Comintern propaganda as the chief oppressors and exploiters of the colonial lands. As Bukharin frankly admitted, the Communists were willing to support the slogan of independence even for "Hottentots, Bushmen, Negroes, Hindus, etc.," precisely because their struggle for national liberation hurt Soviet Russia's main enemy, the British. If the colonial tentacles of the British and the French could be cut in Asia, Africa would follow, and the West, deprived of its sources of raw material and markets, would then become easy prey for domestic proletarian revolution. Since there were only a few industrial workers in Asia and Africa, all impoverished strata of population were declared as "proletarian." In the countries of "the Third World" the most oppressed were the peasants. Because they lacked sufficient political consciousness, they had to be led by the local "revolutionary intelligentsia." Thus orthodox Marxism was bent again to apply it to colonial conditions, while helping the Soviet global strategy.

The Second Congress of the Comintern repeated the anticolonialist slogans of the first and went a step further; it organized the Congress of Peoples of the East in Baku in September 1920. There the Comintern proclaimed itself the champion of the struggle against colonialism. Zinoviev summoned the Muslims to a "holy war" against the Western exploiters and oppressors. He stressed the role of Communism as a natural protector of the suppressed and exploited colonial peoples of the world, especially of Asia.

Afghanistan, Persia, and Turkey

In both Europe and Asia the common denominator of a possible anti-Soviet coalition was Great Britain. Consequently, the entire Soviet policy throughout Asia, not only in the Far East but also in the Near and Middle East, was essentially a struggle against British influence. To create as many difficulties as possible for London was Moscow's chief objective. It is in this light that one should examine the subsequent Soviet policies along the Asian semicircle that stretches from China to Afghanistan, Persia (Iran), and Turkey.

As in the case of China, soon after the seizure of power the Bolsheviks renounced the special position of Imperial Russia in Afghanistan, Persia, now known as Iran, and Turkey, and Moscow signed a series of agreements with these countries. The 1921 treaty with Persia was of particular significance. The Soviets gave up all claims to the railways and military highways the Tsarist authorities had built in northern Persia, then treated as a Russian sphere of influence, Moscow also renounced its rights to all the lands belonging to the Russo-Persian Bank. This contrasted with the attitude of the British, who strictly maintained all the rights and privileges deriving from the treaty of 1907 that had made southern Persia a British sphere of influence. But even at this early idealistic and utopian stage of Soviet policy, Lenin insisted on a quid pro quo in the form of fishing concessions for Russia in the Persian-controlled southern segment of the Caspian Sea (a major source of sturgeon and hence of caviar), and for a voice in determining Persian tariffs. Another interesting aspect of the Soviet-Persian treaty of 1921 was the right granted to Moscow to send their troops into Persia (Iran) should the government in Teheran be unable to prevent a third power from using Persian (Iranian) territory as a base of operation against Soviet Russia. The Treaty was an effort to counterbalance the British presence in the southern part of the country.

In 1921, Soviet Russia also concluded a treaty of "Peace and Friendship" with another country nurturing numerous grudges against the British after World War I, the defeated Turkey. In the treaty, the Soviet Government agreed to give up the Armenian cities of Kars and Ardahan, which Tsar Alexander II had acquired at the end of the Russo-Turkish war of 1877–1878. This dramatic reversal of Moscow's policies toward Turkey was especially noteworthy in view of the implacable and almost continuous hostility that had characterized the relations between the two

countries for over 200 years. In addition to the renunciation of past privileges and territorial concessions, the Bolshevik leadership now offered the Turks their assistance in the Turks' efforts to recover from the catastrophe of the Great War. Reversing the traditional and relentlessly pursued policy of the Tsars, the Bolsheviks insisted that the Turks alone be left as guardians of the strategic Black Sea Straits, the Bosphorus and the Dardanelles. Moscow declared that the Straits were no longer needed for Russia's safety and insisted that Soviet security could be safeguarded as long as free commercial passage from the Black Sea to the Mediterranean would be assured. On the other hand, Moscow urged the closing of the Bosphorus and the Dardanelles to warships of foreign powers wishing to penetrate the Black Sea. The fact that Turkey was dictatorially ruled with an iron fist by Kemal Atatürk and pursued a policy of repression of its native Communists was not considered an obstacle.

Summary

From the beginning, Moscow's attitude to the Communist revolution in Asia was radically different from that in the West. Both the Comintern and the Soviet government viewed the struggle as a socioeconomic conflict, or that of the industrial proletariat against the bourgeoisie, with the peasants acting as a sporadic auxiliary force, since in the East, there were very few industrial workers. Consequently, the Comintern was resolved to support temporarily the "local national liberation" movements, represented mostly by "progressive" bourgeoisie in its opposition to both "Western imperialism" and native feudalism. In the long run, it was calculated in Moscow, the backing lent to the native bourgeoisie by the Comintern would not hinder the eventual destruction of capitalism, but would merely postpone it.

During its first decade, Soviet diplomacy was characterized by a pronounced duality; diplomats often made idealistic gestures, but never entirely forgot Russian national interests; they were simply expressed in the complex Marxist verbiage and in the light of "proletarian internationalism." Soon, however, "proletarian internationalism" changed its meaning entirely. When the great revolutionary expectations and euphoria of 1917–1920 faded away, the Bolsheviks, while still paying lip service to the old slogans, gradually reconciled themselves to existing realities. They accepted the "temporary stabilization" of capitalism, relinquished their revolutionary zeal, and tried to adjust themselves to the facts of international life. The Baku Congress was not reconvened.

Initially, Soviet diplomats were distinguished by a demonstrative "proletarian" and "revolutionary" style; for instance, they used different titles, refused to wear the customary dress uniforms, and so on. Soviet diplomacy, however, little by little, conformed to the alien environment in which it had to function. The outward duality of Soviet foreign policy expressed in the symbiosis of the Narkomindel and the Comintern persisted until the late 1930s, but the center of gravity was dramatically shifting already during the early 1920s toward the conventional style of diplomacy.

Although the Comintern's activities and its export of social revolution occasionally caused a great deal of embarrassment to the Narkomindel, they also paid handsome dividends, for they provided Moscow with excellent sources of intelligence, as well as with an instrument of pressure on other governments. It was largely owing to the Comintern that the Soviet Union, despite its limited postrevolutionary military and economic capabilities, did play the role of a de facto great power by the late 1920s.

Suggested Reading

AGURSKY, MIKHAIL, *The Third Rome: National Bolshevism in the USSR.* Washington, DC: Sidney Kramer Books, 1987.

ANGRESS, WERNER T., *Stillborn Revolution: The Communist Bid for Power in Germany, 1921–1923.* Princeton, NJ: Princeton University Press, 1963.

BORKENAU, FRANZ, *World Communism: A History of the Communist International.* New York: Norton, 1939.

BOROVKIN, VLADIMIR, *Russia after Lenin: Politics, Culture, and Society, 1921–1929.* London: Routledge, 1998.

CARR, E. H., *German-Soviet Relations between the Two World Wars, 1919–1929.* Baltimore, MD: Johns Hopkins Press, 1951.

DALLIN, DAVID J., *The Rise of Russia in Asia.* New Haven, CT: Yale University Press, 1949.

DEGRAS, JANE (ED.), *Calendar of Soviet Documents on Foreign Policy, 1917–1941.* New York: Royal Institute of International Affairs, 1948.

———, *Soviet Documents on Foreign Policy.* New York: Oxford University Press, 1951–1953, 3 Vols.

———, *The Communist International, 1919–1943.* London: L. Cass. 1971.

FISCHER, RUTH, *Stalin and German Communism.* Cambridge, MA: Harvard University Press, 1948.

FREUND, GERALD, *Unholy Alliance: Russo-German Relations from the Treaty of Brest-Litovsk to the Treaty of Berlin.* New York: Harcourt Brace Jovanovich, 1957.

GEONG, SOW-THONG, *Sino-Soviet Diplomatic Relations, 1917–1926.* Honolulu: University of Hawaii Press, 1976.

HESSEN, ROBERT (ED.), *Breaking with Communism: The Intellectual Odyssey of Bertram D. Wolfe.* Stanford, CA: Hoover Institution, 1990.

HILGER, GUSTAV, AND ALFRED G. MEYER, *The Incompatible Allies: A Memoir–History of German–Soviet Relations, 1918–1941.* New York: Macmillan, 1953.

HULSE, JAMES W., *The Forming of the Communist International.* Stanford, CA: Hoover, 1964.

ISAACS, HAROLD R., *The Tragedy of the Chinese Revolution,* Rev. Ed. Stanford, CA: Stanford University Press, 1951.

KENEZ, PETER, *The Birth of the Propaganda State: Soviet Methods of Mass Mobilization, 1917–1929.* New York: Cambridge University Press, 1987.

KENNAN, GEORGE F., *Russia and the West under Lenin and Stalin.* Boston: Little, Brown, 1961.

TANG, PETER S.H., *Russia and the Soviet Policy in*

Manchuria, 1911–1931. Durham, NC: Duke University Press, 1959.

ULAM, ADAM B., *Expansion and Coexistence: The History of Soviet Foreign Policy, 1917–1967.* New York: Praeger, 1968, Chaps. 1–4.

ULLMAN, RICHARD H., *Anglo-Soviet Relations, 1917–1921.* Princeton, NJ: Princeton University Press, 1961–1973, 3 Vols.

WHITE, STEPHEN, *The Origins of Detente: The Genoa Conference and Soviet-Western Relations,* *1921–1922.* Cambridge, Eng., and New York: Cambridge University Press, 1985.

WHITING, ALLEN S., *Soviet Policy in China, 1917–1924.* Cambridge, MA: Harvard University Press, 1954.

ZENKOVSKY, SERGE A., *Pan-Turkism and Islam in Russia.* Cambridge, MA: Harvard University Press, 1960.

Chapter 11

The Formation of the USSR and Lenin's Death

While reorganizing their economy and groping for a new international bearing, Soviet leaders were also reshaping the administrative structure of their state. At the time, Lenin was ailing, and the prospect of his death triggered the first jockeying for position of advantage by potential successors. The constitutional issue and the problem of succession were closely interconnected.

As discussed earlier, the Civil War resulted in the eventual reconquest of the Dnieper Ukraine, most of Belorussia, and the three Caucasian republics—Georgia, Armenia, and Azerbaijan—by what was until 1922 called the Russian Socialist Federal Soviet Republic (RSFSR). Through an agreement with Tokyo, the Far Eastern Province, temporarily a Japanese protectorate, also rejoined the RSFSR in 1922. Meanwhile, at Stalin's insistence and despite the fierce opposition of many Georgian Communists, Georgia, Armenia, and Azerbaijan were merged into a single Transcaucasian Republic. Thus, although a large segment of the multinational western fringe was lost, the remaining core of about 140 million people was about 46 percent non-Russian (64 million people). They represented a bewildering variety of ethnic groups at various stages of cultural and socioeconomic development. While the Great Russian heartland, especially its major cities, was fairly westernized, most of the seminomadic inhabitants of Central Asia, the Muslim tribes of the Northern Caucasus, and the inhabitants of Siberia were mostly backward, illiterate, and lacked a conscious feeling of nationality.

Federalism versus Centralism

How to weld these areas and peoples together again was the subject of lively and often embittered discussion in the Party and in government circles in the early 1920s. The 1918 Constitution had already provided for a federal structure, as favored by Lenin himself. Once again, as with the peasant question, he followed the SR program. On the other hand, people like Trotsky, Stalin, and Dzerzhinsky opposed federalism as making undue concessions to local nationalism and thus being fraught with great danger of encouraging separatist movements. Instead, they favored strict centralism, combined with limited autonomy if local conditions warranted. Yet the emerging Soviet Republic was very similar to the former Imperial Russia, at least in one respect: it was decidedly a multinational empire.

Lenin had observed how shallow and ineffective had been the old imperial policy of Russification, and how difficult it had been to impose Russian-Communist rule on the borderlands during the Civil War. In view of this, federalism seemed a better device to bribe the nationalities of the former Tsarist Empire to adhere to the new Soviet State structure. Lenin believed that federal slogans would soften the impact of the reconquest of non-Russian areas by permitting the continued coexistence of various peculiarities in an ethnically heterogeneous republic, while the existence of an ethnic mosaic of peoples, some of them at a tribal stage of development, without developed national sentiments, provided an opportunity for Communist social engineering. In addition to these not inconsiderable advantages, federalism, if shrewdly presented abroad, would make the Soviet State a structure open to others who might wish to join it in the future.

All these assets were eventually accepted even by the opponents of federalism. On December 27, 1922, the Tenth All-Russian Congress of Soviets accepted Stalin's motion, made on Lenin's insistence, to establish the Union of Soviet Socialist Republics, or USSR. It was originally composed of four member-republics: Russia, the Ukraine, Belorussia, and Transcaucasus. In October 1924, the Russian Republic split and gave birth to two Central Asian Republics: Uzbek and Turkmen. In 1929 these six republics were joined by the Tajik Soviet Republic. Finally in 1936 the Transcaucasian Republic was broken into three segments—Georgia, Armenia, and Azerbaijan—thereby transforming the USSR at that time into a union of nine federated segments. Within most Soviet republics, especially within the RSFSR, settlements of smaller ethnic groups were consolidated into autonomous areas in accordance with the long-range Soviet strategy of playing one ethnic group against another. The RSFSR, for instance, contained twelve regions, including, for instance, a Volga German autonomous republic and the autonomous territory of the Kalmucks.

By 1923, the USSR had framed a new Constitution. Ratified in 1924, it remained in force until 1936. The new charter was merely the former Constitution of 1918 adjusted to the new federal structure of the Soviet State. The 1924 basic law differentiated between the governmental bodies of the USSR, or the Union, and those of the four previously mentioned individual Union Republics then in existence. The All-Union Congress of Soviets was made bicameral and was to be composed of the Council of the Union and the Council of Nationalities. While the Council of the Union was to be selected on the basis of population, the Council of Nationalities was to be composed of five delegates from each Union Republic and each autonomous republic, and one delegate from each autonomous area (*oblast*).

The Constitution provided for three kinds of ministries, then still called commissariats. There was the All-Union Commissariat for the USSR as a whole, and one for each Union-Republic or autonomous republic. The federal, or All-Union, government was given authority in the fields of armed forces, war and peace, foreign relations, foreign trade, and fiscal matters, as well as for economic planning for the USSR as a whole. The authority of the constituent republics was limited to such powers as were not reserved for the All-Union government, and this was precious little.

It is worthwhile noting that the Russian Republic comprised nearly three-quarters of the Soviet Union's territory, and contained its predominantly Great Russian population. Despite this, the Russian Republic had no separate Communist Party organization, no separate Academy of Science, nor many other, outwardly impressive institutions enjoyed by other republics. Moscow was designated as capital of the USSR and not of the Russian Republic. Yet, soon, the term "Russia" became a shorthand for "USSR," and the Russian language became the *lingua franca* of the Union (see Chapters 24 and 25). Nominally, all constituent republics had their individual Communist Parties; these were in fact subordinate to the All-Union, or Soviet Party.

The supreme power of the USSR theoretically was represented by the All-Union Congress of Soviets. The Congress, consisting of delegates from local soviets, was to be summoned every year by its Central Executive Committee. Only the delegates for the lowest tiers in the hierarchical pyramid, the village and city soviets, were to be elected by direct vote. All the higher soviets, the county, province, and republican ones, were composed of delegates selected by the soviets immediately below. However, all elections were strictly controlled by the Soviet Communist Party. The franchise was limited to people over eighteen involved in "productive work"; this included officials and soldiers but excluded former members of the bourgeoisie and priests. The Executive Committee was to be elected by the All-Union Congress from among its members and was to act as a governing body between congresses. The actual governmental functions of the Committee were to be performed by its Presidium, the chairman of which was to act as head of state. The first Chairman of the Presidium was Mikhail I. Kalinin, son of a poor peasant from the Tver province, a metal worker until 1917, and a man of flexible disposition. He was ideally suited to perform this purely symbolic function in full harmony with dictates of the ruling Party, as he was to do for well over twenty years.

Like the Constitution of 1918, the new charter bore only a vague relationship to political realities and power in the USSR and had a strong propagandistic ring. The preamble stated: "The family of brotherly peoples" of the USSR represents a "voluntary union of equal peoples, ready to embrace others who desire such association." The 1924 Constitution went so far as to provide for the right of each republic to secede freely from the USSR. Various semiofficial comments left no doubt, however, that a request for succession would be regarded as a hostile act opposed to the interests of the proletariat represented by the Soviet Communist Party. The Constitution also made specific provision for the admission

Mikhail I. Kalinin, Chairman of the Presidium of the Central Executive Committee of the Soviet State, 1919–1937, and Chairman of the Presidium of the USSR Supreme Soviet, 1937–1946

of "all Socialist Soviet republics, both those now in existence, and those which will arise in the future."

Centripetal Factors

The outward decentralization allegedly resulting from the establishment of the federal system was a daring feat of political engineering devised by Lenin. The operation was made possible by the preservation of the centralized and hierarchically organized All-Union, Soviet Communist Party, which reached from its Moscow headquarters into the remotest provinces, through its national branches, skillful manipulated Moscow. It was the All-Union Soviet Party that formed the firm infrastructure, the reliable nerve center of the USSR. The existence of this dictatorial Party allowed the construction of an alluring and impressive federal facade for the Soviet State, yet simultaneously rendered federalism illusory. Like the 1918 Constitution of the RSFSR, the new charter of the

USSR made no direct reference to the real locus of power.

Another factor that permitted the Bolsheviks to put federalism into practice and implement an outwardly liberal ethnic policy was the overwhelming strength of its Great Russian hard core, the RSFST. In 1923–1924 it comprised about three quarters of the territory of the USSR at that time; slightly over 76 million were Great Russians, who in turn constituted nearly 80 percent of the membership of the Communist Party. Within the territory of the Russian Republic were situated most natural resources including oil, natural gas, gold and diamond mines. Moreover three of the four major industrial centers of the USSR (Petrograd, Moscow, and the Southern Ural region) were located in the ethnically Russian territory. Only the fourth industrial area, the Ukraine, was outside the Russian Republic.

From the Soviet point of view, the establishment of a federal state served several purposes. First, it helped to attract and maintain within the Union those ethnic elements for whom Communism would otherwise have had little appeal, such as the radical yet nationalistic segments of various minority groups. Second, the theoretically generous ethnic policy was a potentially effective instrument of foreign expansion, especially among the states to the west of the Soviet Union like Poland, Romania, Czechoslovakia, and Turkey, where Ukrainian, Belorussian, or Armenian minorities lived without the benefit of a formally generous federal structure. In organizing their outwardly multinational federal state, the Bolsheviks were helped by their Civil War allies among the national minorities. The belief that national emancipation could be achieved through tactical, temporary cooperation with Communism was strong among leftist socialists, and even the radical democrats in various ethnic groups, especially the Ukrainians, the Belorussians, and some Moslems. Typical of them was the Ukrainian nationalist revolutionary leader Volodymyr K. Vinnychenko. He was convinced that by passing through the inevitable stage of "National Bolshevism" the Ukrainians might, perhaps, eventually achieve national independence. Among many Ukrainians this belief was strengthened by the development of their national culture, previously suppressed by the Tsarist administration and now flourishing under Soviet rule.

In the beginning, many of the pro-Bolshevik nationalists had reason to be optimistic because the Communist Revolution, with its principle of expropriation of all the means of production, was initially advantageous to the ethnic minorities, especially the Ukrainians and Belorussians. The upper classes in both regions were either Russian or Polish, and most of the capital, including the land, belonged to foreigners while trade and handicrafts were largely in the hands of the local Jews. During the period of the NEP, there was little forcible collectivization. Many petty traders and small industrialists were natives, and the Communist administration, short of qualified people, had to rely on whatever local talent was available, which often meant overlooking the political views of the people who were not anti-Communists. Economic planning could already boast some achievements. The figures, although often inflated, were outwardly impressive. From 1922 on, Soviet mass media constantly reported the building of new factories, highways, railroads, and canals, like those connecting the Dvina, the Niemen, and the Dnieper with the Volga. Electric light began to appear in the villages.[1]

The NEP was paralleled by the policy of "taking native roots." Lenin in particular was determined to make the Communist system penetrate more deeply into the multinational fabric of the USSR. Consequently, national cultures were encouraged, education was fostered, native literatures were developed, often from scratch among some Central Asian tribes, and native tongues were

[1]While stressing these achievements, the Soviets cleverly manipulated their statistical data so as to keep dark the fact that, despite the expanded acreage, for several years the agricultural harvests were proportionately lower than in 1913.

revived. Lenin was in favor of teaching the national language and culture at State schools to every child of each nationality. On the other hand, he opposed separate political organizations (autonomous Communist parties) for each ethnic group.

Among the people who benefitted from the Leninist ethnic policy were not only Ukrainians and Belorussians, but also some three million Jews, formerly largely restricted to the Pale of Settlement and cramped by its discriminatory legislation. As a result of the liberal revolution, the Jews had already obtained legal equality. The Bolsheviks officially condemned anti-Semitism and made it a punishable offense. Yiddish, the language of most Soviet Jews, was introduced into the Jewish schools. A Jewish press developed rapidly, and as early as the end of 1918, there were eighty-one Yiddish and ten Hebrew newspapers. A first-class Jewish theater was organized in Moscow. At the same time, however, religious Jews suffered from the official atheism of the new regime. Synagogues were being closed and rabbis often had to suffer indignities, not unlike the clergy of other denominations. At the same time, the Soviet regime, with the Jewish section of the Communist Party as its willing tool, was trying to assimilate the Jews into the surrounding population.

One method of assimilation was to diversify the hitherto rather one-sided socioeconomic structure of the Jewish population by encouraging Jews to leave the urban centers, settle in the countryside, and practice agriculture. And indeed, during the 1920s Jewish villages were set up in the Ukraine and in the Far Eastern segment of Birobijan. Jewish culture, like that in the Ukraine and Belorussia, enjoyed a brief period of expansion and flowering. The internationalist aspects of the Communist doctrine greatly appealed to many cosmopolitan Jews, who sincerely believed that they were undergoing a process of genuine amalgamation. They renounced their Jewishness not in order to become Russians or Ukrainians, but to be "New Soviet Men."

During the 1920s the Bolsheviks also paid a great deal of attention to the Muslim peoples, who numbered around 25 million. Kazakhs, Uzbeks, Turkmens, Tatars, and others were united by a common religion and the Arabic script. Mirza Sultan-Galiev, an able imaginative Muslim Volga Tatar and a member of the All-Russian Muslim movement, was largely instrumental in reconquering the Central Asian provinces for the Bolsheviks. Once in control of Central Asia, the Bolsheviks began to pursue a step-by-step policy of gradual secularization and integration of the native population. They gradually cut off the Muslims of the USSR from their brethren who lived south of its borders by discouraging travel and interpersonal contacts, and by replacing the original Arabic script first with the Latin and finally with the Russian. Secularization was fostered, initially without exaggerated zeal and excesses. "Don't paint nationalism red!" Lenin warned his comrades. Local cultures were to be "national in form but Marxist in content."

The Soviet ethnic policy was especially important in the Soviet Ukraine, the largest and most important of the federal republics. As long as Poland, Romania, and Czechoslovakia ruled over the western segments of the Ukrainian people, an outwardly liberal policy could serve as a means of pressure and diversion against these countries. The granting of cultural, if not political, autonomy to the ethnic minorities was also very useful to the Comintern in its propaganda; it could present the USSR as an attractive model for all peoples of the world to join eventually or at least emulate. One of the standard slogans of Soviet propaganda was: "We solved all ethnic problems."

Lenin's Illness

At the time the new Constitution was being formulated, Lenin had been partially paralyzed by his first stroke. His illness generally prevented him from exercising a more vigorous influence on the shape of the charter. For instance, the merger of the three Transcaucasian republics into one was carried out against his wishes, at Stalin's insistence and with Trotsky neglecting to support Lenin. Lenin's illness had far-reaching consequences for the balance of forces within the ruling Party. He was Chairman of the Council of People's Commissars, or in Western terms, the Prime Minister. His authority as the founding father of the Party and the State was enormous. Hitherto, thanks to his exceptional authority and his clever manipulatory tricks, Lenin exercised an overwhelming influence over Party affairs. With his influence gradually fading away from both government and partisan work, a vital linchpin of the still fluid Soviet system was removed. To fill the gap, the ailing Lenin wanted a resolute and resourceful deputy to carry out his functions as chief executive. Twice, in May and December of 1922, he offered the post of Vice-Chairman of the Council of People's Commissars to Trotsky. Trotsky twice refused the offer, pleading ill health.

During Lenin's illness, Trotsky, then Commissar for War and a member of the Politburo, or the powerful committee making most vital policy decisions, was (see below) frequently indisposed and absent from Moscow. The situation created a power vacuum and suggested new arrangements. One of them was to create a post that would effectively coordinate the working of the main Party bodies, like the Political and Organizational Bureaus (colloquially known as the Politubro and Orgburo) as well as the Party Control Commissions, with the fast multiplying State institutions. The name given to the new post established for that purpose was Secretary General of the Central Committee. The post seemed innocuous and was meant to be of a purely bureaucratic nature. The title suggested that the main function of the Secretary General would be to keep the Party records and act as the coordinator of various Party bodies in order to serve better what the by-laws termed the most important body of the Party structure: its Central Committee.

In May 1922, after Lenin's first stroke, Stalin was entrusted with this job. The office did not originally convey any political power or much prestige and was bound to involve a lot of hard, thankless work. Nobody wanted the job except Stalin, who was reputed to be a tireless Party wheel horse. Whether he perceived all the potentialities of the new position is not clear. Whatever his original motives, he did accept the job, and by methodical, patient work began to use it cunningly for his purposes. Since the Secretariat administered the personnel files, Stalin utilized this function to gain the vital power of appointment, and hence of patronage. Under the meticulous management of a man with an immense capacity for work and a lot of patience, the office of Secretary General became a formidable instrument, a reliable base for the expansion of Stalin's personal power. Systematically, he pursued his grassroots work. Imperceptibly, step by step, he began to gather around him his Civil War cronies and all those he could make subservient. At the same time, he was cultivating all who could be useful to him, while ruthlessly undercutting his potential opponents.

Stalin's Ascendance

The bedridden Lenin had noticed the growing power and arrogance of Stalin. He clearly anticipated the struggle for power that was likely to take place after his death, in view of the lack of rules to regulate this unprecedented situation. To provide some guidance for his comrades in their choice of his successor, Lenin wrote a memorandum, dated December 23, 1922, expressing his views about the Party's leading personalities and their possible future roles. Trotsky and Stalin were the two ablest members of the Central Committee, according to Lenin. Despite his high opinion of Stalin's native ability, he warned his Party comrade, "Comrade Stalin, having become Secretary General, has concentrated enormous power in his hands; I am not sure that he always knows how to use that power with sufficient caution." On January 9, 1923, Lenin added a postscript in which he issued another warning: "Stalin is too rude, and this fault, entirely supportable in relations among us

Communists, becomes insupportable in the office of General Secretary." Lenin therefore proposed to find a way to remove Stalin from his position.

Lenin's memorandum, often called his testament, came too late to have a decisive influence on the succession contest. Other factors had intervened. In October 1922, Lenin had recovered sufficiently to resume his active leadership for three months or so. Then, on December 16, came the third and final stroke, which resulted in his total loss of speech and incapacitated him permanently. From then on Lenin was able to communicate only by means of written messages. It was during his brief return to work that his relations with Stalin worsened. The split was triggered by Stalin's rudeness as well as his ruthless way of handling the nationality problem, especially the purge of Communist leadership in his native Georgia. Alarmed by Stalin's high-handed policies, Lenin wrote his "Letter on the National Question" on December 30–31, 1922, in which he criticized Stalin's "Great-Russian chauvinism," as expressed in his merging of the three newly annexed republics—Georgia, Armenia, and Azerbaijan—into a single Transcaucasian Republic. In addition, a few days before his third stroke, Lenin had learned about Stalin's rudeness to Nadyezhda Krupskaya, Lenin's wife since 1898. He wrote a blunt letter threatening to break off all personal relations with Stalin unless he apologized to his wife.

By that time, however, Stalin, supported by two other Politburo members, Zinoviev and Kameniev, felt strong enough to prevent the publication of Lenin's Testament, or even its wider circulation in Party circles outside the top echelons. Zinoviev and Kameniev, both old Bolsheviks and close coworkers of Lenin, were at the head of the Party organization in Leningrad and Moscow, respectively. Both of them, at that time, were more afraid of the brilliant and versatile Trotsky as a potential competitor for Lenin's mantle than of Stalin.

Acting with a mixture of cunning and caution, Stalin continued to work shrewdly behind the scenes by making himself useful to key Party members, thus improving his position within the only body that really mattered. His spade work produced its results at the Twelfth Party Congress, which deliberated from April 17 to 25, 1923. This was the first Congress from which Lenin was absent. Many delegates knew about Stalin's disagreements with the ailing leader over the nationality issue and personal matters. Yet the Congress was so well prepared and manipulated by Stalin that nobody dared to raise either issue. Trotsky, the only man who could have done so, refrained from exploiting these opportunities. Despite his earlier promises to Lenin, he did not take up the problem of Georgia, an issue on which Stalin was rather vulnerable.

Trotsky's disinclination to take advantage of the unique opportunity to present the two issues, the nationality problem and that of succession to a Party Congress not yet completely dominated by Stalin, is an enigma. Later, Trotsky explained that such a step would have been embarrassing to him and beneath his dignity, but such an interpretation carries little conviction. His behavior suggests either lack of judgment or a lapse of will power, or perhaps both. Thus, the course of the succession struggle was largely predetermined before Lenin's death by Trotsky's refusal to challenge Stalin with the authority of the still-living Lenin and with Trotsky's supporters still in control of many vital posts. He himself was then still a member of the powerful Politburo and Commissar for War, thus controlling most of the formidable defense establishment.

Lenin's Death

Trotsky's failure to act at the Twelfth Congress was aggravated by his absence from Moscow during the last days before Lenin's death, recovering from another illness. Lenin died on January 21, 1924. Everyone expected Trotsky to rush back to the capital to attend the funeral. He did not do that, however, for reasons he later tried to explain in various ways; one of them was Stalin's telegram giving him a false, early funeral date and urging him not to interrupt his sick leave. Whatever the real reason, Trotsky was not in Moscow when Lenin's body was buried. The absence of the second most prestigious Bolshevik provided Stalin with an ideal opportunity to present himself as the closest and most loyal lieutenant of the dead leader.

Stalin not only eagerly pontificated over the funeral ceremonies and exploited the situation to the hilt, but he immediately followed it up with a series of moves to consolidate his new place in the Soviet hierarchy. At the meeting of the All-Union Congress of Soviets that was held on January 26 to commemorate Lenin, Stalin pledged to the Party to carry out the deceased leader's presumed will. Each segment of his long, litany-like oration was followed by the rhetorical refrain: "We swear to thee, Comrade Lenin, that we will fulfill with honor thy command!" Stalin's funeral oration, often referred to as the "Lenin oath," tried to sum up, in the form of succinct slogans, the essence of the dead leader's teaching, and further enhanced Stalin's luminous image as his loyal lieutenant.

Immediately after Lenin's death, an officially sponsored cult of his personality was launched. "The cradle of the Revolution," Petrograd, was renamed Leningrad. On the order of a Politburo already largely manipulated by Stalin, the dead leader's corpse was embalmed, like that of an Egyptian pharaoh and placed in an impressive red granite mausoleum built next to the Kremlin in Red Square. Promptly an almost uninterrupted series of pilgrimages was sponsored by the Party to pay homage to the mummy of the founder of the Soviet State and its ruling Party. Soon this became a secular ritual, skillfully exploited for propagandistic purposes of the Communist regime.

After the funeral, the Politburo decided to keep Stalin in his post of Secretary General and not to publish Lenin's "Testament." Trotsky could have insisted on disclosure, but again he refrained. This gave his rival time to consolidate his hold on the increasingly crucial post.

Lenin in Perspective

Lenin's death brought to a close the initial, formative period of the Soviet State, the years 1917–1924. Lenin was the founder, organizer, unquestioned leader, and theoretician of both the Bolshevik Party and the world Communist movement. With the seizure of power by the Bolsheviks, he became the top executive of the Soviet Republic, whose authority, although frequently challenged, was never seriously undermined. His position as founder of the Party, chief architect of its victory in 1917, and father of the Soviet Republic, as well as its savior in times of crisis, gave him a unique place in Soviet history. At least twice his decisions—one to sign the peace treaty with Germany in 1917, and the other to abandon War Communism in 1921, rescued the Soviet regime from catastrophe. Formally, Lenin was merely Chairman of the Council of People's Commissars and one member of the Politburo. Yet his power had a strong individual imprint and was virtually that of a full-scale dictator.

Lenin's achievements were astonishing. An obscure provincial lawyer, he built a small group of revolutionaries into an effective, hierarchical political organization. Out of the twenty or so original members of the Bolshevik Party, he forged an instrument that in fourteen years captured control of the largest country of the world. Despite its utopian goals, cruel methods, and numerous near-catastrophic failures at home, the movement he created soon spread over the entire globe. In its various modified forms, the ideology he developed deeply affected over one-third of the earth for some three generations.

Lenin's personality was very complex. Despite his preoccupation with action he wrote prolifically and produced numerous books as well as innumerable articles and speeches. Yet, his caliber as a philosopher and theoretical political writer remains highly controversial. The most important are his seminal pragmatic works, such as *What Is to Be Done?* which laid down the theoretical

A line of people waiting to visit Lenin's Mausoleum in the Red Square in Moscow, 1924; Saint Basil's Church is in the background.

foundation of the Bolshevik Party. His *Development of Capitalism in Russia* (1899) is a work of factual socioeconomic research. *Imperialism, the Highest Stage of Capitalism* (1916) has been an influential book because of its impact not only on Soviet and Chinese policy but also on the entire revolutionary movement of the Third World.

Despite numerous attempts at theory, Lenin was primarily a practical politician, endowed with an impressive flexibility pos-

sessed by few Soviet leaders. These qualities were revealed many times during his career. The first was when he deemphasized the orthodox Marxist idea that the urban proletariat should be the main carrier of the revolution in predominantly rural Russia, and advocated a boldly revisionist "alliance of workers and peasants." The second was when he took over the agrarian and nationality programs of the Social Revolutionary Party; third, when he accepted the harsh Brest-

Litovsk peace as a precondition of the survival of Soviet dictatorship in Russia; and fourth, when he launched the New Economic Policy. In each case his decision largely determined the fate of the Bolshevik Party and the Soviet State.

As there are few purely theoretical considerations in Lenin's writings, so is there little Marxist orthodoxy in his practice.[2] While constantly paying lip service to the Marxist theory, Lenin, a master manufacturer of pithy slogans, reversed most basic assumptions of the Prophet. Whereas Marx stressed the paramount importance of "objective" socioeconomic conditions, the value of spontaneity, and the crucial role of the masses, Lenin emphasized the organized, willful effort of a small revolutionary group consciously shaping events to fit their authoritarian goals. While Marx hardly ever dealt with organizational matters and tended to dwell in the realm of lofty speculations, Lenin stressed the role of grabbing power. He was preoccupied with military matters; he probably studied as much the works of the German General Karl Clausewitz on strategy, as Karl Marx's *Capital*. While for Clausewitz war was a continuation of politics by other means, Lenin reversed this dictum and considered politics as continuation of war under another guise. He assigned crucial importance to military factors in gaining and keeping power. In Lenin's teachings, the hierarchically structured elitist party was to play the decisive role; it was to overcome the impracticality of the intellectuals, the amorphous, anarchic spontaneity of the masses, and, as "the vanguard of the proletariat," it was to lead the Communist Party to victory. It was the Party that was to be the repository of dictatorial power in the new type of state. The concept of a tightly woven, elitist, Party organized in a military fashion represents the essence of what is called *Leninism*. Leninism

was clearly an anticipation of Stalinism. Under Lenin's dictatorial rule the tentacles of the secret police penetrated most fields of human activity and the first Soviet concentration camps were organized on his personal order.

Another of Lenin's contributions to the Bolshevik rule was another revisionist concept—the adaptation of Marxist doctrine to conditions of a multinational, backward, agrarian country. In Russia this meant acceptance of the peasantry and the ethnic minorities as temporary tactical partners in the struggle against Tsarism. Recognizing the power of the peasantry, Lenin agreed to the highly non-Marxist distribution of land, and in 1922 legalized it by promulgating the Land Code. Whether this compromise was meant to be a temporary or a lasting is a matter of speculation that can not be resolved.

The third revision of Marxism was Lenin's rejection of a two-stage revolution in a developing country. He was impatient with the deterministic approach to history and was often eager to use force to speed up its tempo. He advocated, therefore, an immediate seizure of power by the proletariat—irrespective of its political maturity—by means of an armed insurrection. His saying, "Let's grab political power and then we shall see . . ." is very characteristic. Still, another revision of Marxist doctrine was Lenin's ingenious and bold nationality policy. By his military strategy, combined with his cunning and flexible ethnic strategy, Lenin rescued the bulk of the old Tsarist empire from disintegration and launched its heir, the Soviet Union.

Suggested Reading

ALLWORTH, EDWARD A., *The Modern Uzbeks*. Stanford, CA: Hoover Institution Press, 1990.

DEUTSCHER, ISAAC, *The Prophet Unarmed: Trotsky, 1921–1929*. New York: Oxford University Press, 1959.

DMYTRYSHYN, BASIL, *Moscow and Ukraine, 1918–1953: A Study of Russian Bolshevik Nationality Policy*. New York: Bookman Associates, 1956.

---

[2]One of Lenin's faithful followers, the Soviet historian Pokrovsky, said, "You will not find in Lenin a single purely theoretical work; each has a propaganda aspect." *Molodaia Gvardiia (The Young Guard)*, February–March 1924, p. 248. Both Mussolini and Hitler admired Soviet propaganda techniques and often imitated them.

ELWOOD, R.C., *Inessa Armand: Revolutionary and Feminist.* Ottawa: Carleton University Press, 1992.

FAINSOD, MERLE, *How Russia is Ruled*, rev. ed. Cambridge, MA: Harvard University Press, 1963.

FISHER, ALLAN W., *The Crimean Tatars.* Stanford, CA: Hoover Institution Press, 1978.

KOLARZ, WALTER, *Russia and Her Colonies.* New York: Praeger, 1954.

KUCHEROV, SAMUEL, *The Organs of the Soviet Administration of Justice: Their History and Operation.* Leiden: Brill, 1970.

LENIN, V.I., *Selected Works.* Moscow: Progress Publishers, 1970, 3 vols.

LEVIN, NORA, *The Jews of the Soviet Union.* New York: New York University Press, 1988.

MEYER, ALFRED, *Leninism.* Cambridge, MA: Harvard University Press, 1957.

MOTYL, ALEXANDER J., *Sovietology, Rationality, Nationality: Coming to Grips with Nationalism in the USSR.* New York: Columbia University Press, 1990.

OLCOTT, MARTHA BRILL, *The Kazakhs.* Stanford, CA: The Hoover Institution Press, 1984.

PAGE, S. W., *Lenin and World Revolution.* New York: New York University Press, 1959.

PIPES, RICHARD, *The Formation of the Soviet Union: Communism and Nationalism, 1917–1923.* Cambridge, MA: Harvard University Press, 1954.

PIPES, RICHARD, (ED.), *The Unknown Lenin: From the Secret Archive.* New Haven: Yale, 1996.

RORLICH, AZADEAYSE, *The Volga Tatars.* Stanford, CA: Hoover Institution Press, 1986.

SCHAPIRO, LEONARD, AND PETER REDDAWAY (EDS.), *Lenin: The Man, the Theorist, the Leader—A Reappraisal.* Boulder, CO: Praeger, 1987.

SCHWARTZ, SOLOMON M., *The Jews in the Soviet Union.* Syracuse, NY: Syracuse University Press, 1956.

SOCHOR, ZENOVIA A., *Revolution and Culture: The Bogdanov-Lenin Controversy.* Ithaca, NY: Cornell University Press, 1988.

SULLIVAN, ROBERT S., *Soviet Politics and the Ukraine, 1917–1957.* New York: Columbia University Press, 1962.

TUMARKIN, NINA, *Lenin Lives! The Lenin Cult in Soviet Russia.* Cambridge, MA: Harvard University Press, 1983.

ULAM, ADAM, *The Bolsheviks.* New York: Macmillan, 1965.

VAKAR, NICHOLAS, *Belorussia.* Cambridge, MA: Harvard University Press, 1956.

VOLKOGONOV, DMITRI, *Lenin: A New Biography.* New York: Free Press, 1994.

Chapter 12

The Struggle for Lenin's Mantle: The Stalin-Trotsky Controversy

The Bolshevik Party, despite Lenin's stress on discipline and unity, initially was far from being homogeneous. Actually, in-group fighting was constant. The first postrevlutionary faction, formed in 1918 by Bukharin and known as the "Left Communist Opposition," criticized Lenin for his readiness to sign the Brest-Litovsk treaty. In 1920, a number of prominent Communists, mostly trade union leaders, headed by A. G. Shlyapnikov, Commissar for Labor, and Alexandra Kollontai, Commissar for Social Security, formed the so-called "Workers' Opposition." This group criticized the bureaucratic control of industry and favored a syndicatist solution; they urged the establishment of an All-Russian Congress of Producers to run the economy. The Tenth Party Congress of March 1921 condemned all "factionalism" as incompatible with the principles of democratic centralism. During the years 1919–1922, a group of upper-level Party functionaries called "democratic centralists" favored less censorship and a freer intra-Party regime by urging that democratic centralism be more democratic and less centralist. They too were defeated by Lenin.

As Lenin's illness progressed, factional tendencies again surfaced. During the last two years of his life, an intense feud smoldered between the two personalities designated by the ailing leader as the most able in the Party leadership—Trotsky and Stalin. Since the feud was as much a conflict of ideas and methods of operations as a clash of personalities, a brief examination of the rivals' backgrounds is in order.

Trotsky's Credentials

Leon Trotsky was born Lev Davidovich Bronstein in 1879. He came from the Kherson region of the Ukraine, from a family of prosperous Jewish farmers. His father owned more than 250 acres and was renting some 500 while routinely employing peasant farmers. This small estate had plenty of various livestock and a steam-operated mill. His father was a hard-working man and tended to be a stern disciplinarian toward his children. As Leon was to note later of his early years: "We were not deprived, except of life's generosity and tenderness." He became a revolutionary at the age of nineteen; he was soon arrested and exiled to Siberia, but escaped abroad. It was at that time that Bronstein assumed the name of Trotsky. In 1902 in London he met Lenin. Impressed with the vivacity of his mind as well as his enthusiasm, Lenin invited Trotsky to collaborate on the editorial board of *Iskra*, to which he contributed articles signed with the pseudonym *Pero* (Pen). Despite this early and fairly close association with Lenin, Trotsky was to be critical of him for a long time. He oscillated between the Bolsheviks and the Mensheviks for a decade and a half. In 1904 he went so far as to denounce bitterly Lenin's ruthless authoritarian tendencies. one day, argued Trotsky, these tendencies would lead to a state of affairs in which "the organization of the party takes the place of the party itself; the Central Committee takes the place of the organization; and finally the dictator takes the place of the Central Committee."

Trotsky first became prominent during the revolution of 1905 as Vice-Chairman and then Chairman of the St. Petersburg Soviet. Arrested and exiled once more to Siberia, he again escaped abroad and lived mostly in Austria, France, and finally the United States. His revolutionary activities did not interfere with his earning a living as a journalist, working for the bourgeois Ukrainian newspaper *Kieyvskaia Mysl*; in October 1912, Trotsky was its Vienna correspondent reporting on the first Balkan War. In his dispatches he vividly described the atrocities committed by the Serb soldiers on the Albanian population. After the fall of Tsarism, Trotsky returned to Russia from the United States and only then, in the summer of 1917, formally joined the Bolshevik Party and was soon elected to its Central Committee. After Kornilov's attempted coup, in September 1917, the Bolsheviks won the majority of the Petrograd Soviet and Trotsky was once again elected its Chairman. In October 1917, he also became Chairman of the military Revolutionary Committee, which prepared the Bolshevik seizure of power in the capital. In the first Soviet Government, Trotsky was Commissar for Foreign Affairs. Opposed to the signing of the Brest-Litovsk peace treaty, he argued for "neither peace nor war," but in the end voted with Lenin. From 1918 until 1925, Trotsky was Commissar for War, chief organizer of the Red Army, and one of its leaders during the Civil War.

Trotsky's position was unique. He was a major leader of the Bolshevik Party, second in importance to Lenin. In addition, he was intellectually brilliant. He was a magnetic speaker, bursting with exuberant vitality and wit, as well as the prolific author of articles, pamphlets, and books. But these qualities were coupled with glaring weaknesses; he was vain, self-centered, and self-confident to the point of arrogance, which made him widely disliked and distrusted by many of his comrades. He loved theatrical gestures, tended to be haughty, hated routine work, and lacked consistency and singleness of purpose.

Stalin's Credentials

Trotsky's main rival, Joseph Stalin, born in 1879 as Josip Djugashvili in the village of Gori near Tiflis, was as complete a contrast to Trotsky as one could imagine. Stalin was the son of an obscure Georgian cobbler who was a drunkard and an adventurer and a pious, devoted mother. He was sent, at her insistence, to the Orthodox Theological Seminary in Tiflis. In 1898, he was expelled front the seminary for his revolutionary outlook and activity. In 1903, Djugashvili joined the Bolshevik faction of the RSDWP and later assumed the pseudonym Stalin, or "man of steel."

Until 1913, Stalin worked as an active follower, mainly in the revolutionary underground of Transcaucasia. In 1907 he organized several raids (or "expropriations") on banks to provide funds for the treasury of the Bolshevik Party After the Prague Conference of 1912, Stalin was coopted to the Party's Central Committee by Lenin and Zinoviev, both of whom desperately needed an energetic and systematic co-worker of non-Russian ethnic stock; Stalin fitted this description perfectly. In November 1912, he visited Lenin in Cracow and spent several months in Vienna. It was during this first trip that Stalin, with Bukharin's assistance, wrote his early theoretical work, *Marxism and the National Question*.

According to N. N. Sukhanov, author of *Notes on the Revolution* and its faithful chronicler, when Stalin returned from his Siberian exile to Petrograd in the spring of 1917, he was still merely "a gray blur, which glimmered dimly and left no trace."

From 1917 to 1923, Stalin was Commissar for Nationalities, and from 1919 to 1923, Commissar for State Control. The purpose of the second job was to guard the administrative apparatus against bureaucratization. The combination of these two posts gave Stalin a great deal of political and administrative experience. He became a close co-worker of Lenin's only after the crisis precipitated by the Brest-Litovsk Treaty; unlike Trotsky, Stalin firmly supported Lenin's stand, thus winning his confidence and gratitude. Both Trotsky and Stalin were members of the Politburo from its inception on the eve of the Bolshevik coup d'état.

During the Civil War Stalin, like many other leading Bolsheviks, was a high-ranking political commissar and in this capacity a subordinate of War Commissar Trotsky. In 1919 Stalin was attached to the Red Army group commanded by Voroshilov that successfully defended Tsaritsyn on the Volga (later renamed Stalingrad, and now called Volgograd). It was at that time that the first bitter disagreements arose between Stalin and Trotsky. During the Soviet-Polish campaign of 1920, Stalin was with Budënny's First Cavalry Army, again as Chief Political Commissar of the Western front. During those crucial August days, Stalin advised Budënny to march on Lvov (Lviv) and not on Warsaw, where Trotsky as Commissar for War had wanted to deal the decisive blow to the Poles. Stalin's responsibility for the catastrophe that befell the Red Army at the Battle of Warsaw became a touchy, controversial problem in Soviet politics and historiography.

Stalin versus Trotsky: A Study in Contrasts

It is hard to imagine two more contrasting personalities. Trotsky was well read and widely traveled, cosmopolitan, flamboyant, extroverted, exuberant, and brilliant. Stalin, on the other hand, seemed provincial, introverted, secretive, dull, and, to a superficial observer, might have appeared devoid of outstanding abilities. Trotsky was a scintillating writer, a dramatic as well as a witty orator; Stalin's literary and speaking performances were rather crude and pedestrian. His oratory was down to earth and tended to stress immediate, concrete goals. His typical argument was that with firm establishment of Bolshevik power in Russia "the Socialist system will follow the capitalist, as day follows the night." Trotsky, on the other hand, was inclined to paint an apocalyptic vision, difficult to grasp by ordinary people. For instance, speaking in October 1918 to a large crowd of workers he fulminated: "We, Comrades, love the sun which illuminates us, but if the rich and the oppressors wanted to monopolize the sun, we would say, let the sun go out and let darkness reign in eternal gloom!"

Trotsky's physique was striking: he had a broad chest, high forehead, black fiery eyes, and a mane of black hair. Stalin looked rather insignificant: small with a pock-marked face, a crooked arm, black teeth, yellow eyes, and a half-shy, half-sinister smile under a cockroach mustache. He had a heavy Georgian accent and, unlike Trotsky spoke no foreign language. Trotsky was a mercurial and neurotic intellectual, an inspirational man who tended to react spontaneously, on the spur of the moment, and who experienced frequent emotional ups and downs. Stalin, on the other hand, was steady, systematic, capable of cool judgment, patient planning, and meticulous execution.

By 1922–1923, these two men, the "pen" and the "man of steel," had emerged as the main rivals for the leadership of Soviet Russia. Each had strong and weak points in his respective claim to be Lenin's heir. Trotsky, despite his role during the Revolution and the Civil War, was a latecomer to the Bolshevik Party. Prior to July 1917 he had repeatedly quarreled with Lenin and attacked him on various issues, including that of his arbitrary leadership. Trotsky split with Lenin at the time of the Brest-Litovsk negotiations. He failed to heed Lenin's advice to raise the Georgian question and thus attack Stalin's "Great Russian" chauvinism at the Twelfth Party Congress. Finally, Trotsky twice refused to be Lenin's deputy as Chairman of the Council of People's Commissars. Stalin, on the other hand, while he had never openly embroiled himself in a controversy with Lenin until his illness, was strongly disavowed in Lenin's Testament.

"Troika" versus Trotsky

During the crucial years of 1922–24, Trotsky, who initially appeared to be Lenin's natural successor, was, as has been noted, often ill and absent from Moscow. Supremely self-centered, self-confident, and arrogant, he had few intimate friends. Moreover, after the end of the Civil War, he tended to neglect public relations. On the other hand, Stalin devoted much effort to cultivating political allies and meticulously manipulating the party machine. While his rival was a loner, Stalin worked hand-in-hand with two leading Politburo members, Grigori Zinoviev and Lev Kameniev. This automatically gave him a strong position in the seven-member top policy-making body, for only five members regularly attended the meetings: Lenin was ill and Trotsky often absent.

Zinoviev, a man of middle-class Jewish origin, was Chairman of the Communist International, and as such enjoyed considerable prestige in world revolutionary circles. As head of the Petrograd Soviet, he also had an important power base at home. He was an adroit journalist and a fiery speaker of a rather demagogic brand who lacked both the capacity for systematic work and perse-

verance in his undertakings. Zinoviev's bosom friend, L. V. Kameniev, had a similar background. Under Lenin, Kameniev was Deputy Chairman of the Council of People's Commissars and Chairman of the Moscow Soviet. He excelled in routine administration work, which was Zinoviev's weak point, but he had little talent for writing and speaking. In a way, Zinoviev and Kameniev complemented each other and they soon became the Castor and Pollux of Soviet politics. Both of them, however, lacked Trotsky's rich intellectual endowment. The Troika members—Stalin, Zinoviev, and Kameniev—had been in Lenin's faction since 1902, while Trotsky was a relative newcomer. All three could boast of considerable achievements during the preceding heroic period, yet personally and in their accomplishments, all were overshadowed by Trotsky. It seems likely that it was feelings of inferiority that made the Troika form a tactical alliance against the man they feared and of whom they were jealous; they accused him of harboring "Bonapartist" ambitions. All four contenders probably dreamed of being Lenin's successor, yet none of them would ever publicly admit to harboring such an ambition.

Grigori Y. Zinoviev, a member of the Troika and Chairman of the Executive Committee of the Comintern, 1921–1926.

The Permanent Revolution

The ideological differences between Trotsky and Stalin can be epitomized in two battle cries: "permanent revolution" versus "socialism in one country." The term *permanent revolution* was first used casually by Marx and Engels in their *Communist Manifesto* to describe revolutionary ferment spreading from one country to another. This concept was first elaborated upon by a leftist German Social Democrat, Alexander Helphand, while writing (under the pseudonym of Parvus) an introduction to Trotsky's pamphlet on the domestic situation in Russia at the beginning of 1905. According to Parvus, the Russian proletariat was to make a revolution which, while it may initially have been bourgeois, was not to stop there but would continue "in permanence" until it changed into a world proletarian revolution.

Inspired by Parvus, Trotsky expanded upon his ideas in a collection of essays entitled *Our Revolution*, published in 1905, and in a book, *Results and Prospects*, published in 1906. At that time most Russian Socialists, following Marxist doctrine, were convinced that the forthcoming upheaval in their backward country be confined for a considerable time to its bourgeois stage of development. Trotsky, on the other hand, considered this to be a too literal and formal interpretation of Marxism. As a result of his observation of the events of 1904–1905, Trotsky, came to the conclusion that the Russian bourgeoisie was too weak to keep political power for any appreciable period of time.

The reason Russia was predestined to become the pioneer of Socialism-Communism was to be found in the peculiarities of Russian history: in the endemic indolence of its middle class, its conservatism, timidity, and its dependence on the all-powerful state and upon foreign capital. In view of the lethargic passivity of the Russian bourgeoisie and its political proponents, the Liberals, the tough, young dynamic Russian proletariat was the only force capable of seizing and holding power. Yet because Russia was still an underdeveloped peasant society with a proletariat that amounted to three million people out of a population of 150 million, a workers' government could not survive for long; it would soon be overthrown by a domestic counterrevolution, toppled by foreign intervention, or both. Consequently, the proletarian revolution in Russia could be saved from failure only by extending it to other, more advanced, industrialized countries. Trotsky defined his "permanent revolution" as a process "of which every next stage is anchored in the preceding one and which can end only with the total liquidation of the class society." In this way, the revolutionary spark in Russia would eventually initiate a worldwide conflagration. To succeed, the national Russian revolution must eventually become a world revolution. Russia's primitive economy, argued Trotsky, was not ripe for socialism, but that of Western Europe was. That is why the Bolsheviks, immediately after the seizure of power in their native country, should spread their gospel to the West, especially to Germany. This would assure Russia of adequate resources for the continuing development of socialism in its own country.

Trotsky's theory appeared to be an accurate forecast of events in the fateful years 1917–1919, as revolutionary upheavals occurred not only in Russia, but also in Germany and Hungary. But when in mid-August 1920 the Red Army's westward offensive was smashed at the gates of Warsaw, the chain was broken. For Trotsky, however, the recovery of Western capitalism was merely a temporary phenomenon, a "rotten stabilization." Despite mounting evidence to the contrary, despite the proclamation of the NEP, he continued to preach his unrealistic concept with characteristic zeal and brilliance, arguing that his concept was in accordance with Lenin's teaching and practice. Yet it was increasingly obvious that Trotsky's theory was utopian and rather-alien to most of the party leadership, let alone the masses of the Soviet people exhausted by seven years of war, exertion, and starvation, and eager for return to normalcy.

Socialism in One Country

In his determination to succeed Lenin, Stalin welcomed an opportunity to argue in public about fundamental issues affecting Soviet domestic and foreign policies. As has already been mentioned, after Lenin's death each contender for power took special care to establish his credentials as a "good Leninist" and to stress his special devotion to the deceased founder of the Bolshevik Party and the Soviet State. Here was an opportunity for Stalin to prove that he was a theoretician comparable to Trotsky, and that he would perpetuate Lenin's teachings. A careful search of Lenin's papers resulted in the unearthing of one of his essays of 1915 vintage in which Lenin had anticipated that, in view of the unequal development of capitalism, the proletarian revolution might initially break out in only one country—which one Lenin did not specify—and might not immediately assume an international character. Stalin seized upon this idea of Lenin's and elevated it into a fundamental stance, a beacon for Soviet Russia to follow in the immediate future.

Stalin insisted that it was not only possible but even necessary to construct and consolidate the already existing socialist system in the USSR before starting a series of similar upheavals in the West. To try spreading the proletarian revolution to other countries would be a gamble, because it would invite new foreign intervention and thus jeopardize the very existence of the infant Soviet State. Stalin concluded his argument by saying that the only sensible goal the Bolsheviks could pursue was:

to consolidate the dictatorship of the proletariat in one country, using it as a base for the overthrow of imperialism in all countries.

In March 1925, the Fourteenth Party Conference proclaimed Stalin's theory the official Party line. By this means he had won another round in the struggle for supreme authority, and had not only further identified himself with Lenin, but also established himself as a Party theoretician to be reckoned with. The decision of the Fourteenth Conference was an important turning point in the evolution of Soviet Communism from its originally lofty yet rather utopian international goals, toward national Communist orientation.

Socialism in One Country versus the Permanent Revolution

In opposing Trotsky's theory of permanent revolution, Stalin grasped the mood of the Party leaders more perceptively than his opponent. Many members who were basically sympathetic to Trotsky's stand on the continuation of the heroic period of Bolshevism were asking themselves whether the young Soviet State, ruined, starved, and exhausted, would be courting disaster in undertaking such an adventurous course. The policy of permanent revolution was, moreover, contrary to the NEP's attempts to rehabilitate the country, attract foreign investments, expand trade with the outside world, and obtain diplomatic recognition for the Soviet Union. To these arguments, based on objective considerations, one should add those rooted in psychology. To whom could such an intellectually brilliant, yet rather subtle and highly speculative theory appeal? Certainly neither to the Soviet workers and peasants, nor to the members of the bureaucracy, many of whom were of a parochial background. Just emerging from a cruel seven-year period of trial and tribulation, all were preoccupied with consolidating their gains: the eight-hour working day, the land, or in the case of the Soviet establishment, a newly acquired position of power and prestige. A complex theory of this type could appeal only to internationally minded intellectuals, a small group in a fast-expanding Party composed largely of workers. peasants, and their children. To them Stalin's ideas appeared more in accordance with their immediate interests to consolidate their newly acquired hold on Soviet Russia.

Moreover, by placing Russia's destiny in the hands of foreigners, even if they were

Communists, Trotsky's stand implied that the Russian people were dependent on the outside world, incapable of "going it alone." By saying that socialism could not be built in Russia without outside aid, Trotsky took a psychologically disadvantageous stand. This allowed his rival to represent him as an adventurer, prepared to squander Russia's resources for the sake of spreading Communism abroad while neglecting the country's rehabilitation, rather than successfully proceeding as a result of the NEP. Stalin, asserting that socialism could be built even in one-sixth of the earth isolated from the outside world, assumed a psychologically advantageous position. By 1924, even most of the Party zealots had grown weary of Communist adventurism, of waiting for the long-proclaimed world revolution. Stalin's theory of socialism in one country, therefore, was more attuned to their sentiments; it tended to restore their pride and confidence in their own achievement, the survival of which was not necessarily dependent on outside events, but only on their own strength. To Trotsky's argument that his rival lacked revolutionary zeal, Stalin would answer that Trotsky lacked faith in the future of the Russian Revolution by making its ultimate fate dependent on outside assistance.

The Bolshevik Revolution had been achieved in the name of abstract, universalistic principles or "proletarian internationalism." Yet very early on, the nationalistic undercurrent began to reassert itself. Stalin, although a Russified Georgian, sensed this trend better than any other Bolshevik leader and became its spokesman. By proposing "socialism in one country," he was urging his countrymen not to depend on the world proletarian revolution. Even if it should be delayed, he argued, Russia should be capable of developing its own brand of socialism—Communism. This preaching of self-reliance had a deep meaning for the Russians because it bolstered their latent yet powerful national ego.

The real differences between Stalin and Trotsky were actually small and could be reduced to timing, wording, and emphasis.

Consequently they could be reconciled—provided a modicum of mutual trust and good will existed. What made reconciliation impossible was not so much conceptual differences but rather temperamental incompatibility. Coveting the same prize, they despised each other. They were two stars belonging to different constellations. The two rivals could be compared to two lions who could not share the same den. One had to destroy the other.

Stalin's Power Base

Historians, often fascinated with dramatic, colorful events, have a tendency to imbue political duels between powerful personalities with a romantic aura. This has largely been the case in the feud between Stalin and Trotsky. Aside from the intellectually fascinating theoretical debates, apart from the clash of two irreconcilable personalities, there was often sordid and brutal jockeying for power and behind-the-scene maneuvering and intrigue. While Trotsky believed in the power of the word, either spoken or written, Stalin relied primarily on tangible levers of power: the systematic, day-to-day control of the Party apparatus. Much earlier than his rival he realized that this was the main locus of power, that it was the Party that ultimately controlled the State bureaucracy, the armed forces, and last but not least, the secret police. Beginning in the spring of 1922, when he became Secretary General, Stalin worked very hard to undermine Trotsky's position in the two places where the latter had power: first in the Politburo, and then in the Commissariat for Military and Naval Affairs.

In the Politburo of seven members, as we have seen, this undermining was achieved by the formation of the triumvirate with Zinoviev and Kamenev. The two members who have not yet been accounted for here were Mikhail Rykov and Alexey Tomsky. They tended to be more sympathetic to the moderate line embodied in the NEP, and hence to the slogan "socialism in one country." Consequently, Trotsky was increasingly isolated in the chief policy-making body. Had Trotsky accepted the post of Vice-Chairman of the Council of People's Commissars (cabinet of ministers), twice offered to him by Lenin, he would have been, it is safe to say, Lenin's natural successor as chief executive of the Soviet Union. This would have strengthened his power and prestige and somewhat counterbalanced Stalin's growing influence. But Trotsky's preoccupation with theoretical writing and fear of a new administrative responsibility allowed Stalin to place Rykov, then Deputy Chairman of the Council of People's Commissars, as Lenin's successor in the crucial post. By this means Stalin made Rykov into his ally in the crucial Politburo, and further weakened and isolated Trotsky.[1]

By the winter of 1924, Stalin had further consolidated his already formidable position. No longer was Lenin there to watch him and criticize his arbitrariness, arrogance, and chauvinism. As Secretary General, Stalin increasingly controlled Party machinery through patronage; and through Rykov, he also had a powerful influence over governmental affairs and the everyday functioning of the State apparatus, which the Party ultimately supervised anyway.

Lenin's Testament

One of the decisive moments in the struggle for power came in May 1924, when Lenin's Testament was read aloud to the Central Committee members. Stalin sat silent and embarrassed by Lenin's request that he be removed from his influential post as Secretary General; he actually tendered his resignation. But again Trotsky failed to act, thus missing his last chance to oust Stalin. It was

Zinoviev, who rescued his ally by making a statement that sounded as if he were representing the opinion of the entire Politburo. Referring both to the Testament and to Stalin's funeral oration, known by then as "the Lenin oath," Zinoviev said, "We are happy to say, that in one point Lenin's fears have proved baseless. I have in mind the point about our Secretary General. You all have witnessed our harmonious cooperation in the last few months. . . ." The Central Committee decided not to publish the Testament and to keep Stalin in his post.[2]

Soon after Lenin's death, on Stalin's initiative, the Politburo ordered to launch a recruiting drive. It resulted in the admission of over 200,000 new members; the Party expanded by about one-third. Outwardly, the campaign was conducted to bolster the working class element in the Party ranks. Actually, the Secretariat that controlled the recruitment made sure that only Stalin's supporters were admitted. Consequently, his control of the Party increased dramatically.

Gradually it dawned on his two main allies, Zinoviev and Kameniev, that Stalin was making constant progress and that they were being used by him as pawns in his game. Just when the two were starting to reconsider the value of their association with the increasingly omnipotent and arrogant Secretary General and beginning to grope toward a rapprochement with their alleged enemy, Trotsky committed another crucial mistake. In the autumn of 1924, he published a book entitled *The Lessons of October*. With his usual biting brilliance he attacked Zinoviev and Kameniev as the most reluctant supporters of Lenin's plan of armed insurrection and hence as "defeatists." Stalin grasped the opportunity and came out in support of his allies. He spoke of Trotsky's record both before and after 1917, and especially of his disagreements with Lenin. Thus, instead of winning Zinoviev and Kameniev over to his side and splitting Stalin's majority in the Politburo, Trotsky pushed his potential allies

---

[1] Kameniev, who had presided over the Council during Lenin's illness, was denied the job, at Stalin's suggestion, because of his Jewish origin. As Stalin put it, early revealing his anti-Semitic bias, "We must consider the peasant character of Russia." Rykov was a Russian with a strong peasant background.

[2] The Testament was not published in the Soviet Union until 1956.

back into the arms of his mortal enemy. To take revenge on the man who had tried to denigrate them, both Zinoviev and Kameniev lent their support to a renewed anti-Trotsky drive aimed at discrediting him for having conspired to corrupt the Leninist purity of the party doctrine with the "petty-bourgeois," "Menshevik" doctrine of permanent revolution, which was again condemned as "dynamite under the foundation of the Party," and a threat to its "general line" as embodied in the NEP.

At the peak of the campaign directed against him in September 1925, Trotsky committed another tactical mistake. He tried to conciliate Stalin by, repudiating Lenin's Testament as "evil fantasy." Thus, he lost an excellent opportunity to restore his authority and reassert himself.

Despite, or perhaps because of, this gesture, Stalin pressed his advantage to its logical end. All this time Trotsky, isolated in the Politburo, still controlled an important power base, the Commissariat for Military and Naval Affairs; as such, he was also Chairman of the Revolutionary, Military Council. Trotsky's absenteeism and his neglect of routine work greatly facilitated Stalin's task. In January 1925, on Stalin's initiative, Mikhail Frunze, victor over Kolchak and Wrangel and Chief of Staff of the Red Army, replaced Trotsky in these crucial posts. However, the ambitious and independent Frunze proved less subservient to his promoter than had been expected. He died in October of that same year under mysterious circumstances as a result of a mishandled and essentially unnecessary stomach operation in which an excessive amount of chloroform had been used. The convenient vacancy was filled again, at the insistence of the Secretary General, by Stalin's Civil War companion, Klement Voroshilov. Through the political administration of the Army and the Navy, he made sure that the military were loyal to the Party. Now Stalin could sleep more comfortably, for the Soviet armed forces were under the watchful eye of his crony with no Bonapartist ambitions.

Stalin's power was, by now, concentrated in two executive bodies: the Secretariat and the Politburo. As General Secretary, he could steer the working of the entire Party apparatus. By manipulating the majority of the Politburo he could pass almost any measure he wanted. Through Rykov he influenced the everyday running of the bureaucratic machine of the State. Moreover, the Chief of the Secret Police, Dzerzhinsky, was his friend; so was Voroshilov, the Commissar for Army and Navy. Through Tomsky, he could manipulate the trade unions as well. Thus the decision-making, administrative, and enforcement organs were all ultimately controlled by Stalin.

From the close of 1925, Stalin's struggle against Trotsky proceeded from one success to another. His rival was not only deprived of his power base, but increasingly isolated from his supporters by Stalin's control of all official mass media. Trotsky, a fierce and resourceful fighter, could do little against a systematic campaign of vilification openly waged against him: his pronouncements were ignored by the press; his was a voice crying in the wilderness.

The NEP's Future

One of the important issues in the struggle for power was the domestic program. The main question was, should the NEP, which favored the peasants, be continued, or should it be replaced by a more vigorous industrialization drive? Here Stalin supported by Zinoviev, Kameniev, Rykov, and Bukharin defended the NEP as the only way of preserving the Leninist alliance of workers and peasants. Trotsky, on the other hand, argued for a more energetic collectivization drive to alter the overwhelmingly individual structure of Soviet agriculture, allegedly dominated by the prosperous kulaks. He criticized his opponents as being "pro-kulak and pro-Nepman," giving too much support not only to the peasants but also to light industry, while he believed that a vigorous modernization drive should be based on the quick expansion of heavy industry. But by now Trotksy and the gradually shrinking group of his supporters were denounced as "deviationists" or "Left Opposition" to the only truly Leninist line of policy, that of consolidating the NEP.

The swiftness and smoothness of the Secretary General's victory over Trotsky surprised both Stalin's opponents and allies. Zinoviev and Kameniev now launched a belated attack on the policies they had supported in concert with Stalin. After Trotsky's dismissal, in the same crucial autumn of 1925, Zinoviev published a book entitled *Leninism* in which he condemned the NEP as a "continuous retreat from the original goals set by Marx and Lenin." He insisted on resumption of the socialist offensive, especially in the countryside, to destroy the growing power of the kulak. As Chairman of the powerful Leningrad Soviet, Zinoviev managed to mobilize his local Party organization against the NEP. His close friend Kameniev, the Moscow Party boss, was also uneasy about Stalin's growing power; he backed Zinoviev. Since their theoretical premises were close to Trotsky's, a gradual rapprochement took place among the three. Thus, after having refused an alliance with the powerful Commissar for the Army and Navy, the disgruntled Zinoviev and Kameniev belatedly sided with the now powerless Trotsky and fought a hopeless rearguard action as the leaders of the shrinking Left Opposition.

In December 1925, at the Fourteenth Party Congress, Zinoviev and Kameniev finally launched a frontal attack on Stalin. But since the Congress had been carefully packed by the Secretary General, the attack miscarried. At the Congress Bukharin, Rykov, and Tomsky gave public expression of their full acceptance of "socialism in one country," and consequently became Stalin's allies. The NEP, argued Bukharin, was a slow but sure way for socialist construction, while the policy of the Left Opposition represented adventurism, and threatened with ruin what had been already achieved, the nearly complete restoration of the economy. This implied continuation of the mixed economy, a distinct characteristic of the NEP. In this way the NEP, originally conceived as a temporary tactical retreat, would become a long-range policy. Stalin supported Bukharin, Rykov, and Tomsky, and the Fourteenth Congress ended in another victory for him.

Strengthened by his new triumph, Stalin proceeded to deal with the Left Opposition. The reaffirmation of his slogan "socialism in one country" meant not only continuation of the NEP at home, but also a cautious policy abroad. This in turn had far-reaching implications for the Comintern, still headed by the restless and rebellious Zinoviev. His aggressive policy as Chairman of the Executive Committee of the Comintern was now increasingly out of tune with the party's general pro-NEP line. In October 1926, Zinoviev was removed from his post and replaced by Stalin's new chief supporter and ideological spokesman, Bukharin. At the same time, Zinoviev and Trotsky lost their Politburo posts. The Politburo was reconstructed by the addition of three new members, Kalinin, Molotov, and Voroshilov, all of them devoted to the Secretary General body and soul.

Foreign Political Factors

The struggle for power was closely intertwined with foreign policy. The German fiasco of 1932, which finally shattered Soviet hopes for an early European revolution, gave additional support to Stalin's concept of building socialism in isolation with exclusively native resources. To the failure in Germany were soon added setbacks in Great Britain and Poland, and finally, a debacle suffered by the Chinese Communists. These three fiascoes came as much greater shocks because they had been preceded by a series of apparent Soviet successes.

Initially there were two countries where the united front policy had achieved some success: Great Britain and China. In 1924, the first Labor Government in British history, headed by former trade union leader Ramsay MacDonald, granted *de jure* recognition to the USSR. This, together with the establishment of Soviet diplomatic relations with France, considerably enhanced Moscow's international prestige. In 1925 an Anglo-Soviet trade union committee was established. However, a letter allegedly written by Zinoviev as head of the Comintern was published in the British press. It urged British comrades to spread subversive propaganda in the British armed forces in order to prepare for the forcible overthrow of the London Government. The Conservative opposition exploited the letter to the full and managed to oust the Labor Government. The newly established diplomatic relations between Moscow and London were broken off.

In May, 1926, the outbreak of a general strike in Britain seemed to create a propitious atmosphere for revolutionary agitation. However, the strike soon collapsed and revealed the lack of revolutionary enthusiasm of the partially, Communist-infiltrated coal miners' union, as well as the impotence of the Communist Party of Britain. This failure was paralleled by Pilsudski's *coup d'état* in Warsaw, where the seizure of power by an old antagonist of Soviet Russia had been actively supported by the Polish Communists, who had hoped to be able to use him for their purposes.

This double, almost simultaneous setback was followed by a full-blown catastrophe in China. As was mentioned earlier, the Comintern favored a fairly intimate collaboration between the tiny Communist Party of China and the Kuomintang in order to overthrow the warlords and the weak central government of Peking. They were to be aided by an able and resourceful diplomatic agent, Michael Borodin, who was sent to China in September 1923 as head of a team of Soviet military and economic experts. In exchange, the Kuomintang dispatched to Moscow a group of its officers and officials to study Soviet methods. One of them was a close co-worker of Sun Yat-sen, Chiang Kai-shek. He was soon made an honorary member of the Comintern.

Stalin's objective in China was to establish the "hegemony of the proletariat" within the "bloc of four classes" in the struggle against imperialism. His argument was that China was on the eve of a "bourgeois-democratic" revolution intertwined with a mounting nationalistic revolution against encroachments by foreign imperialists. Soviet Russia, argued Stalin, should use these forces for its purposes and in alliance with the local bourgeoisle, chase the imperialists out of the Chinese subcontinent, thus weakening their hold on the Orient as a whole. Trotsky, on the other hand, denounced any alliance with class enemies as "Menshevism" and urged an immediate offensive by the Communist Party of China to seize power.

Stalin's Failure in China

By 1925 the revolutionary tide in China seemed to be mounting. The Kuomintang Army, reorganized with the assistance of the Soviet experts headed by General Vasily K. Bluecher (known in China as Galen), was ready to march north and seize power in Peking. In March 1926, however, Chiang Kai-shek, who had returned to Canton from Moscow with an extensive knowledge of Soviet methods of infiltration and subversion, decided to regain full control of the Kuomintang's forces before proceeding any further that summer. On March 20, 1926, Chiang arrested the political commissars in his army and placed the Soviet advisers under house arrest. After his successful coup, Chiang insisted on absolute subordination of the Chinese Communist Party to the Kuomintang. This was accepted by the chief of the Soviet advisers, Borodin, with Stalin's approval. The uneasy alliance was now maintained at this price, and soon the military campaign to unite China under Kuomintang rule, the "Northern Expedition," was launched. By April 1927, the combined forces of the Communists and the Kuomintang had reached as far north as Shanghai. There, alarmed by the growing strength and popularity of the Communists, Chiang put a bloody end to the alliance, executing thousands of Communists and their supporters in a reign of terror known as the "Shanghai massacre."

After the Shanghai massacre, the Comintern at first denied its failure, but when the defeat was too obvious to conceal, its mass media tried to minimize the scope and consequences of the debacle in China. Still, the failure of Stalin's policy was striking. By 1928, having also suppressed a Communist uprising in Canton the previous December, Chiang had united most of China under his leadership. Moscow had overlooked the Kuomintang's many sins because it was anti-Western—primarily, anti-British—only to have its policy backfire, thereby delaying the Chinese revolution for a full generation. Virtually silent on foreign policy before the China catastrophe, the Left, inspired by Trotsky, now charged Stalin and his allies with having betrayed the international revolution. From then on, the split between the leadership and the Left Opposition was unbridgeable. Comintern failures were compounded by Soviet diplomatic setbacks. The breaking of diplomatic relations by the Conservative British Government in May 1927 and the assassination of the Soviet ambassador to Warsaw by a White Russian émigré created an acute sense of Soviet isolation that helped Stalin propagate a siege mentality conducive to strengthening his control over all branches of Party and State activities.

The failure of Soviet foreign policy in Britain, Poland, and China made Stalin vulnerable to attacks by the Left Opposition. The Chinese disaster in particular lent itself to a critical reappraisal of his concepts and operational methods. Stalin blamed that defeat on the wrong correlation of class forces and the sabotage of Comintern directives by the leaders of the Chinese Party. In a speech on April 6, 1927, less than a week before the Shanghai massacre, he had defended his policy in China by saying: "Chiang Kai-shek has perhaps no sympathy for the revolution, but he is leading the army and cannot do otherwise than lead it against the imperialists. . . . So [the Rightists] can be utilized to the end, squeezed out like a lemon and then flung away." Trotsky soon pointed out that "a few days later, the squeezed-out lemon seized power and the army." Despite the temporary defeat in China, the original Soviet aim of loosening the grip of the imperial powers on China was

eventually accomplished. But it was in spite of Stalin's policies during the 1920s that the groundwork was laid for the eventual triumph of the Communist cause.

Trotsky's Expulsion and Exile

The alleged threat in 1927 of a new foreign invasion of Russia led by the British allowed Stalin to pounce on the Left Opposition with full fury. Trotsky and Zinoviev, who had voiced bitter criticisms of both his domestic and foreign policies, were denounced by the Secretary General, with Bukharin's support, as a bunch of "petty bourgeois intellectuals, divorced from life, from the Revolution, from the Party and from the working class." The political division between the bulk of the party and the Left Opposition reflected a deep-seated class division, argued Stalin. Any opposition to the vanguard of the proletariat must be bourgeois-inspired. Trotsky defended himself with vigor, pointing out the series of blunders and failures of his opponent, but he was helpless against Stalin's organizational power.

Stalin could have tolerated a meek Trotsky vegetating silently on the fringe of Soviet society. He could not tolerate a triumphant Trotsky constantly engineering acts of defiance and shouting, "I told you so!" In October 1927, on the eve of the tenth anniversary of the Bolshevik Revolution, the leaders of the Left Opposition, driven to desperation by the denial of access to mass media and their expulsion from the Central Committee, staged a series of public demonstrations in the streets of Moscow and Leningrad. Trotsky led the demonstration in the capital in person. All these processions were dispersed by the police. Finally, on November 15, 1927, Trotsky, Zinoviev, and Kameniev were expelled from the Party.

Trotsky refused to accept the decision and loudly protested against it. In response, he was exiled to Alma Ata in Central Asia. Zinoviev and Kameniev, on the other hand, retracted their criticisms of Stalin and submitted to him; they were pardoned and readmitted. As the triumphant Stalin contemptuously put it, "They crawled back into the Party." When from his exile in Alma Ata, Trotsky tried to maintain secret links with his remaining scattered supporters and continued to criticize the Secretary General's policies, he was banished from the USSR to Turkey in 1929.

Abroad, in Western Europe and eventually in Mexico, the exiled prophet published his *Bulletin of the Opposition* and tried to mount a Fourth International, but in vain. On August 20, 1940, a Spanish Communist, Ramon Mercader, who served as Trotsky's secretary, murdered him in Mexico City with an ice pick. He was sentenced to twenty years in prison by a Mexican court, but was decorated *in absentia* by Stalin.

Reasons for Trotsky's Defeat

Stalin's victory over the Opposition was a perfect example of political teamwork and timing skillfully manipulated from behind the scenes. At the beginning of 1925, Bukharin, who had joined the Politburo after Lenin's death, coalesced with Stalin to form a new Party leadership. Their coalition originated in the dissolution of the anti-Trotsky triumvirate, which began to disintegrate in late 1924 and collapsed in 1925, when Zinoviev and Kameniev challenged Stalin's leadership of the Party. At that time seven full members sat on the Politburo: Stalin, Bukharin, Trotsky, Zinoviev, Kameniev, Rykov, and Tomsky. The new duumvirate of Stalin and Bukharin was able to manage the Politburo because it acted resolutely, supported mostly by Rykov and Tomsky; and because the irresolute Left Opposition had failed to unite effectively until the spring of 1926, when it was too late.

Most of the time Trotsky was the soul of the Left Opposition and its driving force. From the perspective of more than seventy years, the reason for his debacle emerges more clearly than before. He was essentially more an intellectual than a man of action. After a meteoric outburst of activity during the Revolution, the Civil War, and in the early 1920s—which is to say, in the decisive opening phases of the struggle for power—Trotsky relapsed into mental pursuits that were probably more congenial to his temperament than routine peacetime duties.

Following Lenin's death, when the fight for leadership was going on, Trotsky was an absentee pretender who believed that Lenin's mantle would automatically fall on his shoulders because of his intellectual and military achievements. He relied too much on his brilliant wit and not enough on well-planned, consistent, and resolute action. He underestimated his opponent and openly called him "the most eminent mediocrity of his Party," thus mistakenly identifying intellectual caliber with political skill. While the proud Trotsky held himself aloof from the menial, humdrum tasks inherent in everyday organizational routine, the initially self-effacing, yet methodical, and indefatigable Stalin was always willing to assume arduous, albeit unglamorous, administrative Party duties. Gathering strength step by step, Stalin built for himself an impregnable position of power in the Party, and indirectly in the State apparatus, armed forces, and secret police. This formidable position no fancy rhetoric of his opponents could destroy.

Besides his outstanding organizational gifts, Stalin, no original thinker. displayed a remarkable talent for popularization of his simple concepts presenting them in the form of simple slogans. Stalin's opponents were misled by his speeches that seemed to them pedestrian, repetitious, and dull. Yet his pronouncements invariably presented the essentials of his point of view in a clear way that was accessible and acceptable to the Party rank and file, most of whom were newly promoted people without much education. In addition to all this, Stalin was endowed with an exceptional gift for behind-the-scenes Machiavellian manipulation and cunning intrigue, which neither Trotsky, nor any other of Stalin's rivals, could match. The Left Opposition's sense of timing was disastrous, while Stalin's was masterful.

Unlike Stalin, the leaders of the Opposition were victims of the Leninist fetish of "Party unity" as the overriding goal. The accepted principles, "Everything for the Party and through the Party," and "The Party is always right," inhibited their struggle against the man who at that time still carefully veiled his personal goals, always acting as a legitimate spokesman for their common, collective hero. While nothing Stalin said, wrote, or did was divorced from some practical purpose, Trotsky often hesitated or indulged in empty phrases and spectacular but inane gestures. To Trotsky himself, after 1921, one may apply his own criticism of Martov: "His thought lacked the mainspring of will." Stalin, on the other hand, exhibited a remarkable tenacity of purpose and an acute alertness to changes in the popular mood. He usually exercised caution and avoided unnecessary tactical risks until his enemies were ripe for a well-timed blow.

Suggested Reading

BOGDANOV, ALEXANDER, *Red Star.* Bloomington: Indiana University Press, 1984.

BRANDT, CONRAD, *Stalin's Failure in China.* Cambridge, MA: Harvard University Press, 1958.

CHESTER, LEWIS, STEPHEN FAY and HUGO YOUNG, *The Zinoviev Letter.* Philadelphia: Lippincott, 1968.

COX, TERRY, *Peasants, Class, and Capitalism.* New York: Clarendon Press, 1986.

DALLIN, DAVID, *The Rise of Russia in Asia.* New Haven, CT: Yale University Press, 1949.

DANIELS, ROBERT V., *The Conscience of the Revolution: The Communist Opposition in Soviet Russia.* Cambridge, MA: Harvard University Press, 1960.

DANILOV, VICTOR, *Rural Russia Under the New Regime.* Bloomington: Indiana University Press, 1988.

DAY, RICHARD B., *Leon Trotsky and the Politics of Economic Isolation.* New York: Cambridge University Press, 1973.

DEGRAS, JANE (ED.), *Soviet Documents on Foreign Policy.* New York: Oxford University Press, 1951–1953, 3 vols.

DEUTCHER, ISAAC, *The Prophet Unarmed: Trotsky, 1921–1929.* New York: Oxford University Press, 1959.

————, *The Prophet Outcast: Trotsky, 1929–1940.* New York: Oxford University Press, 1963.

FAINSOD, MERLE, *How Russia Is Ruled,* 2nd ed. Cambridge, MA: Harvard University Press, 1963.

GORODETSKY, GABRIEL, *The Precarious Truce. Anglo-Stalin Relations, 1924–27.* New York: Cambridge University Press, 1977.

MALIA, MARTIN, *The Soviet Tragedy: A History of Socialism in Russia, 1917–1991.* New York: Free Press, 1994.

MCNEAL, ROBERT H., *Stalin: Man and Ruler.* New York: New York University Press, 1988.

RESHETAR, JOHN, *A Concise History of the Communist Party of the Soviet Union.* New York: Praeger, 1960.

RUBINSTEIN, ALVIN (ED.), *The Foreign Policy of the Soviet Union.* New York: Random House, 1960, Ch. III.

SHAPIRO, LEONARD, *The Communist Party of the Soviet Union.* New York: Random House, 1959.

TROTSKY, LEON, *The Real Situation in Russia.* New York: Harcourt Brace Jovanovich, 1928.

————, *The Revolution Betrayed.* Garden City, NY: Doubleday, 1937.

TUCKER ROBERT, *Stalin in Power.* New York: W. W. Norton, 1990.

ULAM, ADAM, *Stalin: The Man and His Era.* New York: Viking Press, 1973.

VOLKOGONOV, DMITRI, *Stalin: Triumph and Tragedy.* London: Weidenfeld and Nicolson, 1991.

VON HAGEN, MARK, *Soldiers in the Proletarian Dictatorship: The Red Army and the Soviet Socialist State, 1917–1930,* Ithaca, NY: Cornell University Press, 1990.

WHITING, ALLEN S., *Soviet Policies in China, 1917–1924.* New York: Columbia University Press, 1954.

Chapter 13

The Industrialization Debate and the Five-Year Plans

Stalin's triumph over Trotsky and the Left Opposition was made possible by his coalition with Trotsky's opponents, Bukharin, Rykov, and Tomsky. Like the Left Opposition, Stalin's new partnership with the right wing of the Party was held together as much by a fear of common foes as by shared ideas. Yet the partnership survived such bitter factional controversies as the foreign policy crisis of 1926–1927. What scuttled this successful coalition was Stalin's sudden and quite unexpected decision to precipitate a grandiose industrialization scheme.

As early as 1923–1924, when the NEP achieved its first breakthrough, the question arose as to whether it should be regarded as "a tactical retreat" or a long-term strategic guide for Russia's economic future. The problem was not easy to solve. Although the NEP scored many successes, even its supporters could not deny that it suffered from many problems. One of the most crucial was the disparity between the development of agriculture and industry, which resulted in the glaring difference between the prices of foodstuffs and industrial goods.

The gap between rising industrial and low agricultural prices was compared by Trotsky to two blades opening on a pair of scissors. The government's harsh policy was at the root of the crisis, for the State was buying cheaply from the peasants and selling them the often inferior, expensive products of its industry. The difference which was pocketed by the treasury, went to finance further expansion, mostly of heavy industry, which was of no immediate tangible benefit to the average peasant. The term "price scissors" was a graphic metaphor for the growing disparity between the two categories of prices; this disparity was one of the basic contradictions of the NEP.

Agriculture had recovered much more rapidly because its basic capital stock was still there, and the essential skills needed for farming were relatively few. It was different, however, with industry, where retooling the ruined factories and training a skilled labor force were a protracted and costly process. Moreover, a large part of the machinery was of foreign origin, and by the mid-1920s was either used up or obsolete and had to be imported with hard currency, which was not readily available. Moreover, plants were not always utilized to their full capacity; large-scale planning seldom worked in practice.

Finally, overhead expenses were high, and the huge Soviet bureaucracy unwieldy, expensive, and inefficient. As a result of these factors, industrial products were scarce and inferior in quality. A "goods famine" arose.

The Crisis of the NEP

The goods famine was especially true of the basic products most needed in the country-side: farm machinery, domestic utensils, hardware, shoes, clothing, and so on. As a consequence of these scarcities, the peasants were not interested in selling their produce in the cities and tended to consume it them-selves. This amounted to a spontaneous boy-cott of the cities by the peasantry. The revival of the countryside during the NEP had rein-forced the traditional self-sufficiency of Russian villages, while the abolition of the peasants' arrears had given them greater freedom in deciding how much and what to sell. Thus the Soviet regime was kept at bay by the defiant peasants.

By 1927 food production had risen almost to the 1913 level, yet the marketed surplus grain available for urban consumption and export was less than a third of its prewar vol-ume. The easiest means of increasing the supply of agricultural produce was to end the goods famine by offering the peasantry a quid pro quo in the form of suitably priced and properly manufactured cheap consumer goods. However, suspicious of "creeping capi-talism" and the growing peasant power in a country where nearly 80 percent of the pop-ulation lived in the countryside, the Govern-ment purposely refused to give in. As a result, in 1927, State acquisition of grain fell short of the expected minimum by some two million tons. The governmental propaganda apparatus began to proclaim that the cities were threatened with near starvation. This statement was an exaggeration. In 1928 there was only a slight decline in State grain purchases while production of meat, milk, and vegetables continued to increase.

In response to the situation, the Left Opposition launched the slogan, "The kulaks grasped the worker by the throat." The term *kulak* literally means fist; it denotes the tough, hard-working, stingy farmers who were often also tight-fisted local money lenders. By the 1927 census, only 5 percent of the Soviet peasants were in that category because they owned more land than they could cultivate and consequently had to hire labor to exploit their plots efficiently. Soviet propaganda pictured the kulak as a fat-bel-lied usurer, a blood-sucking monster eager to exploit his less fortunate fellow villagers. Actually, most kulaks were peaceful, hard-working, industrious farmers. They used most of the available farming machinery, and most of the market grain came from them.

The Industrialization Debate: Bukharin's Stand

The question of what was to be done, became a subject of protracted, passionate debate between the two rival wings of the Party. "The industrialization debate," as the polemics of the middle 1920s were called, was closely connected with the previously described struggle for power, with the com-ing launching of the First Five-Year Plan, and even with issues of foreign policy. Both the right and the left wings were committed to modernization; their differences were in just how to do it. They argued about the rate of industrialization and the sources of its financing. Both the Right and the Left recog-nized that further economic progress largely depended on expanding and retooling existing plants and on constructing new ones. While the Left insisted on a more rapid and ambi-tious investment program in heavy industry, Bukharin and the Right advised a more cau-tious development. He hoped that the steady growth of the State's consumer goods plants combined with the output of the private sec-tor, including handicraft, would alleviate the growing goods famine.

Bukharin's concept envisaged the contin-uation of two parallel sectors: the public, embracing "the commanding heights" of the economy, and the private, composed of small industry, handicraft, and individual peasant farming. He insisted on a more balanced development. He suggested a variety of practical measures for economizing on capital while still making significant investments in heavy industry. Bukharin also hoped for gradual, "painless" accumulation of capital by encouraging peasants to increase production, make profits, and deposit those profits in State-run banks, which meant putting their savings at the disposal of the State. State intervention through credit investment and control of the "commanding heights," he argued, was more than enough to preserve the balance and the "leading role of the Party." Soviet power's firmest support would be assured by the continuation of the worker-peasant alliance with the workers in the vanguard. Like all other Bolsheviks, Bukharin was far from being a liberal or a democrat. What he wanted was to make the Soviet power more stable by humanizing somewhat the harsh authoritarian system, and thus making it acceptable to the bulk of the population—the peasant masses.

The only sensible way out of the scissor crisis, argued the Right, led by Bukharin, was to cut industrial prices and thus encourage the demand for manufactured goods. This in turn would allow State industry to produce more cheaply. The accumulated industrial profits could enhance industrial growth all along the line. The State monopolistic practices advocated by the Left, such as enforced low prices for food, were rightly decried by Bukharin as a continuation of "War Communism." Such practices would simply stifle incentives for food producers, while at the same time crippling industrial growth for the sake of temporary profit. Given the opportunity to purchase goods they needed, argued the Right, the peasants would increase their supply of food to the urban population. Moreover, the surplus harvest could be used as barter to import the capital goods so badly needed for the expansion of industry. Consequently, the

Construction of a dam on the Volga during the First Five-Year Plan

Right argued for more stability of land tenure, for State credits and tax relief for the peasants, for supplying the countryside with the goods the peasants needed most at a suitable price. Bukharin's stand implied an indefinite continuation of a mixed economy, the essence of the NEP.

The Left Opposition's Stand

This economic program was vitriolically condemned as reactionary by the propaganda of the Left. According to Trotsky and his chief economic supporter, Yevgenii A. Preobrazhensky, all of this meant the appeasement of the petty bourgeois forces represented by the bulk of the peasantry. The Left was unwilling to make concessions to the peasants and insisted upon speedy industrialization above all else, at the same time paying lip service to noncoercive methods. Because there had been little new capital construction since the war, argued Preobrazhensky, the level of technology was relatively low. The size of the capital stock might even diminish as the patched-up machinery started to fall apart. Soviet Russia would therefore be falling further and further behind the advanced, capitalist countries. For these reasons, the Left insisted that immediate, rapid industrial investment was a vital necessity.

Since investment must take place at the expense of consumption, the Left felt that the necessary belt-tightening should be applied first by the peasants, who were living better than ever and consuming most of the surpluses. Collectivization would make the prosperous peasants "disgorge" their surpluses and thus solve the urgent problem of procuring food for the cities. The supervision of some 24 million individual households was impossible; collectivization would not only solve that problem but would also allow for mechanization, so that modern technology would be introduced into the backward countryside. In the long run, ran the argument of the Left Opposition, collectivization would be the best way to ensure that the recalcitrant peasants would supply food regularly and cheaply to the State. The Government could then resell the produce to the urban population. The profit that they would pocket would provide the treasury with the capital necessary for further accelerated development of heavy industry.

"Taxation by price," one of the Left Opposition's formulas, allowed for continued high prices for manufactured goods combined with low prices for agricultural produce. The Left also argued that economic growth would be, in the long run, faster and more solid if investment were directed overwhelmingly to heavy industry. Investment in light industry could only very slowly and indirectly lead to overall economic progress, and at a higher cost. The Soviet Union surrounded by capitalist enemies, allegedly eager to invade it under any pretext, could not afford such a retardation of economic development. It had to modernize at a faster rate than the more advanced bourgeois countries in order to catch up with them. Trotsky maintained that without a solid base of heavy industry Soviet Russia would be unable to

fulfill its revolutionary task as a leader of the world proletariat. It would be "a clawless kitten trying to climb an oak tree."

Besides these economic aspects, the industrialization debate also had ideological implications connected with the clash between Trotsky's "permanent revolution" and Stalin's "socialism in one country." The theoretical controversy was urgently felt because of the growing isolation of the workers' Party in a still overwhelmingly agrarian and partly capitalist country. As Trotsky, paraphrasing Lenin, put it, "A proletarian government cannot function in a country where an overwhelming majority is composed of peasants." It was feared that "creeping capitalist" elements would eventually link up with foreign imperialists and together overthrow the Soviet regime. The growing kulak and Nepman power was regarded by the Left as a serious threat to Soviet power.

Replying to this, largely demagogic, propaganda, Bukharin argued that fair prices of agricultural machinery, combined with an abundance of consumer goods, would entice the peasants to increase steadily the amount of surplus food they brought to market. In 1925 when, despite a good harvest, grain collection fell considerably below official expectations, his warning proved right. Yet it was not heeded and a similar crisis occurred in 1927. Thus the State remained without reserves, unable to provide the villages with enough industrial goods to obtain enough food. Unwilling to disrupt industrial investment plans by raising grain prices sufficiently, Stalin resorted in January 1928 to "extraordinary measures." They involved brutal massive reprisals against the prosperous peasantry, confiscation of the available food produce, and arrest of the owners as "saboteurs" and "speculators." This momentous decision led to the launching of the original inflated version of the five-year plan, which included a scheme of collectivizing 20 percent of the individual farms. This finally precipitated an open break between the Politburo Right and Stalin. It also spelled the end of the NEP.

Soviet Planning

Before analyzing the first two five-year plans, let us examine briefly the role of planning in Soviet theory and practice. State planning has always been an integral part of Marxist thinking; it is inherent in the public ownership of the means of production, which is the essence of Marxist socialism. "Anarchy of production" was, according to Marx and Engels, the inevitable result of an economic system based on the private ownership of capital, the mainspring of which is no satisfaction of human social needs but blind greed. Reliance on the market mechanism as the sole means of equating supply and demand of goods and services was bound to be subject to the violent fluctuations so characteristic of the capitalistic system. To remedy this, an element of rationality ought to be injected, in the form of central planning.

Consequently, planning had been introduced into the Soviet economy almost simultaneously with the nationalization of what Lenin called "the commanding heights"; banks, transport, communication, foreign trade, and, eventually, industry. Since the early 1920s, centralized planning was described as a major coordinating mechanism in the Soviet economy. To charter and coordinate economic planning in 1921, the State Planning Commission (*Gosplan*) was established, directly subordinate to the Council of People's Commissars. The task of the Gosplan was to supervise the allocation of resources and to produce both annual and long-term plans.

The First Five-Year Plan (1928–1933) was more than just a purely technical document; it reflected a certain all-embracing vision of the future. It described in general terms what lay ahead in the planned period in all fields of human activity—not only in the economy, but also in education, science, culture, and on the international scene. Widely publicized in abbreviated forms and slogans, it was also an instrument of intense propaganda that aimed at mobilizing energy and enthusiasm for the realization of certain overall goals, political as well as economic.

As we know, between 1925 and 1928 Stalin supported Bukharin. The fact that Bukharin's moderate theories momentarily meshed better with the policy of "socialism in one country" misled the leaders of the Right. Meanwhile, Stalin often denounced the leftist program as "irresponsible adventurism" that would undermine the Leninist principle of worker-peasant alliance. The reason for this tactical support of the Right was that Stalin needed Bukharin's backing in the struggle against Trotsky. It is worth remembering that on the surface, the power of the Right was impressive and Stalin did not want to alienate it prematurely. At that time, they controlled many levers of power: the premiership (Rykov), the Party theoretical organs and the Comintern (Bukharin), and the trade unions (Tomsky). In addition, many experts of the Gosplan were also close to the Right, and this enhanced their false sense of security. Like Trotsky, in whose final destruction they had acquiesced, the Right forgot where the real locus of power resided.

The First Five-Year Plan

With the smashing of the Left Opposition, however, Stalin's line underwent a rapid change. In November 1928, in the First Five-Year Plan, he forced a huge increase in investment in heavy industry. Disregarding his former condemnation of the Left Opposition's program as "irresponsible adventurism," Stalin imposed on the reluctant experts of the State Planning Commission capital investment goals far higher than Trotsky had ever dared to advocate. The five-year plan adopted by the Sixteenth Party Congress in April 1929 provided for an increase in total industrial output of 250 percent and in heavy industry as much as 330 percent. Coal production was to be doubled, pig iron tripled, and electric energy quadrupled. In an agrarian country, diverting such a huge share of resources to investment in industry could be accomplished only by primitive accumulation at the expense of the peasantry. Here was the great contradiction of the plan: on paper it envisaged collectivization of only 25 percent of the land while providing for an instant increase in food production of 150 percent. How this paradox was to be resolved was a mystery.

Thus in 1929, overriding the vocal opposition of the Right, Stalin precipitated a super industrialization program, his "great leap forward." The rapid tempo of industrialization was predicated on the collectivization of agriculture, in order to squeeze both capital and additional manpower for industrial equipment this could come only from the lifeblood of the peasantry by means of "primitive socialist accumulation."

The First Five-Year Plan, which was to go from August 1928 to August 1933, was forced through over the protests of the Right Opposition. According to Bukharin, the October Revolution was a mixture of proletarian upheaval and peasant mutiny. The Bolshevik victory was a result of an alliance between these two classes. To assure the continuation of Soviet power, the alliance should be strengthened and not weakened; this was, he argued, the essence of Lenin's phrase, "democratic dictatorship of workers and peasants." Launching a forcible collectivization drive would end the cooperation of these two classes and thus endanger the foundations of Bolshevik power. This could plunge the country into another civil war. These arguments were brushed aside by Stalin, who accused the Right not only of dragging their feet on industrialization, but of attempting to "put the brake on the Revolution" and "surrendering the position to the capitalist elements"—the Nepmen and the kulaks.

In November 1929, Bukharin, Rykov, and Tomsky were removed from the Politburo, and Stalin pushed forward with his overly optimistic objective of "putting Soviet Russia in a motor car and the peasant upon a tractor." In his words, "steps [were] to be taken to restrict the development of capitalism in the countryside and guide peasant farming toward socialism." This statement was misleading. The previous decade had demonstrated that no amount of friendly persuasion would "guide" the peasants, fiercely attached to their land, into collective or State farms. Only massive coercion could achieve that target. Since administrative pressure, vigorous propaganda, and administrative prodding failed again, by the autumn of 1929 an embittered struggle was unleashed in the countryside to press the hostile peasantry into the collective farms (*kolkhozy*). The struggle focused on the kulaks. As the Soviet Union put it, the kulaks were to be "liquidated as a class." The term "liquidation" was now assuming an increasingly sinister meaning in the Soviet vocabulary.

In his study of the development of capitalism in prerevolutionary Russia, Lenin crudely defined the poor peasant as one with very little or no land and no horse; the middle peasant as the owner of enough land to support his family and keep one or two horses; and those who had more land and more horses, and hired labor to help them cultivate their plots were denounced as kulaks. Even this far-from-scholarly definition was now brushed aside. Anybody opposed to collectivization, or even to the Soviet regime in general, was accused of being a kulak, hence a member of the exploiting class, and as such declared a "saboteur" or "wrecker." The term kulak, as Soviet officials often admitted quite openly, came to denote not an economic status, or even a social status, but a state of mind.[1]

The first measures applied in the process of *dekulakization* were fiscal. In addition to already high taxes, a special exorbitant household tax was levied on those classified as "exploiters and profiteers," hence "enemies of the people." The high household tax was to be paid in cash and/or food produce, usually within twenty-four hours after its

---

[1] As a British scholar highly sympathetic to Soviet objectives, if not their methods, admitted, "It was not the class analysis that determined policy. It was policy that determined what form of class analysis was appropriate to a given situation." E. H. Carr, *A History of Soviet Russia: Socialism in One Country* (London: Macmillan Press, Ltd., 1953), p. 47.

Harvesting on a collective farm (kolkhoz)

assessment. After the expiration of the time limit, the delinquent's farm was usually raided by members of the "Committee of Poor Peasants" and the Komsomol squads, often backed by the local militia. The farm would be confiscated, the owner arrested and deported. Meanwhile, poorer peasants were allowed to grab the kulak's possessions and pool them in the collective farms then painfully taking shape.

Opposition to collectivization was widespread, by no means limited to real and alleged kulaks. It was so fierce that often even the local militia and the Komsomol were unable to cope with it. Consequently Red Army detachments had to be dispatched. In some cases pitched battles were fought between large army units, occasionally supported by airplanes, and the local resisters. This was, in some localities, like a new civil war. Altogether, some five million

people were deported to Siberia and other distant parts of the Soviet domains, mostly to the far north. Many of those who survived the transport, died of starvation and exposure in the harsh, subarctic environment. Where the opposition in the countryside was only passive, peasant hostility was expressed in acts of sabotage and the application of go-slow methods; many refused to sow and reap and perform other duties on the newly founded collective farms. In many instances wholesale slaughter of cattle and horses, or the destruction of implements, or even the burning of farm buildings would take place. At the peak of collectivization, the peasants' desperate destructive rage assumed massive proportions and thus crippled the productivity of Soviet agriculture for at least two decades. This was especially true in Ukraine, traditionally the granary of the Russian Empire.

Collectivization: A Balance Sheet

Collectivization uprooted and destroyed some 20 to 30 million peasants. The exact figures are still a subject of scholarly dispute. It is difficult to imagine the harshness of the collectivization ordeal especially during the dead of winter. At short notice, people were torn out of their homes, transported in cattle railway cars to distant, deserted places, and ordered to start their lives from scratch. How does one establish a collective farm somewhere in Siberia or Kazakstan with the snow a foot or two deep? As a result of such cruel and wasteful methods, death rates were appalling. The collectivization process was modernization achieved through "primitive socialist accumulation by the methods of Tamerlane," to use a phrase of Soviet economist N. Valentinov. Those peasants who were spared either had to join the kolkhozy immediately or flee to the large cities where, behind a veil of anonymity, they would seek employment in the mushrooming industries. Consequently, collectivization achieved several objectives at one blow: It destroyed a fairly large stratum of prosperous farmers and hence relatively independent and productive people who, through their industry and self-sufficiency, were a challenge to the system. In addition to that, the dispossessed peasants, either as forced labor or as fugitives in the cities, increased the manpower available to the State to achieve its ever-ambitious plans. The millions deported to labor camps and compulsory settlements created a sprawling network of punitive concentration camps, or what Alexander Solzhenitsyn would later on term the *Gulag Archipelago*.[2]

Resistance to collectivization was fiercest in those regions of the USSR that had a strong tradition of individual farming, like Ukraine, Kazakstan, and the northern regions of the Caucasus. The Ukraine was sealed off and the special detachments were to seize every scrap of food they could grab. The aftermath of the dekulakization resulted in a widespread, deliberately created famine that reached its peak in 1932–1933. Many cases of cannibalism were reported to the authorities, but never publicized. The famine was not a result of an actual food shortage. Throughout the First and Second Five-Year Plans the Soviet Union exported considerable quantities of food, some of which could have been diverted to feed the starving millions. The deliberate decision at the top, however, was to punish the widespread resistance to the Kremlin's decrees rather than to diminish the amount of hard currency that food export provided. While Ukraine suffered most, the entire Soviet Union was affected by the dramatic drop in food production during collectivization. The scarcity of food and of consumer goods in general was experienced by everyone, except a small group at the top. Strict food rationing had to be introduced, and it lasted until 1933.

By the end of January 1930, there were slightly over four million peasant families on collective farms. By March 1 of the same year the number had increased to 14 million. This amounted to about 40 percent of all peasant households, more than twice what the plan had anticipated. The terrible tensions generated by forcible collectivization, bordering on open civil war, were threatening to the stability of the regime. By that time it was obvious that things had gotten out of hand, and Stalin finally decided to intervene. On March 2, 1930, Stalin pub-

---

[2] The term *Gulag* is an abbreviation of the Soviet official term denoting "General Administration of Labor Camps." The Gulag's initiator was not Stalin, but Lenin himself. The system reached its peak under Stalin and despite the thaw under Khrushchev, it continued in a diminished size. Lenin laid the foundation of the Gulag shortly after the Bolshevik Revolution by sending thousands of the Revolution's opponents to distant isolated places, mostly in Siberia. Trotsky contributed to the expansion of the concentration camps system in 1921 by dispatching to the camps those participants of the Kronstadt rebellion who were not shot on the spot. Originally, Gulag inmates were not to perform any work except camp service; the main task of the camps was supposed to be political re-education. But, gradually, due to their increasing numbers, the prisoners were used as manpower for timber felling, road building, canal digging and so on. Beginning in 1930, concentration camps were assigned regular quotas of work to be carried out.

lished an article in *Pravda* entitled "Dizzy with Success." He stressed that nearly 50 percent of all farms had been collectivized; this exceeded by 100 percent the goal envisaged in the five-year plan. In his typically repetitious manner, he stressed that "People are often intoxicated by such successes, they become dizzy with success, they lose all sense of proportion, they lose the faculty of understanding realities."

Stalin's article meant that he was now trying to shift the blame for the ruthlessness with which his personal instructions had been executed onto the shoulders of his allegedly overzealous agents, who were then punished for their loyalty to him. Meanwhile, collectivization was to proceed at a slower pace so as not to wreck Soviet agriculture altogether. Soon a series of arrests of the most zealous officials of the Ministry of Agriculture took place. These officials were punished for allegedly sabotaging the process and persecuting innocent people.

Nevertheless, at the Sixteenth Party Congress in June 1930, Stalin triumphantly proclaimed it "the Congress of the sweeping offensive of socialism along the whole front, of the elimination of kulaks as a class...." In 1928, there had been more than 24 million individually owned farms with an average sown area of 11 acres. By the close of 1930, the land was redivided into some 250,000 collective farms (*kolkhozy*) with an average sown area of 1,200 acres. In addition, some 4,000 State farms (*sovkhozy*) cultivated an average of 7,500 acres each. While in 1928 nearly 96 percent of the land was in private hands, by 1938 over 94 percent was, in one form or another, controlled by the State.

The collectivization, completed by 1937–1938, exacted a terrible price. Besides the five million people who perished, one way or another, in the collectivization process and the famine of 1932–1933 that paralleled its middle stages, material losses were staggering. While in 1928 the USSR had 32 million horses, by 1934 only 15 million survived; of 60 million cows, only 33 million remained by 1934; similar figures for sheep are 97 million and 37 million. The overall per capita agricultural production of 1928 was not reached again until 1938, if we are to believe official Soviet statistics.

The Soviet Agrarian System

After having brutally crushed peasant resistance by administrative and fiscal inquisition, starvation, and force of arms, Stalin proceeded to reorganize Soviet agriculture to fulfill his largely politically inspired goals. While State farms were considerably expanded in number and size, it was the collective farm sector that absorbed the bulk of the land and manpower. Sovkhozy were directly operated by the Ministry of State Farms with hired labor, while kolkhozy were supposed to be self-governing cooperatives. They were allegedly voluntarily established agricultural enterprises run by their peasant members. Initially, four types of collective farms were organized; they differed as to the degree of pooling of land and the amount of livestock and implements. In the strictest type of kolkhoz, everything was owned and operated in common. In the loosest type, on the other hand, each peasant family kept title to its own land, livestock, and implements, while joining with other families to cultivate land, purchase seeds and machinery, and market the surplus produce.

Although legally the kolkhoz was a free self-governing agricultural cooperative, in reality it was strictly controlled by the State and the Party. The first instrument of control was the chairmanship of the farm. Theoretically, the kolkhoz chairmen were elected by their members. In reality, they were appointed from above and most were Party members. Through them, the authorities communicated their economic plans and political instructions.

The second instrument of control on the kolkhozy was, until March 1958, the Motor Tractor Station (MTS). Owned by the State, the MTS was to furnish to the collective farms the machinery necessary to sow and harvest the crops prescribed by the current economic plan. For these services the kolkhoz had to pay a fixed high price, most of it in crops. The remaining annual output of the kolkhoz was as a rule divided in the following way. Under Stalin, priority number one was the compulsory quota of grain to be delivered to the State at a price drastically below its market value. When the prescribed allotments had been made for capital and reserve stock, for seeds, fodder, and insurance, the remainder was distributed in accordance with the number of labor days involved in its production. Consequently, the collective farmers were reduced to the level of sharecroppers or residual claimants to the fruits of their labor. Obligations to the State were always to be met first, regardless of the size of the crop. Stalin himself bluntly called compulsory deliveries "something of a tribute" imposed on the newly subdued masses of peasantry to force them to finance breakneck industrialization.

In calculating labor days, almost all emphasis was on the quantity of work performed. As a consequence, by and large, the work on collective and State farms was performed carelessly, as it had been in times of serfdom. This was especially true of animal husbandry, where individual care and attention are preconditions of success. On the other hand, the peasants tended to lavish their labor on the minute patches of land left to them in the form of household plots. Constantly threatened by the State encroachments and restrictive regulations, the household plot, cultivated with love and care by its owners, was an important source of livelihood, not only for collective farmers but also for the rest of the country. In the Soviet system, no amount of moral or material incentives were able to persuade the sullen peasantry to provide enough labor for the collective enterprises to function efficiently. In contrast, privately owned plots, amounting to some three percent of all cultivated land, thrived and produced nearly half of all Soviet meat, milk, and green vegetables.

The purpose of collectivization was threefold. First, it was to assure steady procurement of cheap food without taxing industry too much. Second, collectivization, to be followed by mechanization of the agricultural processes, was to free a considerable number of superfluous peasants who would then be pumped into the urban labor market. Third, collectivization would make it possible to tighten politico-economic controls over a countryside hitherto relatively free from party cells and their supervision. These controls were to assure that the peasant masses would remain politically obedient to the regime's fiat, and that they would deliver the prescribed quotas of produce to the State at fixed, nominal prices. The produce was then to be sold at a much higher price and the difference pocketed by the State to be used for its purposes, largely for further industrialization and rearmament. Thus the burden of the "second revolution" was overwhelmingly shifted onto the shoulders of the peasantry; now they were largely reduced to a status of servitude similar to that existing prior to their emancipation in the 1860s. Individual landlords were replaced by the collective master—the State.

Forced collectivization, completed at a stupendous human and environmental cost, produced immediate benefits to the regime by assuring an adequate supply of food to the expanding city population during the crucial stages of industrialization. But the long-run effects were disastrous. Soviet agriculture was crippled beyond repair.

Industrialization

Parallel to collectivization, the main lines of the industrialization scheme were unfolding. The first two five-year plans had three main industrial objectives: first, to expand and modernize the already functioning industries; second, to construct entirely new branches of industry to complement the existing plants; and third, to alter the USSR's economic geography by relocating those plants that were too close to the exposed western or southern frontiers of the country and placing them further away in more strategically secure places.

The first plan was launched with great fanfare in August 1929 in an atmosphere of officially sponsored optimism. The first apparent successes pushed the leaders even further. The Sixteenth Party Congress, held in June–July 1930, went so far as to adopt the slogan, "The Five-Year Plan in four years." But soon numerous difficulties began to develop. Industrialization was embarked upon too hastily, with insufficient planning and scarce resources, and with a limited pool of skilled labor. Moreover, overcentralized planning did not always work in practice. Untrained workers often could not operate the complicated, largely imported machinery, which was frequently put in unsuitable locations. There were cases of factories provided with the wrong type of equipment, sent to enterprises unable to house it. Information about such cases was suppressed by the censorship following Stalin's battle cry, "There are no fortresses that Bolsheviks could not conquer," shock tactics were applied. Specially mobilized "brigades" of workers and engineers, some of them volunteers from the Komsomol, were dispatched to perform emergency tasks. "Socialist competition of labor" was encouraged, to be rewarded not only with honorific titles, medals, and citations, but also with bonuses and other material benefits. At the end of 1932, it was officially announced that the overall objectives of the First Five-Year Plan had been achieved ahead of time.

According to official Soviet figures, which have been questioned by most Western economists, the output of machinery and electric equipment expanded by 157 percent over the 1929 level, which would represent overfulfillment of the plan. On the other hand, iron and steel production rose only to 6.2 million (instead of 10 million) tons. The output of coal was only 65 million tons instead of 75 million, while consumer goods production increased by only 73 percent. Despite the unreliability of the Soviet statistics, in the industrial field the overall quantitative achievements of the plan were impressive. Two new important industrial centers were established, one in the Urals (Magnitogorsk) and the other in southern Siberia (Kuznetsk).

Entirely new branches of industry were developed, such as aviation, plastics, and synthetic rubber. Consequently, the plan constituted an important milestone in the process of the socioeconomic transformation of Russia.

While the overall achievements appeared impressive, the quality of most goods produced was appalling. In the case of some consumer goods, rejects amounted to 40 percent or more. In view of this, the fundamental task of the Second Five-Year Plan, launched in 1933, was "the completion of the technical construction in the whole of the national economy," and the improvement of the quality of goods produced. The number of failures and nonfulfillments of the first plan compelled Soviet economists to lower some targets of the second. Nevertheless, the second plan also gave priority to heavy industry. The machine tool industry again expanded considerably, and the output of nonferrous metals (especially copper, lead, zinc, aluminum, nickel and magnesium) was increased dramatically.

One of the weaknesses revealed during the First Five-Year Plan was that of the Soviet infrastructure, especially roads, railways, and canals. Consequently, the second plan focused on the them. For instance, it provided for reconstruction and double-tracking of the principal lines starting with the Trans-Siberian Railroad. The Japanese occupation of Chinese Manchuria in 1931 made it of strategically paramount importance. The widening of old canals and the construction of new ones (like the Moscow-Volga Canal) was another vital task assigned to the new plan.

By 1933, the altered international position of the USSR resulting from Japan's aggressive strategy in China, as well as Hitler's seizure of power in Germany, was reflected in a rapid expansion of armament production. During the Second Five-Year Plan the Soviet armament industry was given priority. To enhance centralized structure and to be ready for a quick mobilization of resources in case of a war from now on began to override all other considerations. The armed forces that had emerged from the Civil War

The dam of Dnieprostroi under construction

were being gradually reshaped into an increasingly professional, huge modern fighting machine, comparable to those of other great powers. Between 1933 and 1936, the size of the Red Army almost tripled; from 562,000 it grew to 1.5 million, which exceeded the size of the 1913 Imperial Army. The Soviet armed forces were increasingly mechanized; a powerful air force and a large number of armored units were developed. The Red Army was the first to organize large parachutist units.

As with the First Five-Year Plan, the second was also officially declared completed ahead of time, in 1937. Again, however, not all its goals were achieved. Among the items that surpassed their estimated targets were steel (17.6 million tons instead of the projected 17 million) and the automotive industry, created practically from scratch, could now boast of an eightfold increase. Tanks, airplanes, and armored cars were given priority over civilian vehicles. The most striking failures of the second plan were oil (30.5 million instead of 46.8 million tons), coal (128 million instead of 152 million tons), and consumer goods in general. Cotton in particular fell far behind its relatively modest target.

The Results

Despite many failures, the first two five-year plans increased the industrial capacity of the USSR dramatically in all major fields—steel, coal, electric power—and created new manufacturing sectors indispensable to any great power—automobiles, airplanes, chemicals, and plastics. Consequently, the first two five-year plans laid the foundation of the industrial might of the Soviet Union, especially in the military field.

The first major objective of both plans was expansion and modernization of industry. In 1928, industry's share of total production of the USSR was 58.7 percent, while heavy industry accounted for only 39.7 percent. In 1940, on the brink of the German attack on Soviet Russia in 1941, the share of industry in total production had advanced to 84.7

percent, and that of heavy industry to 61.2 percent. Further expansion was merely a matter of time. Improving the quality of consumer goods, however, was grossly neglected, and the standard of living of the broad masses remained low.

As for the third goal, the relocation of industrial centers, here the successes were also impressive. While in 1929 the USSR had four major industrial centers—Leningrad (metallurgical and machine industry), Moscow (chiefly consumer goods, headed by textiles), the Ukraine (mining, metallurgy, food processing), and the Urals (mining and metallurgy)—by 1937–1938 three new centers were created beyond the Urals, in Central Asia, well away from the vulnerable Western frontiers of the USSR.

Industrial expansion and often forcible relocation involved a massive shift of sometimes unwilling citizens, mostly from the countryside to the cities. One of the traditional Marxist goals, the elimination of differences between town and country, was brought closer to realization. Soviet urbanization policy assumed that the industrial city was the modern sector of socialist society and that urban patterns should triumph over "the idiocy of rural life," as Karl Marx once put it. Here too the progress was striking. While in 1926, out of a total population of 147 million, there were 26 million urban dwellers; in 1939, out of 171 million peoples, 56 million lived in urban centers—a near-doubling of the overall percentage of urban dwellers, from 17.7 to 32.7 percent. This dramatic increase within thirteen years represented in itself a major aspect of the Stalin revolution. Industrialization spelled urbanization and the triumph of a new style of life more in tune with the Marxist-Leninist ethos, and with the lifestyle of the largely Russian cities of Central Russia.

As in the case of collectivization, the ambitious industrial objectives were also achieved at the cost of great human sacrifices and high environmental price. The standard of living of the Soviet population, which by 1928 had begun to approach that of the 1913 level, dropped dramatically during the early 1930s.

This was Soviet Russia's period of great austerity, known as the "iron age." The consumer goods famine was acute, much worse than the grossly over publicized crisis of 1925–1926. This was reflected in a number of popular stories that people usually whispered in secret. One of them is so characteristic of popular mood that it is worth recording: "How do we know that Adam and Eve were Soviet citizens?" "It is obvious. They had nothing to wear, an apple to share, yet they were told they lived in paradise."

The Shortcomings

Breakneck expansion created confusion and an acute shortage of industrial resources and skilled manpower; this resulted in fierce scrambling among plan managers to obtain them at any cost. One has to bear in mind that fulfillment of the Plan (with a capital P) was often a matter not only of advancement, but even of life and death. Under Stalin, failure was not tolerated; nonfulfillment of the prescribed norm was considered sabotage, and saboteurs were treated as "enemies of the people." One day of unjustified absenteeism was cause for dismissal from work, which meant loss of a ration card and housing, with all the grim consequences for individuals now entirely at the mercy of an increasingly brutal, totalitarian regime.

"Socialist competition of labor" led to the establishment of various devices that would assure recognition and reward; they included honorary titles, medals, extra vacations, and, finally, cash awards. For instance, in 1935 a coal miner in the Don basin by the name of Alexey G. Stakhanov organized a team of co-workers who apparently achieved spectacular successes by coordinating and directing their efforts toward a common goal. This resulted in their overfulfilling the standard norm many times over. For this Stakhanov received not only a special bonus, but a number of honors, including the Order of Lenin and the Red Labor Banner. He was declared a "hero of socialist labor," withdrawn from actual physical work, and used as a propagandist of the highly competitive Soviet labor system that became known as Stakhanovism. The example he set was used to justify an increase in production quotas for all workers. This in turn resulted in a considerable revulsion against what came to be regarded as a return to the old capitalist sweatshop system in a new "socialist" guise. In the early 1930s, it was decreed that a worker must go where ordered and carry out tasks prescribed by the authorities at a wage fixed by them. Since collective bargaining had been finally abolished in 1933, by the middle 1930s Soviet workers found themselves at the mercy of the all-powerful State.

As we know, Stalin's industrialization was hastily undertaken by crude, and often cruel methods, without adequate know-how or skilled labor. Capital was forcibly squeezed out of the reluctant population, mainly the peasantry, by the process of primitive accumulation. The arbitrary price system that consequently developed in the USSR was politically motivated. Prices for heavy industrial goods were held down by providing subsidies in the form of operational loans granted without interest. Prices of consumer articles were dramatically increased through the imposition of a turnover tax, a sales tax levied on all goods sold by the State to the people. This served a double purpose: On the one hand, high prices of consumer goods curtailed demand; on the other, the exorbitant turnover tax provided a major source of revenue to the Soviet treasury. By the exercise of ruthless dictatorial power, Stalin diverted a huge percentage of national income to industrial investment mainly for defense purposes.

The first two five-year plans hinged on four fundamental assumptions: first, that collectivization would bolster Soviet agrarian production; second, that the Soviet Union would have ever-increasing trade surpluses with foreign countries; third, that the Soviet cost of production would decrease and individual labor productivity would increase; and fourth, that the percentage of expenditure for national defense would eventually drop.

All these assumptions proved false, partly because of the numerous technical blunders in brutally enforcing the ruined agriculture collectivization. To these factors one should add the rapidly deteriorating international situation. The Japanese invasion of Manchuria in 1931 and Hitler's rise in Germany in 1933 almost simultaneously created a double menace to the USSR. Both these dangers necessitated reshaping of the five-year plans, especially the second one, and increasing military expenditures. Crop failures, high costs of production, and lagging productivity of labor were the result of domestic mistakes and shortcomings of rigid, highly centralized planning.

The program of industrialization was launched by Stalin under the slogan of "catching up with and overtaking the West." Although Soviet modernization was carried out without outside financial aid, it was achieved by importing considerable Western machinery and know-how, as well as by bringing in personnel from Europe and America. The machinery was freely copied by Soviet engineers not hampered by international patent laws. The period of the first two five-year plans paralleled the period of the Great Depression, which started in 1929 and continued throughout most of the 1930s, resulting in mass unemployment in most of the Western countries. Consequently, Western companies welcomed Soviet orders, while many unemployed American as well as West European engineers, especially Germans, flocked to the Soviet Union in search of work. As Stalin was to admit to the United States wartime ambassador in Moscow, Averell Harriman, more than two-thirds of all foreign companies that were involved in building Soviet industrial projects were American. Stalin and other Soviet leaders often highly praised American efficiency, and set it as an example to be emulated by Soviet workers and engineers. This quite naive and uncritical admiration for the "American tempo" often led to blind imitation. What was good for the United States was often assumed to be even better for the

Soviet Union. An example of this gigantomania was Stalin's decision on the level of output of the Magnitogorsk Steel Works. According to one of his close co-workers, Stalin scrapped the elaborate calculations made by his economic experts as "too defeatist." Then Stalin asked him what was the size of American plants of this type. When he was answered that large pig iron works in the United States produced some 2.5 million tons a year, Stalin bluntly ordered a similar plant built in Magnitogorsk. Later on, he insisted, its output must be increased to 4 million tons. At the same time, he ordered the expert to be jailed as a saboteur. At that time even a plant producing 2.5 million tons was actually beyond the capacity of Soviet engineers and managers. Stalin's gigantomania proved very costly to the Soviet economy.

Central planning, which in theory appeared an ideal solution of economic problems, had many inherent shortcomings. First of all, production and distribution were calculated by a distant central planning agency situated in Moscow and then its detailed instructions were sent to specific factories. Without an effective clearing mechanism, such a system resulted in a surplus of unwanted goods and a shortage of products wanted by consumers. Central planning proved unable to adjust such distortions, because the theoreticians in Moscow did not have prompt access to the immediate signals of price changes that rule markets in capitalistic countries. This resulted in all sorts of illegal dealings and in spreading of black market. Secondly, central planning was unable to absorb properly new ideas; this resulted in continuous mass production of the same type of goods of the same, usually low, quality.

Summary

The Stalin revolution of the 1930s precipitated an upheaval far more profound than the Bolshevik revolution of 1917–1921.

Besides greatly expanding and restructuring the Soviet economy, Stalin's arbitrary methods profoundly affected practically every aspect of the life of every individual in the USSR. Internal passports, abolished in 1905, were reintroduced, to remain a standing feature of the Soviet system. Stalin's whim was enforced by ruthless mass reprisals and unbridled terror. This resulted in an unprecedented degree of State control over all fields of human activity. The Stalinist system was characterized by a tight, regimented, centrally planned economy, and rigid thought control, all of which was enforced by an all-pervading, indiscriminate terror (see the next chapter). Within the framework of the command economy, the Party machinery, manipulated by an increasingly omnipotent dictator, combined its monopoly of political power with tight control over practically the entire economy. By 1938, 99.3 percent of national wealth of the USSR was produced by the "socialist sector."

Stalin's grand design stemmed from two traits: a totalitarian imperative nourished by inordinate ambition and paranoia; one should also point out his proclivity to treat people in a manipulative way as means to his ends. To him human beings were no more than Pavlov's dogs, to be drilled by conditioned reflexes to perform the desired tricks. Most historians agree that, if there ever was a command economy and a totalitarian system, it existed in Soviet Russia for more than a quarter of a century under Stalin. His methods for achieving immediate results appeared to be effective. In the long run, however, the price paid by the Soviet people and their environment for the Stalinist revolution proved to be exorbitant. All this took place despite the warnings of Russian and Ukrainian environmentalists. To their entreaties and even protests Vice-Premier Andrei Vyshinsky replied: "We have the Stalin Constitution. That is sufficient to ensure that our public hygiene and public health are the best in the world." Soon after this statement repressions against scientists and doctors criticizing wasteful and dangerous practices were launched and many environmental spokesmen were arrested.

Suggested Reading

ARNOT, BOB, *Controlling Soviet Labor.* New York: M. E. Sharpe, 1988.

ATKINSON, DOROTHY, *The End of the Russian Land Commune, 1905–1930.* Stanford, CA: Stanford University Press, 1983, part V.

BERGSON, ABRAM, *The Real National Income of Soviet Russia Since 1928.* Cambridge, MA: Harvard University Press, 1961.

CAMPBELL, ROBERT W., *The Failure of Soviet Economic Planning: System, Performance, Reform.* Bloomington: Indiana University Press, 1992.

CHAMBERLIN, WILLIAM H., *Russia's Iron Age.* New York: Arno, 1970.

COHEN, STEPHEN F., *Bukharin and the Bolshevik Revolution: A Political Biography, 1888–1938.* New York: Knopf, 1973.

CONQUEST, ROBERT, *The Harvest of Sorrow: Soviet Collectivization and the Terror-Famine.* New York: Oxford University Press, 1986.

DAVIES, R. W., *The Industrialization of Soviet Russia,* 2 vols. Cambridge, MA: Harvard University Press, 1980.

FILTZER, DONALD, *Soviet Workers and Stalinist Industrialization.* New York: M. E. Sharpe, 1986.

FITZPATRICK, SHEILA, *Everyday Stalinism: Ordinary Life in Extraordinary Times: Soviet Russia in the 1930s.* New York: Oxford University Press, 1999.

GELB, MICHAEL (ED.), *An American Engineer in Stalin's Russia.* Berkeley: University of California Press, 1991.

GILL, GREAME, *Stalinism.* New York: St. Martin's Press, 1998.

GRAHAM, LOREN, *The Ghost of the Executed Engineer, Technology and the Fall of the Soviet Union.* Cambridge, MA: Harvard University Press, 1993.

HUNTER, HOLLAND AND SZYRMER, JANUSZ (EDS.), *Faulty Foundations: Soviet Economic Policies, 1928–1940.* Lawrenceville, NJ: Princeton University Press, 1992.

JASNY, NAUM, *The Socialized Agriculture of the USSR.* Stanford, CA: Stanford University Press, 1949.

———, *Soviet Industrialization, 1928–1952.* Chicago: University of Chicago Press, 1961.

———, *The Socialized Agriculture of the USSR.* Stanford, CA: Stanford University Press, 1949.

KUROMIYA, HIROAKI, *Stalin's Industrial Revolution: Politics and Workers, 1928–1932.* Cambridge, Eng.: Cambridge University Press, 1988.

LEWIN, MOSHE, *Russian Peasants and Soviet Power,* (trans. Irene Nove and John Biggart). Evanston, IL: Northwestern University Press, 1968.

NOVE, ALEC, *An Economic History of the USSR.* London: Allen Lane, 1969.

———, *The Soviet Economy.* New York: Praeger, 1961.

PRYOR, L. FREDERIC, *The Red and the Green: The Rise and Fall of Collectivized Agriculture in Marxist Regimes.* Lawrenceville, NJ: Princeton University Press, 1992.

ROSSI, JACQUES, *The Gulag Handbook.* New York: Paragon House, 1989.

SCOTT, JOHN, *Behind the Urals: An American Worker in Russia's City of Steel.* Bloomington: Indiana University Press, 1989.

ZALESKI, EUGENE, *Stalinist Planning for Growth 1933–1952* (Ed. and trans. Marie-Christine MacAndrew and John H. Moore). Chapel Hill: University of North Carolina Press, 1980.

Chapter 14

The Purges

In 1944, Stalin told France's General Charles de Gaulle that the best way to make men achieve things was by instilling fear in them. This axiom he practiced throughout his rule. The second Bolshevik revolution was so profound and extensive that it could be enforced only by inhumanly harsh measures. The full fury of the terror did not come at once, however; it was rather a product of the evolution of the Soviet system, from one in which coercion existed on a large scale but was selective, to a regime where terror became its central feature.

Stalin, of course, did not invent mass reprisals. From the beginning, the Bolsheviks considered human life expendable, subordinate to their ultimate goal. Under Lenin, the Cheka always acted not in accordance with strict legality but by following its "revolutionary conscience," without bothering too much to provide irrefutable proofs to justify its arrests and executions. In 1922 the Cheka (the full name of which was "The Extraordinary Committee for Fighting Counter-Revolution and Sabotage") was euphemistically renamed the GPU, or the Chief Political Administration. Thus the "extraordinary" institution became an ordi-

nary one, an integral part of Soviet system even during the NEP. Its increasingly ubiquitous activity initially affected not so much Party members as actual or suspected enemies of the Soviet regime. Until 1934 the Bolsheviks seldom punished their high-ranking comrades with death; this was reserved for the "enemies of the people." At first, the idea of exterminating one's political opponents within the Party was regarded as unacceptable, and until the mid-1930s there existed an unwritten law that Bolsheviks do not kill Bolsheviks. Even Stalin's archenemy Trotsky, despite his vitriolic attacks against the Stalinist regime, was merely expelled from the Party and exiled in 1929.

But, paradoxically enough, as the Stalin regime grew in strength, so did the intensity and the scope of its repression. The launching of the First Five-Year Plan saw the first trials of economic experts as "wreckers" and "saboteurs," allegedly responsible for the shortcomings that were revealed in the execution of Stalin's various grandiose undertakings. This signaled the beginning of a lengthy process of displacing the old professional cadres trained under the Tsarist regime, and replacing them with the new Soviet intelligentsia.

The Patterns of the Early Purges

Soon a pattern developed according to which, after each political failure or breakdown of production, the "guilty" ones had to be "discovered," charged with their crimes, made to confess, and purged. Soon specific purge institutions developed and a purge ritual was established. According to this ritual, on an appointed day a purging commission would visit a given enterprise, institution, or Party cell. In an open meeting, frequently attended by hundreds of onlookers, the commission would question each employee or Party member. The questions were based on information derived from their autobiographies, from secret police files, or from denunciations by their Party comrades. During the 1920s a mechanism known as self-criticism was developed. Its function, according to an official Soviet definition, consisted in

exposing the deficiencies and errors in the work of particular persons, organizations and institutions, on the basis of free, businesslike discussion by the toilers of all the problems of economic-political work . . . and developing the ability to see, to uncover and to acknowledge one's mistakes. . . .

Such self-criticism was to be practiced regularly by all Soviet citizens, but especially by Party members.

During the Stalin revolution, under pressure from security organs and often supported by mass media, self-criticism was practiced on a large scale. Of course, self-criticism was subject to the limitations inherent in the totalitarian nature of the Stalinist system; it could only deal with mistakes committed by individuals, usually at a lower or middle level, but could never extend to official policies of the regime. While policy itself was taboo, its execution was not; consequently only subordinate officials were the targets of self-criticism and public denunciation, and could be charged with slackness, inefficiency, corruption, or "lack of revolutionary vigilance." This helped the regime to divorce itself from the less popular aspects of its own policies and to shift the blame for their failures onto the shoulders of a few carefully selected "slackers," "wreckers," and "saboteurs." It became Stalin's habit not to let any of his mistakes go unpunished.

After completing the investigation, the purge commission would announce its verdict. In the case of Party members, the sentence would follow one of three sentences: cleared, cleared with a reprimand, or found guilty. Party members who were found guilty not only were expelled from the Party, but lost their jobs as well. In either case, even if the actual sentence was light, being purged was tantamount to losing one's ration card and very often one's lodging. Since by the early 1930s practically the entire economy was already controlled by the State, even the lighter punishment left the victim of the purge and his family homeless and destitute.

The purging of "slackers" and "saboteurs" was soon followed by mopping-up operations aimed at the elimination of both wings of the opposition, ex-Trotskyites and ex-Bukharinites. Throughout 1932–1933, stricter attention was also paid to intellectual and scientific workers, especially those belonging to minority groups. In 1934, the GPU was expanded into the People's Commissariat for Internal Affairs (NKVD). This meant that the secret police was to remain not only a central feature of the regime, but was also to be integrated with one of the key governmental institutions that controlled much of the country's internal life. Moreover, the NKVD was now placed in charge of all existing labor camps. These were increasingly swollen by former kulaks and other "enemies of the people," including selected members of the Party who had become, according to Stalin, "dizzy with success" while carrying out his own orders.

The Kirov Affair

The year 1934 was a turning point of the purges. In June of that year the Soviet regime broke with the Western principles of individual responsibility and the presumption that any accused person is innocent until proven guilty. The question of guilt or innocence was to be predetermined by a preliminary inquiry, as a rule conducted by the police. In the same year, a decree on "counterrevolution and high treason" provided for collective family responsibility in cases of flight by military personnel abroad. Severe penalties were established for failing to inform the authorities about an act of treason, whether actually committed or merely contemplated. A decree of April 7, 1935, extended capital punishment down to twelve-year-olds.

A line of reasoning called "legal analogy"—alien to the legal concepts common to the entire civilized world—was incorporated into Soviet criminal laws. For example, if a workman bungled a job he could be severely punished for sabotage, the analogy being that the damage he had done to the State was equal to what would have been done had he consciously engaged in an act of wrecking "socialist property." Since the standard penalty for sabotage was death, a workman who merely permitted a faulty truck transmission to pass through the inspection line could be executed. During the 1930s, this sort of thing occurred frequently. The denunciation of others was increasingly encouraged by rewards; those who refrained from it for whatever reason were publicly condemned. Reporting on one's fellow citizens or even on family members was pronounced a civic and patriotic duty. One of the heroes of Soviet youth was a small boy, Pavlik Morozov, who did not hesitate to denounce his family as counterrevolutionaries.

Until the close of 1934, the purge, as severe as it appeared, was still selective, directed mainly against actual or potential opposition. As far as the top Party members were concerned, it was on the whole bloodless. What changed the situation entirely was the Kirov affair and its aftermath. Since the personality and activities of Kirov played a central role here, a few words about him are in order. Born Sergei M. Kostrikov, a graduate of a two-year technical school in Kazan, he joined the Leninist faction of the RSDWP in 1905 at the age of nineteen. After the Bolshevik triumph, Kirov took part in the establishment of Soviet power in the Caucasus, where he was a firm supporter of Stalin's cruel methods. Kirov was a fanatically dedicated Party worker who used to repeat: "A Bolshevik should love his work more than his wife!" On the strength of this record, he replaced the demoted Zinoviev in 1926 in the second most important Party district, Leningrad. His purge of the supporters of Zinoviev and Trotsky was as stern as his struggle against "the bourgeois nationalists" in the Caucasus. As a reward, Kirov was promoted to membership in the Politburo in 1930.

Soon, however, the excesses of Stalin's tyranny began to alienate even as tough a man as Kirov. At the Seventeenth Party Congress of 1934, Kirov was already critical of Stalin's personal dictatorship. During the Congress he argued for reconciliation, saying that the class enemies had been routed and the Soviet system was secure and needed all those who were not against it. His speech was applauded and the Seventeenth Party Congress witnessed a major crisis of the regime. In the election to the Central Committee, Stalin received fewer votes than any other candidate, while Kirov was at the top of the list. Stalin was elected only because there were as many candidates as seats in the Central Committee.

Meanwhile, through the secret police, Stalin had learned that many Party members favored his removal from the post of Secretary General and his replacement by the more popular Kirov. The latter, when approached in private, secret conversations, repeatedly rejected the suggestion. What Stalin thought about the matter he never publicly revealed. In any case, on December 1, 1934, Kirov was assassinated in his office in Leningrad under circumstances that pointed at least to criminal negligence on the part of the security organs.

Whatever the final verdict, Kirov's assassination stands as one of the most important landmarks in the history of Soviet Russia. Immediately, and without even a summary investigation, the assassin and forty-nine of his alleged accomplices were shot. Soon after that the available former leaders of the Left Opposition, Zinoviev and Kameniev, were charged with complicity. Although they refused to confess, they were immediately sentenced to prison as co-responsible for the crime. Soon the hitherto selective purge assumed unprecedented mass proportions, and the country descended into a horrible bloody pit. Countless "Kirov's assassins" were arrested and deported without trial to distant parts of the Soviet Union under such inhuman conditions that countless casualties occurred even during the journey to labor and concentration camps. Thus the end of 1934 ushered in the period that was to last four years, known as the *Great Purge*.

The Great Purge

The Great Purge was characterized by unbridled mass terror and punctuated by a series of dramatic public "show trials" that differed markedly from previous affairs of a similar type. The political trials of the late 1920s and early 1930s were directed mainly against the survivors of the old technical intelligentsia, tainted with prerevolutionary spirit and counterrevolutionary in mood. Also hard hit by those trials were members of the historic political parties—the remnants of the Cadets, the SRs, and the Mensheviks—who had not emigrated when the opportunity was still available. Through these means, emigration and trials, by the mid-1930s all former opposition groups had already been broken. Whatever dissatisfaction with Stalin's policies still existed was centered around certain restricted Party circles.

By 1935, with the liquidation of countless "Kirov assassins," the Stalinist system could look back at the completion of its grimly successful mass purging operations. Resistance, even potential, had been broken. Yet it was only then that the Great Purge, having been unleashed, began to acquire a momentum of its own and to turn against the Party itself. In 1935, in a symbolic move signifying the end of one era and the beginning of another, a number of old Communist societies and

associations were abolished on Stalin's order. The first to be dissolved was the Society of Old Bolsheviks, composed of those who had joined the Party prior to 1917; next came the Association of Political Prisoners and the renowned Communist Academy. At the same time, in 1936, a new constitution was promulgated by Stalin, who called it "the most democratic in the world." It contained what appeared on paper as a fairly comprehensive and liberal bill of rights. Yet Article 112 of this constitution subordinated the judiciary to the Supreme Soviet. Since the Soviet was elected from a single list of candidates submitted by the Party, the Constitution thereby rejected an independent judiciary.

At this time the first national anthem of the USSR, the old battle song of the European revolutionary movement, "The Internationale," was replaced by a new song. The new anthem extolled the Soviet Union as the freest of all countries. The first stanza of the new anthem ended with the words, "I don't know any other country where man can breathe so freely."

All the time Stalin kept assuring his subjects at home and his followers abroad that he and his Party were devoted to human welfare above everything else. As he put it in one of his speeches at that time, "People must be tended carefully and lovingly, as a gardener tends a favorite fruit tree." But while paying lip service to loving care, he was increasingly practicing brutal pruning, woodchopping, and even timber-felling on an increasingly massive scale. It was puzzling that the terror of the years 1936–1938 increased in inverse ratio to the existence of internal opposition.

The Moscow Trials

There were three major public show trials in the 1930s. In all of them the main actors were former leading members of the Party and State administration. All the trials were held in Moscow; hence they are often referred to as the *Moscow trials*. The first was held in August 1936 and involved Zinoviev,

Kameniev, and fourteen other leading Communists, all former members of the Left Opposition. All were accused of being part of a "Trotskyite-Zinovievite terrorist center." Within four days the trial was over. All sixteen death sentences were carried out immediately.

Four months later, on November 30, the second show trial took place; it involved seventeen defendants headed by Karl Radek, one of the most enthusiastic and brilliant propagandists of the regime. All of the defendants, despite their initial sympathies with the Trotskyite opposition, had eventually recanted and finally sided with Stalin. Of the seventeen, thirteen were sentenced to death. Radek miraculously escaped execution by conveniently disclosing facts implicating some of the top Red Army commanders allegedly harboring "Bonapartist" ambitions.

Having finished with the Bolshevik Left, Stalin now brought the Right to the courtroom in the third and the last great public Moscow show trial, in March 1938. The trial involved twenty-one of the surviving former members of the Right Opposition, including such masterminds of Soviet Communism as Rykov and Bukharin. The third group also contained a number of Communist leaders from various national republics especially Ukraine. Paradoxically, the trial included as

Karl Radek (1885–1939), editor of *Pravda* and one of the victims of the Great Purge

well the previous purger-in-chief, former head of the NKVD Genrikh G. Yagoda. To the standard accusations of sabotage, spying, and treason was now added a new one: Yagoda was accused of having organized a regular murder laboratory for the purpose of exterminating top Soviet leaders, including the writer Maxim Gorky, who had died in somewhat mysterious circumstances. One of the most grotesque allegations was that Bukharin had plotted the assassination of Lenin and Stalin as early as 1918. The real disagreements between Stalin and Bukharin over the NEP and collectivization were not even mentioned.

The Moscow show trials were not the only blows dealt by Stalin to his political opponents—past, present, and potential. In June 1937, a sudden trial and immediate execution of top leaders of the Red Army also took place. As a result of secret and summary proceedings, three out of five marshals of the Soviet Union were accused of various crimes, including Trotskyism and conspiracy with Germany and Japan. Among the three marshals was one of the principal heroes of the Civil War and the actual Chief of the Soviet General Staff, Mikhail N. Tukhachevsky; Alexander I. Yegorov and Vasily K. Bluecher were also tried.

Following the execution of Tukhachevsky, Yegorov, and Bluecher, the purge of military and naval personnel descended to the lower echelons of the Soviet armed forces. Parallel with the reimposition of stricter controls by the Political Commissars, some 40 to 50 percent of the senior officers were arrested and either shot or deported to various concentration and labor camps run by the NKVD. The Soviet Navy was especially hard hit. Among the lower personnel the purge was less extensive and affected only 20 to 30 percent of the junior officers. The damage the purge inflicted on the Red Army was devastating.

Although the decapitation of the Red Army was not the last dramatic act of what became known as the "Great Purge," in many ways it represented its climactic novelty, and may have been the most original contribution of the Stalinist totalitarian system to the

Marshal Mikhail Tukhachevsky (1893–1937)

evolution of State-sponsored terror. In the past all dictatorships based themselves to a greater or lesser extent on the armed forces and operated in partnership with their leaders. Stalin was the first to prove that his regime was capable of relying on other factors like the Party apparatus and the secret police. By using the Party Political Administration and operating through the network of Political Commissars attached to every unit, as well as through an extensive counter-intelligence organization, Stalin was able to neutralize any possible reaction of the military personnel to his deadly blows; they were surprising and sudden.

The crippling of the Red Army also represented another noteworthy variation in the pattern of the purge. Whereas during the show trials Stalin dealt with already defeated, completely isolated, helpless individuals, here he struck at powerful and popular, idolized men in full command of the armed forces. Both the swiftness and the decisiveness of the blow were revealing. So were the

utter helplessness and passivity of the victims. None of the destroyed Army leaders tried to resist, and their executions did not produce even a ripple in the smooth functioning of the Soviet military machine. Stunned Red Army and Navy personnel meekly followed official instructions to maintain strict discipline and "Bolshevik vigilance." The June 12, 1937, edition of *Pravda* that carried the news of the trial and execution of the three former idols of the Soviet armed forces also included some interesting items about the reaction of aroused military personnel and factory workers: they promptly passed a series of resolutions justifying the allegedly prophylactic measures undertaken against "the mad dogs." "For the dogs—dogs' death" ran a resolution of one of the night shifts of a Moscow factory.

The NKVD's Mistakes

The charges against most victims of the purges were fantastic and often hastily prepared. In some cases their absurdity was apparent almost immediately. For instance, on August 24, 1936, six days after the execution of "the Zinoviev-Kameniev-Trotskyite gang," the Danish paper *Socialdemokraten* pointed out that the Bristol Hotel in Copenhagen, where a representative of the leftist conspirators allegedly had met Trotsky's son Sedov in 1932, had been demolished long before the meeting was alleged to have taken place. Moreover, Sedov could not have been in Copenhagen at that time because on that particular day he was undergoing a written examination at the Berlin Technical College, a fact testified to by the College in a legal affidavit. This example, one of many, revealed the inefficiency of the NKVD and could not go unpunished. And indeed, on September 28, 1936, its head, Yagoda, was dismissed and replaced by Nikolai I. Yezhov.

The trial and execution of the three military leaders is an excellent example of the faulty accusations made by the regime. From German documents captured by the victors in 1945, it is possible to reconstruct the story of

Tukhachevsky and his two comrades. The deputy head of the Gestapo, Reinhardt Heydrich, was familiar with Stalin's morbidly suspicious mind and with Tukhachevsky's outstanding abilities. He decided to create confusion in the ranks of a former ally who was, after 1934, a possible wartime enemy. In 1937, Heydrich forged a letter in Tukhachevsky's name to a former fellow student at a military academy in Berlin. The letter informed his colleague, now a German general, about the mounting opposition to Stalin's personal dictatorship and about Tukhachevsky's plans to overthrow him and reestablish cordial relations with Germany. The forged letter was conveniently sold by the Gestapo to an agent of the Czechoslovak intelligence service in Berlin. Czechoslovak Foreign Minister Edward Beneš, after signing the 1935 alliance with the USSR, was only ingratiating himself to Stalin, and passed on this piece of intelligence to Stalin without first verifying its authenticity. One should not, however, think that Stalin was tricked by Heydrich and Beneš. Although he received the incriminating letter in January 1937, he did not act upon it. The letter did not figure in the trial of the marshal and his colleagues; it was added to the file for good measure only after he had been shot. Clearly, Stalin had been determined to get rid of the popular and potentially dangerous military leader by hook or by crook, whatever the evidence. Any serious examination of the Gestapo-manufactured letter probably would have exposed it as a forgery; its political naiveté was obvious because no Soviet military leader would inform a foreigner living in a capitalist country about a planned *coup d'état* against a well-established, formidable ruler controlling arguably the best and most extensive intelligence network in the world.

Stalin's Motives

Stalin's motives in slaughtering such a vast number of Soviet leaders have been a subject of much debate. One possible explanation for his behavior was given by a Trotskyite writer, Isaac Deutscher, in his admiring biography of Stalin. In case of a German- and/or Japanese-Soviet war—which Stalin as a realistic leader must have envisaged—the Russian opposition leaders might be driven to take action against him, should the course of such a war turn against Russia. To exclude any such possibility, Stalin decided to accuse them of having already entered into a treasonous alliance with the two potential enemies. Thus, according to Deutscher's imaginative reconstruction, Stalin's move was an act of prophylactic political surgery aimed at the physical elimination of all possible alternatives to his rule. Justice was seldom more blindfolded than during the Great Purge, for it was made to serve strictly political purposes having nothing to do with legal order. One of Stalin's dogmas was: "Death solves all problems, no man, no problem."

Another, more plausible explanation, advanced by the former head of Stalin's bodyguard, Colonel Alexander Orlov, is that the Soviet dictator was a secret admirer of Hitler and believed in the possibility, nay necessity, of a new close agreement with the man whom he considered as the only leader in Europe worthy of such a name. Consequently, from 1934 onwards, he set out to destroy all those who would have opposed such an accommodation with an "Arch Fascist." Another explanation ascribes the purges to the necessity of diverting the restless population's attention from economic hardships, the shortages of food, fuel, and other basic necessities, by the tales of sabotage, wreckage, and terroristic attempts perpetrated by a selected group of Stalin's opponents. Every failure or mishap could be conveniently blamed on these scapegoats as "saboteurs," or "enemies of the people." Still another possible explanation of the purge is Stalin's desire to make more room at the top for his own henchmen, the people he had just promoted, and whom he trusted more than the "Old Guard."

In some ways, the Great Purge represented the last phase of the power struggle precipitated by Lenin's demise. Except for the military leaders, the main opponents had all

Andrei Vyshinsky, the Chief Prosecutor of the Moscow trials and Minister of Foreign Affairs, 1940–1949 and 1953–1955

the purge trials was as important as their eventual physical liquidation. Many of the better-known victims in better times had had their pictures displayed in public places, in offices, schools, and barracks. Streets and squares had been named after them; this was especially true of Marshal Tukhachevsky. Now all this had to be erased, places renamed, textbooks withdrawn from circulation and reprinted, and portraits replaced, usually with those of Stalin. During 1936–1938, public adulation of Stalin's personality and achievements reached its peak. There was, finally, nobody to compete with him.

Stalin's purges were an expression of his paranoia, his morbid, irrational suspicion of everyone around him. Consequently, he tended to ascribe to his actual and potential opponents those criminal intentions that he harbored himself. Not to be mistaken, he always preferred to kill ten potential opponents than to miss one real enemy. He would probably agree with his Chinese admirer, Mao Tse Tung: "People are not chives—when you cut their heads, they do not grow new ones."

been either politically destroyed or at least neutralized. One of the purposes of the trials was to dramatize the opponents' downfall to the masses and to destroy their image as good Communists, thereby completing their destruction. Thus the trials represented morality plays. The educational side of the show trials was underscored by the insistence of the chief prosecutor, Andrei Vyshinsky, that the accused confess to the charges against them. Most defendants obliged Vyshinsky and confessed to what were often the most absurd crimes. The reasons why they agreed to this final humiliation varied. Kameniev, for instance, did it for a guarantee that his family and those of other accused victims would not be persecuted. Bukharin confessed to spare his young wife and their child a similar fate. Radek admitted his alleged guilt to save his own skin. But none of Stalin's promises were kept.

The moral destruction of the victims of

The Scope of the Purge

The Great Purge affected not only the Party leaders; it filtered down, spread, and assumed unprecedented proportions. The arrest and deportation and/or execution of one member of a family often resulted in the imprisonment of other family members. Accusations ranged from acts of sabotage and disloyalty to telling unacceptable political jokes. Dissenters who managed to escape to the West to tell the story often mentioned in their testimonies that even trivial incidents could cause severe punishment. A sentence of five years of forced labor camp was considered light. There is a story, that a former inmate of a camp near Novosibirsk was asked by his commander, "What's your sentence?" The prisoner answered, "Twenty-five years." "What for?" "For nothing," answered the prisoner. "You are lying! In our country, for nothing they give you only five years!"

Another authentic report says that one day an old seamstress had been cutting a dress pattern and needed some extra paper for the collar. She reached for a newspaper and, as she was cutting, the tip of her scissors happened to pierce a photograph of Stalin in the paper. Someone saw that and ran off to report to the police. Soon the old lady was hauled off to a camp. It was said that the huge Baltic–White Sea Canal was built by those punished for telling political jokes.

By 1938 the orgy of denunciations, deportations, and executions had reached tidal proportions; some eight million people were crowding the prisons and labor camps of the Soviet Union. The power of the secret police had become so extensive as to frighten Stalin himself. Meanwhile, he must have decided that the purge had gotten out of hand. Had Yezhov been allowed to carry it on at the same rate, he would have brought down the very framework of the Soviet State. Consequently, Stalin decided to call a halt. At the Eighteenth Party Congress in March 1939, he admitted numerous excesses and promised Party members to protect their security. In an effort to divorce himself from the disastrous consequences of the repressions, he declared that it was the NKVD, treacherously infiltrated by enemies of the people, that was responsible for the deplorable excesses that had crippled the Party. Moreover, he pledged never to allow another mass purge. But the disaster that had befallen the Soviet people could not be undone: between seven and eight million people arrested, about one million executed, some eight million in slave labor camps. Many victims were children. Again, as in the past, selected scapegoats had to pay for Stalin's mistakes. In December 1938, the dreaded Yezhov was arrested and soon liquidated, like his predecessor, Yagoda. Yezhov's place was taken by Lavrentii Beria, charged with the task of purging the former purgers.

Thus by the close of 1938, Stalin weathered another crisis. Although in 1937 he had employed the NKVD to crush the Army, in 1938 he combined the forces of the Party, supported this time by aroused public opinion, against the hated secret police. A campaign against the "opportunists," "careerists," "slanderers," and "liars" in the ranks of the NKVD was unleashed, and numerous arrests were made among its ranks. "The purge of the purgers" resulted in numerous former police agents joining their erstwhile victims in prison cells and camps. Several interrogators committed suicide from fear of arrest. On the other hand, numerous survivors who had been apprehended during the Great Purge were released and rehabilitated.

The intensity of the campaign indicated the dictator's determination to dissociate himself from the vast scope and fierce intensity of the purge. Meanwhile, Stalin continued to make pronouncements condemning the nefarious activities of his unruly insubordinates who dared to exceed their orders and assured the people that, "Of all the treasures a State can possess, the human lives of its citizens are for us the most precious."

Historians have been arguing how many people Stalin killed altogether: 20 or 30 million. Whatever the actual figure, it requires seven digits to approximate.

The Uniqueness of the Great Purge

Perhaps the most characteristic feature of the Great Purge was its unprecedented scope and depth. Between 1936 and 1938, nine out of eleven cabinet ministers were executed. So were twenty-seven top political and legal experts who had drafted the Constitution of 1936 with its generous bill of rights. The armed forces were hit harder than any other group. According to the most recent Western estimates not only did 3 out of the 5 Marshals of the Soviet Union perish in the purge, but also 14 of the 16 Army Commanders, all 8 Admirals, 60 of the 67 Corps Commanders, 136 of the 199 Divisional Commanders, and 221 of the 397 Brigade Commanders. All 11 of the Vice-Commissars of Defense and 75 out of 80 members of the Supreme Military Council were also liquidated. Altogether 35,000 officers, about 50 percent of the officers' corps, were affected one way or another by the purge. Not all were shot or perished in the labor camps. Many of them survived the predicament and were rehabilitated in the emergency of World War II. Some of them became national heroes; for example, Marshal of the Soviet Konstantine Rokossovsky. Although the purges did not cripple the Red Army completely, they weakened it considerably on the eve of a great international storm.

The Great Purge was distinct from the preceding phases of Stalinist repression in many respects. Its most striking feature was its unprecedented scope which affected, one way or another, millions of people. Second, the Great Purge either introduced or intensified extraordinary methods for extracting confessions from selected victims at spectacular, carefully rehearsed show trials. These devices combined subtle psychological pressures with the use of naked force. The "conveyor," or continual interrogation in relays by police officers for hours and even days on end, was a classic example. Third, apart from the public show trials, immense, unpublicized operations were conducted through the country to identify, apprehend, and punish millions of human beings who were considered potentially harmful or inconvenient to the regime or were simply, for one reason or another, disliked by its security organs.

Stalin's terror differed from the reprisals of other totalitarian regimes by two additional features. First, most of the Soviet purges were directed not against an outside group but toward their own people, largely Party members. Second, the purges gave their victims no opportunity to exonerate themselves. Guilt and innocence became irrelevant. Individuals were killed or deported not for what they did or said, but for being what they were (for instance, kulaks), or for supposedly harboring disloyal or subversive thoughts.

The Great Purge was for the Soviet people a traumatic experience comparable to World War II. Boris Pasternak put these words into the mouth of one of the characters in his novel *Dr. Zhivago*:

And when the war broke out, its real horrors, its real dangers, its menace of real death were a blessing compared with the inhuman reign of the lie, and they brought relief because they broke the spell of the dead letter.

Terror has always been a by-product of revolutionary upheaval. But mass, unbridled terror of the Stalinist type, indiscriminate and deliberately haphazard, with people arrested even when they were known to be perfectly innocent and harmless, was a novelty. It seems that Stalin purposely tried to create an atmosphere in which no one could feel secure and everybody was vulnerable and at the mercy of the omnipotent dictator, the complete master of everyone's destiny. Many historians and political scientists have tried to rationalize the Stalinist purges, but all their explanations are weak if they do not take into consideration the irrational element of Stalin's psyche—his morbid, vindictive mind, warped by suspicion and permeated by paranoiac fears. During a drinking bout Stalin told his intimates that the greatest joy he could imagine was "to choose one's victim, to prepare one's plans minutely, to slake the implacable vengeance, and then go to bed. . . . There is nothing sweeter in the world." Indeed the saying of the French moralist La Rochefoucauld that "we are seldom able to pardon those we have injured" is fully applicable to Stalin.

The Purge and the Reshaping of the Party

The Great Purge, which destroyed many, opened unexpected avenues of advance for others. For instance, a minor director of a textile factory named Alexei N. Kosygin climbed to the rank of a Deputy Premier of the Russian Federal Republic. A minor engineer in a metallurgical factory named Leonid I. Brezhnev advanced in a few years to become Party boss of a key industrial district, Dnepropetrovsk. A little known regional commander, Gregory K. Zhukov, rose within three years to the post of Chief of the Soviet General Staff, while Nicholas G. Kuznetsov within the same period was promoted from commander of a cruiser to the Chief of the Soviet Navy.

Besides the speeding up of upward mobility, another aspect of the purges of the late 1930s was their impact on the country's economy. They were not the sole or even the main cause of the first serious decline in the rate of growth of the Soviet GNP since the launching of the First Five-Year Plan. Yet it seems beyond doubt that the dislocations they caused in the industrial cadres significantly contributed to the economic slowdown and the decline in labor productivity. In 1939, for instance, pig iron and steel output fell below the 1938 level and did not recover until the beginning of 1941. Production of tractors and automobiles also declined during this period. All this was largely the result of the destruction of the cream of Soviet industrial management.

As has already been mentioned, the Party as a whole was proportionately more affected by the purges than the population at large. By the time Yezhov was dismissed by Stalin in December 1938, Lenin's Bolshevik party of the 1920s had been reshaped so that it was now a different body. Of the 140 members of the Party's Central Committee, 98 were purged; altogether some 70 percent of the Party leadership was affected by the Stalinist reprisals. While in 1935 the Party numbered 2,358,000 people, in 1938 it shrank to 1,920,000 or 438,000 fewer members, this despite constant recruitment of new members.

Besides its numerical contraction, the quality of Party membership had been dramatically altered. Although the organizational framework remained the same, its human content underwent a radical change. The extent of the discontinuity becomes striking when one analyzes the composition of the Seventeenth Congress of 1934 and the Eighteenth Congress of 1939. The latter included less than 2 percent of the rank-and-file delegates of the former. Meanwhile, not only had delegates opposed to Stalin been eliminated, but even those hesitant or potentially mistrustful of him had disappeared from the scene. The delegates to the 1939 Congress were a soulless crowd of automatons hand-picked by the regional bosses. They voted unanimously for the motions presented by the Leader, irrespective of their convictions—if they had any at all. This had been exactly Stalin's goal. As he said bluntly, "A true Communist must be able to agree that two times two is sixteen." Total subordination to Number One, and not the revolutionary, innovative, and restless spirit of the earlier evangelical period, became the supreme criterion for survival and promotion. Consequently, the Party became highly bureaucratized. After 1938, as life gravitated toward totalitarian stability, there was an increasing need for material advantages. Stalin cunningly harnessed these desires. The survivors of the purges were rewarded for their servility with a variety of privileges, including special shops, apartments, cars, country villas, and educational advantages for the children of "the new class," the Party elite, or a sort of Party upper crust, known as *nomenclatura*.[1]

Another change in the Party was of an ideological character. The old Bolshevik "proletarian internationalism," with its universalist supranational outlook, had been discarded in the late 1920s and replaced by a sort of proletarian nationalism that, while paying lip service to the old concept of the international proletarian revolution, increasingly emphasized the domestic interests of the Soviet Union. As a result, during the 1930s, Stalin consummated the marriage of Soviet Communism with traditional Russian nationalism. While the old Bolshevik party had been dominated by a mixed lot of cosmopolitan intellectuals of Russian, Georgian, Jewish, Baltic, and Polish extraction, the

---

[1] *Nomenclatura* is the term for a list of the most important posts and of the names of Party members who are trustworthy enough to fill these posts.

Stalinist Party "of a new type" was increasingly dominated by native Russians; they were members largely of peasant origin and relatively much less interested in the affairs of the outside world. During the 1930s, Stalin's Party started its evolution from proletarian internationalism toward Russian nationalism. These changes in Party composition were paralleled by Stalin's new attitude toward the Soviet nationality problems and foreign affairs.

Suggested Reading

ARMSTRONG, JOHN A., *The Politics of Totalitarianism: The Communist Party of the Soviet Union from 1934 to the Present.* New York: Random House, 1961.

BONNER, ELENA, *Mothers and Daughters.* New York: Alfred A. Knopf, 1992.

BRZEZINSKI, ZBIGNIEW K., *The Permanent Purge: Politics in Soviet Totalitarianism.* Cambridge, MA: Harvard University Press, 1956.

CARMICHAEL, JOEL, *Stalin's Masterpiece, The Show Trials and Purges of the Thirties—The Consolidation of the Bolshevik Dictatorship.* New York: St. Martin's, 1976.

CONQUEST, ROBERT, *The Great Terror.* New York: Oxford University Press, 1990.

———, *Stalin and the Kirov Murder.* New York: Oxford University Press, 1989.

———, *Inside Stalin's Secret Police.* Stanford, Calif.: Hoover, 1985.

COSTELLO, JOHN AND TSAREV, OLEG, *Deadly Illusion.* London: Century, 1993.

DJILAS, MILOVAN, *The New Class.* New York: Praeger, 1957.

FAINSOD, MERLE, *Smolensk under Soviet Rule.* Cambridge, MA: Harvard University Press, 1958.

FRIEDRICH, CARL J., AND ZBIGNIEW K. BRZEZINSKI, *Totalitarian Dictatorship and Autocracy,* 2nd ed. Rev. by Carl J. Friedrich. New York: Praeger, 1966.

GETTY, J. ARCH, *Origins of the Great Purges. The Soviet Communist Party Reconsidered, 1933–1938.* Cambridge, England: University of Cambridge, 1986.

GRAHAM, LOREN, *Soviet Academy of Science and the Communist Party, 1927–1932.* Princeton, NJ: Princeton University Press, 1967.

KATKOV, GEORGE, *The Trial of Bukharin.* New York: Stein and Day, 1969.

LARINA, ANNA, *This I Cannot Forget: The Memoirs of Nikolai Bukharin's Widow.* New York: W.W. Norton, 1993.

MATTHEWS, MERVYN (ED.), *Party, State and Citizen in the Soviet Union.* New York: M.E. Sharpe, 1990.

PARISH, MICHAEL, *The Lesser Terror: Soviet State Security, 1939–1953.* Westport, CT: Praeger, 1996.

REIMAN, MICHAEL, *The Birth of Stalinism: The USSR on the Eve of the "Second Revolution."* Bloomington: Indiana University Press, 1987.

SERGE, VICTOR, *Memoirs of a Revolutionary, 1901–1941.* New York: Oxford University Press, 1963.

SOLZHENITZYN, ALEXANDER, *The Gulag Archipelago.* New York: Harper and Row, 1974, 1975, and 1977, 3 vols.

VAKSBERG, ARKADY, *Stalin's Prosecutor: The Life of Andrei Vyshinsky.* New York: Grove Weidenfeld, 1991.

WEISSBERG, ALEX, *The Accused.* New York: Simon and Schuster, 1951.

Chapter 15

A New Nationality Policy and the Soviet Cultural Revolution

One of the results of the Stalin revolution was such close integration of economic management with the Party-State bureaucracy. Consequently, the two became practically indistinguishable. After the 1930s the Party, supported by the iron hand of the ubiquitous security apparatus, became virtually omnipotent. This naturally had profound repercussions on all aspects of life, including nationality policy, culture, and science.

Stalin's views had manifested themselves in the field of nationality policy before the integrative forces generated by the five-year plans brought about the economic welding together of the USSR's multiethnic segments. The creation of ostensibly sovereign federal republics was largely due to Lenin. This was always resented by a considerable segment of the Party leaders, including the then Commissar for Nationalities, Stalin. He, Trotsky, and the Chief of the Secret Police Dzerzhinsky, were not satisfied even that an impressive measure of economic control was maintained through unified Party supervision. Although after 1924 the constituent republics of the Soviet Union ostensibly preserved their local separate party structures, the tightening of Soviet Party centralizing controls had already begun during the NEP.

Although Stalin was not an ethnic Russian, he was thoroughly Russified. His daughter did not hesitate to say about her father, "I know no other Georgian who had so completely sloughed off his qualities as a Georgian and loved everything Russian."[1] He was always suspicious of local nationalism as a potentially centrifugal force. It was Stalin who ruthlessly repressed all traces of local patriotism, which was condemned as "bourgeois nationalism." All this was done not in the name of Russian national ideas, but in the name of a new homogenized Soviet society, allegedly national in form, but Marxist in content. In order to carry out this process of "social engineering," Stalin purposely deemphasized the Russian character of the Communist Party and stressed the role of the All-Union Communist Party, or the CPSU.

The ethnic pluralism of the Soviet Union, however, was tough to suppress. Manifestations of "bourgeois nationalism" could be

---

[1] Svetlana Alliluyeva, *Twenty Letters to a Friend*, trans. by Priscilla Johnson McMillan (New York: Harper & Row, 1967), pp. 119–120. By permission of Harper & Row.

spotted in various parts of the USSR. The horrors of the collectivization and industrialization carried out by most cruel methods turned the western and southern provinces of the Soviet Union into areas seething with resentment and potential revolt. During this period Stalin could not fail to notice that the opposition to collectivization and other measures was stronger in the multiethnic borderlands than in the Great Russian heartland of the USSR. He obliquely acknowledged it at the Sixteenth Party Congress in 1930: "The survival of capitalism in men's consciousness is much more tenacious in the sphere of national problems than in any other sphere." This observation, combined with his congenital suspicion of ethnic nationalism, made him equate all manifestations of local defiance with irredentism and treason.

Resistance in the Borderlands

Nowhere did the resistance to collectivization and other measures manifest itself more vigorously than among the Ukrainians, whom the Russians traditionally regarded as their "junior brothers." The opposition was also strong among the inhabitants of Belorussia, and the Caucasus, home of Stalin's native Georgia. Consequently, the purges of the 1930s hit these border regions with special ferocity. The heaviest blows fell during the mid-1930s on the second most important and populous federal republic, Ukraine. The great famine, which had affected the Ukrainians most horribly, tried the loyalty even of local Communist zealots. Their policies, which attempted to combine Marxist doctrine with Bolshevik methods and local radical traditions, were increasingly attacked and overruled by Moscow. Two men who embodied this peculiar combination of Communism and nationalism were Alexander Shumsky and Mykola Skrypnik. Both of them had been instrumental in establishing Soviet rule in Ukraine. As successive Commissars for Education, each tried to apply a hybrid policy that combined Communism and local patriotism to their native land. Their policy greatly stim-

ulated the flowering of Ukrainian literature and arts during the 1920s and early 1930s. Many Ukrainian intellectuals—for instance, Mykola Khvylovy—took advantage of the apparently relaxed atmosphere that had prevailed on the Dnieper during the NEP, to voice their nationalistic aspirations. In 1925, Khvylovy established a weekly newspaper in which he assailed the Muscovite centralism now hiding behind the Communist facade, and urged his countrymen to draw closer to the main source of progressive ideas, the West. Khvylovy suspected that social and economic modernization meant not merely Sovietization, but ultimately Russification. Other writers denounced the continuing Muscovite policy of economically exploiting the rich Ukrainian natural resources for the benefit of the Great Russian heartland. Although these voices were promptly silenced, the fairly permissive ethnic policy was continued essentially unchanged under Skrypnik until the early 1930s.

Collectivization was more desperately resisted by the Ukrainian peasants, freer of the Russian communal tradition than anywhere else and more attached to their individual farms.[2] Besides fierce active opposition and passive sabotage, the resistance expressed itself in a series of secret societies, the most important of which was the Union for the Liberation of the Ukraine. The trial of forty-five members of the Union in 1930 spelled the beginning of the end of the policy of "Ukrainization," and hence of the Ukrainian cultural revival. In June 1933, Skrypnik's policy was sharply attacked by Stalin's henchmen, Pavel P. Postyshev—who since 1931 had been Secretary of the Communist Party in the Ukraine—and his associate, Stanislaw Kossior. Skrypnik was denounced for allegedly coddling Ukrainian nationalist deviation and tolerating "bourgeois nationalistic conspirators." Seeing his

---

[2] Collectivization as a political instrument in the struggle against the Ukrainians and the man-made large-scale famine that ensued, are expertly discussed by Robert Conquest in *The Harvest of Sorrow: Soviet Collectivization and the Terror-Famine* (New York: Oxford University Press, 1986), Part III, "Terror-Famine."

policy in ruin, threatened with demotion, and a purge that had meanwhile struck many of his close friends and co-workers, Skrypnik committed suicide. Khvylovy had already done so two months earlier.

The purge of their associates and co-workers, who were being denounced as "traitors," reached a crescendo under Stalin's new proconsul for the Ukraine, Lazar Kaganovich. In 1937, another of the dictator's close allies, Nikita Khrushchev, became a member of a "purge troika" including Vyacheslav Molotov and Nikolay Yezhov, head of the secret police. By 1937–1938, the "liquidation of the enemies of the people" in the Ukraine had reached its peak. Most members of the Ukrainian government, the Ukrainian Central Committee, and the Ukrainian Supreme Soviet were summarily executed. The purge was not limited to Party and State apparatus and to military personnel; it fell heavily on the intellectuals as well. Between 1937 and 1938, all thirteen secretaries of the Ukrainian Academy of Science were arrested. Of the seven rectors (presidents) of Kiev University during the same period, six were liquidated; only one died a natural death. This persecution was paralleled by mass deportations of Ukrainians to various distant parts of the USSR, mainly Siberia and the Maritime Provinces. The flourishing Ukrainian cultural revival was thus aborted.

In the Belorussian Soviet Republic, "bourgeois nationalistic tendencies" were also "unmasked" during the 1930s, and their exponents most cruelly purged. There too the composition of the local top Party and government leadership was changed several times over. By 1938–1939, the former protagonists of the "national Bolshevik" trend in both western border republics had disappeared almost completely. The vacated jobs were gradually handed over to younger people trained entirely in the new school, and new members of the Party *apparat*[3] loyal to the Stalinist way of interpreting the principle

of "proletarian internationalism" which was a cover term for Russian nationalism.

Other Victims

Meanwhile, even more far-reaching changes were taking place in the Central Asian Republics. Until 1928–1929, this region had been only slightly affected by the Soviet system, except for the replacement of the old Arabic script by the Latin in 1925. Otherwise, under the new rubric of Communism the old tribal life went on unchanged. This situation began to alter drastically soon after the launching of the five-year plans. Settlers from Russia were sent to the region in increasing numbers, while local nomadic tribes were forced to settle down and compelled to engage in various pursuits, including agriculture, largely strange to the mostly nomadic and pastoral tribes of Central Asia. A campaign was launched to uproot Islam and the traditional way of life based on the Koran. Both the Arabic and the Latin scripts were forbidden, and the Russian alphabet made obligatory. These policies caused a great deal of resistance, which was ruthlessly repressed, and resulted in heavy loss of life. According to Soviet statistics, during the 1930s the Kazakh population decreased by almost a million and became outnumbered by the Russian colonists. The Volga Kazan Tatars fiercely opposed the "alphabetic revolution" and their leader, Sultan Galiev was tried, condemned for his "bourgeois nationalist deviation," and sent to a concentration camp where he perished.

The Jews also suffered from the new ethnic policy. By 1926, the Jewish Section of the Communist Party (*Yevsektsia*) had already ceased to meet and soon was disbanded. Under the pretext that Jews had no large, compact, rural settlements and no agricultural population, both Lenin and Stalin had denied the existence of Jews as a separate national group. Then, in 1928, Stalin designated the forbidding Far Eastern region of Birobirdzan, part of the Khabarovsk province, as a place for Jewish

---

[3]By *apparat*, one understood the body of paid Party officials employed full time in running the Party machine.

colonization. In 1934, when a considerable number of Jewish settlers had moved in, the region was triumphantly proclaimed the Jewish Autonomous Province. The Jewish population never outnumbered the local settlers and remained essentially urban. Soon Birobirdzan, initially proclaimed as a success in Soviet ethnic policy, disappeared as a subject of official propaganda. This was another trick in Stalin's arsenal of "social engineering" that failed miserably. In 1937, Semyon Dimanstein, the secretary of the Communist Party in Birobirdzan, was purged and accused of "Trotskyism." Similar fates befell many other prominent Jewish Communists, most of them victims of the Great Purge. The 1930s saw the first manifestations of official anti-Semitism in the form of open discrimination against Jews in education and especially in sensitive positions such as the Soviet Armed Forces or institutions maintaining contact with foreign countries.

The Making of the "Soviet Nation"

While pursuing Draconian nationality policies, Stalin launched the new concept of the homogenized "Soviet nation" that would supersede existing ethnic ties and loyalties. He believed that such a policy would assure maximum centralized control. Political unification required unified national culture. The original Leninist formula that culture must be "national in form and socialist in content" was now reinterpreted dialectically. National cultures, it was argued, must first be allowed to develop. Then Marxist "social engineering" would allow them to merge gradually into one common "Soviet culture" with one common language. Given the numerical and historical predominance of Great Russians within the USSR, Soviet national culture must be essentially a Russian one, with slight local variations.

Throwing away caution, advised by Lenin in the touchy ethnic matters, Stalin precipitated a new, radical nationality policy. First of all, during the middle and late 1930s, new directives were issued to educational and cultural institutions. Anything that bore traces of "bourgeois nationalism" was to be suppressed. Museums, State archives, libraries, and reading rooms were searched in order to remove everything that contradicted the new trend. New textbooks were printed to deemphasize the role of local cultures and languages and stress the "leading role," of the "progressive" Muscovite-Russian civilization. National histories were rewritten to emphasize the common destiny of the family of nations now forming the Soviet Union. Using the term "Russification" was forbidden, however. The whole process was conducted in the name of creating "a new Soviet man," allegedly free of all traces of reactionary "bourgeois nationalist deviations."

During the early 1930s, a new linguistic policy was launched in the two Slavic republics, Ukraine and Belorussia. In 1934, Stalin speeded up the process of bringing the Ukrainian and Belorussian idioms closer to the Russian language. Dictionaries were revised, localisms eliminated, and recent borrowings from Western languages replaced with corresponding loan-words from Russian. The use of local vernaculars in literature was discouraged.

A decisive step was taken on March 13, 1938, when a decree made "the study of the Russian language obligatory in schools of all national republics and [autonomous] regions." The local Commissars of Education were instructed "to compile and publish, before the beginning of the next school year, Russian primers, readers and grammars. . . ." The order meant that by September 1, 1938, within about five months, textbooks and equipment had to be made ready and teachers of Russian trained for over 60,000 schools. Because there were not enough teachers at hand, in many cases Russian language, literature, and history had to be temporarily taught by Red Army officers from the local garrisons. Since replacement of the old textbooks was a long, intricate process, schools were often to go without books entirely for months and even years.

Behind the constitutional facade of federalism, Stalin further pursued his new nationality policy. While a sort of "folkore nationalism" was strongly encouraged, an effort was made to eradicate all manifestations of attachment to genuine local patriotism, and to bully ethnic groups into one Soviet mold. The terms "Soviet nationality" and "Soviet patriotism" took on increasingly strong Russian overtones, although the words "Russia" and "Russian" were avoided whenever possible. The same was true as far as separate political institutions of the Russian Republic were concerned. Unlike in other federal republics, for instance Ukraine or Belorussia, in Russia the governmental and quasi-parliamentary, purely ornamental institutions, were left dormant.

To vindicate the new line as the only effective and "progressive" one, Stalin declared that the USSR offered "a system State organization in which ethnic problems and the problem of cooperation among nations have been solved more perfectly than in any other multinational state." Yet from the point of view of the ethnic minorities, Stalin's policy spelled the return of the old Muscovite colonialism in a new Soviet garb.

The Reshaping of Literature

Just as the Marxist concept of economics had a limited effect on Soviet life during the NEP, so the idea of proletarian culture had little actual effect on Soviet art and literature at large. For several years after the Bolshevik Revolution intellectual life of the country was relatively relaxed. In the 1930s, soon after launching the First Five-Year Plan, and upon encountering obstacles to it, the Party resolved to give short shrift to the relatively free intellectual atmosphere of the NEP and undertake a concerted, resolute effort to mobilize all resources to overcome the mounting difficulties. Literature and the arts were to be auxiliary tools in maximizing the modernization drive. In 1928, with official support, the Russian Union of Proletarian Writers had been established to act as the chief spokesmen of the profession. In princi-

ple, this association recognized the rights of non-Communist writers, but in practice it used all sorts of methods to force them to comply with the new official cultural policy line. Because the Union enjoyed government support, it soon achieved a near dictatorial position over Soviet literature. This it repaid with support for Party policies.

The philosophy professed by the leaders of the Union was simple. New socioeconomic conditions and the emergence of the proletariat as mass consumers of culture had created what the leaders of the Association termed a "social command." Writers of the new era should be "engineers of the soul," "craftsmen of words" who ought to satisfy the cultural needs of their new consumers, "the builders of socialism," and help them in their primary task, i.e., production of desired ideas. "Cultural output," like any other type of production, should be planned and carried out according to a plan chartered by the Party. The system of payment to authors was differentiated so as to provide greater rewards to authors who fulfilled their assigned tasks more quickly and better.

On February 10, 1930, the main Party journalistic organ, *Pravda*, began to publish a special literary page devoted to propagandizing the achievements of collectivization and industrialization. The paper launched the slogan, "Proletarian writers should stand shoulder to shoulder with shock workers" or those who consistently exceeded the prescribed work norm because they were the new heroes of the "epoch of socialism." Soon "production conferences" of Soviet writers and journalists were organized to "plan literary output." The "products" of such "planning" were to be delivered by a given date, and writers were to participate in various campaigns "for the liquidation of illiteracy," "against alcoholism," or "for speeded-up spring sowing." It was decided that the task of "building socialism" would be assisted not by writing poetry and fiction, but with biographies of shock workers and heroes of socialist labor; travelogues describing, for instance, collectivization campaigns in Uzbekistan or Siberia; and documentaries reflecting the "objective reality" of "building socialism." All this ought to be presented as a smooth, spontaneous process enthusiastically supported by the people, led by "the great genius of humanity."

Despite all its efforts, the Union did not quite satisfy the expectations of the Party. As a *Pravda* editorial put it, "No Magnitogorsk (i.e., giants) of literature was created," and intellectual dissent still lingered in many quarters. Consequently, on April 23, 1932, the Union of Proletarian Writers was dissolved. The Party decided that in the future there would be no separate literary groups, even if they called themselves "proletarian." From now on all writers would belong to a single centralized organization under the direct supervision of the Party. That year all existing associations were dissolved; the Union of Russian Proletarian Writers was replaced by the Soviet Writers' Union. Similar unions were established for other branches of artistic activity. Artists, writers, and other professional people were compelled to join centralized trade unions, one for each branch, and each one supervised by a Party delegate. Only such membership could confer the status without which no artist could exist or produce, no writer publish, and no musician perform.

Socialist Realism

The year 1934 was in many ways a turning point in the Soviet cultural revolution. That year *socialist realism* was officially proclaimed as the only prescribed mode of artistic expression. Realism, as the term is understood in the non-Communist world, has little connection with the realism that is preceded by the qualifying adjective "socialist." The qualification that the presentation of reality must serve prescribed ideological and didactic purposes makes socialist realism a way of presenting life "in the process of becoming the ideal." The desirable, the postulated, could hardly be distinguished from the real. What Stalin wanted was an art that would reflect reality as it was seen through the Party (that

is, what he hoped the Party would become). The embellishment (or "varnishing") of reality became a standard feature of Soviet literature, as well as of the other arts, during the remainder of the Stalin era.[4]

As another official commentary explained, socialist realism was required to depict "the heroic struggle of the world proletariat . . . the grandeur of the victory of Socialism, and the great wisdom and heroism of the Communist Party." Thus loyalty to the party and willingness to serve as its handmaiden were to be the first hallmark of this concept. In addition, socialist realist art had to be simple and obvious enough to be easily understood by all, even the least educated. The third obligatory principle that gradually came to be accepted in practice by most Soviet writers was the presence of one central "positive" figure in each story, novel, or poem. This figure, "the positive hero," was usually a person of impeccable personal, professional, and ideological credentials, always the first to appear at work in the morning and at the local Party cell meeting in the evening after the working hours. As a rule he not only fulfilled but even exceeded his norm of nuts and bolts, never lied or cheated, and conducted an exemplary personal life. Fiction of the Stalinist period was Puritanical, even Victorian, in its treatment of the sentimental life of its heroes and heroines. Their sex drive was, as a rule, channeled essentially to reproductive purposes, while reproduction took second place to economic production. Finally, the "positive hero" of Soviet literature was always victori-

[4] The attitude of most independently minded Soviet intellectuals toward socialist realism was reflected in the following anecdote circulated among them. "Once upon a time there was a mighty ruler of a powerful country who had no right arm and no right eye and wanted to have his picture painted for official display. One of the artists submitted to him his portrait as he was, without one arm and one eye. He was immediately hanged for 'bourgeois formalism.' Another painter presented his picture of the Dictator with both arms and eyes. He was executed for 'bourgeois idealism.' Finally, the third artist submitted his portrait depicting the tyrant with the left arm and the left eye to the viewer's side. This one was duly awarded the prize for 'socialist realism.'"

Stalin and Maxim Gorky, spiritual father of "socialist realism"

ous in the struggle against the lesser "nega-tive" characters representing either survivals of the reactionary past, "enemies of the peo-ple," "saboteurs," or "foreign spies."

The few works that are worth mentioning as documents of the epoch, despite the application of these rigid rules, are all novels that ignore the rules of "socialist realism" as originated by its spiritual father, Maxim Gorky. One of them is Mikhail Sholokhov's *Virgin Soil Upturned*, which glorifies collec-tivization but makes no attempt to hide its accompanying horrors. Another is a broad panorama that provides fictional back-ground to the five-year plans, Boris Pilnyak's *The Volga Flows to the Caspian Sea*. Fyodor Gladkov's two novels *Cement* and *Energy* focus on the all-pervasive theme of the country's modernization under Communism.

"Socialist realism" also affected perform-ing arts. Stalin was keenly interested in the cinema and the theater because they pro-vided him a window on cultural life and allowed him to control them. In February 1939 the Bolshoi Theater staged the opera of Mikhail Glinka's *A Life for the Tsar*. It had been performed to celebrate the Nicholas II coronation and to mark the tercentenary of the Romanov dynasty. Now it was performed again on the same stage, though under a dif-ferent name. On Stalin's order it was called *Ivan Susanin*. The words which had become the tsarist national anthem, glorifying the tsars, had been changed to "Glory, Glory, to Thee, My Russia!" Stalin came to attend the first performance of the opera, occupying the former imperial box.

Painting also came to serve the regime. Canvases and sculptures were naturalistic in rendering and simplistic in their message. They portrayed cheerful, well-fed collective farmers and their families, workers overfulfilling their norms, rosy-cheeked women shock workers singing and smiling as they drove huge tractors on collective (preferably State) farms. Most painters and sculptors were becoming increasingly nationalistic and the Red Army man became, next to the Stakhanovite hero of labor, their favorite theme. Most of the pictures of those days were actually posters designed for the purpose of teaching, preaching, and propagandizing.

The Soviet Cultural Revolution

The enforcement of socialist realism as the only tolerated artistic form resulted in the stifling and near-extinction of spontaneous, meaningful creativity. State-approved literature consisted mainly of slogans and ideological declarations recited by abstract wooden characters. Lyrical poetry was pushed into the background and replaced by eulogies of Stalin and his accomplishments. More independent Soviet writers increasingly sought shelter in such safe pursuits as editing the approved Russian and foreign classics or translating a limited set of approved, ideologically safe books from foreign languages. This was, for instance, Boris Pasternak's main preoccupation during the later phases of the Stalinist era. While glorifying conspicuous production of steel and kilowatts, Soviet writers were increasingly losing sight of human beings.

As the soviet cultural revolution unfolded, it increasingly stressed the integrating values of Russian nationalism mixed with Communist ideology in order to produce a new human species, the Soviet Man. From 1936 on, the cultural-ideological campaign was steered by Stalin himself. Taking revenge on the Soviet intellectual elite that had hardly noticed him before, he now kept them under his capricious thumb. During the 1936–1937 season, ten out of nineteen new plays in major Moscow theaters were taken off the stage for being "ideologically unsatisfactory."

A similarly arbitrary course was followed regarding other branches of arts. In 1935,

thirty-four movies were stopped in production, thirty-five the next year, and thirteen in 1937. At the same time, on Stalin's instructions the Soviet movie industry undertook the production of a series of historical films about great figures of the Muscovite and Russian past: Alexander Nevsky, Ivan the Terrible, Peter the Great, and Alexander Suvorov. Some of them, for instance Ivan the Terrible, were idealized beyond recognition. The central theme of these movies was the struggle against foreign imperialistic encroachments and the necessary strengthening of autocratic power as the best guarantee of Soviet Russia's unity.

Social sciences and humanities, including history, were subject to a thorough reexamination. Mikhail Pokrovsky's Marxist school was soon discarded and a new interpretation fostered after his disgrace in 1932. Soviet historians were told to rewrite the entire history of mankind to demonstrate that all past events were merely a prologue to the Bolshevik Revolution, steppingstones to the eventual triumph of Communism. Stalin himself revised the history of the Party. Under his supervision, a one-volume compendium known as *The Short Course* was produced. Contrary to the Marxist theory, which claims that not individuals but socioeconomic forces play the decisive role in determining history, glorification of Stalin's achievements was now the major goal of historical teaching and research.

Education and Sciences

The 1930s also saw the extension of new, strict disciplinary methods of thought control in education. Soon after the launching of the First Five-Year Plan, a retreat was sounded from the old permissive ways of "progressive education." From being an experimental educational community, the school returned to being an institution of strict formal learning, with a hearty admixture of Communist indoctrination. School administrators and teachers were ordered to reintroduce the old grading system and militarylike discipline, including uniforms and medals. The old quasi-liberal Anatoly Lunacharsky was replaced at the Commissariat of Education by Andrei Babunov, a former head of the Political Academy of the Red Army. The authority of the teacher was made as strict as during Tsarist times.

Eventually, Party control also included scientific theory and research, which was to be conducted in the spirit of Marxist materialism. While initially, during the years of 1918–1928, Soviet natural scientists enjoyed considerable freedom of scholarly investigation, during the 1930s the Party's grip on them was tightened dramatically. Some of its first victims were biologists. Biology was especially important because of its direct bearing on man's relation to the natural environment, which, according to Marx, is more important than heredity. Biology also bears directly on the control and cultivation of nature for man's sake, especially in the realm of genetics and breeding.

In 1930, an agronomist and biologist of Ukrainian origin, Trofim Lysenko, propounded a theory that claimed that environmentally acquired characteristics of animals and plants could be transmitted genetically to the next generation. Lysenko took over the ideas of a Russian plant-breeder, Ivan V. Michurin, who through skillful crossbreeding managed to create a variety of fruit trees suitable for the harsh climate of central Russia. Lysenko managed to convince Stalin that the application of his theory of the early subjection of seeds to low temperatures in order to hasten their development, or vernalization, could greatly increase crop yields. Lysenko's ideas, although contrary to the scientifically proved Mendelian theory, were couched in Marxist language and fitted Stalin's personal conviction that everything, including human beings, can be manipulated. By cleverly shifting from one nostrum to another—seed preparation, planting methods, use of fertilizer, animal breeding—and by flattering the Party bosses, Lysenko was able to survive in the face of a succession of failures. Most of these failures were not even known, since his methods were not objectively tested until the 1960s.

Since Lysenko's supporters preached collectivized agriculture, they won increasing favor from the regime to which they pandered. In 1938, Lysenko became President of the Academy of Agriculture and virtual dictator in the fields of biology and genetics. he survived Stalin and retained a great deal of influence until 1962. "Lysenkism" was made the officially imposed, obligatory theory to be taught in all educational establishments of the USSR, to the exclusion of all other theories. Competing biological theories were banned, and Lysenko's opponents, especially the founder of the Agricultural Academy, N. I. Vavilov, were persecuted, arrested, and deported. There was also a tendency to condemn the relativity theory in physics through arguments based on dialectical materialism. Only clever maneuvering on the part of a small group of Soviet physicists saved this branch of science from the total disaster that had befallen genetics. A lucky exception was the behavioral psychologist Professor Ivan Pavlov, who was allowed to continue his research undisturbed. In 1926 he published his seminal book, *Conditioned Reflexes.* His work was supported by the Soviet Government because his theory apparently supported the Marxist doctrine of the decisive influence of environment on behavior. Stalin especially liked Pavlov's experiments with dogs because he hoped that, just as Pavlov influenced the dogs' behavior by manipulating proper external stimuli, Stalin could likewise eventually control human beings.

Nothing illustrates better the evolution of Soviet scholarship under Stalin than its attitude toward the Norman thesis of the origin of the Kievan State. This was the theory that the Eastern Slavs had to call on the Norman Vikings to organize them into a viable State. During the 1930s, with the gradual rebirth of Russian nationalism, the old eighteenth-century thesis dear to the Westernizers could not be tolerated any more. If the Eastern Slavs had to bring in the Germanic Normans to establish the foundations of statehood, they were obviously incapable of doing it themselves. This would support Hitler's thesis of the superiority of the Nordic race over the

Slavs. On the Party's instructions, the thesis was discarded and its teaching in Soviet schools forbidden as harmful to the national pride of the Soviet people. The fate of the Norman theory and the acceptance not only of Pavlov's concept but even of Lysenko's theory are striking examples of Stalin's attitude toward knowledge as an instrument for achieving his ends.

Religion

The Stalinist cultural revolution also affected the regime's attitude toward religion, especially the Russian Orthodox Church. Lenin was fiercely opposed not only to all organized churches but to religion as such. Consequently he pursued a double strategy. While persecuting organized churches by all sorts of harsh reprisals, arrests, confiscations, and deportations, he had also encouraged the struggle against religious beliefs by propaganda that tried to ridicule religion as a fraud, "an opiate for the people."[5]

At the same time, Lenin had encouraged various attempts to split the Orthodox Church as well as tactical compromises with what was regarded as its "progressive wing." This encouraged a group of lower clergy seeking a *modus vivendi* with the new regime to denounce the Church hierarchy for its refusal to liberalize Church regulations and liturgy and for its reluctance to make religion an instrument of social change. In 1922, these dissenters formed a splinter church called the *Living Church.* It proclaimed the abolition of the Patriarchate and declared its willingness to reform the old structure and compromise with the Soviet regime. The Living Church was immediately recognized by the Government. The splinter

faction was soon utilized by the secret police, who had infiltrated its leadership in attempts to take over the remaining more conservative, segment of the Orthodox Church. These machinations, as well as internal squabbles among the ambitious and mostly unscrupulous leaders of the Living Church, discredited it, however, in the eyes of believers. The final blow to the faction was dealt in 1927 by the recognition of the Soviet regime by Orthodox Patriarch Sergei, who summoned the clergy and the faithful to accept it as an unchangeable political necessity. This caused the Soviet regime to withdraw its support from the quarreling splinter group, which soon fell apart.

This step by Patriarch Sergei had profound consequences for the whole Russian Orthodox Church. Some people obeyed the call and rendered allegiance to Soviet power as being a lesser evil than the specter of total destruction of what still remained of the old Church. Some clergymen and believers, on the other hand, protested that the move was an abject surrender by the weak Patriarch to a militant atheistic State bent on a slow, methodical destruction of all religion. In time, the intransigent faction gained the support of a considerable segment of Orthodox communicants living abroad, as well as of a die-hard faction of the faithful within the Soviet Union. Both those inside and outside the country have pointed out the gradual penetration of the Russian clergy by agents of the secret police, and the inevitable corruption of the officially tolerated hierarchy.

Despite these internal upheavals and splits, and in spite of intensive State-supported propaganda by the League of the Militant Godless and its vitriolic newspaper, *Bezbozhnik* (the Godless), the Orthodox Church (as well as Islam) retained a considerable hold on the minds of the people. This was regarded as highly unsatisfactory by the former seminarian from Tiflis, Stalin, who fully shared Lenin's idea about religion. Consequently, the First Five-Year Plan was accompanied by a renewed atheistic campaign. The introduction of continuous work abolished Sunday as a day of rest and relax-

---

[5] In 1914 the Russian Orthodox Church claimed 112 million followers, or about 72 percent of the Empire's population. The Church owned some 50,000 buildings housing about 50,000 priests and 95,000 monks and nuns. According to the *Bulletin of the Moscow Patriarchate* of June 1990, between 1918 and 1930 no less than 42,000 of the clergy perished as a result of Lenin's and Stalin's reprisals.

ation and was a part of the campaign. A large number of churches, monasteries, and nunneries were closed and their property confiscated. The Kazan Cathedral in Leningrad was turned into an antireligious museum. The recruitment of members to the League of the Militant Godless was bolstered; in 1932, at the peak of its activity, the League boasted of over five million members and of 3,200 "Godless shock brigades." By that time, the number of Eastern Orthodox parishes had sunk from 50,000 to under 30,000. Many members of the hierarchy, despite their previous declarations of loyalty, fell victim to the Great Purge.

Thus the surrender of Patriarch Sergei did not save the Russian Orthodox Church from the fury of the new antireligious campaign. Sergei's policy, while mitigating only very slightly the attacks on the Church, eroded the credibility of the officially recognized hierarchy as an authentic champion of the surviving religious beliefs of broad masses of people. In February 1930, the official Soviet organ proclaimed that the USSR had already built a "State without God and a government without God's laws." Nevertheless, religious sentiments survived even the shrill propaganda of the 1930s. The 1937 Census revealed that some 40 percent of the population declared themselves believers. The results of the census were never published.

Summary

During the Stalin revolution, the majority of Soviet creative individuals, artists, and scholars were caught between the harsh demands made upon them by the Party and the dictates of their conscience. Under attack for a variety of "ideological errors," most submitted with scarcely a murmur. Some, however, tried to pursue an independent line in defiance of the tyrant's will. Among the writers who took such a stand, one must mention people like Isaac Babel, Anna Akhmatova, Marina Tsvetayeva, and Osip Mandelshtam, who suffered from the Stalinist persecution. Some, like Sergei Bulgakov and Yevgenii Zamyatin, rejected any compromise and emigrated to continue their work abroad. A few broke down under the burden imposed on them by the demonic forces some of them had worshipped and helped to triumph. To this group belonged one hailed by Stalin himself as "the best, most talented poet of the Soviet epoch," Vladimir Mayakovsky. In 1930, he admitted that the Party had "stepped on the throat of his song" and, like Sergei Yessenin before him, committed suicide.

In his efforts to establish total control in all fields of human activity, Stalin needed artists and scholars as instruments of his "social engineering." Reduced to the level of Pavlov's dogs, they were to serve as tools in the grandiose and grim process of the country's fundamental transformation in accordance with Stalin's design. The increasing adulation of the man who allegedly embodied the best features of human nature, the omnipotent and infallible Leader, was the apex of the cult of the "positive hero." This adulation of Stalin, after 1956 euphemistically renamed his "personality cult," had already reached obsessive mass proportions in 1929, when he celebrated his fiftieth birthday. The cult of personality crescendoed until Stalin's death in 1953. Panegyrics extolling him as "the Father of the People," "wisest of leaders," "people's leader of genius," "great helmsman," "reformer of the world," "forger of world peace," and "the brightest sun of mankind" were commonplace. The following verse, taken from a fourth-grade school reader, is typical of the Stalin personality cult in its mature stage:

Thou, our teacher, like the shining sun
Dost open my eyes on heaven and earth;
Light up, my sun, shine in my window,
I see in thee the staff of life.

It is not unusual for the captive and indoctrinated subjects to attribute superhuman qualities to their dictator. But Stalin's cult of personality was unique because of its scope, its intensity, and its all-pervasive character. It penetrated not only political life and the arts but also scholarship, including such branches as linguistics, which would have been considered immune to these encroachments. At the beginning of its existence, the Soviet Union was the first country to consider science a vital national resource, to plan systematically the progress of scientific development, and to formulate science policies. The gains of the 1920s, however, were curtailed by Stalin early in the 1930s, thus dramatically slowing down the country's cultural as well as technological progress.

Strangled by the boa constrictor of totalitarianism, the country's intellectuals became servile, sterile, and inbred. The nation's arts and literature suffered largely from officially imposed uniformity which resulted in conventionality. Social Sciences became primarily propagandistic, with their main purpose the exaltation of the invincible Party and its infallible leader.

Suggested Reading

ANTONOV-OVSEYENKO, ANTON, *The Time of Stalin: Portrait of a Tyranny* (Trans. George Saunders). New York: Harper & Row, 1982.

BENNIGSEN, ALEXANDER, AND CHANTAL LEMERCHIER-QUELQUE JAY, *Islam in the Soviet Union.* New York: Praeger, 1967.

BEREDAY, GEORGE F., ET. AL. (EDS.), *The Changing Soviet School.* Boston: Houghton Mifflin, 1960.

BROWN, EDWARD, *A Proletarian Chapter in Russian Literary History, 1928–1932.* New York: Columbia University Press, 1953.

CARRÉRE D' ENCASSE, HÉLÉNE, *The Great Challenge: Nationalities and the Bolshevik State, 1917–1930,* New York: Holmes Meier, 1992.

CONQUEST, ROBERT, *Breaker of Nations.* New York: Viking, 1991.

DE WITT, NICHOLAS, *Education and Professional Employment in the USSR.* Washington, DC: National Science Foundation, 1961.

DMYTRYSHYN, BASIL, *Moscow and the Ukraine, 1918–1953.* New York: Bookman Associates, 1956.

ELLIS, JANE, *The Russian Orthodox Church: A Contemporary History.* Bloomington: Indiana University Press, 1986.

FITZPATRICK, SHEILA, *The Cultural Front: Power and Culture in Revolutionary Russia.* Ithaca, NY: Cornell University Press, 1992.

GRAHAM, LOREN R., *Science and Philosophy in the Soviet Union.* New York: Knopf, 1970.

JORAVSKY, DAVID, *The Lysenko Affair.* Cambridge, MA: Harvard University Press, 1970.

KAGEDAN, ALLAN, *Soviet Zion: The Quest for a Russian Jewish Homeland.* New York: St. Martin's Press, 1994.

KOCHAN, LIONEL (ED.), *The Jews in Soviet Russia Since 1917.* New York: Oxford University Press, 1970.

KOLARZ, WALTER, *Russia and Her Colonies.* London: George Philip & Son, 1952.

LAND, DAVID MARSHAL, *A Modern History of Soviet Georgia.* New York: Grove Press, 1962.

LUCKYI, GEORGE N.S., *Literary Politics in the Soviet Union, 1917–1934.* New York: Columbia University Press, 1956.

MATOSSIAN, MARY, *The Impact of Soviet Politics on Armenia.* Leiden: Brill, 1962.

MEDVEDEV, ZHORES A., *The Rise and Fall of T. D. Lysenko* (Trans. I. Michael Lerner). Garden City, NY: Doubleday, 1971.

MILLER, FRANK, J., *Folklore for Stalin: Russian Folklore and Pseudofolklore in the Stalin Era.* New York: Sharpe, 1990.

PERIS, DANIEL, *Storming the Heavens: The Soviet League of the Militant Godless.* Ithaca, NY: Cornell University Press, 1998.

PINKUS, BENJAMIN, *The Jews of the Soviet Union.* Cambridge, Eng.: Cambridge University Press, 1988.

SIMMONS, ERNEST J., *Russian Fiction and Soviet Ideology.* New York: Columbia University Press, 1958.

SOYFER, VALERY, N., *Lysenko and the Tragedy of Soviet Science.* New Brunswick, NJ: Rutgers University Press, 1994.

SULLIVAN, ROBERT S., *Soviet Politics and the Ukraine, 1917–1957.* New York: Columbia University Press, 1962.

TOLSTOY, NIKOLAI, *Stalin's Secret War.* New York: Holt, Rinehart & Winston, 1983.

VAKAR, NICHOLAS, *Belorussia.* Cambridge, MA: Harvard University Press, 1955.

WEINBERG, ROBERT, *Stalin's Forgotten Zion: Birobidzhan and the Making of a Soviet Jewish Homeland: An Illustrated History, 1928–1996.* Introduction, Zvi Gitelman. Berkeley: University of California Press, 1998.

WHEELER, GEOFFREY, *The Modern History of Soviet Central Asia.* New York: Praeger, 1964.

Chapter 16

From Isolation to Collective Security

During the 1920s the Soviet Union, although gradually and reluctantly recognized by most great powers (except the United States), lived in relative isolation from the international community. The USSR did not enter the League of Nations and its network of auxiliary international organizations. Quite the contrary; the League was denounced by Party bosses as a capitalist "League of Robbers," a "Holy Alliance of the bourgeoisie for the suppression of the proletarian revolution." The League was regarded by the Kremlin leaders as a conspiracy concocted to petrify the post-Versailles status quo and plot another intervention against "the first Socialist State." On the other hand, the Western powers continued to regard with profound misgivings the godless Soviet State that had abolished private property, refused to pay foreign debts, indulged in systematic and brutal suppression of all political dissent, and sponsored the Comintern with its anticolonialist and subversive propaganda.

Although Great Britain's first Labor Government granted *de jure* recognition of the Soviet Union on February 2, 1924, and was followed by France and Italy a few days later, relations between the Western powers and Moscow remained tense; mutual recriminations were similar to those of the "Cold War" following World War II. Revolutionary agitation in Ireland, India, and Egypt was frowned on even by the British Laborites. The cynical remarks of some Comintern leaders—like Zinoviev's, "We shall support MacDonald [Labor prime minister] as the rope supports the hanged"—did not improve Soviet–British relations either. Memories of the past, especially of the Allied intervention, still lingered and poisoned the atmosphere. The first Soviet ambassador at the Court of St. James was systematically ignored by King George V at all social functions, for he was considered the representative of a regime that had murdered the king's cousin Nicholas II and his family. No agreements were reached with either Paris or London concerning the prerevolutionary debts, or about compensation for French and British property nationalized by the Soviet regime.

The incident of the "Zinoviev letter" (see Chapter 10) contributed to the downfall of the Labor Government, which was defeated in the election of October 1924. Soviet interference with the British coal strike of 1926,

Europe, 1919–1926

as well as frequent Soviet attacks on British statesmen, especially on Winston Churchill as a proponent of a new Western intervention in Russia, both continued to poison relations between Moscow and London. Their low point was reached on May 21, 1927, when British police raided the London premises of the Soviet–British trade company "Arcos." The search resulted in the confiscation of substantial incriminating material that indicated that the company's officials, about a thousand people altogether, were engaging in espionage and subversive propaganda in Britain and its overseas domains. Among the confiscated documents were copies of some of the most confidential talks between British and French general staffs that had been intercepted by Soviet agents. On May 27 London broke off diplomatic relations with Moscow. Soon Canada followed suit. These moves were denounced by Moscow as a first step toward an "international capitalist crusade" against "the first proletarian government in the world."

Threats in Asia and Europe

Meanwhile, Stalin was pursuing his experiments in relative security until the late 1920s. The situation began to change during the early 1930s, both in Asia and in Europe. Thus, by the middle of the decade Moscow was faced with the specter of potential armed conflict on two distant fronts. The first threat of war appeared in the Far East as a result of the Japanese occupation of Manchuria in 1931; the second potential menace to Soviet security came as a consequence of Hitler's triumph in Germany in 1933.

Initially, the Japanese danger appeared more immediate. Tokyo had not recognized the Soviet regime until 1925, largely because of three points of friction that survived the downfall of the Tsarist regime: (1) the issue of the fishing rights of the Japanese in Russian waters; (2) Japanese concessions on the island of Sakhalin, the southern segment of which they had annexed in 1905; and (3) Japan's growing penetration of China, espe-

cially of Manchuria. While the first two issues were of limited significance and were satisfactorily settled between 1925 and 1928, the third was of considerable importance for both powers competing for influence in Manchuria, the most industrialized province of China. Japanese investments were considerable and on the rise. Moreover, the civil war in China was a temptation for the restless Japanese proponents of imperial expansion on the Asian mainland. Taking advantage of the intensifying Chinese civil war, the Japanese gave increasing moral and material support to the irredentist tendencies manifesting themselves among some segments of Manchuria's population, demoralized by years of civil war and by the activities of local warlords. Unrest spilled over from Central China to Manchuria and gave Tokyo a pretext for dispatching troops, allegedly to protect Japanese nationals and their investments. At the end of 1931 the Japanese went so far as to send troops into Manchuria; on February 5, 1932, they occupied Harbin. On March 9 they proclaimed the establishment of an independent Manchurian state called Manchukuo. The League of Nations debated the problem of the Japanese aggression for a long time but did nothing concrete. Moscow limited itself to verbal protests. Yet Tokyo, angered by the League's eventual censure of its policy, left the organization.

The new strategic situation in the Far East necessitated a reorientation of Soviet Russia's policy in that area. Since the USSR had no diplomatic relations with the United States, steps were undertaken to establish them. Meanwhile, the aid of another countervailing force closer at hand had to be found. Forgetting the bitter past, in the spring of 1932 Moscow resumed diplomatic relations with Chiang Kai-shek's Chinese nationalist government in Nanking; official relations had been broken off in 1927. On June 29, Moscow signed a nonaggression pact with Nanking, and a new chapter in relations between the two countries was opened. While normalizing relations with the government at Nanking, Stalin did not care much to safeguard the interests of the

Chinese Communist Party. So Chiang continued to fight the Chinese Communists who had proclaimed their government in the province of Kiangsi in December 1931. To destroy it, Chiang launched a series of mopping-up operations. Although officially considered successful, these never resulted in stopping the spread of the *sui generis* agrarian Communism that had deep roots in China's anomalous, feudal conditions. Despite bitter losses, the Communist forces continued to expand. By 1933, the Chinese Red Army already numbered over 300,000 regular troops and was supported by at least 600,000 partisans, ably organized by the emerging leader Mao Tse-tung.

In the meantime, the consolidation of Japanese influence on the Asian mainland proceeded apace, and the USSR had to face the new situation realistically. In March 1933, Tokyo offered to buy from the Russians the northern branch of the Manchurian, or Chinese Eastern, railroad. Negotiations dragged on for almost two years. Eventually, on March 23, 1935, the line was ceded to the government of Manchukuo for 170 million yen, far below the actual worth of the railway. Meanwhile, in August 1932, new agreements concerning oil concessions and Japanese fishing rights had been concluded, all of them advantageous to Tokyo. These conciliatory gestures, which momentarily relaxed the tension between the two rivals, could not safeguard Soviet security in the Far East. They, however, did not mean definite Russian withdrawal from an area vital to the position of the USSR in the Far East.

Moscow Reacts to the Japanese Menace

A considerable strengthening of the Soviet posture was needed to face Japan's growing appetite for territory and resources. Consequently, while normalizing somewhat its relations with Nanking, Moscow took two steps to cope with the mounting Japanese danger. First, a powerful Far Eastern army was deployed along the Manchurian and Mongolian frontiers and was gradually reinforced and equipped with the best weapons the Second Five-Year Plan could supply. This army was established as a semi-autonomous unit because at that time the Trans-Siberian Railroad still had only one track; supplying the Far Eastern army in case of emergency would have constituted a serious logistical problem. Second, Moscow speeded up its negotiations with Japan's most serious countervailing force, the United States. Stalin well remembered the American intervention in the Russian Civil War, but he was also aware that it was Washington that had prevented the Japanese from establishing themselves permanently on Siberian soil after the civil war. Although the Japanese were supporting the White forces, with which Washington was in basic sympathy, the Americans had insisted on the evacuation of Japanese troops. Despite the fact that Presidents Wilson as well as Harding refused to recognize the Bolshevik regime on the grounds that it advocated subversion and atheism, trade relations were soon resumed. In 1926, American companies obtained gold prospecting concessions in southern Siberia, on the Amur River and the next year Standard Oil signed advantageous contracts with Moscow. Soon General Electric followed suit. By the late 1920s Soviet-American trade was twice what it had been before the war. The USSR of the five-year plans was a fair hunting ground for American engineers and economic experts eager to escape the Great Depression.

President Franklin D. Roosevelt, who came to power in Washington in 1933, was under increased pressure from business circles to resume diplomatic relations with a country that represented a potential market for American goods. This, combined with Washington's suspicion of Tokyo's designs in the Far East, pushed both countries toward a compromise. In November 1933, the United States recognized the Soviet Union *de jure*, in exchange for Soviet promises to refrain from subversive propaganda and to resume talks about indemnifying American citizens whose assets had been confiscated after the Bolshevik revolution. A friend of President Roosevelt, William Bullitt, who had led an exploratory diplomatic mission to Russia in 1919, became the first American ambassador in Moscow. Yet the deal proved somewhat one-sided; trade between the two countries increased only slightly, while Stalin's expectations of American support against Japan were soon to be disappointed. The Soviet pledges concerning Comintern propaganda and the repayments of both private and public debts remained a dead letter.

The Spirit of Rapallo

At the same time, the ominous changes taking place along the eastern approaches to the USSR were paralleled by equally menacing developments in Central Europe. The latent instability of the Weimar Republic was intensified by the economic Great Depression, with its crippling social consequences. During the early 1930s, unemployment in Germany spread rapidly. Soon nearly six million jobless became easy prey for extremist agitation, including the mushrooming Communist Party of Germany and all sorts of paramilitary fighting squads of the Right. Slogans calling for the destruction of the Versailles Treaty and a return to the 1913 frontiers were propounded by numerous spokesmen. The most ruthless, vitriolic, and dynamic of them was a former lance corporal of the Imperial German Army, an Austrian by birth—Adolf Hitler. As head of the National Socialist Workers (Nazi) Party, he preached anti-Semitism, revenge, and the establishment of a millennial Teutonic Empire reaching far to the East, including the Soviet Ukraine. After the elections of July 1932, the Nazis became the largest party in the German Parliament.

Beneath the Soviet–German military and economic collaboration, there were numerous misgivings in Berlin. Western-oriented statesmen, including Gustav Stresemann, Foreign Minister from 1923 to 1929, favored the policy of conciliation with France and Great Britain. It was Stresemann who brought Germany into the League of Nations, guaranteeing that Germany would respect the status quo, but only in the West. Chancellors Heinrich Brünning and Franz von Papen, both Roman Catholics, also could not hide their aversion to cooperation with the Communists. They both stressed that behind them stood Stalin, who, despite his professed friendship, encouraged subversive activities and supported Germany's fast-spreading Communist movement. But all these voices were silenced because of the double pressure from military and industrial circles, which stressed the rich profits to be derived from Germany's special relationship with the USSR, including the value of the burgeoning trade.

Overall, the spirit of Rapallo seemed unimpaired during the early 1930s. Trade relations, guaranteed by so-called "Russian credits" as security to German exporters, were developing satisfactorily; cultural exchanges were flourishing; collaboration between the Red Army and the small German forces went on undisturbed. Throughout this period high Soviet officers attended secret military courses in Germany, while German pilots and tank crews were being trained in the USSR. The peak of this military intimacy was reached in 1931 when a large German military delegation was allowed to attend Soviet maneuvers near Kiev. Observers witnessed a Red Army display not only of a modern, massive tank force, but especially of paratroopers. All this strongly impressed the German military attaché who then urged Hitler to emulate the Soviet performance and develop such airborne detachments on a large scale.

Litvinov's New Course

While the entire strategic situation of the Soviet Union was gradually undergoing change, the management of Soviet foreign relations was handed over to a new team of younger people. In 1930 the main architect of Soviet–German rapprochement, Chicherin, had to resign because of prolonged illness, and his place was taken by his deputy,

Maxim Litvinov. Born in Bialystok in Russian Poland in 1876, the son of a Jewish bourgeois family, Litvinov had joined the RSDWP in 1903 and thus, unlike Chicherin, was an old Bolshevik. Married to an Englishwoman, the niece of newspaper publisher Sir Sidney Low, Litvinov spoke English fluently and was at home in Britain, whose culture he admired. The task of the smiling, smooth-operating new Commissar for Foreign Affairs was to erase the old image of the Soviet Union as a state fighting the post-Versailles system and thus to overcome British and French fears of the "Red menace." Litvinov tackled the task tactfully, with great skill and remarkable persistence.

With the rise of the Japanese menace in the Far East and mounting revanchist, militaristic, and racial agitation in Germany, Soviet foreign policy began to undergo a gradual yet clear reorientation. Step by step, taking advantage of existing geopolitical realities, Litvinov proceeded with his attempt at making more secure the Western approaches to the Soviet Union. The USSR was separated from Germany by a belt of smaller states stretching from Finland to Romania and including the three Baltic Republics and Poland. Since Germany might again become a threat to Soviet security, it was deemed essential to normalize relations with these border states so as to prevent them from being used as bases of an attack against Russia. To turn these Western neighbors into a buffer zone protecting the USSR through a series of diplomatic arrangements now became a major objective of Soviet diplomacy. It was Litvinov's task to negotiate and sign in 1931 and 1932 a series of nonaggression and friendship pacts with all of Soviet Russia's western neighbors, with the exception of Romania. The Soviet-Romanian negotiations broke down because of Moscow's reluctance to accept the incorporation of Bessarabia into Romania at the close of World War I.

The most important of these treaties was with France's chief ally, Poland. The Soviet-Polish nonaggression pact signed on July 25, 1932 was a steppingstone toward a similar

Maxim Litvinov, Foreign Affairs Commissar, 1930–1939

agreement with Paris, which was concluded on November 29, 1932. Meanwhile, nonaggression pacts had also been signed with the three Baltic republics of Lithuania, Latvia, and Estonia.

Stalin and the Rise of Hitler

While Litvinov was working hard to consolidate the Soviet international position, Stalin became especially preoccupied with the changing political scene in Germany. To understand Stalin's attitude toward the rise of Hitler and his Nazi party, one has to go back to the Sixth Congress of the Comintern, which took place from July to September of 1928. Although the Congress deliberated under the chairmanship of Bukharin, its spirit and temper were already thoroughly Stalinist. At the Congress, Stalin declared, "He is a revolutionary who, without reservation, unconditionally and openly . . . is ready to defend the USSR. He who thinks to defend the world revolutionary movement apart from and against the USSR is going against the revolution." The emphasis of the Congress was on thorough "Bolshevization" of all national sections of the Comintern; this implied strict discipline, ideological intransigence, subordination to Moscow and rejection of cooperation with other "anti-Fascist" forces. All previous attempts at forming "united fronts of the working class" together with Social Democrats were to be abandoned. They were too "soft," too "reformist." The only permissible united front, therefore, was to be made from below by wooing away the proletarian masses from "the social-traitors" of the working class—the socialists who had to be "unmasked" as "Judases" and "social fascists." These statements reflected Stalin's contemptuous attitude toward Western Social Democrats who, despite occasional and rather ambivalent sympathy toward the huge Soviet socioeconomic experiment, were still critical of the way it was being conducted. In 1927, while discussing the possibility of collaborating with them and other leftist elements against the bourgeois parties, Stalin said, "Rather let them go to hell, all these liberal-pacifist philosophers with their 'sympathy' for the USSR."

Thus, after the Sixth Congress of the Comintern, the Socialists emerged as the main enemy of the Communists, their chief competitors for control of the working masses. The Great Depression, which played havoc with most Western economies by breeding mass unemployment and ruining world trade, did not much alter the extreme, uncompromising course of the Comintern. If anything, it sharpened it by stressing the Communist parties' intolerance and exclusivism. According to Moscow theoreticians, the final crisis of capitalism was opening marvelous new vistas for hard, determined parties that would use ruthless methods similar to those applied by the Bolsheviks in 1917. This meant going it alone, adopting the most radical positions on practically every issue, and seizing every opportunity to implement them by the most militant methods.

In view of this attitude, any idea of cooperation between the German Communists and the German Social Democrats against the rising specter of Hitlerism was condemned by the Kremlin as unnecessary. In a way, the mushrooming of the National Socialist, or Nazi movement, after 1930 was welcomed by Stalin. The Nazis, Stalin calculated at that time, were after all merely the tools of bankers, large landowners, and capitalists.

Hitler's triumph was bound to be ephemeral, while the consequences of his inevitable doom would be beneficial. By depriving the German masses of their democratic and parliamentary illusions and by finally running the capitalist economy of the country, Hitler (whom Stalin initially regarded as a strange combination of Kerensky and Kornilov) would merely prepare the ground for the Communists. That is why Stalin explicitly forbade the leader of the Communist Party of Germany, Ernst Thaelmann, to cooperate with the Social Democrats against Hitler.

Toward the Break with Germany

When on January 30, 1933, Hitler was appointed Chancellor, Stalin appeared to be indifferent. He simply tried to ignore the event and continue his good relations with Berlin. The subsequent massacre of the German Communist Party was not particularly bemoaned by the Soviet dictator. Although he issued some vitriolic condemnations of the Nazi actions, he did not allow them to upset the smooth functioning of the two countries' close economic and military collaboration. We have to remember that Stalin took a dim view of foreign comrades and considered them expendable; he cared about them only insofar as they could be useful to his purposes. As he said repeatedly, "One Soviet tractor is worth ten thousand foreign Communists."

Meanwhile, as Hitler consolidated his power and watched the passivity of France and Britain, he embarked on open massive rearmament. Soviet airfields were no longer indispensable for the Germans. In addition, continuing German–Soviet collaboration was difficult to justify in view of Nazi propaganda attacks on Communism as an essentially Jewish conspiracy and the main threat to German internal stability.

Stalin was meanwhile increasingly impressed with the German dictator's skill and boldness, and persisted in his efforts to maintain at least a modicum of good relations with Berlin. Speaking at the Seventeenth Party Congress in January 1934, Stalin, who had abandoned his early views of Hitler as a fly-by-night phenomenon, hinted at the possibility of continuing close relations with Nazi Germany. Stressing the primacy of Soviet security over ideological issues, Stalin resolved that the Soviet Union would be ready to consider rapprochement with any country "which is not interested in disturbing peace." As late as May 1933, a high-ranking German military delegation visited Moscow and held talks with representatives of the Soviet General Staff. The delegation was warmly received by distinguished representatives of the Red Army. At the banquet given in honor of the German guests, the Commissar for War, Klement Voroshilov, expressed the desire to maintain friendly links between the two countries. Hitler, however, took a different view from his military advisers. A few weeks later, he formally denounced the Rapallo Treaty. Thus ended a twelve-year period of steady Soviet–German collaboration.[1]

The balance sheet of the Soviet–German collaboration is difficult to assess, for both partners derived significant profit from the cooperative ventures. While Hitler's rapid rearmament in the 1930s would have been impossible without the spade work by German experts working in the privileged sanctuary of Russia, the Red Army learned a great deal from the Germans. Without the Reichswehr's blueprints for tanks, planes, and guns, speedy modernization of Soviet armed forces would have been very difficult.

Stalin's Search for Security

Left out in the cold, the disappointed Stalin had to play the lone wolf. By that time his contempt for the German dictator had already turned into a mixture of fear and grudging admiration. The skill, speed, and

ruthlessness with which Hitler liquidated the radical wing of the Nazi movement impressed Stalin immensely. Stalin had read the German dictator's work *Mein Kampf* (*My Struggle*) in which Hitler openly declared: "If we talk about new soil and territory . . . we can think primarily of Russia and its vassal border states." How to discourage Nazi Germany from carrying out this threat in the East, and redirect it to the West, now became Stalin's major task. Isolated and still largely ostracized in the international arena and increasingly menaced both in Asia and Europe, Stalin began to grope for a reorientation of Soviet strategy. Overcoming this isolation now became an urgent task of Soviet diplomacy.

Some of the preparatory agreements aimed at normalizing relations with the USSR's western neighbors had been achieved between 1930 and 1932 by Litvinov's skillful diplomacy. But these nonaggression pacts were mistrusted by Stalin; he regarded them as only temporary arrangements designed to make more difficult any future attack by a rearmed Germany.

In view of the steady growth of German militancy, these provisional arrangements had to be bolstered by more solid security ties with the Great Powers. What was needed now was a system of alliances, primarily with Paris and London, that would provide the USSR with military assistance against the two expansionist powers in Asia and Europe—Japan and Germany. This quest for security through alliances with Germany's opponents was obviously incompatible with the radical line of policy hitherto pursued by the Comintern. Now, the policy that treated all non-Communist forces as equally evil became an anachronism. As has already been stressed, besides actively spreading subversive propaganda inside both France and Britain and their overseas possessions, the USSR had also opposed the concept of collective security sponsored by these two pillars of the League of Nations. To achieve a rapprochement with Paris and London, Moscow had to overcome the fears generated by the Comintern's explosive revolutionary propaganda and its

[1] For a collection of documents illustrating the evolution of the Soviet diplomatic posture; see Jane Degras (Ed.), *Soviet Documents on Foreign Policy, 1917–1941* (New York: Oxford University Press, 1951–1953).

denunciations of the League as an imperialist instrument of the status quo powers. The virulent antidemocratic and anti-Western campaign of the Comintern had conducted during the previous six years (from 1928) had to be dropped. All of this required radical reorientation of the work of various Communist parties, including soft pedaling anti-League propaganda and shifting the policy of the Comintern to work even more closely with the Narkomindel. If the USSR was to cooperate with the Western democracies against Nazi Germany, the intransigent Left course that the Comintern pursued since 1928 had to be abandoned.

The Great Shift of Soviet Policy

There was no time to lose. The shift came abruptly in 1934, soon after Hitler's denunciation of the Rapallo Treaty. All national sections of the Comintern were ordered to approach the Social Democratic leaders with proposals of cooperation against the common "Fascist menace." The first to obey was the Communist Party of France, weathervane of the Comintern. Despite his previous emphatic declarations that "a marriage between Communists and Socialists is fundamentally alien to the spirit of Bolshevism," the French party boss, Maurice Thorez, after his visit to Moscow, opened negotiations with the French Socialist Party for mutual abjuration of criticism and the eventual establishment of a working-class united front to struggle against the common danger.

In May 1934, Litvinov met in Geneva with French Foreign Minister Louis Barthou. They discussed closer cooperation between the two countries, Soviet Russia's possible entrance into the League of Nations, and a potential Soviet–French alliance providing for mutual aid and assistance in case of unprovoked attack by a third power. Overnight Litvinov became one of the most eloquent defenders of the League and an ardent supporter of the principle of collective security.

The autumn 1934 session of the League of Nations witnessed the Soviet Union's entrance as a full-fledged member with a prominent seat on the League's Council. This step underscored the end both of Moscow's denunciations of the League and its sabotage of the policy of collective security based on the League's Covenant. Russia was once again recognized as a great power interested in preserving the status quo. Entrance into the League facilitated more intimate association with the Western states, who were also frightened by Germany's rearmament, especially France and Britain. The USSR's decision acknowledged the Soviet hope that the League, weakened by the absence of the United States and the desertion of Japan and Germany, could still be a useful international forum and a potential instrument in the struggle against the aggressive designs of its enemies in Asia and Europe.

Soviet Alliances with France and Czechoslovakia

On May 2, 1935, the USSR and France signed a treaty of alliance that pledged both partners to come to each other's assistance "in case of an unprovoked attack on the part of a European state." Meanwhile, instructions had been issued to the Communist Party of France to drop its antimilitaristic propaganda and its policy of sabotaging the French rearmament effort. On May 16, 1935, the world was surprised to read a French journalist's interview with Stalin, who declared his support of "the policy of national defense followed by France so as to maintain her armed forces on the level necessary to maintain national security."

To appreciate how momentous a step this was, one has to recall the history of bitter mutual hostility that had divided the two countries ever since the Communist revolution. Let down by its former ally as a result of the Brest-Litovsk separate peace and despoiled of its huge investments in Russia, France had become the main sponsor of

Allied intervention against the Bolsheviks. In Soviet eyes France was, next to Britain, the embodiment of imperialist, predatory capitalism and the chief symbol of the Versailles peace, which was not only directed against Germany but also designed to surround Soviet Russia with an East European *cordon sanitaire*. In June 1933, with Hitler already a clear menace, Stalin did not hesitate to call France "the most aggressive and militaristic country of all aggressive and militaristic countries of the world." Nothing but fear of Hitler's boundless greed could have brought Paris and Moscow together.

The new Franco-Soviet alliance was much more restrictive than that of 1894. The treaty of May 1935 was limited to Europe and did not provide for French assistance against Japan. Moreover, unlike its nineteenth-century predecessor, it did not envisage the automatic use of force in case of aggression by a third power against one of the contracting parties. The treaty of 1935 spoke only about "mutual consultations" in case of an act of aggression. Moreover, the fact of aggression had to be recognized as such by the League of Nations under Article 16 of its Covenant. Furthermore, the new pact was signed under different geopolitical conditions. Unlike the situation prior to World War I, Russia and Germany were no longer immediate neighbors. They were now separated by a chain of independent states: Romania, Poland, Lithuania, Latvia, and Estonia. The lack of a common border between the USSR and Germany made it necessary to assure the adherence of the intermediary states, or at least Romania and Poland, to the new security arrangements. For the Red Army to render effective assistance to France in case of an attack by Germany, Soviet units would need to have a right of passage through at least some of these states to reach German soil.

Here the key country was Poland, the largest segment of the area. The problem of putting Soviet bases on Polish territory proved to be a deadly obstacle to effective coordination of Soviet and French prepara-

tions. Although allied with the French since 1921 and committed to the Polish-Soviet Nonaggression Pact since 1932, the Poles steadfastly refused to allow the Red Army to be stationed on their territory in peacetime. To French pleas, the Warsaw diplomats would always give a stubborn refusal, one that was grounded in the long history of Russo-Polish relations. Once established the Red Army would never leave Poland alone. As Vice Minister of Foreign Affairs Jan Szembek retorted to a French ambassador in Warsaw, "That's just the way the partitions of Poland began in the eighteenth century."

An equally serious obstacle was the nature of the Franco-Soviet alliance. Any effective military cooperation in wartime presupposes close peacetime exchanges and detailed planning of future moves. Although some preliminary general staff exchanges were conducted between the two allies immediately after the signing of the pact, they were soon interrupted (partly because of the purge of the top Soviet military personnel and partly because of their endemic futility). Consequently, the French-Soviet alliance was only a pale shadow of its 1894 predecessor. All this time mutual suspicion lingered; French inhibitions were reflected in the fact that the French Parliament dragged its feet on ratification of the treaty until February 1936.

A few days after the signing of the Franco-Soviet treaty, France's ally, Czechoslovakia, followed the example of its western protector and signed a similar treaty. The Soviet–Czechoslovak pact, however, included an additional clause worth remembering in view of Soviet behavior during the Munich crisis of 1938: any Soviet aid to Czechoslovakia, in case of war, hinged on a previous French entry into the conflict.

Thus, without a specific, detailed, military convention to provide the alliance with some substance, the pact of 1935 was more a declaration of intention than an effective instrument of defense. What was lacking was not only mutual trust, but also a sense of mutual purpose and the determination to pursue it together.

The Comintern Follows Suit

The dramatic reversals of Soviet policy had immediate consequences for the national standing of French Communism. Hitherto it had been regarded as an alien, antipatriotic force, and the Communists had therefore been ostracized by most of the French, including a large section of the working class that owed its allegiance to the Socialists. This now began to change while the French Communists became increasingly jingoistic. The 1935 spring local elections registered considerable gains by the Communists, who were now working hand-in-hand with the Socialists, whom they had denounced only shortly before as "Social Fascists."

The success of the united front of all "anti-Fascist" forces, led by the Communists, emboldened Maurice Thorez to extend it toward the center to include the Socialist Radical Party which, despite its name, represented mostly middle- and lower-middle-class people. Thus the united front was to be turned into a broader coalition of "all democratic forces," a "popular front." Despite some opposition from the left wing of the Socialist Party, negotiations to this effect were initiated in the name of joint resistance to the mounting wave of domestic right-wing menace and to the threat represented by Nazi Germany.

To appreciate fully the psychological significance of the abrupt about-face of Soviet policy for foreign Communists, one also has to view the shift against the background of Comintern policy in effect since 1928. Between 1924 and 1928, Stalin turned the Comintern into a pliable tool of his policy of socialism in one country; that is, of consolidating and defending Soviet national interests as he interpreted them. Without even so much as consulting its World Congress, he promoted or demoted the chairman and members of the Comintern's executive committees. In 1926, for instance, Stalin removed Zinoviev and appointed Bukharin as the Comintern's Chairman, then used him and the prestige of this office in the domestic struggle against Trotsky. He often referred to the Comintern as "my little shop." The Comintern, he repeatedly stressed, "represents nothing and exists only thanks to our support."

By the mid-1930s, Stalin's control over the Comintern was nearly complete. Consequently, it was a matter of just a few instructions and stepped-up propaganda among the rank and file to alter the leftist course of his "little shop" to a pro-united front line. While the most obedient of all Communist Parties, the French, acted as a harbinger of the new policy, most other parties needed some pressing, but finally all of them submitted to Moscow's newest line. The official proclamation of the new strategy was staged at the Seventh (and last) Comintern Congress, again held in Moscow, in July and August 1935. The dominant figure of the Congress was the Bulgarian leader Georgy Dimitrov, who was elected the Comintern's secretary general. Dimitrov was at that time basking in the glory of the courageous and eloquent stand he had taken at the 1933 Reichstag fire trial in Leipzig. During the trial he had defied the judges and made many Nazi leaders, including Prussian Minister of the Interior, Hermann Goering, a laughingstock by exposing their complicity in the fire, which had been engineered by the Nazis to look like it had been set by the Communists. Soon after the fire, Hitler was proclaimed Honorary President of the Seventh Congress of the Comintern.

Most speakers of the Comintern Congress were seething with hatred and contempt for Germany and Japanese militarists and imperialists. At the same time, many delegates stretched out their hands to "all sincere opponents of Fascism" and "imperialist aggression." Yet despite all these rhetorical exercises the Congress, manipulated by its real master, failed to commit the Communist movement to an irrevocable struggle against Germany. Actually, the stand against Japan seemed to be stiffer than against Germany. While the Chinese Communists were instructed to "extend the front of the struggle for their national liberation," the German Communists were ordered to enter such organizations as the Nazi Labor Front and to work there for higher wages and better labor conditions. Thus, even at the peak of its "anti-Fascist" offensive, the Comintern's policy was highly differentiated. It never completely closed the door to a renewed understanding with one or both of the increasingly aggressive states of Asia and Europe.

Summary

The popular front phase of Soviet foreign policy marked the final downgrading of the Comintern and the ultimate exposing of its role as a mere tool of Moscow's will. The downgrading of the Comintern was also reflected in its calendar. During Lenin's era, the Comintern met five times: once every year from 1919 to 1923. Under Stalin it met only three times in nineteen years: in 1924, 1928, and 1935. To placate his Western allies, Stalin dissolved it altogether in 1943. But meanwhile, especially during the 1930s, it had had to follow the twists and turns of the General Secretary's tortuous "general line," while hailing its capricious infallibility. The Comintern's messianic, evangelical urge became weaker, as foreign Communists became only a means toward strengthening the Soviet State and solidifying the position of its ruling group. By the late 1930s, through corruption and terror, Stalin had imposed the principle that loyal Communists were to have no opinions of their own; they were simply to obey his orders.

In view of this growing corruption of the world Communist movement and its slavish subordination to the whim of the General Secretary of the CPSU, the indignant Trotsky declared in a letter to his American supporter Max Eastman, "Stalinism is the syphilis of socialism."

While downgrading the Comintern, Stalin upgraded the Comissariate for Foreign affairs, or the *Narkomindel*, which, from the middle 1930s, launched a policy of promoting collective security in cooperation with France and Britain.

Suggested Reading

BAER, GEORGE W. (ED.), *A Question of Trust: The Origin of U.S.-Soviet Relations: The Memoirs of Loy W. Henderson.* Stanford, CA: Hoover Institution Press, 1987.

BORKENAU, FRANZ, *World Communism: A History of the Communist International.* Ann Arbor: University of Michigan Press, 1962.

BROWDER, ROBERT P., *The Origins of Soviet–American Diplomacy.* Princeton, NJ: Princeton University Press, 1953.

BUDUROWYCZ, BOHDAN, *Polish–Soviet Relations, 1932–1933.* New York: Columbia University Press, 1963.

CARR, E.H., *Twilight of the Comintern, 1930–1935.* New York: Pantheon Books, 1983.

CRAIG, GORDON, AND FELIX GILBERT (EDS.), *The Diplomats, 1919–1939.* Princeton, NJ: Princeton University Press, 1953.

DEGRAS, JANE, *Calendar of Soviet Documents on Foreign Policy, 1917–1941.* New York: The Royal Institute of International Affairs, 1948.

———, (ED.), *The Communist International, 1919–1943, Documents.* New York: Oxford University Press, 1956, 3 Vols.; Vol. 2 is the most useful.

———, *Soviet Documents on Foreign Policy, 1917–1941.* New York: Oxford University Press, 1951–1953; 3 Vols.; Vol. 2 is the most valuable.

DRAPER, THEODORE, *American Communism and Soviet Russia.* New York: Viking, 1960.

EUDIN, XENIA J., AND ROBERT M. SLUSSER (EDS.), *Soviet Foreign Policy, 1928–1941: Documented Materials,* Vol. 1. University Park: Pennsylvania State University Press, 1966.

FILENE, PETER G., *Americans and the Soviet Experiment, 1917–1933.* Cambridge, MA: Harvard University Press, 1967.

FISCHER, RUTH, *Stalin and German Communism.* Cambridge, MA: Harvard University Press, 1948.

HASLAM, JONATHAN, *The Soviet Union and the Threat from the East, 1933–41: Moscow, Tokyo and the Prelude to the Pacific War.* Pittsburgh, PA: University of Pittsburgh, 1992.

KENNAN, GEORGE F., *Russia and the West under Lenin and Stalin*. Boston: Little, Brown, 1961.

LAQUEUR, WALTER, *Russia and Germany: A Century of Conflict*. New Brunswick, NJ: Rutgers University Press, 1990.

McKENZIE, KERMIT E., *Comintern and the World Revolution, 1928–1943: The Shaping of a Doctrine*. New York: Columbia University Press, 1964.

McLANE, CHARLES B., *Soviet Policy and Chinese Communists, 1913–1946*. New York: Columbia University Press, 1958.

POST, KEN, *Communism and National Socialism: The Foundation of the Century, 1914–1939*. New York: St. Martin's Press, 1997.

RUBINSTEIN, ALVIN Z. (ED.), *The Foreign Policy of the Soviet Union*. New York: Random House, 1960.

ULAM, ADAM, *Expansion and Coexistence. The History of Soviet Foreign Policy, 1917–67*. New York: Praeger, 1968 (mainly Chaps. 4 and 5).

VON RAUCH, G., *The Baltic States: The Years of Independence, 1917–40*. London: Hurst, 1947.

WANDYCZ, PIOTR S., *The Twilight of the French East European Alliances, 1926–36*. Princeton, NJ: Princeton University Press, 1988.

WHITE, D. F., *The Growth of the Red Army*. Princeton, NJ: Princeton University Press, 1944.

Chapter 17

Prelude to World War II

The Soviet foreign policy was soon dramatically changed as a result of a series of external events. On February 26, 1936, after long hesitation, the French Chamber of Deputies finally ratified the Franco-Soviet alliance. Hitler immediately denounced the treaty as an attempt at encirclement of Germany. On March 7 he ordered his troops into the hitherto demilitarized left bank of the Rhine, in blatant violation of the Treaty of Versailles as well as the Locarno agreements. Despite the suggestion of its Polish ally that they jointly challenge Hitler's move, the French government of Prime Minister Pierre Flandin hesitated to act without prior consultation with London. The Conservative cabinet of Stanley Baldwin, however, refused to support the French and the Poles. From captured German documents and from the Nuremberg trial, we know that the small German detachments had been provided with blank ammunition only and ordered to withdraw if the Western powers resisted militarily the German move. Thus France and Great Britain lost the last chance of calling Hitler's bluff before he completed his rearmament plans and when the Third Reich was extremely vulnerable.

Moscow's attitude toward the crisis was diplomatically correct. An official Tass communiqué declared that "Help would be given to France in accordance with the 1935 Treaty and with the political situation as a whole." Since the USSR had neither a common frontier with Germany nor a right of passage over the intervening territories of Russia's western neighbors, the gesture was safe and purely theoretical. During the 1936 crisis, Stalin must have taken a rather dim view of the passive attitude of the two Western powers. If the French would not stand up to the Germans in defense of their own back yard, how would they behave in case of an attack on their distant allies Czechoslovakia, Poland, or Soviet Russia? His doubts as to the real value of his French alliance must have deepened considerably. On the other hand, he must have been impressed by Hitler, who again behaved like a brilliant gambler.

Immediately after the occupation of the Rhineland, Hitler ordered a chain of strong fortifications built all along the Franco-German frontier. This crash program, combined with further expansion of the German air force and armored divisions, all executed with great speed and efficiency, soon altered the balance of forces in Europe. In the future, the French army, even if it were willing to intervene on behalf of its Eastern European allies to fulfill its obligations toward the USSR, Czechoslovakia, or Poland, would be unable to do so effectively because access to the heart of Germany would be denied by the rapidly expanding *Wehrmacht.*

Failure of a Popular Front in France

Whatever Stalin's suspicions concerning the morbid timidity of the Western leaders and the boldness of Hitler, for the time being he persisted in keeping his Western options open. Stalin maintained his policy of collective security combined with the popular front tactic of moderate politics pursued through broad coalitions of the Left and Center. As mentioned in the previous chapter, the tactic was tried almost immediately in France and Spain. In May 1936, the French parliamentary elections resulted in an impressive victory for the coalition of Communists, Socialists, and Socialist Radicals. Five out of nine million voters cast their ballots for this popular front coalition. The number of votes cast for the French Communist party, made respectable by its tricolor flag-waving, was impressive. For the first time in history, the Party garnered more than a million votes, while their Socialist partners made no progress. Nevertheless the French Communist leader, Maurice Thorez, on Moscow's order, kept a low profile and decided not to enter the new cabinet headed by the moderate Socialist Leon Blum. The Communists were to support the new administration, however, on the condition that it would implement the moderate, popular front program, which included a forty-hour work week, collective bargaining, paid vacations for workers, and the like. Soon Socialist and Communist trade unions merged to form the powerful General Confederation of Labor. The French popular front government assumed power on July 5, 1936, just two weeks before the outbreak of the Span-

ish Civil War, which was to usher in a more daring experiment in collaboration between the rivals for control of the working masses.

The honeymoon between the French Communists and Socialists did not last long; lingering suspicions combined with the acute economic crisis that had crippled the French economy, soon upset it. One of the paradoxes that frustrated the coalition was the fact that the top Communist leaders, again instructed by the Comintern to make a show of moderation, were much less eager to foster strikes than their Socialist partners or the Communist rank-and-file workers. Maurice Thorez's attempts to overcompensate for his antimilitaristic stands in the past by now backing rearmament ran counter to the desire of the masses. Consequently, while trying to help the government in its effort to catch up with the breakneck German remilitarization, the French Communist leaders ran into a conflict with their own supporters, who were bewildered by the sudden advocacy of what they had regarded as French jingoism. These contradictions resulted in a most confusing situation. The French rearmament program was bogged down in a flood of uncontrollable wildcat strikes. The mounting conservative backlash resulted in the downfall of the popular front government. After two years in power, it was replaced in 1938 by a more moderate coalition headed by the Radical Socialist politician Edouard Daladier.

Civil War in Spain

While the French popular front coalition was shaken, a civil war broke out in Spain in July 1936. The war represented the delayed aftermath of the 1931 downfall of the Spanish monarchy. From its inception, the Spanish Republic suffered from the antiliberal, antidemocratic heritage of the past, as well as from Spain's age-old socioeconomic backwardness. Taking advantage of the chaos following the establishment of the republican regime, two vigorous autonomist movements in the north and in the east—in the Basque provinces and in Catalonia—immediately reasserted themselves against Madrid's centralist policies. The parliamentary elections of November 1933 produced a rightist reaction. The new conservative government proclaimed a law-and-order policy and often used the army to suppress a series of strikes, mutinies, and uprisings, the most significant of which were the revolt of the Asturian miners and an insurrection in Catalonia.

The iron-fist policies of the government and the spread of a native variety of protofascist groups, the most important of which was the Falange movement, spawned among the leftist elements fears for the fate of the Spanish Republic. In January 1936, they decided to confront the Fascist menace collectively and signed a popular front agreement. The main partners of the coalition were the Republican Left led by Manuel Azaña; the Spanish Socialists; the small but very active Communist Party of Spain; the Workers' Party of Marxist Unity (representing the anti-Stalinist and pro-Trotsky wing of the Communist movement); and the Catalan Left. The less organized but still numerous Anarchists, who were especially strong in Catalonia, did not join the coalition but lent their support to the popular front government, thus making its victory possible. In the February 1936 parliamentary elections, this heterogeneous coalition won a parliamentary majority, but by a very narrow margin; the leftist victory was largely due to electoral geography.

The unexpected triumph of the popular front alarmed the conservative forces of the country, which was soon flooded by a wave of strikes, riots, and assassinations. The rightist opposition was especially militant among the officers stationed in Spanish Morocco. In July 1936, several colonial detachments, led by General Francisco Franco, revolted against the leftist government in Madrid. Military uprisings soon followed throughout Spain. Consequently, by the summer of 1936 Spain was torn between the supporters of the legal government (or Loyalists) and the rightist rebels (or Nationalists).

The Great Powers and the Spanish Civil War

The bloody Civil War in Spain soon became an event of considerable international significance. Separated from France only by the Pyrenees, covering most of the Iberian peninsula and thus a large segment of the western Mediterranean, Spain was also an important source of such vital strategic raw materials as copper, zinc, iron ore, and lead. Traditionally, what was happening south of the Pyrenees was of great significance to the French as well as to their British allies; both countries had considerable investments in Spanish industry and agriculture. Germany and Italy, on the other hand, were eager, for strategic and ideological reasons, to see their fascist kinsmen, the Falangists, win the fight against Madrid's leftist government, which Berlin and Rome declared to be infected by Communism. First, Italy and then Germany lent direct military support to the rebels of General Franco. The Spanish Civil War threatened to turn into a European war. To prevent this, Paris and London tried to localize the conflict by forming the Nonintervention Committee, which was to isolate the war and keep the conflict strictly a Spanish domestic affair.

Moscow's attitude was quite different. There were powerful reasons that argued for quick and active Soviet intervention. Spain was the scene of the second experiment in popular front governments; therefore, it was difficult for the Kremlin, as well as for the leftist forces of the world, to allow such a government to be destroyed by the rightists, increasingly dominated by the fascist Falange and brazenly supported by Germany and Italy.

Here one should add that the Communist party of Spain was initially a small sect with about 1,000 active members in 1931. Yet, it mushroomed in the course of the war to reach 1,000,000 in June 1937[1] Through the

---

[1] Pierre Broué and Emile Temime, *The Revolution and the Civil War in Spain* (Cambridge, Mass.: MIT Press, 1970), p. 229.

united front the Party exercised powerful influence on the larger but much more sluggish Socialist movement, especially on its youth organization, which soon merged with its Communist counterpart. To add to the bewildering complexity of the Spanish vortex, almost from the beginning one segment of the Spanish popular front, the "Trotskyite" Workers' Party of Marxist Unity (*POUM* in Spanish)[2] was in opposition to the Fabian tactics of delay and avoidance of too drastic revolutionary changes pressed by Moscow on Spain's pro-Stalin Communist party. Moreover, in Catalonia the POUM was numerically stronger and by far more dynamic than was the orthodox Communist movement. Often supported by the Anarchists, it successfully pursued its own line: it desired an unbridled revolutionary war. The official line of the Spanish Communist party—to win the war first and only then to restructure the country in a Communist spirit—was decried by the POUM as a Stalinist trick to sabotage the cause of the international proletarian revolution.

If only to counteract Trotsky's accusation about "the betrayal of the Revolution" and to prevent Germany and Italy from scoring a rapid victory, Stalin had to act decisively. On the other hand, to intervene too openly risked alienating France and Great Britain as military partners of Soviet Russia by raising the "Red Specter" in Western Europe. Since the Spanish Civil War could become the first practical test of collective security, Stalin could not afford to boycott the Nonintervention Committee so strongly supported by his main prospective allies. While reluctantly agreeing to participate in the Committee's work, Moscow tried to preserve its revolutionary integrity and minimize its participation in this bourgeois body through a series of militant pronouncements by the Comintern. For both ideological and strategic

reasons Stalin was duty-bound to help the Republic, but power-political considerations dictated moderation. A Communist-influenced, let alone dominated, Spanish government would be likely to drive France and Great Britain into the Hitler-sponsored anti-Comintern coalition.

Another consideration that emerged after the first stages of the fighting was of a logistic nature: Both Axis powers were obviously using the Spanish Civil War as a testing ground for their newly produced war equipment, especially tanks and planes. The Russians could hardly afford to miss such an opportunity to match their newly produced hardware against that of their potential opponents. Italy's and Germany's military assistance to the rebels in violation of the principle of nonintervention could lead to an early victory of the rebels. This was what Stalin hoped to prevent. After three months of hesitation, Stalin decided to lend military support to the Spanish Republic.

Soviet Intervention in the Spanish Civil War

Soviet aid to the Loyalists was granted on four main conditions. First, Spain's pro-Moscow faction of the Communist party was to be given a greater role in the Madrid government. Second, Soviet experts were to have a strong say in the use of Soviet materiel without being compelled to participate in the actual fighting; they were instructed to "keep out of the range of artillery." Third, political commissars would be introduced to all units above the company level. Fourth, arms and supplies were to be paid for in gold from the Spanish National Bank. All these conditions were complied with, and in September 1936 two Spanish Communists entered the popular front government headed by a Socialist. In Catalonia the local Communists merged with the Catalan Socialist Party and formed the United Catalan Socialist Party, which the Communists soon managed to dominate completely. Meanwhile,

[2] The POUM was led by former members of the Spanish Communist Party who had sided with Trotsky and Zinoviev in the late twenties and opposed Stalin as a dictatorial usurper and a traitor of the revolutionary cause.

the USSR helped the Loyalists with arms, munitions, and other equipment under the supervision of a team of Soviet military and political advisers.

At the same time, via the Comintern, foreign Communists were encouraged to enlist in several *International Brigades.* With Soviet aid, these volunteers were trained, equipped, and transported to Spain, where they came to play a vital role in bolstering the Loyalist resistance. One well-known brigade was composed of American volunteers, including the writer Ernest Hemingway, and bore the name of Abraham Lincoln. The International Brigades attracted many prominent foreign Communists who were destined to play an important role during and after World War II; among them were Joseph Broz (Tito) of Yugoslavia. "Ercoli" (Palmiro Togliatti) of Italy, Laszlo Rajk of Hungary, and many others. They were soon backed by numerous radically minded non-Communist leftist intellectuals, such as George Orwell and André Malraux, all eager to participate in, or at least support, a "crusade against Fascism."[3] Altogether the International Brigades numbered between thirty and forty thousand people. The brigades, together with direct Soviet aid, considerably bolstered the Republican forces; without them Madrid would most probably have been captured already by the Nationalist troops of General Franco already in November 1936.

As has been previously mentioned, the official Soviet policy of moderation and of sharing power with other nonsocialist members of the popular front alliance was opposed by the Catalan Trotskyists, Poumists, and Anarchists, who believed that the Civil War in Spain provided an excellent opportunity for an immediate seizure of power by the working class. The establishment of a Communist republic at the other extremity

of the European continent would constitute an ideal launching pad for the further spread of a revolution whose favorable outcome seemed likely in the Western world as a result of the persistent Great Depression. This, however, was one more reason why Stalin was determined to be cautious in aiding the Republican forces. Their triumph, he was afraid, might spell the strengthening not of his brand of national Bolshevism, but of the revolutionary, evangelical Communism preached by his archenemy, Trotsky. At the same time, such a triumph would destroy the incipient common front that he was trying to build with France and Britain based on the status quo.

Stalin realized that Spain had become a focal point for Trotskyist forces throughout the world and that the Loyalist camp was crowded with rivals for control of the world revolutionary movement. While pursuing his other objectives he therefore took the opportunity to destroy his ideological enemies among the Communists. Together with Soviet tanks, planes and Soviet advisers, came a team of NKVD security officers. Their task was to hunt not so much the native pro-Franco elements (this was left largely to the Spanish republican militia), but to destroy the heterodox Communists and real and suspected Trotskyists. Thus the Spanish Civil War soon became a foreign extension of the Great Purge in Soviet Russia.

Soviet assistance, given belatedly and in limited quantity, could not counterbalance the massive systematic aid immediately extended to the rebels by the Axis powers. Italy had sent to Spain several fully equipped army divisions, while the Germans, in addition to the crack "Condor" air force squadron, dispatched a considerable amount of first-class, newly manufactured equipment, tanks, planes, and ammunition. Thus the Civil War in Spain, like later wars in Korea and Vietnam, represented a trial conflict by proxy: the Great Powers not only tested their hardware, but used smaller countries as pawns in their intricate imperial game.

---

[3] Each of the writers mentioned produced a major work based on his experience in Spain; Hemingway wrote *For Whom the Bell Tolls*; Orwell, *Homage to Catalonia*; and Malraux, *L'Espoir (Hope).*

The Spanish Civil War Ends

Supported more consistently by their sponsors, the rebels were gaining the upper hand step by step. The more precarious the situation of the Loyalists grew, the greater became their dependence on their only source of supply; the USSR, and thus the local pro-Moscow Communist Party. By the spring of 1937 it had come to dominate most of the governmental apparatus and through the Political Commissars, the Loyalist armed forces. All this, however, was not sufficient to stem the rebel tide, which advanced slowly but relentlessly toward Madrid.

Meanwhile, in March 1938, having already subverted his native country through its local Nazi movement, Hitler occupied and annexed Austria. France and Britain, and Fascist Italy, meekly accepted this move. As a result of the *Anschluss*, the Third Reich increased its population by about eight million, gained considerable industrial resources and reserves of timber, oil, iron ore, and water power, and came to dominate the middle Danube. With the annexation of Austria the frontiers of the Reich moved considerably to the east, toward the USSR. At the same time the Soviet ally Czechoslovakia became surrounded from the south and increasingly menaced by Hitler's expansionist drive.

As the Czech crisis in Europe was mounting in July and August 1938, tension in Asia escalated as the Japanese intervened more and more openly in the affairs of China, established themselves in Manchuria, and thereby threatened southern Siberia as well as Vladivostok. There were several serious incidents on the Soviet-Manchurian borders that necessitated further reinforcing the Red Army in the Far East, thus making more tangible the connection between Soviet Asian and European defenses. Bitter hostilities between the USSR and Japan required more extensive deployment of Soviet forces in the Far East. While Hitler was exploiting the momentary Soviet weaknesses as well as the timidity of the West, the Japanese were the first to probe militarily Soviet defenses in Mongolia and Siberia. In view of this, the limited Soviet resources were urgently needed in Asia as well as in Central Europe. In November 1938, soon after the partition of Czechoslovakia at the conference of Munich, Moscow recalled the International Brigades from Spain and stopped direct Soviet aid. This was the kiss of death to the tottering Loyalist regime. In February 1939, the forces of General Franco captured Barcelona, the capital of Catalonia. In March, after a prolonged siege, Madrid fell into his hands.

Consequences of the Spanish Civil War

In the spring of 1939 the Spanish Civil War was over. It lasted nearly three years, caused untold suffering, and left over one million dead. Soviet assistance to the Loyalists was just enough to keep the Republicans fighting, but not sufficient to let them win the war. The German planes, tanks, and artillery proved superior to the Soviet models. Soviet experts and advisers did help, but on Stalin's orders, they were generally more eager to fight their ideological rivals (mainly the Trotskyists) than to cope with strictly military matters. The war compelled at least one million supporters of the Loyalist cause to seek shelter abroad. Some of them went to the USSR while some settled in Western Europe, mainly in France.

This setback in Spain was a painful blow to Soviet prestige, but it had its silver lining. Stalin had had the opportunity to test his hardware, for which he was handsomely paid with $500 million in Spanish gold. He also had an opportunity to test the willingness of his Western allies to cooperate against common enemies on his conditions. While apparently manifesting his revolutionary zeal, he had destroyed a large number of his Trotskyite rivals. The main Soviet representative in Spain, a former supporter of Trotsky, Vladimir Antonov-Ovseyenko, was arrested and liquidated soon after the end of this mission, as were most of the Soviet advisers who served in Spain, including some who had advocated a radical modernization and reorganization of Soviet mechanized troops.

Soviet intervention in the Spanish Civil War represented Stalin's last effort to exploit the antifascist cause in Western Europe for his purposes. The effort failed only partly because of France's and Britain's hesitation and passivity; it foundered also because Moscow's objectives in Spain had as much to do with domestic politics as with Russia's international objectives. Moscow's experience in the Nonintervention Committee had made it increasingly suspicious of the Western powers, and was a major factor in the dramatic diplomatic about-face that was soon to follow. As a result of his attempted cooperation with France and Britain, Stalin came to be convinced of the bankruptcy of collective security; he even came to suspect that certain groups among the British Conservatives hoped the Soviet Union and Germany might clash sooner or later, leaving the Western democracies as observers.

On the other hand, the persistence of revolutionary phraseology and terrorist practices applied by Soviet security organs in Spain made many European statesmen doubt the sincerity of Stalin's policy, despite Litvinov's sophisticated eloquence. What damaged the Soviet image still further were the massive domestic purges, deportations, and show trials that paralleled most of the Spanish Civil War. The massive purge of the Red Army leaders dealt a particularly powerful blow to confidence in the USSR as a stable and reliable partner in any coalition. Most Western military experts reached the conclusion that the decapitated Soviet armed forces would be unable, for the time being, to fulfill their numerous obligations in both Eastern Europe and the Far East and that one could not count on them as serious allies.

The Anti-Comintern Pact and the Czechoslovak Crisis

While the Spanish Civil War was going on, the international position of the USSR deteriorated further. On October 25, 1936, Italy and Germany signed an agreement that provided for close cooperation in foreign affairs, especially as far as the "Communist menace" was concerned. In November of that year, Japan, by now master of Manchuria, signed a five-year pact with Germany. The document declared Soviet Communism to be their greatest common danger and bound its signatories to unite their forces to fight "Communist subversive activities." In November 1937, on the first anniversary of the Germany-Japanese pact, Italy joined what became known as the Berlin-Tokyo Axis or the Anti-Comintern Pact. Japan recognized the Italian conquest of Ethiopia, while Rome recognized the state of Manchukuo (Manchuria). Thus came into being the triangular alliance among the three authoritarian and aggressive powers, each of them opposed to Soviet Russia.

At that time, Stalin must have been wondering what the Japanese would do after their conquest of China. Would they turn toward the Soviet protectorate of Outer Mongolia and to Soviet southern Siberia, both of them former segments of the Middle Kingdom? This need for military vigilance in the Far East, for maintaining a powerful, well-equipped army there that was involved in not only intermittent skirmishes but occasional pitched battles with the Japanese, the Far Eastern threat, affected Stalin's ambivalent posture in Europe.

The bloodless occupation of Austria did not end the list of Hitler's territorial demands. The remaining ones appeared one-by-one: the Czechoslovak Sudetenland, Danzig and the Polish Pomerania (often called by German propaganda the Polish Corridor), and the Lithuanian harbor-city of Memel (Klaipeda). Whichever way Hitler advanced would bring him uncomfortably close to the Soviet western borders.

By May 1938, it became quite clear that Czechoslovakia would be Hitler's next target. Austria's annexation extended the frontiers of the Greater German Reich 400 miles to the east. As a result of this encirclement from the South, Czechoslovakia's strategic situation became critical. The republic built by Thomas G. Masaryk and his successor Edward Beneš, like the prewar Hapsburg Empire, contained numerous national minorities, including over three million Germans. They lived in compact areas and were concentrated mostly along its western frontiers, adjacent to Hitler's Reich. After a vitriolic preparatory subversive campaign which lasted throughout the spring and summer of 1938, Hitler vigorously pressed his demand that the Sudeten Germans be given the right of self-determination. Should their right to secede be denied, he threatened war. This was the gist of the militant speech he delivered on September 12, 1938. To dramatize his demands, Hitler openly began to make war preparations.

The Munich Appeasement

The rest of the month of September was marked by acute international tension. Prague, while offering concessions that bordered on granting complete autonomy to its German citizens, ordered the mobilization of its armed forces. France followed suit, promising to fulfill the alliance obligations deriving from the treaty of 1924. Great Britain ordered the partial mobilization of its navy. Thus, Europe was brought to the brink of war.

As discussed earlier, Czechoslovakia was bound by an alliance not only to France but also to the USSR. The Soviet alliance hinged, however, on the prior fulfillment by the French of their obligations. After having publicly renewed their pledges to defend the Czechs in case of a German attack, in May 1938 the French, along with the British, privately began to press Prague to surrender to the ever-growing German demands. Consequently, from a strictly legal point of view, the Russians would be freed from their obligations toward the Czechs. Nevertheless, Litvinov kept on repeating that the USSR was ready to discharge all its duties toward Czechoslovakia "in accordance with the treaty of May 16, 1935," and with the League of Nations Covenant. Despite French refusal to

aid them, the Czechs could have invoked Soviet aid, but they never did, either out of fear of provoking Hitler, or perhaps out of doubt that it would be effective. Would the Soviet armed forces, decimated by the purges, be able to protect Czechoslovakia against the Germans? How would the Red Army reach Czechoslovak territory? Polish territory lay between the two countries, and the Poles, who were making their own demands on Czechoslovakia, refused to let the Russians cross. Even the Romanians, Prague's allies were reluctant to let the Red Army pass. As King Carol II declared to the German ambassador in Bucharest, "I would prefer to see the Germans in Romania as enemies, than the Russians as allies."

After being strongly urged by President Franklin Delano Roosevelt, Mussolini, and British Prime Minister Neville Chamberlain, Hitler finally agreed to attend an international conference to settle the Czech issue peacefully. The conference, which took place at Munich, was attended by the representatives of only four powers: Germany, Italy, Great Britain, and France. The USSR and Czechoslovakia itself were excluded from the deliberations.

At Munich, under the concerted pressure of all the Big Four powers, including its formal ally France, Prague was forced "in the interest of peace" to cede immediately to Germany the Sudeten borderlands whose inhabitants were more than 50 percent German; this area included most of the country's frontier fortifications and most of its industry. All four powers agreed to guarantee the integrity and sovereignty of the remaining rump Czechoslovakia.

The appeasement of Hitler's demands had far-reaching consequences. The Sudeten resources, especially its armament industries, strengthened Hitler's arsenal and prestige dramatically. This led to a political landslide in Eastern and Central Europe that resulted in establishing the Greater German Reich as the predominant military force, not only in that area but on the European continent as a whole. Hitler's next prospective victim, Poland, was not outflanked from the south.

Belying his repeated solemn promises not to seek new territorial gains, a few days after Munich Hitler asked Warsaw for Danzig and the establishment of an extraterritorial highway to connect Berlin with the East Prussian enclave. The Poles refused. Hitler then immediately began preparations for war against Poland.

Moscow and the Munich Pact

The four-power Munich conference was a humiliation of Moscow because it spelled its exclusion from the European concert. The Russians were not consulted by their allies, the French, in vital matters pertaining to their mutual ally, Czechoslovakia. The sacrifice of Czechoslovakia to Hitler's appetites and the conciliatory attitude of the Western powers toward him gave rise to further Soviet suspicions that France and Britain plotted to channel the German expansionist drive eastward toward the Soviet borders. In view of this, Stalin decided to reappraise once more his participation in what had originally been intended as a system of collective security. Faced by growing Nazi pressure on the lands immediately adjacent to his domains like the Baltic states, Poland, and Romania, he had to consider two options. He could either bolster the zone separating him from Nazi Germany in alliance with France and Britain, or he could make a deal with the potential aggressor. Unable to make a reasonable choice, however, Stalin kept both irons in the fire.

The autumn of 1938 marked the peak of France and Britain's appeasement policy, which was based on the delusion that peace could be bought with concessions. One of the premises of the Munich settlement had been that, once having united most ethnic Germans, Hitler would be satiated and hence would no longer seek new conquests. He destroyed this delusion when, on March 15, 1939, German troops occupied Prague and the western remnants of Bohemia and Moravia. Immediately, Hitler declared these lands a German protectorate. Meanwhile,

encouraged by Berlin, Slovakia established itself as a separate state, also under German tutelage. Thus Hitler was caught in a flagrant breach of promise; he disregarded the declarations he made when he said that he merely wanted to unite the German people. The second Czechoslovak crisis was still more ominous from the Soviet point of view. Paris and London, unprepared to act in fulfillment of their Munich guarantees, again merely issued diplomatic protests.

It became obvious that their policy of appeasement was now in ruins. Paris and London decided to switch to a policy of containing Hitler. While they were busy consulting with each other and with Poland, the next prospective victim of Hitler's aggression, Lithuania, was forced to cede to Germany the port of Memel (Klaipeda) on March 27. This brought the Third Reich still closer to Soviet borders.

Moscow's apparent aloofness in the spring of 1939 could only camouflage its profound mistrust not only of Hitler's intentions but also of the Western powers' hesitating attitude. The establishment of the German protectorates of Bohemia and Moravia and the separation of Slovakia, which now became a German military jumping-off ground to the East, all moved German influence beyond the middle Danube. Hungary had already been penetrated by the Nazis, while the Balkan countries, from Romania to Greece, had been under increasing economic and political pressure from Berlin since Austria's annexation in March 1938. The German pincers were crawling inexorably eastward toward the Soviet western frontiers, both along the Danube and the Baltic. The snowballing German might and the whetting of the Nazi appetite for further conquest made the German threat a clear and present danger not only to the Soviet Union's interests, but to its very existence. Should the Soviet Union's largest western neighbor, Poland, be conquered, the situation of the USSR, in the middle of its great socioeconomic experiment and still recovering from the collectivization and the Great Purge, would become critical. This necessitated an urgent reappraisal of Soviet foreign policy. Should Moscow establish closer military ties with Paris and London and bolster Warsaw's determination to oppose Hitler's expansionist drive? Or should the Soviets seek other ways to protect their security?

Molotov Replaces Litvinov

While Hitler was preparing his final annexation of Bohemia and Moravia, the Eighteenth Soviet Party Congress (the first in more than five years) was gathering in Moscow on March 10, 1939. A posture of diplomatic flexibility permeated the speeches of its main orators, who were as much anti-German as anti-Western. In his general report Stalin restated his pet thesis that Britain and France, by sacrificing Czechoslovakia, wanted to divert Hitler's attention from the West and encourage his eastward expansion toward the USSR. He admonished France and Britain that the Soviet Union would not "pull the chestnuts out of the fire for them," and that it stood "for peace and the strengthening of business relations with all countries." The accent was on *all*. Although warning that the Soviets were ready to defend themselves, Stalin offered the Germans the benefits of expanded trade.

While the Eighteenth Congress was still in session, Hitler occupied Prague on March 15 and forced the Lithuanians to cede the port city of Memel a few days later. These continuous acts of German aggression alarmed London. At the end of March, the British replied by offering guarantees of Poland's sovereignty and integrity in case they should be threatened by Germany. Soon London made a similar pledge to Romania, the main repository of European oil resources. France associated itself with these guarantees. Poland and Romania now became a sort of buffer: any German attack on the USSR would involve a violation of these guarantees and hence a war with Britain and France.

Hitler obviously was looking for another pushover. Furious at Poland's refusal to sur-

Vyacheslav M. Molotov, Soviet Foreign Minister, 1939–1946 and 1953–1957

render, on April 28 he denounced the German-Polish nonaggression pact of 1934, claiming that it had been violated by Warsaw's acceptance of London's "provocative" guarantees. In this speech there were none of his customary vitriolic denunciations of the Soviet Union. Stalin understood the hint.

An impending shift of the Kremlin's policy was foreshadowed by a change of its pilot. On May 2, Litvinov, whom the Germans had ostracized as a Jew, was replaced as Minister for Foreign Affairs by an ethnic Russian, Molotov. For the first time since Trotsky's resignation from that post on the eve of the Brest-Litovsk treaty, Soviet foreign policy was in the hands of a full member of the Politburo, Stalin's close co-worker, as well as Prime Minister of the Soviet government. The change of the Soviet Foreign Minister had a beneficial effect on the intermittent secret talks that Soviet diplomats had been conducting with their German counterparts since the event of Munich.

While pursuing these negotiations, the Kremlin tried to probe the extent of the unprecedented British commitment to Eastern Europe. Did the British really intend to go to war in defense of Poland and Romania? The apparently serious nature of this inquiry seems to indicate that the British involvement was a welcome novelty. On April 18, Litvinov had suggested to the British ambassador in Moscow that France should join in these pledges. The three powers, he urged, should guarantee militarily all the "East European states situated between the Baltic and Black seas and bordering on the USSR." The three powers were to hold staff talks as to the details of such help and pledge not to conclude a separate peace in case of war. To negotiate the details of the proposed cooperation, British and French military missions were sent to Moscow in May. However, the fact that they traveled by boat created an impression of a lack of zeal on the part of both London and Paris to cooperate with the USSR.

During the talks the Russians were in a hurry to conclude the negotiations. Two serious barriers seemed to impede them at every step: the right of passage of Soviet troops through Poland, Romania, and the Baltic states. All three Baltic republics—Lithuania, Latvia, and Estonia—refused to accept the extensive Soviet guarantees which involved stationing of Soviet troops on their territory, even in case of a threat of an "indirect aggression," an extremely vague term. They interpreted it as a blanket Western consent for the Russians to do as they wished in the Baltic area. The Western powers were hesitant as to whether they could impose such a drastic solution on sovereign pro-Western states. On the other hand, when the French and British delegates promised to press Poland, Romania, and the Baltic states to be more flexible, the Russians immediately put forward another issue, that of establishing their bases on Finnish soil. Consequently, the frustrating negotiations dragged on throughout the hot, tense summer of 1939. Meanwhile secret German-Soviet talks had been going on in Berlin under the guise of trade negotiations; soon they revealed that Hitler was willing to share Poland and the Baltic states with Stalin and would even offer him the Romanian province of Bessarabia for good measure, as a price for his cooperation in attacking Poland.

The Stalin-Hitler Pact

Stalin, with both sides competing for his favors and with plenty of time to choose the highest bidder, was in a more advantageous position than Hitler. Hence he was in no hurry to decide what to do. Hitler, on the other hand, eager to pounce on Poland before the autumn rains would make his tanks useless, was getting restless. On August 2, German Foreign Minister von Ribbentrop held out the bait to Stalin. He suggested a joint partitioning of Poland and an offer of German intervention in Tokyo to stop the Soviet–Japanese clashes then going on along the Manchurian and Mongolian borders. The Russians, however, were still hesitant; the legacy of years of mutual suspicions was hard to overcome: they suspected a trap. Since Stalin did not react to his previous overtures, on August 3 Hitler ordered the German ambassador in Moscow, Count von Schulenburg, to assure Molotov that Berlin was also resolved to respect fully the vital Soviet interests in Estonia, Latvia, and Lithuania. Stalin, however, was still reluctant to commit himself; he pondered the risks involved in a decision that would amount to giving a green light to a German attack on Poland; this would demolish the territorial buffer zone separating Germany from the USSR, and involve him in conflict with France and Britain. Now Hitler became angered by the lack of Stalin's reply. On August 20, he insisted that his Foreign Minister, von Ribbentrop, be invited to Moscow within twenty-four hours; otherwise the whole planned deal of sharing Eastern Europe would be off. This was a virtual ultimatum and Stalin gave in.

On August 23, von Ribbentrop flew to Moscow for a brief but momentous visit. The same day at the Kremlin, in an atmosphere of cordiality, he and Molotov, with Stalin supervising, signed two crucial documents: an open declaration of nonaggression, friendship, and cooperation; and a secret protocol. This protocol, the more important of the two documents, divided Eastern Europe into two spheres of influence: Estonia, Latvia, Poland east of the Vistula, and Bessarabia were to be left to the Soviet Union; Lithuania and Poland west of the Vistula were to remain within the German hegemonial sphere. Each side was given a free hand in its respective sphere. The nonaggression pact provided that both parties would refrain from attacking one another in case one of the signatories should be invaded by a third party. Both promised to refrain from any activity aimed directly or indirectly at the other party.

The signing of these two agreements, which were to enter into force immediately, was followed by a lavish banquet at the Kremlin. Both sides were elated. Ribbentrop slapped Molotov on the back and said he felt as if he were among "old revolutionary comrades" now struggling together against a common enemy, the "Western capitalists." Von Ribbentrop told Stalin a German joke:

Stalin at the Kremlin raises his glass of champagne to drink to Hitler's health.

Soon the Soviet Union would join the Anti-Comintern Pact. Stalin was not amused and refused to laugh. Nevertheless, he gave his "word of honor" that the Soviet Union would not betray Germany. He raised his glass of champagne and drank a toast to Hitler's health and success: "I know how much the German people love their Führer."

The Outbreak of World War II

The Stalin-Hitler Pact hit the world like a blast of dynamite. The Soviet diplomatic about-face had been suspected by only a few more perceptive Western observers. Their warnings, however, had met with the skepticism of all those who had reasoned in purely ideological terms that the Communist-Nazi hostility was unbridgeable. Hardly had the outside world had time to analyze the full implications of the pact when, on September 1 at 4:00 A.M., German troops attacked Poland. On September 3, Britain and France reluctantly declared war on Germany. World War II was on.

The German troops made rapid progress in Poland and soon occupied even large stretches of land originally assigned by the secret protocol to the Soviet partner. Yet, despite repeated urgings, Stalin refused to openly enter the fray. All the time he was anxiously watching the situation in Western Europe and in the Far East. The fact that neither France nor Britain undertook any major military operations in defense of Poland emboldened Stalin: he was uncertain about the situation in the Far East. During the first stages of the Polish campaign, the Red Army was engaged in a series of savage encounters along the Manchurian border. Finally, by mid-August, commander of the Soviet Far Eastern forces, General Georgi K. Zhukov, launched a crushing blow against the Japanese that knocked their shattered Sixth Army back into Manchuria. The effect of the Soviet victory on the Japanese was so severe that the Tokyo General Staff had to rethink its original plan of conquering Southern Siberia. This defeat of the Japanese Army gave the upper hand to the Japanese naval establishment, eager to spread the "Asian Co-prosperity Sphere" in Southeast Asia instead.

September 15, the same day that the Soviet-Japanese armistice in the Far East was signed, the Red Army was ordered to march into Eastern Poland. On September 17, six Soviet armies, numbering nearly a million soldiers, crossed the Riga frontier to "liberate Russia's Ukrainian and Belorussian brethren." The Soviet invasion met with hesitant resistance from the Polish forces; all the time they were fighting alone, without the promised assistance of their Western allies, and they had been badly mauled by the Germans. By the beginning of October, the Red Army took some 200,000 POWs, of whom 15,000 were officers.

By the end of September, German troops had occupied large stretches of Central Poland originally allotted to the USSR and refused to withdraw. This necessitated a revision of the deal of August 23. By a supplementary agreement of September 28, the Germans gave up Lithuania in exchange for the Polish lands west of the rivers Narev, Bug, and San. This redistribution still left the Soviets 48 percent of Poland's territory, with nearly 13 million inhabitants.

Throughout this period the Soviet media followed a rigidly pro-German line. Their anti-Western campaign was supported by the whole apparatus of the Comintern. On September 29, a joint Soviet-German declaration held London and Paris responsible for the continuation of the "imperialistic" war. When the last traces of Polish resistance collapsed at the beginning of October, Stalin sent Hitler personal congratulations which ended with the words, "Our alliance has been sealed in blood."

The Winter War with Finland

In October 1939, while the Russians were establishing military bases in Lithuania, Latvia, and Estonia, and stern political controls in Eastern Poland, they opened negotiations with their northern neighbor, Finland. Unlike the three small Baltic republics which had submitted to the Soviet ultimatums without firing a shot, the stronger and strategically better-situated Finns squarely opposed most of the Soviet demands that would leave them at Moscow's mercy. These demands focused around the Karelian isthmus, including the Finnish fortifications (the "Mannerheim line"), Western Karelia, Petsamo (the ice-free Finnish port on the Arctic Sea), the several islands controlling the approaches to Leningrad, and leasing of the strategic Hangoe peninsula. The Soviet argument was that the Mannerheim line was only twenty miles north of the outskirts of Leningrad, while the strategically vital railroad connecting Leningrad with the Soviet ice-free port of Murmansk had to be protected to a wider belt of Karelian territory. The Finns sought a compromise solution and offered considerable territorial readjustment in favor of the Soviet Union, including ceding four islands and moving their frontier thirteen miles further north of Leningrad; but they refused cession of their system of fortifications protecting their southern approaches, and disarming their armed forces. Neither would they permit the establishment of Soviet military bases on their territory. The long drawn-out negotiations broke down on November 13. Suddenly, on November 28, after a provoked border incident, a Soviet frontier guard was killed under mysterious circumstances. Two days later, some thirty Soviet divisions attacked the Finns in eight places simultaneously. At the same time, in the border village of Terijoki, the "Karelo-Finnish Soviet Socialist Republic" was established, headed by a veteran Finnish Communist Otto Kuusinen, who promptly acceded to all Soviet demands.

The war between the Finnish David and the Soviet Goliath raged in snows five to six feet deep, with temperatures often dropping to thirty and forty degrees below zero. The Finns defended themselves with skill and tenacity. At the same time the Helsinki Government appealed to the League of Nations;

KEY:

▓ Soviet Union
█ Territories Ceded to the Soviet Union
░ Swedish & Norwegian Territories
○ Swedish Iron Ore Mines of Kiruna & Galivare
⚓ Soviet Navel Base at Hangoe
── Narvik-Lulea Railroad
▭▭ Mannerheim Line

The Soviet-Finnish Treaty of Moscow, March 1940

on December 14, the League declared the USSR the aggressor and expelled it from the League. The sympathy of the whole civilized world was overwhelmingly on the Finnish side and Western volunteers flocked to Finland. In the course of murderous fighting that lasted through January 1940, the Red Army managed to advance between fifteen and forty miles, depending on the sector. Only on February 21, after ten days of storming by twenty-seven Soviet divisions and after having suffered 48,745 dead and 159,000 wounded, according to official Soviet figures, did the Russians break the Finnish resistance. Finnish casualties amounted to 24,923 killed and 43,557 wounded.[4]

The peace treaty was concluded in Moscow in March 1940; the treaty compelled Finland to cede the Karelian isthmus, including the town of Viborg, a naval base at Hangoe, the region north of Lake Ladoga, a peninsula in the north of Murmansk, and a group of several islands controlling the Gulf of Finland—altogether over 16,000 square miles and containing a population of 420,000.

The "Winter War" considerably strengthened the Soviet strategic position in the Eastern Baltic and made Leningrad more secure. But the price, moral and material, was very steep. The USSR eventually committed to the Finnish campaign about one million men, 3,000 planes, and almost as many tanks. Yet this huge mass was for some three months bogged down by a tiny Finnish force. The bitter experience of the Finnish campaign dramatized to the Soviet leadership the necessity of military reforms.

The setbacks of the "Winter War" compelled the Red Army to modernize. First, unified command was reintroduced and political commissars were made subordinate

to field commanders; field officers were made solely responsible for all military decisions. Second, cooperation among different branches and services of the armed forces was updated. Third, training of troops under winter conditions was improved, and field regulations were revised to make them correspond more to the demands of modern warfare. The most important improvement was a vigorous effort at resupplying the Red Army and Air Force with modernized weapons. While adopting some of the Finnish innovations, like the "Molotov cocktails" and the wooden boxes to hide land mines, Red Army researchers promptly developed an array of new weapons, including massed rockets. Another improvement was application of newly developed lubricants that allowed their weapons, tanks, artillery, and aircraft to function in frigid temperatures. In marshal Zhukov's words, 1940 was for the Red Army the year of "the great transformation."

The Soviet strategic and economic gains in the Baltic region were counterbalanced, however, by political and moral liabilities. The Finns, while nursing their wounds, were contemplating how to recover their painful losses. Soviet incompetence greatly encouraged Hitler to plan his invasion of Russia. In his opinion, it would be a walk-over that would last only a few months.

The Stalin-Hitler Pact: An Appraisal

Many factors contributed to Stalin's deal with Hitler. One of them was the menacing situation in the Far East and Soviet fears of being involved in a two-front war. Another was Stalin's growing disillusionment with the prospects of French and British military cooperation against Germany. The tardiness with which the British, and especially the French, entered the war, along with their lack of effective help to Poland, both reinforced Stalin's conviction that the West lacked the will to fight.

From the Soviet point of view, the pact with Hitler must have appeared to be the least dangerous of available alternatives.

---

[7] According to recent Finnish research, Soviet losses were actually much higher, amounting to 230,000 to 270,000. Despite these high numbers, Finnish losses were disproportionally much higher. In 1939–1940 the population of Finland was less than four million. By way of comparison, if the same percentage of losses had been sustained by the United States in 1940, it would have been the equivalent of 2.6 million casualties.

A German military delegation visits Brest Litovsk, October 1939.

Stalin's tactic was to keep his country out of the war as long as possible, even at the price of destroying the belt of buffer states, Poland and Baltic Republics, which hitherto separated the USSR from the menacing Third Reich. While the two brands of almost equally dangerous capitalist camps were to massacre each other, the Russians were to remain on the sidelines as vigilant observers, ready to enter the fray at the last, decisive stage. The Stalin-Hitler deal was not the determining cause of the war, yet it considerably encouraged Hitler to unleash the war. By securing Germany's eastern flank, Stalin removed the last obstacle to Hitler's attack on Poland.

Was Stalin's decision a rejection of the ideological premises of the Communism and a shift to the traditional Russian imperialist position? There were certainly some such elements visible in his calculations in 1939. The loss of the broad belt of territory in the west to Russia's smaller neighbors after 1917

was painfully felt by all Great Russian nationalists, with whom Stalin gradually came to identify himself. These losses, a humiliating reminder of Russia's defeat in World War I, also made the Soviet strategic situation precarious. One has to bear in mind that, in 1939, three of the USSR's major ports were virtually frontier cities: Leningrad was only twelve miles from the Finnish border, Odessa was about twenty miles from the Romanian boundary, and Murmansk was separated by only fifty miles of tundra from Finland.

To the strategic and political factors must be added economic considerations. Stalin believed that the acquisition of better warm-water ports—Tallin, Riga, or Liepaja—would improve Soviet access to the world's sea routes, as well as allow him to eventually control the Baltic Sea. He remembered that a hostile power could reach Archangel, located in the desolate and sparsely populated Sub-Arctic region, several months a year via the open sea. These political, strategic, and economic motifs were closely intertwined with another of Stalin's ambition, the achievement by his Russia of a leading position among world powers.

All these geostrategic considerations, however, do not necessarily prove that nationalism was Stalin's main motivating force, and that he definitely rejected the ideological premises of Communism. His appetite for old Tsarist lands and international prestige, it can be argued, did not affect his basically Marxist analysis of the world situation. Stalin did not distinguish between capitalistic states, democratic or totalitarian: they were all "imperialist enemies"; a war between the two brands of capitalist and hence necessarily imperialist powers would speed up the ongoing disintegration of the Western world and thus enhance the chances for further Soviet gains. That is why Soviet Russia, Stalin believed, should not be reluctant to fan the conflagration and intervene only at the last stage in order to impose Soviet peace on the exhausted foes.

Suggested Reading

BROUÉ, P., AND E. TEMINE, *The Revolution and the Civil War in Spain.* Cambridge, MA: MIT Press, 1970.

CATTELL, DAVID T., *Communism and the Spanish Civil War.* Berkeley: University of California Press, 1955.

————, *Soviet Diplomacy and the Spanish Civil War.* Berkeley: University of California Press, 1957.

EHRENBURG, ILYA, *Eve Of War, 1933–1941.* London: MacGibbon and Kee, 1963.

ERICKSON, JOHN, *The Soviet High Command.* New York: St. Martin's, 1962.

FEDOTOFF-WHITE, DIMITRI, *The Growth of the Red Army.* Princeton, NJ: Princeton University Press, 1944.

GARLIŃSKI, JÓZEF, *The Enigma War.* New York: Charles Scribner's Sons, 1979.

HERLING, GUSTAV, *A World Apart.* London: Heinemann, 1957.

HILGER, GUSTAV, AND ALFRED G. MEYER, *The Incompatible Allies.* New York: Macmillan, 1953.

HOCHMAN, JIRI, *The Soviet Union and the Failure of Collective Security, 1934–1938.* Ithaca, N.Y.: Cornell University Press, 1984.

JAKOBSON, MAX, *The Diplomacy of the Winter War: An Account of the Russo–Finnish War, 1939–1940.* Cambridge, MA: Harvard University Press, 1961.

KAHN, DAVID, *The Codebreakers.* New York: Macmillan, 1967.

————, *Hitler's Spies.* London: Hodder and Stoughton, 1978.

KENNAN, GEORGE F., *Russia and the West under Lenin and Stalin.* Boston: Little, Brown. 1961.

MARTEL, GORDON (ED.), *The Origins of the Second World War Reconsidered.* Boston: Allen and Unwin, 1986.

NAMIER, LOUIS, *The Diplomatic Prelude.* New York: Macmillan, 1948.

ORWELL, GEORGE, *Homage to Catalonia.* New York: Harcourt Brace Jovanovich, 1952.

PAANEN, LAURI, *The Winter War, the Russo–Finnish Conflict, 1939–1940.* New York: Scribner's 1973.

TANNER, VAINO, *The Winter War, Finland against Russia, 1939–1940.* Stanford, CA: Stanford University Press, 1950.

TARULIS, ALBERT, *Soviet Policy toward the Baltic States, 1918–1940.* Notre Dame, IN: University of Notre Dame Press, 1959.

THURSTON, ROBERT W., *Life and Terror in Stalin's Russia, 1934–1941.* New Haven, CT: Yale University Press, 1996.

TROTTER, WILLIAM, R., *A Frozen Hell: The Russo–Finnish War Of 1939–1940.* Chapel Hill: University of North Carolina Press, 1991.

ULAM, ADAM, *Expansion and Coexistence: The History of Soviet Foreign Policy, 1917–1967.* New York: Praeger, 1968. Chapters 5 and 6 in particular.

VON RAUCH, GEORGE, *The Baltic States: The Years of Independence, 1917–1940.* Berkeley: University of California Press, 1974.

WEINBERG, GERHARD, *Germany and the Soviet Union, 1939–1941.* Leiden, Neth.: Brill, 1954.

ZAWODNY, J. K., *Death in the Forest: The Story of the Katyn Forest Massacre.* Notre Dame, IN: University of Notre Dame Press, 1962.

ZHUKOV, GEORGI K., *Marshal Zhukov's Greatest Battles.* New York: Harper & Row, 1969.

————, *The Memoirs Of Marshal Zhukov.* New York: Delacorte Press, 1971.

Chapter 18

"The Great Patriotic War"

The bolstering of the Russian geostrategic position in the Baltic that resulted from the Winter War against Finland and the establishment of Soviet bases in the three Baltic states was no source of comfort to Hitler. Nevertheless, he had to accept it as the price of Stalin's benevolent neutrality, since he was too busy putting out peace feelers while preparing his Western drive. Germany, now under the Allied blockade, badly required supplies of Soviet raw materials. Hitler's Reich profited from the Soviet deliveries of such raw materials as oil, iron ore, and timber, as well as from the cessation of Communist subversion, which Stalin imposed on the Moscow-controlled parties of the German-occupied territories. Communist propaganda blamed the Anglo-French alliance for the continuance of "the senseless, imperialistic war," which was "nothing else but a crusade of the Western capitalists" against Germany. Moreover, the Hitler-Stalin Pact of 1939 had permitted the Germans to withdraw most of their troops from the East in order to use them successively against Denmark, Norway, Holland, Belgium, France, and Britain.

The news of the German attack against these countries in the spring of 1940 was received at the Kremlin with relief. It was perceived by Stalin as the beginning of a long and exhausting war that would be conducted far away from Soviet frontiers. While the capitalists were tearing each other to shreds, the Red Army would wait for the moment to enter the war to destroy the exhausted temporary victor. The softness of the Western resistance, revealed by the speedy collapse of France in June, shocked Stalin profoundly. Britain's decision to continue the war alone was regarded by him with reluctant admiration but with constant fear of a negotiated peace between two capitalist rivals. Altogether the sudden shift in the European balance of power could augur no good for Russia.

Incompatible Allies

Meanwhile, taking advantage of Hitler's temporary involvement in the West, Stalin tried to make up for Germany's gains by consolidating the Soviet position on the Baltic-Black seas isthmus. In June 1940, Soviet intelligence had conveniently discovered a secret plot allegedly hatched by the governments of Lithuania, Latvia, and Estonia, directed against their eastern protector. The plots gave the Red Army the convenient pretext they needed to occupy militarily all three Baltic states. Soviet troops brought in their baggage trains teams of Communist agents who, together with local supporters, established new governments "friendly to the USSR." Soon, as a face-saving device, hastily prepared plebiscites ratified these regimes. The fact that the plebiscites were thoroughly forged did not bother Stalin who said: "It doesn't matter how they vote, only how votes are counted." By these means, by July 1940, the three Baltic states were incorporated into the USSR as its fourteenth, fifteenth, and sixteenth republics.

After securing the northwestern regions of his realm, Stalin decided that he must safeguard Russia's interest not only in the Baltic but also all along the southern approaches of the Soviet Union. From his vantage point he decided that he must have full control of the Black Sea littoral and the mouth of the Danube River to counterbalance the enormous German gains in Western Europe, resulting from the conquest of Denmark, Norway, Holland, Belgium, and France. In a note to Bucharest on June 26, 1940, Moscow insisted that "in the interest of justice" the provinces of Bessarabia and Northern Bukovina be ceded to the USSR. The latter demand was stretching the secret protocol, for while Bessarabia had been a part of the deal, Northern Bukovina had never been mentioned. The Soviet demands made King Carol II of Rumania appeal to Berlin for help, but Hitler, still busy in France and contemplating an invasion of Britain, advised compliance with both requests. With the occupation of Northern Bukovina, former Habsburg lands, Stalin for the second time pushed beyond the old boundaries of the Tsarist Empire, Eastern Galicia, which, like Northern Bukovina, had belonged to the Hapsburgs until 1918 was now annexed to round up the Ukrainian

domains of Stalin. While Bessarabia was declared the Moldavian Soviet Socialist Republic, Northern Bukovina was incorporated into the Soviet Ukraine. The annexation of these two former Romanian provinces extended the Soviet frontiers to the crest of the Carpathian Mountains to threaten the Danubian valley.

Hitler, angered by the Soviet violation of the secret protocol of September 1939, reasserted German hegemony in the Danube region by rewarding his Hungarian and Bulgarian allies. On August 30, 1940, in Vienna, he compelled the Romanians to cede Northern Transylvania to Hungary and later on Southern Dobrudja to Bulgaria. Moreover, the Soviet Union was not invited to the reconstituted Danube Commission. Simultaneously, on September 27, 1940, Germany, Italy, and Japan issued a solemn declaration in Berlin dividing the world into three "natural spheres of interest." Europe was to be Germany's sphere and Africa Italy's, while Southeast Asia was allotted to Japan. The three anti-Comintern powers undertook "to assist one another with all political, economic and military means" should one of the contracting powers be attacked by a country "not at present involved in the European war, or in the Sino-Japanese war."

The aggressive restlessness of the Axis powers and the repeated exclusion of the Russians from decisions concerning the Balkan and Danubian regions created a great deal of anxiety in Moscow. Moreover, a deal concerning the stationing of German troops in such countries as Slovakia, Finland, and Romania generated further friction between Moscow and Berlin and precipitated a series of sharp Soviet protests. To cope with the mounting tension and to explain to Moscow the meaning of the tripartite declaration, Hitler invited Molotov to visit Berlin on November 12 and 13.

Molotov's visit was the first official call by a Soviet foreign minister on the Nazi capital. Lack of mutual confidence was reflected in the fact that Molotov insisted on eating only the food prepared by the cook he brought with him from Moscow. During the negotiations, Hitler made an offer to the Soviet Union to participate in the repartitioning of the world, foreshadowed by the Tripartite Pact. They suggested that Russia redirect its interests away from the Balkan-Baltic area and toward the Middle East, Iran, Afghanistan, and the Indian Ocean, which comprised the British sphere of influence. While accepting German recognition of Soviet interests in the Persian Gulf and the Middle East, Molotov repeatedly stressed the primacy of Russia's European security perimeter stretching from Finland to Turkey. Moreover, he asked a series of embarrassing questions. How can the presence of German military instructors in Romania be explained? Against whom were the Romanian borders guaranteed? And what about the German threat to the Soviet security zone in the Balkans, Bulgaria, and Turkey, where the Soviets wanted to establish their bases? During Ribbentrop's speech, in which he proposed jointly partitioning the British Empire and asserted that the war against England was really over, an air alarm was sounded because of a massive British air raid over Berlin. Molotov asked, "If Britain is finished, whose bombs are falling on us?" There was no answer, and the negotiations soon broke down. They merely revealed the widening gap separating two partners.

Molotov's stubbornness finally convinced Hitler that he would have to prepare for a military showdown with Russia. On December 18, 1940, he issued directives for an operation to be called "Barbarossa." The very cryptonym was significant: the German Emperor, Frederick I, called Barbarossa, was a symbol of the Teutonic expansion to the East. The planned operation was to be a short, swift campaign against Russia, to open in May 1941 and end in September or October. The spring of 1941, however, brought two surprising events that, at least indirectly, upset Hitler's calculations; one resulted from Japan's growing disillusionment with Germany's increasingly independent policy, while the other took place in the Balkans.

On the Eve of the Invasion

One event to bear in mind, the fall of France, was followed by a diplomatic landslide. The small states of formerly pro-Western Eastern Europe, one by one, starting with Romania, sought protection of the now-dominant Germany. Yugoslavia, a former ally of France, was no exception. With the dispatch of German troops to Bulgaria on March 2, 1941, the government of Prince Paul, regent for the sixteen-year-old King Peter, succumbed to Axis pressure and in April adhered to the Tripartite Pact. This shocked many traditionally anti-German Serb patriots. During the night of March 26–27, a *coup d'état* overthrew the regency and established the youthful King Peter on the throne in Belgrade. On April 4, the new government, while outwardly adhering to the Tripartite Pact, reestablished close relations with Britain, and even concluded a friendship agreement with the USSR. Two days later the furious Hitler ordered twelve German divisions "to punish the Yugoslavs" for their "breach of faith." The order was executed with ruthless efficiency. Within a fortnight, Yugoslavia was overrun by the Wehrmacht, supported by the troops of Italy, Hungary, and Bulgaria.

Meanwhile, the steady growth of Hitler's power in the Danubian basin had alarmed not only the Russians, but Mussolini as well. On October 28, 1940, using their Albanian bases, the Italians suddenly attacked Greece. After a few initial successes, the Italian forces were bogged down and had to beg their German allies for help. Hitler decided to oblige and divert from the Russian front considerable forces to subdue the Greeks. The Yugoslav campaign, however, together with German intervention in Greece on behalf of the indolent Italian allies, resulted in some twenty German divisions being tied down in the Balkan peninsula, thus weakening his armies which he planned to launch against the Soviets.

Another factor that intervened on behalf of the USSR was the shifting attitude of

Japan. Offended by the unilateral and quite unexpected signing of the Hitler-Stalin Pact while the allied Japanese troops were still fighting the Red Army in the Far East, the Japanese were sulking. The fact that Tokyo was not consulted, as well as the impressive performance of the Red Army in the Far East in the summer of 1939, determined the subsequent decision in Tokyo. As a consequence of this, despite gestures of outward solidarity with the Anti-Comintern Pact, the Japanese began to pursue their own policy which was to be directed eventually not against Russia, but against the United States. The result of this policy was the nonaggression pact which Japanese Foreign Minister Matsuoka signed with the USSR during his visit to Moscow on April 13, 1941. In case of an attack by a third power against one of the signatories, the other was to remain neutral. The Soviet-Japanese neutrality agreement was an unexpected blessing to Stalin because it freed him of the risk of a two-front war in case of a possible conflict with Germany.

Meanwhile, relations between Germany and the Soviet Union were becoming strained. The steady concentration of German and satellite troops (Finnish, Romanian, Hungarian, and Slovak) along the western approaches of the USSR from Bulgaria to Finland was no secret to anyone. Not only Soviet intelligence but many outside sources (including President Roosevelt and British Prime Minister Winston Churchill) kept sending Stalin warnings about an impending German attack on Russia. Stalin, however, was as much suspicious of Britain's intentions as of those of Hitler. Stalin's suspicions of London were deepened by the sudden landing of Hitler's deputy, Rudolf Hess, in Scotland, allegedly at the invitation of Lord Hamilton, who actually acted on behalf of British intelligence. Stalin had learned about Hess's visit from his British secret agents. The Hess episode reawakened Stalin's pathological suspicion of a possible separate peace and of an Anglo-German crusade against Soviet Russia—an idea allegedly harbored by "the men of Munich"—deepened his suspicion.

Meanwhile, to oblige Hitler and fulfill his part of the bargain, Stalin leaned over backward to maintain good relations with Berlin. As a rule, Soviet deliveries of large amounts of raw materials were made more punctually than those coming from Germany. The Soviet supplies were dispatched up until the last moment, despite constant delays from the German partner. Whatever partial Soviet mobilization measures were undertaken, they were carried out as discreetly as possible in order "not to provoke the Germans." Most of the surviving German Communists who had found shelter on Soviet soil were handed over to the Nazis. Referring to some 80 warnings about the impending German invasion, Stalin said to the then-General (later on Marshal) Zhukov: "You see, *they* are trying to frighten us with the German menace, while the Germans are being scared with the Soviet menace. *They* want to pit us against each other."

Five days before the German attack, on June 18, when Zhukov described in great detail the concentration of enemy forces along the Soviet frontiers, Stalin became irritated and declared "Have you come to scare us with war? Or do you want a war, as you are not sufficiently decorated, or your rank is not high enough?" One of the few visible signs of Stalin's concern was the fact that on May 6 he took over from Molotov the premiership of the USSR while remaining the Party's Secretary General. Thus the two supreme offices of the country were officially united in the hands of its actual ruler.

The First Blow

The German attack on Russia had already started on the night of June 21–22, 1941, when the German ambassador in Moscow, Count von Schulenburg, handed Molotov the official declaration of war. Molotov's reaction was most revealing: "Can it really be that we have deserved all that?" Berlin's note justified the invasion with the pretext that the Russians "were about to attack Germany from the rear" while Germany was getting

German Invasion of Soviet Russia, June 22–December 6, 1941

ready for its final blow at Great Britain. The unpreparedness of the Soviet forces at the time of the invasion and Stalin's obsequious helpfulness toward Hitler were the best refutation of the German claims.

The battle of Russia was the largest, bitterest, and bloodiest campaign of World War II. Hitler's objective was to crush Soviet Russia in one swift blow before the close of 1941. Then, with the resources of the USSR at his disposal, he would return to the West for a showdown with Britain. Consequently, the success of his plan hinged on the speed of the advance of the 154 German and satellite divisions he had deployed along the more than 1,200-mile front from the Baltic to the Black seas. They were facing some 170 Soviet divisions.

The Soviet forces, like the invaders', were organized into three army groups (in Russian terminology, "fronts")—Northern, Central, and Southern. They were commanded by Stalin's cronies, Kliment Voroshilov, Semyon Timoshenko, and Semyon Budënny, respectively. Although the Red Army had numerical superiority not only in men but also in guns, tanks and planes, it was stretched in linear formation along the borders; moreover the attackers enjoyed an undoubted technical superiority compounded by the advantage of strategic initiative. The Soviets' crash modernization program, started after the Finnish campaign, had hardly begun to produce its first fruits.

Stalin himself had little to do with the first few days of the Soviet war effort. When Stalin awakened on the morning of June 22, he refused to take seriously the report of the enemy attack and called it a "rumor spread by *agents provocateurs.*" By midday, when the news was confirmed by innumerable Soviet sources, he lost his nerve. For several days he plunged into a drunken orgy, punctuated by violent outbursts of anger and self-pity. The first official announcement and war appeal was made by Molotov. Only on July 3 did Stalin address the Soviet people in a broadcast speech, making an effort to justify the pact with Hitler as having provided both the time and space necessary "for preparing our

forces to repulse Fascist Germany." Stalin deemphasized Marxist ideology and appealed to traditional Russian sentiments, calling on the population to "fight our patriotic war of liberation against the Fascist enslavers," even using scorched earth tactics if necessary.

From then on the Soviet war effort was directed by a State Defense Council presided over by Stalin himself, assisted by Voroshilov for military problems, Molotov for diplomatic issues, Lavrenty Beria for security matters, and a younger member of the Politburo, Gregory M. Malenkov, for technical equipment of the armed forces as well as various party matters.

By the time Stalin resumed leadership, the three German army groups had broken through the surprised Soviet forces and made deep inroads on all three sectors, but especially in the south. There, the mostly Ukrainian units, commanded by the old, incompetent Marshal Budënny were either surrendering in large masses or retreating in confusion. The Germans again applied the methods of the "lightning war" (*Blitzkrieg*) that they had perfected during the Polish and French as well as Balkan campaigns; this combined the use of armored and mechanized units capable of deep penetration into enemy territory with devastating air raids, not only against military targets but also against the civilian population, thus causing panic and disorganizing troop and supply deliveries.

The German tactics were facilitated by the fact that the Red Army divisions were, as a rule, strung out along the new, still largely unfortified, western frontiers. The Soviet troops had been moved as much as 250 miles to the west in 1939 and 1940. Commanded for the most part indifferently by survivors of the purges, the Red Army suffered from extended communication lines stretching back to their old supply bases. This made them especially vulnerable to concentrated German thrusts. Once through the Soviet defenses, the Wehrmacht would encircle the Soviet units and then destroy them or make them capitulate. To slow down their onslaught, the desperate Stalin ordered the Soviet troops to engage the enemy piece-meal, in increments of brigades and divisions. When Soviet units were surrounded by the enemy, they were ordered to stand fast. The mostly young and inexperienced commanders, who still remembered what had happened to their predecessors during the Great Purge, obeyed orders from Moscow under the watchful eye of the Political Commissars, whose full powers had been reinstated just a few weeks before the attack.[1]

The rapidity of the Germany advance all along the front was disconcerting. Their Army Group North, after having captured all naval bases valiantly defended by the Soviet navy, and having destroyed the Soviet units in the Baltic area, besieged Leningrad by the beginning of September. The city could then communicate with the rest of the country only through Lake Ladoga, which mercifully froze earlier than usual. The German Army Group South swept like a tornado through the Western Ukraine, took masses of POWs, and pushed irresistibly toward Kiev, and then beyond the Dnieper, thus achieving by far the greatest territorial advances, and taking the most prisoners. Kiev was lost on September 19, together with 600,000 Soviet soldiers captured by the Germans. The Soviet southern front almost collapsed; Odessa and Sevastopol held out heroically. The Army Group Center, which had the strongest concentration of tanks, took about 300,000 POWs and pushed through Minsk and Smolensk toward Moscow. It seemed that the Soviet capital would be conquered by September or October.

The Battle of Moscow

The rapid advances along all three sectors made Hitler overconfident. He took it for granted that he could have Moscow any time

he wished. In August his Propaganda Minister, Joseph Goebbels, ecstatically announced to the world, "We have smashed the Red Army to splinters. Russia lies like a limp virgin in the arms of the German Mars." In the meantime; however, the huge Nazi war machine, operating largely on costly synthetic gasoline and limited European oil supplies, was getting dangerously low on fuel. Consequently, to reach the oil of the Caucasus seemed to Hitler a more vital target than capturing Moscow. On August 3, despite the urging of his military advisers, Hitler ordered one segment of the best armor dispatched to the south to get him the Caucasian oil; at the same time, some units were to be diverted to the north to seize Leningrad before it could be resupplied through the frozen Lake Ladoga. This momentous decision caused a major crisis. Utterly bewildered and frustrated by Hitler's order, many senior officers sabotaged his instructions, considering them senseless; some of them resigned in protest. As a result, while the northern and southern sectors of the German front were not reinforced in time to reach the oil fields, the central group was weakened enough to slow down its advance on Moscow. This happened at the time when the Soviet capital was plunged into panic and its defenses in disorder.

While Hitler was rearranging his schedule, the weather worsened dramatically; the October mists and rain, mixed with wet snow, turned the Russian plain into a sea of mud. Tanks, artillery, and transport vehicles sank deep into the boggy ground. By November heavy snows were falling throughout the area and the temperature sank below zero. The German soldiers, prepared only for a short, swift summer campaign, were frequently victims of frostbite and other winter ailments. On December 2, when Hitler finally ordered an all-out assault on Moscow, the mercury stood at 40 degrees below zero. The breechblocks of rifles froze solid, oil in the tanks and trucks had the consistency of tar, the drag on dynamos made it impossible to start their engines, cylinder blocks were split open, and axles refused to turn. The

---

[1] The problem of responsibility for the Soviet lack of preparedness has been discussed in Vladimir Petrov and A. M. Nerrich, *June 22, 1941: Soviet Historians and the German Invasion* (Columbia: University of South Carolina Press, 1968).

Moscow's anti-aircraft defenses in action in October 1941

forest around Moscow limited the mobility of the German tanks while increasing the effectiveness of highly mobile Soviet cavalry and the increasing number of partisans. In these circumstances bayonets and grenades were the only effective weapons, and in the hand-to-hand fighting the Red Army's mostly peasant boys proved superior. Moreover, the frozen and exhausted Wehrmacht now had to face the first large units of the Soviet Siberian Army, which Stalin had begun to withdraw from the Far East soon after signing the nonaggression pact with Japan in April.

By December, when the battle for Moscow was at its peak, about twenty Siberian divisions, all in fine condition, and equipped for winter warfare with 1,700 tanks and 1,500 aircraft, were already at the crucial Moscow sector. By December 1941, every third defender of Moscow came from the Siberian units. Whereas German motorized communications were often paralyzed

because of deep snow, the Red Army kept their communication lines opened partly due to the small, tough, shaggy Siberian horses, which were used to such conditions; the horses' phenomenal capacity of survival, even when they were given next to nothing to eat except conifer twigs or root-straw, allowed such cavalry units to penetrate deep behind enemy lines, causing havoc among the unsuspecting German rear echelons. Dressed in white, quilted uniforms, with felt boots and fur caps, the Siberian units now faced the shivering, exhausted German soldiers of the Central Army Group. During the battle of Moscow, instances of individual heroism were especially striking and frequent. For instance, on December 6, eighty miles to the east on the highway connecting Volkolamsk with Moscow, twenty-eight soldiers of the Panfilov division held up the enemy advance on the capital for a whole day. Only three of the twenty-eight warriors survived, but they had destroyed eighteen out of fifty German tanks before being overwhelmed.

Meanwhile, the Soviet commanders, under the experienced eye of the veteran commander of the Far Eastern Army, General Zhukov, were learning how to use effectively a few weapons that from the beginning of the campaign proved superior to their German counterparts: the Soviet T-34 tank and their batteries of rockets. The Soviet air force, decimated mostly on the ground by the early German surprise attacks, was resupplied and reorganized. After repeated, bitter attempts to break through the Moscow front, on December 8 the German Army Command announced suspension of military operations "because of the severe conditions." Moscow was saved.

Failure of the Lightning Campaign

To the military factors responsible for the German failure to score a quick victory, one must also add the changing political climate inside the Soviet Union. Hitler had entered the USSR with the slogan of abolishing its Communist system and liberating its oppressed national minorities, especially the Ukrainians, Belorussians, and the Baltic peoples. That is why, at the beginning of the invasion, the German soldiers were often greeted by the population of the western borderlands with the traditional welcoming gestures of bread, salt, and flowers, while many Soviet units composed of recruits of these nationalities, especially the Ukrainians from the western segments of the republic, were surrendering in large masses. Yet none of the original German promises were carried out. Brushing aside the various national committees he himself had helped create, Hitler promptly established his own centralized administration in the conquered areas; his deputies soon ran them with an iron fist in accordance with racist Nazi doctrine and for the sole benefit of the German Reich. The primarily Slavic inhabitants of these

lands were treated as inferior creatures, almost like colonial slaves. The Jewish population of the conquered areas was ruthlessly exterminated. In addition, some of the most hated Soviet institutions, like the collective and State farms, were preserved; they were now to be used by German authorities to exploit the resources of the occupied areas. Some three million workers were forcibly conscripted to slave in Germany factories and mines while being treated like subhuman creatures. Finally, over four million Soviet POWs were mistreated in blatant disregard of the Geneva Convention pertaining to treatment of prisoners of war. Well over two million of them were surrounded by barbed wire and either allowed to starve or otherwise destroyed. Soon it became obvious to the people of the German-occupied areas that Hitler had nothing to offer to the Soviet people, but a still worse form of oppression and exploitation. Consequently, by the autumn of 1941 instances of terror, sabotage, and even organized armed resistance to the invaders became more and more frequent.

As the German occupation continued, a full-scale partisan movement developed. The first bands were formed by Communist Party activists and by Red Army soldiers caught behind the lines by the German advance. The partisan units could communicate with Moscow by radio and air, and so could coordinate their activities with the regular army. While the partisans lived off the land, they were often supplied with arms and munitions by air drops. They were able to harass the German troops, sometimes seriously disrupting their lines of communication.

When the news about Nazi cruel policies, especially the inhuman treatment of POWs, filtered back behind the Soviet lines, resistance to the invaders began to stiffen dramatically. This was reflected in the attitude of both the Soviet front-line soldiers and the populations of the occupied areas. At the same time, Stalin had aroused the patriotic feelings of the Russian people. In this he was aided by the Russian Orthodox Church. From the day of the German attack, the leaders of the Church urged the faithful to support the regime in its efforts to repel the invaders. The head of the Russian Church went as far as to acclaim Stalin as "the divinely anointed leader of the nation." The population of the occupied areas was threatened with excommunication if they collaborated with the Nazis. Meanwhile, the Communist Party and State put an end to the persecution of the Church. The Orthodox Church and the atheistic State worked together throughout the war to whip up patriotic fervor.

At the same time, Stalin salvaged some of the surviving victims of his purges from the concentration camps and had them rehabilitated and put into a number of key jobs,

Life in the besieged Leningrad. The slogan above the poster proclaims: "Death to the murderers of children!"

civilian as well as military. Several of them, like Konstantin Rokossovsky, became "heroes of the Soviet Union." The first months of the terrible ordeal proved to be a good school, particularly for many Soviet commanders, who were quickly learning on the job the secrets of modern warfare. This was already evident by late autumn of 1941, during the battle of Moscow, when instances of growing military sophistication, were especially numerous and striking. By the end of 1941, the desperate and often chaotic retreat had turned into a patriotic war in which the home front played as important a role as did the soldiers at the front lines. The places of the mobilized men were taken by Soviet women, who often proved as tough as their male counterparts. Some of them volunteered as pilots and parachutists and served with courgae and distinction.

Formation of the Grand Coalition

The checking of the German onslaught on Moscow coincided almost to the day with another major turning point of World War II—the Japanese attack on Pearl Harbor in December 7, 1941. The attack was greeted in Moscow with a sigh of relief. Now pushed into the war, the United States became a partner of the USSR in the war against the Axis powers. Meanwhile, immediately after the German invasion of Russia, Great Britain, disregarding Stalin's previous close collaboration with Hitler, had spontaneously offered its unconditional aid to the Soviet Union. In a radio speech on June 22, Winston Churchill declared, "Any man or state who fights against Nazidom will have our aid." However, the generous but limited help of Britain, itself under German air attacks, fighting a desperate battle in the Atlantic, and dependent on the United States, could not be substantial. The entry of the United States into the war in December 1941, multiplied the resources of the anti-Axis coalition dramatically. By extending "lend-lease" assistance to both Britain and Russia, the United

States soon became the arsenal of the anti-Axis coalition.

Even before the Japanese attack on Pearl Harbor, on August 14, 1941, President Roosevelt had met with Winston Churchill aboard a battleship in mid-Atlantic, where they issued a joint declaration of basic principles that underlied their approach to the war. The Atlantic Charter, as the declaration was to be called, promised "a better future for the world . . . after the final destruction of Nazi tyranny," and that "sovereign rights and self-government" would be "restored to those who had been forcibly deprived of them." Both countries "hoped to see established a peace which will afford to all nations the means of dwelling in safety within their own boundaries, and which will afford assurance that all the men in all the lands may live out their lives in freedom from fear and want."

Soviet Russia's position within the grand coalition was ambiguous from the very beginning. Stalin did not join the partnership against the Axis as a willing ally but as a betrayed accomplice of Hitler. Having committed numerous acts of aggression in collaboration with him, the Soviet dictator had been guilty of many violations of these very human rights extolled by the Atlantic Charter. Consequently, Soviet entry into the anti-Axis alliance posed questions: How would it affect the Atlantic Charter and the moral posture of the anti-Axis coalition in general? Would Stalin subscribe to the Charter? And if so, would he respect its principles in practice?

In 1941 the Western allies were in no mood to ask such embarrassing questions. Seeing the Soviet soldiers bearing the brunt of Hitler's onslaught, they did not put any conditions on their aid. Unable to match Russia's massive contribution to the land war or satisfy Stalin's urgent requests for the immediate establishment of a "second front" on the continent of Europe, the Western allies were glad to buy Stalin's cooperation with military and economic aid, as well as with initially vague but momentous political

promises. Most of these promises were made at the expense of their weaker allies like Poland and China.

The Black Summer of 1942

During 1941 the Germans had captured large stretches of land and inflicted tremendous losses on Russia, but they were unable to win the war. Besides the lost battle for Moscow, there were other factors aiding the successful Soviet resistance. Many factories and some rolling stock had been successfully evacuated beyond the Volga to the Urals and even to Central Asia. Thanks to this gigantic operation, often paralleled by the superhuman sacrifices of numerous individuals, by the spring of 1942 most of these factories had started production on their new sites. Together with British and American aid, which was increasing as time went by, they began resupplying the Red Army with new equipment. Once Hitler had lost his chance of winning a quick victory by the autumn of 1941, the superior Soviet and Allied manpower and resources, gradually reinforced by those of the United States, slowly began to shift the balance against the German invaders.

Despite the lost battle of Moscow the German Army was still a formidable fighting machine that was getting ready for another assault in the spring of 1942. Disregarding the advice of his main military expert, the overconfident Stalin ordered a spring counteroffensive in May 1942. Its main objective was to free the industrial district of Kharkov from enemy occupation. The offensive was badly planned and poorly executed, and ended in one of the worst disasters of the war. Again, the Red Army suffered its heaviest losses in the Ukrainian sectors. In July the Germans captured Sevastopol and the entire Crimea. Pressing their gains, the Germans reoccupied Rostov-on-the-Don, which had been momentarily recovered by the Red Army, and continued their spectacular sweep toward the key area of the lower Volga and the Caucasus. By the end of August the German troops were on the northern slopes of the Caucasus, near the oil fields of Grozny. The industrial and communications center, Stalingrad, was Hitler's next target. The Germans also made impressive gains during July and August in the northern and central sectors. Again the surrender and rout of entire units assumed epidemic proportions. The specter of a total collapse again appeared on the horizon. The period of July to August was aptly called the Red Army's "Black Summer."

In this desperate situation, Stalin resorted to a series of Draconian measures. Special NKVD detachments were to follow front-line units and shoot on sight all those retreating and even hesitating soldiers. Summary executions for disobeying orders or for cowardice now became a standard procedure; several generals were among those shot. A special anti-espionage organization was created under the code name, "Death to the Spies" (*Smersh*). The hate-the-Germans campaign was stepped up and reached unprecedented intensity. At the same time the Russian patriotic propaganda further replaced the Communist slogans. The military oath pledging the soldier to struggle for the emancipation of workers was replaced by a new one making it his primary duty to fight for the Motherland. The dual command, reinstated on the eve of the German invasion, was abolished definitively; the political commissars were now turned into officers in charge of political education, propaganda, and welfare, and forbidden to interfere with military decisions of the field commanders. Former distinctions of rank and old military titles were reintroduced: these included the gold and silver braided shoulder straps abolished by the Bolshevik Revolution. In January 1942, a new magazine, *Slovyanye* (Slavs), was established in Moscow to present the war as a Slavic crusade against the Teutonic invasion. This was followed by a series of Slavic congresses and conferences. Concessions were made to the religious sentiments and atheistic propaganda was soft-pedaled.

The Battle of Stalingrad and Its Consequences

Throughout the summer of 1942, the German juggernaut resumed its seemingly unstoppable drive toward the mother of Russian rivers, the Volga, a vital supply route. By September 4 the offensive of the crack Sixth Army of General Friedrich Paulus had reached the outskirts of Stalingrad. On August 25 Hitler issued a personal order to capture the city and to cut the oil supply line linking the Caucasus with Moscow. The battle of Stalingrad, one of the most cruel of the campaign, lasted for almost five months. The period from mid-September to mid-November was its peak. Soon, the fierce street fighting turned the city into a heap of ruins. Although several times the Germans were half a step from capturing the headquarters of the Soviet commander, each time they were frustrated by the dogged resistance of the Red Army men. By November 19, the exhausted Sixth Army had to give up because of intolerable losses and the onset of winter. At the same time, Paulus's supply lines had been cut by a broad encircling movement of three Soviet reserve armies, assembled by Zhukov, totaling one million men. Paulus wanted to retreat, but was forbidden to do so by Hitler, who ordered him to fight to the bitter end. Meanwhile, several German attempts at cutting the Soviet ring failed.

While the Sixth Army stuck to the smoking debris of Stalingrad, the Red Army prepared a mighty counteroffensive. Ably assisted by his Deputy Supreme Commander Zhukov, Stalin plotted his counterstroke; it involved three armies amounting to some eighty divisions of nearly one million men, supported by 13,500 guns and mortars and 1,100 aircraft. The Soviet counterattack started on November 19. First, a powerful army group hit the poorly armed Romanian troops on the Don covering the northwestern approaches to Stalingrad. Overnight, the flimsy Romanian contingents collapsed and their divisions surrendered. At the same time, from those Don bridgeheads that still

Street fighting in Stalingrad, November 1942

remained in Soviet hands, Red Army tanks pounded on the remnants of the German Sixth Army. Simultaneously, the mechanized forces of General Fedor Tolbukhin carried out a broad enveloping movement from the south. The Soviets then moved swiftly from north and south through the breach to exploit their gains. Within four days, the German Sixth Army with its 200,000 men was cut off by this brilliant envelopment. With the outflanking of the Sixth Army by November 23, the German position in the northern Caucasus became untenable. The agony of the Sixth Army grew so severe that finally on February 3, 1943, Paulus felt compelled to surrender. Some 91,000 frostbitten and half-starved survivors of the once-elite Sixth Army trudged into Soviet POW camps. The captured included Field Marshal Paulus himself, twenty-three generals, and 2,500 other officers. Some 140,000 German and satellite soldiers had died fighting and from hunger and disease. More than a decade later, in 1955–1956, only about 6,000 of these survivors finally returned to their homeland.

The Soviet booty was impressive. It included 750 planes, 1,550 tanks, 480 armored cars, 8,000 guns and mortars, 61,000 trucks, 235 ammunition dumps, and a vast quantity of other equipment and the remaining reserves of food, including large quantities of champagne that the farsighted German command had shipped to celebrate its victory.

Was Stalingrad worth the price Hitler was willing to pay for it? Stalingrad did not completely control use of the Volga waterway, on which oil as well as Anglo-American war aid were shipped northward.[2] Through stubborn sacrifice, the Red Army successfully drew the vast bulk of German resources on the southern front into the Stalingrad meatgrinder.

---

[2] From June 1941 to April 1944, the Red Army received by way of the Volga 4,292 British tanks, 3,734 American tanks, and 1,400 tanks from Canada. By mid-1943 the Americans had shipped in over 900,000 tons of steel, 1.5 million tons of food, 138,000 trucks and jeeps, as well as boots, industrial equipment, and raw materials—in all a highly variegated military-industrial shipping list that included 12,000 tons of butter sent for Soviet troops convalescing in hospitals. However, it was not for the tanks or the aircraft that Stalin pressed; it was mostly for the food and industrial supplies, metals, chemicals, machine tools, and lorries.

Psychologically, Stalingrad spelled an end to the myth of the Third Reich's invincibility and the start of another myth, that of Stalin's military genius.

The vigorous Soviet drive that followed the Stalingrad victory soon resulted in the recovery of Kharkov and the German withdrawal from the Northern Caucasus. The situation changed all along the front. In the northern sector the Russians relieved the siege of Leningrad after 900 days of murderous attacks, by cutting a gap seven miles wide between Lake Ladoga and the German lines. This made the life of the surviving 600,000 inhabitants easier.

The climax of the battle of Stalingrad was preceded by the halting of the Japanese advance in the Pacific by the American Navy in the summer of 1942 and the victory of the British Eighth Army at El Alamein in North Africa, which stopped the advance of Marshal Rommel's African Corps on Cairo at the end of October 1942. That November the landing of British and American forces in the then-French protectorate of Morocco and Algeria established a firm Allied base for an invasion of southern Europe. In May 1943 the German and Italian forces in Tunisia capitulated. These events, which succeeded each other kaleidoscopically, marked a decisive turning point in World War II. While the battle of Moscow indicated that Hitler could not knock down the Russians instantly, the battle of Stalingrad and the Allied successes in North African raised the question of whether he could win the war at all.

The Battle of Kursk

The issue of the Russian campaign was basically settled during the summer of 1943. Faced with disaster at the beginning of 1943, Hitler ordered total mobilization of all the resources at the command of all his satrapies, then covering most of Europe from the Dnieper to the Pyrenees and from Norway to Greece. This extraordinary effort produced a panoply of new weapons by the summer. They were to be used in an unprecedented concentration in the central Russian sector around the city of Kursk, an important point welding the central and southern sectors of the front. The Russians, forewarned about Hitler's plans by their intelligence network inside Germany, had fortified the area around Kursk for about sixty-five miles in depth, using some 300,000 workers, mostly women. At the same time Zhukov, by now promoted to the rank of Marshal, had massed large quantities of tanks and approximately 20,000 guns of all calibers. In sectors where the attack was expected, an average of 4,000 antitank and antipersonnel mines were laid per mile. The battle of Stalingrad had not only lifted the Red Army's morale but had also given it invaluable battle experience, which was fully applied at Kursk. Fresh divisions had also been trained. By the spring of 1943 large quantities of American lend-lease supplies, especially trucks, had reached the Soviet front line and made the Red Army more mobile and much better equipped than it had been at the beginning of the war.

To split the central sector of the front and capture Moscow was Hitler's order to his crack force, which included as many as seventeen armored divisions. They were provided with over 2,000 of the most modern tanks and supported by nearly 2,000 of the newest planes. The Germans launched their formidable offensive on the night of July 4. Fighting with great skill and determination, they penetrated the Soviet defenses to a depth of between ten and thirty miles.

At that critical moment, as if to prove that nothing fails like failure, Hitler's grand coalition began to crumble. After the Stalingrad defeat, practically all his allies (the Italians, the Romanians, the Hungarians, the Slovaks, and the Finns) began to negotiate secretly with his enemies about leaving the leaky ship. As the Battle of Kursk was reaching its climax on July 10, the Western Allies landed their forces on Sicily. Moreover, on July 12 the Russians launched a diversionary counteroffensive toward Orël and cut the rear of the German Ninth Army, the backbone of the Kursk drive. The Italians had meanwhile

Soviet artillery in the battle of Kursk, July 1943

failed to stop the Allied advance. To prevent a complete collapse of the Axis southern front, Hitler had to stop the Kursk offensive and hastily send several of his elite divisions south of the Alps.

Thus ended Germany's supreme effort in Russia. In the process of this greatest tank battle, the Nazis had suffered crippling losses in their elite troops and in their newest war materiel that could never be made up by the Reich's already shrinking resources. Kursk put an end to Hitler's hopes of winning the war in the east. From now on the Germans could wage only a defensive war, and the strategic initiative fell into the Russians' hands. Advancing steadily despite stubborn German delaying tactics, the Red Army gradually reconquered the area around Leningrad and the Ukraine. By January 1944, the pre-1939 frontiers of the USSR had been crossed and the conquest of East Central Europe began.

In 1943, Stalin assumed the title of "Generalissimo," donned a Marshal's uniform, and began to stress more and more his role as the proclaimed mastermind behind the victorious Soviet strategy. Several of the most successful field commanders, including Zhukov, Rokossovsky, Rodion V. Malinovsky, and Vasily D. Sokolovsky, were granted the title Marshal of the Soviet Union. New military decorations to be awarded to officers only were now created, among them the old imperial orders of Suvorov, Kutuzov, and Alexander Nevsky. A new parade uniform was introduced for the Red Army and Navy. In October 1943, the restored Patriarchate of Moscow was recognized as the sole legal representative of all Orthodox Christians of the USSR and was granted the right to own property.

Wartime Diplomacy

Entry of the Red Army onto the pre-war Polish territory in January 1944 raised a series of highly sensitive political problems. As long as the Russians were fighting a life-and-death struggle, military issues overshadowed everything else. But with the military climax behind them and with the Germans retreating from Soviet lands and the Red Army approaching the contested areas of East Central Europe, political problems began to loom larger and larger. One of them was the

Soviet-Polish controversy. In July 1941, under British pressure, the Polish Government in London reestablished diplomatic relations with Moscow. A Polish Army was to be organized from among the Polish POWs in the USSR and the deportees from the Soviet-occupied eastern provinces of old Poland, who were now released from various camps. However, the army desperately needed the 15,000 officers captured in 1939, and Soviet authorities were unable to explain their absence. "Maybe they have fled to Manchuria," Stalin once tried to explain. The problems of the former Polish eastern provinces, the future of the Polish government-in-exile, and the issue of the missing officers constantly plagued Polish-Soviet relations.

In April 1943, the Germans had discovered graves of several thousand Polish officers in the Katyn forest near Smolensk. They had apparently been executed in the spring of 1940, a year or so before Hitler's attack. When the Polish government in London asked the International Red Cross to investigate the issue, Moscow broke off diplomatic relations with the "London Poles," accusing them of slandering the Soviet Union.[3] At the same time Stalin began to gather the surviving veterans of the old, once-dissolved Communist Party of Poland and other pro-Soviet elements from all over East Central Europe and coach them for their future role as rulers of their perspective countries. These issues, as well as the problem of the second front, necessitated top-level consultation.

In May 1943, Stalin dissolved the Comintern and declared that it was no longer needed. By appearing to abandon the worldwide ambitions of militant Communism, he hoped the West would be more trusting of his future intentions. By 1943, Moscow had achieved such far-reaching control over other Communist parties that the old, rusty, cumbersome machinery of the Comintern seemed unnecessary. Leaders of the Communist underground movements in all Axis-occupied lands were instructed to achieve rapprochements with the local forces of "anti-Fascist resistance" in order to form a "broad national front." In June 1943, a "Union of Polish Patriots in Russia" was created to rival the Polish government in London. In July 1943, a "Free Germany Committee" was organized from among the captured German POWs, including the captured Marshal Paulus. Working hand-in-hand with veterans of the old Comintern like Walter Ulbricht, the Committee began to act not only as an instrument of propaganda and political diversion, but also as the nucleus of a future pro-Soviet German government.

These skillful moves and the almost uninterrupted series of Soviet victories that had carried the Red Army to the old boundaries formed the background of the first summit conference at Teheran; at that time the capital of Iran was under Allied British, U.S., and Soviet occupation. With a record of spectacular Soviet successes that the Western Allies could not match—even with Italy's capitulation in September and their further victories in the North Atlantic and the Pacific—Stalin could negotiate from a position of strength. By that time the Western Allies were already preparing to launch their invasion of Hitler's "Fortress Europe" in the spring of 1944, but no one could guarantee its success. The lack of a second front imbued both Roosevelt and Churchill with a guilt complex, and Stalin seldom missed an opportunity to exploit it. He was determined to exact political quid pro quos in form of control over East Central Europe. Supported by American Chief of Staff General George C. Marshall, he vigorously opposed the idea of the Allies attacking the Axis's "soft underbelly," the Balkans, which would probably have resulted in the arrival of British and American troops in Sofia, Belgrade, Bucharest, Budapest, and Vienna before the Red Army. Stalin insisted instead on the scheduled cross-channel invasion of the European continent. And indeed,

---

[3] When, in 1990, Soviet leader Mikhail Gorbachev, pressed by the new non-Communist government of Poland, ordered an investigation of the Katyn affair, it was revealed that the Polish POWs were shot at Stalin's personal order; for the full treatment of the problem: J. K. Zawodny, *Death in the Forest: The Story of the Katyn Massacre* (New York: Hippocrene Books 1988).

at Teheran the Western Allies agreed to jettison the Balkan landing and promised to carry out Operation Overlord in 1944.

At the conference the Big Three recognized the partisans of Joseph Broz—Tito—as the most effective resistance group in Yugoslavia and therefore most deserving of Allied support. Roosevelt and Churchill also agreed to discuss with Stalin the highly explosive Polish problem. This was done without consulting their ally, the Polish Government in London, which was firmly supported by a strong underground resistance movement in Poland, as well as by considerable armed forces fighting alongside the Western Allies. Stalin, claiming the principle of self-determination, insisted that Poland's eastern provinces should be allotted to the USSR as they were largely composed of Belorussians and Ukrainians. Churchill and Roosevelt agreed "in principle" to Stalin's demands, President Roosevelt wanted his acquiescence kept secret until after the 1944 presidential election so as not to lose the Polish vote in the United States. Since the Poles had been the first to fight Hitler in September 1939, had suffered enormous losses, and had remained loyal allies of the West, Churchill agreed to the idea that Poland be compensated at the expense of Germany's former Slavic eastern provinces—East Prussia, Pomerania, and Silesia—to resettle the Polish population to be evacuated from the former eastern marches.

Assuming a posture of moderation, Stalin did not seek at Teheran formal and final recognition of all his territorial claims in East Central Europe. By frustrating the Balkan landing and obtaining firm assurances of an invasion of Western Europe, he merely created a situation in which his ambitions would be safeguarded. And through his promise to help the United States against Japan and through his apparent willingness to support Roosevelt's idea of a new international security organization to replace the old League of Nations, Stalin won the American President's gratitude. The way in which the Americans and the British treated their Polish ally bolstered Stalin's opinion that Eastern Europe was of marginal importance to Washington and London and that they were more interested in the facades of the future Eastern European governments than in their real democratic contents.

The Crucial Year of 1944

With this conviction in mind, Stalin was driving his battered but reinvigorated troops first through the Baltic states, and then through Poland, Romania, and Hungary. Throughout 1944 the by-now crippled Wehrmacht was unable to stage anything but a series of desperate delaying actions at the eastern front. In the west, however, Hitler's position was still strong; protected by formidable fortifications, he confidently awaited an Allied invasion.

The long-delayed landing in Normandy, France came on June 6, 1944. The successful invasion was greeted by Stalin with great relief. The supporting Soviet summer offensive was launched, symbolically enough, on June 23—one day after the third anniversary of Hitler's attack. The result was a series of almost uninterrupted Russian victories. From then on, in every offensive the Red Army had a decisive superiority not only in men, but also in tanks, artillery, and aircraft. While in the west the Allies occupied most of Italy, France, and the Low Countries up to the Rhine, the Red Army reached the Vistula and the heart of Romania. When an uprising exploded in Warsaw on August 1, the commander of the Soviet First Belorussian Front, Marshal Konstantin Rokossovsky, stopped the advance on Stalin's order. For sixty-three days, while the Polish freedom fighters struggled against the overwhelming German forces, the Red Army remained inactive, watching as the flower of the Polish resistance movement was crushed. Consequently, the bulk of the non-Communist forces was destroyed. This allowed the Communist-dominated "Polish Committee of National Liberation" to be proclaimed the Provisional Government of Poland on January 1, 1945.

During the crucial summer of 1944, while

purposely delaying its offensive on the Polish front and thus postponing its march toward Berlin, the Red Army advanced rapidly in the Danubian valley and in the Balkans. The first country to be occupied was Romania, where the pro-Nazi regime of Marshal Antonescu had been overthrown. King Michael not only surrendered his country to the Russians on August 23, but also declared war on Germany. The traditionally pro-Russian Bulgarians, who had never been in a state of war with the USSR, were now anxious to capitulate to the Western Allies. To prevent the possibility of the appearance of British or American troops in the Balkans, Moscow declared war on Bulgaria on September 5. The reluctant Bulgarians therefore had to surrender to the Russians. Pushing rapidly forward, the Red Army linked up with Marshal Tito's Yugoslav partisans, who had meanwhile liberated most of their country themselves. On October 20 the Soviet and Yugoslav troops jointly entered Belgrade and, ignoring the royal government of King Peter, established a Communist-dominated administration.

In Hungary, however, Soviet progress was much slower. There on October 15, the Regent Admiral Nicholas Horthy tried to emulate the Romanian example and surrendered his country first to the Western Allies and then to the Soviets. His attempts were frustrated, however, by the local fascist movement which collaborated with the Germans. Horthy was imprisoned. During the late autumn and winter of 1944, the Red Army advanced to the heart of Hungary, and besieged Budapest. Meanwhile, a pro-Soviet coalition government was set up in Debreczen; on January 20, 1945, it signed an armistice with Moscow and declared war on Germany. On February 15, Budapest capitulated and the Debreczen government was installed in the Hungarian capital. In the autumn of 1944 there was also an uprising in Slovakia, directed against the local Fascist regime and the Germans. Like in Warsaw, the Slovak upsurge received no assistance from the Russians, who were eager to see the non-Communist forces exterminated.

Thus by the close of 1944 Hitler had lost all his satellites, while his forces, outnumbered and outweaponed, were fighting a desperate delaying struggle; finally, they fell back to their bombed and exhausted homeland. Facing disaster, Hitler changed his earlier policies; in September 1944 he allowed the formation of a "Russian Liberation Army" from among the surviving Soviet POWs, under General Andrei A. Vlasov. The Army was to fight for the "creation of a new People's political system without Bolsheviks and exploiters." This desperate move came too late to affect the course of the war.

Hitler's last effort to wrest the initiative from the Western Allies and compel them to begin separate negotiations with him took place in December 1944, when he launched a sudden, powerful counteroffensive in the Ardennes. The surprising blow forced British and American troops to retreat. On January 10, 1945, while the "Battle of the Bulge" was hanging in the balance, Winston Churchill sent an urgent personal message to Stalin requesting "a major Russian offensive on the Vistula" during January to relieve the German pressure in the West. Stalin promised to oblige. And indeed, on January 12, the Soviet drive was resumed. The ruined Warsaw was captured by Marshal Rokossovsky's First Belorussian Front, which included units of the Soviet-sponsored Polish Army, meanwhile formed in Russia.

The Yalta Conference

On January 29, on the eve of the twelfth anniversary of Hitler's seizure of power, the massive Soviet juggernaut crossed the pre-1939 Polish-German boundaries and penetrated into the German province of Brandenburg. Berlin lay beyond the last natural obstacle, the Oder. At the same time that the Red Army was pushing along the Danube valley toward Bratislava and Vienna, the Western Allies were bogged down in the Italian Apennines and on the Rhine. It was against this background of practically uninterrupted Soviet triumphs that the second summit conference gathered at Yalta in the Crimea at the beginning of February 1945.

In October 1944, between the Teheran and the Yalta conferences, Winston Churchill visited Moscow. On the night of October 9, after a long wrangle about their respective spheres of influence, the British Prime Minister scribbled on a scrap of paper the following suggestions for dividing the spheres of influence in Eastern Europe.

Romania: Russia 90 percent, the others 10 percent
Greece: Great Britain and the United States 90
    percent, Russia 10 percent
Yugoslavia: 50–50
Hungary: 50–50
Bulgaria: 75 percent Russia, the others 25 percent

Then Churchill pushed the sheet across the table toward Stalin, who examined it, put a check mark on it, and passed it back. The matter was settled. Later, in view of the rapid advance of the Red Army, the Hungarian formula was revised, at Molotov's insistence, to 75–25 and the Bulgarian to 80–20, both in the Soviet favor.[4]

While the Russians negotiated Yalta from a position of strength, the Western powers were inhibited not only by the temporary stalemate in Europe, but also by uncertainties in the Far Eastern theater of war. On the way to the Crimea, President Roosevelt had been informed that an invasion of the Japanese home islands "might be expected to cost over a million casualties to American forces alone." The Yalta decisions pertaining to both Poland and China were largely influenced by these grossly exaggerated apprehensions.

The Yalta Conference took place in two palaces that had formerly belonged to Tsar Nicholas II and his cousin Prince Yusopov, Rasputin's assassin. The Conference confirmed the Churchill-Stalin deal of October 1944 and resulted in a common understanding for enforcing the unconditional surrender of Germany and its occupation by the three Great Powers—the Soviet Union, the

United States, and Great Britain. (France was allowed to share in the allied occupation regime only after the war.) Germany was to be disarmed, its war industries dismantled, and its general staff abolished. German society was to be de-Nazified. Those responsible for war crimes were to be tried and punished. The Germans were to pay reparations to the victorious powers. For ceding nearly half of its prewar territory to the Soviet Union, Poland was to be compensated with the southwestern segment of East Prussia and with territories east of the Oder-Neisse Rivers.

The Yalta agreement also contained a provision concerning the terms under which the USSR would join the war against Japan. This was to be carried out no later than three months after the end of the war in Europe. In exchange Stalin was assured of generous benefits. The status quo in Outer Mongolia, formerly a segment of China but by then a full-scale satellite of the USSR, was to be maintained. Southern Sakhalin, lost to Japan in 1905, was to be restored to Russia; the Kurile Islands, never a Russian possession, were added for good measure. The Chinese port of Dairen (Dalny) was to be internationalized, and Soviet interests there were to be recognized as preeminent. China was also to be persuaded to lease to the USSR a naval base in Port Arthur, and the Chinese-Eastern and Southern Manchurian railroads were to be jointly operated by a Soviet-Chinese company.

From Yalta the Big Three issued the "Declaration on Liberated Europe." Invoking the Atlantic Charter, the declaration announced that in any country "where in their judgment conditions require," the Soviet Union, the United States, and Great Britain would "jointly assist" the people concerned to establish domestic peace, to set up "interim governmental authorities broadly representative of all democratic elements," and to hold free elections. The declaration made no distinction between the allied countries—Poland, Czechoslovakia, Yugoslavia, and Greece—and the enemies—Germany, Italy, and their satellites, Hungary, Romania, and

---

[4] Winston S. Churchill, *Triumph and Tragedy* (Boston: Houghton Mifflin Company, 1962), p. 197.

Generalissimo Stalin and Prime Minister Churchill at the Yalta Conference

Bulgaria. Since the October 1944 deal between Churchill and Stalin made Western influence in Eastern Europe vestigial in nature. The Yalta declaration was merely a face-saving device that resulted in handing over East Central Europe to Soviet hegemonial power. What was outlined at Teheran was more specifically spelled out and confirmed at Yalta.

German Capitulation and the Potsdam Conference

The last great battle of World War II in Europe, the storming of Berlin, started on April 16, 1945, from the bridgehead on the River Oder which was forced by the armies of the most successful of all Soviet commanders, Marshal Zhukov. At the same time his

rival, Marshal Ivan Koniev's troops, after capturing Vienna and Prague, swept toward the German capital from the south. The Western Allies were also pushing toward Berlin from the west. On April 25, a United States patrol from the 96th Division encountered a Soviet horseman at the river Elbe. Later on the same day another American patrol made its way across the damaged bridge over the Elbe at Torgau. There the GIs met and briefly fraternized and drank toasts with a group of Red Army men. Hitler had committed suicide in his underground bunker on April 30. On May 2 came the capture of Berlin by Soviet troops. The Germans capitulated on May 8.

While preparing for another top-level interallied conference and a campaign in the Far East, on June 24 Stalin staged a spectacular victory parade in Moscow's Red Square at which over 200 captured German

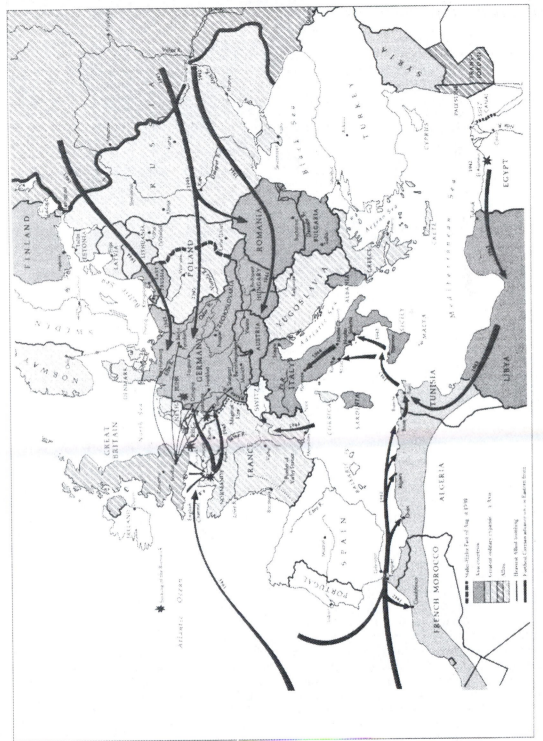

European and Mediterranean Theaters in World War II, 1939–1945

Moscow, June 24, 1945: The Victory Parade on the Red Square. Standards and banners of the German Army were thrown at the feet of Stalin

banners were thrown at the feet of the triumphant Generalissimo. From then on Stalin insisted he be honored not only as a great, progressive statesman, but also as mankind's most brilliant military leader. At a lavish reception at the Kremlin following the parade, Stalin drank his toast to "the leading nation" of the USSR, the Great Russian nation, which he feted as "remarkable for its clear mind, its patience and its firm character." This singling out of one out of over 100 Soviet ethnic groups by the leader of a Party dedicated to the "Leninist principle of proletarian internationalism" and equality of all nations of the USSR; this marked another step toward the encouraging of Russian nationalism, smarting under the cover term of Sovietism.

The end of the hostilities in Europe was followed by the last summit meeting of World War II. Potsdam, a small garrison town now in the Soviet sector and a symbol of Prussian militarism, was decided on because no suitable premises could be found in the vast, once proud, but now devastated German capital. The most logical choice, Hitler's Chancellery, was no more; the tri-

umphant Russians had razed it to the ground. Soon the area was covered with sod, leaving a grassy mount where rats and rabbits roamed over the symbol of the Nazi Reich that was to have lasted for a thousand years.

The Potsdam Conference (July 17–August 2, 1945) revealed once more the brittleness of the wartime alliance. Mutual distrust resulting from different philosophies and postwar objectives was surfacing more and more. Aware of this, Stalin, always a meticulous planner, tried to arrange every detail of the conference; he wanted to preserve the partnership that had contributed to his victory. He still hoped to persuade his allies to resume lend-lease supplies to his war-ravaged country and finance its reconstruction with Western credit. After inspecting the hall in which the deliberations of the Big Three were to take place, he immediately ordered that the ceiling, which depicted a sailing ship surmounted by a dark cloud, be redecorated; to replace this ill omen, the Soviet host ordered a star, a symbol common to the heraldry of both the Soviet Union and the United States, to be painted shining over the ship.

Despite these efforts, the divergent interests of Soviet Russia and the Western powers cropped up at every step. President Roosevelt had died in the interim, and Winston Churchill was at Potsdam only until his defeat in the British parliamentary election of July 28. This left Stalin as the only veteran of the two previous summit meetings, those of Teheran and Yalta. Faced by two novices in international affairs—President Harry Truman and the head of the new Labour government, Clement Attlee—Stalin proved more than ever that he was the most resourceful and determined of all the wartime Allied leaders.

The main task of the Potsdam Conference was to establish the frontiers and the occupation regime of the defeated Germany. The country was split: the Elbe valley, Upper Saxony, and all of Thuringia were to be occupied by Soviet troops; the area to the west was to be shared by the United States, Britain, and, later on, by France. Berlin was to be jointly occupied by the four powers, and the economic policy to be applied to all zones of the Allied occupation was to be collectively determined. After having made the gesture of consulting with the representative of the new, Communist-dominated Warsaw regime, the Big Three decided that lands east of the Oder-Western Neisse rivers were to be put "under the administration of the Polish State." The two million Germans remaining in this area were to be transferred to the Soviet and Western occupation zones. The Allies put at Polish disposal enough transport facilities to carry out this operation as quickly as possible.

By this time, after the withdrawal of the German troops from Czechoslovakia, the Czechs had expelled from the Sudetenland practically all the Germans, numbering some three million people. Since, at the same time, numerous although more limited deportations of Germans had taken place in Romania, Yugoslavia, and Hungary, the ethnic map of Eastern Europe, now under Soviet hegemony, had undergone a further radical change. To Hitler's mass extermination of the Jews, or the Holocaust, was now added the expulsion of most Germans. By sponsoring the transfer of the Germans as well as by encouraging their Polish allies to push their boundaries so far to the west, the Russians achieved three interlocked objectives: first, they reduced the territorial base of their potential future enemy; second, they denied as much land and as many resources as possible to the Western powers; third, they supported their control over the heart of the former Reich by a broad belt of buffer states that depended on Soviet sponsorship in various ways. All this was backed by stationing a powerful army between the Elbe and the Oder, as well as on the territories of their clients.

Japan's Surrender and the End of World War II

Before the Big Three finished with the German problem, they had to deal with another partner in the Axis triangle. In the summer of 1945, Japan was still fighting a bloody delaying action both on the Asian mainland and on the Pacific islands. On July 26 the Big Three issued a declaration threatening Japan with annihilation unless the Japanese surrendered unconditionally and immediately. The Tokyo government, while officially rejecting the Potsdam declaration, asked Moscow for mediation. Stalin did not inform either Washington or London about this proposal to conclude a negotiated peace. As a consequence, President Truman, determined to avoid a costly invasion of Japan, ordered the first atom bomb to be dropped on the naval and military base of Hiroshima on August 6. This resulted in 135,000 casualties (66,000 killed and 69,000 wounded) and the utter destruction of the city. When the Japanese continued to fight, another bomb was dropped a few days later on the city of Nagasaki.

Meanwhile, on August 9, the USSR had launched its land offensive against the Japanese armies in Manchuria and Korea. Within ten days the Soviet Far Eastern force, about one-and-a-half million men, smashed the Japanese forces.. Pursuing the retreating enemy, the Red Army entered northern

China and Korea. The devastating results of the first military application of nuclear weapons had shattered Japanese morale. On August 14, Tokyo accepted the Potsdam declaration and asked for peace. On September 2, 1945, General Douglas MacArthur, accompanied by Soviet representatives, received Japan's capitulation. World War II was over.

At the time of the armistice the Soviet troops pursuing the Japanese in Korea had reached, roughly speaking, the 38th parallel, which was then designated as the demarcation line between the American and Russian occupation zones. Korea, like Germany, was split between its Communist-dominated northern part and American-controlled southern segment along the 38th parallel; another great prize of World War II, Japan, avoided division because of Washington's stubborn opposition. As in the case of another Axis partner, Italy, no Soviet soldiers were admitted on Japanese soil. Thus, despite Soviet protests, Japan remained a United States preserve. This became another bone of contention between the two rivals for the control of the globe and contributed to the mounting tensions. Without the integrating pressure of wartime necessity, the facade of Allied unity disintegrated. Nevertheless, despite its short and largely superfluous contribution to the Far Eastern war, the USSR obtained practically everything it had been promised at Yalta and Potsdam; this more than reversed the 1905 settlement.

The end of World War II witnessed a far-reaching rearrangement in the ranking of great powers. France lost this status as a result of its humiliating defeat in 1940. Italy was disqualified by 1941 because of its inability to cope even with small Greece, let alone with Great Britain. Britain, exhausted by six years of continuous fight against heavy odds, had to limit drastically its global commitments soon after the war. This left the United States and the Soviet Union as the only global super powers. Almost immediately after they finished with Japan, the former allies turned into deadly rivals in the struggle for the control of the world.

Suggested Reading

ALTSHULER, MORDECHAI, *Soviet Jewry on the Eve of the Holocaust: A Social and Demographic Profile*. Jerusalem: The Centre for Research of East European Jewry, 1998.

ANDERS, WLADYSLAW, *Hitler's Defeat in Russia*. Chicago: Regnery, 1953.

ANDREYEV, CATHERINE, *Vlasov and the Russian Liberation Movement*. Cambridge, Eng.; Cambridge University Press, 1987.

ARMSTRONG, JOHN A., *Ukrainian Nationalism, 1939–1945*. New York: Columbia University Press, 1955.

——— (ED.), *The Soviet Partisans in World War II*. Madison: University Of Wisconsin Press, 1964.

BIALER, SEWERYN (ED.), *Stalin and His Generals: Soviet Military Memoirs of World War II*. New York Praeger, 1969.

CHUIKOV, VASILI I., *The Battle for Stalingrad*. New York: Holt, Rinehart and Winston, 1964.

———, *The End of the Third Reich*. London: MacGibbon and Kee, 1967.

CIECHANOWSKI, JAN, *The Warsaw Rising of 1944*. New York: Cambridge University Press, 1974.

CLARK, ALAN, *Barbarossa: The Russian-German Conflict, 1941–1945*. New York: Morrow, 1965.

CLEMENS, DIANE SHAVER, *Yalta*. New York: Oxford University Press, 1970.

CONQUEST, ROBERT, *The Nation Killers: Soviet Deportation of Nationalities*. New York: Macmillan, 1970.

COOPER, MATTHEW, *The Nazi War against Soviet Partisans, 1941–1944*. New York: Stein And Day, 1979.

DALLIN, ALEXANDER, *German Rule in Russia, 1941–1945*. New York: Macmillan, 1957.

DEANE, JOHN R., *The Strange Alliance*. New York: Viking, 1947.

DJILAS, MILOVAN, *Conversations with Stalin*. New York: Harcourt Brace Jovanovich, 1956.

DOBROSZYCKI, LUCJAN, AND JEFFREY S. GUROCK (EDS.), *The Holocaust in the Soviet Union*. Armonk, NY: M. E. Sharpe, 1993.

DUFFY, CHRISTOPHER, *Red Storm on the Reich*. New York: Atheneum, 1990.

DZIEWANOWSKI, M. K., *War at any Price: World War II in Europe, 1939–1945*. Upper Saddle River, NJ: Prentice Hall, 2nd Ed., 1991.

ERICKSON, JOHN, *The Road to Stalingrad*. London:

Weidenfeld and Nicolson, 1975. New York: Harper & Row, 1975.

————, *The Road To Berlin.* Boulder, CO: Westview Press, 1983.

————, *The Soviet High Command.* New York: St. Martin's Press, 1962.

EUBANK, KEITH, *Summit at Teheran.* New York: Morrow, 1985.

FEIS, HERBERT, *Between War and Peace: The Potsdam Conference.* Princeton, NJ: Princeton University Press, 1960.

————, *Churchill, Roosevelt and Stalin: The War They Waged and the Peace They Sought.* Princeton, NJ: Princeton University Press, 1957.

GORODETSKY, GABRIEL, *Grand Delusion: Stalin and the German Invasion of Russia.* New Haven, CT and London: Yale University Press, 1999.

GOURÉ, LEON, *The Siege of Leningrad.* Stanford, CA: Stanford University Press, 1962.

HERRING, GEORGE, C., JR., *Aid to Russia, 1941–1946.* New York: Columbia University Press, 1973.

KOLARZ, WALTER, *Russia and Her Colonies.* Hamden, CT: Shoe String, 1967.

KORIAKOV, MIKHAIL (Trans. Nicholas Wreden), *I'll Never Go Back: A Red Army Officer Talks.* New York: Dutton, 1948.

LIDDELL-HART, BASIL H., *The Soviet Army 1946 to the Present.* Gloucester, MA: Peter Smith, 1956.

————, *History of the Second World War.* New York: Putnam, 1971.

NERRICH, ALEXANDER M., *June 22, 1941: Soviet Historians and the German Invasion.* Columbia: University of South Carolina Press, 1968.

———— (Trans. George Saunders). *The Punished Peoples: The Deportation and Fate of Soviet Minori-ties at the End of the Second World War.* New York: Norton, 1978.

NEWTON, VERNE W., *The Cambridge Spies.* Madison, WI: Madison Books, 1991.

NOGGLE, ANNE, *A Dance with Death: Soviet Airwomen in World War II.* College Station: Texas A & M University Press, 1994.

PAVLOV, DMITRI V. (Trans. John C. Adams), *Leningrad, Nineteen Hundred Forty One: The Block-ade.* Chicago: University of Chicago Press, 1965.

REESE, ROGER R., *Stalin's Reluctant Soldiers: A Social History of the Red Army, 1925–1941.* Lawrence: University Press of Kansas, 1996.

SALISBURY, HARRISON E., *The 900 Days: The Siege of Leningrad.* New York: Harper & Row, 1969.

SEATON, ALBERT, *The Russo-German War, 1941–1945.* New York: Praeger, 1970.

VARDYS, STANLEY (ED.), *Lithuania under the Soviets.* New York: Praeger, 1965.

WEINSTEIN, ALLEN, AND ALEXANDER VASSILIEV, *The Haunted Wood: Soviet Espionage in America—The Stalin Era.* New York: Random House, 1999.

WIECZYNSKI, JOSEPH, L. (ED.), *Operation Barbarossa: The German Attack on the Soviet Union.* New York: Norman Ross Publishing, 1993.

ZAWODNY, J. K., *Nothing but Honour: The Story of the Warsaw Uprising, 1944.* Stanford, CA: Hoover Institution, 1978.

ZHUKOV, GEORGE K. (Trans. Theodore Shabad). *Marshal Zhukov's Greatest Battles,* Edited with an Introduction and Explanatory Comments by Harrison E. Salisbury. New York: Harper & Row, 1969.

Chapter 19

The Aftermath of the War: Rehabilitation and Retrenchment

The clashing objectives of the two main victors of the war were obvious from the very beginning, both in Europe and Asia. Consequently they looked at each other with suspicion. The Soviet garrison was stationed in the heart of Europe, in Berlin. Because of the forcible incorporation of the three Baltic states, Lithuania, Latvia, and Estonia, as well as the gain of Koenigsberg, the Baltic Sea became almost a Soviet lake. In East Central Europe and in the Balkans, the Soviet Union was now the dominant force. In the Far East, because of Japan's crushing defeat and the continuing civil war in China where the Communists became a major force, Moscow's position was also paramount.

In East Central Europe, with the exception of Finland and Central Poland, the USSR had directly incorporated all the land that had ever belonged to the Tsarist Empire. In the cases of the northern segment of former East Prussia, Galicia, Northern Bukovina, and Carpathian Ruthenia (which Czechoslovakia had been compelled to relinquish), Stalin went beyond the old imperial borders. The incorporation of the last three provinces finally gathered all the Ukrainian-speaking people under Soviet rule. The grand total of Soviet territorial acquisitions amounted to 265,850 square miles with a population of 23,477,000. In addition to these direct gains, Moscow extended its writ over a large slice of Germany, along with Poland, Czechoslovakia, Hungary, Romania, Yugoslavia, Bulgaria, and Albania in Europe; and Northern Korea and Outer Mongolia in Asia. All these states, numbering some 120,000,000 inhabitants, were now clients of the Kremlin.

In terms of the sheer increment of material power and prestige, the outcome of the war brought to the Soviet Union gains without parallel in modern history. Yet even this unprecedented triumph did not satisfy Stalin. When Averell Harriman, then the United States Ambassador in Moscow, asked him whether he was happy now that his soldiers were in Berlin, the Soviet dictator answered wistfully, "Yes, but those of Alexander I were also in Paris."

Rehabilitation and Recompression

Despite these unprecedented gains the USSR, while it had achieved great prestige, was economically exhausted by the autumn

A Soviet tank in front of the ruined German Parliament Building (*Reichstag*)

of 1945. Its war damages were staggering. The population losses, if one counts the decline in the birth rate caused by the hostilities, may be estimated at from twenty-five to thirty million. Most of the western and southwestern provinces of the USSR were in ruins. Some 1,700 towns and cities and 70,000 villages were either razed to the ground or severely damaged. So were about 35,000 plants and factories and over 6,000,000 buildings of all sorts, while nearly 25,000,000 people were left homeless. By 1945, about a quarter of the capital assets of Soviet industry had been destroyed, and industrial production had dropped by about 30 percent as compared with 1940. Starvation was rampant and cases of cannibalism not infrequent. Yet the people, elated by their victory, set out to rebuild their war-ravaged country, their unbroken spirit overcoming their numerous disappointments.

The reconstruction plan was based on the theory that the Communist institutions, political as well as economic, had passed the grim test of the war with flying colors. The triumph was to be attributed solely to the Communist system, masterfully orchestrated by "the greatest statesman and leader of all time." All vestigial, criticism of the regime was therefore once again silenced and regarded as treason. Any notion of economic reform was rejected by the triumphant Stalin. At the close of the war he emerged not only in his restored glory as the wise teacher and most farsighted statesman, but also as the Generalissimo, the organizer of victory, and the greatest military leader of all time. The cult of personality was intensified. A monumental, multivolume history of the "Great Patriotic War" commissioned by Stalin attributed to him an allegedly masterful plan of luring the invaders deep into the territory of the USSR to destroy them more thoroughly. The chief hero of the "Great

Soviet Territorial gains in Europe, 1939–1945

Patriotic War," the man actually responsible for the victories of Moscow, Stalingrad, Kursk, and Berlin, Marshal Zhukov, was soon relegated to a provincial command and then retired.

Immediately after the war Stalin proceeded to reassert ruthlessly the shaken politi- cal controls. Security measures were always his first priority. As a historically minded man, Stalin remembered that political agita- tion had almost invariably followed foreign wars. The Decembrist revolt of 1825 was a dis- tant echo of the Napoleonic campaigns and the wide-ranging presence of Russian soldiers in Europe. The Great Reforms of the 1860s were largely a result of the Crimean War. The revolutionary populism of the 1880s was attributable to the Russo-Turkish War of 1877–1878. The connection between the revolutions of 1905 and 1917 and the two wars that had preceded them was a part of Stalin's own life experience. He was aware of how much the dislocations resulting from the German invasion had contributed to the relaxation of political control over the fluid, shifting, and hence unmanageable population. He was also aware of the ferment generated by the soldiers, forced laborers, and former POWs now returning from the West, where they saw that the standard of living was so much higher than in the "paradise of the proleteriat."

To reimpose the old controls over those that had strayed, now became Stalin's paramount task. The returning POWs and Soviet laborers from the West had to go through reindoctrination camps, and many of them did not escape deportation either. The former soldiers of the Russian Liberation Army of General Vlasov were punished with the usual severity: Vlasov himself was hanged.

During the war some ethnic groups that were suspected by Stalin of disloyalty were deported to distant locations of the huge empire. Of these the most important group was the Volga Germans, who were deported in the summer of 1941 to Central Asia, and dispersed there. Between October 1943 and May 1944, six other ethnic groups were driven out of their original locations as punishment for alleged wholesale collaboration with the Germans. Among these groups were the Crimean Tatars, the Kalmyks of the lower Volga, and four North Caucasian peoples: Chechens, Ingush, Karachay, and Balkars. These mass deportations, which affected 1,250,000 men, women, and children, were extremely costly in human lives.

After the war the restless Ukrainians were next on Stalin's list, but as he admitted frankly to his then close co-worker, Secretary of the Communist Party Nikita S. Khrushchev, there were not enough trains in the whole country to transport some 40 million people from their homeland to the wastes of Central Asia and Siberia. Nevertheless, the reprisals against Ukrainian collaborators and anti-Soviet partisans were massive and extraordinarily harsh. Stalin's main problems were the new western fringes of his vast empire. Eastern Galicia, Northern Bukovina, and Carpathian Ruthenia, which formerly belonged to Poland, Romania, and Czechoslovakia respectively, had been the mainstay of the Greek Catholic (Uniate) Church that combined fidelity to the Greek Orthodox liturgy with allegiance to the Pope. Fearing this foreign connection, Stalin ordered an enforced merger of the Uniate Church, a bastion of Ukrainian nationalism, with the Orthodox Church of Russia. Surprisingly enough, the outwardly atheistic Soviet State threw all of its authority behind the proselytizing activities of the Orthodox clergy, which was mostly Great Russian. The largely recalcitrant Uniate hierarchy was deported, while Church property was confiscated or handed over to the Orthodox clergy. At the same time the familiar Soviet institutions, including land collectivization, were promptly extended to all the newly incorporated territories, including the three Baltic states. They had enjoyed two decades of independence, democracy, and relatively high standard of living. In formerly Polish eastern Galicia, now Western Ukraine, the resistance was as fierce and protracted as in the Baltic provinces; 260,000 Lithuanians, over 100,000 Latvians, and 80,000 Estonians were deported. Their place was occupied by Soviet colonists. Despite these measures, Western Ukraine and the former Baltic Republics became a constant source of unrest.

Economic Reforms and the Fourth Five-Year Plan

Soviet Russia's postwar economy was in shambles and called for radical rehabilitation. The war had been largely financed by printing paper rubles, great quantities of which found their way into the countryside in payment for extremely scarce produce. The money was usually kept by the peasants not in the form of savings accounts but in their coffers and mattresses. Stalin was determined to cut down this excess of cash, while increasing the supply of labor. In 1947 the people were ordered to exchange ten old rubles against one new ruble. This 1,000 percent devaluation had a double effect: It at once wiped out wartime cash savings and encouraged persons who were idle to re-enter the labor market. Both consequences severly affected the rural population. The extensive process of illegal land seizure by the peasants, who during the wartime relaxation of controls in the countryside enlarged their private plots at the expense of the collective farms, was stopped and then reversed. In the summer of 1946 the authorities also tightened severe measures to combat the wartime laxity that prevailed in many factories. "Labor discipline" was strictly enforced again. Absenteeism and similar offenses were to be severely punished as of old. To tighten political controls and increase administrative efficiency, many collective farms were merged; two, three, or four of them were pooled and reorganized around what became known as "agrarian towns." These operations were carried out under the supervision of the rising star of the Politburo, Nikita S. Khrushchev.

The magnitude of the war damage was such that it soon became obvious that some form of outside aid had to be considered, even by the autarkic-minded Stalin. The lend-lease deliveries had been discontinued in the spring of 1945 while the United States-sponsored Marshall Plan was rejected by Stalin as politically too dangerous; any hope for foreign loans was fast fading because of the rapidly developing tension between the Soviet Union and the United States. Consequently, the USSR relied on war booty, reparations, tribute in cash, and forced delivery of goods from the countries East Germany, Poland, Czechoslovakia, Hungary, Yugoslavia, and Bulgaria. Forcible delivery from these satellites of the Soviet Union had to supplement the ruthless mobilization of all

"Don't be a fool!" In this Soviet cold war poster, a Soviet soldier warns Uncle Sam holding an atom bomb

native resources as the immediate instruments of the rehabilitation of the USSR. Combined with patriotic exhortations, these measures proved on the whole successful, and the rehabilitation of the ravaged country proceeded at a faster pace than had been expected by Western economists. Later, a series of highly advantageous trade agreements and other economic arrangements (such as joint stock companies) between Moscow and its client states of East Central Europe were to augment the German war reparations. Yet, from the beginning, the old mistaken trust in the central planning was an original sin of the whole scheme of reconstruction. Its symbol was the Fourth Five-Year Plan, launched in 1946 and expected to end in 1950. Its purpose was to make up for the losses suffered during the hostilities, and to exceed the 1940 economic level. The Fourth

Five-Year Plan followed the well-established tradition of focusing on heavy industry, which was rebuilt according to the old, i.e., mostly 1930–1940 pattern. This meant the new factories were obsolete before they were finished. The prewar command economy was soon restored and even reinforced. The emphasis was again on quantity and not on quality, on more rather than better. The industrial targets were achieved, and in 1950 the output of heavy industry doubled. At the same time, agriculture, saddled with compulsory deliveries, lagged behind.

The whole life was further militarized. The top echelons of the armed forces became further separated from the rank and file by increased privileges and perks.

The Anti-Western Campaign

By 1945, after one of the great victories of all time, the veterans of Stalingrad, Kursk, and Berlin were longing for a respite from their exertions. Their lingering hopes for a fuller, freer, and more prosperous life were shattered by Stalin's radio address of February 9, 1946. In this speech, Stalin extolled the virtues of the Soviet system and proclaimed a program of austerity, hard work, and discipline. He attributed World War II to the political and socioeconomic forces behind Western monopoly capitalism. Quoting Leninist doctrine, Stalin pointed out that "the capitalistic system of world economy conceals elements of crisis and war." (The documents discovered in Soviet archives indicate that he expected a war between the United States and Britain.) Stalin stressed that "so long as capitalism existed, the world would not be free from the threat of war." His conclusion was that while the war against Facism was over, the danger of a clash with the Western capitalists and imperialists was ever-present. Therefore, the Soviet people should be ready to make more sacrifices.

Stalin's appeal for vigilance was applied immediately. Soon there began a full-blown campaign against cultural and intellectual "rootless cosmopolitans." The term was broadly used to describe those who tended

Andrei A. Zhdanov, member of the Politburo since 1939 and virtual dictator of the ideological front between 1945 and 1949

to glorify Western ideas and ways, but soon it became obvious, that it was largely directed against Jews. Slogans like "toadying to the West" often appeared in newspaper headlines. The Museum of Modern Western Art was closed to the public. Books by contemporary Western authors were denounced as "seditious" and "subversive," while jazz, as the music developed in the United States, was banned. Many intellectuals, many of them Jewish, were arrested and the more independent professors were removed from their chairs, often on the basis of student denunciations that had been officially encouraged. "Socialist realism" was reimposed as the prescribed norm of artistic creativity.

The anti-Western drive was conducted under another close co-worker of Stalin's, Andrei A. Zhdanov, a man who in 1934 had replaced Kirov as head of the Leningrad Party district and now emerged as the dictator's heir apparent. In the sphere of culture he ruled supreme. He sharply criticized three of the best Soviet composers—Sergei Prokofiev, Dmitri Shostakovich, and Aram Khatchaturian—for "formalistic deformations" and "encouraging antidemocratic tendencies in contemporary Soviet music." Their work, thundered Zhdanov, reflected "too closely the spirit of the modern bourgeois music of Europe and America." In such an atmosphere, original creativity was stifled. When the leading Soviet poet and novelist, Boris Pasternak, told an American journalist that he was engaged exclusively in translating foreign writers—mainly Shakespeare—the American asked him, "Aren't you writing anything original?" Pasternak replied, "Writing original works *these days*? One would have to be crazy . . . !"

The Anti-Zionist Drive

Under Zhdanov's supervision the Soviet authorities radically switched their previously benevolent attitude toward the Jews who survived the German invasion and the atrocities that followed. This shift was officially justified by many considerations. One was that there had been a large number of defections to the West by Red Army soldiers of Jewish extraction stationed in the Soviet zone of occupation. Stalin had come to believe that many of those who had been active on behalf of the USSR in organizing the Jewish international assistance during the war in the West, especially in the United States, had established secret links abroad. Stalin's suspicion of foreign espionage and subversion was thus further aroused. Consequently, he ordered the removal of Jews from most positions of power, especially from jobs involving security matters. Another reason for official encouragement of anti-Semitism, camouflaged by terms "anti-Zionism" or "cosmopolitanism," was the accusation that the Jews wanted to detach the peninsula of Crimea and establish there their own state. Finally there was the desire to divert away from itself the growing popular resentment against the tightening of political and economic controls.

The factor that finally made Stalin launch an open, massive "anti-Zionist" campaign was the establishment of the State of Israel in the spring of 1948. Initially, nothing seemed to forecast such a negative attitude on the part of the Soviet dictator. In 1946–1947, Stalin supported the Jewish struggle against the British mandate, which he saw as a form of colonialism; hence the generous Soviet supply of weapons to the Israelis as long as they were fighting the British rule in Palestine. When the State of Israel was established, the USSR was the first to recognize it *de jure*. Moreover, hoping that Israel, largely founded by Russian Jews of radical socialist proclivities, would turn to Moscow for guidance, Stalin continued his material and diplomatic assistance. However, he was soon disappointed by the Israeli government, which leaned more and more heavily on the West, especially on the United States.

The final blow was the enthusiastic greeting extended by the Jewish public to the first Israeli ambassador in Moscow, Golda Meir. The sight of Soviet Jews openly manifesting their devotion to a foreign envoy angered Stalin; he launched a thorough purge of the Jewish cultural institutions and other organizations still tolerated by the State. From then on, Jews were purged from most responsible posts in the Party and governmental apparatus. Jewish cultural life suffered cruel losses because of the widespread arrests of leading intellectuals and professional people. Altogether the purge affected several hundred people; many leading Jewish intellectuals were executed, while others deported to various concentration camps. In August 1948, Zhdanov, then at the peak of his prestige and power, died suddenly. Nevertheless, the anti-Western, and anti-Semitic campaign continued.

The Start of the Cold War

Theoretically, the decisions of the Teheran and Yalta summit conferences were reached by Soviet Russia, the United States, and Great Britain unanimously. But at Potsdam it was already obvious that the Soviet Union and the United States were highly suspicious of the other's goals; they were the only surviving powers who commanded enough resources to compete for the control of the globe. This bipolarity of power, coupled with sharp ideological antagonisms between capitalist United States and the bastion of Communism, were the contributing causes of a series of diplomatic clashes and military confrontations that soon came to be called the *Cold War.*

The main stake of the Cold War in Europe was its heartland—Germany. In Asia the apples of discord were Japan, the main industrial power of the area, and China, the world's most populous country. The signing of a peace treaty with Germany, which at Potsdam was thought to be an event that would take place in the near future, was postponed indefinitely in view of the growing clashes between the two main victors of World War II.

Germany, after satisfying the territorial claims of its neighbors, was divided among the Soviet Union, the United States, Britain, and France into four zones of occupation. Similar arrangements were carried out in Austria. The fourfold military occupation of Germany was initially intended by the Western powers as a temporary solution. This was, however, not Stalin's goal. From his point of view the stationing of the Red Army on German soil, especially in Berlin, had a double purpose. First, the USSR wanted to deny at least a segment of the German territory and resources to the West while exploiting them for Soviet purposes. Second, the occupation satisfied Soviet pride and prestige: the presence of the Soviet soldiers in Berlin symbolized the scope of the Russian victory.

One of the more divisive issues at Yalta was the question of postwar Germany reparations; it was finally settled by President Roosevelt's agreeing to an overall sum of $20 billion, of which the USSR would be entitled to half. The cessation of lend-lease and the fading hopes for an American loan made Stalin determined to squeeze the maximum in reparations out of Germany. Since the devastated country was unable to pay in cash, the Russians set about removing whatever they

could in the way of capital equipment from their own zone and wanted to extend the same policy to the Western zones in order to get their share.

Already by the beginning of 1946 Stalin had repeatedly violated the Potsdam agreements by sealing off his occupation zone economically as well as politically. In reply, in July 1946, Britain and the United States had agreed on a complete economic fusion of their zones. Both the British and the Americans were supplying reparations to the USSR from their zones while also pouring money into Germany in an attempt to set up a viable economy there. Such a state of affairs was untenable in the long run. Therefore in September 1946, when Secretary of State Byrnes spoke at Stuttgart—one of the main industrial cities of southern Germany—he confirmed the policy of suspending reparations from the American zone and denounced the plan of dismantling German industry. Moreover he promised American support for German economic reconstruction. By 1947, "Bizonia"—created from the fusion of the British and American zones—was already a political and economic reality. As time went on, the differences between the occupying powers were widening. The only tangible fruit of an interallied policy in Germany was the jointly staged trial of the major Nazi war criminals at Nuremberg. Twelve chief defendants were sentenced to death by hanging.

Both antagonists in the *Cold War* were meanwhile preparing to set up their "own" Germany as a stepping stone for the eventual unification of the country, each one hoping it would be under their guidance and supervision. Throughout the years 1945–1948, the political situation in war-ravaged Western Europe was highly dangerous. After the war the French and Italian Communist parties, then still fully subservient to Moscow, emerged as powerful political instruments and could be relied upon to support any Soviet move. Although Stalin never used them as such, and they even participated in the French and Italian governments until 1946, the Western fears of Communism persisted. One has to bear in mind that, while the Western armies had been demobilized, the Red Army remained partly on war footing and in 1947 still exceeded its 1941 size.

The documents, discovered in Soviet archives after the downfall of Communism in Russia, have confirmed the suspicion that Stalin had constantly in mind a march of the Red Army toward the Atlantic.

Sovietization of East Central Europe

To the east and southeast of the Soviet zone in Germany, between the Baltic, the Adriatic, and the Black seas, stretched a belt of states which the Red Army had occupied at the closing stages of the war: Poland, Czechoslovakia, Romania, Hungary, Bulgaria, Yugoslavia, and Albania. These countries, containing altogether some 100 million people, commanded important strategic bases as well as natural resources. Stalin regarded this area as a buffer zone that was to cushion any possible attack on the part of any future remilitarized Germany or a state allied with Germany. Consequently, he was determined to control these countries by means of "friendly" governments that would be allied with the USSR and would put their respective territories at its disposal allegedly only for "guarding Soviet communication lines" with the strong Red Army bases in Germany. And indeed, with the baggage trains of the Red Army came teams of native Communists who, together with Soviet agents—local politicians sympathetic to the Soviet point of view—formed a series of governments which called themselves "people's democracies."

While Yugoslavia and Albania had been freed from Axis occupation largely owing to the effort of local Communists, the other aforementioned countries were occupied by the Red Army at the end of the war. Only Finland escaped Soviet occupation; it remained an independent country, merely tied to the USSR by a defensive treaty that obliged the Finns to stand by the Soviet Army in case of an attack coming through Finnish territory. While the Communists takeover was immediate in Yugoslavia, Albania, and Bulgaria, where the Communist

movements had deeper native roots, the traditional monarchy in Romania and the Western-type democracy in Czechoslovakia survived for a while. The Romanian coalition government, however, was from the beginning under the thumb of the local Communists backed by the Soviet garrisons. In June 1947, the National Peasant Party was suppressed. King Michael was forced to abdicate and leave the country. In Hungary, a coalition government of four democratic political parties lasted for about three years. In Poland the process of Sovietization was much shorter; after the rigged elections of February 1947. Poland was, as the official slogan proclaimed, already a people's democracy, "a transition form between bourgeois democracy and a Soviet type of government." The last country to succumb to undisguised Communist domination was Czechoslovakia. By early 1948, all the countries of East Central Europe were under Moscow's control.

During the years 1945–1948, the process of *Sovietization*—gradual assimilation of local political, socioeconomic, and cultural patterns—was going on throughout this part of Europe at various speeds. The dosage of violence inherent in this process was determined by circumstances and local conditions. The general pattern, however, was clear everywhere. First, the remaining large landed estates were divided among the land-hungry peasants. This was conducted with an eye to eventual collectivization; the parcels of land were small and the necessary credits, implements, and cattle were not always provided. While this neutralized the peasant masses during the crucial stages of the Communist takeover, the reform was intended to demonstrate the alleged absurdity of individual farming. At the same time, propaganda drives extolled "socialist farming." The collectivization process was speeded up during the 1950s. By the time Stalin died in March 1953, collective and State farms amounted to approximately 20 percent of all farms in Poland and Romania, 30 percent in Hungary, 43 percent in Czechoslovakia, and 62 percent in Bulgaria. These results were achieved by means of intensive

Soviet Marshal Konstantin K. Rokossovsky in the uniform of Commander-in-Chief of Poland's Armed Forces

agitation mixed with fiscal harassment and threats of violence.

In a second step toward Sovietization, all banks, credit and insurance companies, and large industrial and commercial enterprises were taken over by the State. Eventually, only the small service and artisan shops were left in private hands as a vestigial, barely tolerated form of private ownership. The third part of Sovietization involved the cultural patterns of each country, which underwent intensive reshaping in order to emphasize atheistic education, socialist realism, and folklore elements in art. These last were seen as embodying people's art, as contrasted with the decadent, Westernized art of the former ruling bourgeoisie. Close cultural and trade relations were imposed by the countries of East Central Europe with the USSR. In all of them the local Commu-

nist parties, each acting under a different cover name, were the driving force for the changes that were eventually to make the people's democracies more similar to the superior Soviet model. The Social Democratic movements were compelled to merge with the Communists.

In exchange for "Soviet fraternal aid" in "liberating" and rehabilitating their respective countries, the new regimes granted generous economic concessions to the USSR, either directly or through the intermediary of "joint stock companies," which were run as a rule for the benefit of the Soviet partner. The net of reciprocal military alliances that soon linked the people's democracies with the center allowed for the stationing of Soviet garrisons on the territories of their respective countries: Yugoslavia and Czechoslovakia, traditionally pro-Russian, were so trusted that no Soviet troops were stationed there. Foreign trade was reoriented eastward. At the same time Western contacts were discouraged, if not forbidden outright.

So it was that between 1945 and 1948 the area east of the Elbe and the Adriatic became separated from the rest of Europe, not only by barbed wire fences guarded by armed sentries, but by a less tangible, but nevertheless real, psychological barrier of mistrust and even outright hostility toward things Western. Before the term "Iron Curtain" was coined by Winston Churchill in March 1946, it had already become more than a propaganda slogan.

The Berlin Blockade and the Two German States

While this was going on, Stalin observed the differences among the Western powers, especially the British-American and French attitudes toward Germany, and decided to attack the West's weakest point. This was the Berlin enclave, separated from the Western powers by 110 miles of Soviet-occupied territory. Stalin hoped to use the vulnerability of the Western position in Berlin and to blackmail the West into legitimizing the new *status quo* and prepare the further Soviet expansion westward.. He must have seen the spring of 1948 as a propitious moment to challenge the Western position by means of a series of combined military and political operations that would be effective, yet gradual enough so as not to warrant a nuclear response. On June 24, 1948, after months of intermittent Soviet harassment, all railroad connections to Berlin from the West were cut off by the Soviets on grounds of "technical difficulties."

Washington, while reluctant to resort to its overwhelming nuclear arsenal, was inferior in conventional weapons. On the other hand, it saw in Stalin's challenge an ominous step toward ousting the Western powers from Berlin, destroying their political and military credibility, and eventually pushing them, step by step, beyond the Rhine, if not further. The Americans feared that, if the technical know-how of a united Germany were ever combined with Soviet manpower and natural resources, Soviet Russia could become a power superior to the United States.

To prevent the creation of a dangerous aggregate of military and economic power, Washington decided to accept the Soviet challenge. Rejecting the initially considered use of American atom bombs, the Western Allies, led by President Truman, decided nevertheless to reassert their right of passage to the former German capital. An air lift was organized, chiefly with American resources, to maintain vital supply lines and defy the Soviet land blockade. At the same time Washington initiated military consultations with most of its wartime allies in the Western hemisphere—the countries of the North Atlantic area—to organize an integrated Western defense system. On April 4, 1949, the North Atlantic Treaty Organization (NATO) was established (see page 276). This firm stand, combined now with the military potential of NATO, combined with the success of airlift, compelled the Russians to lift the Berlin blockade and to open negotiations for new traffic regulations.

Meanwhile, during the blockade, from June 1948 to May 12, 1949, Soviet authorities had converted their zone of occupation, containing 17 million people, or less than half of the West German population, into a separate entity called the German Democratic Republic. Thus, while demonstrating Soviet inability to oust forcibly the Western powers from Germany, the Berlin blockade also contributed to laying the foundations of a separate East German state. The new state was run by a Communist party that used the name Socialist Unity Party. It was headed by a Comintern veteran, Walter Ulbricht, a man entirely subservient to Moscow.

Persia, Greece, and Turkey

While these events were taking place in Central and Eastern Europe, a critical situation was unfolding in the Near and Middle East, in Iran, Turkey, and Greece. During the war Soviet Russia, Great Britain, and the United States had occupied Iran to assure oil supplies for their war machines and to remove the pro-Axis Shah. They all agreed to leave the Iranian territory simultaneously soon after the end of hostilities. The two Western powers complied with these conditions, but the Russians did not. They not only stayed beyond the agreed deadline, but they tried to engineer a rebellion against the government of Teheran in the province of Azerbaijan, the northern segment of Iran adjacent to the USSR; they even set up a pro-Soviet Azerbaijani government there. Blackmailing the central Iranian authorities with this instrument of pressure, in 1946 the Russians extracted from that government a series of oil-exploitation rights in Northern Persia. The Iranian government of the 1940s was not the ruthless body of the 1970s or 1980s. It seemed, for a while, that a Soviet takeover of Iran would soon follow those already accomplished in East Central Europe. Seeing their vital oil supplies threatened, the United States and Great Britain had the Soviet machinations in Iran condemned by the United Nations as an interference in the internal affairs of a member state. At the same time, Washington threatened Moscow with military action. Faced with these determined measures, Stalin backed down and ordered Soviet withdrawal from Northern Persia.

The Iranian experience served as a guide for Western behavior in adjacent Turkey and in Greece. During the Italian and German occupation of Greece, the local Communists managed to organize a strong underground movement. In September 1941 a popular-front coalition based on a broad understanding among most anti-Axis political groups had been established by the Communist Party of Greece, which, as the coalition's best organized and most disciplined segment, dominated the front. While fighting the Germans and the Italians, the Communists never lost sight of their ultimate objective of seizing power. And indeed this almost took place in October 1944, before British forces from North Africa could land in Greece and install a pro-British government.

Meanwhile, Stalin acted judiciously. Having conceded Greece as a Western sphere of influence, he refrained from assisting or even encouraging the Greek Communists.[1] But Stalin's Yugoslav, Bulgarian, and Albanian henchmen had no such inhibitions; they eagerly sent volunteers and weapons to the Greek Communist partisans. With this considerable outside aid and with a fair amount of local support, the Communists in Greece were gradually getting the upper hand. The British, who tried to bolster anti-Communist resistance, had been so weakened by their war efforts from 1940 to 1945, followed by the crises in Palestine and India, that they were in no position to continue their assistance to the royalist Greek government.

The Communist subversion of Greece was paralleled by an almost equally menacing situation in the formerly nonbelligerent

---

[1]In his war memoirs Churchill remarked that, while there was protest within Britain against the British landing in Greece, Stalin adhered faithfully to the October, 1944 agreement; during the long weeks of fighting in Greece, no reproach came from Moscow. Winston Churchill, *Triumph and Tragedy* (Boston: Houghton Mifflin Company, 1962), p. 197.

Turkey. Continuing the traditional Russian attempts to obtain a foothold in the Eastern Mediterranean, soon after the war Stalin began to insist on naval and military bases in the Black Sea straits, the Bosphorus, and the Dardanelles. While peaceful Turkey was in much better shape than the war-exhausted Greece, the scope and persistence of Soviet diplomatic pressure, supported by a massive concentration of Red Army near the Turkish border, was such that Ankara's resistance to it might have crumbled if it had not been bolstered from outside. The threatening double surrender in Greece and Turkey would overnight have turned the Eastern Mediterranean into a Soviet sphere of influence, threatened the oil supplies of the Middle East, and thus undermined the whole Western position in this strategically important area.

This prospect was intolerable to President Harry Truman. In a message to the Congress on March 17, 1947, he announced the American determination to grant moral and material aid to "countries whose political stability was threatened by Communism," and asked for $400,000,000 in military and economic aid to Greece and Turkey. Moreover, he ordered military and naval advisers sent to both countries. Although the Soviet Union was not mentioned by name, the resulting *Truman Doctrine* was obviously directed at its expansion beyond the lines agreed upon during the wartime conferences.

The proclamation of the Truman Doctrine was merely the first step in the American global strategy of opposing Communist encroachments on the Western sphere of influence agreed upon at Yalta. In June 1947, United States Secretary of State General George C. Marshall proposed a plan of massive economic aid to Europe. The European Recovery Plan (also called the *Marshall Plan*) invited all European countries without distinction to appraise their need for help and their attitude toward broad economic cooperation to rehabilitate the war-ravaged continent. This plan, an American instrument in the global competition with Soviet Russia, constituted a momentous step in bolstering the tottering economies of Western Europe and initiated a process not only of rehabilitation but even of dynamic expansion. Surprisingly enough, on June 27, 1947, Soviet Foreign Minister Molotov, then attending a conference of allied foreign ministers in Paris, expressed the USSR's qualified readiness to participate in the plan. So did the foreign ministers of Czechoslovakia and Poland on behalf of their countries. On July 2, however, the suspicious Stalin ordered Prague and Warsaw to reverse their stand and condemned the Marshall Plan as "an infringement on European state sovereignty."

Containment and the Soviet Reaction

The Truman Doctrine and the Marshall Plan were complementary moves on the chess board of the Cold War. But Western morale was still shaky and the fear of a "Soviet march to the Atlantic" was paralyzing economic reconstruction. To bolster Western resistance and to demonstrate American interest in defending the Western hemisphere, Washington decided to prove its determination to confront Soviet Communism, arms in hand if necessary. As has been already mentioned, on April 4, 1949, twelve Western European countries and the United States joined together to form NATO, the North Atlantic Treaty Organization. Within days, substantial American air forces were being redeployed to bases in Western Europe.[2]

The launching of the Marshall Plan and the establishment of NATO were two major turning points of the Cold War in Europe. The fact that the standard of living of the Western European workers was steadily rising—it soon exceeded its prewar level—tended to mitigate the militancy of such powerful Communist parties as those of Italy and France, and gradually forced them to

function within the democratic framework of their respective states, with no immediate hope of gaining power.

If the Truman Doctrine and the Marshall Plan created the material preconditions for West European recovery, the head of the State Department's planning staff, George Kennan, provided the theoretical framework for the new long-range United States strategy toward Soviet Russia. In a 1947 article in *Foreign Affairs* signed "Mr. X" and entitled "The Sources of Soviet Conduct," Kennan stressed that the basic antagonism between the USSR and the United States would continue, whether in the foreground or the background, until the internal nature of Soviet power was fundamentally altered. In these circumstances, Kennan suggested that the main element of future United States policy toward Soviet Russia must be a patient, determined containment of the Soviet expansive drive.

Moscow replied to the policy of containment with two moves. On October 5, 1947, the Party press organ *Pravda* revealed that a conference of delegates of nine Communist parties (the USSR, Poland, Czechoslovakia, Hungary, Romania, Yugoslavia, Bulgaria, France, and Italy) had taken place in September in Poland and established a new coordinating body, the Communist Information Bureau (Cominform), which was to coordinate various activities of the several Communist parties. Later on, in January 1949, the Soviet Union initiated the establishment of another coordinating body, the Council of Mutual Economic Assistance (COMECON). The Council included the USSR, Poland, Czechoslovakia, Hungary, Romania, Bulgaria, and Albania. The constituent document reiterated the refusal of "the Socialist countries to submit to the dictates of the Marshall Plan," and announced their commitment to the "exchange of experience in the economic field and mutual assistance in regard to raw materials, foodstuffs, machinery and equipment. . . ." The seat of COMECON was to be in Moscow. Conspicuous by its absence from the Council was Yugoslavia.

---

[2] In 1951, Greece and Turkey joined the original twelve nations and in 1955 West Germany (or the Federal Republic of Germany) was also admitted to NATO.

Tito's Yugoslavia

Among the Soviet Eastern European client states, Yugoslavia was in many respects an anomaly. It had been liberated in 1944, earlier than most other countries of the area, which was largely due to the native partisan Communist-controlled forces of Marshall Broz-Tito, supported by the Western allies. The Soviet troops that did help withdrew very early, leaving Tito's victorious partisans to establish a highly regimented Communist dictatorship. Real power was in the hands of the Communist minority, though the fiction of a coalition was maintained. Thus, the Yugoslav people, like all other Eastern Europeans, really had no chance to create the democratic institutions of their choosing provided for in the Yalta Declaration. The Yugoslav Communists, largely Moscow-trained veterans, were among the most pro-Russian of the whole world movement. The cult of Stalin was fanatical and widespread. At one time one of Tito's lieutenants, Edward Kardelj, insisted that the country should become one of the constituent Soviet republics. Yet, in the end, Yugoslavia was the first country to oppose the Soviet designs to turn the country into a meek satrapy of Moscow.

To understand this paradox, one has to examine Yugoslav-Soviet relations during and immediately after the war. In 1942 and 1943, Stalin was much more inclined to reach a compromise with the British and Americans. He was willing to support the Yugoslav royalist *Chetniks* of Colonel Dražha Mikhailovich rather than Tito's partisans, who then constituted an unknown force. Tito's successes, against both the Axis powers, as well as against the Chetniks, were thus scored partly with native resources. When it seemed that Tito, as Churchill put it, was "killing more Germans" than his rival Mikhailovich, the Western powers were the first to extend to the Communist partisans significant support, which was only then followed by much smaller Soviet aid. The fact that Tito had won his local civil war, largely by his own effort, combined with foreign aid, made Stalin suspicious: he did not like people who were too independent of him.

After the war there were numerous points of friction in Soviet-Yugoslav relations. The Russian representatives made it clear that they had orders to found such Soviet-Yugoslav joint-stock companies in Yugoslavia as would give the Soviet Union a monopoly in whole branches of industry and mining, especially tin, copper, and bauxite. The handsomely paid Soviet experts were proud and rigid; they wanted to transplant everything as it was in the Soviet Union, making no allowance for specific conditions in Yugoslavia. The camel's back was broken by Stalin's attempts to fill most of the key positions, especially in the army, the security apparatus, and the Party machine, with his agents. Seeing his newly conquered power undermined in his own bailiwick, Tito was reluctantly compelled to fight back for his own political survival and, probably, his neck. He began to cancel ruinous economic contracts and dismiss both Soviet experts and secret agents. In reply, the angry Stalin summoned a meeting of the remaining members of the newly founded Cominform to try the Yugoslav comrades as "deviationists" and "traitors." On June 28, 1948, the Cominform condemned Yugoslavia and expelled it from that body. Simultaneously, Stalin appealed to the Yugoslav Party to overthrow Tito. The armies of the neighboring satellites—Hungary, Romania, Bulgaria, and Albania—had meanwhile been massed along the Yugoslav borders. At the peak of his power Stalin was supremely self-confident and said, "It is enough for me to lift my little finger and Tito will be no more."

The Yugoslav Communists, however rallied around Tito. They resisted the Soviet political pressure, which was vigorously supported by an economic boycott and various military threats. The rigid controls that Tito had established, combined with an upsurge of patriotic and anti-Soviet sentiments, allowed him to suppress the few native supporters of the Cominform. For the first time, Stalin made a frontal attack on a determined opponent who knew how to turn his own methods

Marshal Broz-Tito in 1945 as leader of the Yugoslav partisans

against him. The toughness of Tito and the favorable geopolitical situation of the country, which had territorial and maritime contacts with the West, all greatly helped Yugoslavia to survive this critical period. Another vital factor was the promptness of American aid. Brushing aside ideological considerations and forgetting Tito's past provocative policies, including his confiscation of American property, Washington promptly decided to aid the Communist rebel and send him food, fuel, and arms. At the time of its expulsion from the Cominform, Yugoslavia had oil supplies left for only eight days.

Yugoslavia's banishment from the Soviet camp was the first major breach in the hitherto monolithic structure of Stalin's empire in Eastern Europe. This was a painful blow to Soviet prestige and to its strategic position in the Mediterranean. Communist Albania, with its Soviet maritime bases, was now isolated from the rest of the bloc. Moreover, Belgrade overnight became a center of attraction for many restless Communists who, despite the long years of Stalinist brainwashing, still preserved a certain independence of mind and favored autonomy of national Communist movements. Soon they began to journey to Yugoslavia in search of

shelter, support, and enlightenment. This made Stalin more angry. One of the consequences of Tito's expulsion was the tightening of police regimes in the satellite countries. All symptoms of sympathy with Tito's "national Bolshevik" views, or "Titoism," were spotted by Soviet intelligence. Those Communists who were suspected of favoring the type of national Communism more attuned to particular native conditions, like Laszlo Rajk in Hungary or Wladyslaw Gomulka in Poland, were arrested. In the case of Rajk, his trial and execution soon followed. Gomulka, on the other hand, owing to a set of favorable circumstances, survived to play a crucial role in the process of political decompression that was to take place in Poland after Stalin's death in 1953.

Another result of Tito's expulsion was the defeat of the Communist guerrillas in Greece. Beleaguered and fighting for survival, Yugoslavia was unable to spare any more resources for the Greek partisans. The other two major suppliers, Bulgaria and Albania, were now busy blockading their new ideological enemy, were also incapable of aiding the Greek Communist forces. Deprived of outside assistance, they were crushed by the superior British- and American-trained troops supporting the royalist government. Thus, the survival of the rebel Yugoslavia, achieved partly thanks to American aid, constituted a major setback for Moscow in what was now turning into the Cold War in Europe.

The Communist Victory in China

The situation in Asia initially seemed less promising. According to Lenin's theory of combating imperialism, the last stage of capitalism must be broken at its weakest links—the colonial areas. To achieve this objective, Asian Communists, supported by Moscow to varying degrees, played a leading role in a series of "national liberation struggles" that followed World War II. While in Europe the Cold War between the superpowers was played in conformity with certain ground rules that excluded the overt use of force, in Asia the situation was different. There pent-up socioeconomic forces, intermingled with bitter racial hatreds, tended to form a highly explosive mixture. The native radical anti-colonial forces, aided by the Soviet Union, more often than not resorted to violence. While in Europe Moscow was, on the whole, not effective beyond the boundaries fixed at Teheran, Yalta, and Potsdam (that is, Iran, Turkey, and Greece), "the national liberation wars" in Asia were by and large much more successful. This was especially true of China and Indochina.

Throughout the Chinese civil war (1946–1949), Stalin was less interested in the local Communist cause than in immediate economic and strategic gains. That disposition was reflected in particular in the bargain that Stalin struck with Chiang Kai-shek on August 14, 1945, which legitimized the arrangements formulated at Yalta. Chiang thereby sanctioned paramount Soviet influence both in Manchuria—China's most industrialized province and the strategic center of Northeast Asia—and in Outer Mongolia. In exchange Stalin agreed to do business in China with the anti-Communist Chiang Kai-shek's government only and to aid the eventual restoration of Kuomintang authority in Manchuria. During the war, at Stalin's directive, the Chinese Communists, led by Mao Tse-tung, had adopted a sort of truce arrangement with Chiang Kai-shek, which was to last as long as the hostilities against Japan were going on. While pursuing a policy of limited cooperation with Kuomintang forces in resisting the Japanese invasion, the Communists never abandoned their ultimate objective of grasping power. When the Japanese troops in the Far East surrendered in August 1945, the Big Three provided that in China the Japanese should yield to Chiang's forces with two exceptions. Japanese forces in Manchuria and North Korea north of the 38th parallel were to capitulate to the Red Army.

The suspicious Stalin repeatedly urged the Chinese Communists to disband their partisans, forget about the social revolution, and join Chiang Kai-shek's government. Mao would have none of it since his basic principle was that "the seizure of power by armed force is the central task and the highest form of revolution." Fortunately for him, many Red Army commanders acting on their own did hand to the Chinese Communists much of the weaponry taken from the Japanese Kwantung Army. During the years 1946–1949, this equipment, together with superior organization, morale, and leadership of Mao, greatly helped the Chinese Communists to defeat the Kuomintang forces. They skillfully applied partisan warfare based in the countryside, where they were supported by the land-hungry peasantry. By October 1949 Mao had chased the remnants of the Kuomintang forces to the island of Formosa (Taiwan) and a series of minor off-shore islands. Thus, the most populous country in the world, comprising nearly one-fourth of humanity, was now under Communist control. This seemed like the peak of the Communist influence in the world. Altogether about one-third of humanity now lived under the Marxist dictatorship!

Soon after they had seized power, the Chinese Communists launched a series of radical revolutionary reforms. To surpass his Soviet comrades, Mao attempted to encapsulate over two decades of their experiment into a few years. This was an adventurous policy which was a premature challenge to the Soviet leadership of the world Communist movement.

During the first several years the new masters of China, friendless and isolated, desperately needed outside aid for their country, ruined by nearly four decades of civil war. Since help could come only from the USSR, Mao had to adopt a humble posture despite his grudge toward Stalin, who regarded him as a potential rival. During Mao Tse-tung's first long visit to Moscow, which lasted from mid-December 1949 to February 1950, he was treated shabbily, like a poor cousin. He was given accommodations in a hotel, not in one of the palatial residences usually assigned to foreign dignitaries. He had to wait for several weeks to be received by

Stalin. But in the interim he did some very tough bargaining with condescending minor Soviet officials. In exchange for a token loan of $300,000 (a pittance in comparison with China's enormous needs!), the Soviets were allowed to retain temporarily their positions in Manchuria and the Kwantung peninsula, including such strategic harbors as Port Arthur and Dairen. Moreover, joint Russian-Chinese companies, with the Russians in control, were established to exploit Sinkiang's oil and mineral resources. These arrangements were not much different from the kinds of deals Standard Oil or Shell Petroleum made with Arab sheiks or colonial chieftains. Yet the exhausted Chinese had to suffer such indignities for the time being in order to survive the critical transition period.

What was a great triumph for world Communism proved a setback for Russia as a state—instead of a weak neighbor she now had a potential rival harboring inveterate territorial claims, centering on southern Siberia.

Wars in Korea and Indochina

Korea constituted another Asian front in the Cold War. In December 1945, some four months after Japan's surrender, a joint Soviet-United States commission tried to establish a provisional government for the whole country, but the plans never materialized. The Soviet military authorities, who controlled the area north of the 38th parallel, never permitted the commission to set foot on their territory. By February 1946 they were sponsoring their own North Korean government, headed by a Moscow-trained Communist, Kim Il Sung. In view of this, American authorities in the South decided to establish their own client administration. Thus Korea was divided into two segments along the 38th parallel, and like Germany, each was organized along different, mutually exclusive, and antagonistic principles. By June 1949 both protecting powers, believing that their tasks were finished, withdrew their forces—the Americans to Japan, and the

Russians to their Siberian and Manchurian bases.

For a year or so, Stalin sought to participate in the occupation and postwar control of Japan, no doubt anticipating the role it would eventually play in Asia. Frustrated by Washington opposition, he encouraged Kim Il Sung to absorb South Korea and the Chinese to help him. Stalin most probably calculated that a united Communist Korea would affect the Asian balance of power, but especially the still fluid situation in Japan. And indeed on June 25, 1950, following a speech by United States Secretary of State Dean Acheson, who had failed to mention South Korea as a part of the American defense perimeter in Asia, the Soviet-trained and equipped North Korean forces invaded South Korea without any provocation. Soon most of South Korea was in their hands.

In reply to this attack, President Truman ordered the American armed forces in the Pacific to come to the aid of South Korea. At the same time he submitted the case of the North Korean aggression to the United Nations Security Council, composed of delegates of five powers: the United States, the Soviet Union, Britain, France, and China. It happened that at that time the Soviet delegate was absent from the Council because he had walked out in protest at the refusal of the United Nations to admit Communist China. As a result, the USSR could not exercise its absolute veto power to block the Council's resolution condemning North Korea and ordering United Nations members to aid in resisting the aggression. Many countries responded and supported efforts by the United States to check the progress of the invasion. By the end of the year, the North Koreans had been repelled as far as the Yalu River, which forms the Korean-Chinese frontier. China responded to the possible security threat by sending in some 200,000 "volunteers." Together with the regrouped North Korean troops, the Communist forces regained most of the land and even recrossed the 38th parallel. They were soon pushed back, thanks to the American counteroffensive. By July 1951, truce negotiations were opened at Panmunjon. For two years the negotiations dragged on because of the controversial problem posed by the Korean and Chinese POWs. While the Western side wanted the voluntary principle to govern their reparation, the Communist representatives insisted that they be sent back home without asking them about their preferences.

As events in China and Korea were unfolding, still another Cold War front was taking shape in a former French colony, Indochina. There French rule lasted until May 1945, when the Japanese decided to occupy Indochina militarily, only three months before their own capitulation. This brief overthrow of the French colonial rule brought to the surface the native anti-Japanese, as well as anti-French, resistance movement led by a Paris-educated intellectual, Ho Chi Minh. In accordance with the armistice agreement, Kuomintang Chinese troops took over Northern Indochina, which had been a former dependency of Peking. Chiang Kai-shek, who opposed the restoration of French rule, generally cooperated in this task with Ho's partisans. While in Southern Indochina the British forces handed over their administration to the returning French colonial authorities, Chiang's reluctance to let the French officials in allowed Ho to consolidate his hold on the countryside and form a popular-front government. By February 1946, when the Chinese Nationalists, under the pressure of the Western powers, finally did allow the French to return to Northern Indochina, Ho was already well-established. Soon numerous points of friction between the old bureaucracy—which was most interested in protecting the French economic interests and those of the local landowners—and Ho's revolutionary movement resulted in a series of clashes between the French troops and the local partisans. By the end of 1946, the country was in a state of war. The first stage of this conflict was to last for eight years and to end with a French withdrawal. This in turn led to numerous complications that affected the relations among Moscow, Peking, and Washington for years to come.

Stalin and American Nuclear Monopoly

The Soviet-sponsored invasion of South Korea that followed the Berlin blockade, the formation of a Communist East German state, and the spectacular triumph of the Communists in China all alarmed the West. Moscow's influence in the world seemed to be at its peak. Washington interpreted the North Korean attack not in the local Asian context, but as an indication of escalated global Soviet militancy. By the mid-1950s, American leaders came to suspect that the pattern of the Korean "aggression by proxy" might be repeated to unite Germany under Communist rule, and thus threaten Western Europe. The aroused American sense of global insecurity precipitated two Washington decisions: first to rearm the Federal Republic of Germany and then to strengthen Japanese defenses by the formation of a native territorial army. At the same time, the program of American domestic rearmament was speeded up to cope with new prospective tasks and multiplying military commitments. This in turn further intensified the already formidable tension prevailing between the two superpowers and their respective allies and clients.

One factor seems particularly responsible for the successful containment of the intermittent Soviet encroachment on the Western sphere of influence in Europe and the Middle East (Berlin, Iran, Turkey). This factor was the initial monopoly of nuclear weapons by the West, especially the United States. By the early 1950s, the United States had acquired an enormous arsenal of offensive weapons, both nuclear and conventional, which were deployed at home, in Europe, in East Asia, and on the high seas in such a way as to be able to attack and destroy almost any other country on earth. On the basis of capability, if not intent, the United States was thus perceived by Stalin as a deadly threat. It was during the 1950s that the Cold War entered its most intense phase. Through his British and American spies, Stalin knew about the atom bomb already while at the Potsdam Conference, but pretended not to be impressed. It was no coincidence, however, that ten days after Hiroshima and Nagasaki the Gosplan was instructed by him to go full speed ahead with incorporating many military and civilian projects that would be helpful in furthering the development of Soviet nuclear weapons. At the same time, Stalin strained his intelligence network to achieve two purposes: first, to detect any symptoms of a possible enemy attack; second, to obtain further secrets of the atomic bomb from the West, and the United States in particular. When his hopes of sharing nuclear weapons with the United States were frustrated, he decided to combine whatever scientific know-how was available at home with secrets obtained abroad and begin a crash program to build his own atom bomb at any price. The main Soviet atomic polygons were the vast steppes of Kazakhstan.

For four years or so the United States had a monopoly on the atom bomb, and hence the capacity to obliterate Soviet cities and defense installations. Moscow, on the other hand, despite its huge military establishment kept on a partial war footing, would not be able to retaliate in kind. Projecting his own way of reasoning, Stalin expected an American-instigated invasion of the Soviet Union before it could develop its own nuclear weapons. The system of global alliances so rapidly built up by Washington since 1947 confirmed his suspicion. As Nikita Khrushchev reported in his memoirs, Stalin lived in constant terror of an American attack and kept the anti-aircraft guns around Moscow on a twenty-four hour alert. Since during the 1940s and 1950s, before the full-scale development of rockets, the main military threat was from manned bombers carrying nuclear weapons, the greatest possible depth for defense seemed vital. Hence Stalin's emphasis on the rapid consolidation of a vast buffer zone of Communist-dominated satellite states. The existence of uranium mines in some of them, like Czechoslovakia, made it doubly necessary to keep the area under tight military and political control. At the same time, he ordered a redoubling of the Soviet spying activity in the West, especially in the United States, to obtain as many details of the nuclear secrets as possible.

Meanwhile, NATO came into being in the spring of 1949, the economic recovery of Western Europe was well under way, and the situation in the West became stabilized. In Greece the Communist partisans had been crushed, West Berlin had been successfully defended, and Yugoslavia had become independent. The Western ascendancy did not last for long, however. No sooner had the North Atlantic Treaty been ratified than, at the end of August 1949, a United States aircraft flying over the Pacific collected a radioactive air sample; this was fallout from a recently exploded Soviet atom bomb. This meant that the Russians had managed to explode it three years ahead of the schedule anticipated by the Pentagon. This momentous event, followed by Mao's triumph over Chiang Kai-shek's forces on the mainland of China, further escalated international tensions.

The unexpectedly rapid development of the Soviet atomic bomb was followed by the completion of deliverable hydrogen warheads during the early 1950s. Both these events took the West by surprise. The USSR's very possession of nuclear weapons profoundly affected the global rivalry between the superpowers. From then on, what Winston Churchill termed the "balance of terror" became a dominant factor in the strategic situation.[3] For some 40 years the Soviet Union and the United States watched each other like two scorpions in a bottle.

[3] Only in 1990 did the Soviet Union admit that their bombs exploded in 1953, had no deliverable hydrogen warheads. It was, therefore, no military threat; it weighed sixty-five tons and no airplane was big enough to carry it. The United States exploded the world's first hydrogen bomb in November 1952.

Suggested Reading

BANAC, IVO, *With Stalin against Tito.* Ithaca, NY: Cornell University Press, 1988.

BRZEZINSKI, ZBIGNIEW, *The Soviet Bloc: Unity and Conflict,* 2nd ed. Cambridge, MA: Harvard University Press, 1961.

COUNTS, GEORGE S., *The Country of the Blind: The Soviet System of Mind Control.* Westport, CT: Greenwood, 1959.

DEDIJER, VLADIMIR, *Tito.* New York: Arno, 1972.

DJILAS, MILOVAN, *The New Class: An Analysis of the Communist System.* New York: Praeger, 1957.

FEIS, HERBERT, *The China Tangle: The American Effort in China from Pearl Harbor to the Marshall Mission.* Princeton, NJ: Princeton University Press, 1953.

GROSS, JAN T., *Revolution from Abroad: The Soviet Conquest of Poland's Western Ukraine and Western Belorussia.* Princeton, NJ: Princeton University Press, 1988.

HAHN, WERNER G., *Postwar Soviet Politics: The Fall of Zhdanov and the Defeat of Moderation, 1946–1953.* Ithaca, NY: Cornell University Press, 1982.

HAYNES, JOHN EARL, AND HARVEY KLEHR, *Venona: Decoding Soviet Espionage in America.* New Haven, CT: Yale University Press, 1999.

HOFFMAN, GEORGE W., *Yugoslavia and the New Communism.* Millwood, NY: Kraus, 1962.

HOLLOWAY, DAVID, *Stalin and the Bomb: The Soviet Union and Atomic Energy, 1939–1956.* New Haven, CT: Yale University Press, 1994.

KERSTEN, KRYSTYNA, *The Establishment of Communist Rule in Poland, 1943–1948.* Berkeley: University of California Press, 1991.

LAFEBER, WALTER, *America, Russia, and the Cold War, 1945–1971,* 2nd ed. New York: Wiley, 1972.

LEE, WILLIAM T., AND RICHARD F. STARR, *Soviet Military Policy Since World War II.* Foreword by William R. Van Cleave. Stanford, CA: Hoover Institution, 1986.

LEVIN, NORA, *The Jews in the Soviet Union: A History from 1917 to the Present.* New York: New York University Press, 1988.

LISKA, GEORGE, *Russia and World Order: Strategic Choices and the Laws of Power in History.* Baltimore, MD: Johns Hopkins University Press, 1980.

MASTNY, VOJTECH, *Russia's Road to the Cold War: Diplomacy, Warfare and the Politics of Communism, 1941–1945.* New York: Columbia University Press, 1979.

MCLANE, CHARLES B., *Soviet Strategies in South East Asia: An Explanation of Eastern Policy under Lenin and Stalin.* Princeton, NJ: Princeton University Press, 1966.

MIKOLAJCZYK, STANISLAW, *The Pattern of Soviet Domination.* London: Sampson Low, Marston, 1948.

NAMARK, NORMAN M., *The Russians in Germany: A History of the Soviet Zone of Occupation, 1945–1949.* Cambridge, MA: Harvard University Press, 1995.

NETTL, J. P., *The Eastern Zone and Soviet Policy in Germany, 1945–1950.* New York: Oxford University Press, 1951.

RAACK, R. C., *Stalin's Drive to the West, 1938–1945: The Origins of the Cold War.* Stanford, CA: Stanford University Press, 1995.

REMEIKIS, THOMAS, *Opposition to Soviet Rule in Lithuania, 1945–1980.* Chicago: Institute of Lithuanian Studies Press, 1980.

RORLICH, AZADE-AYSE, *The Volga Tatars.* Stanford, CA: Hoover Institution, 1986.

STARR, RICHARD F., *Poland 1944–1962: The Sovietization of a Captive People.* Baton Rouge: Louisiana State University Press, 1962.

SUDOPLATOV, PAVEL AND ANATOLI SUDOPLATOV, *Special Tasks: The Memoirs of an Unwanted Witness— A Soviet Spymaster.* Boston: Little, Brown, 1994.

ULAM, ADAM B., *Dangerous Relations.* New York: Oxford University Press, 1983.

———, *Titoism and the Cominform.* Westport, CT: Greenwood, 1971.

VAKSBERG, ARKADY, *Stalin Against the Jews.* New York: Vintage, 1995.

ZINNER, PAUL E., *Communist Strategy and Tactics in Czechoslovakia, 1918–1948.* New York: Praeger, 1963.

ZWASS, ADAM, *The Council for Mutual Economic Assistance.* Armonk, NY: M. E. Sharpe, 1989.

Chapter 20

Stalin's Death and the Twentieth Party Congress

During the postwar years, Stalin continued his life style: hard work during the day, heavy drinking at night. All the time he was preoccupied with his place in history. Would he be considered greater than Peter the Great? What achievements would testify to his superiority? This obsession with the future made Stalin launch a series of gigantic projects that were to leave his name permanently engraved on the face of the country and thus testify forever to his might. Officially these projects were aimed at "transforming nature," yet they were really to serve as Stalin's memorials. Huge dams, canals, and hydroelectric stations were to be constructed on the Dnieper, the Don, and the Volga. Enormous skyscrapers to rival those of Manhattan were to be erected in Moscow. The fact that the sandy and often marshy soil of the region did not lend itself to this sort of building was overlooked. All these projects were on such a gigantic scale as to eclipse the most impressive kinds of similar accomplishments in the rest of the world, even the Egyptian pyramids.

Biology and Linguistics

The intensely transformist outlook of Stalin's last years was reflected in the 1948 debate about biology. The debate centered mostly around two individuals and their allegedly scientific theories: Ivan V. Michurin and Trofim D. Lysenko. While "Michurinism" and "Lysenkism" were officially supported even before the war, in 1948 Stalin went so far as to formally outlaw Gregor Mendel's classic theory, which emphasized the decisive importance of hereditary as opposed to environmental influences. By 1948, all agricultural and genetic research and all teaching were to conform to Michurinism-Lysenkism. The new theory about the possibility of inheriting acquired characteristics and consequently of transformation of species was enforced.

The Lysenko affair was characteristic of the aging dictator's growing megalomania. His manipulative approach was imposed on many areas of Soviet thought. Stalin interpreted the theories of Michurin and Lysenko as containing a doctrine of the transformation of organisms on the biological level. His materialistic view of human beings made him wonder whether these discoveries could also be applied to society. If Michurinism–Lysenkism could produce new species of plants, might it not be used as an instrument of creating a new species: Soviet men and women?

This concept haunted the Soviet leader more and more. In the process he came to rediscover the teachings of Ivan Pavlov about conditioned reflexes. The Pavlovian theory fitted well Stalin's mentality and his conviction that human beings are kin of signal-receiving robots. He decided that the Pavlovian theory should be applied not only in physiology and medicine, but also in education. Here was a formula that seemed ideally suited to the process that would mold human beings in accordance with a set of well-coordinated verbal commands to create a new person—Soviet man. This was connected with Stalin's attitude toward linguistics. The ringing of a bell was sufficient in the case of Pavlov's dogs to make their saliva flow in anticipation of being fed. Human beings, however, needed a more complex set of signals to follow their Master's will, concluded Stalin; so he began to study ways to use language as a vital instrument of political indoctrination.

As a result of these reflections, in 1950 Stalin initiated a public debate on the relationship between Marxism and the theory of language. Prior to that time the officially accepted theory was that of Soviet linguist, Nikolai Marr, who considered language part of the superstructure of society. It was a central theorem of Marxism that a society's superstructure is determined by its economic base. Consequently, as society's socioeconomic base was fundamentally reshaped by Socialism-Communism, the linguistic superstructure must also change. When Communism would triumph on a world scale, these changes were bound to be reflected in a new global *lingua franca*, the "language of Socialism." This theory was now rejected by Stalin as too mechanical and cosmopolitan. Stalin declared that language was not only inde-

pendent of socioeconomic changes; it was even capable of influencing them profoundly. He rejected the idea of a merger of languages and declared that in a Communist world federation, one superior language would triumph. The promotion of Russian as the language of Communism was in line with the spreading glorification of all things Russian and the growing emphasis on the universal significance of the Soviet State, led by its most worthy component, the Great Russian stock.

The Nineteenth Party Congress

Meanwhile, adulation of Stalin continued to grow.[1] It reached its peak during the last major public affair attended by the dictator, the Nineteenth Party Congress. The Congress, the first in thirteen years, gathered in Moscow on October 5, 1952. By that time Stalin was seventy-three years old. He was present at the deliberations but took no active part in them; like a silent demigod he remained in the background.

The main report at the Congress was delivered by his henchman, Gregory M. Malenkov. He was the first person other than Stalin to do so since 1923. The report faithfully echoed the master's main ideas. The slogan "struggle for peace" was featured prominently not only in most key speeches, but also in many resolutions. The international "peace offensive" that Stalin had launched immediately after the war was to redouble its efforts. The offensive represented an attempt by the Soviets to blame the Western powers for the Cold War; the offensive was intended to foster pro-Soviet,

---

[1]An American correspondent in Moscow, Harrison Salisbury, reported that at the Soviet Art Exhibit of 1949 at the Tretyakov Galleries, nearly 70 of the 600 works entered in the exhibition depicted some aspect of Stalin's life. Salisbury stressed that the Soviet censor removed from his dispatch to New York the words "nearly 70 of," thus leaving the impression that all were devoted to Stalin. Harrison Salisbury, *Moscow Journal* (Chicago: University of Chicago Press, 1961), p. 82.

but not necessarily pro-Communist, sentiments among leftist and pacifist elements in the West.

The Congress also belatedly sanctioned the Fifth Five-Year Plan (1951–1955), which focused on the final rehabilitation of war damages and the assimilation of the newly incorporated territories as well as those of the vassal states of East-Central Europe. The Fifth Five-Year Plan was based on old patterns: It anticipated the further rapid expansion of heavy industry; it continued to neglect agriculture and the need for consumer goods.

By a show of hands, the delegates unanimously rubber-stamped a radical reshuffling of the Party's top structure. The Politburo and the Orgburo were merged and renamed "Presidium of the Party Central Committee." The Presidium was enlarged: it was to be composed of twenty-five members, not eleven, as in the past. Another attempt to water down the old top Party apparatus was made by expanding the Central Committee's Secretariat from five to ten members. Prior to the Congress, the Secretariat (besides Secretary General Stalin) was composed of five members: Gregory M. Malenkov, Deputy Premier of the USSR; Averky R. Aristov, Secretary of the Chelyabinsk province, or *oblast*; Nikita S. Khrushchev, first Secretary of the Moscow oblast; Mikhail A. Suslov, editor of *Pravda* and the Soviet delegate to the Cominform; and Pantaleymon K. Ponamarenko, the former premier of Belorussia and since 1950, Soviet Minister of Supplies. To this old team were now added five younger, little-known people. Among them was Leonid I. Brezhnev, a Party member only since 1931, an engineer by profession, First Party Secretary in the Moldavian Soviet Republic since 1950, and not yet a member of the other key Soviet body, the Politburo.

The reorganization of the top Soviet governing bodies was a reflection of Stalin's paranoid mistrust of the small group of his closest co-workers, like the eleven-member Politburo. He wanted to weaken their established position by watering down the body's membership with younger bureaucrats entirely drilled in Stalin's school of silence, obedience, and strict discipline. Parallel with these changes in the internal Party machinery were changes in its external appearance. The term "Bolshevik," which had followed in brackets the words "Communist Party of the Soviet Union," was now dropped. This, together with suppression of the traditional terms Politburo and Orgburo represented further attempts to discard the past and create a new image of the Soviet Union.

Because Stalin had designated Malenkov to deliver the main report at the Nineteenth Party Congress, and Malenkov, as Deputy Premier, was the dictator's closest co-worker, his eventual assumption of power was taken for granted. After all, Malenkov was also a member of both the newly created Presidium and the expanded Secretariat. Only Khrushchev, also a member of both key bodies, could match his accumulation of political power.

Stalin's Death

Following the noisy celebration of his seventieth birthday on December 21, 1949, Stalin became more and more sullen, suspicious, and isolated—even from his close co-workers. He excluded them from important decision making, often insulted them, and even threatened his close henchmen; for instance, shortly before the Nineteenth Party Congress, Stalin publicly called Molotov and Voroshilov British spies, and Mikoyan (who was an Armenian) a Turkish spy. Soon Molotov lost his ministry of foreign affairs for he had incurred Stalin's displeasure because of his Jewish wife, who was sent, without her husband's protest, to a labor camp. Even Stalin's closest henchmen like Voroshilov and Beria were not entirely free from danger. Not until Khrushchev's speeches of February 25–26, 1956, did the outside world learn that most of the Leningrad party leadership associated with the former virtual dictator of the ideological sector, Zhdanov, had been destroyed in the secret purge known as the "Leningrad affair." In 1949, the life of future Soviet prime minister Alexei Kosygin was, as Khrushchev, put it, "hanging by a thread." The Leningrad purge apparently had been arranged by Beria and Malenkov to eliminate a group of potential contenders for power. Between 1946 and 1953, selective arrests had again become a standard feature of Stalin's last phase.

Since 1939, Beria had been the chief of the security apparatus and hence the main instrument of Stalin's repressive policies. Yet, after the Nineteenth Congress, in November 1952, Beria was mysteriously implicated in a "nationalistic plot in Mingrelia," a province of Georgia and Beria's native region, where he had many intimate ties. The discovery of the "Mingrelian plot" was followed by the arrest of several of Beria's close associates. All of the arrests were carried out on Stalin's orders. Since it was his habit eventually to turn all his past chiefs of police into scapegoats of one sort or another, these arrests could be interpreted by Beria only as ominous signs.

Meanwhile, the anti-Zionist campaign continued. There is some evidence that Stalin intended to deport Jews from the great urban centers of the European USSR to Siberia. On January 3, 1953, nine distinguished doctors, most of them of Jewish extraction were arrested. They soon allegedly confessed that they had murdered Zhdanov and other high Soviet dignitaries at the instigation of the CIA. "The doctors' plot" seemed to be concocted to justify the planned mass deportations of the Jewish population.

Amidst the rumors accompanying these plots, faked accusations, and arrests, it was suddenly announced on the night of March 4, 1953, that Stalin had suffered a massive brain hemorrhage and as a result was losing the power of speech. On March 5 came the solemn announcement. As the official communiqué declared: "The heart of the comrade-in-arms and brilliant continuer of the work of Lenin, of the wise leader and teacher of the Communist party and the Soviet peo-

The official picture of Stalin circulated on May Day, 1953

ple—Joseph Vissarionovich STALIN—has ceased to beat." Four days later he was buried with great pomp in the Lenin mausoleum in Red Square. The tomb was immediately renamed the Lenin-Stalin mausoleum. To show that from now on there would be no personal dictatorship, but a collective leadership, three speakers in succession bade farewell to their former boss: Molotov, Malenkov, and Beria. The latter's well-armed and ubiquitous security forces, massively displayed during the burial ceremonies, controlled the situation in the capital.

Stalin's disappearance from the scene represented an event of the first magnitude. Since the mid-1920s, he had become *the* central institution of the Soviet Party-State, linked so closely with the image of the USSR that many outsiders had come to identify the two. After almost three decades of his rule, most people had gotten used to their terrible master. Up until March 1953, everything had been enacted and justified in Stalin's name. Suddenly this seemingly immortal deity vanished, creating a huge power vacuum. The official communiqué of Stalin's death was intended to console the people. It stated: "The immortal name *Stalin* will always live in the hearts of the Soviet people and of all progressive mankind."

The Emergence of Khrushchev

During the transition period following Stalin's death, power was indeed in the hands of the three members of the Presidium who had given his funeral oration: Malenkov, also a deputy premier and the Party's senior secretary; Beria, chief of state security; and Molotov, a one-time foreign minister, who immediately aligned himself with Beria. Forgetting the lesson of nearly three decades, hypnotized by Stalin's recent practice of stressing governmental instruments of power rather than party institutions, his successors focused their attention on what seemed to them the main prize: the premiership of the USSR.

The day after the announcement of Stalin's death, a joint meeting of the Central Committee, the Council of Ministers, and the Presidium of the Supreme Soviet, at Beria's suggestion, designated Malenkov as Prime Minister. Malenkov repaid the favor by proposing a merger of the recently split ministries of Internal Affairs (MVD) and State Security (MGB) into one ministry with Beria as its head. Molotov became First Deputy Premier while regaining control of the Ministry of Foreign Affairs. Voroshilov became chairman of the Presidium of the Supreme Soviet or official Head of State. Marshal Zhukov, perhaps the most popular man in the country, was recalled to active duty and made Minister of Defense. At the same time, the Presidium of the Central Committee was reduced to fourteen members and candidates to resemble the old Politburo. Full voting members were listed in the following order: Malenkov, Beria, Molotov, Voroshilov, Khrushchev, Bulganin, Kaganovich, Mikoyan, Saburov, and Pervukhin. This meant that Khrushchev, then fifty-nine years old, was only in fifth place.

Yet as early as March 14, 1953, the world was surprised to learn that the Central Committee accepted Malenkov's sudden resignation from the position of First Secretary of the Party's Central Committee so that he could devote himself to governmental work as Prime Minister. Khrushchev, the only

Party secretary who was also a member of the Presidium, took over Malenkov's Party post as First Secretary of the Party, the main locus of power.

Khrushchev was born in 1894, the son of a small farmer from the Kursk province in southern Russia, bordering Ukraine. He went through only three years of formal schooling and initially eked out a living as a miner and locksmith. In 1918, at the age of twenty-four, he joined the ranks of the Bolshevik Party and fought in the Civil War. Soon he caught the attention of Stalin's proconsul in the Ukraine, Kaganovich, who enlisted him for organizational work. In 1929, Khrushchev was rewarded for his loyal services by being transferred to Moscow to study at the Industrial Academy while doing work in the central Party apparatus. Vigorous, loquacious, sly, and ruthless, Khrushchev rose swiftly. In 1931, he was already Party Secretary of the largest and most crucial Moscow city district. In 1934, he was elected a member of the Central Committee

Nikita S. Khrushchev, member of the Politburo since 1938 and Secretary of the Central Committee since 1949

and four years later was entrusted with the responsibility for Party work in the entire Moscow province. In 1938, he became an alternate member of the Politburo; the next year he was promoted to the crucial post of a full-fledged member. After being Stalin's cruel emissary in Ukraine between 1938 and 1949, while intermittently acting as a high-ranking political commissar during the war, Khrushchev returned to Moscow. During the period 1947–1949, he quarreled with his former protector, Kaganovich, who had accused Khrushchev of "insufficient vigilance" toward Ukrainian nationalism. Stalin's death found Khrushchev occupying three strategic posts, all crucial in the coming struggle: He was not only Party Secretary of the Moscow province, but also a member of the two key bodies, the Presidium and the Secretariat of the Party. These posts provided him with a firm triple power base. Yet, it appeared that he could never aspire to supreme power because of his simplistic mind, lack of serious theoretical training, and extreme crudeness of manner. Consequently, he was generally underestimated.

The Thaw and the Downfall of Beria

While avoiding open criticism of the late dictator, yet wanting to contrast the "new course" with his policies and practices, the collective leadership initiated a series of small concessions, step by step. On April 3, Beria himself declared that the "doctors' plot" had been a hoax, charged one of his assistants, M. D. Riumin, with responsibility for it, and had him arrested. Beria further admitted that "inadmissible" methods had been used by State security agents in interrogating suspects. The doctors, as well as those implicated in the "Mingrelian plot," were released and rehabilitated. These events were sensational. For the first time Soviet security organs were apologizing and going back on their word. The concessions announced by Beria were soon emulated by a move of Premier Malenkov. He ordered wider distribution of food, especially grain,

and promised the Soviet people more consumer goods "in two or three years."

These concessions were paralleled by a slight relaxation of censorship and regulations concerning foreign travel. All of these moves instantly created a new political and moral climate. The mood of hope and the sense of relief felt by many people in the spring and summer of 1953 were captured by a perceptive observer of the Soviet scene, Ilya Ehrenburg, in a novel bearing a significant title, *The Thaw*. This title gave a name to the immediate post-Stalin period.

In the ongoing popularity contest, Khrushchev remained initially a spectator. Yet he was soon to enter the race with a trump card of his own, the spot of the First Secretary of the Central Committee. His first step was the removal of his most dangerous rival, Beria.

Although in theory the Soviet Union was controlled by the Party, Beria's ubiquitous system of State security, which had previously been subordinate only to Stalin himself, cast a sinister shadow over everybody. After Stalin's death, Beria reorganized his now all-encompassing controls by uniting in his hand two key ministries: Internal Affairs and State Security. It soon became obvious to everybody, even to his friend Malenkov, that Beria was determined to use his power to further his own ambitions. At the time of Stalin's burial, Beria ordered several divisions of the Ministry of Internal Affairs to the city to maintain order. After the funeral these divisions were not sent back to their regular garrisons. Shortly after Stalin's death, a general amnesty had been declared for prisoners serving sentences of less than five years. While this did not include most political prisoners, whose minimum term was normally from eight to twenty-five years, it applied mostly to common criminals. Thus thousands of criminals appeared in Moscow and other cities, and the crime rate soared and caused general public indignation. This, in turn, gave Beria an excuse to retain his large contingents in the capital.

These and other similar measures alarmed his former allies and precipitated a plot; it was organized by Khrushchev and supported by the military establishment, including Marshals Zhukov and Koniev. The conspirators acted with remarkable speed and determination. On June 28, 1953, Beria's guards at the Kremlin and the Central Committee building were suddenly replaced by regular Army sentries. Meanwhile, Army units surrounded and blockaded the key buildings in Moscow. Trapped in the Kremlin, Beria was arrested by two marshals, summarily tried, and soon executed. Over a period of several days most of Beria's henchmen and regional security officials were also arrested and shot.

Beria's downfall meant cutting down to size the Secret Police, which was now purged and reorganized and subordinate to the Party rather than a potential menace to its primacy. Soon after Beria's execution, some of his trusted men in various Soviet satrapies were removed from their key positions one by one. This resulted in a considerable weakening of the whole Soviet security network not only in the Soviet Union, but also in Eastern Europe where its branches were totally dependent on Moscow.

The investigation of Beria's activities revealed his monstrous crimes and the scope of reprisals that surpassed even the imagination of the former conspirators, no strangers to Stalin's system of bloody repression. Meanwhile, the courts were flooded with millions of appeals for review of the mostly fabricated cases of people still in prisons and camps. The country's judicial apparatus could not deal with so many requests. Yet, of the 12 to 13 million people who had been in concentration camps during Stalin's time, only about 4,000 were released in 1953, but even this small trickle from the "Gulag Archipelago" was to have a great impact on the climate of public opinion. Those released were mostly people with political connections; consequently, they generated more pressure for the further release or rehabilitation of the surviving political inmates. This led to the creation of the Special Investigating Committee and a net of extraordinary,

temporary judicial commissions to deal with between five and six million cases.

The Virgin Lands' Campaign

The removal of the most vicious rival in the struggle for power, the Soviet "godfather," narrowed the competition to two men: Malenkov and Khrushchev. Since it was Khrushchev who had initiated and engineered Beria's demise, the former's position was now bolstered. On the other hand, the position of Malenkov, who had been much more closely associated with Stalin, was weakened.

While the problem of the "excesses of the past period" was being investigated, the most immediate issue was that of food shortages caused by the lamentable state of Soviet agriculture. The 1953 harvest was exceptionally poor. In September 1953, Khrushchev delivered a major public address sharply criticizing the condition of the Soviet countryside. He pointed out its sorry state and admitted that the total number of cattle was now lower than in 1916, the third year of the devastating World War I. Stating that the "agriculture" had become a major bottleneck for further development, he promised its reorganization along more efficient lines. Since Malenkov had been, during the postwar years, mainly responsible for the whole economy, including its agrarian sector, the target of Khrushchev's accusations was unmistakable. To provide more incentives to the apathetic collective farmers, Khrushchev decreed three immediate measures. First, prices for compulsory deliveries of food were to be considerably increased; second, the criminal prosecution for nonfulfillment of compulsory norms was now to be replaced by fines; and third, taxes on the output of household plots were dramatically lowered.

In February 1954, Khrushchev announced that to end the chronic grain shortage the available arable land of North Kazakhstan and West Siberia should be plowed. Using various methods, mixing encouragement with coercion, he dispatched to those lands thousands of young peasants and party workers to turn the "virgin lands" into a "new granary of the Soviet Union." This mass migration of mostly Russian people altered the entire composition of North Kazakstan; the local population was overwhelmingly swamped by a wave of Slavs, numbering 1 to 1½ million. The first harvest seemed to justify fully the great drive. By 1956, the tilled land of the USSR had increased by some 87 million acres, or nearly 50 percent. In January 1955, Khrushchev launched another drive for the cultivation of more corn, or "the sausage on a stalk," as he put it. The expansion of corn fields from 10 to 70 million acres was to provide the main source of concentrated fodder for Soviet cattle. By 1970, argued Khrushchev, the USSR should "overtake the United States in meat and milk production per capita." One of the chief supporters of Khrushchev in his effort to farm the virgin lands was the then First Party Secretary in Kazakhstan, Leonid Brezhnev (see Chapter 21).

Relaxation of the cruel Stalinist rule at home and a series of Soviet concessions abroad had numerous repercussions in the USSR and throughout its satellite empire. In the spring of 1953 there was an uprising of the inmates of the huge Vorkuta and Karagand labor camps and minor riots in various Czechoslovak industrial centers. In June East Berlin workers rose in revolt against the high labor norms prescribed by the State and inhuman working conditions in their factories. All these disturbances were brutally put down. In the case of the East Berlin rebellion, Soviet troops and tanks helped the East German army and the security apparatus to suppress the revolt. At the same time, symptoms of dangerous intellectual unrest could be observed in Hungary and Poland.

Malenkov Replaced by Bulganin

In December 1954 and January 1955, the conflict between the Prime Minister, Malenkov, and the First Party Secretary,

Khrushchev, intensified. It first surfaced in the form of a press polemic in which *Izvestia*, the State newspaper, and *Pravda*, the Party paper, took opposite points of view for the first time in Soviet history. While *Izvestia* stressed the need for more consumer goods, *Pravda* denounced such tendencies as a "rightist deviation" reminiscent of the revisionist "Bukharinism." This was a unique event: nothing of this sort had occurred in Soviet Russia for over a quarter of a century.

It was obvious that the press debate was an outward symptom of a behind-the-scenes struggle for power. An official communiqué issued on February 8, 1955, announcing Malenkov's resignation as Premier of the USSR. In an unusually frank public self-critique, Malenkov repudiated his former ideas about producing more consumer goods and confessed his "inexperience" in the affairs of State. Malenkov went so far as to assume full responsibility for "the unsatisfactory state of affairs in agriculture." Malenkov, although demoted from premiership, still retained his post in the policy-making Presidium. On Khrushchev's motion, the Supreme Soviet elected Minister of Defense Marshal Nikolai A. Bulganin as Premier.

Bulganin was another classic product of the Stalinist *nomenklatura*. One year younger than Khrushchev, he had joined the Bolshevik Party in 1917, a year before Khrushchev, and since 1922 had devoted his energies to administrative work. In 1934, he became a member of the Central Committee, and in 1948 was selected by Stalin for membership in the Politburo. Simultaneously, from 1937 to 1938, Bulganin was Premier of the Russian Republic. During the war, promoted to the rank of general, Bulganin had acted as a junior member of the top defense council and also, since 1944, as a political commissar on several fronts and as the Deputy People's Commissar for Defense. At the end of the war he was made a marshal. From 1947 to 1949 and from 1953 to 1955, he acted as Defense Minister and at the same time, between 1947 and 1955, as Deputy Premier of the USSR. Khrushchev had probably selected Bulganin as his partner because of his wide administrative background and varied connections with the bureaucratic machine, the "military-industrial complex," and the security apparatus. He had experience but lacked brilliance, and was familiar with administrative routine without having real political ambition. He could act as Khrushchev's solid alter ego without threatening him or outshining his histrionic and mercurial personality.

Thus the "collective leadership" underwent further transformation; it was now led by Khrushchev and seconded by Bulganin; Malenkov, Molotov, and others were relegated more and more to the background. Despite his downfall, Malenkov suffered no hardships. The fact that he was not killed was a novelty in the hitherto deadly game of Soviet politics.

Foreign Policy of the Collective Leadership

Soon the "collective leadership" initiated a conciliatory foreign policy that would reduce the main points of friction between the USSR and its Western opponents. One of the first steps was the agreement to sign the Korean armistice in July 1953. The conclusion of the armistice, which reconfirmed the 38th parallel as the line dividing South Korea from North Korea, was made possible by Soviet, North Korean, and Chinese acceptance of Washington's demand that the repatriation of POWs be voluntary. This was a bitter pill to swallow, for some three-quarters of the Chinese "volunteers" who had fought on the side of the North Koreans decided not to return home but to go to Taiwan.

In January 1954, the Council of Foreign Ministers convened again in Berlin, after years of inactivity, to discuss peace treaties for Germany and Austria. While nothing was accomplished as far as the German treaty was concerned, the council decided to hold a conference in Geneva to deal with Austria and with the problems created by the French withdrawal from Indochina. The

participants confirmed the partitioning of the former French colony. It was agreed that Ho Chi Minh's forces controlled the north, but his Communist partisans were to be withdrawn from the south. At Geneva, Soviet Foreign Minister Molotov supported the Chinese, who urged Ho to stabilize the area. In September 1954, Khrushchev and Bulganin traveled to Peking, where a second Sino-Soviet treaty returned Manchuria to Chinese sovereignty and promised to do the same to Port Arthur. This the Soviets did by May 1955. The scope of Soviet assistance to China was expanded, but Peking still had to pay for it.

Meanwhile, after protracted negotiations, in May 1955 the Russians promised to withdraw their forces from Austria, provided that the Western powers did likewise; moreover, they agreed to the permanent neutralization of that country. The Austrian treaty considerably relaxed international tensions and resulted in the first meeting of top Soviet representatives with their Western counterparts in neutral Switzerland. In July 1955, Khrushchev and Bulganin traveled to Geneva to meet United States President Dwight Eisenhower and Secretary of State John Foster Dulles, British Prime Minister Anthony Eden, and Premier Edgar Faure of France. Although such crucial questions as disarmament and the reunification of Germany were discussed without success, some progress in East-West trade and cultural exchanges was made. The summit meeting in Geneva was followed by the abandonment of the Soviet naval base in Porkkala near Helsinki; in September 1955 it was handed back to the Finns, albeit in a state of utter devastation. These achievements, preceded by the signing of the Austrian peace treaty, were hailed as the dawn of a new era of peaceful coexistence. The "spirit of Geneva" became a slogan used to designate the momentary relaxation of the tensions so characteristic of the previous decade.

While making these concessions, the Khrushchev-Bulganin team undertook some measures to strengthen the inner structure of the Soviet camp. At a meeting in Warsaw in

May 1955, representatives of the USSR and its satellite countries, Albania, Bulgaria, Czechoslovakia, the German Democratic Republic, Hungary, Poland, and Romania signed an agreement that would coordinate their defense preparations and place their forces under the command of Marshal Koniev. The *Warsaw Pact* was Moscow's response to progressive remilitarization of West Germany and the resulting strengthening of NATO. By playing up the issue of alleged West German revanchism, Moscow hoped to achieve a measure of popular support in countries like Poland and Czechoslovakia, where the threat of possible German territorial vindications was still a useful instrument of Soviet control. The main advantage of the Warsaw Pact, however, was that it provided an additional contractual basis for the continued stationing of Soviet troops in some of the satellites. As a result of the Warsaw Treaty, the USSR gained another degree of control over its East Central European neighbors. They were now not only economically linked to the USSR by the Council of Mutual Economic Assistance, but also by the umbrella of the multilateral Warsaw Treaty, which was superimposed over the original military arrangements of the immediate postwar period.

The year 1955 also witnessed the first Soviet steps toward extending the geographical range of Soviet foreign policy beyond its traditional continental orientation. Khrushchev made bold attempts at penetrating the Middle East by exploiting the tensions resulting from the Arab-Israeli armistice of 1949. Here his efforts to emancipate Egypt from Western tutelage stood him in good stead. The emergence of Colonel Gamal Nasser as an ambitious leader anxious to modernize the country and regain full sovereignty over the vital Suez Canal was skillfully exploited by Khrushchev. In the summer of 1955, the new Soviet Foreign Minister, Dmitri T. Shepilov, who had replaced Stalin's old crony, Molotov, visited Cairo and offered Nasser economic and military assistance, which the West had been hesitant to provide. Meanwhile, Khrushchev and Bulganin made a triumphant journey through India, Burma,

and Afghanistan. Thus, while proclaiming "peaceful coexistence," they bolstered the Soviet influence in the "Third World."

Reconciliation with Tito

The most dramatic reversal of Stalin's foreign policy, however, concerned Yugoslavia. During the early 1950s, after two or three years of resistance to Moscow, Tito—motivated overwhelmingly by his desire to stay in power—began to change his strategy. Unable to find ideological justification for his disobedience to the Center, and with his protestations of loyalty scorned by Moscow, he reoriented his line, domestic as well as foreign. Suspended between the Soviet and Western camps, like Mohammed between heaven and earth, Tito decided to rationalize his precarious situation by devising the theory of "active neutrality." He proclaimed his position as uncommitted to either side and promised to pursue a policy of defending the interests of the Third World against both West and East. Soon Tito attacked every aspect of Soviet policies, both foreign and domestic. He accused the Soviet Union of having transformed the "once independent East European states . . . into mere colonies in the heart of Europe." He placed full responsibility upon the USSR for having "pushed Northern Korea into an aggressive war." He bewailed the fact that some of the non-Russian nationalities were "erased from the earth's surface."

These attacks were combined with liberalization of the Yugoslav political and economic system. Economic planning was decentralized. Most of the collectivized land was gradually returned to the peasants, self-government in the form of workers' councils was instituted in the factories, and later some elements of a market economy were introduced. All this had a demoralizing effect on other Eastern European Communists, smarting under Moscow's rigid control, and envying Tito's freedom. What was worse, Yugoslavia, threatened by its Communist neighbors Albania, Bulgaria, Romania, and

Hungary, began to draw nearer to Greece and Turkey, both members of NATO.

Concluding that Stalin's mistaken policy toward Yugoslavia was increasingly counterproductive, Khrushchev decided to change it and woo Tito back to the Soviet fold, whatever the price. The price was stiff. The long list of conditions that Belgrade submitted to Moscow included the acceptance of the right of different nations to build socialism in their own way; the rehabilitation of the executed or jailed "Titoists" and the ousting of their jailers and executioners still in power in Eastern Europe. These demands, rather arrogant when one considers that they were made by a small country to a mighty superpower, were nevertheless accepted by Khrushchev, who hoped to have Yugoslavia back in the Soviet camp and thus consolidate his hold on the Balkans. With this objective in mind, he went to Belgrade to seal the reconciliation with Tito. The June 1955 journey of the future dictator of one-sixth of the earth to visit the triumphant Balkan chieftain at his capital to seek forgiveness for the admitted errors of Stalin was an almost unparalleled historical event. It was almost as if the pope of Rome had canceled the excommunication of Martin Luther and gone to Germany on a pilgrimage to apologize to him and offer his readmission into the Catholic Church.

After having accepted the Soviet recantations and thereby scoring an immense political success, Tito abruptly refused to return to the Soviet camp. This triumph of the former heretic, the public and solemn Soviet acceptance of his peculiar position toward socialism-communism, was bound to have profound repercussions throughout the entire Communist world. This was especially true in East Central Europe, still suffering from the years of oppression. Moreover, the now legitimized principles of separate, national roads to socialism-communism were in the long run bound to affect the Communist parties of the West as well. The Stalinist principle of the universality of the Soviet experience lay in ruins.

The Twentieth Party Congress

During its first three years, the collective leadership was silent about the enormity of Stalin's crimes. Nobody dared to attack openly "the period of mistakes and aberrations."

This was the situation on the eve of the Twentieth Party Congress, which gathered in February 1956 in Moscow. As with all such major public manifestations of the past period, it was a strictly structured and carefully staged performance that seemed to contain few surprises. It started with a traditional tribute to the deceased "Great Leader and Teacher." It was only three years after Stalin's death, and he still seemed to overshadow the Soviet scene from his grave. His monuments were visible everywhere, while only 12,000 out of the 5 or 6 million political prisoners had been freed.

In his report that opened the Congress, Khrushchev revised somewhat the Leninist thesis that war was inevitable "as long as imperialism exists." He ventured to say that imperialism had ceased to be "an all-embracing world system" because one-third of the world already lived under Communism, and the rapid process of decolonization made further expansion of the socialist system very likely in the future. Moreover, the steady strengthening of the "antiwar forces" made the outbreak of a world conflict less likely. This meant that there was a chance for "peaceful coexistence between states of various political and social systems." While the "final triumph of socialism" was inevitable, there were various roads leading to its achievement.

On the last day of the Congress, February 23, after all the routine work had been accomplished, Khrushchev suddenly convened an extraordinary session. No foreign observers were admitted. At this secret session he delivered a long, passionate speech about four and a half hours long, in which he denounced Stalin's personality, methods, and policies in a resolute and often spiteful way seldom encountered even among the most violent Western anti-Communists.

Although he did not spare the late tyrant's harmful policies, Khrushchev mainly emphasized his personal shortcomings, his thirst for power, his sadism, and his increasing paranoia. "The negative characteristics of Stalin, which, in Lenin's time, were only incipient, transformed themselves during the last years into a grave abuse of power which caused untold harm to our Party. . . ." The audience, not prepared to hear such shocking denunciations, was petrified and listened to their new leader in complete silence.

Among the main targets of Khrushchev's denunciations were the mass purges and show trials of the 1930s and their crippling effect on the functioning and morale of the Party. He admitted that all the old Bolsheviks' confessions had been false, and that many critical comments made about the Moscow trials abroad were actually true, and often rather understated. "When the cases of some of these so-called 'spies' and 'saboteurs' were examined it was found that all their cases were fabricated." Then he went on, "Many thousands of honest and innocent Communists have died as a result of this monstrous falsification of such 'cases.'"

Despite his furious onslaught, Khrushchev did not blame the late dictator's crimes on the Communist system as such, but rather on one man's vicious character. Stalin, according to Khrushchev, was a man of incredible criminality, a pathological paranoiac who suffered from an acute persecution mania caused both by hereditary predisposition and corruption induced by the unlimited power he had appropriated through flagrant violations of the principles of "socialist legality." The Communist system and the CPSU were not to be blamed for one man's mistakes, he thundered. While Stalin was bad, Communism was good; it should simply be cleansed and consolidated.

Khrushchev closed his "secret speech" by praising some of Stalin's achievements and said that despite his numerous mistakes, he had "performed great services to the Party, to the working class and to the international [Communist] movement." In the name of

Lenin, Khrushchev summoned the Party to do away with "the cult of personality" and urged a return to "the Leninist principle of socialist democracy."

One of the most striking features of Khrushchev's speech was its selectiveness. It denounced mainly the crimes directed against certain Party members, not against the people at large. While he exonerated Rykov and Tukhachevsky, he completely omitted Trotsky, Zinoviev, Kameniev, and their followers. They still remained not only "enemies of the people" but "unpersons," to use George Orwell's words. The selectiveness of Khrushchev's attack can be seen in the events that took place after the speech. Following the Congress, while several million inmates of prisons and labor and concentration camps were gradually freed, several categories of political prisoners were not rehabilitated, even though they had been released. Finally, neither the rehabilitation commissions, nor the procurator, nor the Party dared to prosecute those guilty of the monstrous crimes committed under Stalin. Neither were the chiefs of jails and camps tried and punished, nor were the names of slanderers and informers revealed, nor were the interrogators responsible for torturing people prosecuted.

Yet despite these inconsistencies, and even glaring mistakes, the secret speech was an event of the highest significance. By denouncing Stalin as a blood-stained maniac, the violator not only of the Marxist–Leninist principles of "socialist legality" but of basic human rights, Khrushchev performed a dramatic operation the consequences of which were soon visible. He destroyed the myth of Stalin's infallibility as an interpreter of orthodox Marxism-Leninism. By so doing, Khrushchev cast doubt upon the legitimacy of any leader or regime trying to govern in the name of similar principles. As a consequence, Khrushchev seriously undermined the foundations of Communist rule in the USSR and severely damaged its international image. If a sadistic monster could rule supreme in Soviet Russia for nearly three decades in the name of Marxist-Leninist doctrine, how reliable could these principles be? And how trustworthy were the methods by which Stalin's successors have been selected?

Why the Secret Speech?

Khrushchev's speech initially discredited only Stalin; in so doing, however, it placed a time bomb under the foundations of the world Communist movement. The Soviet regime was an ideocracy in which the leader of the Party was also the chief theoretician, the keeper of the Word, and its sole interpreter. The General Secretary of the ruling Party was the Emperor as well as the Pope, both the Sultan and the Caliph. Knowing the Truth was the Soviet leader's main claim to total power and the reason for enforcing his subjects' total obedience. In such a system, the top dog was also the top dogmatist. Once this myth was broken, the system became open to challenge.

The question of what moved Khrushchev, a former henchman of the late dictator, to the eloquent, although incomplete, exposure of his former master's crimes, is still controversial. It was certainly not squeamishness about Stalin's bloody record, for as Stalin's delegate in the Ukraine during the Great Purge, Khrushchev had stained his own hands with the blood of countless innocent victims. A better explanation would be his conviction that the rule of unmitigated terror was in the long run a dangerous way of ruling the country because of the revulsion it had produced. The experience of World War II, including the defection of such an old Communist as General Vlasov, must have been of crucial importance. As Stalin's proconsul in the Ukraine, Khrushchev had witnessed the near-collapse of most of the southern front because of mass desertion by the recruits, who were largely members of various non-Russian minorities, especially the Ukrainians and the Moslems. Moreover, Khrushchev was also aware that brutal compulsion was not the best economic incentive. He must have concluded that the Stalinist system of terror was counterproductive. By making his "secret speech," he was actually defending his own rule, as well as stability of a system that urgently required more effective ways of managing and motivating people.

Still another motive to Khrushchev's speech must have been the pressure of the Party apparatus. The Stalinist purges had been a traumatic experience that haunted the Soviet people, including the Party oligarchy. By 1955–1956, everyone was yearning for security, stability, and the cry "Never, never again!" could be heard also in many Party circles. The political balance of forces in the Party must have been such that its leader had no alternative but to expose his predecessor's misdeeds to preserve the vital support of the apparatus. If he did not do it, one of his rivals would. To keep power, Khrushchev had to exorcise Stalin's ghost once and forever and promise to the "new class" or the Soviet Party apparatus that the horrors of the purges would never be repeated again.

Thus Khrushchev, who had assumed Stalin's office, came to preside over the initial dismantling of the Communist regime in the Soviet Union. This made the Twentieth Congress one of the most momentous events of Soviet history. By his secret speech Khrushchev, without ever planning it that way, opened up for discussion the fundamental premises of Communism and thereby started a crisis more profound than any previously experienced by the Communist Party.

Stalinism as a Historic Phenomenon: Four Soviet Views

Stalin was the most powerful personality of Soviet Russia and the world Communist movement for over twenty-nine years, from Lenin's death in January 1924 to March 1953. Even in death, Stalin overshadowed the Soviet political scene for a long time. The formative period of Soviet history was shaped by his personality and his way of governing, some of which he inherited from Lenin. Stalinism is thus the central problem of Soviet history, and an explanation of its complexities is in order.

Stalin and his system have been the subjects of numerous debates, both in the Soviet Union and abroad. Let us now examine four Soviet views of the problem, followed by three main Western schools of thought. The first approach that must be analyzed is the official Soviet one. It is embodied in Stalin's speeches and official declarations; it is encapsulated in one authoritative book entitled *History of the Communist Party of the Soviet Union (Bolsheviks), Short Course*, edited by Stalin himself and published in many editions up to his death, and in various revised versions under his successors. *The Short Course*, as the work is usually called, represents the authentic interpretation of Stalinism directly from the horse's mouth. If we are to believe this version, the history of the USSR during Stalin's rule was a record of far-sighted policies formulated by a wise, benevolent leader and carried out enthusiastically by the Soviet people, with only a few exceptions. Those who did oppose the Great Helmsman's policies were mostly traitors, saboteurs, and foreign agents. They were punished, and rightly so. Most were relegated to corrective labor camps. Some of the more vicious ones had to be removed altogether for the sake of State security. On the whole, however, the political and socioeconomic transformation of the USSR was conducted most successfully. The correctness of these policies was tested during the "Great Patriotic War," which finally validated the wisdom of the Leader's policies and consolidated the position of the Soviet Union as "the main progressive and peace-loving force" of humanity and as one of the two superpowers.

The official Stalinist version of Stalinism has been challenged not only by most Western scholars, but also by some independent Soviet minds. The earliest major critic of Stalin was, of course, his main rival, Leon Trotsky. Most of Trotsky's writings after his removal from power in 1926 actually focused on criticism of Stalin. Trotsky was a prolific and brilliant writer; his views changed as the

situation in the Soviet Union and the international arena fluctuated; they may be telescoped here only briefly. The gist of Trotsky's and his followers' basic analysis may be summarized as follows. Classical, Western European Marxism was a model designed for a developed, industrialized, homogeneous country, whereas what happened in Russia was the triumph of socialism-communism in a backward, multinational empire that happened to constitute the weakest link in the capitalist chain. Therefore, Stalinism was a product of the anomaly that, after the failure of the revolution in the West, primitive, unindustrialized Russia had to assume the role of vanguard in the march toward the international proletarian revolution. While Marx had said that the revolution should be preceded by industrialization, in Russia it was the other way around. This unnatural reversal of the sequence was bound to produce Stalinism, a degeneration of the original Marxist idea, a Russian form of "Bonapartism." As Trotsky put it, "Stalinism is the syphilis of Socialism." Similar explanations of Stalinism has been continued in the works of numerous Trotskyists.

Another interpretation of Stalinism as a spoiler of the Good Thing that is Communism was embodied in the aforementioned Khrushchev speech and the Twentieth Party Congress. Khrushchev's interpretation, however, differed from Trotsky's in its heavy emphasis on Stalin's morbidly suspicious personality as a quintessential part of the process of corruption of the essentially correct theory of Marxism-Leninism. While Trotsky, especially in his biography of Stalin, also emphasized the personality factor, he never considered Stalin's criminal lust for power, his vindictiveness, and his sadistic proclivities as decisive factors. It was Khrushchev who graphically analyzed the cult of personality and its consequences for the Party and the country at large in terms of the idiosyncrasies and perversion of a "giddy despot." Besides presenting a rather simplistic and highly un-Marxist interpretation of Stalin, Khrushchev left aside many problems that were often raised not only by Western historians but also by some representatives of Soviet historiography. One of them is that it was perhaps Lenin himself who had prepared the ground for Stalinism by smashing the old administrative and legal system in a country where the elemental notions of law and legality had only recently begun to germinate. Khrushchev's approach suggested that Stalin only perfected and used for his own ends Lenin's concept of the omnipotence of the unfailing Party.

Leaving aside these broad historiographic issues, let us examine the fourth approach to Stalinism as represented by a Soviet historian, Roy Medvedev. In his book *Let History Judge—The Origins and Consequences of Stalinism*, Medvedev has accused Stalin of corrupting Marxism-Leninism by unbridled application of terror because of a pathological thirst for personal power. Here Medvedev, a product of Soviet environment, leans toward Khrushchev's view that Stalinism was not a cancer in the Soviet body politic, but a skin-deep disease on the essentially healthy idea, a disease that should and could have been removed in due time by a cosmetic operation before it spread deeper. Using some of Trotsky's original arguments as well as Khrushchev's reasoning, Medvedev represents a crossbreed between the two schools of thought, while leaning toward the psychohistorical approach. Instead of analyzing in a Marxist way the political, social, and economic roots of the Stalinist phenomenon, both Khrushchev and Medvedev preferred to stress the sins of the tyrant's personality. Both of these professed Marxists, therefore, reduced a complex historic phenomenon to highly subjective factors. Of course, Stalinism was marked by the personality of the dictator, more than any other totalitarian movement; hence Stalin's psyche is of considerable importance. Yet to ascribe decisive importance to his heredity and mental makeup obfuscates rather than clarifies the essence of the phenomenon. The question: Did Stalin create his system, or did the Communist system, as shaped by Lenin, create Stalinism, is crucial to this controversy.

Stalin: Some Non-Soviet Views

Non-Soviet views of Stalinism can be boiled down to three main currents. The first should be called a historical school because it stresses the roots of Communism in the Russian past, in the peculiarities of the Muscovite-Russian development that contributed to the triumph of Bolshevism in the former Tsarist Empire. Typical representatives of this school believe that Communism, including its Stalinist variety, was a unique product of peculiarly Russian historic conditions. Such typical representatives of the historical approach as Nicholas Berdiaev (*The Origin of Russian Communism*), Jan Kucharzewski (*From the White Tsardom to the Red, The Origins of Modern Russia*), Tibor Szamueli (*The Russian Tradition*) or Robert V. Daniels (*Russia: The Roots of Confrontation*) stress the continuity of the Muscovite-Russian development. They all argue that the retarded amorphous Muscovite-Russian state, bent on foreign conquests, was bound to produce a despotic government and that when Tsarism went bankrupt only another type of despotism could replace it. Communism, therefore, was nothing but a mutation of the Tsarist autocracy in a new, Marxist garb—a red Tsardom. By extension, Stalinism was a historically conditioned, warped phase of the system Muscovy-Russia had already experienced, in a different guise, under Ivan the Terrible, Peter the Great, and Nicholas I.[2]

On the other hand, the traditional liberal school of thought finds the roots of the Stalinist tyranny in the suppression of political liberty compounded by the destruction of private property. Private property is the foundation of individual liberty, argue such conservatives as Friederich Hayek (*The Road to Serfdom*) or Richard Pipes (*Russia Under the*

[2] Daniels goes as far as to write, "In terms of the revolutionary process, by exirpating the spirit of revolutionary innovation and liquidating the vast majority of the makers of the Revolution, Stalinism became the functional equivalent of a royal Restoration." Robert V. Daniels, *Russia: The Roots of Confrontation.* (Cambridge, Mass.: Harvard University Press, 1985) p. 21.

Bolshevik Regime). If one replaces private property with State property, everybody becomes a slave of an omnipotent monster. By controlling both political power and all material resources, rulers exercise total control over each individual. As long as a measure of private initiative and property was still tolerated under the NEP, Soviet Russia was merely a harsh authoritarian police state of a new type. It became a totalitarian structure only as a result of the Stalin revolution, which wiped out the remnants of private property, even in land ownership.

The third popular non-Soviet approach to Stalinism was represented by the supporters of the "industrialization theory." Its spokespersons found a coherent explanation of the Communist experiment, especially of its Stalinist stage, in Russia's economic retardation. According to them, Stalinism was Russia's response to the challenge of industrialization under the peculiarly stern conditions of political isolation, the threat of renewed foreign intervention, and a shortage of native capital, as well as the know-how. Menaced by foreign powers, with no chance for foreign aid, the Communist rulers of Russia decided to pull themselves up by their own bootstraps. Facing both external and internal dangers to the newly established regime, they decided on the desperate, cruel measures to which the western Sovietologists applied the blanket term of Stalinism. The industrialization theory was represented by a plethora of works: Barrington Moore's *Soviet Politics: The Dilemma of Power* or Walt Rostow's *Dynamics of Soviet Society* are perhaps the most representative of this approach.

This basic typology simplifies and telescopes a broad spectrum of views that includes various shades of opinion. These theories often overlap and/or supplement each other. No single theory comes near to the full interpretation of the complex historical phenomenon of Stalinism. Even their combination falls short of adequately explaining its astonishing "success." Was Stalin "the greatest reformer of all times," as

Isaac Deutscher called him, or was he the most monstrous criminal of all times, comparable only to Hitler?

Without embracing either of these positions, one should try to draw up a balance sheet of Stalin's rule of nearly three decades. On the negative side one should put the establishment of the strictest and harshest police regime on record, the stifling of individual initiative in all fields, including intellectual activity, the ruining of native agriculture, the thorough bureaucratization and militarization of society, and the slaughter of some twenty to thirty million people, including most of his close friends and co-workers. Even if one puts on the positive side the turning of Soviet Russia into the second military power of the world, the winning of World War II, and the expansion of Soviet frontiers, even beyond those of the Tsarist Empire—the achievements that so flattered the Russian national ego—there always remains the problem of the monstrous human and environmental price paid for these successes. Stalin was the only ruler in history who exterminated more of his own people than did all of his country's enemies put together. It is worth noting that all the positive or allegedly positive achievements have to do with State power and prestige, while most of the negative ones pertain to the lot of the individual.

Suggested Reading

ADAMS, ARTHUR E., *Stalin and His Times*. New York: Holt, Rinehart and Winston, 1972.

ALI, TARIQ (ED.), *The Stalinist Legacy: Its Impact on Twentieth-Century World Politics*. Boulder, CO: Lynne Rienner Publishers, 1984.

ARMSTRONG, JOHN, *The Politics of Totalitarianism*. New York: Random House, 1961.

COLBURN, FORREST D. (ED.), *Everyday Form of Peasant Resistance*. Armonk, NY: M. E. Sharpe, 1986.

CRANKSHAW, EDWARD, *Khrushchev: A Career*. New York: Viking, 1966.

DANIELS, ROBERT V., *The Stalin Revolution: Founda-*

tions of Soviet Totalitarianism. Lexington, MA: Heath, 1972.

DAVIS, L. E., *Cold War Begins: Soviet–American Conflict over Eastern Europe.* Princeton, NJ: Princeton University Press, 1974.

DELLENBRAND, JANE AKE, *The Soviet Regional Dilemma.* Armonk NY: M. E. Sharpe, 1986.

GIBIAN, GEORGE, *Interval of Freedom: Soviet Literature During the Thaw, 1954–1957.* Minneapolis: University of Minnesota Press. 1960.

HALPERIN, ERNST, *The Triumphant Heretic: Tito's Struggle against Stalin.* London: Heinemann, 1958.

HINGLEY, RONALD, *Joseph Stalin: Man and Legend.* New York: McGraw-Hill, 1974.

HOCHSCHILD, ADAM, *The Unquiet Ghost: Russians Remember Stalin.* New York: Viking, 1994.

JORAVSKY, DAVID, *The Lysenko Affair.* Cambridge, MA: Harvard University Press, 1970.

KNIGHT, AMY, *Beria: Stalin's First Lieutenant.* Princeton, NJ: Princeton University Press, 1994.

KOREY, WILLIAM, *The Soviet Cage: Anti-Semitism in Russia.* New York: Viking, 1973.

KULSKI, WLADYSLAW W., *Peaceful Co-Existence.* Chicago: Regnery, 1959.

LEONHARD, WOLFGANG, *The Kremlin Since Stalin.* New York: Praeger, 1962.

MCCARLEY, MARTIN, *Khrushchev and the Development of Soviet Agriculture: The Virgin Land Program.* New York: Holmes and Meier, 1976.

MEDVEDEV, ROY, *Let History Judge: The Origins and Consequences of Stalinism.* New York: Columbia University Press, 1989.

———, AND ZHORES A. MEDVEDEV, *Khrushchev: The Years in Power,* New York: Columbia University Press, 1976.

MEDVEDEV, ZHORES A., *The Rise and Fall of T. D. Lysenko* (Trans. I. Michael Lerner). Garden City, NY: Doubleday, 1971.

PORTER, BRUCE D., *The USSR in the Third World Conflicts.* Cambridge, Eng.: Cambridge University Press, 1984.

RANDALL, FRANCIS, *Stalin's Russia.* New York: Free Press, 1965.

RIGBY, T. H. (Ed.), *Stalin.* Upper Saddle River, NJ: Prentice-Hall, 1966.

RUBINSTEIN, ALVIN L., *Red Star over the Nile.* Princeton, NJ: Princeton University Press, 1977.

RUSH, MYRON, *The Rise of Khrushchev.* Washington, DC: Public Affairs Press, 1957.

SCHWARTZ, HARRY, *The Soviet Economy Since Stalin.* Philadelphia: Lippincott, 1961.

SOUVARINE, BORIS, *Stalin: A Critical Survey of Bolshevism.* New York: Octagon, 1972.

SWAYZE, HAROLD, *Political Control in Literature in the USSR, 1946–1959.* Cambridge, MA: Harvard University Press, 1962.

URBAN, G. R., (ED.), *Stalinism: Its Impact on Russia and the World.* New York: St. Martin's, 1982.

VAKSBERG, ARKADY, *Stalin Against the Jews.* New York: Vintage, 1994.

VOLKOGONOV, DMITRI, *Stalin: Triumph and Tragedy.* London: Weidenfeld and Nicolson, 1992.

WOLFE, BERTRAM D., *Khrushchev and Stalin's Ghost.* New York: Praeger, 1957.

Chapter 21

The Khrushchev Years: The Upward Trend

During the last two or three years of Stalin's rule, the whole immense machinery of the Soviet State had been in danger of running itself into the ground because of the growing senile rigidity and arbitrariness of its dictator. The fundamental problem faced by Stalin's heirs could be summed up in one sentence: how to release the country's productive and creative forces from the Stalinist ice age without losing control. Two people, Malenkov and Khrushchev, were determined to implement a reform program. Both of them perceived that the apparatus of power forged by Stalin could not indefinitely rely on terror alone. Both understood that the old machine required for its functioning a reasonably well-fed and well-housed labor force that could put its heart into the tasks at hand without constant threat of arrest and deportation. The open question was who would lead this process.

The more practical Malenkov had run the Party for years on Stalin's behalf. Having packed its top echelons with Stalin's yes-men, Malenkov acquired a deep contempt for the servile, slovenly *apparatchiki*. On the other hand, as vice-premier in charge of the economy, he came to value some of the more efficient government bureaucrats and technocrats like Minister of Finance, Alexei Kosygin. As a result of this, Malenkov came to the conclusion that cultivating government forces, rather than the more corrupt Party apparatchiki, would better guarantee the success of his reform program. Hence his willingness to relinquish the post of senior Party secretary to Khrushchev while keeping the premiership.

Khrushchev, on the other hand, never forgot where the locus of power resided. At the end of 1953 and the beginning of 1954, the story of Stalin and Trotsky's struggle for power was reenacted in miniature, thus opening a new phase in the saga of Soviet succession struggles. After having first denounced Malenkov's reform program, Khrushchev adopted it and began to peddle it with the zeal and exuberance so characteristic of this human dynamo.

The first major test came at the end of the Twentieth Congress. Khrushchev's speech debunking Stalin was intended as another blow to his chief enemy, who had been Stalin's closest henchman. At first, as mentioned earlier, the speech was intended to be secret and only the Party's top echelon was to have heard it. Soon, however, the gist of Khrushchev's denunciations filtered down to the masses and leaked abroad, where its full text was published in June 1956 by the United States State Department. While the speech may have had a beneficial effect on the Soviet people and on Khrushchev himself, the shattering contents of this pronouncement were bound to produce profound repercussions both in the Soviet Union and in the Soviet satellite empire.

One result of the speech was the release of millions of former political prisoners, who soon began to look for work. Another consequence was the beginning of political and intellectual ferment in the Soviet Union. The great debate on Stalin's crimes inevitably resulted in people's questioning the very foundations of the Soviet regime. This debate was the origin of the dissent movement. Its danger had been anticipated by Khrushchev's hard-line opponents, and the early manifestations of political and intellectual unrest were immediately blamed on him.

While the traditionally subservient Soviet people were relieved by the break with the past and limited their show of discontent to a few mutinies in labor camps—in Vorkuta, for instance—the reaction of the newly subdued peoples of East Central Europe was much deeper, more dramatic, and widespread. There, the vestiges of Western liberalism and democracy and the traditions of the national independence these people had enjoyed during the two interwar decades were fairly strong. These traditions, combined with resentment against the harsh Soviet overlordship, created a highly explosive situation in at least three countries: East Germany, Poland, and Hungary. The situation in that area should be viewed against the background of the general evolution of the foreign policy initiated by the collective leadership.

The Thaw Spreads to the Satellite Empire

The last three or four years of Stalin's rule had been the bleakest in the history of the Soviet hegemonial sphere. Arbitrary arrests and show trials of "Titoists" and "Zionists" were increasingly frequent in Eastern Europe. Gradually the stern, stifling atmosphere of Stalinist dogmatism had enveloped life in the buffer-zone countries. Literature was muzzled and along with all the other arts fell victim to socialist realism. In all writings, at least lip service had to be paid to Soviet achievements.

During this period all people with Western links or sympathies were under suspicion in East Central Europe. This group included Communists of Jewish extraction, who were increasingly regarded as security risks. As in the USSR, in the satellite countries the new anti-Semitic line was camouflaged by the euphemisms "the struggle against cosmopolitanism" and "anti-Zionism." Such Jewish Communists as Ana Pauker in Romania and Rudolf Slansky in Czechoslovakia, who had been used by Stalin as instruments of Sovietization, were purged. While Pauker was merely exiled, Slansky was hanged for being a "Zionist" as well as an "agent of the CIA." Hundreds of lesser leaders of Jewish background were also purged. The struggle against organized religion continued; it was especially vicious as far as Roman Catholicism was concerned, because it had ties beyond the limits of the Soviet sphere. Numerous members of the Catholic hierarchy were arrested and tried, including Cardinal Mindszenty in Hungary and Archbishop Beran in Czechoslovakia. The religious persecution survived even Stalin's demise; the Primate of Poland, Cardinal Stefan Wyszynski, was arrested in September 1953.

Stalin's death and the struggle for power that followed were bound to have considerable impact on the whole Soviet orbit. The slight domestic thaw that could be observed in the Soviet Union during the years 1953–1955 was reflected almost immediately in the revolt of East Berlin workers in June 1953. Its suppression was followed, nevertheless, by a political ferment in Hungary and Poland. One of the factors that precipitated it was the July 10, 1953, Soviet announcement of Beria's liquidation; this brought about at least a temporary disorganization of the Soviet security network in Eastern Europe, with which all East European secret police systems had been intimately linked. From then on events in Hungary and Poland, both of which had a long tradition of independent statehood and defiance to foreign domination, snowballed.

In July 1953, the most cruel of all East European dictators, Hungary's Matyas Rákosi, had to yield the premiership to a representative of a milder variety of Hungarian Communism, Imre Nágy. Rákosi, however, kept the post of First Secretary of the Party. Nágy tried to placate consumers and inaugurated a "new course" in Hungary. Nágy went further and released a number of political prisoners, permitted peasants to leave collective farms and relaxed censorship somewhat. As a result, a number of debating and literary groups were formed, the most significant of which was the Petöfi Club, named after the great Hungarian poet of the "Spring of Nations" era of the 1848 revolution. By 1954–1955 Hungary was in a state of ferment. In the spring of 1955 came Khrushchev's visit to Belgrade with his acceptance of the "national" approach to Socialism-Communism.

In Poland the event that unleashed a series of dramatic incidents was the flight to the West in December 1953 of a high official of the Ministry of Public Security, Joseph Swiatlo. His revelations of the corruption of the "new class" (as Milovan Djilas called the party *apparat*) and the bestiality of its secret police were broadcast by Western radio systems in 1954 and 1955. These disclosures increased the existing tensions and precipitated a purge of numerous discredited security officers and Party dignitaries. At the same time, Imre Nágy's Polish counterpart, Władysław Gomułka, was released from detention and

became the object of considerable attention from various factions. While the Party's Stalinist wing wanted to win him over to bolster their tottering ascendancy, the more "liberal" faction hoped to use him as the standard bearer for a reformed, watered down, "humanized" Communism more attuned to the sentiments of the broad masses.

The crisis at the top was, in Poland as in Hungary, accompanied by growing unrest among the youth and the intellectuals, eager for more freedom of expression. Soon many basic tenets of Marxism were openly criticized, and the universality of the Soviet experience openly challenged.

The "Polish October"

In February of 1956 came the Twentieth Soviet Party Congress and Khrushchev's secret speech. The speech put both the Hungarian and the Polish party bosses, Matyas Rákosi and Boleslaw Bierut, on the spot; both of them, but especially Rákosi, had been as guilty of brutal, arbitrary rule as Stalin himself. Bierut was so shocked that he died of a heart attack. The debunking of Stalin amounted to undermining the Communist grip in the satellite area; for most East Europeans, Stalinism and Communism were indistinguishable from each other.

In Poland the gist of Khrushchev's speech promptly filtered down to the masses and produced a sharp reaction. On June 28, during the yearly international fair at Poznan, Polish factory workers staged a demonstration. Their slogan was, "We want bread and freedom." The demonstrators instantly clashed with the police, who were supported by army detachments with tanks. According to official figures, 53 people were killed and some 300 wounded.

After the Poznan riots, events in Poland gathered momentum. In August, the leader of the right wing faction, Gomułka, had been readmitted to the United Polish Workers' Party, and on October 19 was chosen as the Party's First Secretary. In his acceptance speech, Gomułka submitted the "past period" to searching and vehement criticism and promised broad reforms that would make the Communist system of Poland more democratic, and less dependent on Moscow. One of his decisions was to send packing Marshal Konstantin Rokossovsky, whom Stalin had made Commander-in-Chief of the Polish armed forces. The same order was given to several hundred Soviet officers who had occupied most of the key positions in the Polish defense establishment. Most collective farms were dissolved. Optional religious teaching was permitted in schools.

Hardly had Gomułka undertaken these steps when Khrushchev, at the head of a large military and civilian Soviet team, descended upon Warsaw uninvited. Despite strong Soviet pressure supported by threats of a full-scale military intervention, Gomułka boldly stood by his decisions. In a stormy interview he managed to persuade Khrushchev that a firmly Communist but semiautonomous Poland loyal to the Warsaw Pact obligations and maintaining its membership in the CMEA would be a more reliable ally of the USSR. The Polish armed forces, now under native command, overwhelmingly supported Gomułka, and the people of Poland, especially workers and students, manifested their solidarity with his attempts to gain at least a modicum of domestic independence from Russia.

Faced with the resolute stand of Gomułka, supported by the masses of Polish people, while reassured about the preservation of a vital triple link with the Center (the party's leading role, and military as well as economic ties), Khrushchev accepted the compromise, which was fully in accordance with the principle of separate roads to socialism he had proclaimed in Belgrade in 1955.

Meanwhile the highly explosive situation in the Middle East and the mounting crisis in Hungary put Poland on the back burner of Soviet global priorities. Here again the events of October-November 1956 have to be viewed in light of the secret speech. In Hungary, Khrushchev's revelations precipitated the downfall of the cruel Stalinist satrap Rákosi, who had to relinquish his last stronghold, the post of First Secretary, to a less compromised man, Ernö Gerö. Under public pressure Gerö in turn had to rehabilitate Lazlo Rajk, who had been executed as a Titoist traitor in 1949. The solemn reburial of Rajk's body on October 6, 1956, turned into a silent but impressive mass demonstration by the people of Budapest.

The Hungarian Revolt

The peaceful triumph of Gomułka in Poland triggered a revolutionary situation in Hungary. There the mixture of suppressed patriotic longings of the twice defeated and humiliated nation and inveterate socioeconomic grievances was even more potent than in Poland. Because of traditional friendly ties between the two countries, the Polish events were closely watched by the Hungarians. On October 23 a demonstration was organized in Budapest in support of the Poles—then already celebrating their limited but enviable success. The next day a similar manifestation occurred in front of a Budapest radio building to press the government for a reformed party. While most of the leaders of the demonstration were willing to preserve all existing links with the USSR, Nágy insisted on complete independence of Hungary and its neutrality. The severing of all existing political, military, and economic links with the USSR was obviously a serious matter for Moscow. A neutral Hungary would separate Czechoslovakia from Romania and thus split the Soviet satellite empire, setting a dangerous precedent for other nations of the bloc. For a few days Khrushchev hesitated over what action to take. While the Hungarians and others in the Soviet empire were celebrating their apparent victory, the reinforced Soviet troops swept back into the country in the early hours of November 4. Despite massive Hungarian resistance, the superior forces of the Red Army crushed the insurgents within a few days. Nágy sought shelter in the Yugoslav Embassy while protesting Soviet violation of

The Soviet Bloc in 1956

Hungary's neutrality and vainly appealing to the United Nations. Meanwhile, the victorious Soviet army installed the subservient János Kádár as First Party Secretary and Prime Minister. The armed resistance collapsed.

The Hungarians paid a high price for their attempts at freedom. Some 3,000 people perished during the uprising and its aftermath, while nearly 15,000 were imprisoned. Over 200,000 Hungarians left the country and settled in the West, about 40,000 of them in the United States. This was a terrible bloodletting for a nation of some eight million people that was already suffering from a declining birth rate. All this, however, was soon forgotten by the West, as if to confirm the saying of the French moralist de la Rochefoucauld that "We have always enough strength to bear the misfortunes of others."

The reasons for Western indifference were numerous and complex. One of them was the international situation. In the midst of the Hungarian uprising, the world's attention was diverted to the Middle East. On October 29, Israeli troops, acting in concert with the French and the British, who were smarting over Nasser's nationalization of the Suez Canal, attacked Egypt. The Israeli, French, and British troops were about to capture the canal when the Soviet Union issued a stern protest and demanded immediate international action to stop the invasion of Egypt. Khrushchev's intervention included a threat to use the Soviet nuclear weapons to enforce the Israeli-French-British withdrawal.

Almost at the same time the United States also took a determined stand against the triple invasion of Egypt. This parallel action of the two superpowers, hitherto bitter opponents in the Cold War, brought about an instant armistice and the withdrawal of the Israeli, French, and British forces. The unexpected cooperation of the two global rivals dramatized their role as guardians of the status quo created by World War II. This was underscored by the fact that Washington, despite its often vigorous advocacy of slogans of "the liberation of Eastern Europe from the Soviet yoke" and "rolling back the Iron Curtain,"

now refused to respond to the appeals of the Hungarian rebels for help. Quite the contrary, the United States repeatedly reaffirmed its adherence to the status quo created by the wartime agreements of Teheran, Yalta, and Potsdam.

The suppression of the Hungarian uprising had numerous consequences for the Soviet domestic situation and for its international prestige. The United Nations, despite angry Soviet protests, denounced Moscow's highhanded action in Hungary as an act of naked aggression. Among more liberal-minded and humanitarian Communist intellectuals, the Soviet action provoked protests and encouraged desertion from the Party ranks. For instance, such Marxist writers as Jean-Paul Sartre in France and Howard Fast in the United States tore up their Communist Party cards.

While the world soon forgot about the fate of Hungary, the 1956 events in Eastern Europe, combined with some Soviet domestic events, seriously threatened Khrushchev's newly established predominant position at the Kremlin. His opponents blamed the ferment in Poland and Hungary on his rash acceptance of Tito's independent line and on Khrushchev's liberal attitude toward the manifestations of Communist heterodoxy in other dependent countries. To this criticism of his foreign policy, domestic arguments were also added.

Khrushchev's Tactics

To understand Khrushchev's domestic policy, one must consider the events of the early years of the post-Stalin era. The first in importance was cutting the security apparatus down to size and returning to what was termed "socialist legality." Then came the rehabilitation of several million political prisoners and deportees. These people and their families and friends automatically became Khrushchev's supporters. From the ashes of Beria's autonomous Ministries of State Security (MGB) and of the Interior (MVD) arose the Committee of State Security (KGB), which was directly subordinate to the Council of Ministers and hence ultimately to the Party. The KGB ruled with an iron hand, but arbitrary mass arrests and deportations without trial were things of the past. In comparison with the unbridled reign of terror, this was a great improvement. Censorship was relaxed and books like Vladimir Dudintsev's *Not by Bread Alone*, which was strongly critical of the Soviet regime, could see the light of day. Poetry and public balladeering began to flourish again, and artists like Yevgenii Yevtushenko and Bulat Okudzhava made public appearances, often presenting their verses and songs to thousands of eager listeners. By the spring of 1956, Khrushchev had already become a folk hero in the eyes of a sizable majority of the Soviet people, including many of the Party rank and file. The magnitude of the reform process and its far-reaching consequences made most people forget how selective these rehabilitations actually were.

Second in importance among Khrushchev's reforms were raising of the standard of living. The suppressed popular disenchantment with Stalin's postwar economic policies was rooted in an abysmally low level of consumption that was only partly caused by objective necessities of the postwar period. The austerity of this period had been largely imposed by Stalin's inordinate desire to make the USSR a military power far beyond its means. Enormous resources had been channeled toward nuclear research projects, most of them carried out on a crash basis. The huge network of concentration and labor camps, or the Gulag Archipelago, had expanded under Stalin like a cancerous growth.

The main victims of Stalin's repressive economic policies were the Soviet peasants. In rehabilitating the country, Stalin had again turned his back on the villages, and overwhelmingly focused on rebuilding the cities and creating heavy industry, starting with those primarily serving defense. Consequently, the countryside, ravaged and depopulated, was far behind in regaining even its miserably low prewar productive capacity. Many former peasants, discharged from the armed forces, did not want to return to the semiserfdom of the collective or State farms, where they were legally tied to the land like serfs. Instead, they rushed to better-paying and more mobile urban jobs that held some prospect of advancement.[1] As this trend brought about a further decline in the young, able-bodied rural population, it also increased the need for greater food production for the expanding cities. Yet Soviet agriculture, operating under a system of sui generis peonage, starved of fertilizers and modern machinery, and harassed by rising taxes and delivery quotas, was stagnating. By 1953 it was on the verge of collapse. The prices paid by the State for the products of collective farms often amounted to only a fraction of their production costs. After 1946, taxes on household plots began to exceed the point at which it would be worthwhile to increase their cultivation. Fines and criminal charges were again imposed on those who were in arrears. Since for tax purposes the household plots were assessed on their output rather than their size, the peasants not only stopped cultivating them, but often destroyed what they had planted. Fruit trees were chopped down to avoid the exorbitant taxes on them, and pigs, cows, and poultry were slaughtered. By the early 1950s, potatoes had become the main crop, because their quota and taxes remained fairly reasonable. As Khrushchev admitted in September 1953, the per capita grain production of that year was lower than in 1913.

Stalin had never cared to visit a collective farm and was blind to the plight of the peasantry. He had no idea whatsoever about farming, and mistrusted peasants as greedy "petty bourgeois." Most of his henchmen, like Zhdanov and Malenkov, tended to assume a similar attitude, either because of ignorance or to please Stalin. Among the people around Stalin, Khrushchev was the only one born and bred on a farm and he preserved some sympathy for the downtrodden and exploited peasants.

---

[1] People working in a town or city were registered with the police and had internal passports for identification. Peasants had no passports, only identification papers from their respective collective or State farm authorities. These papers did not entitle them either to travel beyond a certain narrow radius or to work anywhere else.

By the spring of 1953, Khrushchev quickly grasped that the rescue must come swiftly and that rescue of the country's agriculture was his number one priority. One of his first steps, therefore, was to lower delivery quotas and taxes on household plots, and to increase dramatically the prices to be paid by the State to the peasants. Prices for meat and poultry were augmented 550 percent, for milk and butter 200 percent, and for vegetables, 40 percent. Old debts of the collective farms were canceled. These reforms immediately brought some relief of the economic plight of the peasantry and an improvement in their morale. For the first time in a quarter of a century, the squeeze on them had been not only halted, but even reversed.

While in 1953 almost a quarter of the 20 million peasant families did not have a cow, by 1959 virtually every family had at least one cow. The number of sheep more than doubled, while poultry and pigs also multiplied. Orchards and vegetable gardens slowly revived. The 1956 harvest was the best in Soviet history. All this represented, on balance, a modest progress that did not radically remedy the nationwide shortage of food, especially of milk, meat, fruit, and vegetables; but in comparison with the near-disastrous situation in the early 1950s, it resulted in an improvement in the people's diet and mood.

Khrushchev was also responsible for the considerable expansion of housing construction. To speed it up, he ordered the application of new methods of prefabrication. Despite the fact that he lacked scientific training and had only a rather rudimentary education, he displayed a keen interest in technology. One of his favorite pastimes was to watch technical documentary films, especially those on American agricultural methods. During his 1959 journey to the United States, Khrushchev was fascinated by the efficiency of American farming. After his trip, Khrushchev was more determined than ever to rescue Soviet agriculture from its slovenly backwardness by using selected capitalist technological methods, including intensive fertilizing.

Khrushchev at Bay

What delighted the average Soviet citizen and even most Party members, appeared, however, as anathema in the eyes of a small group of *apparatchiki*, who had been Stalin's closest henchmen. These were people who had been intimately connected with his criminal acts and who resented Khrushchev's growing popularity. This small group of diehard Stalinists was determined to oust him. The hard core of this faction centered around Malenkov, Molotov, and Kaganovich. All of them, to a greater or lesser degree, bore some responsibility for Stalin's excesses. Moreover, they resented being eclipsed by the "upstart" former laborer whom they regarded as their inferior. This clique was soon joined by a small but influential segment of the Party machine as well as by some bureaucrats who had been planted in high State positions by Malenkov. The opposition also included the surviving former members of the old security network. All of these people felt threatened by the ongoing process of liberalization and were looking for a chance to strike back at Khrushchev.

One has to bear in mind that during his rule of nearly three decades, Stalin had instilled certain habits and conditioned reflexes difficult to eradicate. Some of them had deep roots in Russian history, while others were of fresher vintage. The domestic ferment, including the first public political dissent, shocked the Communist fundamentalists used to absolute obedience. The unrest in Eastern Europe, the worsening relations with Mao, who disapproved of the secret speech and refused to accept Khrushchev's leadership of the world Communist movement—all this was now blamed on Khrushchev's unorthodox methods, exuberant pronouncements, and rash reforms.

By the spring of 1957, despite his popularity with the masses, Khrushchev's Party position was shaky; he was under constant pressure and unsure as to how quickly he could proceed with his reforms. Meanwhile, however, the first indications of a bountiful harvest in the newly opened virgin lands bolstered his position dramatically by vindicating one of his pet schemes. The apparent successes of the corn-growing emboldened Khrushchev. Now, with exuberance exceptional even for him, he put forward two new schemes. One established a number of regional economic bodies called "People's Economic Councils." This, he argued, would cut through red tape by decentralizing economic planning and thus it would engage local talent and initiative. The scheme, while offering the promise of promotion to thousands of local Party men, was a heavy blow to the central ministries.

Khrushchev's successes were quick and tangible. His second scheme was to make the Soviet Union take a "great leap forward" as far as the diet of its citizens was concerned. In May 1957, he put forth a gigantic plan for greatly expanding Soviet production of meat, milk, and butter. By 1960–1961, the USSR was to surpass the United States in these three fields. Overtaking the United States in butter production was quite possible, since its consumption of this item was rapidly declining as a result of increased marketing of vegetable oil and margarine. In meat production, however, the USSR lagged so far behind its rival that Khrushchev's scheme bordered on lunacy. At that time the United States produced more than twice as much meat as the Soviet Union. Consequently, Khrushchev's idea was decried as fantastic even by many of his supporters. Yet he stuck to his guns, despite the objections of most of the Presidium and many of his economic advisers, whom he had not consulted before his speech.

Defeat of the Anti-Party Group

Both schemes served to precipitate a bitter inner-Party clash. His opponents concocted a plot to unseat Khrushchev. While he and Bulganin were on a state visit to Finland, the conspirators finished their preparations. On June 18, the day after his return from Helsinki, Khrushchev had to face a critical majority of the Presidium, which denounced him as an irresponsible adventurer leading the country to ruin and ridicule. His suggestions for hasty reforms were outvoted eight to four. His only supporters were Mikhail S. Suslov, Anastas I. Mikoyan, and his own "lady friend," Katerina A. Furtseva, Minister of Culture. Malenkov, Molotov, and Kaganovich were joined by Voroshilov, First Deputy Premier and Chairman of the State Planning Committee Mikhail G. Pervukhin, Maxim Z. Saburov, another First Deputy Premier, and Dmitri T. Shepilov. At the last moment even his alleged friend Bulganin also sided with the plotters. Having outvoted Khrushchev by two to one, the conspirators insisted on his instant resignation from the post of First Secretary of the Central Committee. Khrushchev, however, objected. Arguing that the "rules of arithmetic do not always apply in politics," he appealed from the Presidium to a plenary meeting of the Central Committee, whose members, after all, had elected him as their Secretary. This was a legally justified demand: According to Soviet Communist Party bylaws, the First Secretary was elected and/or removed by the plenum of the Central Committee.

At that time Leningrad was celebrating the 250th anniversary of its founding by Peter the Great, and many members of the Central Committee were gathered there. Informed about the situation, Minister of Defesne Marshal Zhukov, grateful to Khrushchev for recalling him from retirement, put military jet planes at his disposal. By June 21, over 100 members of the Committee, more than a third of the entire body, had arrived at the Kremlin to insist on their statutory right to decide the fate of their First Secretary. Most Central Committee members were regional Party functionaries whose power and sense of security were increased by Khrushchev's plans to decentralize the central authority. During the June 22–23 session, they outvoted the conspirators. Out of 309 present, 215 voted for Khrushchev and only a few abstained.

The conspirators, decried by their opponents "the anti-Party group," were denounced and punished. The three main ringleaders—Malenkov, Molotov, and Kaganovich—were expelled from the Presidium and the Central Committee. Shepilov was deprived of his alternate Presidium membership and his place at the Party's Secretariat as well as in the Ministry of Foreign Affairs, where he was now replaced by his deputy, Andrei Gromyko. For reasons of expediency and decorum, Bulganin's and Voroshilov's punishment was delayed.

Khrushchev's victory was followed by a far-reaching reshuffle of the apex of the power pyramid. The four main leaders of the anti-Party group were not given a capital punishment that would have been their lot under Stalin. Malenkov, once in charge of the whole of Soviety industry, was appointed manager of a power station in a remote corner of Central Asia where he, eventually, underwent a religious conversion and even joined a local Orthodox church choir. Molotov was made ambassador to the distant satellite republic of Mongolia. By these relatively mild reprisals, Khrushchev was trying to show that terror was no longer needed to run the country.

Meanwhile, the Presidium was packed with Khrushchev's supporters. Four candidates were raised to full membership. One of them was Leonid Brezhnev, then First Party Secretary of the Kazakhstan Republic and a man who had been very helpful in launching the virgin land project in his bailiwick. Another noteworthy promotion to full membership in the Presidium was that of Marshal Zhukov, who was now rewarded for his prompt support in suppressing the "anti-Party" conspiracy. Zhukov's political role did not last very long, however. His insistence on further downgrading the political commissars' role ran counter to the concept of strict Party control of the armed forces. In October 1957, after his return from a visit to Yugoslavia, Zhukov was dismissed from the post of Minister of Defense. He was replaced by Marshal Rodion Malinovsky who had been closely associated with Khrushchev during the Stalingrad battle.

After smashing the anti-Party group, Khrushchev abandoned the pretense of collective leadership and adopted a dictatorial manner. This became especially true when, in 1958, both the premiership and the post of First Secretary were united in his hands. Now a new sort of personality cult, more subdued than under Stalin, yet pronounced enough, began to develop around him. Khrushchev's picture began to appear everywhere.

In 1959, Khrushchev made a thirteen-day tour of the United States. He visited factories and farms, paying special attention to American agricultural techniques, which he secretly envied and admired. He also visited universities and film studios, and in Hollywood he raised hell with one of the directors, sternly admonishing him that the can-can was obscene and immoral.

Khrushchev's Apogee

Khrushchev reached his apogee in the years 1957–1959. Radiating vitality and exuberance, he traveled throughout the country, mixing with ordinary people as no Soviet leader had done before. Among the faceless and colorless Soviet chieftains, he stood out as a colorful, dramatic, and witty personality, an

Andrei A. Gromyko, Foreign Minister, 1957–1985

accomplished actor, although frequently one of a somewhat clownish variety. Even his controversial and coarse pronouncements were greeted as a welcome relief from the unbearable banality of other Soviet bureaucrats. His populist-like pronouncements, emphasizing the importance of non-Party people, were greatly appreciated by the Soviet masses. Khrushchev tried to foster his popularity by a series of small but significant gestures. For instance, he opened the Kremlin to visitors for the first time since 1930. Ordinary citizens were now allowed to enter freely the old fortress, its churches and palaces, and to see national treasures. After Stalin's haughty and unapproachable manner and his isolation behind heavily guarded Kremlin walls, most people liked to see Khrushchev laughing and mixing freely with the people.

In the scientific field, Khrushchev's liberalizing attitude toward non-Party scholars, especially technicians, paid rich dividends. Under Stalin about half of all scientific projects pertaining to nuclear and space research had been conducted by political prisoners who in everyday life had been distinguished specialists in their fields. They worked in closely guarded institutes controlled by the MGB or MVD. Khrushchev freed most of them and showered them with favors. He ordered the construction of an "academic city" at Novosibirsk and allowed the study of cybernetics. A few years of this policy produced beneficial results. In October 1957, Soviet space scientists successfully launched the first artificial earth satellite, *Sputnik*, or Co-traveler; *Sputnik II* followed in November. The West was struck dumb by the Soviet technical achievements. Followed by a series of other brilliant experiments in space, all these successes had a stunning impact on the morale of the Soviet people. Communism and not capitalism appeared to them as the wave of the future. The international prestige of the Soviet Union now skyrocketed. The USSR seemed to have demonstrated its superiority over its main rival in the field of technical education, especially in the vital sphere of space technology. Peace-

ful competition among nations would decide the course the world would take. As a result of this competition the Communists will bury their capitalist rival proclaimed Khrushchev. "We can produce rockets like sausages!"

The launching of the Sputniks was also a great personal victory for Khrushchev. After all, it was he who had given high priority to space research in general and to missiles in particular. One has to remember that the chief designer of the Sputnik, Sergei P. Korolev, had been arrested before the war on Stalin's orders for allegedly sabotaging work on standard aircraft. As a result, he had spent years in the Kolyma gold mines as punishment. Khrushchev freed Korolev and made him chief designer of the Soviet space program. The two Sputniks, which ushered in the space age, created in the United States and throughout the West a crisis of confidence in the capitalist system. Profoundly scared by the Soviet successes in space, the

A Soviet cosmonaut in his space ship

United States launched its own program of crash research, to beat its rival in the cosmic competition.

Suggested Reading

BRANT, STEFAN, *The East German Rising.* New York: Praeger, 1957.

BREZEZINSKI, ZBIGNIEW, *The Soviet Bloc: Unity and Conflict*, 2nd Ed. Cambridge, MA: Harvard University Press, 1961.

COHEN, STEPHEN F., ALEXANDER RABINOWITCH, AND ROBERT SHARLET (EDS.), *The Soviet Union Since Stalin.* Bloomington: Indiana University Press, 1980.

CRANKSHAW, EDWARD, *Khrushchev: A Career.* New York: Viking, 1966.

DALLIN, ALEXANDER, ET AL., *The Soviet Union, Arms Control and Disarmament.* New York: Columbia University Press, 1964.

DJILAS, MILOVAN, *The New Class: An Analysis of the Communist System.* New York: Praeger, 1957.

DZIEWANOWSKI, M. K., *The Communist Party of Poland: An Outline of History*, 2nd Ed. Cambridge, MA: Harvard University Press, 1976, Chs. 12–16.

GADDIS, JOHN LEWIS, *The Long Peace: Inquiries into the History of the Cold War.* New York: Oxford University Press, 1987.

——— (ED.), *Cold War Statesmen Confront the Bomb: Nuclear Diplomacy Since 1945.* Oxford and New York: Oxford University Press, 1999.

HILDEBRANDT, RAINER, *The Explosion.* New York: Duell, Sloan and Pearce, 1955.

KANET, ROGER K. (ED.), *The Soviet Union, Eastern Europe and the Third World.* Cambridge, Eng.: Cambridge University Press, 1987.

KHRUSHCHEV, NIKITA, *Khrushchev Remembers.* Boston: Little, Brown, 1971.

———, *Khrushchev Remembers: The Last Testament.* Boston: Little, Brown, 1974.

LEONHARD, WOLFGANG, *The Kremlin Since Stalin.* New York: Praeger, 1962.

LINDEN, CARL A., *Khrushchev and the Soviet Leadership, 1957–1964.* Baltimore, MD: Johns Hopkins University Press, 1966.

MACINTOSH, J. M., *Strategy and Tactics of Soviet Foreign Policy.* New York: Oxford University Press, 1963.

MATTHEWS, MERVYN, *Education in the Soviet Union: Policies and Institutions Since Stalin.* Winchester, MA: Allen & Unwin, 1982.

REMINGTON, ROBIN, *The Warsaw Pact: Case Studies in Communist Conflict Resolution.* Cambridge, MA: MIT Press, 1971.

RUSH, MYRON, *Political Succession in the USSR.* New York: Columbia University Press, 1965.

SAGDAEEV, RONALD Z., *The Making of a Soviet Scientist: My Adventure in Nuclear Fusion and Space from Stalin to Star Wars.* New York: John Wiley and Sons, 1994.

SCHOLMER, JOSEPH, *Vorkuta.* New York: Holt, Rinehart and Winston, 1955.

SCHWARTZ, HARRY, *The Soviet Economy Since Stalin.* Philadelphia: Lippincott, 1965.

STEHLE, HANS JAKOB, *The Independent Satellite.* New York: Praeger, 1965.

SWEARER, HOWARD R., *The Politics of Succession in the USSR.* Boston: Little, Brown, 1964.

SYROP, KONRAD, *Spring in October: The Polish Revolution of 1956.* New York: Praeger, 1958.

TATU, MICHEL, *Power in the Kremlin: From Khrushchev to Kosygin.* New York: Viking, 1969.

ULAM, ADAM, *New Face of Soviet Totalitarianism.* New York: Praeger, 1965.

VALI, FERENC A., *Rift and Revolt in Hungary.* Cambridge, MA: Harvard University Press, 1961.

WESTAD, ODD ARNE, *Brothers in Arms: The Rise and Fall of the Sino-Soviet Alliance, 1945–1963.* Washington, DC: Woodrow Wilson Center Press and Stanford, CA: Stanford University Press, 1998.

WHITNEY, CRAIG R., *Spy Trader: Germany's Devil's Advocate and the Darkest Secrets of the Cold War.* New York: Times Books and Random House, 1993.

ZINNER, PAUL E., *Revolution in Hungary.* Plainview, NY: Books for Libraries, 1962.

Chapter 22

Khrushchev's Decline and Fall

While Khrushchev was basking in the light of his apparent successes, the consequences of his rash policies were accumulating. In October 1964, when he was overthrown, a saying was coined in the diplomatic and journalistic quarters of Moscow that he had lost power because of three "Cs": China, Cuba, and corn. As with most epigrams of this sort, this one reduces a complex set of causes to a witty alliteration. But if Cuba is meant to cover the totality of Soviet-American relations, if corn stands as a symbol of Khrushchev's domestic politics, and China for the quarrel with Peking, then the saying acquires some real meaning. Applying the formula of the triple "Cs," therefore, let us examine the causes of Khrushchev's decline and fall.

The Chinese Problem

The launching of two Sputniks, months before similar ventures in the United States, seemed to have opened an era of Soviet ascendance in space and the apogee of Communism. The fact that these achievements took place when Moscow was celebrating the fortieth anniversary of the Bolshevik revolution lent them a symbolic significance. The Chinese were even more impressed by the Soviet space feats than the rest of the world. In November 1957, Mao, forgetting his previous differences with Khrushchev concerning the de-Stalinization campaign, attended the celebration in Moscow to persuade Soviet leaders to take advantage of this apparent Communist advantage over the decadent capitalistic world. The first step in this direction, he argued, should be a challenge to the United States in the Far East; with the support of the Soviet Navy (and nuclear weapons if necessary), Mao Tse-tung planned an invasion of Taiwan and the offshore islands of Quemoy and Matsu. The USSR, master of the hydrogen bomb, now overshadowed the Americans in intercontinental missiles. Soon Mao began to argue that the socialist camp would triumph over the imperialists in every way. He claimed that the United States was a "paper tiger" and that "the East Wind" was prevailing "over the West Wind." In a talk with a Yugoslav delegation in Peking, Mao went as far as to say that a nuclear war would mean the end of capitalism but not of Communism: even if 300 million Chinese were killed, there would still be 300 million left alive.

Khrushchev was shocked by Mao's argument. The USSR was building up a fully developed Communist society, not inviting its destruction, he retorted. His ballistic missiles were instruments of Soviet State power. He had not the slightest intention of placing his nuclear weapons at the disposal of China. Moreover, he refused Peking's request to instruct the Chinese technicians in how to make them. This refusal was soon followed by theoretical disputes concerning Soviet Russia's and China's stages of historic development. After his return from the November 1957 Communist rally, the offended Mao launched a new program aimed at demonstrating not only China's self-reliance but even its superiority in the march toward Communism. Within a short period of time, Peking announced that some 90 percent of the Chinese peasantry had joined rural communes in which private property and the family were nearly obliterated in favor of a strictly regimented communal life style. This was combined with a new crash program of industrialization, epitomized by the hasty support to the cottage industries, symbolized by the small "back-yard blast furnaces." As a result of this attempted "great leap forward," argued Mao, China was to overtake its Russian comrade.

Initially, Soviet leaders had cautiously praised the experimental policy of the Chinese. This changed, however, when Peking proclaimed that it was about to pass the Socialist stage of development and achieve full Communism. Such a proclamation constituted an open challenge to the Soviet leadership of the Communist camp; the Chinese claim that Mao had found a short-cut to the final goal, and thus had overtaken the Soviet Union in its march toward Utopia, was a serious blow to Khrushchev's claim to leadership of the world Communist movement. The claim was based not only on Moscow's "revolutionary seniority," but also on the axiom that the Soviet Party headed the most

advanced society, one that had already constructed mature Socialism and was well along the way to Communism.

Initially, the Sino-Soviet dispute was purely theoretical, conducted in strictly Marxist terms. But by the early 1960s, with the emergence of a bitter territorial conflict, the power-political factors altered the nature of the conflict.

The Sino-Soviet Split

During the late 1950s, Khrushchev ignored the repeated requests of his Chinese Communist comrades for more military aid against America's protégé, Chiang, who was firmly entrenched on the island fortress of Taiwan, and for more economic aid to stave off the catastrophic failure of Mao's "second revolution." Khrushchev blatantly disregarded China's warning not to consort with the "capitalist imperialists" and pursued his policy of peaceful coexistence. The highwater mark of these efforts was his 1959 trip to the citadel of capitalism, a visit which Khrushchev enjoyed immensely. In October of 1959, after his American trip, Khrushchev flew to Peking to celebrate the tenth anniversary of the Communist triumph in China. At that time the artillery duel between the Chinese People's Liberation Army and the Nationalist forces, who successfully defended the offshore islands separating Taiwan from the mainland China, was still going on.

Mao ignored Khrushchev throughout his brief stay in Peking. The Soviet leader responded by leaving the Chinese capital before the conclusion of the anniversary celebration. The snub was followed by the further worsening of Sino-Soviet relations. After his return, Khrushchev ordered the withdrawal from China of most of the Soviet military, economic, and scientific experts who were helping their comrades in a variety of fields. This further damaged the already shaky relations between the two Communist colossi.

Until 1960 the depth of Sino-Soviet disagreements was carefully camouflaged. In June of that year, however, at the conference of Communist leaders in Bucharest, Khrushchev for the first time openly leveled bitter words of criticism of Chinese behavior. He attacked the absent Mao for his ignorance of modern warfare, especially of the dangers inherent in nuclear weapons; he upbraided him for his domestic politics that were not only "un-Leninist," and "left-revisionist," but also totally detached from the realities of the modern world. The head of the Chinese delegation in Bucharest indignantly retorted by accusing Khrushchev of having sabotaged the Chinese economic plans and having conspired with the "American imperialists" against China's vital interests concerning the reunion of the irredentist Taiwan with Mainland China. He charged the Soviet leader with total blindness to the dangers of imperialism. The Communist delegates present in Bucharest supported Khrushchev's agrument. Only Albania's leader, Enver Hoxha, openly sided with Peking.

Despite attempts at papering over the Sino-Soviet dispute, it went from bad to worse. In August 1960, the remaining Soviet students, scholars, and experts were promptly evacuated from China. Peking reciprocated. While most of their experts were safely released from the Soviet Union, the departure of the Chinese nuclear specialists studying at various Soviet atomic centers (mainly at Dubna near Moscow) was delayed for a long time. Soviet authorities refused to accept Peking's offer of military planes to transport the Chinese experts and insisted on sending them back in their own aircraft. When they were finally dispatched in a Red Army transport plane, it exploded in midair. There were no survivors. The Soviets explained the accident as "engine failure."

The conflict between the United States and Cuba in October of 1962 further complicated relations between Moscow and Peking. During the Sino-Indian war, which broke out in the meantime, the Soviet Union assumed a "neutral" position, which was immediately denounced by the Chinese as tacit support of a "bourgeois" country against a Communist one, and hence a flagrant violation of "proletarian solidarity." From then on, Sino-Soviet relations continued to deteriorate rapidly. Charges of mutual "betrayal," "perfidy," and "duplicity" appeared more and more often in ongoing, acerbic polemics. In March 1963, relations were further embittered by Peking's territorial demands. The Russians were reminded that the Soviet Maritime Provinces in the Far East and the whole valley of the Amur River had once belonged to China and that they had been wrested away as a result of the "unequal treaties" imposed on Peking by the Tsars.

Tension along the common frontier mounted and resulted in a series of large-scale bloody incidents. The signing by the USSR of the international partial nuclear test ban treaty in July 1963 brought relations between Moscow and Peking to their lowest point yet. The Chinese bitterly denounced the agreement as "a capitulation to United States imperialism," and a "dirty fraud" calculated to prevent all the threatened peace-loving countries, including China, from increasing their defense capabilities by acquiring their own nuclear weapons.

The Sino-Soviet cold war gradually spread all over the world. The Chinese, using their Albanian allies as an instrument of propaganda, launched a sharp campaign against the Soviet domination of Eastern Europe. Skillfully, they made numerous attempts at splitting other Communist parties. Soon every party in the world had its pro-Chinese as well as pro-Soviet faction. The Romanians, without openly siding with Peking, tended to assume an increasingly neutral position by publishing official communiqués of the two rivals side by side.

It is probable that the Sino-Soviet split was inevitable in the long run. But it is certain that it was precipitated and made more ferocious than it needed to be by Khrushchev's arrogance. For instance, Khrushchev often referred to Mao as "a racist," "a mixture of petty bourgeois adventurist, a great-power chauvinist," and a "worn-out galosh."

Khrushchev thus unnecessarily embittered the quarrel by adding personal factors to the already potent ideological and power-political differences.

Moscow and the Third World

The second cause of Khrushchev's mounting troubles was the lost Cuban gamble of 1962. The Cuban crisis must be viewed against the broad background of Soviet-United States as well as Soviet-Chinese relations, Khrushchev's inner admiration for American drive and efficiency was enhanced by his 1959 trip to the United States. Good relations with the United States, which still enjoyed definite nuclear superiority, fitted his doctrine of the peaceful coexistence of states with different sociopolitical systems, since it made a virtue out of necessity. Khrushchev's quest for better relations with the United States was hampered, however, by the growing Soviet drive for influence in underdeveloped countries, especially in Latin America, Africa, and Southeast Asia, coupled with repeated challenges to the Western position in Germany. Competitive coexistence suited Soviet objectives because it allowed the still militarily weaker of the two Cold War rivals to make peaceful, and often not so peaceful, penetration of the other side's perimeter without the risk of armed confrontation.

In the aftermath of World War II, the Western powers had granted independence to most of their former colonies. This opened the way for the two superpowers to extend their influence into these newly emerging unstable countries. Khrushchev revised Stalin's doctrine, which was based on the assumption that all nations newly freed from Western bondage, but still preserving ties with their former colonial masters, were in fact "cryptocolonial." Thus, Khrushchev assumed the existence of a new vast sphere of political neutralism, the *Third World*, where competitive coexistence could be tested fairly safely. He was ready to bid against the West by sending material and diplomatic aid to nationalist anti-Western regimes, whenever he wanted to create an opening for Soviet influence.

Soviet assertiveness in the countries of the Third World found its theoretical expression on December 6, 1960, in the form of a "Declaration of Representatives of the Communist and Workers' Parties" signed in Moscow by representatives of eighty-one Communist parties. The declaration formally announced that the Communist world aimed to step up its offensive "by all means" and to follow a more militant policy in underdeveloped countries in order to subvert all Western influence in these areas. The Communist parties were to support politically, economically, and even militarily all anti-Western forces in underdeveloped countries and rebuff interference in the affairs of the people of any country that had risen in revolution against Western colonialism. All these points were incorporated into the new Soviet Party program adopted by the Twenty-Second Party Congress in October 1961, which thereby formally endorsed this new Communist support to "wars of national liberation."

The new Soviet militancy in the Third World was soon to manifest itself in the formerly French and Belgian sub-Saharan Africa. In Africa it centered around the Congo (now Zaire), hastily emancipated from Belgian rule. The Soviets were attracted to the Congo by its strategic location, its vast mineral resources, as well as the amenability of one of the Congo leaders, Premier Patrice Lumumba, to Soviet persuasion. During the summer of 1960, Moscow made a vigorous but unsuccessful attempt to support Lumumba and the radical forces he led. The attempt backfired, however, because of the intervention of United Nations forces, supported by Washington. By September 1960, Lumumba was driven out of office. In February 1961, he was assassinated by his opponents.

Moscow blamed UN Secretary General Dag Hammarskjöld for Lumumba's death, and refused to pay its share of the UN's Congo expedition. Moscow recognized the pro-Soviet regime of Antoine Gizenga in Stanleyville as the legal government of the Congo and threatened to intervene on his behalf. All that remained of the Congo adventure was the renaming of a University for the Friendship of Peoples, which was established in Moscow in February 1960 as the Patrice Lumumba University. The school was set up to train three to four thousand students from Africa, Asia, and Latin America.

In the meantime, Khrushchev's anti-UN offensive continued. Late in 1960 the Soviets started a forceful offensive to undermine and discredit that world body. Speaking as the head of the Soviet delegation to the Sixteenth General Assembly of the United Nations in October 1960, Khrushchev argued that a true world organization must reflect the actual distribution of world power, which he believed to consist of the Communist, the Western, and the uncommitted nations. He insisted that the office of Secretary General be replaced by a three-man directorate, a *troika.* At one point in his forceful speech, Khrushchev went so far as to emphasize a point by pounding his desk with his shoe. This behavior tarnished both the Soviet world image and Khrushchev's personal prestige.

The Berlin Crisis

The marked deterioration of Soviet relations with the Western powers did not stem exclusively from Moscow's repeated attempts to win over the countries of the Third World, nor from the continuing Communist anti-Western propaganda. In addition, Khrushchev stepped up his efforts to dislodge the Western powers from Germany. Relations with Washington got still worse when in May 1960 an American U-2 reconnaissance plane was shot down over Sverdlovsk, deep inside the USSR. President Dwight Eisenhower first claimed that the U-2 was an unarmed weather plane.

To the amazement of the entire world, Khrushchev produced the captured pilot,

Khrushchev examines the United States U-2 spy plane shot down over Soviet territory in May 1960

Francis Gary Powers, thereby forcing Washington to admit that the U-2 was not a weather plane but a high-flying craft on an espionage mission. This incident doomed the planned Khrushchev-Eisenhower summit meeting. Khrushchev insisted that the President publicly acknowledge that the United States had committed an act of aggression against the USSR, apologize for it, and punish all those responsible.

The U-2 incident was followed in June by the Soviet shooting down of another American plane, an RB-47, in the Arctic Ocean. Both incidents created frigid Soviet-United States relations, which remained in that state until well after the election of John F. Kennedy in November 1960. Khrushchev sent the President-elect a congratulatory message and in January 1961, as "a gesture of "friendship," ordered the release of the imprisoned fliers of the RB-47 plane. Early in June 1961, the two leaders met in Vienna to examine their respective positions on world problems. From Khrushchev's point of view the meeting was to be exploratory in nature. The new President, scion of a wealthy family and a young man of little international experience, must have appeared to Khrushchev as a playboy with a toothpaste-advertising smile. During the meeting, Khrushchev handed to Kennedy an eight-point memorandum outlining the Soviet view of the German situation and insisting on Western withdrawal from Berlin. On June 17, the United States replied with a detailed outline of its negative response to the Soviet proposal, stressed its determination to maintain a Western position in Berlin. At the same time, President Kennedy alerted Western garrisons in the divided city, which was surrounded by the East German territory and powerful Soviet garrisons.

On August 13, 1961, the international situation took a turn for the worse. To prevent further massive East German escapes to the West, East German leader Walter Ulbricht ordered the construction of a concrete wall across Berlin and began to tamper with Allied traffic within the city. This challenge, combined with numerous incidents along the border, made Berlin the most explosive spot in the world. Early in September 1961, abandoning his self-imposed moratorium on thermonuclear atmospheric tests, Khrushchev ordered resumption of Soviet nuclear tests. Throughout the rest of 1961 and most of 1962, both sides confronted each other with open preparation for what appeared like an approaching nuclear war.

The Berlin crisis soon became intertwined with another critical situation centering around Cuba.

The Cuban Missile Crisis

In 1959, relations between Washington and Havana deteriorated rapidly as a result of the seizure of power in Cuba by a radical leader, Fidel Castro. He not only nationalized the holdings of United States citizens, but insisted on the return to Cuba of the United States naval base at Guantánomo Bay. At the same time, Castro systematically developed a close collaboration with the Soviet Union. In February 1960, he signed a trade agreement with the USSR and was given a loan equivalent of $100 million. From that time on, Soviet influence over the island proceeded apace, to the extent that on December 2, 1961, Castro openly declared himself a "Marxist-Leninist." In June 1960, a new economic agreement provided for the exchange of Soviet iron ore for Cuban sugar. The Cuban army was gradually equipped with Soviet weapons, including tanks and planes. Further help, including rockets, was promised "if the aggressive forces of the Pentagon should dare to start an intervention against Cuba." These steps, paralleled by Castro's vigorous anti-United States propaganda campaign, which found a measure of support in many other Latin American countries, resulted in the rupture of diplomatic relations with Washington. In April 1961, the United States backed attempts by some anti-Communist Cuban refugees to overthrow the Castro regime;

John F. Kennedy, Nikita S. Khrushchev, and Andrei A. Gromyko in Vienna, June 1961

the attempt, known as the Bay of Pigs invasion, failed miserably.

While Washington was gradually reconciling itself to the idea of having a Communist island ninety miles off the Florida coast, the Castro regime proceeded to develop still more intimate military ties with the Soviet Union. In July and August 1962, Fidel's brother, Raúl Castro, who was the Cuban War Minister, and Che Guevara, the Minister of Industries, visited Moscow and concluded an agreement that provided for the dispatching of Soviet personnel and sophisticated offensive equipment. An agreement which Khrushchev kept secret even from his KGB boss, intermediate ballistic missiles were also included.

United States intelligence promptly spotted these arrangements. On October 22, President Kennedy in a televised speech warned the Cubans and their Soviet allies against the dangers of constructing launching pads for such weapons as ballistic missiles on an island so close to American shores and declared a quarantine on Cuban waters as of October 24. At the same time, Washington submitted to the UN Security Council proof of the construction of the Cuban nuclear missile bases by Soviet rocketry specialists. The evidence was angrily denied by the Soviet delegates. Meanwhile, on October 23, all military leaves for Soviet defense personnel were canceled, and the Supreme Commander of the Warsaw Pact countries put their forces on alert. Thus, in addition to the Berlin crisis, another highly explosive situation was now created in the Caribbean only 90 miles south of Florida. The two superpowers found themselves on the verge of a nuclear war. At that time there were forty-two nuclear missiles in Cuba fully ready for action, manned mostly by Soviet personnel.

One cannot fully understand Khrushchev's Cuban or German gambles without taking into consideration the rapidly widening Sino-Soviet split. By 1962, Khrushchev was under strong pressure to reassert the prestige of the Soviet Union both as a state and as the headquarters of the world revolution. The reckless Chinese talk about the hollowness of the American threat, about the cowardice of all those Communists who were afraid of a showdown with the craven capitalist "paper tiger," impressed some radical

Communists all over the world. In Cuba there seemed to be an excellent opportunity to throw Moscow's generous support to a fledgling Communist regime and thus belie Peking's accusation of Moscow's betrayal of the proletarian revolution in the interests of a temporary detente with the citadel of capitalism. Khrushchev came to the conclusion that the price of reasserting the Kremlin's revolutionary role, while at the same time bolstering the Soviet position toward the United States, was worthwhile. In the back of his mind he must have mistakenly thought that "the playboy" President, soon to face another presidential campaign, would never risk the danger of nuclear incineration of millions for the sake of a few missiles on Cuban soil. Surprised by the American readiness to fight Khrushchev got scared and began to hesitate.

The Compromise

At this critical point, at the end of October 1962, UN Secretary General U Thant offered a suggestion that led to an exchange of letters between the leaders of the rival superpowers. As a result of that exchange, it was revealed that Khrushchev was willing to compromise and dismantle the missile bases in Cuba in exchange for the withdrawal of U.S. missiles from its bases in Turkey as a face-saving measure. President Kennedy rejected this proposal, which was made on October 26. The next day he ordered further military preparations, including the mobilization of United States paratroop reservists. The Cuban missile crisis had reached its peak.

At this moment of supreme danger, around noon on October 28, Radio Moscow made public another letter from Khrushchev to the White House. This letter, without insisting on the previously proposed exchange of bases, offered to dismantle unconditionally the Soviet missile installations on the Cuban soil. The sudden Soviet surrender was a tacit acknowledgment of U.S. strategic superiority over the Soviet Union. Khrushchev was obviously unable to

back his Cuban gamble with sufficient naval and air support. Contrary to Mao's allegation, America was not a "paper tiger," or at least, as Khrushchev pointed out later, it was a "paper tiger with nuclear claws." The opposite view was taken by Fidel Castro. He urged Khrushchev to launch a preemptive strike against the United States regardless of the consequences of such action.

As a result of the Soviet capitulation, the threat of thermonuclear holocaust was averted. From a historical perspective, the Cuban missile crisis appears as a major turning point in the mounting global crisis generated by the two superpowers. Faulty perceptions and miscalculations among the three nations involved led to a situation that none of the three had either foreseen or desired. Castro saw American-sponsored counterrevolution and a new invasion of Cuba as the greatest threat to his regime. Exploiting this suspicion, Khrushchev placed Soviet missiles within range of the United States. This could partially offset American nuclear superiority by placing middle-range rockets on the territory of the first Communist state in the western hemisphere, close to the shores of the United States. This Washington regarded as a mortal threat.

The crisis ended with a compromise imposed on all three sides by the fear of a ghastly nuclear devastation. Khrushchev, who had miscalculated President Kennedy's determination, withdrew from the Cuban adventure without catastrophic consequences for his country, while extracting a qualified U.S. guarantee of respect for Cuba's independence. Washington was relieved to see the missiles withdrawn, its strategic superiority confirmed, and the Monroe Doctrine at least partially reasserted. Finally, Castro, although disappointed by the Soviet capitulation, profited from a promise that the United States would not again sponsor an invasion of Cuba.

The Cuban confrontation, besides discrediting Khrushchev as an irresponsible gambler, tarnished Soviet international prestige. The crisis dramatically revealed the Soviets' naval weakness that prevented Moscow from projecting its power faraway from its shores. After the Suez crisis of 1956, the energetic Admiral Sergei G. Gorshkov had started to expand the Soviet naval forces initially neglected by Khrushchev, but this crash effort came too late to counterbalance the preexisting American naval superiority. His effort was hampered by the geostrategic position of the Soviet Union surrounded by four separate maritime spaces: Baltic and Black Seas in the West, and Arctic and Pacific Oceans in the North and East. This made an especially heavy drain on the limited economic resources of the Soviet Empire.

The Cuban crisis, during which Khrushchev acted without sufficient consultation with his defense experts, further alienated the military establishment from the leader, whose ill-considered moves brought about humiliation to the country's armed forces.

The removal of the danger of Soviet nuclear blackmail and the gradual relaxation of tension in Berlin that soon followed led to an improvement in relations between Moscow and Washington. The Cuban crisis dramatized the danger of the hitherto slow conventional diplomatic channels in an age when the fate of the world could be decided in a matter of seconds. As a result of this realization, on June 20, 1963, the two superpowers agreed to establish a direct communication link between the White House and the Kremlin called the "hot line." Moreover, frightened by the spiraling atomic arms race, on July 25, 1963, the USSR, the United States, and the United Kingdom successfully negotiated a partial nuclear test ban treaty. The three powers pledged to stop test explosions of nuclear weapons in the atmosphere, in outer space, and under water, but not under ground. The signatories reserved the right to propose amendments to the treaty, as well as the right to withdraw from its obligations should any one of them feel that its vital interests had been jeopardized. They invited all other powers to join the ban. Many states expressed their readiness to be a party to the treaty, but neither China nor France subscribed to it; both continued to experiment with all sorts of nuclear weapons, despite numerous international protests.

Domestic Difficulties

During the early 1960s, while Khrushchev was busy with foreign affairs and Soviet cosmonauts continued to make history in space, the Soviet economy deteriorated. Industrial growth was slowing down, and consumer goods were still in short supply and poor in quality. The collectivized agriculture was the festering wound of the economic illness. Even the triumphal flight of half a dozen Soviet spaceships could not obscure the fact that the Soviet people were shortchanged of those boastful promises that Khrushchev had repeatedly made in the past.[1]

While propagandizing the space achievements as "new triumphs of Lenin's ideas" and a manifestation of "the invincible might of Socialism," Khrushchev had to eat his words and renege on his 1957 pledge of overtaking the United States. The harvests of both 1959 and 1960 proved to be bad; the latter was as much as 20 million tons of grain short of what had been expected. At the same time, the livestock situation also deteriorated: in 1960 almost 10 million sheep starved and the number of cattle also decreased greatly. Khrushchev blamed the failure not so much on climatic conditions as on the poor, obsolete organization of agricultural administration, the backwardness of Soviet agrotechnology, and the large-scale pilfering of grain before and during the harvest. To correct this, he pledged to divert a larger share of capital investment to agriculture. At the same time, the death penalty was ordered for several categories of "economic crimes." Between May 1961 and May 1964, several thousand people were reprimanded and jailed for such crimes, and about 200 were sentenced to death by shooting.

Despite these Draconian measures, the

---

[1] During the late 1950s and early 1960s Soviet cosmonauts successfully completed at least six spectacular feats. A direct (unmanned) landing on the moon was made by a Soviet spaceship on September 12, 1959, and pictures of the moon's hidden side were taken. On April 12, 1961, a major in the Soviet Air Force, Yuri A. Gagarin, achieved the first manned orbital flight around the earth aboard the spaceship *Vostok I.*

food crisis continued, further undermining Khrushchev's already precarious position.

The Twenty-Second Party Congress

Meanwhile, in October 1961, the Twenty-Second Party Congress, solidly packed with Khrushchev's supporters, unanimously approved a new Party program, the third in its history.[2] The program anticipated that "the building of the foundations of Communism" in the Soviet Union would be completed by 1980. At that time the principle "from each according to his abilities, to each according to his needs" was to be implemented. This objective was to be reached in two stages: from 1961 to 1970 the country was to create a material and technical base for Communism, improve the living standards of the people, and surpass the United States in per capita production. From 1971 to 1980, the USSR was to achieve "a gradual transition to a single form of public ownership."

For agriculture this Twenty-Year Plan had a twofold aim: to provide an abundant supply of food and to obliterate "the distinction between town and country." To attain these goals Soviet agriculture was expected to achieve a high degree of mechanization, irrigation, and a "scientific system of land cultivation and animal husbandry." The Plan postulated that the extension of "the luxury of city living" to the countryside would make household peasant plots economically "obsolete" and unprofitable and that the peasants would "give them up of their own accord." By 1980, the total volume of production was to increase by 250 percent; grain output was to double, milk to triple, meat to quadruple, and the productivity of agricultural labor was to rise by between 400 and 500 percent. The Twenty-Second Party Congress was notable for its abandonment of the term "dictator-

ship of the proletariat" in favor of a new populist slogan calling the Soviet regime as "a state of the whole people."

At the Congress, for the first time in public, Khrushchev called Stalin a murderer, an instigator of mass repression against Communist leaders, and a man who had flagrantly violated Lenin's principles by criminally abusing power. Many Congress delegates seconded Khrushchev's charges against Stalin. On October 30, 1961, the delegates voted unanimously to remove Stalin's body from the Lenin mausoleum in Red Square for reburial alongside the Kremlin wall; Stalin's name was to be erased from the tomb. Shortly after this gesture, the city of Stalingrad was renamed Volgograd. Soon other cities, streets, collective farms, mountains, canals, factories, and the like throughout the USSR and its European dependencies—save for Albania, led by staunch Stalinist Enver Hoxha—followed suit. Khrushchev went so far as to suggest that a monument to Stalin's victims be erected in the heart of Moscow. All these measures, while accepted by the Twenty-Second Party Congress, caused dissatisfaction among the diehard Stalinists.

The Ups and Downs of De-Stalinization

The resolutions of the Twenty-Second Congress were not easy to realize. Soon food prices increased substantially in order to shift some of the cost of intensifying agricultural production to the urban population, as Khrushchev explained. On June 1, 1962, the mass media announced that the retail price of meat was to be increased 30 percent and that of butter 25 percent. This staggering price rise coincided with a State-sponsored "economy drive," which had already reduced the take-home pay of workers by approximately 10 percent. In reply to these measures, widespread riots, sit-down strikes, and mass demonstrations broke out among Soviet workers. For instance, in Novocherkask, a city of 100,000 residents, these riots lasted over a week and cost hundreds of lives. Street protests also flared up in Moscow, Groznyi,

---

[2] The original program of the movement was adopted at the Second Congress of the Russian Social Democratic Workers' Party in London in 1903. The second was adopted at the Eighth Party Congress in March 1919.

Gorkii, Krasnodar, Donetsk, Iaroslavl, and Zhdanov. Massive sit-down strikes occurred in Leningrad, Krivoi Rog, Omsk, and several cities in the Urals. The disastrous harvest of 1963 resulted in panic buying of food.

The Twenty-Second Party Congress was followed by a partial relaxation of controls over intellectuals. The most outstanding example of this freedom was the publication in the November 1962 issue of *Novyi Mir* of the novel *One Day in the Life of Ivan Denisovich* by Alexander Solzhenitsyn, a former inmate of a labor camp. The work describes the phantasmagoric life of prisoners in a forced labor camp under Stalin—a world apart ruled by its own unwritten cruel laws—which reflected the Soviet reality of those days. The work of Solzhenitsyn was published in book form as a result of Khrushchev's personal decision. It is paradoxical that the man who in 1958 had been shocked by Boris Pasternak's relatively mild indictment of the Soviet regime in his epic Nobel Prize-winning novel, *Doctor Zhivago*, now sponsored the incomparably more traumatic story of Ivan Denisovich.

Meanwhile, some Soviet intellectuals, encouraged by the momentary loosening of ideological supervision over published material, began to press for further concessions, including the abolition of censorship. Following the release of Solzhenitsyn's book, Soviet publishers and editorial offices were flooded with thousands of similar accounts. All of this frightened Khrushchev and made him clarify the Party's position in the matter of freedom of expression.

At a series of conferences between Party leaders and intellectuals during the first half of 1963, liberal intellectuals suddenly found themselves face to face with angry Party leaders. As always at such affairs, the principal spokesman was Khrushchev himself. At one of them, he went back on his previously lenient position and warned "the smiths of the human psyche" that freedom had its limits and that the Party was still determined to delineate them. He warned the artists not to expend their energies on "one-sided" presentations of such aspects of Soviet reality as "lawlessness, arbitrary reprisals and abuse of power" during "the years of the personality cult." The Hungarian uprising, he said, would never have occurred if the Budapest government had had the courage to shoot a few of the rebellious writers in good time. Should a similar situation occur in Moscow, he would know what to do: "My hand would not tremble."

As Khrushchev's domestic and international difficulties increased, and the opposition of the hard-line Communists began to grow in intensity, he began to softpedal his anti-Stalin campaign and resorted himself to some of the harsh practice usually associated with the late tyrant. The tightening of censorship and wider application of the death penalty for "economic crimes" were examples of his growing intolerance.

The Agrarian Crisis

The showdown with the liberally inclined intellectuals and artists was paralleled by the deepening of the economic crisis. By the spring of 1963 it became evident that the goals set by Khrushchev were far beyond the reach of the Soviet economy: Its rate of growth was declining steadily. The 1963 harvest, despite the fact that that year the USSR had the largest sown area in its history (some 350,000,000 acres), was disastrous. Consequently, Moscow had to negotiate two huge grain purchases. One was from Canada and involved 6.5 million tons; the other, amounting to 1.6 million tons, was from Australia. The extent of Soviet grain purchases abroad in 1963 reflected the magnitude of the failure of the Soviet collectivized system and resulted in a catastrophic setback to Khrushchev's image. Taking advantage of these setbacks, the suppressed opposition raised its head and began to attract people hitherto devoted to Khrushchev.

To understand the reasons for Khrushchev's failures, we have to examine more closely his erratic economic policies. According to Khrushchev, overtaking the United States in per capita production should occur first in the production of food, where Soviet Russia would be less handicapped by its backward technology, and where it would have both a considerable reservoir of rural manpower and large reserves of unutilized land in Southern Siberia and Central Asia, especially the steppe areas of Kazakhstan. Hence Khrushchev's two pet projects: the virgin land campaign and the corn campaign.

The initial success of the virgin land campaign, which produced the bountiful harvest of 1956, made him expand the existing acreage. Everything—manpower, machinery, and fertilizers—was poured into the new agricultural regions, to the neglect of the old, vital grain-producing areas like the Ukraine or the Northern Caucasus. Yet throughout the entire Seven-Year Plan of national development (1958–1965), in only one of those years was the government's grain quota for the virgin lands fully met. This was the result of a variety of factors which were rashly overlooked by Khrushchev, who was hellbent on immediate, spectacular success. As a result of hasty plowing, not deep enough, soil erosion rapidly increased. Consequently, most of the virgin lands became an ecological disaster by the early 1960s. Some experts had predicted that this would happen and warned Khrushchev of the folly of superficially plowing millions of hectares of open steppes unprotected by forests. He had dismissed these experts as "pessimistic scarecrows." The hasty cultivation of the virgin lands could have been less disastrous if some attempt had been made to apply well-proven methods (proper crop rotation, animal husbandry, and so forth). But with shallow plowing, combined with inadequate fertilizer, and periodic erratic mobilizations of labor recruited for a month or two, this was impossible. Not only were fertile lands plowed, but so were saline areas and large expanses of light sandy loams which were soon blown away by the wind. During the dry summer of 1962, wind erosion struck at several million hectares, and this was only the beginning. In the spring of 1963, wind storms (with winds up to ninety-five miles an hour) blew away millions of

tons of fertile soil. This amounted to a full-scale ecologic disaster.

The "Corn Campaign"

Another of Khrushchev's pet projects was planting corn, both as a supplement to human diet and as fodder crop for livestock. The initial small increase of corn acreage in 1954 did not satisfy Khrushchev. And although the necessary seed, fertilizer, machinery, silos, and experience were lacking, he issued an order: Corn acreage must be substantially expanded in almost all agricultural areas. This meant a reversal of the newly adopted system of agricultural planning whereby collective farms would be permitted to decide for themselves what crops to raise. Now they were ordered to plant corn, corn, and more corn. As a result of this pressure, the amount of corn cultivation rose dramatically. Soon everyone jumped on the corn bandwagon. In 1954, the corn area had increased to 4.3 million hectares (one hectare equals two and a half acres). By 1955, under Khrushchev's relentless pressure, it was expanded to 18 million hectares. Yet he was not satisfied with these advancements and he pressed for further expansion of corn planting. By 1960, corn acreage had risen to 28 million hectares and in 1962 it reached 37 million hectares.

Having staked his prestige on tripling meat production, Khrushchev felt that only corn could guarantee the livestock herds he desired. He failed to consider that corn requires not only great inputs of labor and fertilizer, but also hot weather and rich soil. The obsession with corn and the pouring of vast manpower and technical resources into its cultivation inflicted heavy injury on the entire agricultural sector and consequently retarded economic progress of the entire country. Lest the kolkhozniks turn back their hay making, the government halted the manufacture of equipment for improving and maintaining natural meadows. As a consequence wild weeds overgrew the pastures. Thus, one-third of all meadowland was almost completely abandoned. The average annual production of hay dropped from 64 million tons in 1953 to 47 million tons in 1965. The cattle suffered and meat production dropped dramatically. Thus, the "corn campaign" was a catastrophe and added to the nation's agricultural woes.

Khrushchev's Style of Leadership

To complete the examination of the reasons for Khrushchev's downfall, we should say a few words about his leadership style. A typical authoritarian personality brought up in the Stalinist school of absolute obedience, he liked arbitrary one-man decisions. He consulted only those whom he personally trusted, and suffered no outside criticism. Moreover, Khrushchev had a tendency to surround himself with random advisers who had no official role in the Party or government. In many cases he relied on the advice of these personal friends as aides rather than on the recommendations of members of the Presidium and the Politburo, or the cabinet ministers. This bypassing of the Party and government hierarchy made him many additional enemies. Khrushchev also traveled a great deal, both within the Soviet Union and abroad, making bombastic speeches. Moreover, he frequently made decisions during these travels when only his own coterie was available for consultation. Gradually, there formed around him something like an "inner cabinet," a clique consisting of his closest cronies. They tended to operate quite independently of the Council of Ministers or the Presidium. As the influence of the "inner cabinet" increased, Khrushchev's relations with members of the government and of the Party steadily eroded. Emboldened by the abandonment of the old style "liquidation," his opponents began to form conspiratorial preparations to overthrow him.

Khrushchev's style of leadership threatened the Party top apparat with marginalization. The personality cult that had developed around him, a sign of which was the press constantly inundated with exaggerated reports about his alleged successes, made him a laughingstock in the eyes of the opposition.

To the dissatisfaction that permeated the Party network was added Khrushchev's loss of popularity with the military establishment because of his unilateral decision to reduce the size of the Soviet Armed Forces and cut down the military budget. This resulted in the premature retirement of thousands of career officers, which diminished their pensions.

Aware that his popularity among Communist elite had plummeted, Khrushchev launched three policies likely to endear him to the Stalinist hard liners: a renewed, vigorous antireligious campaign, the curtailment of the growth of private peasant household plots, and a drive to turn kolkhozes into State farms. This policy was especially dear to Khrushchev, who was fond of the grandiose and was dreaming of merging all agrarian land into huge agrotowns. But the policy backfired. The resistance of the peasants, fiercely attached to their highly productive household plots, cut down food production and increased the provisioning difficulties in the cities. As a result of the renewed antireligious drive, some two thousand churches, many of them valuable historic relics, were closed. Religious persecution increased in 1961 due to the enactment of the new Criminal Code of the Russian SSR. Article 227 of that Code declared criminal any religious activity that might cause citizens "to reject socialist activity or the performance of their duties as citizens," as well as "the enticement of minors into a [religious] group." This meant that even parents were now forbidden to give their children religious instruction, even at home. This decreased his popularity in the countryside, where religious sentiments were still rather strong.

Khrushchev and the Party

The restless Khrushchev tried to modify Party rules, as well as to recast its program. Under the new rules, which were applicable to governing Party bodies, and even to the Central Committee itself, it became mandatory for one-third of the members of each committee to be replaced by new Party workers at each election. Theoretically this rule could be applied to the Presidium too, but Khrushchev exempted himself from it. The new rules meant that there would be a periodic evaluation of the performance of people in office. While the new rules enabled Khrushchev to remove those he disliked, they deprived most of the Party apparat of the sense of security they had enjoyed since 1953.

In November 1962, Khrushchev, without consulting the Party Congress, made a move that was to precipitate another crisis. He decreed a radical reshaping of both Party and government structures. This reorganization reversed the decentralization measures of 1957 and concentrated all economic planning in the USSR in the Supreme Economic Council (SEC). Directly below the SEC were two pivotal agencies: the Gosplan, which was responsible for the current plan, and the National Building Agency. The new reform resulted in the division of the unitary Party into two sections, one for agriculture and one for industry. A Central Committee Bureau for Industry and a Central Committee Bureau for Agriculture were formed. At the same time, the Russian branch of the Communist Party of the Soviet Union, neglected by Stalin, was reactivated. Although at the top the industrial and agricultural Party hierarchies were subordinate to one head, the First Secretary, virtually the entire Party structure was now split into two independent constituents.

These reforms reduced the authority of the provincial Party secretaries, who comprised the bulk of the Central Committee. By alienating such a substantial portion of the Soviet *nomenklatura*, Khrushchev gravely weakened his own political base. Soon an undercurrent of tension arose between Khrushchev and the secretaries of the regional committees, who in large measure formed the membership of the crucial Central Committee. This tension was skillfully exploited by his rivals.

As the failure of the reforms became more and more visible and the mounting chaos submerged the Party apparatus, Khrushchev's opponents gathered strength. While industry was less affected, agriculture staggered under new handicaps. For instance, agricultural sections had no power to recruit urban factory or office workers for seasonal agricultural labor in case of emergency, and emergencies were almost constant. The industrial sections, now free of responsibility for agriculture, were no longer interested in lending thousands of their workers to mow hay, bring in the harvest, or dig potatoes. Without this assistance, agricultural quotas were impossible to fulfill. The shock of the Party split, compounded by the agricultural failures, compounded by the gigantic grain purchases abroad, galvanized Khrushchev's rivals into action.

Khrushchev's Downfall and His Place in History

The splitting of the Party into two sections was the proverbial straw that broke the camel's back. In October 1964, while Khrushchev was away from Moscow on vacation, those who opposed him ganged up to bring him down. The opposition, centering around his wartime comrade and protégé, Leonid Brezhnev, enjoyed the support of the dissatisfied marshals as well as the head of the secret police, Alexander N. Shelepin. Summoned by the Presidium back to Moscow on "urgent business," the surprised Khrushchev had to face a formidable barrage of criticism on the part of a hostile Presidium. This time his old trick of appealing from the Presidium to the Central Committee did not work. By that time, even most of its members had been alienated by his innumerable "hare-brained schemes," his erratic and irresponsible style of leadership.

Although the overthrow of Khrushchev was officially described as a "resignation," there was never any doubt that it was more of a palace revolution preceded by a sharp power struggle. On October 17, 1964, the main Party daily *Pravda*, reflected the debates that led to Khrushchev's fall by accusing him of "wild schemes; half-baked conclusions and hasty decisions and actions divorced from reality; bragging and bluster; attraction to rule by fiat; unwillingness to take into account what science and practical experience have already worked out. . . ."

Khrushchev's downfall introduced several elements of novelty into the annals of Soviet history. Khrushchev was the first top Soviet leader without prerevolutionary experience. He was also the first true proletarian Party boss. In addition, he was the first ruler in Russia's history to be deposed by being outvoted by a process that at least vaguely resembled Western parliamentary procedure. He lost power, but not his head. He became an un-person, but not a corpse. The deposed leader was kept under close supervision in his summer home near Moscow until his death in 1971 at the age of 77. His son,

Sergei, emigrated to the United States and became a professor at Brown University.

Khrushchev's most important historic role was that he presided over the first stages of destruction of the Stalin myth and the partial dismantling of the Great Tyrant's inhuman system. Thanks to Khrushchev, millions of survivors of the Gulag Archipelago returned to more or less normal life. Despite his denunciation of the Stalinist harshness, however, Khrushchev occasionally relapsed into the old, heavy-handed methods; yet his reprisals could never compare with Stalin's savage mass terror. Khrushchev suffered also from Stalin's mania of launching crash programs, which resulted in throwing massive resources into one great drive after another with its concomitant inevitable waste and chaos.

Yet Khrushchev must be given credit for alleviating the rigors and drabness of the rural life and for supplying at least a trickle of consumer goods to the average Soviet citizen. Not

A view of Moscow in 1959 from the top of the University building

the least of his achievements was a vast program of housing construction. Poor in quality, these hastily prefabricated dwellings soon turned into slums; but in comparison with the shocking neglect of the problem under Stalin, even this was noteworthy progress.

Scientists, scholars, and intellectuals in general owed a debt to Khrushchev. Under his rule cultural exchanges with the West were resumed after two decades of Stalin's ban on such contacts. At least some Soviet scholars and artists were once again permitted to publish, travel abroad, and renew their participation in international scientific conferences, contributing to a partial reintegration of Soviet scholarship into the world academic community. These were modest gains, but they have to be judged against the nightmare of domestic thought control and the almost complete isolation from abroad that Stalin had imposed on Soviet intellectuals.

Khrushchev as a statesman has to be viewed from a broad historic perspective. This unprecedented sequence of traumatic experiences—stretching over three generations—profoundly scarred the psyche of the Soviet people. Khrushchev, in spite of all his grave errors, gave the Soviet people some relief from their sufferings and tried to heal their wounds as best as he could. There is no doubt that Soviet Russia, after 1964, was a better place to live than before 1953, that is, in comparison with the Stalinist period.

Suggested Reading

BESCHLOSS, MICHAEL R., *The Crisis Years: Kennedy and Khrushchev 1960–1963*. New York: Harper-Collins, 1991.

BLOOMFIELD, LINCOLN P., ET. AL., *Khrushchev and the Arms Race: Soviet Interests in Arms Control and Disarmament, 1954–1964*. Cambridge, MA: MIT Press, 1966.

BOFFA, GIUSEPPE, *Inside the Khrushchev Era*. New York: Marzani & Munsell, 1963.

BROMKE, ADAM (ED.), *The Communist States at the Crossroads: Between Moscow and Peking*. New York: Praeger, 1965.

BROWN, J. F., *The New Eastern Europe: The Khrushchev Era and After*. New York: Praeger, 1966.

BRZEZINSKI, ZBIGNIEW (ED.) *Africa and the Communist World*. Stanford, CA: Stanford University Press, 1963.

———, *Dilemmas of Change in Soviet Politics*. New York: Columbia University Press, 1969.

COHEN, STEPHEN F. (ED.), *An End of Silence: Uncensored Opinion in the Soviet Union; From Roy Medvedev's Underground Magazine, Political Diary*. Translated by George Saunders. New York: Norton, 1982.

CONQUEST, ROBERT (ED.), *Agricultural Workers in The USSR*. New York: Praeger, 1969.

———, *Russia after Khrushchev*. New York: Praeger, 1965.

CRANKSHAW, EDWARD, *The New Cold War: Moscow vs. Peking*. Plainview, NY: Books for Libraries. 1963.

DINERSTEIN, HERBERT S., *The Making of a Missile Crisis: October 1962*. Baltimore, MD: Johns Hopkins University Press, 1976.

FISCHER-GALATI, STEPHEN, *Eastern Europe in the Sixties*. New York: Praeger, 1963.

JOHNSON, PRISCILLA, *Khrushchev and the Arts: The Politics of Soviet Culture, 1962–1964*. Cambridge, MA: MIT Press, 1965.

KASER, MICHAEL, *Comecon: Integration Problems of the Planned Economics*, 2nd Ed. New York: Oxford University Press, 1965.

KHRUSHCHEV, NIKITA S., *Khrushchev Remembers*. Boston, MA: Little, Brown, 1971, 1974.

KHRUSHCHEV, SERGEI, *Nikita Khrushchev and the Creation of a Superpower*. University Park: Pennsylvania State University Press, 2000.

———, *Khrushchev on Khrushchev: An Inside Account of the Man and His Era*. Boston: Little, Brown, 1990.

MACGWIRE, MICHAEL, KEN BOOTH, AND JOHN McDONNELL, *Soviet Naval Policy: Objectives and Constraints*. New York: Praeger, 1975.

McCAULEY, MARTIN (ED.), *Khrushchev and Khrushchevism*. London: Macmillan, 1987.

MEDVEDEV, ROY (Trans. Brian Pearce). *Khrushchev*. Garden City, NY: Doubleday, 1983.

PLOSS, SIDNEY L., *Conflict and Decision-Making Process in Soviet Russia: A Case Study of Agricultural Policy, 1953–1963*. Princeton, NJ: Princeton University Press, 1965.

RUSH, MYRON, *Political Succession in the USSR*, 2nd Ed. New York: Columbia University Press, 1965.

SALISBURY, HARRISON E., *War Between Russia and China.* New York: Norton, 1969.

SMITH, STANTON GERALD, *Songs to Seven Strings: Russian Guitar Poetry and Soviet "Mass Song."* Bloomington: Indiana University Press, 1985.

TATU, MICHEL, *Power in the Kremlin: From Khrushchev to Kosygin.* New York: Viking, 1969.

TOMPSON, WILLIAM J., *Khrushchev: A Political Life.* Basingstoke: Macmillan, 1997.

VALKENIER, ELIZABETH K., *The Soviet Union and the Third World: An Economic Bind.* New York: Praeger, 1983.

ZAGORIA, DONALD S., *Vietnam Triangle: Moscow, Peking, Hanoi.* New York: Pegasus, 1967.

Chapter 23

Soviet Russia Under Brezhnev's Rule

The Khrushchev spoils were divided between Leonid I. Brezhnev, who took over the post of the Party's First Secretary, and Alexei Kosygin, a former Finance and Consumer Goods Industry Minister and First Vice-Premier, who now became Prime Minister. The new leaders pledged not to follow in the footsteps of their predecessor and to observe the rules of collective leadership.

Son of Russian working-class parents, Leonid Brezhnev was born in December 1906 in Kamenskoe (later renamed Dneprodzerzhinsk), in the Northern Ukraine. According to his official biography, he was a graduate of a classical high school. In 1923, the young Brezhnev joined the Komsomol and was sent to take a land surveyor's course, which enabled him to enter public administration in 1927. In 1931, he joined the Party and entered the metallurgical institute, from which he graduated in four years. After serving as a political commissar in World War II under Khrushchev, Brezhnev left the military service in 1946 as a major general. Soon he became Party chief in Zaporozhye, where his energy in rebuilding a hydroelectric station and a steel plant was evidenced. In the early

1950s, he served as Party chief in Moldavia and then in Kazakhstan, both good schools of political-administrative work. While Party boss in Kazakhstan, Brezhnev was very helpful to Khrushchev in launching his pet virgin lands scheme. The excellent harvest of 1956 rescued Khrushchev from his predicament. To reward Brezhnev for this service, Khrushchev made him a Secretary of the Central Committee and a member of the Politburo. In 1960, he became titular president of the USSR, which enabled him to travel abroad and familiarize himself with foreign affairs.

Brezhnev's ascent to supreme power was more rapid than that of Khrushchev. The Twenty-Third Party Congress (March–April 1966) recognized Brezhnev's preeminence and awarded him the prestigious title of Secretary General, which had not been in use since Stalin's death. By the early 1970s, Brezhnev was also a leading spokesman in foreign affairs. On official visits abroad he began to be received with the ceremonial protocol due a head of state. By the fall of 1967, he dominated celebrations of the fiftieth anniversary of Bolshevik power.

From the middle 1970s on, Brezhnev's

Leonid Brezhnev (1906–1982) as a young member of the Politburo

unquestioned supreme power was underlined by a series of exceptional honors bestowed on him by the Supreme Soviet. On May 8, 1976, he was elevated from the rank of five-star general of the army to marshal. Gradually, a cult of personality also developed around Brezhnev.

Brezhnev and Kosygin's Attempted Reforms

The paramount initial task of the new leaders was to put some order into the administrative chaos inherited from Khrushchev. They had to discard, first of all, his most unpopular policies, starting with the split of the Party into two sections. The Khrushchev-initiated campaign to eventually transform all collective farms into unwieldy State farms was suspended. Private plots owned by collective farmers were restored to their previ-

ous size, assistance was again offered to collective farmers in acquiring livestock, and the tax on cattle owned by city dwellers was repealed. Yet in 1965 the proposed doubling of state investment in agriculture was shelved. Most of the funds were shifted to the armament industries.

In 1965, Kosygin tried to decentralize Soviet industrial planning by allowing more play in the forces of supply and demand. Wages for both managers and workers would depend on profit, that is, on the actual sale of products, not on the fulfillment of prescribed quantitative norms. As in Yugoslavia, the Soviet economy would become a "market socialism"; supply and demand would again play their role, and suppliers and manufacturers would deal directly with one another rather than going through central ministries.

Soon, however, the attempted innovations were aborted by opposition from hard-line Pary bureaucrats. First, they watered down the reforms by reinstating the principle of strict central planning; then they slowed down their implementation. The reasons for this sabotage of Kosygin's reform were quite clear. The conservative Party opposition realized that to free managers from central tutelage would reduce the power of the Moscow bureaucracy. The local Party boss exercised his power the same way the old Tammany Hall man did his, simply by virtue of the fact that his word was law. The Party chieftain had the final say on jobs, rents, and who got what reward in his bailiwick. Every far-reaching economic reform raised the issue of how far the Party could allow liberalization to go without losing the political supervision necessary to maintain its hold on the country. One may imagine the following case: A factory director who under a new decentralized system has authority to hire and fire, uses his power and dismisses a man who had obtained his job as a reward for Party work. Who was to decide whether the man was to go or to retain his job? Consequently, the old pattern, which strongly favored heavy industry, was maintained.

The worsening situation in the countryside alarmed Kosygin who considered the farm sector as a rat hole. His remedy was more mechanization. Yet, despite considerable investment in machinery and fertilizers, agriculture remained the Achilles heel of the Soviet economy. The annual harvest continued to fluctuate. A poor crop in 1972 depressed the rate of economic growth to 1.7 percent; the good harvest of 1973 raised it momentarily to 7.5 percent. Crop failures in 1963 and 1972 resulted in repeated shortages of bread and flour. In 1972, the USSR purchased as much as $750 million worth of grain from the United States. Despite an excellent harvest of 222.5 million tons of grain in 1973, a large part of it was wasted because of poor transport facilities and lack of proper silos. Consequently, the USSR did not achieve self-sufficiency in grain and fodder. Later harvests were much poorer. Actually per capita agricultural production in the USSR during the 1960s and 1970s was rising only about 1 percent annually. Small private plots continued to provide about one-third of gross Soviet agricultural output.

Between 1976 and 1980 no less than 474,000 new tractors and combines were supplied to the collective and State farms. The lack of maintenance, however, devastated them and 322,000 were soon written off as unusable.[1]

The Arms and Space Races

Despite the shrinking Gross National Product, the growth of the Soviet armed forces continued. The defense budget increased rapidly, in order to allow Moscow to project its might to distant parts of the globe. Altogether, between 1966 and 1982, the Soviet

military budget expanded from 13 billion rubles to well over 20 billion rubles. These official figures were incomplete, however, because the published defense expenditures included only a portion of the overall Soviet military expenditure. The actual figure for defense, space, and nuclear-energy programs had been estimated by Western experts to be as high as 30 to 40 percent of the country's GNP, which amounted to less than half of that of the United States. As a result of their mounting allocation of funds to defense-oriented heavy industry, the Soviet armed forces also increased their stockpiles of intercontinental ballistic missiles. At the same time they were building up their conventional forces into the world's largest standing army, achieving nuclear parity with the United States, as well as making the Soviet Union the world's second naval power, a ruinous task in view of the much smaller resources and its geostrategic position.

The new leadership also continued the space effort of its predecessor and tried to overshadow the United States in cosmic accomplishments. One of the more spectacular Soviet space achievements was the September 1970 soft landing and return of a robot craft; not only did it land on the moon, but it also brought back three-and-a-half ounces of its surface dust. This was followed in November of the same year by the soft landing of an eight-wheeled moon-rover (*Lunakhod*), the first self-propelled vehicle to ride on the lunar surface. Impressed by these brilliant achievements, the United States agreed to cooperate with the USSR in space experiments. In July 1975, the USSR and the Americans staged a joint venture; the Soviet space ship *Soyuz* (Union) had a rendezvous with an American ship, *Apollo*. In 1983, two Soviet astronauts established the world endurance record in space by orbiting the earth for 185 days.

The impressive Soviet successes in space were due to a variety of factors. The Russians, traditionally good in theoretical mathematics, had also been paying a great deal of focused attention to rocketry since the

---

[1]Agricultural land area of the former Soviet Union was about 70 percent greater than that in the United States, but used more than seven times the manpower, with about one-third the tractors and trucks. Although the former USSR number some 42 million cows, twice as many as the United States, Soviet milk production was only slightly higher than American.

beginning of the century. The Soviet government took over and intensified these prerevolutionary efforts. It was quick to perceive the connection between rockets and their significance for military weaponry; consequently the Soviet governments put considerable resources into further research in the field. Because the program was defense related, it was provided all the financial support it needed. Prestige and propaganda considerations also played a major role in furthering the ambitious space programs. The enormous defense and space effort, however, resulted in lamentable sacrifices in all nondefense-oriented branches of an economy that was starved of badly needed investment funds, especially in agriculture.

Domestic Recompression

The Brezhnev-Kosygin team also had to cope with the manifold consequences of Khrushchev's de-Stalinization campaign. By destroying the legend of Stalin, Khrushchev destroyed the myth of Party infallibility and thus weakened its hold on the people's minds. Some of the more daring individuals who had not lost the capacity to ask pertinent questions, especially the youth less inhibited by memories of the Stalinist terror, began to query the hitherto unquestionable Communist dogmas and practices. This ferment was especially striking in intellectual circles, where the liberalization process had considerably loosened the ideological pressure; this was especially true of artists, writers, and scholars, who were no longer required to pay lip service to socialist realism and dialectical materialism.

The mounting political unrest made the collective leadership nervous. Bent on Party controls, they were very concerned with the effect of intellectual opposition to ideological orthodoxy. By 1965 the trend of de-Stalinization had been reversed; for instance, memoirs of leading World War II military leaders began to praise Stalin's contribution to wartime achievements, and Brezhnev made repeated laudatory references to the role played by the late dictator. Alexander M. Nekrich's book about the initial military blunders of Stalin (entitled *June 22, 1941*) was banned. In 1970, Stalin's grave at the Kremlin wall was provided with a marble bust.

The trend toward partial revindication of Stalin as a meritorious statesman encountered outspoken criticism among an important segment of the Soviet intelligentsia. Chief spokespeople for the opposition, which manifested itself especially strongly in academic circles and among the technological elite, included some of the leading minds of the USSR. Notable critics of the new trend were Pyotr Kapitsa, the dean of Soviet physicists; Andrei D. Sakharov, the father of Soviet-controlled thermonuclear bombs; and Zhores A. Medvedev, a geneticist and the author of a major work in the sociology of science.

The most daring, courageous, and persistent critic of the re-Stalinization attempts was Sakharov, who in 1968 published a significant document entitled "Thoughts on Progress, Peaceful Coexistence and Intellectual Freedom." In this eloquent manifesto he advocated permitting genuine freedom of thought in the Soviet Union. According to Sakharov, such freedom was indispensable for the full development of science and hence for solving the most urgent problems facing Soviet society. Sakharov repeatedly condemned the monopoly of power by the Communist Party, dominated by "hypocrites and demagogues." He criticized the Party's continued preaching of class struggle and the Marxist-Leninist assumption that world ideologies and nations are incompatible and clash eventually. Stressing the danger of nuclear war to mankind, Sakharov urged Soviet-American cooperation to save civilization. He argued that the Soviet and American systems, borrowing from each other, should eventually end up with triumph of democratic socialism. Sakharov bluntly warned Soviet leaders that unless secrecy were removed from science and technology, the USSR would become a second-rate power. As a result, he pleaded for an end to bureaucratic despotism and censorship and urged a liberal-democratic reform of the Soviet regime.

The Dissent Movement

Late in 1970, Sakharov established the Human Rights Committee in the USSR. The declared aim of the committee continued for several years "to give consultative aid to the organs of power in applying guarantees of human rights" theoretically granted by the Soviet Constitution of 1936 but not respected in practice. In 1975, Sakharov was awarded the Nobel Peace Prize, but was refused permission to leave his country to receive the award from fear of not being permitted to return.

While opposition in top scientific circles was less exposed to ruthless Soviet "administrative measures"—not only because of the continuing need of the regime for the expertise of some of the leading dissenters—this

Andrei Sakharov (1921–1989)

has not been the case with other protesters. The artistic and literary wing of the opposition originally was centered around a former inmate of concentration camps, Alexander Solzhenitsyn, author of *One Day in the Life of Ivan Denisovich, Cancer Ward,* and *The First Circle,* and the recipient of the 1970 Nobel Prize for literature. His bold criticism, not only of vicious practices of the Soviet regime but of Marxism as alien and harmful to the Russian ethos, soon made him subject to harassment and persecution. When in 1974 he began to publish abroad his monumental, multivolume work *The Concentration Camps,* soon to be referred to as the "Gulag Archipelago," as he dubbed the huge, sprawling prison system, Moscow reacted. In 1975, Solzhenitsyn was expelled from the USSR. Eventually, he settled in the United States, where he continued his bitter criticism of Communism, while presenting his own vision of Russia's future.

Hampered by rigid censorship, the dissenters tried to spread their ideas in a variety of ways, ranging from protest demonstrations and the circulation of privately printed, uncensored publications, to the smuggling of literary works abroad. Among the most significant phenomena in this sphere was the emergence of an underground periodical entitled *Chronicle of Current Events,* which made its debut in the spring of 1968. The bimonthly *Chronicle* carried information on the latest arrests and imprisonments of anti-Soviet dissenters; the periodical also printed texts of vital documents and letters of protest about official persecution of ethnic and religious minorities (Jews, Ukrainians, Crimean Tatars, Lithuanians, Estonians, Baptists).[2] Until his confinement to an insane asylum in February 1969, one of the most prominent contributors to the *Chronicle* was former Major General Pyotr Grigorenko, a highly

[2] The underground publications were usually referred to by the Russian term of *samizdat. Samizdat* is a play on words. *Gosizdat* is a telescoping of *Gosudarstvennoye Izdatelstvo,* the name of the monopoly-wielding State Publishing House. The *sam* part of the new word means "self." The whole—*samizdat*—translates as "we publish ourselves"— that is, we the people.

decorated World War II hero of Ukrainian descent. In the spring of 1978, while visiting the United States, he was deprived by Moscow of his Soviet citizenship, military rank and medals; thus he was forced to become a political exile.

Soviet authorities treated dissenters either as dangerous elements they deported abroad (as in the case of Solzhenitsyn and another outspoken dissenter, Vladimir Bukovsky), or simply as traitors. In some cases they were classed as mentally deranged persons requiring treatment in mental institutions. This last was the fate of an increasing number of dissenters, including Alexander Yesenin-Volpin. According to a statement by Yuri Andropov, then Chairman of the Soviet State Security Committee and therefore boss of the KGB apparatus, the failure to endorse Soviet Communism was in itself a sign of a serious mental illness and could only be cured by psychiatric treatment.

During the 1960s, 1970s, and 1980s, a number of prominent Soviet citizens defected from the USSR and sought political asylum in the West. The most sensational among them was Stalin's only daughter, Svetlana Alliluyeva, who, after settling in the United States, published several revealing accounts of her relations with her father. Other prominent defectors who reinforced the emigration ranks included the two leading Russian writers, Solzhenitsyn and Siniavsky, and leading Soviet ballet stars Rudolph Nureyev and Mikhail Baryshnikov.

Some Soviet dissenters, known as "culturalists," adhered to the Russian tradition of oppositionists as morally motivated fighters; many of them wanted to include the Orthodox Church as an integral part of the Russian tradition. Many of them were ready for endless, and perhaps hopeless, sacrifices to fight for their moral imperative. While most dissenters, including Sakharov, did not emphasize religion, a large segment of the dissent movement did reveal a strong religious coloring. A considerable segment of that movement, especially its Social Christian wing, stressed a deep interest in the Russian past, including prerevolutionary art, especially ikons and old architecture. The rediscovery of old Russia, partly through field trips to remote places to study surviving historic monuments and old handwritten documents, became a passion with many dissenters, for it provided them with a live contact with the roots of their native tradition.

Ethnic Ferment

Closely related to the political and intellectual dissent was the surfacing of a powerful wave of national awareness among non-Russian ethnic minorities. Constituting nearly half of the total population, these minorities pressed to claim those rights theoretically granted by the Soviet Constitution. The predominance of Great Russians in most top Party and Government posts, along with the pressure to impose Russian culture on non-Russians under the guise of Sovietization, were increasingly criticized. A significant external factor that stimulated unrest was the worldwide decolonization and the birth of new independent states in Asia and Africa out of the ruin of Western empires.

Ethnic ferment was already apparent in the Khrushchev era. To pacify the restless Ukrainians, Khrushchev offered them a gift in the form of the peninsula of Crimea in 1954. From then on it was to form an integral part of the Soviet Ukrainian Republic. After the Twentieth Party Congress of 1956, several national minorities formerly accused of collaboration with the Germans and banished from their homelands (Kalmyks, Chechens, Kabardinians, Balkarians, Ingush, Volga Germans, and Crimean Tatars) were rehabilitated and partly allowed to return to their national territories. This was done immediately for most of the groups, who were sent back to their former settlements. The rehabilitation of the Volga Germans and the Crimean Tatars, however, dragged on until 1967.

In the vanguard of the agitation for the implementation of human rights for all ethnic groups was the Jewish minority, which numbered nearly two million people. Stalin never openly preached anti-Semitism as a theory, but it was inherent in his practice and, as his daughter Svetlana testified, in private he often gave vent to his violent anti-Semitic sentiments. Khrushchev was more outspoken in his anti-Semitism. The publication in 1962 of Yevtushenko's poem "Babi Yar," dedicated to over 100,000 Kiev Jews massacred during the war, revived the issue. This precipitated Khrushchev's angry insistence that "We do not have a Jewish question." Nevertheless, he maintained that it is better for Jews not to hold high posts in government, for this only stirs up further popular resentment.

The growing exclusion of Jews not only from politically sensitive posts, but also from most good jobs in general increased their opposition to the Soviet regime. There is considerable evidence that, like their Tsarist counterparts, Soviet officials singled out Jewish, as well as Ukrainian and Baltic dissenters, for unusually harsh treatment. Anti-Semitic policies in turn created increasing resentment on the part of Soviet Jews and led many of them to press loudly for strict application of those human rights that the Soviet Constitution promised them. The focal point of the Jewish demands was the right to emigrate to Israel. Initially, Soviet authorities denied this right, describing it as a form of "desertion of the Soviet fatherland." Under pressure of world opinion, however, Moscow began to allow thousands of Jewish dissenters to leave the country. Under Brezhnev, Jewish emigration reached its peak in 1979 when 51,320 Jews left the USSR. Thereafter, it dropped below 22,000 in 1980 and to 894 in 1984.

While the Jewish agitation, despite its unpleasant international repercussions, did not threaten the internal stability of the USSR, the ferment in the western borderland union republics, especially in the Ukraine and the Baltic countries, Lithuania, Latvia, and Estonia, was treated as a potential threat to the integrity of the USSR. Hence a series of purges of leading spokesmen of the "bourgeois nationalistic" deviationists. The

reprisals hit especially hard leading Ukrainian freedom fighters, including Valentin Moroz, Ivan Dziuba, Viacheslav Choronvil, and Ivan Svetlichny. In April 1966, two Ukrainian critics, Svetlichny and Dziuba, were accused of smuggling "nationalist" verses to the West. Chornovil, a courageous journalist who denounced the Russification reflected in shocking discrimination against the Ukrainian culture, was sentenced to forced labor. Similar purges took place in Azerbaijan, and Kazakh republics in the early 1960s, and in the Estonian, Latvian, Lithuanian, Ukrainian, Armenian, and Georgian SSRs in 1972 and 1973. Out of nearly 4,000 arrested dissidents, most were members of national minorities; about 60 percent of them were Ukrainians.

Brezhnev-Kosygin Foreign Policy

While in domestic politics the collective leadership rejected many of their predecessor's measures, in the field of foreign policy there was no significant break with the expansive line pursued by Khrushchev. After having criticized him for the break with China, neither Brezhnev nor Kosygin, who visited Mao in 1965 and again in 1969, were able to improve relations with Peking. Early in 1965, Sino-Soviet relations became strained by the increased military involvement of the United States in South Vietnam, where both Communist powers competed for predominance. In April 1965, in an effort to make their military assistance to North Vietnam more effective, Moscow asked Peking for the use of two airfields in southwestern China for air transit rights, and for the right to use harbor facilities in southern China. All the Soviet requests were turned down by Peking, jealous over Russia's influence in Southeast Asia.

During the period of the Chinese Cultural Revolution (1965–1969), Sino-Soviet relations deteriorated still further. In March 1969, the Moscow-Peking dispute erupted in a violent clash between Soviet and Chinese armed forces along the Ussuri River and later extended to other points along the 4,000-mile Sino-Soviet frontier. Both sides suffered heavy casualties; as in the past, each country held the other responsible for starting the conflict.

Chinese dialogue with the United States that began in 1971 and Peking's admission to the United Nations later that year did not improve Sino-Soviet relations either. Quite the contrary, it embittered them still further by inciting both sides to accusations of plotting nuclear attack against one another with the tacit support of an "imperialist silent partner." Neither the death of Mao in September 1976 nor the message of greetings sent by the People's Republic of China to the Soviet Union on the sixtieth anniversary of the Bolshevik revolution improved significantly relations between the two Communist giants.

The deployment of some forty army divisions, as well as considerable nuclear forces along the Sino-Soviet border, only slightly diminished Soviet pressure on Western Europe. However, the specter of a possible two-front war made legal confirmation of the territorial status quo in Europe a major and pressing objective of Moscow's foreign policy. In pursuit of that goal, Brezhnev renewed the call for a European conference to be followed by a European security pact that would reaffirm the frontiers established after World War II. The first step in that direction was the signing in September 1970 of a treaty of friendship with the government of West Germany. The treaty, followed by a similar pact between Warsaw and Bonn concluded in December of that year, ratified the 1945 status quo in Eastern and Central Europe. But the Soviet leaders continued to press for broader and more solemn confirmation of their wartime territorial gains by a European Security Conference. This they finally obtained through the Helsinki agreement in 1975.

Meanwhile, Moscow expressed interest in becoming a major participant in West European trade. For this purpose it concluded several agreements for marketing Soviet oil as well as natural gas abroad. Another urgent goal was to obtain superior Western technology. For instance, Moscow purchased a license from the Italian Fiat Company to produce its cars in Russia. For this purpose a new city was constructed on the banks of the Volga; the city was called Togliatti, in honor of the leader of the strongest Communist Party in Europe.

Soviet oil pipeline supplying the satellite countries of East Central Europe under construction

The Soviet Union and East Central Europe

Soviet leaders worked hard by various means to make permanent their control over the satellite countries of East Central Europe. One form of consolidating their hold was the establishment within the framework of the Council of Mutual Economic Assistance (CMEA or COMECON) of several supranational corporations to integrate the East European economies with that of the USSR. Other Soviet steps aimed at making East Central Europe more dependent on the USSR included the foundation of the International Bank for Economic Cooperation and the construction of the "Friendship Oil Pipe Line," which supplied Soviet oil to East Germany, Poland, Czechoslovakia, and Hungary at reduced prices.

Soviet attempts at economic integration with Eastern Europe were problematic. The foremost difficulty was an inability to resolve satisfactorily the problem of joint investment, prices, currency, and convertibility. The increasing pressure on Moscow's satellites resulted in two upsets. One of them was the opposition of oil-rich Romania to Moscow's integrative drive. This opposition, which had already manifested itself in 1963,

assumed new forms during the middle and late 1960s. Romania's ambitious leader, Nicolas Ceausescu, refused to submit to many Soviet demands, not only in the economic but also in the military sphere. While brutally tightening his domestic controls, Ceausescu pursued a largely independent line of foreign policy; for instance, Romania maintained an attitude of noncomment in the raging Sino-Soviet dispute and even went so far as to openly support Peking's point of view from time to time.

Another country that came to oppose the tightening of Soviet controls over its hegemonial sphere during the late 1960s was Czechoslovakia. Quiescent and submissive until 1964, the Czechs, but especially their junior partners, the Slovaks, gradually began to be affected by the political winds coming first from Tito's Yugoslavia, and then from Gomuľka's Poland after 1956 when that country began to enjoy considerable domestic autonomy. In 1964, the huge statue of Stalin, which for well over a decade had spoiled the beautiful panorama of "golden Prague," was toppled. Public opinion began to force partial concessions from the reluctant regime of the staunch Stalinist leader, Antonin Novotny. He tried for four years to channel the mounting discontent, but in

NATO   **WTO**

Soviet and Western systems of alliances in 1968

December 1967 he was dismissed from his post as First Secretary of the Czechoslovak Party. In January 1968, Novotny was replaced by Alexander Dubček, a reform-minded Slovak. Under the mounting pressure of public opinion, Dubček tried to liberalize the system and replace the lingering Stalinism with what he called "socialism with a human face." He abolished censorship, rehabilitated many victims of "the past period of mistakes," and even toyed with the idea of legalizing non-Communist political groups. He also showed considerable sympathy for various projects directed at loosening the Warsaw Treaty Organization and putting the Czechoslovak-Soviet military and economic relations on a more equitable basis. All this was accompanied by improving Czechoslovak relations with the West, including the Federal Republic of Germany, from which Dubček expected credits and technical aid to modernize the faltering economy of his country. The series of liberalizing political and economic reforms constituted the essence of what came to be called the "Prague Spring" of 1968. Dubček's efforts immediately aroused the suspicions of Moscow, which saw in them a threat to three main pillars of its control: the "leading role" of the Communist Party, the Warsaw Pact, and the CMEA, or COMECON.

Soviet response to the Prague Spring escalated through a series of warnings and preparatory military moves. At first Moscow tried to persuade Czechoslovak leaders to slow down the tempo of the reforms. When that failed they issued strong public protest and sought, in a series of top-level meetings, to persuade Dubček to stop the avalanche of changes that were affecting both the internal structure of Czechoslovakia and its international position as an integral segment of the Communist camp. When all these warnings failed, on August 21, 1968 the Soviets struck. With impressive speed and efficiency, Soviet, East German, Polish, Hungarian, and Bulgarian forces invaded and occupied Czechoslovakia. Dubček and his immediate associates were arrested and brought to Moscow in chains. There they were branded as traitors to international Communism and blackmailed into surrender.

Meanwhile, the invading forces encountered no active organized resistance and occupied the whole country. A new government run by a hardliner, Gustav Husák was imposed upon the country. His government signed a "Treaty of Friendship" that gave the Soviet forces the right of indefinite presence as well as the freedom to enter Czechoslovakia at will.

What motivated Brezhnev's violent reaction? An important factor behind the Soviet intervention was Moscow's fear that the triumph of the "liberals" in Czechoslovakia would destabilize the rest of the Soviet hegemonial sphere in East Central Europe, and eventually affect the Western fringes of the USSR, especially the restless Western Ukraine. The downfall of Novotny and the emergence of Dubček were for Brezhnev a signal of ferment in East Central Europe. All the Czech assurances of loyalty to the Warsaw Pact and the CMEA notwithstanding, Brezhnev, as a man schooled in Marxist dialects, must have interpreted Prague's "economic opening to the West" as the first step toward deeper cooperation between Czechoslovakia and the strongest European member of NATO. Consequently, Brezhnev must have viewed Czechoslovakia's experiment as representing not only the danger of capitalist contamination, but also a potential threat to the existence of the Communist system.

At the Polish Party Congress of December 1968, Brezhnev justified the military intervention as an exercise of the Soviet Union's right to protect "the achievements of the socialist construction" in other Communist states when they are threatened unrest. This concept was often called in the West the "Brezhnev doctrine."

Moscow and the Third World

After World War II, as European colonial empires collapsed one after another, the bitter conflicts among nations and tribes in Africa provided fertile ground for Moscow's intervention on behalf of the newly established, unstable governments. The Soviet backing of a mosaic of Third World regimes, "one-party democracies," guerrillas, and "national liberation movements" allowed the Kremlin to project its image as the main champion of colonial peoples. While Stalin had limited his expansion to the countries adjacent to the Soviet Union, which he could control with the bayonets of the Red Army, Khrushchev and Brezhnev began to project their rapidly expanding military and naval might into the most remote corners of the globe. This they tried to achieve by offering economic as well as military aid to a plethora of developing nations.

For instance, until 1965, Moscow continued to supply Indonesia with credits and economic assistance as well as liberal quantities of all sorts of weapons. As a reaction to the threat of Communist domination, the 1965 military coup overthrew President Sukarno. The upheaval was paralleled by a massive purge of the Indonesian Communists, then the largest nonruling Communist Party in the world. The establishment of a Western-oriented regime ended the spread of Communist influence in this oil-rich Indonesian archipelago. Also in Ghana the pro-Soviet regime of Nekumah was replaced by an anti-Communist military government in 1965. Neither this double defeat, nor a similar blow that in 1973 overthrew the Marxist coalition government of Salvador Allende in Chile, stopped Soviet attempts to penetrate and subvert the developing countries of the Third World.

Until 1972, the focal points of Soviet penetration in the Near and Middle East were Iraq, Syria, and Egypt, particularly the last. Strategically situated at the juncture between the African and Asian continents and controlling the Suez Canal, Egypt's role in the Soviet strategy was initially paramount. To strengthen Egypt's dependence on the USSR, a team of Soviet engineers helped to complete both the Aswan Dam on the Nile and the Helwan iron and steel complex near Cairo. Success in both fields bolstered Moscow's prestige considerably. While help-

ing Egypt's economy, the Soviets also lavishly supplied the country with tanks, planes, and rockets, as well as several thousand Soviet military advisers. After the large-scale destruction of the Egyptian arsenal during the Arab-Israeli War of June 1967, Moscow not only resupplied Egypt, but also installed many sophisticated surface-to-air missiles and radar stations and provided Soviet crews to man them. Thus, operating from Egyptian naval and air bases, the Soviets could challenge American control of the Eastern Mediterranean and easily move farther, to Aden, Sudan, or Libya.

The death of President Gamal Nasser in 1970 and his replacement by Colonel Anwar Sadat altered the Soviet position in the Middle East. Sadat believed that he could achieve his objectives—modernizing his country and regaining some of the Egyptian land lost to Israel—with American diplomatic support only. Consequently, in July 1972 Sadat expelled most of the Soviet advisory personnel from his country and made overtures to Washington to gain its support for his cause. Despite this gesture, Moscow tried to maintain its influence in Egypt, if only to assure the advantages its treaty of friendship with Cairo had given it at the Alexandria naval base. Yet, Soviet reluctance to rearm fully the Egyptian forces with the most sophisticated weapons, along with Moscow's insistence on prompt payment of the old debts, caused still further strains in the relations of the formerly close partners. President Sadat's cancellation of Egypt's friendship treaty with the Soviet Union and the subsequent liquidation of the Soviet naval bases in March 1976 caught Moscow by surprise. The Soviet Mediterranean squadron was suddenly compelled to anchor in international waters.

A major point of friction between the Soviet Union and the United States continued to be their conflicting attitudes toward the state of Israel. These differences repeatedly resulted in some highly explosive situations at the peak of the Egyptian-Israeli conflict of 1973, known as the Yom Kippur War. The Soviets readied an airborne division as Israeli troops broke across the Suez Canal and encircled an entire Egyptian Army corps. Washington's response to the impending Soviet military intervention was a worldwide alert of American military forces. This confrontation was only gradually diffused, thanks to the restraint shown by both sides and owing to the existence of the direct hot line between the Kremlin and the White House. The Russians, while reluctantly accepting the existence of Israel, supported the Arab's demands: total withdrawal from Arab territories occupied in the 1967 war, acceptance of Palestinian rights, including the right to statehood, and recognition of the Palestine Liberation Organization as the sole legitimate representative of the Palestinian people.

Moscow gave the Arab cause a great deal of diplomatic and military support. Its principal partners were Syria and Libya. Iraq was also linked with the Soviet Union by a Treaty of Friendship and Cooperation. All of these partners required assistance of one kind or another. During the 1970s, the USSR and Eastern European nations provided almost 90 percent of the military technicians in Africa. At the end of Brehzhev's rule, Moscow provided no less than foreign aid programs, for not only Communist states but also strategic allies like India and Egypt, countries it tried to manipulate.

This projection of power to the distant countries of the Third World was a considerable drain on its limited resources without bringing any tangible profit to the people.[3]

This trend to expand Soviet influence overseas was punctuated by the Soviet-Cuban intervention in the former Portuguese colonies of Angola and Mozambique, and by the grand design that Moscow tried to implement in Northeast Africa. Seldom in history has a great power made a bolder bid for establishing its influence than Brezhnev did

in 1977–1978, when he attempted to control the whole of the Suez Canal–Red Sea trade routes between Europe and Asia. At the end of 1976, with Libya and Somalia under their control and with military advisers and technicians entrenched in Sudan and Ethiopia, Moscow began to press into Chad in the heart of Africa. By the summer of 1977, Soviet forces were threatening the defiant Egypt with encirclement and had a chance to bring the whole Northeastern African region within Soviet sphere of influence. Brezhnev's costly gamble, supported by Cuba, staked Soviet prestige and billions in arms to build a pro-Soviet coalition out of the volatile situation in Africa's Horn, constructing a bloc that would offset the militarily weak pro-Western Saudi Arabia, as well as the mostly conservative Arab emirates in the Red Sea area. Moscow's plan called for forging Ethiopia, Somalia, Sudan, Djibuti, and South Yemen into a pro-Soviet constellation. Meanwhile, however, through a combination of excessive ambition and ineptness, the Russians suffered a sharp diplomatic setback. On November 5, 1977, encouraged by the United States, Somalia ordered all Soviet advisers to leave the country, ended the Soviet use of naval facilities on the Indian Ocean, and broke off diplomatic relations with Cuba. Not since 1972, when the Egyptians similarly expelled the Russians, had Moscow been dealt such a blow.

Another area of Soviet diplomatic activities was the Indian subcontinent. Trying to bolster India as a bulwark against China, Moscow viewed with unease the Indo-Pakistani war of 1965 and successfully mediated its prompt end. Early in 1966 Premier Kosygin met with leaders of both states in the capital of the Soviet Uzbek republic, Tashkent, and arranged a peaceful settlement that greatly enhanced Russia's image in Asia. While putting the main emphasis on India, which the Soviets had generously supplied with economic as well as military aid, Moscow also sought to establish good relations with Pakistan, whose friendship with Peking and proximity to Soviet borders were significant strategic factors. During the early

---

[3] To assure adequate yearly import of grain to the Soviet Union, Cuba, Vietnam, North Korea, and Mongolia, Moscow had to sell some 15 million tons of oil and 397 tons of gold a year. All this was only partly counterbalanced by the Soviet export of arms.

1970s, under Indira Gandhi's premiership, India's dependence upon Soviet industrial, military, and diplomatic support reached its zenith. Using Indian naval bases, Soviet warships in the Indian Ocean were able to challenge the Western preponderance in that geostrategically crucial area and to outflank China.

After the withdrawal of the Soviet ICBMs from Cuba in 1962, the regime of Fidel Castro continued to receive not only liberal financial subsidies and economic aid from Moscow, but also military assistance. In return for the aid that cost the Soviets up to five billion dollars per year, Castro sided with the Soviets in their quarrel with the Chinese. He also opened Cuban ports to Soviet naval units, and assisted Soviet efforts to establish a foothold in Angola by sending his troops to successfully support the local pro-Soviet "national liberation movement" against its rivals in the civil war that broke out when the Portuguese withdrew from Angola and Mozambique in 1975. Cuba's acceptance as a member of CEMA in 1972 marked its further integration into the Soviet camp. These were symptoms of the "Cold War" waged throughout the world between the Soviet Union and the United States.

Toward Detente

Despite these bold ventures, Brezhnev avoided any open confrontation with the United States, fearful of a possible nuclear Armageddon. That is why he made occasional attempts to seek the relaxation of tensions or a *detente*. To cope with these highly explosive issues, in July 1967 Kosygin met with President Johnson at Glassboro, New Jersey. Partly as a result of these talks, in August the two governments signed a treaty to check the spread of nuclear weapons.

The Soviet-led invasion of Czechoslovakia in August 1968 put a momentary damper on the attempts at detente. Early in 1969, however, relations improved somewhat when Moscow suggested ratification of the nuclear nonproliferation treaty and proposed that

the two powers begin discussions on a strategic arms limitation treaty (SALT). A new phase in the process of relaxation of tensions was reached as a result of the visit of President Richard Nixon in Moscow in May 1972. The most significant result of the Nixon-Brezhnev summit was the signing of a document called "Basic Principles of Relations between the USA and the USSR." By this declaration the two leaders agreed to develop normal relations "based on the principles of sovereignty, equality, [and] noninterference in internal affairs," while exercising restraint in order to avoid military confrontations. The two superpowers promised to cooperate in defusing dangerous tensions, to exchange views on mutual problems, and to limit their armaments. The meeting also included agreements that pledged the two countries to develop close economic relations and to cooperate in scientific, technological, and cultural fields.

Soviet-American relations were further strengthened by Nixon's June 1974 visit to the USSR and by President Gerald Ford's meeting with Brezhnev in Vladivostok that November. At Vladivostok the two powers set a ceiling on the number of offensive missiles for each side at 2,400. Soviet-American cooperation also increased in space and environmental research.

Meanwhile, in July and August 1975, thirty-five countries from Europe and North America convened at Helsinki and signed a document entitled the "final Act of the Helsinki Conference on Security and Cooperation in Europe." In effect, the document amounted to official Western recognition of the inviolability of the existing boundaries in Europe, thus legalizing the frontiers of Europe as established as a result of World War II, in 1945.

Initially, the Helsinki conference seemed to Soviet leaders like the fulfillment of their dreams, a true blessing. Yet, to obtain this coveted prize, they reluctantly accepted the so-called *third basket* of the Helsinki declaration. It included respect for human rights, the flow of information across borders, the right to travel, and even promises to extend "freedom of thought, conscience, religion or belief," as well as "the freedom of the individual to profess and practice, alone or in community with others, religion or belief, acting in accordance with the dictates of his own conscience." The third basket gave considerable stimulus to the Soviet dissent movement. Taking advantage of the momentary thaw, some courageous dissenters organized a net of civic committees to monitor the compliance of their government with the provisions of the "third basket." These so-called "Helsinki committees" became a vital factor in the spread of opposition to the Communist regime.

The military parade at the Red Square in Moscow during the sixtieth anniversary of the Bolshevik Revolution

The Constitution of 1977

On November 7, 1977, Soviet Russia celebrated its sixtieth anniversary with pride, pageantry, and fanfare. The huge, carefully orchestrated birthday party thrown by the regime was marked by two steps: a new constitution and a new national anthem that eliminated all mention of Stalin. The preamble of the 1977 Constitution described the USSR as "a society of mature socialist social relations" in which "the concern of all for the welfare of each and the concern of each for the welfare of all" was to be a guiding principle. Thus, the USSR was no longer officially defined as a dictatorship of the proletariat.

After thirteen years of leadership of the Party, while promulgating the new Constitution, Leonid Brezhnev was vested with the position of Chairman of the Supreme Soviet, or nominal Chief of State, while remaining the Party's Secretary General. No such precedent had existed in the Soviet Union. After Khrushchev was overthrown in October 1964, the Party resolved that the two posts could not be held simultaneously, but this restriction was not extended to the chairmanship of the Supreme Soviet. Brezhnev became the first leader to be both Soviet Chief of State and Chief Leader of the Party. The logic of the Soviet political mechanism, superimposed on the Russian inveterate tradition, combined with a deep psychological need of seeing a strong father figure at the apex of the power pyramid, pushed Brezhnev to the top.

The new Constitution formally endorsed the leading role of the Communist Party. In the 1936 Stalinist document, the Party was mentioned almost in passing in Article 126. A new preamble, as well as Article 6, now enshrined the Party as the guiding spirit in the Soviet State. While stating that "all power in the USSR is vested in the people," the new Constitution stressed that it was the Party that was the driving force behind all public bodies. The year 1977 seemed like the apex of Breznev's ascent to supreme power and prestige. Soon after that his health began to deteriorate. His loss of concentration and lapses of memory were often alarming. Not infrequently he would fall asleep at important Politburo meetings or read a speech twice.

Death of the Detente

The early and middle 1970s were the years of Soviet-American detente, which culminated in the Helsinki declaration of 1975, and the signing of the SALT II agreements in Vienna in 1979. While the West understood the term detente to mean a relaxation of international tensions, followed by expansion of trade and cultural exchange, Moscow adopted a much more tricky interpretation of the term. The Kremlin used the accompanying Western euphoria as an opportunity to expand in the Third World and undermine the United States position in Europe. The Soviets also intensified their attempts to weaken Western Europe's ties with NATO with the purpose of turning one European country after another into neutral, noncommitted buffer states.

These efforts, along with repeated Soviet military intervention in Africa, strained the detente, but did not ruin it altogether. What dealt the fatal blow were the events in 1979. The sequence started with the installation of new Soviet medium range SS-20 missiles in the Western regions of the USSR, as well as in East Germany and Czechoslovakia. Targeted on the main urban and industrial centers of Western Europe, the SS-20 more than doubled the Soviet strike capacity. Their installation meant that from well inside the Soviet orbit the Soviet missiles could reach NATO command posts and launching sites, while their own were out of reach of NATO's intermediate range missiles. Together with the marked Soviet superiority in conventional weapons, especially tanks and artillery, the SS-20 rockets threatened to destabilize the military situation in Europe.

The worsening of the strategic balance in Europe was paralleled by the overthrow of the pro-American ruler of Iran, the Shah Riza Pahlevi in the beginning of 1979. Suddenly, the pro-American establishment in Teheran was replaced by a fiercely anti-Western regime headed by a radical, fanatical Muslim leader, the Ayatollah Khomeini. His supporters not only sent the American military advisers packing, but also captured the United States embassy and kept its personnel as hostages for well over a year. The Ayatollah was certainly not pro-Soviet, but the Shah had been so pro-Western that his replacement amounted to a serious setback to Washington. Thus the upheaval in oil-rich Iran unsettled the Western position in the Middle East. As a result of the turmoil in

Iran, a dangerous power vacuum was created in the geostrategical area of the Persian Gulf. The damage of the West's position in the region implied a significant advantage to the Soviets. They saw a new opportunity to enhance their influence in the oil-bearing area adjacent to their southern border. This is why the Kremlin initially supported the Islamic revolution, even though it feared its impact on its adjacent Muslim Central Asiatic provinces. It was hoped in Moscow that the Tudeh Communist Party, banned under the Shah, could gain enough popular support to play a dominant role once the Ayatollah Khomeini, already over 80 years old, was no longer in control. The Khomeini forces initially exploited the Communist support, but they saw it as a danger to themselves. Consequently, the Ayatollah banished the Tudeh Communist Party in May 1983.

Meanwhile, in December 1979, with Iran hovering on the brink of chaos, and before SALT II could be ratified by the U.S. Senate, Soviet troops invaded Afghanistan. The reasons for the Kremlin's military move at that particular moment are still unclear. Brezhnev ordered the Soviet troops into Afghanistan to establish in Kabul a government completely subservient to Moscow. He calculated that the power vacuum created by the downfall of the pro-American Shah was too good an opportunity to be missed. If the Americans were to establish in Iran a military dictatorship replacing that of the Shah, he probably calculated, the result could be the establishment of United States bases on the Soviet border; with a hostile China stretching along most of the remaining Soviet frontier in Asia, and only a turbulent Afghanistan in between, this might have created a dangerous situation for the Soviets. On the other hand, Russian direct control of Afghanistan could eventually bring about a partition of Iran into spheres of influence, as had been the case in 1907 and during World War II. Or perhaps the Kremlin feared the birth of a radical Islamic fundamentalist regime in Afghanistan, a regime that could undermine its own Central Asiatic republics.

Whatever the real motives, conquest of

Afghanistan in 1979, a stepping stone of the Soviet drive toward the Indian Ocean

Afghanistan could offer a route to the waters of the Arabian Sea and the Indian Ocean. Moreover, in the process, the Soviet Union could acquire a land rich in iron ore, copper, uranium, and natural gas. Soviet military control of Afghanistan could considerably improve Moscow's strategic position toward the West as well as China, while directly threatening Iran and Pakistan. A substantial Soviet military presence would be placed not only at the Khyber Pass (the gateway from Central to South Asia) but beyond it. Should the gamble succeed, the Soviet forces would advance over the great divide of the Hindu Kush to within less than 500 miles of the Persian Gulf and the critical Strait of Hormuz, threatening oil routes of the Arabian Sea.

After the invasion, ruthless "pacification operations" were launched by the Soviet occupation army of over 100,000 men against the widespread Afghan resistance movement. The construction of numerous military bases and large, modern airfields seemed to indicate that the Soviet forces were planning to stay for good. At the same time, they engaged in a major effort to train Afghans in the Soviet Union to run the half-conquered country. Moscow's propaganda machine tried to explain the "pacification" of Afghanistan as a fight against an "imperialist" attempt to overturn the native "people's revolution."

The Soviet invasion of Afghanistan had several negative effects for the USSR. First, President Carter reacted to the act of naked aggression by shutting off the flow of high-technology items and grain to the Soviets and proclaimed a United States boycott of the 1980 Olympic Games in Moscow. Moreover, the Afghan resistance was unexpectedly strong and widespread and soon the invaders were entrapped in tricky guerrilla warfare, resembling the United States fight in Vietnam: The Soviet soldiers were able to hold cities, control main lines of communication, and carry out their own version of search-and-destroy missions. Yet the Soviet invaders stopped far short of "pacifying" the entire countryside; despite killing some 9 percent of the Afghan population and exiling some nearly 5 million, mostly to Pakistan and Iran. The invasion alerted Washington to recognize the necessity of improving American military readiness in the Persian Gulf and Indian Ocean areas. To protect their vital oil routes, to the naval and air base on the small but strategically vital island of Diego Garcia, the United States added new defense facilities in Egypt, Oman, Somalia, and Kenya.

Finally, the invasion of Afghanistan pushed the United States to develop closer ties with Peking, which included supplying American military-related technology to the Chinese armed forces. The invasion destroyed any hope that the United States Senate would ratify the SALT II treaty, signed in Vienna in the summer of 1979 by President Carter. The Soviet aggression also resulted in a far-reaching alienation of public and government opinion in much of the Third World, particularly in Muslim countries. Last, but not least, the invasion of Afghanistan helped to elect the militantly anti-Communist Ronald Reagan to the office of United States President. He called the USSR "the focus of evil in the modern world" and stimulated an abrupt rise in U.S. defense spending, which included considerable aid to the Afghan guerrillas. Thus, the war in Afghanistan resulted in a dangerous increase in international tensions and the drain on the Soviet resources was not compensated by any tangible gains.

To the end of his rule, Brezhnev continued the effort to extend Soviet influence deep into the Third World. This included not only Asia and Africa, but also Central America and the Caribbean region. In Latin America, Moscow focused its attention primarily on San Salvador and Nicaragua and on the little Caribbean island of Grenada, thus threatening the United States position in the vital region of the Panama Canal.

On the African continent, in 1975, Soviet weapons and technical and economic aid, as well as contingents of Cuban soldiers, brought Marxist revolutionaries to power in the former Portuguese colony of Angola. In Ethiopia, they helped the Castro-type Communist military regime to fight the rebels in Eritrea and the Ogadan desert. Thanks to Soviet and Cuban allies, by 1979 Ethiopia was able to reverse the initially unfavorable tide of rebellion and secure a precarious control over Eritrea, a strategically vital region at the Red Sea.[4]

For Moscow, the setback of the anti-Ethiopian rebellion in Eritrea was followed by a sudden shift of Soviet support from the equally Marxist rebels in Eritrea and Ogadan to the central government of Ethiopia, considered a more important ally of the USSR. Once Ethiopia had secured Eritrea's Red Sea ports, Massawa and Assab, the Soviets acquired two excellent naval bases along a 1,000 mile coastline. These harbors seemed to compensate the Soviets for their expulsion from the Somali port of Berbera in 1978. Thus, by scoring another victory by proxy, the Soviet Union momentarily became a leading maritime power in the Indian Ocean, across which so much of the West's oil must travel.

In November 1978, the Soviet Union signed a "friendship" treaty with Vietnam that committed the partners to maintain friendly relations for 25 years. Moscow agreed not only to consult with Vietnam in all matters pertaining to its region, but also to take "appropriate effective measures" if either partner were attacked or threatened with attack. A similar clause had been included in the Soviet-Indian Treaty of 1979.

Meanwhile, the United States, feeling threatened by the Soviet expansion in Asia and Africa, continued its policy of improving relations with China, which President Nixon had initiated in 1972. At the end of January 1979, the Chinese Deputy Prime Minister, Teng Hsiao-ping, arrived in Washington. He brought a long list of goods and services that the Chinese wished to obtain from the United States, as well as advice on how the United States should proceed in its dealings with the Soviet Union. The talks resulted in some U.S. assistance to help China in its modernization programs. On April 3, 1979, Peking, whose treaty with Moscow dated

---

[4]Eritrea, an Italian colony from 1890 to 1941, was joined to Ethiopia in a United Nations-sponsored federation in 1952. Without the Eritrean ports of Massawa and Assab, Ethiopia would have no access to the sea.

back to 1950, gave notice of its formal cancellation.

The Polish Crisis

What further aggravated the East-West tension was the crisis in Poland, which surfaced during the summer of 1980. Ever since 1956, Poland had been a maverick of the Communist camp. With the agricultural land overwhelmingly in the hands of individual farmers, the Polish People's Republic sharply contrasted with all of its partners. Moreover, Poland had relatively liberal cultural and religious policies. In exchange for the loyal support given by the Polish leaders first to Khrushchev and then to Brezhnev in all matters of foreign policy, Moscow reluctantly tolerated these peculiarities.

Encouraged by this tolerance, Edward Gierek, Party boss since the end of 1970, ventured even further. With Soviet encouragement, he framed an economic policy that was to use Western technology, which was to lead to a rapid expansion of Polish exports to the West, while, at the same time, supplying enough consumer goods to appease the restless population. By the mid-1970s, however, difficulties began to mount. The growing personal incomes generated by politically motivated higher earnings could not be offset by adequate supplies of consumer goods, especially food, for the domestic market and for export to the Soviet Union, thus leading to inflation.

Opposition to Gierek's policies first surfaced in 1975 when he proposed amendments to the Polish Constitution that would legitimize the leading role of the Party and "unshakeable bonds with the Soviet Union." Faced with widespread protests from the people, the Polish Party was forced to modify these ambitious goals. By the summer of 1980, the deepening economic crisis and food shortages had become so acute that the government made an attempt to impose drastic price increases. In response, in mid-August workers in the Gdansk shipyards conducted a sit-down strike. By the end of that month, the strikes spread throughout the country and soon received backing from the Church hierarchy and many intellectuals. Led by a dynamic electrical worker, Lech Walesa, representatives of various regional striking committees formed a massive trade union.

On August 31, 1980, the Polish Communist Party was forced to concede to the workers not only the right to strike, but also to form an autonomous trade union free from government and Party control, known as "Solidarity." The helpless Gierek was eventually replaced by General Wojciech Jaruzelski, Minister of Defense and Commander-in-Chief of Poland's armed forces. Thus, for the third time in the history of Communist Poland, a workers' revolt resulted in a change in leadership. On this occasion, however, unlike in 1956 and 1970, the workers caused the change by nonviolent means. By the beginning of 1981, the autonomous trade unions had about 10 million members enrolled, which represented, with their families, the great majority of Poland's population of 36 million. Nearly one-third of the Polish United Workers' Party (PUWP) members joined the Solidarity movement. All this impacted greatly on the lingering Soviet dissent movement.

The rise of a powerful, autonomous, democratically elected, non-Communist trade union in a key country of the Warsaw Pact confronted the Kremlin with an agonizing problem. Here was a classic spontaneous, peaceful, mass proletarian movement led by a genuine working class people, who were antagonistic to Communism. The cherished Soviet myth, that there are no conflicts between a working class party and the workers, was dramatically exploded. The Kremlin was alarmed. All verbal warnings and threatening gestures made by Moscow, including military demonstrations, proved ineffective.

Confronted with the choice of military intervention on the Czechoslovakian model or allowing things to drift, Brezhnev hesitated. While the rest of the world was wondering what Moscow would do next, martial law was suddenly declared throughout the country by General Jaruzelski on December

31, 1981. With the tacit approval of Moscow, he assumed virtual dictatorial power at the head of a Military Council. Personal freedoms were drastically curtailed, universities were closed, activities of all organizations were suspended, and starting with the Solidarity leadership, over 5,000 persons were interned. Addressing the nation, Jaruzelski, in veiled language, justified the crackdown as having been necessary to forestall direct Soviet intervention in Poland. The Polish revolt was outwardly suppressed, but its long-range consequences for the entire Soviet empire were long lasting.

The End of the Brezhnev Era

On November 10, 1982, Brezhnev died at the age of 75 from "heart disease and respiratory troubles." His rule of eighteen years in office was second longest after that of Stalin. The Brezhnev era covered the length of five American presidencies: those of Johnson, Nixon, Ford, Carter, and part of Reagan's. In domestic politics, Brezhnev was a highly conservative defender of vested interests of the increasingly corrupt Communist elite. He had seized power with the support of the military establishment, kept it largely thanks to their backing, and loyally repaid his debt of gratitude by satisfying its often exorbitant claims. Under his rule, defense spending nearly doubled, increasing by some 4 percent a year up to 1976 and decreasing only slightly even when the Soviet GNP began to plummet alarmingly.

The price of the systematic increase of military investments and lavish aid to the Soviet vassal states resulted in tremendous strain on the economy; suffering from obsolate technology, it entered a period of stagnation. By 1981 it entered the period of negative growth. Agriculture, despite attempts to streamline the existing system, remained the weakest area of the system. Supplying the population with food, especially meat, became increasingly difficult. In the 1980s, four disastrous grain harvests in a row forced huge purchases abroad. Food imports cost $700 million in 1970 and as much as over $12 billion in the early 1980s.

In some ways, Brezhnev was Stalin's epigone: He, too, emphasized power over ideology and industry over agriculture, ignoring human rights. But while Stalin was feared but respected to the end, at the close of his rule the senile Brezhnev became a laughingstock because of his vanity; he collected innumerable racing cars as well as titles, ranks, and decorations of all sorts, including those especially invented for him.

Brezhnev's era was crowded with contradictions. He was an architect both of detente and of a massive Soviet military build-up. While preaching "peaceful coexistence," he ordered the invasion of both Czechoslovakia and Afghanistan. He both signed the Helsinki Accord and deployed the Soviet Union's advanced medium-range missiles against Western Europe. He was instrumental in trying to make the USSR a superpower rivaling the United States, thus extending Soviet resources beyond the breaking point. He presided over an ailing economy showing signs of immobility and even regress. His name is likely to go down in history as the father of the overambitious "Brezhnev doctrine." From a historic perspective, Brezhnev's rigidity in economic matters and his imperial overreach contributed to the decline and eventual disintegration of the USSR.

Suggested Reading

BARGHOORN, FREDERICK C., *Détente and the Democratic Movement in the USSR.* New York: Free Press, 1976.

BLOCH, SIDNEY, AND PETER REDDAWAY, *Psychiatric Terror.* New York: Basic Books, 1977.

BOCHAROV, GENNADY, *Roussian Roulette: Afghanistan Through Russian Eyes.* New York: Harper-Collins, 1990.

BROWN, J.F., *Relations Between the Soviet Union and Its Eastern European Allies.* Santa Monica, CA: Rand Corporation, 1975.

CHERNOVIL, VIACHESLAV, *The Chernovil Papers*. New York: McGraw-Hill, 1968.

CLARK, WILLIAM A., *Soviet Regional Elite After Khrushchev*. New York: Praeger, 1989.

DORNBERG, JOHN, *Brezhnev: The Mask of Power*. New York: Basic Books, 1974.

DRACHMAN, EDWARD, *Challenging the Kremlin: The Soviet Jewish Movement for Freedom, 1967–1990*. New York: Paragon House, 1992.

DUNLOP, JOHN B., *The New Russian Revolutionaries*. Belmont, MA: Nordland, 1976.

DZIUBA, IVAN, *Internationalism or Russification?* London: Weidenfeld and Nicolson, 1968.

FREEDMAN, ROBERT O., *Soviet Policy Toward the Middle East Since 1970*. New York: Praeger, 1975.

GAIDUK, ILYA V., *The Soviet Union and the Vietnam War*. Chicago, IL: Ivan R. Dee, 1996.

GOLDMAN, MARSHALL I., *The Enigma of Soviet Petroleum: Half Empty or Half Full?* Winchester, MA: Allen & Unwin, 1980.

HAMMOND, THOMAS T., *Red Flag over Afghanistan: The Communist Coup, the Soviet Invasion, and the Consequences*. Boulder, CO: Westview Press, 1983.

HAYWARD, MAX (ED.), *On Trial: The Soviet State Versus Abram Tertz and Nikolai Arzhak*. New York: Harper & Row, 1966.

———, AND WILLIAM C. FLETCHER (EDS.), *Religion and the Soviet State: A Dilemma of Power*. New York: Praeger, 1969.

HERSPRING, DALE R., *The Soviet High Command, 1967–1989*. Princeton, NJ: Princeton University Press, 1990.

KHODOROVICH, TATYANA (ED.), *The Case of Leonid Plyushch*. Boulder, CO: Westview Press, 1976.

LANE, CHRISTEL, *Christian Religion in the Soviet Union*. Albany: State University of New York Press, 1983.

LAPIDUS, GAIL W. (ED.), *Women, Work and Family in the Soviet Union*. Armonk, NY: M.E. Sharpe, 1982.

LISANN, MAURY, *Broadcasting to the Soviet Union: International Politics and Radio*. New York: Praeger, 1975.

LOWENTHAL, RICHARD, *Model or Ally? The Communist Powers and the Developing Countries*. New York: Oxford University Press, 1976.

PANISH, PAUL, *Exit Visa: The Emigration of the Soviet Jews*. New York: Coward, McCann and Geoghegan, 1981.

PORTER, BRUCE D., *The USSR in Third World Conflicts: Soviet Arms and Diplomacy in Local Wars, 1945–1980*. New York: Cambridge University Press, 1984.

RUBINSTEIN, ALVIN Z., *Red Star on the Nile*. Princeton, NJ: Princeton University Press, 1977.

RYWKIN, MICHAEL, *Moscow's Muslim Challenge: Soviet Central Asia*. Armonk, NY: M. E. Sharpe, 1982.

SAKHAROV, ANDREI, *Memoirs*. New York: Alfred A. Knopf, 1990.

———, *Progress, Coexistence and Intellectual Freedom*. New York: Norton, 1968.

SHEVCHENKO, ARKADY N., *Breaking with Moscow*. New York: Knopf, 1985.

SIMMONDS, GEORGE (ED.), *Nationalism in the USSR and Eastern Europe in the Era of Brezhnev and Kosygin*. Detroit: University of Detroit Press, 1977.

STARR, S. FREDERICK, *Red and Hot: The Fate of Jazz in the Soviet Union, 1971–1980*. New York: Oxford University Press, 1983.

YANOV, ALEXANDER, *The Russian New Right: Right-Wing Ideologies in the Contemporary USSR*. Berkeley: University of California Press, 1978.

Chapter 24

Gorbachev: *Glasnost* and *Perestroika*

Within forty-eight hours after Brezhnev's death, Yuri V. Andropov, age 68, was chosen as the Party's General Secretary. Seven months later, on June 15, 1983, he assumed the Soviet presidency in addition to the leadership of the Communist Party. In comparison, it had taken Brezhnev thirteen years as party leader to achieve the same position. Undoubtedly his KGB connection helped him to consolidate his power.

From 1953 to 1957 Andropov was the ambassador to Hungary, and in the decade following 1957 he directed the Socialist countries' sector of the Central Committee. From 1967 to 1982, he functioned as head of the KGB. Since 1973, he was also a member of the Politburo. On May 25, 1982, Andropov stepped down as chief of the KGB, two days after being appointed one of the ten permanent secretaries of the Central Committee. Although his tenure in the KGB of fifteen years was not marked by the bloody mass terror of the Stalinist type, under Andropov the KGB expanded its functions and became a more sophisticated means of enforcing nearly absolute political control, outwardly emasculating the lingering Soviet

dissent movement. Even jokes critical of the regime became a risky thing. As a contemporary saying went: "Comrade Andropov collects not only political stories, he also collects people who tell them."

Andropov began his tenure with a call for prompt action to improve the deteriorating economic situation. On November 22, 1982, in his first major policy speech, he emphasized the need to raise labor productivity by tightening discipline and controlling drunkenness.[1]

With regard to the crucial arms control problem, Andropov proved to be a tougher negotiator than Brezhnev. When the November 1981 Intermediate-Range Nuclear Force (INF) talks began in Geneva, Andropov firmly opposed any deployment of the new American medium-range missiles and condemned them as "dangerous provocation" because the Pershing IIs in West Germany

---

[1] Unofficial sources spoke of 40 to 45 million alcoholics in the former Soviet Union (out of a population of some 286 million), with total damage caused by alcohol-related problems estimated at 180 billion rubles—nearly one-third of the USSR's GNP. Russian drinkers guzzle 83 percent of the world's vodka production.

and the cruise missiles in Britain and Italy would be able to reach well into the Soviet Union, covering an arc that extended from the mouth of the Dnieper to Leningrad. Consequently, they could hit Soviet military bases and command centers just short of Moscow. As a gesture of protest, in December 1983 the Soviet delegation left the Superpowers' Strategic Arms Reduction Talks (START) in Geneva and ended the mutual and balanced force reduction negotiations in Vienna. As a result, the world entered an uncharted period in which no nuclear control talks went on for two years.

Andropov was a very intelligent and well-informed leader who realized that the Soviet Union suffered from corruption, nepotism, and economic regress. But his planned reforms were limited only to attempts at streamlining the existing system, of making it function more efficiently. But suffering for a long time from diabetes and kidney disease, Andropov was unable to implement even the planned, limited reforms. His death was officially announced on February 5, 1984. Andropov remained in power only for fifteen months, and for over five months of that period he was bedridden. During his brief stewardship, he achieved no more than a marginal improvement of Soviet productivity. In foreign affairs Andropov held tightly to Soviet positions in Vietnam and Afghanistan, thus failing to improve the tense relations with either China or the United States.

The Chernenko Interlude

Andropov's recommendation to make the relatively young Mikhail Gorbachev his successor was disregarded by the jealous members of the Central Committee. As a result of ingenious intrigue, the 72-year-old Konstantin V. Chernenko was elected. This surprising choice was the triumph of the senile members of the Politburo. Chernenko had been the Second Secretary of the Committee and thus the second ranking member of the Politburo. With his selection as their boss, the guardians of the old system had reasserted themselves. Gerontology at the Kremlin reached its peak. Until 1985, the average age of Politburo members had constantly gone up. In 1919, the average age was about 40; in 1934, it had risen to 48. In the last years of the Brezhnev era and during the Andropov and Chernenko interludes, the average age of Politburo members was around 70. The election of Chernenko was the old guard's last hurrah.

Continuing his predecessor's negative attitude toward the West, Chernenko rolled himself into the defensive posture of a bristling porcupine. He decided to boycott the 1984 Olympic Games in Los Angeles. When the White House sent General Brent Scowcroft to Moscow with a personal letter from President Reagan, Chernenko simply refused to receive the envoy.

Chernenko died on March 11, 1985, after barely thirteen months in office. He was a clumsy, stubborn, bureaucratic nonentity with no objective qualities for leadership, let alone an ability to develop a "personality cult." As one of his comrades remarked: "There can be no personality cult where there is no personality." Like Brezhnev, Chernenko, by his arrogant intransigence, tried to make the hollow shell of the Soviet Communist State appear as solid as the rock of Gibraltar.

On March 12, a mere four hours after the news of Chernenko's death, Radio Moscow interrupted solemn music to announce the election of Mikhail S. Gorbachev, Andropov's close co-worker and protégé, as General Secretary of the CPSU. This was the quickest and smoothest transition of power in Soviet history.

Gorbachev in Power

Mikhail S. Gorbachev was born in March 1931, the son of a kolkhoz peasant in the Stavropol region in Northern Caucasus. He ascended to the top post at the age of 54. He studied law and agriculture and joined the

Party in 1952, starting his career already in the post-Stalin era. His first important job was that of regional Party boss at Stavropol, capital of the fertile region of the same name, an area in Caucasus with a mild climate and luxuriant vegetation. In Stavropol Gorbachev gained the reputation of an efficient administrator. Loquacious, adaptable and charming, in 1971 he became a member of the Party's Central Committee. Northern Caucasus was favored by the Kremlin elite because of its numerous summer resorts blessed with warm springs. The exclusive spas were often patronized by the Soviet elite; this allowed Gorbachev to establish good contacts in Moscow. As the local Party boss, Gorbachev eagerly played host to Andropov, the KGB boss under Brezhnev. Gorbachev and his wife Raisa befriended Andropov and turned him into their ally. In 1979, on his protector's initiative, Gorbachev was called to Moscow and joined the Politburo as a nonvoting candidate member. In October 1980, he became a full member, and as a close associate of Andropov, he was thus privy to KGB intelligence.

In the summer of 1983, supported by Andropov and taking advantage of the senile passivity of his colleagues, Gorbachev gradually gathered responsibility for cadres, ideologies, and consumer industries in addition to agriculture. This was a formidable accumulation of power, unrivaled by any other member of the mostly passive members of the Politburo. Once elected General Secretary, Gorbachev lost no time in trying to reshape the country's ailing economy. He attempted to put his reform plans into practice in close alliance with a new, personally selected team of like-minded comrades. On April 22, 1985, the 115th anniversary of Lenin's birth, the Politburo met in the Kremlin's Contress Palace in accordance with a carefully arranged hierarchical order. But by the next day, this order was upset by the addition of three new men. Two of them, Yegor Ligachev and Nikolai Ryzhkov, had not even been candidate members of the Politburo. The third, Viktor Chebrikov, head of the KGB, had become a candidate member not long before.

The next big change came on July 1, nine weeks later, when Gorbachev's rival, Grigori Romanov, until then a full Politburo member and Central Committee Secretary for Heavy and Defense Industries, as well as the Leningrad Party boss, was forced into retirement. The very next day, July 2, the twenty-eight year career of the world's longest-serving Foreign Minister came to an end when Andrei Gromyko, a stubborn Stalinist, was kicked upstairs to the symbolic post of Chairman of the Presidium of the Supreme Soviet, or the nominal President of the USSR. At the same time, one of Gorbachev's confidants from his *Komsomol* days in the Caucasus, Edvard Shevardnadze, previously Party boss of Georgia and candidate member of the Politburo, was promoted to its full membership and became the new Foreign Minister. Aleksander Yakovlev, former ambassador to Canada, a man with broad Western experience, was put in charge of propaganda. For the first time since 1961, a woman was allowed to join the top leadership when Aleksandra Biryukova was added to the Central Committee Secretariat. On September 27, the seventy-nine-year-old Prime Minister Nikolai Tikhonov retired and was replaced by Gorbachev's younger supporter and economic expert, Nikolai I. Ryzhkov. Hardly two-and-a-half weeks later, on October 14, Gorbachev removed the Chairman of the State Planning Commission, whom he considered a major stumbling block to his plans. Thus, in seven months, Gorbachev restructured and rejuvenated the Soviet top leadership more quickly than any of his predecessors, Stalin not excluded.

The opening stages of Gorbachev's rule were marred by three accidents; all took place in 1986. The first was the near meltdown at the Chernobyl (Ukraine) nuclear energy station in late April. The meltdown affected large areas and proved the largest nuclear catastrophe in history. The second accident occurred with the collision and sinking of the Soviet passenger ship "Admiral Nakhimov" in the Black Sea on August 31, with the loss of more than 100 lives. The third blow to Soviet pride came on October 3 in the form of the acknowledgment that a Soviet submarine, carrying ballistic missiles, had caught fire and sunk off the coast of Bermuda. Gorbachev remained undisturbed by these blows to the Soviet prestige and symptoms of bad management practices. Nevertheless, he continued to press the urgency to lift the Soviet Union from the bog of stagnation that had marked the late 1970s and early 1980s.

In the course of a vigorous barnstorming campaign, Gorbachev attacked the shocking corruption and inefficiency of the huge bureaucratic apparatus. He pointed out that since the late 1970s, the growth of the Soviet GNP, which in 1966–1970 had exceeded 5 percent, was alarmingly plunging downward. Moreover, he argued, the resources of the most economically advanced western parts of the Soviet Union were yielding less and less. Oil production showed a steady decline since 1984. The processing industry could receive less and less investment, as more and more capital had to be applied for the extraction of raw materials in inaccessible parts of Siberia. The birth rate in the most heavily industrialized segments had been declining for years and the problem was compounded by the poor health of young workers. He ascribed the lower productivity of Soviet workers to inefficient management and rampant alcoholism, a truly national catastrophe. The balance between heavy and light industries was badly upset. Whereas in 1960 only 18 percent of heavy industry work was for the military establishment, by 1976–1977 this figure exceeded 25 percent, about four to five times larger than that in most Western countries. Military manufacturing drained much of the industrial production of the Soviet Union, thus starving the supply of consumer goods and vital services. This allowed the USSR to remain a military superpower for the time being, but in the long run the prospects were dim. To save the Soviet global position, Gorbachev argued, the country must modernize quickly. The reforms in China that significantly lifted the standard of living of its population, together with the simultaneous rise of Japan as an economic giant, had made the Soviet decline more striking. Gorbachev's conclusion was: "We must hurry up. We don't have much time left."

Gorbachev's Plans

Gorbachev presented his reform plans with amazing frankness. He declared that the old overcentralized economic model was not only a serious impediment to progress but to the very survival of the Soviet Union as a global power. This he illustrated with numerous facts and figures stressing the shocking inefficiency in industry and especially the service sector. Yet he did not dare launch a plan of a radical reform of the Communist system as such. State ownership of the means of production, including the land, and the State's central role in economic planning were still unshakable dogmas. This meant that Gorbachev's economic plans, despite their radical rhetoric overtones, were, in reality, less extensive than Lenin's NEP, let alone the Chinese reforms.

Gorbachev's scheme of economic reconstruction (*perestroika* in Russian) could not be carried out without far-reaching political changes that would affect the Party and State bureaucracy, or some 18 million people. To cope with the threatening bureaucratic opposition to his plans, Gorbachev resorted to another slogan, that of *glasnost*, which in Russian means both openness and publicity. *Glasnost* allowed the Soviet media and intellectuals to debate frankly many shortcomings and ills of the Soviet society. Thanks to *glasnost*, the press began to attack not only the shocking arrogance of the civilian bureaucracy, but also the complacency and inefficiency in the military establishment. The media openly criticized poor discipline, which allowed brutal hazing practices that resulted in many deadly accidents, the existence of military schools that were simply camps for the privileged, favoritism in appointments, and the need for younger people in top command posts. The main target of the liberalized mass media was

Gorbachev, at the I. Likhachev Auto Works in Moscow, discusses the factory's retooling

the dragging war in Afghanistan. Gorbachev approved of most of this criticism, especially of the Afgan war. He went as far as to call it "a bleeding wound."

Initially the withdrawal from the costly venture was opposed by the hardliners and by the military establishment. The Soviet armed forces were a formidable presence; they had emerged from World War II with a greatly enhanced prestige. Stalin had tried to play down this esteem for the military by attributing the victory in "the Great Patriotic War" to his own unique strategic genius, but his successors could not ignore the high status of the marshals. Under Khrushchev and Brezhnev, the military elite considered themselves legitimate bearers of the national will and guardians of its destiny. The military top brass was the only organized body of people with an espirit de corps comparable to that of the Party.

Nomenklatura, the "new class" of high officials in the Party, was also a powerful obstacle; it shared with the top of the military establishment numerous privileges that were threatened by Gorbachev's stress on austerity. An entire department of the Party Central Committee provided for a variety of services not only to the *nomenklatura,* but also to the big brass and their families. The department operated and equipped exclusive apartment houses, country dachas, government palaces, special rest homes, and car pools, and maintained squads of security-trained servants. A network of unmarked stores without display windows catered to the Soviet top Party as well as military hierarchy, offering choice delicacies like caviar, smoked salmon, export brandies, vodka, exotic wines, and liqueurs. The Soviet elite indeed enjoyed many of the privileges of the former ruling Tsarist aristocracy.

So in addition to the highly privileged Party *apparat,* the military high command was bound to be affected by Gorbachev's scheme of shifting priorities away from the heavy defense-oriented industry toward consumer goods. The growing power of the Soviet military establishment had been reflected in the constantly expanding defense appropriations; under Brezhnev, for more than a decade, the USSR had been increasing its defense spending by 3 to 4 percent a year in real terms.

In dealing with the military lobby, Gorbachev was helped by a unexpected quirk of fate. On May 27, 1987, a youthful West German amateur flier, Matthias Rust, evading allegedly impregnable Soviet air defense systems, landed in Moscow's Red Square, near the Kremlin's walls, after an audacious five-hour flight. This was an unheard of scandal that revealed the complacency of the high command responsible for the country's air defense. The incident gave the General Secretary his chance to rejuvenate the top military establishment. The aging Defense Minister, Marshal Sergei Sokolov, was dismissed and replaced by a younger man, General Dmitry T. Yazov. Yazov had headed two of the Soviet Union's sixteen military districts, the Far East and Central Asia, and commanded Soviet troops in Czechoslovakia. His commands had thus far faced both NATO and China, and they seemed to provide him with unique breadth of experience.

Attempts at Reforming the Soviet Economy

At the Twenty-Seventh Party Congress (February 25–March 6, 1986), Gorbachev launched his scheme of *perestroika*, which he termed a "radical reform of the economy." For instance, he promised to give the enterprises more independence and to increase their interest in the final products but only "within the framework of the planned economy." Gorbachev intended to achieve a major redistribution of power from central planning bodies and ministries to factories and enterprises by 1991. The *Gosplan* was instructed to lay down general guidelines only, while local managers would make their own detailed plans and set their own wages. Inefficient installations were to go bankrupt. State-dictated pricing systems were to be eliminated; the maze of subsidies that had distorted the whole economy, making it cheaper for Soviet farmers to feed pigs with state-produced bread than grain, was to be dropped. The reform was to affect some 60 percent of all enterprises.

By far the greatest obstacle to reforming the entire economy was its rural sector, which Gorbachev's reform plan grossly neglected. Since the 1930s, some 27,000 collective farms and 21,000 gigantic State farms were both organized in a way that hampered effective production. As in industry, the collective and State farms had been shackled by a system of norms set arbitrarily by Party-appointed bureaucrats. Under Khrushchev and Brezhnev, enormous funds were invested in the modernization of both types of farms to provide them with new costly machinery. Although Soviet agricultural output had increased about 10 percent during the 1970s, it did not correspond to the enormous amount of resources devoted to it. For instance, in the Eleventh Five-Year Plan (1981–1985), 40 percent of investments in the countryside were allocated to all agricultural machinery and the construction of grain silos and other storage facilities. Yet, as Gorbachev admitted, the quality of the agricultural machines was often abysmal and storage unavailable. Many farms often could not start sowing on time because the necessary machines stood around idle for want of spare parts. A large part of agricultural produce spoiled as a result of delayed transportation and lack of proper care. Consequently, the amount of produce that actually reached the stores was very low; the grain output per hectare was only about one-third of that achieved in the United States. As a result, over the years grain imports had accumulated a Soviet hard currency debt exceeding $80 billion. It was estimated that about 20 percent of the value of all foodstuffs consumed in the Soviet Union was imported, thus draining the gold and hard currency reserve of the Soviet State Bank.

While in charge of agriculture, before he had become General Secretary, Gorbachev had tried to remedy some of these shortcomings. For instance, in March 1983, he had sanctioned breaking up large farms into autonomous segments cultivated by small units or "brigades." It had become official policy to pay these groups according to their output. Gradually the "brigades" were allowed to be responsible for large tracts of land. Once attaining the post of General Secretary, Gorbachev continued his efforts, going a step further. In August 1987 agricultural contracting was expanded to include family contracts. Moreover, family contracting was broadened to include the leasing of land to individual families for twelve to fifteen years. Nevertheless, leasing operated outside the collective farm structure and employing workers from outside the family unit were still illegal. The long-term leasing of land affected only a limited number of peasants. In essence, it was Gorbachev's policy to tolerate small-scale private agriculture under the heading of leasing, while basically sticking to the Communist standard—collectivized farming. Thus, agriculture contracts were a lame compromise.

As we see, Gorbachev's plans for economic reform stressed a change in the industrial management system without altering basic property relations, especially in the crucial agricultural sector, where successes could have been achieved much more cheaply and quickly than in industry. His plans included only limited, half-hearted toleration of private enterprise and market-oriented mechanisms. Gorbachev could have drawn from the successful Chinese example of starting economic restructuring with privatization of agriculture and then addressing the rest of the economy, but that model was ignored. Gorbachev forgot that bread had been the staff of life for the Russian masses for centuries and that, without first solving the problem of food, no other issue could be resolved.

Deteriorating Quality of Life

Meanwhile, the mass media, encouraged by *glasnost,* continued to reveal various alarming aspects of Soviet life. Besides quoting disquieting figures about the rapidly declining of GNP, the press revealed numerous menacing symptoms of a fast deteriorating quality of life. After rising steadily after 1953, the quality of life began to level off in the late 1970s and had stagnated ever since. This was camouflaged by official Soviet statistics until *glasnost* allowed publication of some shocking figures. For instance, the February 17, 1988 issue of the daily *Socialist Industry* noted that education expenses constituted 6.7 percent of the national budget in 1964, but had declined to 4.2 percent by 1982. The same article reported that in 1983 UNESCO had ranked the Soviet Union third in a table of different nations indicating the proportion of young people engaged in higher education. Since that time Soviet ranking kept on declining. By 1990 the USSR occupied the 42nd position. Meanwhile, it was officially admitted that air, soil, and water pollution had reached frightening dimensions, especially in some European urban areas and throughout Central Asia. For instance, the Aral Sea had shrunk to some 60 percent of its former surface area as a result of irrigation and industrial projects that had siphoned off its water while poisoning the lake. Many large cities, including Moscow, were threatened with ecological disaster.

Another menacing factor was striking demographic trends, mainly among Slavic population groups. The traditionally strong Russian family had been undermined by deteriorating morals, as well as by unfavorable socioeconomic factors. The main threats were the alarmingly high growth of alcoholism, narcomania, divorce caused in part by the lack of adequate housing. The media revealed that by 1980, the national divorce rate had reached 40 percent, and exceeded 50 percent in large urban areas. In almost half of the cases, the husband's drunkenness was cited among the reasons for divorce. Among the other causes mentioned were adultery, violence, and cramped living conditions. Since World War II, there were far more women than men, while an increasing number of single males refused to marry for one reason or another.

At the same time, the reservoir of the available labor force was practically exhausted. The fact that Soviet men were permitted to retire at 60 and women at 55 did not help matters; various incentives offered to workers by the authorities to remain in the work force produced only limited results. Meanwhile, the Soviet population was aging very fast. The median age was 24 in 1950 but rose to 30 by 1990. The declining birth rate had been paralleled by a growing number of abortions. The media debates soon made public that there were about twice as many abortions as live births, up to 6 million annually. Although no information was published on infant mortality in the USSR for more than a decade following the reported 20 percent increases of the 1971–1974 period, in October 1986, Soviet sociologists pointed out that infant mortality rates were then higher than they had been in 1971. Already on November 9, 1987, Minister of Health Evgenii Chazov admitted that the USSR currently stood fiftieth in the world in terms of infant mortality, behind many countries of the Third World. The shrinking Russian population is bound to affect the control over such thinly settled regions as, for instance, the Far Eastern provinces.

One factor behind the demographic crisis was the alarming state of medical services, once the pride of the Soviet regime. The right to free medical care was written into the 1977 Soviet Constitution. Statistically, in the USSR there were three times as many hospital beds and twice as many doctors per 10,000 people as there were in the United States. Yet Soviet spending on health care per capita was the smallest among the industrialized nations. In the 1980s, life expectancy in the USSR was a dozen years shorter for males than females. Some sociologists attributed this unusually wide gap to the much higher rates of alcoholism and tobacco smoking among Soviet men. In addition, a sharp increase in deaths among urban residents from hypertension, heart disease, and cancer was also noted. The declining quality of health care was one by-product of the high level of defense spending, which stripped resources away from the civilian sector of the economy. With a GNP less than half that of the United States, Gorbachev admitted, the Soviet Union could not afford to invest at least a quarter of its resources on military and space budgets, while at the same time supporting very extensive welfare benefits.

Women and Youth

The rapidly declining quality of life hit the female majority of the Soviet population much harder for a variety of reasons. Traditionally, Russian women had always performed heavy and dirty tasks both on the farm and in urban households. To these tasks, the Soviet regime had added brutal work conditions. From 1928 on, Stalin sent women to construction sites to build factories and dams, to operate drill presses and lathes, to pour cement and asphalt, and to dig ditches and canals. Millions of them paid for this with their health and often their lives. After Stalin's death, voices were raised in protest against this cruel inhuman exploitation of women at the expense of their family duties. In 1981, decrees were enacted banishing the employment of women in 460 heavy and hazardous jobs. Despite these reforms, Soviet women still had to work harder and longer than their male counterparts. In the early 1990s, nearly 70 percent of all Soviet women 16 or older worked full-time, while a similar figure for the United States was 51 percent. By 1985, over 72 percent of all working people were women; they dominated such professions as teaching, medical services, and, of course, most sorts of secretarial and lower administrative duties. On the other hand, men held nearly three-quarters of the important pedagogical, medical, and political posts in the country.

In addition to their regular work at offices, schools, hospitals, and factories, women had to carry on their domestic chores. Married women usually spent some thirty to thirty-five hours per week on various household chores including shopping, often a most exhausting task because of long lines in front of shopping places. Their life was so crowded with everyday chores, from standing in lines to buy necessities to finding practically nonexistent electricians or plumbers, that they had little time for systematic organizing and forming effective pressure groups. Feminism of the Western type, let alone a women's liberation movement, until recently was in its infancy in the former Soviet Union. Most Soviet women had to think simply in terms of survival.[2] This has affected their willingness to bear children. As a result, the Russian birthrate has been declining dramatically.

Here came the growing Western influence with its radio and television. It was easier to seal Soviet boundaries against foreign invaders during World War II than to prevent the gradual infiltration of Western culture, fads, and mores in the USSR. Jamming foreign broadcasts, strict censorship, all sorts of "administrative measures" and intense pro-

paganda drives by the Party and the *Komsomol* proved of no avail. Throughout the Gorbachev years, Western concepts and attitudes continued to affect the people. Even the *Komsomol* leaders had to admit privately that Communist ideology was quickly losing its hold on Soviet youth, male and female. This was reflected in the *Komsomol's* dwindling membership; its rank and file, taking advantage of *glasnost*, openly criticized the top strata of the organization as too stuffy, doctrinaire, and bureaucratic. Another consequence of *glasnost* was the emergence of unofficial political clubs and debating societies, some of which, eventually, transformed themselves into political parties. Their nuclei, under various covers, were springing up throughout the country. Dissatisfaction with the war in Afghanistan was spreading more rapidly among the youth who were facing the draft than among the older generations, and speeded up the protest movement against the political establishment.

[2] The plight of Soviet women was graphically described by Francine du Plessix Gray in *The Soviet Woman: Walking the Tightrope* (New York: Doubleday, 1990).

Street sweeping Moscow style by an elderly women with an old fashioned broom: a frequent sight in most Soviet cities

Young women were full participants in this cultural revolt. Being better educated than their male counterparts and, by and large, more sober, women made up the vanguard of the spontaneous movement that threatened to upset whatever remained of the established values of male-dominated Russian society. The Communist Party constituted a mighty bastion of male hegemony. Only a handful of women were members of the Central Committee; only one reached the Politburo.

Culture and Religion

Glasnost also resulted in a slow but far-reaching reexamination of Soviet history. Yuri Afanasiev, Rector of the Moscow State Historico-Archival Institute, called the reexamination of the painful Soviet past "an awakening from a prolonged mythological dream," that had lasted for over seventy years. Rehabilitation of many individuals previously regarded as "non-persons" was welcomed by most historians. Two schools of thought soon emerged regarding the past. One stressed the need to analyze frankly past mistakes in order not to repeat them, while the other expressed fear that a wholesale repudiation of official history would destroy the Communist Party's legitimacy and thus undermine the very existence of the Soviet regime.

Parallel with the revision of the past, a more open approach to Soviet as well as foreign literature became evident. Works by some of the century's finest writers—Boris Pasternak, Anna Akhmatova, Michail Bulgakov—were published for the first time after delays of up to sixty years. Other disgraced or ignored writers—satirist Mikhail Zoshchenko and poets Osip Mandelshtam (who died in a concentration camp in 1938), Marina Tsvetayeva (who committed suicide in 1941), and Nikolai Gumilov (who was shot in 1921), were republished. Emigré writers like Vladimir Nabokov and 1987 Nobel laureate Joseph Brodsky published to much acclaim. The 1980s saw a flood of long-suppressed works by many Soviet filmmakers. And in art, Marc Chagall finally received official recognition with a major exhibit in Moscow.

Another important topic, although hardly mentioned in Gorbachev's speeches, was religion. Yet it was widely known that a considerable number of Soviet citizens, despite over seventy years of persecution, believed in God and carried on various religious practices often independently of the official hierarchy tainted by its collaboration with the KGB. The tradition bound Russian Orthodox Church was by far the largest denomination, with a membership estimated at about fifty to sixty million. It should be noted, however, that large segments of the nominally Orthodox population of the Western Ukraine, annexed from Poland after World War II, were Greek Catholics, or Uniates, who recognized the supremacy of the Pope of Rome. To a lesser extent it was also true of the population of Western Belorussia. They had been brutally forced by Stalin to submit to the Moscow Patriarchate in March 1946. Yet most Ukrainians regarded the suppression of their church as one of many aspects of a Moscow-inspired policy of Russification and remained Uniates at heart.[3]

The next largest religious group of the Soviet Union were the Muslims, numbering forty-five to fifty million and located mostly in Soviet Central Asia and the Caucasus. All these areas were situated in the vicinity of other Muslim countries, Turkey, Iran, Afghanistan, and Pakistan. Their proximity to other Muslim peoples helped to stimulate a fundamentalist revival among the Soviet Muslim population. To these religiously oppressed groups one must add an estimated over six million Roman Catholics, mostly in the western borderlands, Lithuania, Latvia, and in the former eastern provinces of Poland, now known as Western

---

[3] At the time of its suppression after World War II, the Greek Catholic Church numbered 2,772 parishes, nearly as many priests, eight bishops, and more than four million followers, largely of Ukrainian, and partly of Belorussian stock.

Belorussia and Western Ukraine. The Catholics, in turn, were affected by events in East Central Europe and the election of a Pole, John Paul II, a "Slavic Pope" to the Vatican as well as the phenomenal growth of the "solidarity" movement in Poland. Protestants were clearly in the minority, numbering altogether between four and five million. A major subgroup of Protestants were Lutherans, largely living in the Baltic provinces of Latvia and Estonia. There were also some two million Jews scattered all over the USSR, but living mainly in the cities, and some 500,000 Buddhists in the Soviet Far East. Other localized groups included the Georgian Orthodox Church in Georgia and the Armenian Church in Armenia.

Thus, out of some 286 million Soviet citizens, over 100 million people—well over one-third of the entire population—were, for religious reasons, in bitter opposition to the atheism that had been ruthlessly imposed by the State for some seventy years. A confirmed atheist, Gorbachev initially changed little in Soviet ecclesiastical policy. Looking for support for his program of *perestroika*, however, Gorbachev had to set aside his personal beliefs gradually. First of all, some paragraphs of the Criminal Code were revised to increase the civil rights of hitherto discriminated religious groups and to revise restrictions on religious cults. The existing laws had banned activity by any congregation until it was registered with and approved by the authorities, and also prohibited teaching religion to children outside the family. One by one, Gorbachev dropped these limitations. The most important measure declared that membership in a religious group was not to be an obstacle to professional advancement. The 1988 anniversary of the millennium of the conversion of Kievan Rus to Christianity was celebrated without hindrance, highlighting the new changes. Many foreign delegations, including that of the Vatican, participated in the celebratory festivities.

While all of these reforms were significant, the true turning point of Gorbachev's religious policy occurred when he visited Pope John Paul II at the Vatican on November 25, 1989. The Pope's precondition to reestablishing diplomatic relations with Moscow, that had been broken in the 1920s, was complete religious freedom for the country's Catholics of both rites, Western and Eastern. The Pope also demanded freedom to appoint bishops wherever they were needed. Old habits die hard, however. Not until October 1, 1990, did the Supreme Soviet pass a bill that provided full freedom to all religious denominations and all individuals to practice their respective cults without any restrictions. Houses of worship that had been closed or confiscated were to be returned to their rightful owners. The bill also legalized religious education, including church schools, ecclesiastic seminaries, and theologic academies. The notorious State Committee on Religion, an organization widely regarded as an instrument of KGB, was abolished under the new law. The decree served to formalize what was already largely an accomplished fact—the widespread, elemental revival of religious belief and practices throughout the Soviet Union. Within the next year or so, some five to six thousand houses of worship that had been often used as warehouses or "museums of atheism" were returned to the believers of various denominations.

Effects of Glasnost and Perestroika

Gorbachev's economic reforms won only faint support from the broad masses of people used to the old system for nearly three generations. From the beginning the Soviet people sensed that changes in business management and alteration of work norms might result not only in lower wages and higher prices, but also in unemployment and inflation. Only a tangible rise in the standard of life, especially the availability of more plentiful food and fuel, might have persuaded the silent majority to alter its sullen, passive attitude. The most consistent supporters of *perestroika* and *glasnost* were Soviet intellectuals, university professors, writers, and artists, mainly in the great urban centers of Moscow, Leningrad, and Kiev. Although rather pampered economically for decades, the intellectuals had been smarting under tight censorship. Consequently, they greeted *glasnost* with enthusiasm.

A more realistic attitude toward the reform was taken by some members of the Politburo, especially by Boris Yeltsin, a former Party boss from Sverdlovsk in West Siberia. This powerfully built, silver-haired son of a peasant, was born in 1930 in the village of Burko in the Ural mountains. During World War II, the eleven-year-old Yeltsin picked up a grenade which then exploded, causing him to lose the forefinger and thumb of his left hand. Despite these handicaps, he went on to graduate form Ural Politechnical Institute in 1955, with a degree in construction engineering. Gregarious, boisterous, and flamboyant, Yeltsin worked hard in the construction field, while steadily rising in the Communist Party ranks. He was brought by Gorbachev into the body as candidate member of the Politburo, in February 1986, soon, however, Yeltsin became critical of Gorbachev's style of leadership and complained that an entrenched bureaucracy had stalled Gorbachev's efforts to modernize Soviet society. He repeatedly urged Gorbachev to speed up his economic restructuring of the country by definitely switching to a free market economy. He warned that otherwise Gorbachev would face "a revolution from below," a revolt of workers eager to taste tangible results of *perestroika*, and various ethnic groups eager to turn the sham Soviet federation into a legitimate union. The angry Gorbachev fired Yeltsin from the Politburo under humiliating circumstances, on November 11, 1987.

Yeltsin's warnings proved prophetic: The economic revolution that Gorbachev himself initiated soon began to spill over into other areas throughout the USSR. Economic problems, especially rapidly shrinking food, fuel, and other necessary consumer goods, were compounded by highly explosive ethnic issues. From the Baltic republics, especially restless Lithuania, to the tinderbox of the Caucasus and Ukraine, people were awakening from prolonged lethargy to an active political civic life.

The Revolt of Industrial Workers and the Ethnic Fringe

Gorbachev's political troubles were compounded by a mounting wave of strikes that affected many branches of industry, especially the coal mines. To the economic difficulties was added the ethnic unrest that swept the western and southern borderlands of the USSR, primarily the Caucasus and the Baltic republics. Lithuania was the first of the three Baltic republics to formally challenge the legitimacy of Soviet rule, and Estonia and Latvia soon joined Lithuania. In all three Baltic republics, popular front movements with commanding public support pressed for greater economic and political independence, including the option of secession, if their craving for sovereignty could not be satisfied within a Soviet sham federation. In 1988, repeated violent clashes between the Christian Armenians and Moslem Azeris took place; the apple of discord was the Armenian enclave of Nagorno Karabakh, situated in the Western segment of Azerbaijan. The disturbances were brutally suppressed by the KGB and the army. The repressions caused hundreds of casualties. On September 23, 1989, the fiftieth anniversary of the Stalin-Hitler pact, the Lithuanian legislature declared that the annexation of the three Baltic republics had been an act of aggression and pronounced the incorporation of Lithuania into the USSR invalid. This was supported even by many local Communists. Lithuanian Communist Party newspapers published a draft plan to declare the Lithuanian Party's independence from the Soviet Communist Party in Moscow.

These bold steps further stimulated the lingering irredentist sentiments of Azerbaijan and in Stalin's native land, the federal republic of Georgia. In November, 1989, the Georgian parliament declared that the republic had been annexed by military force in 1921 and reasserted its constitutional right to secede from the USSR. The republic's Supreme Soviet voted to give itself the right to veto Soviet laws and regulations "if it consider[ed] that they run contrary to Georgian interests."

These irredentist moves had to be viewed as the failure of Stalinist nationality policy. Although the policy outwardly aimed at "Sovietization" of all ethnic groups, reshaping them in the spirit of Communist ideology, its net result was superficial. One of the paradoxes of the USSR was that while pursuing in foreign policy a strongly anti-colonialist line, it remained the last great colonial empire. The Soviet Union not only subjugated within its borders well over a hundred minority ethnic groups, some 140 million people, but also dominated about 100 million people of East Central Europe.

It was the inclusion of the Western-oriented countries of East Central Europe into the overstreched Soviet Empire that proved, in the long run, to be a time bomb. In those countries, a spirit of revolt kept on shaking the Soviet hegemonical sphere through a series of outbursts. Ever since Yugoslavia's expulsion from the Cominform in 1948 the national ferment spread wider and wider. The first was the uprising of East German workers in 1953; this was followed by the revolts of the Poles and Hungarians in 1956; then came the defection of the Albanians in 1960; Romania's persistent independent line in foreign policy that surfaced in 1963 came next; the Czechoslovak Prague Spring of 1968 followed. Finally, the deep and protracted Polish crisis of the 1980s, triggered by the birth of the "Solidarity" movement, could be seen as the capstone of thirty-five years of nationalism throughout East Central Europe. This one eventually triumphed. In 1989, Poland openly seceded from the Warsaw Pact and CEMA, or COMECON, and became a sovereign state. This set the example for the remaining satellites of the USSR; Czechoslovakia, Hungary, East Germany, Romania, and Bulgaria. In 1988–1989, revolts in these countries had a profound impact on the nationalities of the Soviet Union, especially in Ukraine and the Baltic Republics.

The Constitution of 1977 had stressed that the USSR was a voluntary union of equal nations working harmoniously to consolidate the already well-established socialist society. In the days of Lenin, it was widely assumed among Communists that Marxism would be the doctrine that would unite in common purpose the plethora of 100 or so different peoples, who lived in equality, harmony, and brotherhood. The events of the late 1980s proved that, despite the claims of Soviet leaders that Communism had solved all ethnic problems, this was far from true. Russian nationalism had been on the rise since the "Great Patriotic War"—a victory that Stalin attributed to the unique, superior qualities of the Great Russian stock: courage, persistence, and singleness of purpose. The mounting trend toward Russian chauvinism provoked strong criticism, especially among the Jews. Many Jewish leaders, as well as those of other Soviet ethnic groups, insisted on the political equality and racial justice promised to them by the Constitution. Despite these promises, anti-Semitism, which had been condemned as a crime already in the first year of the Soviet regime soon became endemic. Tsarist Russia had been the traditional source of this prejudice, giving rise to hundreds of pogroms, and many of Hitler's anti-Semitic fables were partly drawn from Muscovite sources. Since the war and the establishment of Israel in 1948, anti-Semitism had been encouraged by official propaganda suggesting that the State was merely opposing the racially inspired ideology of "Zionism." These sentiments and the growing discrimination had pushed Soviet Jews toward mass emigration, although under Brezhnev attempts by Jews to leave the Soviet Union were denounced as treason.

The ethnic issue proved to be the USSR's most highly explosive internal problem. The problem was made more and more serious because the Great Russian stock had gradually been losing its numerical preponderance. The main threat came from the fast multiplying Muslims. In Central Asia, the problem soon assumed a racial aspect: Slavs versus non-Slavs. The Muslim population of Central Asia was less affected by consumerism, secularization, and the spread of contraception, and retained its traditionally high fertility rate as well as cohesiveness. The Muslim people were relatively young; in 1990 some 50 percent of them were under fifteen years of age, while the corresponding figure for the Russians was only 28 percent. With some 50 million Muslims, the USSR ranked as the fifth largest agglomeration of this religious group, after Indonesia, India, Pakistan, and Bangladesh.

Stalin had ruthlessly eradicated "feudal" and "national bourgeois" elites through forcible industrialization and the spread of literacy among the masses. By this means, however, both socioeconomic and cultural preconditions were created for the emergence of truly modern nations. While destroying the traditional native political elites, usually very small and isolated from the masses, Stalin created new Communist elites, skillfully manipulated by Moscow. The Communist Party's Central Committee Secretariat in Moscow usually made sure that Russians (or at least subservient Slavs, Ukrainians, or Belorussians) were placed in key positions in the Union republics. Since Stalin's time, a pattern had been formed in which the first secretary in each Union republic was to be a member of the local nationality, while the second secretary and the head of the local KGB branch were usually Russian or at least Russified Slavs. The second secretary was typically in charge of cadres, and it was he whose influence was usually decisive. But while Russians tended to dominate the USSR politically and culturally, their numerical predominance was now threatened by demographic realities. The declining birth rate had severely affected all Slavs, but it was most dramatic among the Great Russians.

By establishing sham national republics, providing them with political and cultural institutions, Stalin had unwittingly released strong forces of social integration and nation-building—forces that over time developed a powerful momentum. Although the new national elites were by and large corrupt, obsequious, and compelled to pay lip service to Russian hegemony, they grew deep, native roots. The revolts that began in 1987 in Georgia, Armenia, and Azerbaijan are good examples of this phenomenon. Given all these centrifugal tensions, Gorbachev's liberalization policies quickly undermined the USSR.

Foreign Policy

The Soviet invasion of Afghanistan that had taken place some years before Gorbachev came to power proved to have a powerful impact on domestic unrest in the USSR. The invasion also profoundly worsened the Soviet Union's international position as well. As noted in the previous chapter, the result for this aspect was virtual diplomatic isolation of Moscow and the worsening of relations with the United States, China, Western Europe, and most Muslim countries. From the beginning of his rule, Gorbachev tried to end this isolation. From his point of view, the most crucial consequence to Soviet Russia of the Afghanistan war was losing access to Western technology so essential for economic modernization. Hence Gorbachev tried to improve Soviet-American relations and to restrain the increasingly costly arms race. He rightly grasped that the defense budget was the heaviest single drain on the country's rapidly dwindling resources. This burden not only prevented the Soviet Union from moving forward economically but even threatened to turn it into a Third World country as far as quality of life was concerned. This fear helps explain Gorbachev's persistent arms control initiatives in all directions.

He began with China. After being repeatedly rebuffed by Beijing, Gorbachev turned westward and resumed broken off arms control and troop reduction negotiations in Geneva and Vienna. He also arranged a series of summit meetings with U.S. presidents, first with Ronald Reagan and then with his successor, George Bush. The American-Soviet disarmament negotiations had a long and complex history behind them. With nuclear destruction having been closely averted on several occasions, both sides were eager to improve their relations. Now, in the late 1980s, far-reaching changes were taking place in the global balance of power, and the nature of arms negotiations changed too. Gorbachev decided to withdraw from Afghanistan and offered to reduce drastically his arsenal of threatening weapons. After much effort and cost, the two nuclear superpowers concluded first in 1987 an agreement eliminating intermediate nuclear weapons in Europe, and then pursued sweeping cuts in other fields of their nuclear arsenals. These cuts created a new political aura.

At the same time, the nationalistic ferment that started in Poland in the 1980s gradually spread to the rest of East Central Europe. By 1989 Poland was already an independent state. This, in turn, encouraged Hungary and Czechoslovakia to follow suit. Moreover, the Baltic countries were further emboldened to protest openly against the Soviet yoke. When the revolt reached East Germany, the discontent assumed the proportion of a tidal wave and threatened Soviet control over the entire hegemonial sphere that Stalin had erected in Eastern Europe after World War II. On November 9, 1989, the Berlin Wall, constructed in August 1961 to protect the Communist controlled East Germany from the West, was destroyed and the eastern segment of the country merged with the Western Federal Republic.

Initially, Gorbachev refused to accept the idea of German unification, which would rip the heart of the Soviet security system and destroy the gains of World War II. His opposition was momentarily bolstered by the advice of the Romanian dictator, Nicholas Ceausescu, who went as far as to offer his armed forces to suppress the German reunification drive. After some reflection however, Gorbachev reluctantly accepted the Fourth

Reich as a fact of international life. He bargained only with Bonn for economic advantages to be granted in exchange for the eventual withdrawal of the Soviet garrison from the former East Germany.

Meanwhile, the economic catastrophe threatening the Soviet Union compelled Gorbachev to tolerate the centrifugal forces increasingly active on the tottering empire's periphery. The economic weakness had also its repercussion in all sectors of foreign affairs. The previous main stumbling block in the disarmament agreement with Washington was Gorbachev's efforts to insert a set of constraints on the United States scheme of deploying a protective umbrella against a possible Soviet first-strike capacity. (Officially, this space shield was called the Strategic Defense Initiative, or SDI, but was denounced by its American opponents as "Star Wars.") Eventually, however, Gorbachev had to overlook even this seemingly unsurmountable obstacle in order to get at least some Western economic and technical aid to the crumbling Soviet economy.

Soviet military impotence was clearly revealed during the Persian Gulf crisis in 1990–1991. When in August 1990, Iraq, a former Soviet client, invaded the emirate of Kuwait, Gorbachev tried to mediate to prevent an American-led coalition from intervening militarily. He was incapable of achieving any results, however. The resulting January 1991 "Desert Storm" operation smashed Iraq's armed forces, trained for years by Soviet military experts. Much of Iraq's equipment was of Soviet making and proved ineffective when confronted with superior Western hardware. For Moscow, this represented another striking humiliation.

The dramatic events in East Central Europe and in the Persian Gulf further pushed the Soviet Union and the United States toward reexamining their two systems of military alliances, the North Atlantic Treaty Organization and the Warsaw Pact. With Moscow's reluctant acceptance of the sweeping democratic changes in East Central Europe and with East-West tensions easing, the role of these two coalitions was subject to gradual reconsideration.[4] Both sides decided on troop reduction, as well as destruction of a considerable amount of military equipment.

Thus, at the beginning of the last decade of the twentieth century the status quo created by World War II in Europe underwent fundamental changes. The divisions that had emerged from the war in 1945 were blurred, and the fissures that had marked the postwar partition of the continent into rigid spheres of influence were reduced.

The Rise of Yeltsin

Unable to provide the Soviet people with foreign successes or with sufficient material goods, Gorbachev tried to appease them with an expanded sphere of political freedom, at least within the framework of the Communist Party. With his encouragement various discussion groups were gradually formed within the Party; Gorbachev believed that these groups, composed mostly of younger members, would help him to stimulate the stagnating economy. The clubs had different names, like for instance: "Perestroika Club," "Popular Action Club," "The Democratic Platform," or the most radical of them, known as "Memorial." Soon these groups coalesced and formed a sort of liberal wing of the Party, supporting Gorbachev's reform initiatives. The hardliners denounced the clubs as a sort of camouflaged "revisionism," aiming at undermining the Party and finally turning Russia into "an American colony." Confident in the support of the clubs, Gorbachev decided to hold open elections to the Soviet Congress of People's Deputies. And indeed, on March 26, 1989, the first popular election ever for the Congress of People's Deputies took place throughout the USSR. Fifteen-hundred delegates were elected by the people, while another 750 were appointed by Communist Party and Party-affiliated organizations. As the Congress represented the country's first popularly elected national legislature since 1917, it presented the first chance to render a verdict on its rulers. Despite the careful preparations, the long-awaited elections delivered a strong anti-establishment punch. The results showed a consistent pattern of nationwide losses for the Party machine, a steady round of defeats for senior dignitaries, military officers, and outright victories for or unexpectedly good performances by independent candidates.

The fairness of the pluralistic vote was demonstrated by the election of Boris Yeltsin, who won despite Gorbachev's strong opposition. Yeltsin had campaigned openly against the deadening power of Communist Party officials and the slowness of Gorbachev's reform. In his struggle for power, Yeltsin decided to utilize to the utmost the high explosive value of Russian nationalism. Many Russian patriots were, for a long time, dissatisfied with the ways Stalin and his successors tried to manufacture an artificial Soviet identity, while manipulating some trappings of Russian heritage. Yeltsin now began to insist on the creation of a separate Russian Communist Party, as well as a series of other institutions, like, for instance, the Russian Academy of Sciences. The establishment of such institutions was in reality an expression of revolt against Gorbachev's unitarian policy still insisting on the Soviet centralism. For the time being, Gorbachev still dominated the Soviet Congress of People's Deputies and its smaller superstructure, the Supreme Soviet and Yeltsin was forced onto the defensive. When veteran of Soviet politics Andrei Gromyko retired, the Congress elected Gorbachev to the post of President of the USSR. The post of Vice-President went, on Gorbachev's recommendation, to the head of the trade unions, Genady Yanayev. Thus, Gorbachev united in his hands two of the most important posts, that

[4]For an analysis of the disintegration of the Soviet empire, see Robert Cullen, *Twilight of Empire: Inside the Crumbling Soviet Bloc* (New York: The Atlantic Monthly Press, 1991).

of the General Secretary of the CPSU and head of the Soviet State.

The results of the relatively free elections to the Soviet Congress of People's Deputies were bound eventually to threaten the Communist monopoly of power. Although 86 percent of the deputies were still Party members, they soon split into several informal groups and did not vote as a block, thus violating the old rules banning "factions." In the early 1980s a number of Party groups, or "informals," had begun to shape, despite the efforts of the security apparatus to repress them. Some informals formed a loose coalition under the name of the "Inter-Regional Group." Many ethnic groups organized their own parties and joined the Group, hence the name of the coalition. The Group, however, proved to be only a small minority and was not well prepared for the job of effectively challenging the Communist majority. For this the Group needed at least tactical unity and proper leadership. Such leadership was temporarily provided by Andrei Sakharov, who had been freed by Gorbachev from house arrest in Gorky. Initially, he emerged as the most eloquent spokesman of a Duma coalition called the Inter-Regional Group and as its moral patriarch. Soon, however, his advanced age and declining health limited his political effectiveness.

After Sakharov's death in December 1989, Yeltsin was recognized as the actual leader of the opposition. In this role, he pressed for a more speedy transformation of the Communist system by breaking the monopoly of state ownership and permitting private property in land and free market. He also pushed for another goal: to make it impossible for any ruler to have too much power. What good, he argued, are a multiparty political system and a free market economy, if everything depends on the whim of one all-powerful President, who is also General Secretary of the only legally tolerated party? The democratic opposition took up these demands, which were supported by repeated mass demonstrations in Moscow and other Soviet cities.

Pressed by the mounting wave of strikes and protest demonstrations that was spreading throughout the Soviet Union, Gorbachev came to the conclusion that the Leninist doctrine of Communist monopoly of power had to go. On his initiative, on February 7, 1990, the Supreme Soviet discarded Article 6 of the Soviet Constitution, which had legally safeguarded this monopoly. This represented a dangerous gamble, since it opened the possibility of the CPSU being ousted from power, the way its fraternal Communist parties of Poland, Czechoslovakia, Hungary, and East Germany had been relegated to the status of opposition groups. The move drew vitriolic criticism on the part of hardline Communists, who accused Gorbachev of betraying Leninist principles. He replied that rather than relying on constitutional guarantees, the Party must prove its worthiness to govern by coping more effectively with the country's dire economic situation and the fast spreading ethnic dissent. Gorbachev rejected the accusation that his liberalization was to blame for the ouster of Communist regimes of Eastern Europe. He pointed out that those regimes had been toppled by democratic opposition groups no longer willing to tolerate coercion.

Yeltsin immediately took advantage of the reduced status of the Communist Party of the USSR. He insisted that parliamentary elections be held in all fifteen Soviet republics to which Gorbachev agreed. Meanwhile, on March 4, 1990, voting was held for the new Congress of People's Deputies of the Russian Republic, with no reserved proportion of seats for Communist deputies. This resulted in the election of over 50 percent of reformers supporting Yeltsin who proclaimed his wish to be President of the Russian Republic.

In other republics, notably in Lithuania, Latvia, and Estonia, popular fronts also swept aside the local Communists. The multiparty system had in effect arrived. While the Baltic republics continued their struggle for full independence, Yeltsin focused all his attention on reasserting the long-effaced identity and full sovereignty of the Russian Republic, the largest of all federal republics of the USSR and now his effective power base. A separate identity for Russia was to be Yeltsin's jumping-off point in his struggle for power against the still outwardly strong Gorbachev. Hence Yeltsin's effort to exploit his impressive triumph in the first truly free multiparty election in Russia. He promptly reactivated such institutions as the Russian Supreme Soviet and the Council of Ministers of the Russian Republic, both of them dormant since the time of Stalin. Sensing the mounting wave of Russian nationalism, Yeltsin was determined to exploit the discontent of many patriots who, like Alexander Solzhenitsyn, viewed Russia not as the driving force of international Communism, but as its main victim. Solzhenitsyn had maintained that declining economic performance under Brezhnev had made many Russians feel that other ethnic groups had exploited Russia's overwhelming resources by profiting from its cheap oil and natural gas, thus lowering the Russian standard of living. Many similar-thinking nationalists also believed that Russian cultural identity had been sacrificed in favor of a Soviet identity, which they considered a Marxist hoax and "Stalinist window dressing." Another example of this perception was found in the theories of the popular painter Ilya Glazunov. He had once pointed out that, on a poster displaying children from all fifteen Soviet republics, all of the children wore traditional folk costumes except for the Russian boy, who was clad in the red hat and scarf of the Communist Pioneers.

To foster his struggle with Gorbachev, who underrated the dynamic power of the renascent Russian nationalism, Yeltsin was determined to arrange for a fully democratic election of a Russian President. This would contrast with Gorbachev's presidency. After all, argued Yeltsin, Gorbachev owed all to a still largely Communist Soviet Congress of People's Deputies, who selected him to the post vacated by the Stalinist stooge, Andrei Gromyko. And indeed, in June 1991, Yeltsin was elected President of the Russian Repub-

lic, by an overwhelming democratic vote. On July 10, he was installed in his office in a festive, jubilant ceremony held at the Kremlin Palace of Congresses. The ceremony emphasized a return to tradition. The portrait of Lenin which had previously hung on a red curtain forming the background of the stage, was removed and replaced by the old Russian flag—white, blue, and red horizontal stripes introduced by Peter the Great. Nothing marked the change of era more strikingly than the appearance of Alexis II, the Patriarch of the Russian Orthodox Church, in his magnificent golden cape. Alexis, who sat on the stage behind Yeltsin, concluded his frankly political address condemning "seven decades of destruction of Russia's spiritual order" by the "Godless Communist regime."

Taking advantage of his enhanced political position, Yeltsin renewed his attacks on Gorbachev, and stressed that unlike Gorbachev, he had been democratically chosen by the overwhelming majority of the Russian people. Yeltsin also emphasized that he represented the largest federal republic, which produced 90 percent of the USSR's oil and 76 percent of its natural gas, as well as most of its gold and diamonds. He decried *perestroika* as a ridiculously slow, "pseudo-reform." Gorbachev, Yeltsin pointed out, while paying lip service to democratic slogans, had created an artificial hierarchy in which only the President of the USSR need not stand for election. Yeltsin criticized this "benevolent despotism" and argued that Gorbachev had more power than any Tsar and was surrounded by a personality cult, similar to that of Stalin. Yeltsin also urged letting the Baltic republics attain full independence without any hindrance from Moscow.

These pronouncements put Yeltsin again on a collision course with Gorbachev. The mounting wave of criticism on the part of the democratic opposition was manifested through a wave of worker's strikes in various parts of the country and mass ethnic riots in Ukraine and the Baltic Republics. In the forefront of the ferment were the Lithuanians, led by Vitavstas Landsbergis, who, from a leader of the freedom movement, advanced to the post of President of the Lithuanian Republic. This astute and energetic former professor of music proved to be a resourceful organizer. He boldly established customs posts along the Lithuanian frontier and proceeded to drill a local militia to replace the Soviet troops, on the prompt withdrawal of which he insisted. Soon the demands of independence spread not only to the other Baltic states, Latvia and Estonia, but also the Caucasian republics, Georgia, Armenia, and Azerbaijan, and finally to Ukraine. In Kiev, many local Communists, pressed by the coalition of nationalist groups known as "*Rukh*" sided with the growing irredentist trend. The pro-Moscow, Volodymyr Shchebicky was compelled to resign from the top party post in Ukraine, after seventeen years of lording over the land. This resulted in significant curbing of the harassment of

Ukrainian freedom fighters, which in turn increased their activities aimed at reclaiming the long suppressed national identity. This drive assumed openly irredentist character in the western provinces of Ukraine. There the independence movement stressed not only bold political demands, but also insisted on legalization of the Eastern Rite Catholic (Uniate) Church, brutally suppressed by Stalin in 1946.

From Ukraine, the ethnic ferment spread to the Central Asiatic, overwhelmingly Muslim, republics of Kazakhstan, Uzbekistan, Tadjikistan, Turkamenia, and Kirgizia—thus far regarded as rather passive. The strongest movement was that of Kazakhstan. There, matters were complicated not only by the fact that many of these republics had strong Russian minorities, but also by internal quarrels over conflicting economic interests, religious differences, and border disputes. For instance, Uzbekistan witnessed several clashes with Kirgizia in June 1990, with over 100 casualties

A mass protest of the angry Ukrainian crowd in Kiev against the Soviet rule

resulting. Though directed against other Asian groups, such disturbances took on an anti-Russian character as well.

Frightened by ethnic unrest in the Baltic republics, the Caucasus, Central Asia, and Ukraine, Gorbachev decided to cut his losses while saving at least the original Soviet Union. He agreed to full independence for the three Baltic countries, while focusing on preserving the remaining twelve republics under Moscow's aegis. His pet idea was to reconstruct the sham federation engineered by Lenin and Stalin as a union of sovereign entities, joined mainly by common economic and defense interests. He suggested that "USSR" would now stand for Union of *Sovereign* Socialist Republics. Gorbachev chose not to acknowledge, however, that by peddling such a concept he would alienate most of the pillars of the Communist system, with which he still fully identified at heart. And indeed his idea of the new Union clashed not only with the centralist sentiments of the Communist Party hardliners, but also with the military establishment and the KGB. The leaders of these three key institutions soon began to conspire against Gorbachev.

Repeated warnings against a military plot reached Gorbachev from many sides. In December 1990, his minister of foreign affairs, George Shavernadze, resigned and warned that the Soviet Union was threatened with a right-wing dictatorship. Similar warnings were issued by other cautious domestic, as well as foreign, observers of the Soviet scene. These included the president of the United States, George Bush. Basking in his popularity in the West, however, Gorbachev, ignored these repeated warnings because, as he said, "only a madman" would try to overthrow his government. Confident in the soundness of the proposed solution as the only one capable of preventing the old Soviet Union from final disintegration, Gorbachev went on with his zigzagging plans of economic reform and ethnic reconstruction.

Preoccupied by the prospect of a formal signing of a treaty establishing a new Union of twelve republics, on August 20, 1991, Gorbachev left Moscow to enjoy a yearly summer vacation at his luxurious Crimean villa on the Black Sea.

Suggested Reading

ANDREW, CHRISTOPHER, AND OLEG GORDIEVSKY, *KGB: The Inside Story of Its Operations from Lenin to Gorbachev.* New York: HarperCollins, 1991.

BESCHLOSS, MICHAEL R., AND STROBE TALBOTT, *At the Highest Levels: The Inside Story of the End of the Cold War.* Boston, Toronto, London: Little, Brown and Company, 1993.

BOROVIK, ARTYOM, *The Hidden War: A Russian Journalist's Account of the Soviet War in Afghanistan.* New York: The Atlantic Monthly Press, 1991.

BROWNING, GENIA, *Women and Politics in the U.S.S.R.: Consciousness Raising and the Soviet Women.* New York: St. Martin's Press, 1987.

CARRÉ D'ENCAUSSE, *Decline of an Empire: The Soviet Socialist Republics in Revolt.* New York: Newsweek Books, 1979.

CLEMENTS, BARBARA EVANS, ET AL. (EDS.), *Russia's Women.* Berkeley: University of California Press, 1991.

COHEN, STEPHEN F. (ED.), *An End to Silence: Uncensored Opinion in the Soviet Union. From Roy Medvedev's Underground Magazine "Political Diary."* New York: Norton, 1982.

CORDOVEZ, DIEGO, AND SELIG S. HARRISON, *Out of Afghanistan: The Inside Story of the Soviet Withdrawal.* New York: Oxford University Press, 1996.

CULLEN, ROBERT, *Twilight of Empire: Inside the Crumbling Soviet Bloc.* New York: Atlantic Monthly Press, 1991.

DIBB, PAUL, *The Soviet Union: The Incomplete Superpower.* Urbana: University of Illinois Press, 1986.

DUNLOP, JOHN, *The Faces of Contemporary Russian Nationalism.* Princeton, NJ: Princeton University Press, 1984.

ELLIS, JANE, *The Russian Orthodox Church: A Contemporary History.* Bloomington: Indiana University Press, 1986.

FESHBACH, MURRAY, *The Soviet Union: Population Trends and Dilemmas.* Washington, DC: Population Reference Bureau, 1982.

GOLDMAN, MARSHALL I., *USSR in Crisis: The Failure of an Economic System.* New York: Norton, 1983.

————, *What Went Wrong with Perestroika.* New York: W. W. Norton, 1991.

GOURÉ, LEON, *The Role of Nuclear Forces in Current Soviet Strategy.* Washington, DC: Center For Advanced International Studies, 1974.

MATLOCK, JACK F., JR., *Autopsy on an Empire: The American Ambassador's Account of the Collapse of the Soviet Union.* New York: Random House, 1995.

MEDVEDEV, ZHORES A., *Soviet Science.* New York: Norton, 1978.

————, *Andropov.* New York: Norton, 1983.

————, *Soviet Agriculture.* New York: Norton, 1987.

MICKIEWICZ, ELLEN, *Changing Channels: Television and the Struggle for Power.* Durhamand London: Duke University Press, 1999.

ODOM, WILLIAM E., *The Collapse of the Soviet Military.* New Haven and London: Yale University Press, 1998.

SAIKAL AMIN, AND WILLIAM MALEY (EDS.), *The Soviet Withdrawal from Afghanistan.* New York: Cambridge University Press, 1980.

SCHMIDT-HAUER, CHRISTIAN, *Gorbachev: The Path to Power.* London: I. B. Tauris, 1986.

SENN, ALFRED ERICH, *Lithuania's Awakening.* Berkeley: University of California Press, 1990.

SINGLETON, FRED (ED.), *Environmental Misuse in the Soviet Union.* New York: Praeger, 1976.

SOLZHENITSYN, ALEXANDER, ET AL., *From Under Rubble* (Trans. A. M. Brock). New York: Bantam, 1976.

STEWARD, JOHN MASSEY, *The Soviet Environment: Problems, Policies, and Politics.* Cambridge, Eng.: Cambridge University Press, 1991.

SWEARINGEN, RODGER (ED.), *Siberia and the Soviet Far East: Strategic Dimensions in Multinational Perspective.* Stanford, CA: Hoover Institution, 1987.

ULAM, ADAM B., *The Communists: The Story of Power and Lost Illusions: 1948–1991.* New York: A Robert Steward Book/Charles Scribner's Sons, 1992.

WHITE, STEPHEN, *Gorbachev and After.* Cambridge, Eng.: Cambridge University Press, 1991.

YELTSIN, BORIS, *The Struggle for Russia.* (Translated by Catherine A. Fitzpatrick). New York: Belka Publishing Company/Times Books/Random House, 1994.

Chapter 25

The Collapse
of the Soviet Union

The Coup of August 1991

While Gorbachev was basking in the sun at his Crimean *dacha*, in Moscow a group of eight of his closest co-workers were preparing a long-premeditated plot. At the head of the conspiracy was his Vice President, Genady Yanayev. He was helped in his plans of a military coup by the Minister of Defense, General Dmitri Yazov; chief of the KGB, Vladimir Kruchkov; Minister of the Interior, Boris Pugo, and three other prominent Communist leaders. Soon after Gorbachev's arrival in Crimea his villa was surrounded by KGB special detachments and his communications with the outside world carefully screened.

On Monday, August 19, Gorbachev was planning to return to Moscow the next day in order to sign the Union treaty of the twelve remaining Soviet federal republics, thereby implementing his cherished dream of preserving most of the Soviet Union by binding the remaining republics through confederate ties based mainly on mutual economic interests. But when Gorbachev lifted his telephone receiver to contact Moscow, he

was shocked to learn that he was cut off from the outside world altogether. He had become a hostage in his own home. Meanwhile, six of the General Staff, responsible for the President's control of strategic nuclear weapons, left the Crimean villa for Moscow, taking with them the briefcase containing the crucial codes.

While the General Secretary, as helpless as a turtle turned on its back, was struggling with dead telephones and trying to receive outside contact through radio and television, the plotters announced to the Soviet people and the world that President Gorbachev's sudden illness had created an "extraordinary situation" and that the power in the Soviet Union was to be taken over by the "State Council" headed by Vice President Yanayev and seven of his close co-workers.

The sudden announcement of the seizure of power by the self-styled State Council caught most Soviet people by surprise. In Moscow and Leningrad, the main stages of the drama, the presence of tanks and large numbers of troops quickly brought home what the term "extraordinary situation" meant. While the masses of ordinary people remained passive, a few courageous Muscovites challenged some commanders leading a parachutist detachment unit marching to seize the building of the Russian parliament, colloquially called the "White House." Meanwhile, however, Boris Yeltsin, warned by his supporters of the plot, barricaded himself with a team of his closest supporters in the White House. Through radio and television, he appealed to the Soviet people to defend their newly won freedom, which was now threatened by a clique of die-hard Communists eager to turn the clock back and reestablish a dictatorial regime. In a televised address, Yeltsin declared himself Commander-in-Chief of the armed forces of the Russian Republic, appealed to the soldiers to disobey orders of the coup leaders, and declared a general strike. Soon several thousand people, mostly of the younger generation, voted with their feet and, chanting the

Russian President's name, gathered around the White House. They were ready to defend the democratically elected President and his program of quick, radical reform. In an hour or so, makeshift barricades were erected and then reinforced with overturned buses and other vehicles around the parliament building. An attack by the massive military detachments was expected at any moment.

The White House was in peril of an assault by thousands of soldiers, guns, and tanks until the afternoon of Tuesday, August 20. Yet the expected storming of Yeltsin's headquarters did not materialize. The secret of this surprising passivity of the elite units loyal to the rebels was soon revealed. Most officers of the special KGB detachment simply refused to carry out Kruchkov's order to attack the White House and capture the leader of the resistance, Boris Yeltsin, dead or alive. This revolt of the crack unit spread

Moscow, August 19, 1991: Boris Yeltsin addressing the crowd in front of the Russian parliament building

to the guards' parachutist division, another elite detachment of the Red Army. There were a few scattered skirmishes between some of the soldiers surrounding the Parliament building, but no full-scale attack. Although three defenders of the White House were killed as a result of the clashes, it was obvious by the afternoon of Tuesday, August 20, that the poorly prepared plot was a miserable failure.

Aware of the collapse of the coup, its leaders tried to negotiate with Gorbachev for a compromise solution, but he remained unyielding. On August 22, he was brought back to Moscow in a plane sent by the triumphant Yeltsin, who had become the hero of the hour. While Gorbachev physically survived the coup, politically he became a marginal figure. Restored by Yeltsin's grace to his office of President of the crumbling USSR, Gorbachev was now discredited: all eight leaders of the coup had been hand-picked for their high offices by him because of their alleged personal loyalty. All of them had plotted Gorbachev's overthrow for a long time.

Despite this compromising fact, after his return to Moscow, Gorbachev tried to reassert himself. Surprisingly enough, he declared himself still a faithful Communist and tried to defend the crumbling Party's key position in the country. He thus revealed a lack of understanding of the radically altered political climate and committed political suicide.

Yeltsin, on the other hand, grasped the meaning of the new situation. At once he snatched from Gorbachev full initiative and thus the mantle of leadership. Yeltsin's bold behavior during the coup endowed him with impressive moral authority and wide popularity. By making challenging speeches from the top of a tank, urging resistance to the troops surrounding the White House, Yeltsin had created the image of a courageous and resourceful leader, ready to face any danger and any problem. He had early anticipated that the Party was an obstacle to democracy, and had left it. By this means he established

his reputation as a populist tribune expressing the yearnings of the Russian masses for more political freedom. During the three days of the coup, Yeltsin appeared not only as a personification of resistance to Communist dictatorship, but as a national hero. Gorbachev, by contrast, was blamed for his political naiveté and his passivity, and was accused, even by his own supporters, for lacking in resolution and for failing to break with his old Party cronies. His personal weakness and political miscalculation, especially his insistence on retaining the Party hardliners despite numerous warnings, was generally condemned as fatal flaws of judgment and character.

The "Soviet Disunion"

A few days after the failure of the coup, its consequences became obvious. The ruble plummeted and the Soviet economy slid into a free fall. With an empty treasury, the former Soviet Union faced bankruptcy. Facing a default on foreign debt, Yeltsin took the initiative once more and accepted responsibility for the payments of foreign debts in exchange for a year's grace. At the same time, the national republics of the Soviet Union, confronted with chaos and haunted with the spread of starvation and possible civil war, began, one by one, to reassert their independence.

Meanwhile, Yeltsin ordered immediate arrest and trial of the leaders of the plot. On August 24, he banned all activities of the Communist Party in the territory of Russia, dissolved the dreaded KGB, ordered creation of a separate Russian territorial army, and carried out confiscation of the Party's assets and suspension of all its papers and broadcast facilities.

The rapidly progressing disintegration of the Party compelled Gorbachev to step down as its head. At the same time, he called on former rank and file Communists to form a new party, permeated with socialist as well as democratic ideals. This was another fatal mistake. By that time, Communist Party members were thoroughly demoralized, and Party opponents had taken the offensive. This was manifested by the destruction of numerous Communist monuments, starting with that of the dreaded founder of Cheka, Felix Dzerzhinski, in front of the KGB's Moscow headquarters and the monuments of Lenin. This was followed by the restoring to Leningrad of its old name, St. Petersburg. The banner of the hammer and sickle was discarded and the ancient national flag, introduced by Peter the Great, white, blue, and red appeared in Moscow streets and in other Russian cities and towns; so did the black doubleheaded imperial eagle with Saint George on its breast.

The subsequent rapid liquidation of the Communist Party's activities in Russia dissolved the iron corset that held the Soviet Union together. Ukraine declared its independence three days after the failure of the coup, on August 24, Belorussia, Kazakhstan, Georgia, Azerbaijan, and other republics followed the example. Leonid Kravchuk, a long-time Ukrainian Communist and former Secretary of the local party, hitherto rather subservient to Moscow, promptly adopted the nationalistic slogans thus far peddled by the *Rukh*. Refusing to be outdone by other national leaders, he placed himself at the head of the irredentist movement. The Ukrainian declaration of independence unleashed a chain reaction. Soon other federal republics, and even autonomous territories, like the Tatarstan on the middle Volga, began to voice their economic, ethnic, and religious grievances against the Russian domination. The Tatars, for instance, demanded that their oil-bearing fields be handed over to their control. This, and many similar ethnic claims, reminded Yeltsin of the bitter truth that just as the USSR was an amalgam of fifteen constituent federal republics, so the core of the former Soviet imperial structure, the Russian republic, was a conglomeration of a host of autonomous ethnic regions and districts. One of them, the Chechen territory situated in the Caucasus, between the Caspian Sea and Georgia, went so far as to

declare its complete independence from Russia and insisted on the Soviet garrison to leave the Chechen territory. Soon armed clashes turned into a full-scale war.

After the disastrous August coup, Yeltsin completely overshadowed Gorbachev. Cashing in on the moral authority he had earned during the coup, Yeltsin moved rapidly to impose control by issuing a string of decrees, establishing his agents in key Kremlin offices, and sending his proconsuls across Russia to enforce his orders. Yeltsin also pressed for rapid economic reforms, while the Russian parliament gave him a free hand to cope with the mounting shortages of basic necessities, including bread. His efforts were not quite successful. Also unsuccessful were his attempts to mediate peace between Azerbaijan and Armenia and to suppress the irredentist drive of the Chechen partisans.

Despite these setbacks Yeltsin remained as confident as ever. He was the unquestionable democratically elected leader of the Russian Republic some 148 million people, or more than half of the whole population of the former USSR. Moreover, the territory of the Republic commanded overwhelming natural resources, including some 90 percent of oil reserves, 76 percent of natural gas and most of the mines of gold, diamonds, and other precious and semi-precious metals. Trusting in his popularity, the resources and commanding geostrategic position of his republic, Yeltsin acted more and more boldly and often without previous consultation with the helpless and confused Gorbachev.

By the autumn of 1991, the main objective of the increasingly lonely Gorbachev was to reestablish a "single economic space" within the borders of what still remained from the former Soviet Union. His chief argument was that such a new Union of twelve independent states would be firmly based on economic interdependence. From the beginning, however, Gorbachev encountered serious difficulties because the prospective members sharply criticized the Union treaty's proposed text. Most of the constituent republics insisted that the proposed treaty be phrased in more general terms, along the lines of the international agreements that had established the European Economic Community and not those of the dead Warsaw Pact, or the CEMA. The fledgling new states insisted on recognition of their full sovereignty as a precondition for signing the treaty proposed by Gorbachev. Thus, his efforts to regather the rebellious republics by imposing on them strong ties binding them to Moscow, led him into a blind alley. Meanwhile, inflation was spiraling by more than 250 percent; production of both industrial goods and agricultural produce was rapidly falling. The dollar that in 1990 could be bought for about one rubel was now worth 270 rubels. The Soviet National Bank was unable to service the foreign debt of some $80 billion. Staples like sugar, eggs, and even bread and milk could not be found in many stores. Hoarding them had become a widespread practice.

Seeing the futility of Gorbachev's efforts to establish his Union, Yeltsin once more acted on his own and declared that the Russian Republic would sell oil and natural gas at world market prices for convertible currency only. That threatened to take most of the other republics out of the competitive market for these goods, but also enhance Russia's position as a real economic hub of the area.

The final blow to Gorbachev's efforts at regathering the old Soviet Union was dealt on December 1, 1991. On that day the Ukrainians reaffirmed by a popular plebiscite their resolve for final separation from Russia and refused to sign the Union treaty. Boris Yeltsin immediately declared that if Ukraine did not sign the treaty, his republic would not sign either. The loss of some 53 million people, who produced annually about a quarter of the total agricultural output of the former Soviet Union, a fifth of its consumer goods, and controled some 15 percent of its nuclear arsenal, evoked sharp protests among many Russian leaders. The most dramatic protest came from Gorbachev himself. Anticipating collapse of the Union, he warned of possible civil war and a "catastrophe for all mankind" if his Union treaty were not signed promptly.

Trying to counterbalance Gorbachev's pessimism, Yeltsin urged the Russian people to rally for a prompt transition from a Communist to a capitalist and democratic system, promising that by the end of 1992 their food basket would be "two-thirds full." This "leap into capitalism," however, disregarded the grim reality of empty pantries, grain elevators, and gas tanks. Russia's leap into capitalism has proved extremely difficult. One has to bear in mind that Russia's modest experience in capitalism under Witte and Stolypin, had been brutally interrupted by Stalin's thorough extermination of most experienced business people and most efficient farmers. For over seventy years the only democracy Russia had known was the democracy of poverty, and the inequality of wealth was traditionally confronted with envy. Yeltsin's task has been, therefore, formidable: he had to encourage the people to rebuild capitalism in a country where it had been, for two generations or so, equated with gangsterism, private property with theft, and profit with exploitation.

Gorbachev's warning of impending doom should the old Soviet Union fall apart had little effect. Ukraine refused to sign the draft Union treaty proposed by him. Yeltsin made it clear that he did not regard the new Union as feasible without Ukraine's participation, and subsequently recognized the independence of the Ukrainian and Belorussian republics. Other countries, including the United States and Canada, also granted recognition to the new government in Kiev, provided it would honor the disarmament agreements previously signed by Moscow, respect human rights and the existing borders. By promptly accepting Ukraine's and Belorussia's independence, Yeltsin tried to exorcise, at least for the moment, the ghost of the old Russian imperialism. On December 8, 1991, he lured both Ukraine and Belorussia into signing a treaty of alliance with the Russian Republic. The Commonwealth of Independent States he now sponsored, soon joined by other non-Slavic lands of the former Soviet Union,

Students of the military academy in Kiev take an oath of allegiance to the Ukraine (January 1992)

the Soviet people suffering the miseries of their daily existence. Among the ordinary Soviet people, he was not popular, except with a handful of intellectuals who greatly enjoyed the leeway granted them by *glasnost*. For most of the other segments of his people, his *perestroika*, was a lamentable failure. Freedom without bread, however, was meaningless for the broad masses of the frozen and starving crowd, condemned to wrangle for basic necessities standing in increasingly long lines in front of half-empty food shops and closing stores. A report by the Soviet State Planning Committee predicted that Soviet GNP would fall 20 percent in 1991, industrial production more than 20 percent, and agricultural output about 5 percent. This rapid crumbling of the economy could have been remedied as early as 1986–1987 by a prompt and radical structural reform of the Soviet agriculture, beginning with a return of the land to the peasants. But Gorbachev, brought up from childhood as an orthodox Communist, could not reconcile himself to a complete return to private property. Instead, he continually tried half-measures. Instead of dissolving the 27,000 collective and 21,000 State farms step by step, he procrastinated. His proposal to introduce agricultural contracts to be offered to peasant families, was in fact a small step forward, a lame compromise. In essence, it was Gorbachev's policy to tolerate small-scale private agriculture under the heading of leasing, while basically sticking to the Communist taboo—lamentably inefficient collective farms.[1]

including the Muslim republics of Central Asia, Kazahkstan, Uzbekistan, Kirgizia, Turkamania, Tadzikistan, and Georgia. From Yeltsin's bold initiative, Gorbachev lost most of his leverage and remained more like a vocal political observer than a major actor of the political stage.

Gorbachev: A Political Obituary

For over six years, with the dexterity of a daring acrobat in a circus, Gorbachev walked a tightrope without a safety net. It was a most dazzling performance. His performance fascinated more the outside world than it did

Yet, in the crucial agricultural sector, rapid successes could have been achieved much more quickly than in industry. Gorbachev willfully ignored the successful Chinese

---

[1]For instance, the summer of 1990 yielded a bumper crop. Yet the harvest was largely wasted. Some grain and vegetables perished, rotting in the fields uncollected by the apathetic collective farm peasants, while some were lost because of inefficient transport and lack of adequate storage facilities. As a consequence, the Soviet treasury had to deplete its rapidly shrinking reserves of gold and hard currency for continued import of produce from abroad.

example of starting economic restructuring with privatization of agriculture and then proceeding to deal with the rest of the economy. Shortages of food became more and more acute and unleashed waves of strikes and mass demonstrations. Without adequate supplies of food, all other economic reforms were threatened. No wonder, therefore, that Gorbachev's reforms won only hesitant support of the broad masses who "found no calories" in *perestroika*.

Meanwhile, the openness of *glasnost* unleashed the potent forces of religion and nationalism, both often tinged with xenophobia. The best example of this type of national exclusivism was the movement known as *Pamyat*. Although the word literally means "memory," it is more frequently interpreted as revenge. *Pamyat* was outwardly dedicated to the recovery of a genuine Russian past. With its young members dressed in black shirts, emblazoned with the seal of the ancient Kremlin bell, the movement staged public demonstrations, organized lectures, and generally proclaimed that Russian history had been deflected from its true course by the "Masonic Zionist" conspiracy.

By proclaiming *glasnost*, Gorbachev unleashed powerful forces hitherto suppressed by forcible indoctrination and terror. A mounting wave of criticism of the past led to a questioning of Communist legitimacy and of the entire Leninist-Stalinist experiment. Many critics concluded that over seventy years of Communist Utopia had proved to be a road to nowhere. This, in turn, led to a search for alternative pluralistic values. Gorbachev's tinkering with democracy in a country with no democratic tradition produced meager results and only introduced a state of dangerous instability. The seamless robe of the Communist totalitarian system was torn apart.

From the beginning of Gorbachev's reforming activities, it was obvious that his political base was narrow. Both Lenin and Stalin started with small but highly dedicated teams ready to risk anything fighting for their cause. Both Lenin and Stalin brutally purged large numbers of their opponents and replaced them with loyal partisans of the new order. Gorbachev relied more on persuasion than on compulsion, which proved ineffective. Soon it became obvious that the Communist system in Russia could not last for long without terror.

Despite these mistakes, Gorbachev will likely go down in history as a courageous statesman of broad international vistas who was, however, too steeped in Marxist economic doctrine to cope with Soviet domestic crisis. Making virtue out of necessity, Gorbachev put an end to the Cold War, which the increasingly weakening and the already highly unstable Soviet Union, in the long run, could not support anyway. The disintegration of the Soviet Empire radically altered the political climate of the world and opened a new era in the history of the modern world.

The Great Debate

The downfall of the Soviet regime unleashed a great debate among leading specialists in the field. In the vanguard of the discussion was Zbigniew Brzezinski, who actually anticipated this event in his broad analytical study entitled, *The Grand Failure: The Birth and Death of Communism in the Twentieth Century* (New York: Charles Scribner's Sons, 1989). He predicted that Communism, not only in Russia but throughout the world, would fail, because it contained the seeds of its own destruction. Without underrating the vital role played by the United States' policy of containment and the fact that the Soviet Union lost the Cold War, Brzezinski pointed out that, already by the early 1980s, the Soviet Union was facing a mortal crisis because of its internal contradictions and the changing international situation. By the time Gorbachev came to power in 1985, the citadel of world Communism was already in ideological, political, economic, and moral crisis beyond remedy. By rejecting basic moral values and stressing crude materialism, the Soviet leaders made their success dependent on the economic performance of the USSR. Yet they totally failed to appreciate the vital link between spiritual and political freedom and scientific creativity, with its boost to economic productivity; this induced a state of inertia bordering on paralysis. As a result of this lethargy, the democratic, capitalistic societies outperformed the Communist ones, thus discrediting Communist claims to be in the vanguard of human progress and a model worthy of imitation.

A similar line of argument was followed by Professor Richard Pipes in his essay entitled, *Communism: The Vanished Specter* (Oxford: Scandinavian University Press and Oxford University Press, 1994). After a detailed analysis of the Communist leaders' brutal attempts at manipulating human beings, whom Trotsky called "tailless apes," who had to be "driven to happiness by force," Pipes concluded that the Soviet regime failed because it endeavored to suppress two basic human needs: to own private property and to express oneself freely. While successfully eliminating "any possibility of organizing active resistance, the Soviet system never devised effective means of combating its passive manifestations; it learned to perfection how to fend off assaults, but not how to arrest erosion." The passive resistance of the enslaved masses resulted in the progressive loss of creative capacity, including technological inventiveness. Consequently, the Soviet Union, despite the fact that in the 1980s it was the leading producer of oil, cement, and steel, found itself being overtaken economically by the West and rapidly losing its standing as an industrial, and hence military, superpower.

Similar conclusions were reached by Robert V. Daniels in his seminal book, *The End of the Communist Revolution* (London and New York: Routledge, 1993). Daniels stressed not only political and economic factors, but also ideological decay, as a cause of the failure of the Communist utopia. Here Daniels was close to the concepts of Martin Malia, expressed in his monograph, *The Soviet Tragedy: A History of Socialism in Russia, 1917–1991* (New York: The Free Press,

1994). Malia paid a great deal of attention to the ideological meanderings of successive phases of the Communist regimes in Russia, as well as in the captive countries of East Central Europe, and their failure to build truly socialist societies. By contrast, John B. Dunlop, in his study, *The Rise of Russia and the Fall of the Soviet Empire* (Princeton, New Jersey: Princeton University Press, 1993), generally limited his story to strictly political factors. The problem of "the dream that failed" was confronted by John Arnason in his, *The Future that Failed: Origins and Destinies of the Soviet Model* (New York: Routledge, 1993). His analysis was undertaken primarily from the standpoint of the economic and sociological theory of modernization. He ascribed the grand failure to the Stalinist self-destructive focus on military priorities, which put control ahead of innovation, thus condemning the Soviet economy to progressive obsolescence. Stalin's successors duplicated this pattern, which in the long run proved so disastrous. By the 1970s, the Soviet economy had become decrepit, and in the 1980s it went into an irreversible decline. An analogous approach was taken by Moshe Levin in his autopsy of the Soviet economic policies, entitled *Russia/USSR/Russia: The Drive and Drift of a Superstate* (New York: The New Press, 1995). According to Levin, it was the failure of the planned economy that sealed the fate of the Soviet regime, unable to compete in the postindustrial world. The revolt of the non-Russian nationalities, a crucial development at the final stages of the disintegraiton of the USSR, was a side effect of the economic crisis, resulting from the unworkability of the excessively regulated economy. The longer the shop shelves remained bare, the lower fell the prestige of the communist regimes. It was the rising hope for a consumer society during the 1960s and 1970s that hastened the downfall of the Communist regimes in Russia and its East Central European satellites. As multifaceted as it seems, the debate neglected on the whole the role of the Cold War, which the Soviet Union unleashed but failed to win and, last but not least, the role of the lost war in Afghanistan that affected so much the morale of the Russian people.

The above survey represents only an abbreviated and highly selective summary of a larger and constantly growing body of works pertaining to the downfall of the Soviet regime. One of the common features of the debate is the surprise of most of the participants at the ease and speed of the disintegration of the USSR. They point out that by the late 1980s, even the Communist hardliners had lost their nerve. Contrary to general expectation, they did not put up a determined resistance to the democratic demands of an increasingly sophisticated and vociferous urban dissent. By 1990, there were none of the expected vigorous attempts by the *apparat* to crack down on the anti-Communist forces, especially in the multinational borderlands. For the first time, the hitherto ruthless Soviet leaders peacefully backed down before the spontaneous revolt of their own people. Even the attempted coup of August, 1991, was doomed by the almost farcical lack of will on the part of the plotters; they represented a demoralized Party that ceased to believe in the slogans they had proclaimed. Almost all latter-day Sovietologists agree that the leadership's cynicism was a major cause of its utter ineffectiveness, exposing the ruling clique as an empty shell. When a determined use of available military force could have saved, at least momentarily, the old regime, the hesitant plotters did not muster the nerve to use it, and accepted their defeat with fatalistic resignation.

The USSR from a Historic Perspective

When the red and gold hammer and sickle flag was lowered from the top of a Kremlin tower on December 25, 1991, it marked the end of the Soviet experiment. Created after the Bolshevik coup d'état in November 1917, the first Communist State started with an aim to remake the man; in Trotsky's words, it was determined to "overturn the world" and cre-

ate a new type of human being. The Communist dictatorship was challenged by a plethora of opposition groups, but the Bolsheviks muddled through one of the most bloody and devastating civil wars in history, lasting from 1918 to 1921, and imposed the "dictatorship of the proletariat" on the overwhelmingly rural society inhabiting one-sixth of the globe.

Proclaimed as the voluntary union of over 100 ethnic groups, the sham federation was named in 1922 the Union of the Soviet Socialist Republics, the first Communist State in the world. Its avowed aim was to be the bastion of international Communism and the pioneer of progress, enlightenment, and modernization—"the Rome of the proletariat" to use the expression of the French writer André Gide. This utopian vision crumbled under the cruel totalitarian rule of Lenin and Stalin who destroyed the budding civil society, that had been augured by the constitutional period of 1905 to 1917 and the democratic Duma election of December of that year. During the 1920s, the Soviet Union impressed most of the world by its fast progress in liquidating illiteracy, its daring experiments in arts, especially cinema, its electrification of the country, and its dismantling of social barriers. At the price of untold sufferings, Stalin expanded the Soviet economic base. In the 1930s, at a terrible cost in human lives, he managed to collectivize agriculture and build an outwardly impressive industrial base, as well as the largest armed forces in the world. During the Second World War (1939–1945), these forces defeated, with the help of the Western Allies, the most formidable fighting machine ever created, Hitler's Wehrmacht.

After the war, the USSR emerged as one of the two global superpowers, master of a vast East European satellite system. When Mao Tse Tung seized control of China in 1943, the global triumph of Communism appeared to be only a matter of time. Together with North Korea, North Vietnam, Cuba, and the satellite states of East Central Europe, the Soviet type dictatorships covered about one-third of the globe. At the same time, the growing power of French and Italian parties was a menace to Western Europe. In 1950 the Soviet Union acquired nuclear weapons and soon after that impressed the world with its space achievements, while threatening it with its formidable military might.

For forty years the Soviet Union was locked in a most dangerous conflict with the nations of the West, organized under the name of NATO, led by the United States of America. This latent conflict, known as "the Cold War," repeatedly brought the world to the brink of an atomic Armageddon. Moscow's great power arrogance was soon demonstrated in various parts of the Third World, from Cuba to Ethiopia. Confident in its allegedly invincible armed forces, Brezhnev mindlessly plunged into a military adventure in Afghanistan in December 1979. The war initially appeared as a "small colonial expedition." Its aim was to conquer this potentially rich and strategically located country, to bring the Communist colossus closer to the warm waters of the Indian Ocean and the Persion Gulf. Yet the costly conflict dragged on for some nine years, and ended with a stalemate that amounted to virtual defeat of the Red Army by primitively scattered bands of Afghan guerrillas. This humiliating failure of the mighty Soviet military machine demonstrated the weakness of the proverbial "giant with feet of clay."

At the same time, the 1970s and 1980s witnessed the surfacing of a small but vocal Soviet domestic opposition. The parallel mounting ferment in the satellite states of East Central Europe revealed the brittle nature of the Soviet "hegemony without security." This ferment eventually resulted in the vassal countries breaking away from Moscow in 1989, starting with Poland. Meanwhile, the deepening economic disorder inside the USSR pushed the Soviet leadership, headed by Gorbachev, to undertake a series of attempted reforms, known under the name of *perestroika*, or reconstruction. Their initial aim was to retrench and streamline the Communist system and make it function more efficiently. Soon, however, the

reforms were bogged down in bureaucratic inefficiency, graft, and corruption. By 1990–1991, many initial promoters of the reform, like Yeltsin, concluded that a genuine reform was impossible as long as the monopolistic Communist Party ruled supreme. After leaving the Party, Yeltsin challenged Gorbachev's "pseudo-reforms" and launched a bold program based on free market and a fundamental reconstruction of the tottering Soviet Union.

The failure of *perestroika*, revealed the ideological failure of Communism as well as the economic bankruptcy of the Soviet system. It spent more than a quarter of its GNP on the armed forces and enormous sums of money on its clients and national liberation movements of the Third World. As a dynamic, evangelical force communism had been dead for at least a generation or so, since the revelation of Stalin's terrible crimes in 1956. The Communist regime survived in the Soviet Union until 1991, supported by the formidable apparatus of propaganda and coercion. When both weakened, the regime began to disintegrate. The failure of the ineffective coup of August 1991 encouraged the ethnic minorities, for years in revolt against the system of forcible "Sovietization." Some of them stepped forward and claimed full independence from Moscow. The process was started by Lithuania and the remaining two Baltic countries, Latvia and Estonia.

The aftermath of the coup August 1991 witnessed rejection of Gorbachev's scheme to salvage the old Union of Soviet Socialist Republics by turning it into a new Commonwealth of Independent States, or CIS, the heart of which was to be the Russian Federation. The elemental drive toward independence was taken advantage of by Yeltsin, who offered to the rebellious nationalities a more palatable solution: voluntary alliance connected with the Russian republic by common economic interests.

The collapse of the USSR confirmed some of the basic patterns of modern Russian history. The first and the most striking pattern shows that all basic attempts at reform came from above: the "great reforms" of Tsar

Alexander II, those of Witte and Stolypin, Lenin's "New Economic Policy," and Gorbachev's *perestroyka*; the second that most upheavals were triggered by lost foreign wars. The abolition of serfdom followed the disastrous Crimean War of 1853–1855. The liberalization of the autocratic Tsarist system and the constitutional manifesto of October 1905 were a result of the lost Russo-Japanese War. The downfall of the Tsarist system and the triumph of the Bolsheviks in the 1917 revolution were precipitated by the catastrophe of World War I. Is it possible to ignore the role of the Afghan War, while examining the timing and outcome of Gorbachev's attempts at humanizing the Communist regime?

Suggested Reading

ARBATOV, GEORGI, *The System: An Insider's Life in Soviet Politics*. New York: Times Books/Random House, 1995.

CLEMENS, WALTER C., *Baltic Independence and Russian Empire*. New York: St. Martin's Press, 1991.

HOSKINS, GEOFFREY, *The Awakening of the Soviet Union*. Cambridge, MA: Harvard University Press, 1990.

HYLAND, WILLIAM G., *The Cold War Is Over*. New York: Times Books, 1990.

KNIGHT, W. AMY, *The KGB: Police and Politics in the Soviet Union*. Boston, MA: Unwin and Hyman, 1991.

KORT, MICHAEL, *The Soviet Colossus: The Rise and Fall of the USSR*. New York: M.E. Sharpe, 1992.

KOTKIN, STEPHEN, *Armageddon Averted: The Soviet Collapse, 1970–1999*. Oxford: Oxford University Press, 2001.

LOURIE, RICHARD, *Predicting Russia's Future*. New York: Whittle Direct Books, 1991.

MANDELBAUM, MICHAEL, *The Rise of Nations in the Soviet Union: American Foreign Policy and the Disintegration of the U.S.S.R.* New York: Council on Foreign Relations Press, 1991.

MATTHEWS, MERVIN, *Poverty in the Soviet Union*. Cambridge, Eng.: Cambridge University Press, 1987.

MEDVEDEV, GRIGORI, *The Truth about Chernobyl*. New York: Basic Books, 1991.

NAHAYLO, BOHDAN AND VICTOR SVOBODA, *Soviet Disunion: A History of the Nationalities Problem in the USSR*. New York: The Free Press, 1990.

NOVE, ALEX, *Glasnost in Action: Cultural Renaissance in Russia*. Boston: Unwin Hyman, 1989.

ODOM, WILLIAM E., *The Collapse of the Soviet Military*. New Haven, CT: Yale University Press, 1998.

RIORDAN, JIM (ED.), *Soviet Youth Culture*. Bloomington: Indiana University Press, 1989.

SHAVERNADZE, EDWARD, *The Future Belongs to Freedom*. New York: The Free Press, 1991.

SHIRLEY, EUGENE B., JR., AND MICHEL ROWE (EDS.), *Candle in the Wind: Religion in the Soviet Union*. Lanham, MD University Press of America, 1989.

VOLKOGONOV, DMITRII ANTONOVICH, AND HAROLD SHUKMAN, *Autopsy for an Empire: The Seven Leaders Who Built the Soviet Regime*. New York: Free Press, 1998.

ZASLAVSKAYA, TATIANA, *The Second Socialist Revolution*. Bloomington: Indiana University Press, 1990.

Chapter 26

The Commonwealth of Independent States and the Russian Federation

The Commonwealth of Independent States, or the C.I.S., was proclaimed by Yeltsin in 1991 as a loose structure composed of eleven former Soviet Republics: the Russian Republic, Ukraine, Kazakhstan, Belorussia, Armenia, Azerbaijan, Georgia, Uzbekistan, Turkmenistan, Kirgistan and Tajikistan. The C.I.S. has been built around bilateral agreements between Moscow and the new states. This new hub-and-spoke structure was reminiscent of the old Council of Mutual Assistance and the Warsaw Pact; such an arrangement was meant from the beginning to be a way of projecting Russia's influence throughout the area, with a perspective of eventually reestablishing Moscow's control. Although the main instrument of Soviet domination, the net of Communist parties, had largely disintegrated, its functionaries, the old *nomenklatura,* has remained largely intact, and so did the old economic and communication infrastructure, thus allowing the Russian Republic, which has officially assumed the name of Russian Federation, to reassert its influence over most of the lands of the former USSR. This could be facilitated by the disparity between the size, resources, and population of the Federation; as com-

pared with those of the remaining smaller members of the C.I.S.; with the exception of Ukraine and Kazakhstan, they were all relatively small entities, lacking significant natural resources.

The Russian Federation has remained a huge entity; it stretches from the Kaliningrad enclave on the Baltic Sea to the Bering Strait between Siberia and Alaska. The Federation covers over 17 million square kilometers of territory and remains the largest state of the world; the Federation is divided into 89 administrative regions. Almost as much as the defunct Soviet Union, the Federation is a multiethnic state, although the great majority of its population of 147 million, or about 82 percent, is Russian. Last, but not least, the Russian Federation is rich in oil, coal, and timber, as well as gold and all sorts of metals. Yet there are as many as twenty-one ethnically based small republics within the Federation, such as Tartarstan on the Middle Volga. Thus the Russian Federation is a multinational organism as well as a national state.

Despite the loss of the Baltic provinces, the Caucasus, most of Central Asia, and especially of Ukraine, the Russian Federation has remained a potentially powerful

Commonwealth of Independent States

383

state. The Federation inherited about 70 percent of the Soviet Union's nuclear arsenal, which has remained a potential threat to the rest of the world because of the internal instability of the Federation, as well as volatility of its leaders.

Most leaders of the member states of the C.I.S., who, in general, were former Soviet officials, found themselves quite unprepared for independence. Brought up in the Communist school of absolute obedience to Moscow, they have been embarrassed in their new roles as leaders of independent states. Consequently, since 1992, each state has been undergoing a deep identity crisis and has hesitated as to the best means of cutting the umbilical cord that still connected it to the hegemonial center of power. Most of the republics, especially Ukraine, Belorus and Kazakhstan, had to take into account the presence of a large segment of the Russian diaspora, numbering altogether some 25 to 26 million people, scattered throughout the entire former USSR. These people, whom Russians call "the near abroad," have considerably hampered the process of nation building of most members of the C.I.S. Belorus, Kazakhstan, and Ukraine, the former Soviet Belorussian Republic, are all burdened with an especially large Russian minority. Consequently, all three have attempted to form their state identities on a territorial basis, rather than on ethnicity.

Another problem represented the regional differences; Ukraine's drive to full national independence, for instance, has been more pronounced in its western, formerly Polish, provinces, while its eastern, more Russianized part, with Kharkov as its center, has been gravitating toward reunion with the Russian Federation. Belorus lacks the equivalent of the fiercely nationalistic Western Ukrainian segment to bolster its aspirations to full independence. Consequently, Belorus has been undergoing a process of disintegration as a separate state; the political passivity of its citizens and its lack of natural resources have pushed its leaders first to agree to a monetary union with the Russian Federation, then to joint military control of external borders, and finally, at the end of March, 1996, to virtual union with Russia. This has been proclaimed as a great success of President Yeltsin, a vital argument in fighting his jingoist opponents on the right as well as on the left.

Also, the multinational southern fringe of the Commonwealth has provided the Russians ample opportunity to reassert their influence. The Russian military establishment, humiliated by its withdrawal from most of its World War II conquests, welcomed such opportunity, taking advantage of the constant ethnic strife that surfaced after the removal of Soviet shackles. This has been especially true of the Caucasus region. By supporting the Communist and post-Communist factions, the Russian military forces have tried to revive Moscow's influence over the multiethnic area. This was, for instance, the case in the protracted war between Armenia and Azerbaijan over the Upper Karabakh region. In the third Caucasian republic, Georgia, the former KGB general and Soviet foreign minister, Edward Shevardnadze, who had been elected president of his native country, seemed, initially, an instrument of Russian influence. By adroit maneuvering of local political factions, however, he soon reasserted his authority, and became a bold champion of Georgian independence. In Tajikistan, a Central Asiatic Republic bordering on Afghanistan, the Russian armed forces have supported the northern, pro-Communist clans; this intervention has radicalized the southern clans that might, in the future, seek Islamic fundamentalist sponsors in Kabul, Teheran, and Islamabad. The Russian military establishment has bolstered the Trans-Dniester Republic, the northern splinter of the former Moldavian Soviet Republic. The commander of the Russian troops in Trans-Dniesteria, General Alexander Lebed, by his stubborn stand in defense of the Slavic population of the area, has been elevated to the status of national hero by a large segment of the Russian public, who encouraged him to step into the political arena and seek the presidential post.

While, generally speaking, the Russian

policy in the region of the Caucasus has been partly successful, the glaring exception to this rule has been the small autonomous region of Chechnya; inhabited by some one million people, with Grozny as its capital, Chechnya proclaimed itself a republic independent of the C.I.S. To the proclamation Moscow reacted by sending a strong force to reassert its sovereignty. Chechnya possesses considerable oil and gas resources and is strategically located at the crossroads of gas and oil pipelines and Russia's only railroad connection with Azerbaijan. Control of Chechnya has been perceived by Russian leaders as crucial for Russia's influence in the entire Transcaucasian region, threatened by penetration of Western investors, eager to gain access to the enormous oil reserves of the Caspian Sea.

Despite the display of overwhelming forces, the Russian soldiers have been unable to score a decisive military victory. Attempts at negotiating various compromise options have failed, as did numerous ceasefire agreements. The war in Chechnya has revealed the military weakness of the Russian Federation. Its armed forces are, on paper, a formidable fighting machine. Yet, demoralized by the series of humiliating withdrawals from the lands conquered during World War II and by the critical economic conditions at home, the Russian soldiers have suffered from poor morale and inferior leadership. The fact that the Chechen region, a backward land of just over one million inhabitants, could defy an overwhelmingly stronger elite detachment of the Russian Army reveals a measure of the rapid deterioration of the fighting capacity of the once invincible force that had crushed Hitler's Wehrmacht. The persistence with which the Russians have tried to subdue the Chechen irredentist movement has been a sign of their determination to keep the region as an integral part of the Russian Federation.

The dragging war in Chechnya has been only a small part of Moscow's attempts to reassert its direct control over the lands of the former Soviet Union. These efforts have been made largely ineffective by the economic paralysis that followed the collapse of the Russian economy. The beginning of this phenomenon was already visible at the last stages of the existence of the USSR, but its full scope was revealed when a group of young reformers, like Anotoly Chubais, Ygor Gaidar, and Grigory Yavlinsky, launched a hastily conceived and badly prepared scheme of free market reforms. Instead of improving the performance of the ailing economy, they plunged it into chaos.

From Anarcho-Capitalism to Criminal Capitalism

From the beginning of his tenure as president, Boris Yeltsin was committed to free market economic reform. Yet he barely understood its nature, let alone the long-range consequences for the country's crumbling economy. The sudden shift from a command economy to one propelled by market forces, and based on private ownership and initiative, has proved extremely painful. This is no surprise in a country where private ownership had been ruthlessly suppressed for over seven decades. The Stalinist model of forced industrialization and rigid centralized control of the entire economy brutally destroyed all those elements that espoused the virtues of thrift, hard work, and economic discipline necessary for the development of native capitalism. This left Russia at a disadvantage in terms of promptly, as well as effectively, implementing radical market reform.

For such a transformation Russia has lacked the uninterrupted tradition of private ownership needed to achieve this goal; despite the privatization of large segments of all enterprises, mostly small and middle-level ones, the old giant factories have remained State owned, as well as most of the land. This half-house system has suffered from many handicaps. First of all, the Federation thus far has failed to introduce adequate protection of private-property rights. Another handicap has been the lack of a modern credit system and yet another has been the weakness of the consumer-goods industries. The command economy, which overwhelmingly focused on heavy industries, especially those supporting the military establishment, has failed to supply enough consumer products. As a result, many consumer goods available on the Russian market have been imported, with understandable consequences for the country's negative foreign trade balance and its budget.

Perhaps the most significant obstacle to the introduction of a sound economic system has been psychological. In the Soviet system, all industries were organized as virtual monopolies, and their output and prices were regulated by the State. In 1992, the *nomenklatura* eagerly grabbed the ownership of most of the industrial jewels sold to them by the State at ridiculously low prices. The new owners have not been interested in real competition, or closure of inefficient large enterprises, but rather seek to continue their largely parasitic existence. Thus, the old controls have been removed, while the discipline of the market has not replaced them. Genuine capitalist reform requires liquidity of the labor force, and this precondition has been conspicuously lacking. The new entrepreneurs and managers of both privatized and State-owned companies have tended to operate according to old Stalinist methods; they seek to preserve their labor force and to retain control of large stocks of raw materials and huge numbers of workers, thereby maintaining their political clout. Moreover, the new pseudo-capitalists have surpassed their nineteenth-century Western models in ruthlessness; they have dealt with each other in a brutal and often even a criminal way. Instead of investing their profits, they have been looting the country without scruple.

In addition to these handicaps, the hesitant and zigzag efforts at economic reform have been severely complicated by the rise of vicious and rapidly expanding mafias. They have not only penetrated various state enterprises, but have also terrorized small private enterprises by extorting large profits from them; many managers of State-controlled, as well as newly created or privatized enterprises, have been cooperating with organized crime and even themselves acting as mafiosi. According to government estimates, about 40 percent of Russian businesses have been a part of the organized crime that has often punished those who dare to oppose its extortive methods. Paying bribes and protection money has become a standard practice, a regular part of business expenses. Hundreds of so called "contract killings" have taken place every year since 1992. This spread of overt crime and corruption, combined with the failure to establish effective rule of law and hence of civil society, has transformed a system which has been dubbed by some economists as "anarcho-capitalism," into virtual criminal capitalism.

The Duma against the President

From the beginning of its existence, the Russian Federation has been beset not only by economic anarchy but also by a sharp conflict between its legislative and executive branches. The Congress of Peoples' Deputies, or the Russian makeshift parliament, which Yeltsin inherited from the ruins of the USSR, stubbornly opposed the President's market reform policies as well as the concentration of executive power in his hands, as attempts to establish a "presidential republic." This opposition compelled the President to dismiss his acting Prime Minister, Yegor Gaidar, the chief proponent of "shock therapy" in establishing a free market economy; his place was taken by Viktor Chernomerdin, a former manager of the Soviet oil trust and a supporter of a slower tempo of economic transformation. This did not appease the Congress largely composed of Communist deputies. They resented Yeltsin's vast presidential prerogatives, including that of power of dissolving the Congress. Yeltsin, anxious to have his dominant position as Head of State confirmed by a new charter, insisted on a constitutional referendum that would legitimize his powers. Here again he clashed with the Duma opposition, which was supported by his deputy, the Vice President, former Air Force General Alexander Rutskoy, one of the heroes of the Afghan war. After protracted squabbling, and the threat of dissolution, the Congress agreed to a referendum that took place in April 1993. The referendum basically confirmed Yeltsin's project, which proposed to establish a presidential republic with a bicameral legislature and independent judiciary. The lower house, bearing the traditional name of Duma, would be composed of 450 deputies elected by democratic vote. The upper chamber, the Council of the Federation, was to be composed of two parts, with each of the 89 members of the Russian Federation (federal republics and autonomous administrative regions) sending two representatives; the balance of the Council was to be made up of presidents of the federal republics and heads of their governments.

The majority of the Congress of Peoples' Deputies opposed the constitutional project. In response, the infuriated Yeltsin dissolved the Congress and called for elections to the new legislative bodies to take place in October 1993. The Congress, supported by Vice President Rutskoy, denounced this dictatorial move and overwhelmingly called for Yeltsin's resignation on September 22, 1993. When he refused, the opposition declared him deposed by a great majority of the Duma deputies. The opposition then summoned the people to civil disobedience and street demonstrations in support of its demand. A large number of the opposition deputies, as well as hundreds of their Muscovite supporters, barricaded themselves in the parliament building (colloquially called the "White House"). For a few days the issue hung in the balance. Everything depended on the attitude of the armed forces. The standoff was resolved by the army and the police, most of which remained loyal to the President. On Yeltsin's order, elite units of airborne troops, supported by tanks and airplanes, stormed the "White House" and captured it on October 4. Leaders of the revolt, including Rutskoy, were arrested.

Yeltsin triumphed, but at the cost of numerous casualties on both sides. At least 176 people were killed and hundreds injured. Yeltsin justified his highhanded action by arguing that, he, being the democratically elected Head of State, had supreme authority over a rebellious body that was in reality simply a posthumous relic of the discredited totalitarian regime.

To counter this blow to his standing as a democratic leader, Yeltsin kept his promise to carry out fully democratic parliamentary elections. They took place on December 11, 1993. This was the first genuinely free expression of public opinion since December 1917, when the democratically elected Duma deliberating in Petrograd was dispersed by Bolshevik soldiers, on Lenin's orders. The 1993 elections were full of surprises, and contradictions. Over 57 percent of the electorate of 105 million people approved Yeltsin's constitutional draft and thus accepted his presidential system. None of the prerevolutionary political parties appeared on the surface; the new ones were all hastily improvised. The greatest surprise was that nearly 24 percent of all the votes were cast for a semi-fascist and violently anti-Semitic party led by a little known politician, Vladimir Zhirinovsky, who, paradoxically, named his faction the "Liberal Democratic Party." The success of the relatively obscure leader was ascribed not only to the desperate economic situation of about half of Russia's population, but also to Zhirinovsky's skillful use of the mass media in his election propaganda. His demagogic appeal to the broad masses of the people was based largely on wildly nationalistic and shocking racial slogans. He had campaigned on a platform of restoring Russia's imperial rule by reclaiming the lands of the pre-1914 Tsarist Empire; this would include all of Finland, the Baltic states of Estonia, Latvia and Lithuania, and central Poland. Zhirinovsky criticized the allegedly premature withdrawal from Afghanistan and insisted Russia must break through to the Indian Ocean at any cost, without specifying whether or not the Russian drive would involve Afghanistan, Pakistan, and Iran to allow Russian soldiers to "wash their boots in the warm waters of the Indian Ocean." Zhirinovsky went as far as to threaten to bomb Japan as a way to settle, once and for all, the two countries' dispute of the Kuril islands. While denying his racism, Zhirinovsky declared, "Although we are not anti-Semitic, we won't tolerate an increase in the strength of the Jews. Countries that expelled Russians should be threatened with the persecution of their nationals within the boundaries of the Russian Federation."

The main reform coalition, known as "Russia's Democratic Choice," followed the "Liberal Democratic Party" with 14.5 percent of the ballots. The new Communist Party of the Russian Federation (C.P.R.F.) made a surprisingly strong showing by gaining 14 percent of the votes. Among the other parties that passed the 5 percent threshold required to seat their deputies in the Duma was the "Yabloko" ("Apple") bloc of go-slow reformers.

The Duma opened its deliberations on January 11, 1994, dominated by Zhirinovsky's ultranationalists, the Communists, and their minor leftist allies. The downfall of the Soviet superpower was a rude shock to Russian patriots. Unable to analyze the factors underlying the historic process of disintegration of the anachronistic last colonial empire, they began to ascribe it to a sinister C.I.A. plot and treacherous machinations of "western capitalists" eager to grab the profitable Russian market and the country's still unexploited or mismanaged national resources. Complaining that the United States has reserved for Russia the role of a mere regional power and a supplier of cheap raw materials, the frustrated Communists and nationalists canvassed for backing across the political spectrum. They have found many supporters among people looking back nostalgically at the "good old days" when the Soviet Union was a superpower, and Soviet ambassadors were actually running the vassal countries of East Central Europe. This feeling of nationalistic frustration has been widespread. Even former advocates of democratization and peaceful cooperation with the West repeatedly declared the right of defending Russia's "area of historic influence," a euphemistic cover for its former imperial status.

Foreign Policy

To satisfy this sentiment and to preserve his popularity, Yeltsin had gradually assimilated some of the arguments. To emphasize growing dissatisfaction with the West, he had a tough attitude on two issues. First of all, he initially tried to maintain an independent stand toward the civil war in the former Yugoslavia, strongly favoring Russia's traditional allies, the Slavic Serbs, as against the restless, largely Moslem Albanians of Kosovo and Bosnia-Herzegovina. Moreover, he voiced his opposition to the admission to NATO of former Russian vassal countries: Poland, Hungary, Slovakia, and the Czech Republic, as an alleged threat to the Federation's security.

The most essential controversial point of friction between the Russian Federation and the United States has been the problem of disarmament. Despite the progressive dismantling of strategic weapons, the Federation still possesses thousands of nuclear warheads and considerable stores of chemical and biological weapons; to this arsenal should be added huge stores of ingredients necessary to manufacture them. There has been a serious danger of proliferation of these weapons to rogue countries like Iran, North Korea, or China. A good example of the transfer of high technology was the selling of a nuclear reactor, submarines, and other military materiel to Iran. This transaction, carried out despite repeated vigorous protests from Washington, has threatened the stability of the Persian Gulf region, so vital to the West as the main source of oil. The deal was concluded in order to bolster Russia's balance of trade and to emphasize its position as a great power, capable of acting independently from the West. By this gesture of defiance, President Yeltsin has tried, before the presidential election of June, 1996, to outsmart his ultranationalist and Communist rivals and to ingratiate himself with the increasingly vocal military establishment.

Another example of Russia's growing defiance could be observed in the field of conventional disarmament. In 1992, Moscow, together with twenty-nine other countries, signed the Conventional Forces in Europe (C.F.E.) treaty limiting such military units and their armament on the continent. The signatories agreed to destroy thousands of heavy weapons, to permit detailed on-site inspections and to limit troop and weapons deployment, thus effectively diminishing the threat of sudden invasion in Europe. Yet, the C.F.E. treaty was sharply criticized by Russian hawks, especially those of the reviving Communist movement headed by Gennady Zyuganov, as being too restrictive.

The mounting anti-Western sentiments erupted dramatically in the spring and summer of 1999 when NATO decided to bomb Slavic Serbia to stop it from committing mass reprisals against the largely Moslem Albanian population in the Yugoslav province of Kosovo. President Yeltsin saw behind it a U.S. manipulation to reassert American global hegemony and declared: "Some nations are trying to build a world order that would be convenient only for them, ignoring that the world is multipolar." At the end of August, he met with the Chinese president, Jiang Zemin, to forge a closer alliance counterbalancing the U.S. global clout. These efforts did not produce many results because of the chronic internal weakness of the Russian Federation, suffering from political and economic crisis.

The Crisis

Unable to cope with the obstacles constantly thrown in his path by the opposition, after two years of fruitless bickering, Yeltsin dissolved the Duma and decreed new elections to take place on December 17, 1995. This time, about 64 percent of the eligible voters battled blizzards and storms to cast their ballots in another democratic parliamentary election. It resulted in dramatic gains for the Communist Party of the Russian Federation (C.P.R.F.) which won 22.3 percent of the popular vote. Led by an experienced and eloquent former middle-level apparatchik from Oriol, Gennady Zyuganov, the Communists took full advantage of the country's economic plight, deepened by the worst harvest in thirty years, as well as by the skyrocketing crime rate, and the lingering war in Chechnya. By dramatically expanding its electoral base, the party emerged as the strongest faction in the Duma. With 157 deputies in a chamber of 450, the C.P.R.F., reinforced by other leftist groups, has gained a commanding position in the lower chamber.

The main surprise of the 1995 election was the drop in popularity of Zhirinovsky's "Liberal Democratic Party." He failed to repeat his 1993 successes and saw the number of his party's seats cut nearly in half; with just under 14 percent of the vote, he found himself far behind Zyuganov. The mildly reformist pro-government party, "Our Home is Russia," created and led by Prime Minister Victor Chernomyrdin, received less than 10 percent of the votes. The outspokenly reformist faction, "Yabloko," headed by Gretory Yavlinsky, secured only 8.4 percent of the ballots.

The outcome of the 1995 elections was as much a triumph of the reconstituted Communist movement as a no-confidence for Yeltsin. The threat now came from the C.P.R.F., by far the best organized and disciplined political group, supported by some 580,000 card-carrying members. The party's core has been made up of former apparatchiki, middle-age citizens and older pensioners who have felt most severely the negative impact of the capitalist economic reforms. While not overly stressing the old doctrine of a single-party dictatorship,

Gennady Zyuganov, 1996.

to strengthen Russia's influence within the C.I.S., but also to reestablish Russia's great power status.

The 1995 parliamentary elections were a prelude to the spring 1996 presidential contest. No fewer than ten candidates competed in the campaign, but the main attention was focused on Yeltsin and Zyuganov. During the campaign Zyuganov vitriolically lashed out at Yeltsin for his political as well as personal failures. Yeltsin's hasty free market reforms, argued Zyuganov, have resulted in Russia's productive capacity being cut by half; they had impoverished the masses, forcing many people to sell family belongings on the street, while enriching beyond measure the few well-connected plutocrats, a stratum of newly rich individuals, including many governmental officials close to the President and his camarilla. "Can Russia afford another four years of unbridled, rapacious capitalism?" thundered Zyuganov. He accused Yeltsin of halving the country's intellectual, financial, as well as moral reserves, and thus decreasing its overall well being. His political reforms created an imperial presidency and a new mammoth central bureaucracy, while neglecting the periphery of the Federation that, meanwhile, has been drifting away from Moscow. The establishment of the overly strong Council of the Federation in which not only each federal republic but also each autonomous region has two representatives has had negative results. The Council, endowed with considerable power, has brought to the surface not only the latent irredentist trends but also sharpened the competition of various regions for higher status within the Federation, thus also threatening its cohesiveness. Some regions, which had had less power than the republics, but were larger and richer in natural resources, attempted to bolster their status. For instance, several of them drew up their own charters, imposed their own taxes, and even established diplomatic relations with neighboring countries. As an example, Zyuganov cited the Far Eastern region, which promptly proclaimed itself a republic, claiming "economic necessity" as its main reason, initiated close ties with Japan and other coun-

Zyuganov has alluded to a desire to preserve political pluralism and a "mixed economy." On the other hand, the idea of restoring the old USSR as a great world power has been proclaimed quite openly. In one of Zyuganov's speeches, he urged the Russian patriots to prevent the "further breakup of the country and its final transformation into a Western colony," dominated by the "cosmopolitan oligarchy," where the Jewish influence was "growing literally not by the day but by the hour."

The 1995 elections produced several significant results. First of all, they catapulted the reformed Communist, Gennady Zyuganov, fifty-one years of age, into the political arena as a major player. Second, the election displayed the organizational and ideological weakness of the Russian liberal and reformist movement, helplessly split into feuding factions unable to establish a coalition to oppose the Communists. Third, the election evidenced a remarkable increase in nationalistic rhetoric, urging the next president not only tries of the Pacific Rim. Even Yeltsin's native land, the Sverdlovsk region, demanded greater autonomy from Moscow and proclaimed itself the Ural Republic.

The Communist propaganda, although restricted by various governmental regulations, has also submitted Yeltsin's personal record to vitriolic criticism. Zyuganov, himself a modest and rather abstemious man by Russian standards, took advantage of Yeltsin's conspicuous personal weakness—his frequent wild drinking bouts—and the conspicuously exuberant, near monarchical style of his presidency. There were many jokes about Yeltsin's irresponsible behavior. A popular Communist argument in the presidential campaign was borrowed from one of the provincial leaders: "Can the vehicle of the Russian Federation be entrusted again to a drunken driver?"

The ailing Yeltsin launched an American style electoral campaign by proclaiming himself the only guarantor of political stability and the main shield against the return of the brutal Communist rule. He argued that his reelection was necessary for the continuity of the reforms that are about to produce beneficial results. He pointed out that in nearly every city young families were building new homes and were opening new businesses. He and his spokesmen repeatedly stressed that the election of a Communist president would mean confiscation of private property, reestablishment of a police state, i.e., a return to a totalitarian system with its terror, which would precipitate a civil war. This rhetoric was meant to invoke in the minds of the electorate a red specter and the ghost of the fratricidal struggles that had devastated the Russian society in 1918–1921.

At every turn, Yeltsin was opposed by the Duma. To counter the criticism that he had allowed the C.I.S. to disintegrate, Yeltsin engineered an agreement about a "deepening of economic and humanitarian integration" between Russia, Belorus, Kazakhstan and Kirgistan; the text of the agreement stressed full sovereignty of Kazakhstan and Kirgistan, but not of Belorus which, meanwhile, has been implementing a union with the Russian Federation. After this gesture aimed to appease the proponents of expansion and tightening of the C.I.S., he made a move to win over the broad strata of Russian society. To belie the accusation that he had initiated the military intervention in Chechnya without being able to bring it to a successful conclusion, Yeltsin signed another ceasefire with the rebels at the end of May; the agreement provided for withdrawal of the Russian troops within two weeks, just a couple of days before the presidential election of June 16. Finally, he stunned his opponents by announcing his plans to abolish conscription and turn the Russian armed forces into an efficient professional machine. This decision, which runs counter to long-standing Russian tradition, provoked an immediate protest from most of the military establishment. "It is a purely populist decree and nothing will be achieved," said Aleksandr L. Lebed, the retired general and one of the ten presidential candidates. "In order to have a professional army, one must have a powerful economy. Our economy is half-alive, semi-collapsed and down on its knees." Despite this, Yeltsin compelled the director of the National Bank of the Russian Federation to put at his disposal $10 billion to oil the machinery of his presidential campaign by making good some of his most urgent promises to pay out long-overdue wages to officials and workers. Under pressure, the loan was granted, despite the bank director's warning the loan may wreck the state budget, trigger super-inflation and, in general, play havoc with the national economy.

On Sunday, June 16, 1996 70 million or nearly 70 percent of the eligible voters, faced a choice of ten candidates. Despite the advantages of the incumbency, which included a most extensive privileged use of mass media, Yeltsin failed to win the necessary majority of votes as prescribed by the constitution of 1993; he scored barely 35 percent, as against Zyuganov's 32 percent. The third strongest candidate, General Lebed, received as much as 15 percent.

The muddled results of the first round

The triumphant Boris Yeltsin in 1996.

until the year 2000. Meanwhile, however, the epidemic of nonpayment of taxes, the rapid criminalization of a large segment of the population, and the failure of the still overwhelmingly collectivized agriculture to provide enough food, compelling the country to spend large sums for importing even grain and fodder from abroad, precipitated a dangerous economic crisis, deepened by the falling prices of Russia's main exports, oil and natural gas. In the summer of 1998, the Russian currency, the ruble, had to be devaluated by 34 percent, and the Moscow Stock Exchange virtually collapsed. The Russian Federation had to suspend payment of its foreign debt. As a consequence, the bold structure of reforms, hastily planned by the group of West-oriented young economists, crumbled overnight. The financial and economic crisis has had a devastating effect on the Russian Federation, as well as on many neighboring states, especially former segments of the Soviet Union still suffering from their economic dependence on the former heartland of the Empire. The weakness of Russia has seriously threatened any possibility of economic reintegration of the Commonwealth of Independent States into something resembling the old USSR.

A series of quickly changing Prime Ministers proved unable to cope with the critical financial situation and its social consequences that deeply affected an overwhelming majority of the country's population. In August 1999, the mounting dissatisfaction and unrest compelled the increasingly incapacitated Yeltsin to appoint a little-known former KGB officer, Vladimir Putin, as Prime Minister.

made a run-off election a constitutional necessity. Immediately both leading rivals, Yeltsin and Zyuganov, began to grab for the tails of the strongest competitor, General Lebed, who had received some 11 million votes. Yeltsin won the race by offering the General the post of the head of the State Security Council with extended powers, including the right to control the police force as well as the intelligence service. Dissatisfied with these extensive privileges, Lebed immediately began to claim also the recently abolished post of Vice President. This put him on a collision course with Chernomerdin who, as Prime Minister, had been constitutionally designated as the President's deputy.

The alliance with Lebed and the fear of the Communists regaining power pushed the minor reformist groups to back Yeltsin. On July 3, in the second round of the electoral process, he scored a decisive victory by winning 54 percent of the votes cast. Thus he became the head of the Russian Federation

Exit Boris Yeltsin—Enter Vladimir Putin

Putin was born in 1952, in Leningrad (now St. Petersburg); he has two degrees, one in law, another in engineering, as well as a black belt in judo and karate. He planned to be a teacher of chemistry but was picked up by a KGB recruiting agent in 1975: subse-

Vladimir Putin

ters, President Yeltsin chose Putin as the new head of government, on August 9, 1999. When two months later, on October 9, Yeltsin was hospitalized again, with cold and flu, Putin became acting President of the Russian Federation.

Thus ended the era of Boris Yeltsin, which had lasted for over a decade. Yeltsin embodied a host of contradictions: a hardline Communist who once oversaw Brezhnev's order to bulldoze the house in which Nicholas II and his family had been murdered, and then cried presiding over their ceremonial burial. He was a Party aparatchik who smashed the Communist Party and helped to initiate capitalist reforms that privatized most of the economy and left Russia with a rudimentary network of banks and millions of small businesses. In 1991, when the Stalinist mafia tried to restore the old system, Yeltsin mounted an armored vehicle and challenged the coup at the head of a small group of courageous people who turned the mass of the Muscovites against the coup. Yet, this self-styled democrat did not hesitate to send tanks to storm his own parliament in 1993, capture its building, at the cost of more than 176 corpses. Being really a sort of democratic autocrat, he personalized power, manipulated the media, and bullied no less than four Prime Ministers to follow his often erratic and contradictory policies. He laid the foundation of what could be called an electoral democracy, rather than liberal democracy. Whatever his shortcomings, his stand in August 1991, saved Russia from relapsing into totalitarian Communism and set an example of a peaceful transition of power. By storming the Duma in 1993 he probably prevented a civil war in Russia.

The December 19, 1999, Duma election was full of surprises, the hastily but skillfully welded progovernment block called Unity, supported by the centrist coalition and the right-wing forces, gained over 44 percent of the vote. Yet, despite its electoral defeat, the Communist Party remained the largest single faction in the Duma. Another surprise was another poor showing of the xenophobic movement of Vladimir Zhirinovsky, whose

quently, he was carefully trained in one of its espionage schools, and sent to East Germany to watch over German-Soviet Societies in Dresden. One of his tasks was to create a network of secret agents that could survive the already expected downfall of East Germany's Communist regime. After the collapse of the Berlin Wall, Putin returned to Leningrad with a bronze medal from his Stasi, or the East German secret police, and was first assigned to counterintelligence work at his old university; in the early 1990s, however, he was called on to use his legal training and his knowledge of German to negotiate with foreign investors and to unravel the Gordian knot of Russian bureaucracy that hampered establishment of joint ventures; then he returned briefly to Federal Security Service and became its chief. His success in both fields attracted the attention of the Kremlin. After dismissing four ineffective Prime Minis-

Liberal Democratic Party scored only 6 percent of the vote. The reformist, promarket group of Grigory Yavlinsky, a vigorous opponent of the Chechnya war, made an even poorer showing with less than 6 percent of the ballot.

Putin's presidential election started almost the moment Yeltsin appointed him Prime Minister, on August 9, 1999, and actually gave him his blessing as Russia's President. Putin's team relied on a blitz of overwhelmingly biased news coverage on two major television channels, both controlled by the financial mogul, Boris Berezovsky, one of Russia's most powerful and richest men. Putin was invariably presented as a "positive hero." This public relations job was bolstered by Putin's dramatic flight on a two-seated fighter plane into Chechnya in flames. Speaking to frontline soldiers, he urged them to continue the fighting, with fierce abandon, the Chechen guerillas, whom he denounced as "terrorists."

Putin completed his rise to power by decisively winning the March 26, 2000, presidential election; he was inaugurated as the second President of the Russian Federation in a splendid ceremony reminiscent of the imperial times.

Soon after his inauguration he tried to curtail the growing power of provincial governors. To gain control over the provinces, he created seven regional districts. He also reorganized the Federal Council and established the State Council. He decreed a radical reform of the complex tax collecting system, thus dramatically increasing the income of the Federal Treasury. This reform, together with the rising prices for oil and natural gas, greatly improved the Russian financial situation. While muzzling the Russian press and TV, he tried to curtail the activities of various mafia gangs, and the influence of the most powerful tycoons, known as "oligarchs." This, while increasing internal stability, greatly intensified encroachment by law and security organs on the freedom of conscience and the right to spread information. This has aroused new fears among liberals, who have been asking themselves: "Is there such a phenomenon as a *former* KGB man?"

The terrorist attack that struck New York and Washington on September 11, 2001, saw a sudden reorientation of Russian position in the international arena. Putin, who hitherto tried to mount an anti-American coalition of the so-called "rogue states," North Korea, China, Iraq, and Iran, immediately reversed his attitude and declared his readiness to put Russia's intelligence bases and equipment at the disposal of Washington to fight Bin Laden and the Taliban which sheltered and supported him. This made Putin an associate, actually a linchpin, of the group of countries fighting terrorism. This opened the gates for renewed international efforts to help Russia with economic aid and technical assistance so badly needed by the Putin regime.

Russia at the Beginning of the Twenty-First Century

Since the collapse of the Soviet Empire in 1991, the Russian Federation is no more a superpower, but it still remains one of the most important countries of the world because of its size, population, and national resources; its position, spanning two continents, guarantees its continual influence over global affairs. This is a result of the geopolitical changes that took place during the last decade of the twentieth century.

The collapse dramatically altered the geopolitical situation of the main entity that emerged from it in the shape of the Russian Federation; its access to the Baltic Sea was reduced to a narrow strip around St. Petersburg (formerly Leningrad) and the precarious enclave of Kaliningrad. The Black Sea littoral also shrunk because of the establishment of the Ukrainian State and the rebirth of the three Caucasian republics, Armenia, Georgia, and Azerbaijan. The proclamation of independence by Kazakhstan, Uzbekistan, Turkmenistan, Kyrzistan, and Taijikistan reduced tremendously Russian influence not only in Europe, but also in Central Asia. Russia in 1991 resembled the Muscovite State at the end of the seventeenth century.

Although the present picture of Russia appears as rather shaky, one should not forget the assets she has at her disposal. On the economic side of the ledger one has to put her natural resources: She still produces nearly 17 percent of world crude oil, 25–30 percent of natural gas, and 10–20 percent of nonferrous metals; she is the second largest producer of brown coal, third in timber logging, fourth in electric energy output, cast iron and steel, fifth in the production of black coal, mineral fertilizers and nuclear energy. The Russian scientists have a brilliant record as explorers of both outer space and rocketry in general. The Russian Federation has inherited from the USSR a nationwide system of primary, secondary, and higher education. Despite the continuing brain drain, Russia still possesses a large pool of well-educated scientists, managers, engineers, and doctors, who, if properly rewarded and directed, could bridge the technological gap that was one of the causes of the catastrophe that befell the USSR in the 1980s and 1990s. The crux of the problem is not with the availability of the material resources, but with their effective use. It seems that much depends on the quality of leadership of President Vladimir Putin and his and his successors' ability to revive the Russian economy, while restoring domestic stability. Whether a sound economy should precede a stable government, or vice versa, has been a chicken-and-egg problem. Only the future can resolve this crucial dilemma.

Suggested Reading

ANDERSON, JOHN, *Religion, State and Politics in the Soviet Union and Successor States*. New York: Cambridge University Press, 1994.

DAWISHA, KAREN AND BRUCE PARROTT, *Russia and the New States of Eurasia. The Politics of Upheaval*. New York: Cambridge University Press, 1994.

EINKELMAN, DALE, F. (ED.), *Russia's Muslim Frontiers. New Directions in Cross-Cultural Analysis*. Bloomington: Indiana University Press, 1993.

HANDELMAN, STEVEN, *Comrade Criminal: Russia's New Mafia*. New Haven, CT: Yale University Press, 1995.

HUBBS, JOANNA, *Mother Russia. The Feminine Myth in Russian Culture*. Bloomington: Indiana University Press, 1988.

KLEBNIKOV, PAL, *Godfather of the Kremlin: Boris Berezovsky and the Looting of Russia*. New York: Harcourt, 2000.

KNIGHT, AMY, *Spies Without Cloaks. The KGB's Successors*. Princeton, NJ: Princeton University Press, 1996.

KOLSTOE, PAUL, *Russians in the Former Soviet Republics*. Bloomington: Indiana University Press, 1995.

KOSALS, L., *Why Doesn't Russian Industry Work?* New York: St. Martin's Press, 1994.

KRAMER, MARK, *Travels with a Hungry Bear. A Journey to the Russian Heartland*. Boston, MA: A Richard Todd Book—Houghton Mifflin Company, 1996.

KUZIO, TERRAS AND ANDREW WILSON, *Ukraine. Perestrojka to Independence*. New York: St. Martin's Press, 1995.

LANDAU, JACOB M., *Pan-Turkism. From Irredentism to Cooperation*. Bloomington, IN: Indiana University Press, 1995.

ORTTUNG, ROBERT, *From Leningrad to St. Petersburg*. New York: St. Martin's Press, 1995.

PILKINTON, HILARY, *Russia's Youth and Its Culture: A Nation's Constructors and Constructed*. New York: Routledge, 1994.

PUTIN, VLADIMIR, *First Person: An Astonishingly Frank Self-portrait by Russia's President Vladimir Putin*, with Nataliya Gevorkyan, Natalya Timakova, and Andrei Kolesnikov; translated by Catherine A. Fitzpatrick. London: Hutchinson, 2000.

RAGSDALE, HUGH, *The Russian Tragedy: The Burden of History*. New York: M.E. Sharpe, 1996.

RANDOLPH, ELENOR, *Waking the Tempests. Ordinary Life in the New Russia*. New York: Simon & Schuster, 1996.

SOLCHANYK, ROMAN, *Ukraine. The Road to Independence*. New York: St. Martin's Press, 1995.

VOLKOV, SOLOMON, *St. Petersburg. A Cultural History*. Translated by Antonina W. Bouis. New York: The Free Press, 1996.

WEBBER, MARK, *The International Politics of Russia and the Successor States*. New York: St. Martin's Press, 1996.

Appendix

Emperors of Russia, House of Romanov

Peter I	1682–1725	Catherine II	1762–1796
(Emperor in 1721)		Paul	1796–1801
Catherine I	1725–1727	Alexander I	1801–1825
Peter II	1727–1730	Nicholas I	1826–1855
Anna	1730–1740	Alexander II	1855–1881
Ivan VI	1740–1741	Alexander III	1881–1894
Elizabeth	1741–1761	Nicholas II	1894–1917
Peter III	1761–1762		

Chairmen of the Council of People's Commissars (Prime Ministers after 1946)

V. I. Lenin	1917–1924	N. S. Khrushchev	1958–1964
A. I. Rykov	1924–1930	A. N. Kosygin	1964–1980
V. M. Molotov	1930–1941	N. A. Tikhonov	1980–1985
J. V. Stalin	1941–1953	N. I. Ryzhkov	1985–1990
G. M. Malenkov	1953–1955	V. S. Pavlov	1990–1991
N. A. Bulganin	1955–1958		

General and First Secretaries of the Party's Central Committee

J. V. Stalin, General Secretary, April 1922–March 5, 1953

G. M. Malenkov, First Secretary, March 5, 1953–March 15, 1953

N. S. Khrushchev, First Secretary, March 15, 1953–October 14, 1964

L. I. Brezhnev, First Secretary, October 14, 1964–March 1966; General Secretary, April 8, 1966–November 10, 1982

Y. V. Andropov, First Secretary, November 11, 1982–February 5, 1984

K. V. Chernenko, First Secretary, February 13, 1984–March 11, 1985

M. S. Gorbachev, General Secretary, March 12, 1985–December 31, 1991

Congresses of the Russian Social Democratic Workers' Party (RSDWP), Russian Communist Party (Bolshevik) (RCP-B) since March 1918, Communist Party of the Soviety Union (Bolshevik) (CPSU-B) since December 1935, and Communist Party of the Soviety Union (CPSU) since October 1952.

Russian Social Democratic Workers' Party (RSDWP)

I Congress	Minsk	March 1–3, 1898 (Old Style)
II Congress	Brussels and London	July 17–August 10, 1903
III Congress	London	April 12–27, 1905
(Bolshevik faction only)		
IV Congress	Stockholm	April 10–25, 1906
V Congress	London	April 30–May 19, 1917

RSDWP (Bolshevik)

VI Congress	Petrograd	July 26–August 3, 1917

Russian Communist Party (RCP) (Bolshevik)

VII Congress	Petrograd	March 6–8, 1918 (New Style)
VIII Congress	Moscow	March 18–23, 1919
IX Congress	Moscow	March 29–April 5, 1920
X Congress	Moscow	March 8–16, 1921
XI Congress	Moscow	March 27–April 2, 1922
XII Congress	Moscow	April 18–25, 1923
XIII Congress	Moscow	May 23–31, 1924

Communist Party of the Soviet Union (CPSU) (Bolshevik)

XIV Congress	Moscow	December 18–31, 1925
XV Congress	Moscow	December 2–19, 1927
XVI Congress	Moscow	June 26–July 13, 1930
XVII Congress	Moscow	January 26–February 10, 1934
XVIII Congress	Moscow	March 10–21, 1939

CPSU

XIX Congress	Moscow	October 5–15, 1952
XX Congress	Moscow	February 14–25, 1956
XXI Congress	Moscow	January 27–February 5, 1959
XXII Congress	Moscow	October 17–31, 1961
XXIII Congress	Moscow	March 29–April 8, 1966
XXIV Congress	Moscow	March 30–April 9, 1971
XXV Congress	Moscow	February 24–29, 1976
XXVI Congress	Moscow	March, 1981
XXVII Congress	Moscow	February–March, 1986
XXVIII Congress	Moscow	July–August 1990

Congresses of the Communist International (Comintern)

First	Moscow	March 2–6, 1919
Second	Moscow and Petrograd	July 19–August 7, 1920
Third (United Front)	Moscow	June 22–July 12, 1921
Fourth	Moscow	November 5–December 5, 1922
Fifth	Moscow	June 17–July 8, 1924
Sixth (Ultra-left tactics)	Moscow	July 17–September 1, 1928
Seventh (Popular Front)	Moscow	July 25–August 20, 1935

Presidents of the Russian Federation

Boris Yeltsin	1989–1999
Vladimir Putin	1999–

ETHNIC COMPOSITION OF THE USSR IN 1926, 1979 AND 1989:
THE LARGEST NATIONALITY GROUPS (IN THOUSANDS)

Nationalities	Census of 1926 147.028	Percent of the Population	Census of 1979 262.085	Percent of the Population	Census of 1989 286.717	Percent of the Population
Russians	77.791	52.9	137.397	52.4	145.743	50.8
Ukrainians	31.195	21.2	42.347	16.2	44.186	15.5
Uzbeks	3.989	2.7	12.456	4.8	16.698	5.8
Belorussians	4.739	3.2	9.463	3.6	10.036	3.5
Kazaks	3.989	2.7	6.556	2.5	8.136	2.8
Azerbijanis	1.713	1.2	5.477	2.1	6.770	2.4
Armenians	1.568	1.1	4.151	1.6	4.623	1.6
Georgians	1.821	1.2	3.571	1.4	3.981	1.4
Moldavians	279	0.2	2.968	1.1	3.352	1.2
Tadziks	981	0.7	2.989	1.1	4.215	1.5
Lithuanians	41	0.0	2.851	1.1	3.067	1.1
Turkmanians	764	0.5	2.008	0.8	2.729	1.0
Germans	1.239	0.8	1.936	0.7	2.039	0.7
Kirgizians	763	0.5	1.906	0.7	2.529	0.9
Jews	2.672	1.8	1.811	0.7	1.449	0.5
Chuvashi	1.117	0.8	1.751	0.7	1.842	0.6
Latvians	151	0.1	1.439	0.5	1.459	0.5
Bashkirs	714	0.5	1.371	0.5	1.449	0.5
Mordvinians	1.340	0.9	1.192	0.5	1.154	0.4
Poles	782	0.5	1.151	0.4	1.126	0.4
Estonians	155	0.1	1.020	0.4	1.027	0.4

Source: Paul E. Lydolph. *Geography of the USSR.* Fifth Ed., (Elkhart Lake, Wis.: Misty Valley Publishing, 1990.)

Statistical Survey of the Russian Federation

Area, Population and Density

Area (sq km)	17,075,400*
Population (census result)	
12 January 1989	147,400,537†
Population (official estimate at 1 January)	
1991	148,485,000
Density (per sq km) at 1 January 1991	8.7

* 6,592,812 sq miles
†The *de jure* population was 147,021,869 (males 68,713,869; females 78,308,000)

Republics Within the Federation
(census of 12 January 1989)

Republic	Area (sq km)	Population ('000)	Capital (with population, '000)
Adygheya*	7,600	432	Maikop (149)
Altay*	92,600	192	Gorno-Altaysk (40‡)
Bashkortostan	143,600	3,952	Ufa (1,083)
Buryatia	351,300	1,042	Ulan-Ude (353)
Chechen Republic-Ichkeria†	n.a.	n.a.	Grozny (401)
Chuvashia	18,300	1,336	Cheboksary (420)
Daghestan	50,300	1,792	Makhachkala (315)
Ingushetia†	n.a.	n.a.	Nazran (n.a.)
Kabardin-Balkaria	12,500	760	Nalchik (235)
Kalmykia	75,900	322	Elista (120)
Karachay-Cherkessia*	14,100	418	Cherkessk (113)
Karelia	172,400	792	Petrozavodsk (270)
Khakassia	61,900	569	Abakan (153)
Komi	415,900	1,263	Syktyvkar (233)
Mari-El	23,300	750	Yoshkar-Ola (242)
Mordovia	26,200	964	Saransk (312)
North Ossetia	8,000	634	Vladikavkaz (300)
Sakha (Yakutia)	3,103,200	1,081	Yakutsk (187)
Tatarstan	68,000	3,640	Kazan (1,094)
Tyva	170,500	309	Kyzyl (n.a.)
Udmurt Republic	42,100	1,609	Izhevsk (635)

*Under the terms of the 1992 Federation Treaty, these former autonomous oblasts (regions) were granted the status of republic.
† Until 1992 the territories of the Republic of Chechnya and the Ingush Republic were combined in the Chechen-Ingush autonomous republic.
‡ At 1 January 1976

Principal Towns
(estimated population, in '000, at 1 January 1990)*

Moskva (Moscow the capital)	8,801	Astrakhan	510
		Naberezhnye Chelny*	507
Sankt Peterburg (St. Petersburg)*	4,468	Tomsk	506
Nizhny Novgorod*	1,443	Tyumen	487
Novosibirsk	1,443	Viyatka*	487
Yekaterinburg*	1,367	Ivanovo	482
Samara*	1,258	Murmansk	472
Omsk	1,159	Bryansk	456
Chelyabinsk	1,148	Lipetsk	455
Kazan	1,103	Tver*	454
Perm	1,094	Magnitogorsk	443
Ufa	1,094	Nizhny Tagil	440
Rostov-na-Donu	1,025	Kursk	430
Volgograd	1,005	Cheboksary	429
Krasnoyarsk	922	Arkhangelsk	419
Saratov	909	Kaliningrad	406
Voronezh	895	Grozny	401
Vladivostok	643	Chita	372
Izhevsk*	642	Kurgan	360
Tolyatti	642	Ulan-Ude	359
Simbirsk*	638	Vladimir	353
Yaroslavl	636	Smolensk	346
Irkutsk	635	Orel	342
Krasnodar	627	Sochi	339
Khabarovsk	608	Makhachkala	327
Barnaul	603	Stavropol	324
Novokuznetsk	601	Komsomolsk-na-Amure	318
Orenburg	552	Saransk	316
Penza	548	Kaluga	314
Tula	543	Cherepovets	313
Ryazan	522	Tambov	307
Kemerovo	521	Belgorod	306
		Vladikavkaz*	303

*Some towns that were renamed during the Soviet period have reverted to their former names: St. Petersburg (Leningrad); Nizhny Novgorod (Gorky); Yekaterinburg (Sverdlovsk); Samara (Kuybyshev); Izhevsk (Ustinov); Simbirsk (Ulyanovsk); Naberezhnye Chelny (Brezhnev); Viyatka (Kirov); Tver (Kalinin); Vladikavkaz (Ordzhonikidze).

The tables on pps. 400 and 401 are reprinted by permission of Europa Publications from their book *Eastern Europe and the Commonwealth of Independent States,* Second Edition, Europa Publications, London: 1996, p. 560.

Administrative Divisions of the Russian Federation

Photo Credits

Photographs on pages 35, 38, 43, 53, 67, 87, 95, 137, 146, 152, 158, 180, 189, 192, 214, 231, 233, 237, 258, 268, 269, 273, 278, 288, 310, 319 are used with the permission of the National Archives.

Photographs on pages 22, 59, 171, 203, 287, 311, 317, 331, 337, 343 are reproduced from the Collection of the Library of Congress.

Photographs on pages 246, 248, 251, 253, 354, 368, 372 are used with the permission of the Russian Embassy, Washington, D.C. Photograph on page 390 is from Ria "Novosti," photographer V. Federenko, and on page 401 is from Ria "Novosti," and these photos are used with permission of the Russian Embassy, Washington, D.C.

Photograph on page 175 is used with the permission of the United Nations.

Photograph on page 265 is used with permission of the German Information Center.

Photographs on pages 124 and 358 are used with permission of Leslie Deeb.

Photograph on page 376 is used with permission of *The Ukrainian Weekly*.

Photographs on pages 61, 77, 85, 107, 190, 334 are from the collection of the Russian Academy of Sciences.

Index